ALTERNATIVE INVESTMENTS AND PORTFOLIO MANAGEMENT

CFA® Program Curriculum
2017 • LEVEL II • VOLUME 6

Photography courtesy of Hector Emanuel.

ISBN 978-1-942471-78-3 (paper)
ISBN 978-1-942471-99-8 (ebk)

10 9 8 7 6 5 4 3 2 1

Please visit our website at
www.WileyGlobalFinance.com.

FSC
www.fsc.org
MIX
Paper from
responsible sources
FSC® C101537

CONTENTS

⊙ indicates an optional segment

◙ indicates an optional segment

Portfolio Management

◙ indicates an optional segment

⧉ indicates an optional segment

Contents

◙ indicates an optional segment

How to Use the CFA Program Curriculum

Congratulations on reaching Level II of the Chartered Financial Analyst® (CFA®) Program. This exciting and rewarding program of study reflects your desire to become a serious investment professional. You are embarking on a program noted for its high ethical standards and the breadth of knowledge, skills, and abilities it develops. Your commitment to the CFA Program should be educationally and professionally rewarding.

The credential you seek is respected around the world as a mark of accomplishment and dedication. Each level of the program represents a distinct achievement in professional development. Successful completion of the program is rewarded with membership in a prestigious global community of investment professionals. CFA charterholders are dedicated to life-long learning and maintaining currency with the ever-changing dynamics of a challenging profession. The CFA Program represents the first step toward a career-long commitment to professional education.

The CFA examination measures your mastery of the core skills required to succeed as an investment professional. These core skills are the basis for the Candidate Body of Knowledge (CBOK™). The CBOK consists of four components:

- A broad outline that lists the major topic areas covered in the CFA Program (www.cfainstitute.org/cbok);

- Topic area weights that indicate the relative exam weightings of the top-level topic areas (www.cfainstitute.org/level_II);

- Learning outcome statements (LOS) that advise candidates about the specific knowledge, skills, and abilities they should acquire from readings covering a topic area (LOS are provided in candidate study sessions and at the beginning of each reading); and

- The CFA Program curriculum, which contains the readings and end-of-reading questions, that candidates receive upon exam registration.

Therefore, the key to your success on the CFA examinations is studying and understanding the CBOK. The following sections provide background on the CBOK, the organization of the curriculum, and tips for developing an effective study program.

CURRICULUM DEVELOPMENT PROCESS

The CFA Program is grounded in the practice of the investment profession. Beginning with the Global Body of Investment Knowledge (GBIK), CFA Institute performs a continuous practice analysis with investment professionals around the world to determine the knowledge, skills, and abilities (competencies) that are relevant to the profession. Regional expert panels and targeted surveys are conducted annually to verify and reinforce the continuous feedback from the GBIK collaborative website. The practice analysis process ultimately defines the CBOK. The CBOK reflects the competencies that are generally accepted and applied by investment professionals. These competencies are used in practice in a generalist context and are expected to be demonstrated by a recently qualified CFA charterholder.

The Education Advisory Committee, consisting of practicing charterholders, in conjunction with CFA Institute staff, designs the CFA Program curriculum in order to deliver the CBOK to candidates. The examinations, also written by charterholders, are designed to allow you to demonstrate your mastery of the CBOK as set forth in the CFA Program curriculum. As you structure your personal study program, you should emphasize mastery of the CBOK and the practical application of that knowledge. For more information on the practice analysis, CBOK, and development of the CFA Program curriculum, please visit www.cfainstitute.org.

ORGANIZATION OF THE CURRICULUM

The Level II CFA Program curriculum is organized into 10 topic areas. Each topic area begins with a brief statement of the material and the depth of knowledge expected.

Each topic area is then divided into one or more study sessions. These study sessions—17 sessions in the Level II curriculum—should form the basic structure of your reading and preparation.

Each study session includes a statement of its structure and objective and is further divided into specific reading assignments. An outline illustrating the organization of these 18 study sessions can be found at the front of each volume of the curriculum.

The readings and end-of-reading questions are the basis for all examination questions and are selected or developed specifically to teach the knowledge, skills, and abilities reflected in the CBOK. These readings are drawn from content commissioned by CFA Institute, textbook chapters, professional journal articles, research analyst reports, and cases. All readings include problems and solutions to help you understand and master the topic areas.

Reading-specific Learning Outcome Statements (LOS) are listed at the beginning of each reading. These LOS indicate what you should be able to accomplish after studying the reading. The LOS, the reading, and the end-of-reading questions are dependent on each other, with the reading and questions providing context for understanding the scope of the LOS.

You should use the LOS to guide and focus your study because each examination question is based on the assigned readings and one or more LOS. The readings provide context for the LOS and enable you to apply a principle or concept in a variety of scenarios. The candidate is responsible for the entirety of the required material in a study session, which includes the assigned readings as well as the end-of-reading questions and problems.

We encourage you to review the information about the LOS on our website (www.cfainstitute.org/programs/cfaprogram/courseofstudy/Pages/study_sessions.aspx), including the descriptions of LOS "command words" (www.cfainstitute.org/programs/Documents/cfa_and_cipm_los_command_words.pdf).

FEATURES OF THE CURRICULUM

OPTIONAL
SEGMENT

Required vs. Optional Segments   You should read all of an assigned reading. In some cases, though, we have reprinted an entire chapter or article and marked certain parts of the reading as "optional." The CFA examination is based only on the required segments, and the optional segments are included only when it is determined that they might help you to better understand the required segments (by seeing the required material in its full context). When an optional segment begins, you will see an icon and a dashed vertical bar in the outside margin that will continue until the optional segment ends, accompanied by another icon. *Unless the material is specifically marked as optional, you should assume it is required.* You should rely on the required segments and the reading-specific LOS in preparing for the examination.

END OPTIONAL SEGMENT

End-of-Reading Problems/Solutions   *All problems in the readings as well as their solutions (which are provided directly following the problems) are part of the curriculum and are required material for the exam.* When appropriate, we have included problems within and after the readings to demonstrate practical application and reinforce your understanding of the concepts presented. The problems are designed to help you learn these concepts and may serve as a basis for exam questions. Many of these questions are adapted from past CFA examinations.

Glossary and Index   For your convenience, we have printed a comprehensive glossary in each volume. Throughout the curriculum, a **bolded** word in a reading denotes a term defined in the glossary. The curriculum eBook is searchable, but we also publish an index that can be found on the CFA Institute website with the Level II study sessions.

Source Material   The authorship, publisher, and copyright owners are given for each reading for your reference. We recommend that you use the CFA Institute curriculum rather than the original source materials because the curriculum may include only selected pages from outside readings, updated sections within the readings, and problems and solutions tailored to the CFA Program. Note that some readings may contain a web address or URL. The referenced sites were live at the time the reading was written but may have been deactivated since then.

LOS Self-Check   We have inserted checkboxes next to each LOS that you can use to track your progress in mastering the concepts in each reading.

DESIGNING YOUR PERSONAL STUDY PROGRAM

Create a Schedule   An orderly, systematic approach to exam preparation is critical. You should dedicate a consistent block of time every week to reading and studying. Complete all reading assignments and the associated problems and solutions in each study session. Review the LOS both before and after you study each reading to ensure that you have mastered the applicable content and can demonstrate the knowledge, skill, or ability described by the LOS and the assigned reading. Use the LOS self-check to track your progress and highlight areas of weakness for later review.

As you prepare for your exam, we will e-mail you important exam updates, testing policies, and study tips. Be sure to read these carefully. Curriculum errata are periodically updated and posted on the study session page at www.cfainstitute.org.

Successful candidates report an average of more than 300 hours preparing for each exam. Your preparation time will vary based on your prior education and experience. The 2017 Level II curriculum has 17 study sessions, so a good plan is to devote 15–20 hours per week for 17 weeks to studying the material. Use the final four to six weeks before the exam to review what you have learned and practice with topic tests and mock exams. This recommendation, however, may underestimate the hours needed for appropriate examination preparation depending on your individual circumstances, relevant experience, and academic background. You will undoubtedly adjust your study time to conform to your own strengths and weaknesses and to your educational and professional background.

You will probably spend more time on some study sessions than on others, but on average you should plan on devoting 15–20 hours per study session. You should allow ample time for both in-depth study of all topic areas and additional concentration on those topic areas for which you feel the least prepared.

An interactive study planner is available in the candidate resources area of our website to help you plan your study time. The interactive study planner recommends completion dates for each topic of the curriculum. Dates are determined based on study time available, exam topic weights, and curriculum weights. As you progress through the curriculum, the interactive study planner dynamically adjusts your study plan when you are running off schedule to help you stay on track for completion prior to the examination.

CFA Institute Topic Tests   The CFA Institute topic tests are intended to assess your mastery of individual topic areas as you progress through your studies. After each test, you will receive immediate feedback noting the correct responses and indicating the relevant assigned reading so you can identify areas of weakness for further study. For more information on the topic tests, please visit www.cfainstitute.org.

CFA Institute Mock Exams   The three-hour mock exams simulate the morning and afternoon sessions of the actual CFA examination, and are intended to be taken after you complete your study of the full curriculum so you can test your understanding of the curriculum and your readiness for the exam. You will receive feedback at the end of the mock exam, noting the correct responses and indicating the relevant assigned readings so you can assess areas of weakness for further study during your review period. We recommend that you take mock exams during the final stages of your preparation for the actual CFA examination. For more information on the mock examinations, please visit www.cfainstitute.org.

Preparatory Providers   After you enroll in the CFA Program, you may receive numerous solicitations for preparatory courses and review materials. When considering a prep course, make sure the provider is in compliance with the CFA Institute Prep Provider Guidelines Program (www.cfainstitute.org/utility/examprep/Pages/index.aspx). Just remember, there are no shortcuts to success on the CFA examinations; reading and studying the CFA curriculum is the key to success on the examination. The CFA examinations reference only the CFA Institute assigned curriculum—no preparatory course or review course materials are consulted or referenced.

SUMMARY

Every question on the CFA examination is based on the content contained in the required readings and on one or more LOS. Frequently, an examination question is based on a specific example highlighted within a reading or on a specific end-of-reading question and/or problem and its solution. To make effective use of the CFA Program curriculum, please remember these key points:

1   All pages of the curriculum are required reading for the examination except for occasional sections marked as optional. You may read optional pages as background, but you will not be tested on them.

2   All questions, problems, and their solutions—found at the end of readings—are part of the curriculum and are required study material for the examination.

3   You should make appropriate use of the topic tests and mock examinations and other resources available at www.cfainstitute.org.

4 Use the interactive study planner to create a schedule and commit sufficient study time to cover the 17 study sessions, review the materials, and take topic tests and mock examinations.

5 Some of the concepts in the study sessions may be superseded by updated rulings and/or pronouncements issued after a reading was published. Candidates are expected to be familiar with the overall analytical framework contained in the assigned readings. Candidates are not responsible for changes that occur after the material was written.

FEEDBACK

At CFA Institute, we are committed to delivering a comprehensive and rigorous curriculum for the development of competent, ethically grounded investment professionals. We rely on candidate and member feedback as we work to incorporate content, design, and packaging improvements. You can be assured that we will continue to listen to your suggestions. Please send any comments or feedback to info@cfainstitute.org. Ongoing improvements in the curriculum will help you prepare for success on the upcoming examinations and for a lifetime of learning as a serious investment professional.

Alternative Investments

TOPIC LEVEL LEARNING OUTCOME

The candidate should be able to analyze and evaluate real estate and private equity using appropriate valuation concepts and techniques.

15

Alternative Investments

This study session discusses the following categories of alternative investments: real estate, private equity, and commodities. Real estate investments, both private investment and investment through publicly traded securities, are described, and methods for analysis and evaluation are presented. Private equity, including venture capital and leveraged buyouts, is examined from the perspectives of a private equity firm evaluating equity investments for its portfolio and an investor evaluating participation in a private equity fund. The study session concludes with a discussion of commodities and commodity derivatives.

READING ASSIGNMENTS

Reading 43	Private Real Estate Investments by Jeffery D. Fisher and Bryan D. MacGregor, PhD, MRICS, MRTPI
Reading 44	Publicly Traded Real Estate Securities by Anthony Paolone, CFA, Ian Rossa O'Reilly, CFA, and David Kruth, CFA
Reading 45	Private Equity Valuation by Yves Courtois, CMT, CFA, and Tim Jenkinson, PhD
Reading 46	Commodities and Commodity Derivatives: An Introduction by David Burkart, CFA, and James Alan Finnegan, RMA, CFA

READING

43

Private Real Estate Investments

by Jeffrey D. Fisher and Bryan D. MacGregor, PhD, MRICS, MRPTI

Jeffrey D. Fisher (USA). Bryan D. MacGregor, PhD, MRICS, MRTPI, is at the University of Aberdeen, Scotland (United Kingdom).

LEARNING OUTCOMES

Mastery	The candidate should be able to:
☐	a. classify and describe basic forms of real estate investments;
☐	b. describe the characteristics, the classification, and basic segments of real estate;
☐	c. explain the role in a portfolio, economic value determinants, investment characteristics, and principal risks of private real estate;
☐	d. describe commercial property types, including their distinctive investment characteristics;
☐	e. compare the income, cost, and sales comparison approaches to valuing real estate properties;
☐	f. estimate and interpret the inputs (for example, net operating income, capitalization rate, and discount rate) to the direct capitalization and discounted cash flow valuation methods;
☐	g. calculate the value of a property using the direct capitalization and discounted cash flow valuation methods;
☐	h. compare the direct capitalization and discounted cash flow valuation methods;
☐	i. calculate the value of a property using the cost and sales comparison approaches;
☐	j. describe due diligence in private equity real estate investment;
☐	k. discuss private equity real estate investment indices, including their construction and potential biases;
☐	l. explain the role in a portfolio, the major economic value determinants, investment characteristics, principal risks, and due diligence of private real estate debt investment;
☐	m. calculate and interpret financial ratios used to analyze and evaluate private real estate investments.

1 INTRODUCTION

Real estate investments comprise a significant part of the portfolios of many investors, so understanding how to analyze real estate investments and evaluate the role of real estate investments in a portfolio is important. Real estate investments can take a variety of forms, from private equity investment in (ownership of) real estate properties (real estate properties, hereafter, may simply be referred to as real estate) to publicly traded debt investment, such as mortgage-backed securities. While this reading discusses the basic forms of real estate investments and provides an overview of the real estate market, its focus is private equity investment in commercial (or income-producing) real estate.

Private equity investment in real estate is sometimes referred to as direct ownership, in contrast to indirect ownership of real estate through publicly traded equity securities, such as real estate investment trusts (REITs). Similarly, lending in the private market, such as mortgage lending by banks or insurance companies, is sometimes referred to as direct lending. **Mortgages** are loans with real estate serving as collateral for the loan. Publicly traded debt investment, such as mortgage-backed securities (MBSs), are sometimes referred to as indirect lending. Each form of real estate investment has characteristics that an investor should be aware of when considering and making a real estate investment. Also, real estate has characteristics that differentiate it from other asset classes.

Private real estate investments—equity and debt—are often included in the portfolios of investors with long-term investment horizons and with the ability to tolerate relatively lower liquidity. Examples of such investors are endowments, pension funds, and life insurance companies. Other real estate investors may have short investment horizons, such as a real estate developer who plans to sell a real estate property to a long-term investor once the development of the property is complete. Publicly traded, pooled-investment forms of real estate investments, such as REITs, may be suitable for investors with short investment horizons and higher liquidity needs.

Valuation of commercial real estate properties constitutes a significant portion of this reading. Regardless of the form of real estate investment, the value of the underlying real estate is critical to its value. The concepts and valuation techniques described in this reading are generally applicable to global real estate markets. Valuation of the underlying real estate is of importance to private real estate equity and debt investors because the value of each type of investment is inextricably tied to the value of the underlying real estate. Also, because real estate properties do not transact frequently and are unique, we rely on estimates of value or appraisals rather than transaction prices to assess changes in value over time. However, transaction prices of similar properties can be useful in estimating value. In creating real estate indices that serve as benchmarks for performance evaluation, appraised values—rather than transaction prices—are often used. In recent years, several indices based on actual transactions have been developed. Both types of indices are discussed in this reading.

The reading is organized as follows: Section 2 describes basic forms of real estate investment, covering equity and debt investments and public and private investments. Section 3 discusses characteristics of real estate and classifications of real estate properties. Section 4 focuses on private equity investment in real estate. It discusses benefits of and risks associated with investing in real estate. The main types of commercial real estate markets and characteristics of each are covered. Section 5 introduces the appraisal (valuation) process and the main approaches used by appraisers to estimate value. Section 6 discusses the income approach, and Section 7 discusses the cost and sales comparison approaches. Section 8 discusses reconciling the results from these three approaches. Section 9 discusses the due diligence process typically followed when acquiring real estate investments. Section 10 presents a brief international perspective. Section 11 considers real estate market indices. Section 12 discusses some aspects of private market real estate debt. A summary and practice problems complete the reading.

REAL ESTATE INVESTMENT: BASIC FORMS

2

Investment in real estate has been defined from a capital market perspective in the context of quadrants, or four main areas through which capital can be invested. The quadrants are a result of two dimensions of investment. The first dimension is whether the investment is made in the private or public market. The private market often involves investing directly in an asset (for example, purchasing a property) or getting a claim on an asset (for example, through providing a mortgage to the purchaser). The investment can made indirectly through a number of different investment vehicles, such as a partnership or commingled real estate fund (CREF). In either case, the transactions occur in the private market. The public market does not involve such direct investment; rather, it involves investing in a security with claims on the underlying position(s)—for example, through investments in a real estate investment trust (REIT), a real estate operating company (REOC), or a mortgage-backed security.

The second dimension, as illustrated in the examples above, is whether the investment is structured as equity or debt. An "equity" investor has an ownership interest: Such an investor may be the owner of the real estate property or may invest in securities of a company or a REIT that owns the real estate property. The owner of the real estate property controls such decisions as whether to obtain a mortgage loan on the real estate, who should handle property management, and when to sell the real estate. In the case of a REIT, that control is delegated to the managers of the REIT by the shareholders. A "debt" investor is in a position of lender: Such an investor may loan funds to the "entity" acquiring the real estate property or may invest in securities based on real estate lending. Typically, the real estate property is used as collateral for a mortgage loan. If there is a loan on the real estate (mortgage), then the mortgage lender has a priority claim on the real estate. The value of the equity investor's interest in the real estate is equal to the value of the real estate less the amount owed to the mortgage lender.

Combining the two dimensions, we have four quadrants: private equity, public equity, private debt, and public debt, as illustrated in Exhibit 1.

Exhibit 1	Examples of the Basic Forms of Real Estate Investment	
	Equity	**Debt**
Private	Direct investments in real estate. This can be through sole ownership, joint ventures, real estate limited partnerships, or other forms of commingled funds.	Mortgages
Publicly traded	Shares of real estate operating companies and shares of REITs	Mortgage-backed securities (residential and commercial)

Each of the basic forms of real estate investment has its own risks, expected returns, regulations, legal structures, and market structures. Private real estate investment, compared with publicly traded real estate investment, typically involves larger investments because of the indivisibility of real estate property and is more illiquid. Publicly traded real estate investment allows the real estate property to remain undivided but the ownership or claim on the property to be divided. This leads to more liquidity and allows investors to diversify by purchasing ownership interests in more properties than if an entire property had to be owned by a single investor and/or to diversify by having claims against more properties than if an entire mortgage had to be funded and retained by a single lender.

Real estate requires management. Private equity investment (ownership) in real estate properties requires property management expertise on the part of the owner or the hiring of property managers. Real estate owned by REOCs and REITs is professionally managed and requires no real estate management expertise on the part of an investor in shares of the REOCs and REITs.

Equity investors generally expect a higher rate of return than lenders (debt investors) because they take on more risk. The lenders' claims on the cash flows and proceeds from sale must be satisfied before the equity investors can receive anything. As the amount of debt on a property, or financial leverage, increases, risk increases for both debt and equity and an investor's—whether debt or equity—return expectations will increase. Of course, the risk is that the higher return will not materialize, and the risk is even higher for an equity investor.

Debt investors in real estate, whether through private or public markets, expect to receive their return from promised cash flows and typically do not participate in any appreciation in value of the underlying real estate. Thus, debt investments in real estate are similar to other fixed-income investments, such as bonds. The returns to equity real estate investors have two components: an income stream resulting from such activities as renting the property and a capital appreciation component resulting from changes in the value of the underlying real estate. If the returns to equity real estate investors are less than perfectly positively correlated with the returns to stocks and/or bonds, then adding equity real estate investments to a traditional portfolio will potentially have diversification benefits.

Real estate markets in each of the four quadrants in Exhibit 1 have evolved and matured to create relatively efficient market structures for accessing all types of capital for real estate (i.e., public and private debt and equity). Such structures are critical for the success of the asset class for both lenders and equity investors. The categorization of real estate investment into the four quadrants helps investors identify the form(s) that best fit(s) their objectives. For example, some investors may prefer to own and manage real estate. Other investors may prefer the greater liquidity and professional management associated with purchasing publicly traded REITs. Other investors may prefer mortgage lending because it involves less risk than equity investment or unsecured lending; the mortgage lender has a priority claim on the real estate used as collateral for the mortgage. Still other investors may want to invest in each quadrant or allocate more capital to one quadrant or another over time as they perceive shifts in the relative value of each. Each quadrant offers differences in risk and expected return, including the impact of taxes on the return. So investors should explore the risk and return characteristics of each quadrant as part of their investment decisions. The balance of this reading focuses on private investment in real estate—particularly, equity investment.

EXAMPLE 1

Form of Investment

An investor is interested in adding real estate to her portfolio for the first time. She has no previous real estate experience but thinks adding real estate will provide some diversification benefits. She is concerned about liquidity because she may need the money in a year or so. Which form of investment is *most likely* appropriate for her?

A   Shares of REITs

B   Mortgage-backed securities

C   Direct ownership of commercial real estate property

Solution:

A is correct. She is probably better-off investing in shares of publicly traded REITs, which provide liquidity, have professional management, and require a lower investment than direct ownership of real estate. Using REITs, she may be able to put together a diversified real estate investment portfolio. Although REITs are more correlated with stocks than direct ownership of real estate, direct ownership is much less liquid and a lot of properties are needed to have a diversified real estate portfolio. Also, adding shares of REITs to her current portfolio should provide more diversification benefits than adding debt in the form of mortgage-backed securities and will allow her to benefit from any appreciation of the real estate. Debt investments in real estate, such as MBSs, are similar to other fixed-income investments, such as bonds. The difference is that their income streams are secured on real estate assets, which means that the risks are default risks linked to the performance of the real estate assets and the ability of mortgagees to pay interest. In contrast, adding equity real estate investments to a traditional portfolio will potentially have diversification benefits.

REAL ESTATE: CHARACTERISTICS AND CLASSIFICATIONS

3

Regardless of the form of investment, the value of the underlying real estate property is critical to the performance of the investment. If the property increases in value, the equity investor will benefit from the appreciation and the debt investor is more likely to receive the promised cash flows. If the property declines in value, however, the equity investor and even the debt investor may experience a loss.

3.1 Characteristics

Real estate has characteristics that distinguish it from the other main investment asset classes and that complicate the measurement and assessment of performance. These include the following:

■ *Heterogeneity and fixed location*: Whereas all bonds of a particular issue and stocks of a particular type in a specific company are identical, no two properties are the same. Even identically constructed buildings with the same tenants and leases will be at different locations. Buildings differ in use, size, location, age, type of construction, quality, and tenant and leasing arrangements. These factors are important in trying to establish value and also in the amount of specific risk in a real estate investment.

■ *High unit value*: The unit value of a real estate property is much larger than that of a bond or stock because of its indivisibility. The amount required to make a private equity investment in real estate limits the pool of potential private equity investors and the ability to construct a diversified real estate portfolio. This factor is important in the development of publicly traded securities, such as REITs, which allow partial ownership of an indivisible asset.

■ *Management intensive*: An investor in bonds or stocks is not expected to be actively involved in managing the company, but a private real estate equity investor or direct owner of real estate has responsibility for management of the real estate, including maintaining the properties, negotiating leases, and collecting rents. This active management, whether done by the owner or by hired property managers, creates additional costs that must be taken into account.

■ *High transaction costs*: Buying and selling of real estate is also costly and time consuming because others, such as appraisers, lawyers, and construction professionals, are likely to be involved in the process until a transaction is completed.

■ *Depreciation*: Buildings depreciate as a result of use and the passage of time. A building's value may also change as the desirability of its location and its design changes from the perspective of end users.

■ *Need for debt capital*: Because of the large amounts required to purchase and develop real estate properties, the ability to access funds and the cost of funds in the credit markets are important. As a result, real estate values are sensitive to the cost and availability of debt capital. When debt capital is scarce or interest rates are high, the value of real estate tends to be lower than when debt capital is readily available or interest rates are low.

■ *Illiquidity*: As a result of several of the above factors, real estate properties are relatively illiquid. They may take a significant amount of time to market and to sell at a price that is close to the owner's perceived fair market value.

■ *Price determination*: As a result of the heterogeneity of real estate properties and the low volume of transactions, estimates of value or appraisals rather than transaction prices are usually necessary to assess changes in value or expected selling price over time. However, the transaction prices of similar properties are often considered in estimating the value of or appraising a property. The limited number of participants in the market for a property, combined with the importance of local knowledge, makes it harder to know the market value of a property. In a less efficient market, those who have superior information and skill at evaluating properties may have an advantage. This is quite different from stocks in publicly traded companies, where many buyers and sellers value and transact in the shares in an active market.

The above factors fundamentally affect the nature of real estate investment. To overcome some of these problems, markets in securitized real estate, most notably through REITs, have expanded. REITs are a type of publicly traded equity investment in real estate. The REIT provides or hires professional property managers. Investing in shares of a REIT typically allows exposure to a diversified portfolio of real estate. The shares are typically liquid, and active trading results in prices that are more likely to reflect market value. A separate reading discusses REITs in greater detail.

EXAMPLE 2

Investment Characteristics

An investor states that he likes investing in real estate because the market is less efficient. Why might an investor prefer to invest in a less efficient market rather than a more efficient market?

Solution:

In a less efficient market, an investor with superior knowledge and information and/or a better understanding of the appropriate price to pay for properties (superior valuation skills) may earn a higher return, provided that market prices adjust to intrinsic values, by making more informed investment decisions.

3.2 Classifications

There are many different types of real estate properties. One simple classification distinguishes between residential and non-residential properties. Another potential classification is single-family residential, commercial, farmland, and timberland.

Residential properties include *single-family houses* and *multi-family properties*, such as apartments. In general, residential properties are properties that provide housing for individuals or families. Single-family properties may be owner-occupied or rental properties, whereas multi-family properties are rental properties even if the owner or manager occupies one of the units. Multi-family housing is usually differentiated by location (urban or suburban) and shape of structure (high-rise, low-rise, or garden apartments). Residential real estate properties, particularly multi-family properties, purchased with the intent to let, lease, or rent (in other words, produce income) are typically included in the category of **commercial real estate properties** (sometimes called income-producing real estate properties).

Non-residential properties include commercial properties other than multi-family properties, farmland, and timberland. Commercial real estate is by far the largest class of real estate for investment and is the focus of this reading. Commercial real estate properties are typically classified by end use. In addition to multi-family properties, commercial real estate properties include office, industrial and warehouse, retail, and hospitality properties. However, the same *building* can serve more than one end use. For example, it can contain both office and retail space. In fact, the same building can contain residential as well as non-residential uses of space. A property that has a combination of end users is usually referred to as a *mixed-use development*. Thus, the classifications should be viewed mainly as a convenient way of categorizing the use of space for the purpose of analyzing the determinants of supply and demand and economic performance for each type of space.

- *Office* properties range from major multi-tenant office buildings found in the central business districts of most large cities to single-tenant office buildings. They are often built to suit or considering the needs of a specific tenant or tenants. An example of a property developed and built considering the needs of prospective tenants would be a medical office building near a hospital.

- *Industrial and warehouse* properties include property used for light or heavy manufacturing as well as associated warehouse space. This category includes special purpose buildings designed specifically for industrial use that would be difficult to convert to another use, buildings used by wholesale distributors, and combinations of warehouse/showroom and office facilities. Older buildings that originally had one use may be converted to another use. For example, office space may be converted to warehouse or light industrial space and warehouse or light industrial space may be converted to residential or office space. Frequently, the conversion is based on the desirability of the area for the new use.

■ *Retail* properties vary from large shopping centers with several stores, including large department stores, as tenants to small stores occupied by individual tenants. As indicated earlier, it is also common to find retail space combined with office space, particularly on the ground floor of office buildings in major cities, or residential space.

■ *Hospitality* properties vary considerably in size and amenities available. Motels and smaller hotels are used primarily as a place for business travelers and families to spend a night. These properties may have limited amenities and are often located very close to a major highway. Hotels designed for tourists who plan to stay longer usually have a restaurant, a swimming pool, and other amenities. They are also typically located near other attractions that tourists visit. Hotels at "destination resorts" provide the greatest amount of amenities. These resorts are away from major cities, where the guests usually stay for several days or even several weeks. Facilities at these resort hotels can be quite luxurious, with several restaurants, swimming pools, nearby golf courses, and so on. Hotels that cater to convention business may be either in a popular destination resort or located near the center of a major city.

■ *Other types* of commercial real estate that can be owned by investors include parking facilities, restaurants, and recreational uses, such as country clubs, marinas, sports complexes, and so on. Retail space that complements the recreational activity (such as gift and golf shops) is often associated with, or part of, these recreational real estate properties. Dining facilities and possibly hotel or residential facilities may also be present. A property might also be intended for use by a special institution, such as a hospital, a government agency, or a university. The physical structure of a building intended for a specific use may be similar to the physical structure of buildings intended for other uses. For example, government office space is similar to other office space. Some buildings intended for one use may not easily be adapted for other uses. For example, buildings used by universities and hospitals may not easily be adapted to other uses.

Some commercial property types are more management intensive than others. Of the main commercial property types, hotels require the most day-to-day management and are more like operating a business than multi-family, office, or retail space. Shopping centers (shopping malls) are also relatively management intensive because it is important for the owner to maintain the right tenant mix and promote the mall. Many of the "other" property types, such as recreational facilities, can also require significant management. Usually, investors consider properties that are more management intensive as riskier because of the operational risks. Therefore, investors typically require a higher rate of return on these management-intensive properties.

Farmland and timberland are unique in that each can be used to produce a saleable commodity. Farmland can be used to produce crops or as pastureland for livestock, and timberland can be used to produce timber (wood) for use in the forest products industry. While crops and livestock are produced annually, timber has a much longer growing cycle before the product is saleable. Also, the harvesting of timber can be deferred if market conditions are perceived to be unfavorable. Sales of the commodities or leasing the land to another entity generate income. Harvest quantities and commodity prices are the primary determinants of revenue. These are affected by many factors outside of the control of the producer and include weather and population demographics. In addition to income-generating potential, both farmland and timberland have potential for capital appreciation.

Commercial Real Estate Segments

Commercial real estate properties are *most likely* to include:

A   residential, industrial, hospitality, retail, and office.

B   multi-family, industrial, warehouse, retail, and office.

C   multi-family, industrial, hospitality, retail, and timberland.

Solution:

B is correct. Commercial real estate properties include multi-family, industrial, warehouse, retail, and office as well as hospitality and other. Residential properties include single-family, owner-occupied homes as well as income-producing (commercial) residential properties. Timberland is a unique category of real estate.

PRIVATE MARKET REAL ESTATE EQUITY INVESTMENTS

4

There are many different types of equity real estate investors, ranging from individual investors to large pension funds, sovereign wealth funds, and publicly traded real estate companies. Hereafter, for simplicity, the term *investor* refers to an equity investor in real estate. Although there may be some differences in the motivations for each type of investor, they all hope to achieve one or more of the following benefits of equity real estate investment:

- *Current income*: Investors may expect to earn current income on the property through letting, leasing, or renting the property. Investors expect that market demand for space in the property will be sufficient to produce net income after collecting rents and paying operating expenses. This income constitutes part of an investor's return. The amount available to the investor will be affected by taxes and financing costs.

- *Price appreciation (capital appreciation)*: Investors often expect prices to rise over time. Any price increase also contributes to an investor's total return. Investors may anticipate selling properties after holding them for a period of time and realizing the capital appreciation.

- *Inflation hedge*: Investors may expect both rents and real estate prices to rise in an inflationary environment. If rents and prices do in fact increase with inflation, then equity real estate investments provide investors with an inflationary hedge. This means that the real rate of return, as opposed to the nominal rate of return, may be less volatile for equity real estate investments.

- *Diversification*: Investors may anticipate diversification benefits. Real estate performance has not typically been highly correlated with the performance of other asset classes, such as stocks, bonds, or money market funds, so adding real estate to a portfolio may lower the risk of the portfolio (that is, the volatility of returns) relative to the expected return.

Exhibit 2 shows correlations of returns, for the period 1978–2009, between several asset classes in the United States based on various reported indices. The indices used are the National Council of Real Estate Investment Fiduciaries (NCREIF) Property Index for private real estate equity investments, the S&P 500 Index for stocks, the

Barclays Capital Government Bond for bonds, the National Association of Real Estate Investment Trusts (NAREIT) Equity REIT Index for publicly traded real estate investments, 90-day T-bills, and the all items US Consumer Price Index for All Urban Consumers (CPI-U).

Note that the correlation between the NCREIF index and the S&P 500 is relatively low and the correlation between the NCREIF index and bonds is negative. This indicates the potential for diversification benefits of adding private equity real estate investment to a stock and bond portfolio. Also note that publicly traded REITs have a higher correlation with stocks and bonds than private real estate, which suggests that public and private real estate do not necessarily provide the same diversification benefits. When real estate is publicly traded, it tends to behave more like the rest of the stock market than the real estate market. However, some argue that because the NCREIF index is appraisal based and lags changes in the transactions market, its correlation with stock indices that are based on transactions is dampened. This issue is discussed in more detail later in the reading. As a final note on the correlations, note that the NCREIF index had a higher correlation with the CPI-U than the other alternatives with the exception of T-bills. This suggests that private equity real estate investments may provide some inflation protection.

Although the correlations discussed above are based on US data, evidence suggests that real estate provides similar diversification benefits in other countries.

Exhibit 2	Correlation among Returns on Various Asset Classes (1978–2009)					
	CPI-U	**Bonds**[a]	**S&P 500**	**T-Bills**	**NCREIF**[b]	**REITs**[c]
CPI-U	1					
Bonds	−0.2423	1				
S&P 500	0.0114	0.0570	1			
T-bills	0.4885	0.1586	0.0953	1		
NCREIF	0.3214	−0.0978	0.1363	0.3911	1	
REITs	0.1135	0.1258	0.5946	0.0602	0.2527	1

[a] Barclays Capital Government Bond
[b] National Council of Real Estate Investment Fiduciaries Property Index (NPI)
[c] National Association of Real Estate Investment Trusts Equity REIT Index

▪ *Tax Benefits*: A final reason for investing in real estate, which may be more important to some investors in certain countries than others, is the preferential tax benefits that may result. Private real estate investments may receive a favorable tax treatment compared with other investments. In other words, the same before-tax return may result in a higher after-tax return on real estate investments compared with the after-tax return on other possible investments. The preferential tax treatment in the United States comes from the fact that real estate can be depreciated for tax purposes over a shorter period than the period over which the property actually deteriorates. Although some real estate investors, such as pension funds, do not normally pay taxes, they compete with taxable investors who might be willing to pay more for the same property. Publicly traded REITs also have some tax benefits in some countries. For example, in the United States, there is no corporate income tax paid by the REIT. That is, by qualifying for REIT status, the corporation is exempt from corporate taxation as long as it follows certain guidelines required to maintain REIT status.

EXAMPLE 4

Motivations for Investing in Real Estate

Why would an investor want to include real estate equity investments in a portfolio that already has a diversified mixture of stocks and bonds?

Solution:

Real estate equity offers diversification benefits because it is less than perfectly correlated with stocks and bonds; this is particularly true of direct ownership (private equity investment). In other words, there are times when stocks and bonds may perform poorly but private equity real estate investments perform well and vice versa. Thus, adding real estate equity investments to a portfolio may reduce the volatility of the portfolio.

4.1 Risk Factors

Investors want to have an expected return that compensates them for incurring risk. The higher the risk, the higher should be the expected return. In this section, we consider risk factors associated with investing in commercial real estate. Most of the risk factors listed affect the value of the real estate property and, therefore, the investment—equity or debt—in the property. Leverage affects returns on investments in real estate but not the value of the underlying real estate property. Following are characteristic sources of risk or risk factors of real estate investment.

- *Business conditions*: Fundamentally, the real estate business involves renting space to users. The demand for space depends on a myriad of international, national, regional, and local economic conditions. GDP, employment, household income, interest rates, and inflation are particularly relevant to real estate. Changes in economic conditions will affect real estate investments because both current income and real estate values may be affected.

- *Long lead time for new development*: New development projects typically require a considerable amount of time from the point the project is first conceived until all the approvals are obtained, the development is complete, and it is leased up. During this time, market conditions can change considerably from what was initially anticipated. If the market has weakened, rents can be lower and vacancy higher than originally expected, resulting in lower returns to the developer. Alternatively, the demand can be greater than was anticipated, leading to a shortage of space to meet current demand. These dynamics tend to result in wide price swings for real estate over the development period.

- *Cost and availability of capital*: Real estate must compete with other assets for debt and equity capital. The willingness of investors to invest in real estate depends on the availability of debt capital and the cost of that capital as well as the expected return on other investments, such as stocks and bonds, which affects the availability of equity capital. A shortage of debt capital and high interest rates can significantly reduce the demand for real estate and lower prices. Alternatively, an environment of low interest rates and easy access to debt capital can increase the demand for real estate investments. These capital market forces can cause prices to increase or decrease regardless of any changes in the underlying demand for real estate from tenants.

- *Unexpected inflation*: Inflation risk depends on how the income and price of an asset is affected by unexpected inflation. Fixed-income securities are usually negatively affected by inflation because the purchasing power of the income decreases with inflation and the face value is fixed at maturity. Real estate may offer some inflation protection if the leases provide for rent increases due to inflation or the ability to pass any increases in expenses due to inflation on to tenants. Construction costs for real estate also tend to increase with inflation, which puts upward pressure on real estate values. Thus, real estate equity investments may not have much inflation risk depending on how net operating income (NOI) and values respond to inflation being higher than expected. In a weak market with high vacancy rates and low rents, when new construction is not feasible, values may not increase with inflation.

- *Demographics*: Linked to the above factors are a variety of demographic factors, such as the size and age distribution of the population in the local market, the distribution of socio-economic groups, and rates of new household formation. These demographic factors affect the demand for real estate.

- *Lack of liquidity*: Liquidity is the ability to convert an asset to cash quickly without a significant price discount or loss of principal. Real estate is considered to have low liquidity (high liquidity risk) because of the large value of an individual investment and the time and cost it takes to sell a property at its current value. Buyers are unlikely to make large investments without conducting adequate due diligence, which takes both time and money. Therefore, buyers are not likely to agree to a quick purchase without a significant discount to the price. Illiquidity means both a longer time to realize cash and also a risk that the market may move against the investor.

- *Environmental*: Real estate values can be affected by environmental conditions, including contaminants related to a prior owner or an adjacent property owner. Such problems can significantly reduce the value because of the costs incurred to correct them.

- *Availability of information*: Of increasing importance to investors, especially when investing globally, is having adequate information to make informed investment decisions. A lack of information to do the property analysis adds to the risk of the investment. The amount of data available on real estate space and capital markets has improved considerably. While some countries have much more information available to investors than others, in general, the availability of information has been increasing on a global basis because real estate investment has become more global and investors want to evaluate investment alternatives on a comparable basis. Real estate indices have become available in many countries around the world. These indices allow investors to benchmark the performance of their properties against that of peers and also provide a better understanding of the risk and return for real estate compared with other asset classes. Indices are discussed in more detail in Section 11.

- *Management*: Management involves the cost of monitoring an investment. Investment management can be categorized into two levels: asset management and property management. Asset management involves monitoring the investment's financial performance and making changes as needed. Property management is exclusive to real estate investments. It involves the overall day-to-day operation of the property and the physical maintenance of the property, including the buildings. Management risk reflects the ability of the property and asset managers to make the right decisions regarding the operation of the property, such as negotiating leases, maintaining the property, marketing the property, and doing renovations when necessary.

- *Leverage*: Leverage affects returns on investments in real estate but not the value of the underlying real estate property. Leverage is the use of borrowed funds to finance some of the purchase price of an investment. The ratio of borrowed funds to total purchase price is known as the loan-to-value (LTV) ratio. Higher LTV ratios mean greater amounts of leverage. Real estate transactions can be more highly leveraged than most other types of investments. But increasing leverage also increases risk because the lender has the first claim on the cash flow and on the value of the property if there is default on the loan. A small change in NOI can result in a relatively large change in the amount of cash flow available to the equity investor after making the mortgage payment.

■ *Other risk factors*: Many other risk factors exist, such as unobserved physical defects in the property, natural disasters (for example, earthquakes and hurricanes), and acts of terrorism. Unfortunately, the biggest risk may be one that was unidentified as a risk at the time of purchasing the property. Unidentified risks can be devastating to investors.

Risks that are identified can be planned for to some extent. In some cases, a risk can be converted to a known dollar amount through insurance. In other cases, risk can be reduced through diversification or shifted to another party through contractual arrangements. For example, the risk of expenses increasing can be shifted to tenants by including expense reimbursement clauses in their leases. The risk that remains must be evaluated and reflected in contractual terms (for example, rental prices) such that the expected return is equal to or greater than the required return necessary to make the investment.

EXAMPLE 5

Commercial Real Estate Risk

An investor is concerned about interest rates rising and decides that she will pay all cash and not borrow any money to avoid incurring any risk due to interest rate changes. This strategy is *most likely* to:

A reduce the risk due to leverage.

B eliminate the risk due to inflation.

C eliminate the risk due to interest rate changes.

Solution:

A is correct. If less money is borrowed, there is less risk due to the use of financial leverage. There is still risk related to changes in interest rates. If interest rates rise, the value of real estate will likely be affected even if the investor did not borrow any money. Higher interest rates mean investors require a higher rate of return on all assets. The resale price of the property will likely depend on the cost of debt to the next buyer, who may be more likely to obtain debt financing. Furthermore, the investor may be better off getting a loan at a fixed interest rate before rates rise. There is still risk of inflation, although real estate tends to have a low amount of inflation risk. But borrowing less money doesn't necessarily mean the property is less affected by inflation.

4.2 Real Estate Risk and Return Relative to Stocks and Bonds

The characteristics of real estate and the risk factors described above ultimately affect the risk and return of equity real estate investments. The structure of leases between the owner and tenants also affects risk and return. More will be discussed about the nature of real estate leases later in this reading, but in general, leases can be thought of as giving equity real estate investment a bond-like characteristic because the tenant has a legal agreement to make periodic payments to the owner. At the end of the lease term, however, there will be uncertainty as to whether the tenant will renew the lease and what the rental rate will be at that time. These issues will depend on the availability of competing space and also on factors that affect the profitability of the companies leasing the space and the strength of the overall economy in much the same way that stock prices are affected by the same factors. These factors give a stock market characteristic to the risk of real estate. On balance, because of these two influences (bond-like and stock-like characteristics), real estate, as an asset class, tends to have a risk and return (based on historical data) profile that falls between the risk and return profiles of stocks and bonds. By this, we mean the risk and return characteristics of a portfolio of real estate versus a portfolio of stocks and a portfolio of bonds. An individual real estate investment could certainly have risk that is greater or less than that of an individual stock or bond. Exhibit 3 illustrates the basic risk–return relationships of stocks, bonds, and private equity real estate. In Exhibit 3, risk is measured by the standard deviation of expected returns.

| Exhibit 3 | Returns and Risks of Private Equity Real Estate Compared with Stocks and Bonds |

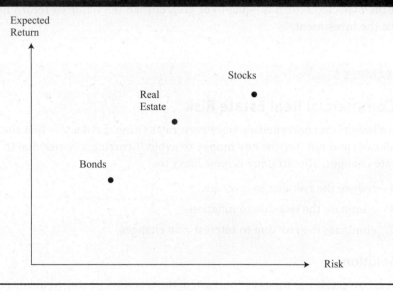

EXAMPLE 6

Investment Risk

Which is a riskier investment, private equity real estate or bonds? Explain why.

Solution:

Empirical evidence suggests that private equity real estate is riskier than bonds. Although real estate leases offer income streams somewhat like bonds, the income expected when leases renew can be quite uncertain and depend on market conditions at that time, which is unlike the more certain face value of a bond at maturity.

4.3 Commercial Real Estate

In this section, the main economic factors that influence demand for each commercial real estate property type and typical lease terms are discussed. It is important to discuss lease terms because they affect a property's value. The main property types included in institutional investors' portfolios are office, industrial and warehouse, retail, and multi-family (apartments). These property types are often considered the *core* property types used to create a portfolio that is relatively low risk, assuming the properties are in good locations and well leased (fiscally sound and responsible tenants, low vacancies, and good rental terms). Another type of property that might be held by an institutional investor is hospitality properties (for example, hotels). Hotels are usually considered riskier because there are no leases and their performance may be highly correlated with the business cycle—especially if there is a restaurant and the hotel depends on convention business.

For each property type, location is a critical factor in determining value. Properties with the highest value per unit of space are in the best locations and have modern features and functionality. Moderately valued properties are typically in adequate but not prime locations and/or have slightly outdated features. Properties with the lowest values per unit of space are in poor locations and have outdated features.

4.3.1 *Office*

The demand for office properties depends heavily on employment growth—especially in those industries that use large amounts of office space, such as finance and insurance. The typical amount of space used per employee is also important because it tends to increase when the economy is strong and decline when the economy is weak. There also has been a tendency for the average amount of space per employee to decrease over time as technology has allowed more employees to spend more time working away from the office and less permanent space is needed.

The average length of an office building lease varies globally. For example, leases on office space average 3–5 years in the United States and around 10 years in the United Kingdom. However, lease lengths may vary based on a number of factors, including the desirability of the property and the financial strength of the tenant as well as other terms in the lease, such as provisions for future rent changes and whether there are options to extend the lease.

An important consideration in office leases is whether the owner or tenant incurs the risk of operating expenses, such as utilities, increasing in the future. A "net lease" requires the tenant to be responsible for paying operating expenses, whereas a "gross lease" requires the owner to pay the operating expenses. The rent for a net lease is lower than that for an equivalent gross lease because the tenant must bear the operating expenses as well as the risk of expenses being higher than expected.

Not all office leases are structured as net or gross leases. For example, a lease may be structured so that in the first year of the lease, the owner is responsible for paying the operating expenses and for every year of the lease after that, the owner pays for expenses up to the amount paid in the first year. Any increase in expenses above that amount is "passed through" to the tenant as an "expense reimbursement." That is, the tenant bears the risk of any increase in expenses, although the owner benefits from any decline in expenses. In a multi-tenant building, the expenses may be prorated among the tenants on the basis of the amount of space they are leasing. While having a small number of tenants can simplify managing a property, it increases risk. If one tenant gets into financial difficulties or decides not to renew a lease, it can have a significant effect on cash flows.

There are differences in how leases are structured over time and in different countries. It is important to have an understanding of how leases are typically structured in a market and to stay informed about changes in the typical structure. Lease terms will affect the return and risk to the investor. For example, in the United Kingdom, until the early 1990s, lease terms averaged about 20 years in length, but they have now fallen by nearly half. Rents are typically fixed for five years and then set at the higher of the then market rent or contract rent upon review; these are known as upward-only rent reviews. Leases are typically on a full repairing and insuring (FRI) basis; the tenant is responsible for most costs. Therefore, detailed cost (expense) analysis is much less important in deriving net operating income—a critical measure in estimating the value of a commercial property—in the United Kingdom than in markets where operating costs are typically the responsibility of the owner.

EXAMPLE 7

Net and Gross Leases

What is the net rent equivalent for an office building where the gross rent is $20 per square foot and operating expenses are $8 per square foot?

Solution:

On a gross lease, the owner pays the operating expense, whereas on a net lease the tenant pays. So we might expect the rent on a net lease to be $20 − $8 or $12 per square foot. Because the risk of change in operating expenses is borne by the tenant rather than the owner, the rent might even be lower than $12.

4.3.2 *Industrial and Warehouse*

The demand for industrial and warehouse space is heavily dependent on the overall strength of the economy and economic growth. The demand for warehouse space is also dependent on import and export activity in the economy. Industrial leases are often net leases, although gross leases or leases with expense reimbursements, as described above for office properties, also occur.

4.3.3 *Retail*

The demand for retail space depends heavily on trends in consumer spending. Consumer spending, in turn, depends on the health of the economy, job growth, population growth, and savings rates.

Retail lease terms, including length of leases and rental rates, vary not only on the basis of the quality of the property but also by the size and the importance of the tenant. For example, in the United States, the length of leases for the smaller tenants in a shopping center are typically three to five years and are longer for larger "anchor" tenants, such as a department store. Anchor tenants may be given rental terms designed to attract them to the property. The quality of anchor tenants is a factor in attracting other tenants.

A unique aspect of many retail leases is the requirement that the tenants pay additional rent once their sales reach a certain level. This type of lease is referred to as a "percentage lease." The lease will typically specify a "minimum rent" that must be paid regardless of the tenant's sales and the basis for calculating percentage rent once the tenant's sales reach a certain level or breakpoint. For example, the lease may specify a minimum rent of $30 per square foot plus 10 percent of sales over $300 per square foot. Note that at the breakpoint of $300 per square foot in sales, we obtain the same rent per square foot based on either the minimum rent of $30 or 10 percent of $300. This is a typical way of structuring the breakpoint, and the sales level of $300 would be referred to as a "natural breakpoint."

EXAMPLE 8

Retail Rents

A retail lease specifies that the minimum rent is $40 per square foot plus 5 percent of sales revenue over $800 per square foot. What would the rent be if the tenant's sales are $1,000 per square foot?

Solution:

The rent per square foot will be $40 plus 5% × ($1,000 − $800) or $40 + $10 = $50. We get the same answer by multiplying 5% × $1,000 (= $50) because $800 is the "natural breakpoint," meaning that 5 percent of $800 results in the minimum rent of $40. A lease may not have the breakpoint set at this natural level, in which case it is important that the lease clearly defines how to calculate the rent.

4.3.4 *Multi-Family*

The demand for multi-family space depends on population growth, especially for the age segment most likely to rent apartments. In other words, population demographics are important. The relevant age segment can be very broad or very narrow depending on the propensity to rent in the culture. Homeownership rates vary from country to country. The relevant age segment for renters can also vary by type of property being rented out or by locale. For example, in the United States, the typical renter has historically been between 25 and 35 years old. However, the average age of a renter of property in an area attractive to retirees may be higher.

Demand also depends on how the cost of renting compares with the cost of owning—that is, the ratio of home prices to rents. As home prices rise and become less affordable, more people will rent. Similarly, as home prices fall, there may be a shift from renting to owning. Higher interest rates will also make homeownership more expensive because for owners that partially finance the purchase with debt, the financing cost will be higher and for other homeowners, the opportunity cost of having funds tied up in a home will increase. This increase in the cost of ownership may cause a shift toward renting. If interest rates decrease, there may be a shift toward homeownership.

Multi-family properties typically have leases that range from six months to two years, with one year being most typical. The tenant may or may not be responsible for paying expenses, such as utilities, depending on whether there are separate meters for each unit. The owner is typically responsible for the upkeep of common property, insurance, and repair and maintenance of the property. The tenant is typically responsible for cleaning the space rented and for insurance on personal property.

EXAMPLE 9

Economic Value Determinants

1   The primary economic driver of the demand for office space is *most likely*:

   A   job growth.

   B   population growth.

   C   growth in savings rates.

2   The demand for which of the following types of real estate is likely *most* affected by population demographics?

   A   Office

> **B** Multi-family
>
> **C** Industrial and warehouse
>
> **Solution to 1:**
>
> A is correct. Job growth is the main economic driver of office demand, especially jobs in industries that are heavy users of office space, such as finance and insurance. As jobs increase, companies need to provide office space for the new employees. Population growth may indirectly affect the demand for office space because it affects demand and job growth. Growth in savings rates affects consumer spending and the demand for retail space.
>
> **Solution to 2:**
>
> B is correct. Population demographics are a primary determinant of the demand for multi-family space.

5

OVERVIEW OF THE VALUATION OF COMMERCIAL REAL ESTATE

Regardless of the form of real estate investment, the value of the underlying real estate is critical because the value of any real estate investment is inextricably tied to the value of the underlying real estate. Commercial real estate properties do not transact frequently, and each property is unique. Therefore, estimates of value or appraisals, rather than transaction prices, are used to assess changes in value or expected selling price over time. Appraisals are typically done by individuals with recognized expertise in this area. These can be independent experts hired to do the appraisals or in-house experts.

5.1 Appraisals

Appraisals (estimates of value) are critical for such infrequently traded and unique assets as real estate properties. For publicly traded assets, such as stocks and bonds, we have frequent transaction prices that reflect the value that investors are currently placing on these assets. In contrast, commercial real estate, such as an apartment or office building, does not trade frequently. For example, a particular building might sell once in a 10-year period. Thus, we cannot rely on transactions activity for a particular property to indicate how its value is changing over time.

There are companies, such as real estate investment trusts, that invest primarily in real estate and have publicly traded shares. REITs are available in many countries around the world. REIT prices can be observed as with any publicly traded share. REITs are businesses that buy and sell real estate; often do development; decide how properties are to be financed, when to refinance, and when to renovate properties; and make many other ongoing management decisions that determine the success of the REIT. Therefore, the prices of REIT shares reflect both the performance of the management of the company that owns the real estate and the value of the underlying properties.

Thus, although it is useful to know how the values of REIT shares are changing over time as an indicator of changing conditions in the real estate market, it does not substitute for the need to estimate the value of individual properties. In fact, knowing the appraised value of properties held by REITs is helpful in estimating the value of the REIT, although, as suggested above, many other factors can affect REIT share prices over time.

Appraisals can be used to evaluate the performance of the investment or to determine an estimate of price or value if a transaction is anticipated. Even if there has been a recent transaction of the property, because it is only one transaction between a particular buyer and seller, the transaction price at which the property sold may not reflect the value a typical investor might place on the property at that time.[1] There may be circumstances under which a buyer may be willing to pay more than a typical buyer would pay or a seller may be willing to accept less than a typical seller would accept. Thus, even when there is a transaction, an appraisal is often used as a basis for estimating the value of the property rather than just assuming that the agreed upon transaction price equals the value. For example, an appraisal is likely to be required if the purchaser of the property wants to finance a portion of the purchase with debt. The lender will typically require an independent appraisal of the property to estimate the value of the collateral for the loan. Even if the purchaser is not borrowing to finance a portion of the purchase, the purchaser may have an appraisal done to help establish a reasonable offer price for the property. Similarly, the seller may have an appraisal done to help establish the asking price for the property.

Properties are also appraised for other reasons. Another important use of appraisals is for performance measurement—that is, to measure the performance of real estate that is managed for a client. For example, a pension fund may have decided to invest in real estate in addition to stocks and bonds to diversify its portfolio. It may have invested directly in the real estate or through an investment manager that acquires and manages the real estate portfolio. In either case, the pension fund wants to know how its real estate investments are performing. This performance can be evaluated relative to the performance of stocks and bonds and against a benchmark that measures the performance of the relevant real estate asset class. The benchmark is used in the same way that a stock index might be used as a benchmark for measuring the performance of a stock portfolio.

Measuring the performance of a real estate portfolio requires estimating property values on a periodic basis, such as annually. Although more frequent measures may be desirable, it may not be practical because appraising property values is a time-consuming and costly process. It may involve an independent appraisal by a firm that specializes in appraising investment properties, or it may be done by an appraiser who works for the investment management firm. In either case, the appraiser is tasked with estimating the value of the property.

5.1.1 *Value*

The focus of an appraisal is usually on what is referred to as the *market value* of the property. The market value can be thought of as the most probable sale price. It is what a *typical* investor is willing to pay for the property. There are other definitions of value that differ from market value. For example, *investment value* (sometimes called worth) is the value to a *particular* investor. It could be higher or lower than market value depending on the particular investor's motivations and how well the property fits into the investor's portfolio, the investor's risk tolerance, the investor's tax circumstances, and so on. For example, an investor who is seeking to have a globally well-diversified portfolio of real estate that does not already have any investments in New York City and Shanghai may place a higher value on acquiring a property in either of those locations than an investor who already has New York City and Shanghai properties in his or her portfolio.

---

1 The term special purchaser is used in some countries, such as the United Kingdom, to refer to purchasers who are not typical.

There are other types of value that are relevant in practice, such as *value in use*, which is the value to a particular user—for example, the value of a manufacturing plant to the company using the building as part of its business. For property tax purposes, the relevant value is the assessed value of the property, which may differ from market value because of the way the assessor defines the value. In most cases, the focus of an appraisal is on market value.

Potential sellers and buyers care about market value because it is useful to know when negotiating price. The market value may differ from the value that the potential buyer or seller originally placed on the property and from the price that is ultimately agreed upon.[2] A seller in distressed circumstances may be willing to accept less than market value because of liquidity needs, and a particular buyer (investor) may be willing to pay more than market value because the worth (investment value) to that buyer exceeds the value to a typical investor.

Lenders usually care about market value because if a borrower defaults on a mortgage loan, the market value less transaction costs is the maximum that the lender can expect to receive from the sale of the property. But there are some exceptions. In some cases, the lender may ask for a more conservative value, which can be referred to as a *mortgage lending value*. For example, in Germany the mortgage lending value is the value of the property which, based on experience, may throughout the life of the loan be expected to be generated in the event of sale, irrespective of temporary (e.g., economically induced) fluctuations in value on the relevant property market and excluding speculative elements. In determining the mortgage lending value, the future saleability of the property is to be taken as a basis within the scope of a "prudent valuation," taking into consideration the long-term, permanent features of the property, the normal regional market situation, and the present and possible alternative uses. Some have argued that over the decades in which it has been applied, the mortgage lending value has helped mortgage lending in Germany to have a stabilizing effect on the German real estate market by evening out current, possibly exaggerated market expectations. The mortgage lending value contrasts with the notion of "mark-to-market" or "fair value" accounting, which would value an asset at its market value at the time the loan is made.

EXAMPLE 10

Market Value

A property that was developed two years ago at a cost of ¥60.0 million, including land, is put on the market for that price. It sells quickly for ¥50.0 million. After the closing, the purchaser admits he would have paid up to ¥65.0 million for the property because he owned vacant land next to the property purchased. A very similar property (approximately the same size, age, etc.) recently sold for ¥55.0 million.

1 The purchaser is *most likely* a:

   A typical investor.

   B particular investor.

   C short-term investor.

2 The market value of the property is *closest* to:

   A ¥50.0 million.

---

2 For further discussion of the various definitions of value, refer to such publications as the "Uniform Standards of Professional Appraisal Practice," the Royal Institution of Chartered Surveyors (RICS) *Red Book*, and "The International Valuation Standards."

    B ¥55.0 million.

    C ¥65.0 million.

3 The investment value of the property to the buyer is *closest* to:

    A ¥50.0 million.

    B ¥60.0 million.

    C ¥65.0 million.

Solution to 1:

B is correct. This investor may be willing to pay more than the typical investor because of his particular circumstances.

Solution to 2:

B is correct. The purchaser paid ¥50.0 million rather than the ¥65.0 million he was willing to pay for the property. However, we have to be careful about using a transaction price as an indication of market value because the market may have been thin and the seller may have been distressed and willing to accept less than the property would have sold for if it had been kept on the market for a longer period of time. The quick sale suggests that the price may have been lower than what a typical investor may be willing to pay. There was a comparable property that sold for ¥55.0 million. Combining these facts and based only on this information, it is reasonable to assume that the market value is closest to ¥55.0 million. Note that what it cost to develop the property two years ago is not particularly relevant. Markets may have deteriorated since that time, and new construction may not be feasible.

Solution to 3:

C is correct. The investment value of the property is ¥65.0 million. The purchaser was willing to pay up to ¥65.0 million, suggesting that his investment value was higher than the amount paid. He paid only as much as he had to, based on negotiations with the seller.

5.2 Introduction to Valuation Approaches

In general, there are three different approaches that appraisers use to estimate value: the **income approach**, the **cost approach**, and the **sales comparison approach**. The income approach considers what price an investor would pay based on an expected rate of return that is commensurate with the risk of the investment. The value estimated with this approach is essentially the present value of the expected future income from the property, including proceeds from resale at the end of a typical investment holding period. The concept is that value depends on the expected rate of return that investors would require to invest in the property.

    The cost approach considers what it would cost to buy the land and construct a new property on the site that has the same utility or functionality as the property being appraised (referred to as the *subject property*). Adjustments are made if the subject property is older or not of a modern design, if it is not feasible to construct a new property in the current market, or if the location of the property is not ideal for its current use. The concept is that you should not pay more for a property than the cost of buying vacant land and developing a comparable property.

    The sales comparison approach considers what similar or *comparable properties* (comparables) transacted for in the current market. Adjustments are made to reflect comparables' differences from the subject property, such as size, age, location, and condition of the property and to adjust for differences in market conditions at the times of sale. The concept is that you would not pay more than others are paying for similar properties.

These approaches are unlikely to result in the same value because they rely on different assumptions and availability of data to estimate the value. The idea is to try to triangulate on the market value by approaching the estimate three different ways. The appraiser may have more confidence in one or more of the approaches depending on the availability of data for each approach. Part of the appraisal process is to try to *reconcile* the differences in the estimates of value from each approach and come up with a final estimate of value for the subject property.

5.2.1 *Highest and Best Use*

Before we elaborate on the three approaches to estimating value, it is helpful to understand an important concept known as *highest and best use*. The highest and best use of a vacant site is the use that would result in the highest value for the land. This concept is best illustrated with an example. Suppose you are trying to determine the highest and best use of a vacant site. Three alternative uses—apartment, office, and retail—have been identified as consistent with zoning regulations and are financially feasible at the right land value. The physical characteristics of the site make construction of buildings consistent with each of these uses possible. Exhibit 4 summarizes relevant details for each potential use:

Exhibit 4	Highest and Best Use		
	Apartment	**Office**	**Retail**
Value after construction	$2,500,000	$5,000,000	$4,000,000
Cost to construct building	(2,000,000)	(4,800,000)	(3,000,000)
Implied land value	$500,000	$200,000	$1,000,000

The value after construction is what the property would sell for once it is constructed and leased. The cost to construct the building includes an amount for profit to the developer. The profit compensates the developer for handling the construction phase and getting the property leased. Subtracting the cost to construct from the value after construction gives the amount that could be paid for the land. In this case, the retail use results in the highest price that can be paid for the land. So retail is the highest and best use of the site, and the land value would be $1 million.

The idea is that the price would be bid up to that amount by investors or developers who are competing for the site, including several bidders planning to develop retail. Note that the highest and best use is not the use with the highest total value, which in this example is office. Even though office has a higher value if it is built, the higher construction costs result in a lower amount that can be paid for the land. A developer cannot pay $1 million for the land and build the office building. If they did, they would have a $5.8 million total investment in the land and construction cost but the value would be only $5 million. So that would result in an $800,000 loss in value because an office building is not the highest and best use of the site.

The theory is that the land value is based on its highest and best use *as if vacant* even if there is an existing building on the site. If there is an existing building on the site that is not the highest and best use of the site, then the value of the building—not the land—will be lower. For example, suppose that a site with an old warehouse on it would sell for $1.5 million as a warehouse (land and building). If vacant, the land is worth $1 million. Thus, the value of the existing building (warehouse) is $500,000

(= \$1,500,000 − \$1,000,000). As long as the value under the existing use is more than the land value, the building should remain on the site. If the value under the existing use falls below the land value, any building(s) on the site will likely be demolished so the building that represents the highest and best use of the site can be constructed. For example, if the value as a warehouse is only \$800,000, it implies a building value of negative \$200,000. The building should be demolished, assuming the demolition costs are less than \$200,000.

EXAMPLE 11

Highest and Best Use

Two uses have been identified for a property. One is an office building that would have a value after construction of \$20 million. Development costs would be \$16 million, which includes a profit to the developer. The second use is an apartment building that would have a value after construction of \$25 million. Development costs, including a profit to the developer, would be \$22 million. What is the highest and best use of the site and the implied land value?

Solution:

	Office	Apartment
Value on completion	\$20,000,000	\$25,000,000
Cost to construct building	(16,000,000)	(22,000,000)
Implied land value	\$4,000,000	\$3,000,000

An investor/developer could pay up to \$4 million for the land to develop an office building but only \$3 million for the land to develop an apartment building. The highest and best use of the site is an office building with a land value of \$4 million. Of course, this answer assumes a competitive market with several potential developers who would bid for the land to develop an office building.

We will now discuss each of the approaches to estimating value in more detail and provide examples of each.

THE INCOME APPROACH TO VALUATION 6

The **direct capitalization method** and **discounted cash flow method** (DCF) are two income approaches used to appraise a commercial (income-producing) property. The direct capitalization method estimates the value of an income-producing property based on the level and quality of its net operating income. The DCF method discounts future projected cash flows to arrive at a present value of the property. Net operating income, a measure of income and a *proxy for cash flow*, is a focus of both approaches.

6.1 General Approach and Net Operating Income

The income approach focuses on net operating income[3] generated from a property. There are two income approaches, each of which considers growth. The first, the direct capitalization method, capitalizes the current NOI using a growth implicit **capitalization rate**. When the capitalization rate is applied to the forecasted first-year NOI for the property, the implicit assumption is that the first-year NOI is representative of what the typical first-year NOI would be for similar properties. The second, the DCF method, applies an explicit growth rate to construct an NOI stream from which a present value can be derived. As we will see, there is some overlap because, even for the second method, we generally estimate a terminal value by capitalizing NOI at some future date.

Income can be projected either for the entire economic life of the property or for a typical holding period with the assumption that the property will be sold at the end of the holding period. We will see that there are many different ways of applying the income approach depending on how complex the income is for the property being valued. But no matter how the approach is applied, the concept is that the value is based on discounting the cash flows, typically represented by NOI in real estate contexts. The discount rate should reflect the risk characteristics of the property. It can be derived from market comparisons or from specific analysis; we will examine both cases.

When the property has a lot of different leases with different expiration dates and complex lease provisions, the income approach is often done with spreadsheets or software.[4] At the other extreme, when simplifying assumptions can be made about the pattern of future income, simple formulas often can be used to estimate the value.

To value a property using an income approach, we need to calculate the **net operating income** for the property. NOI is a measure of the income from the property after deducting operating expenses for such items as property taxes, insurance, maintenance, utilities, repairs, and insurance but before deducting any costs associated with financing and before deducting federal income taxes. This is not to suggest that financing costs and federal income taxes are not important to an investor's cash flows. It simply means that NOI is a before-tax unleveraged measure of income.[5]

There may be situations where the lease on a property requires the tenants to be responsible for some or all of the expenses so that they would not be deducted when calculating NOI. Or they might be deducted, but then the additional income received from the tenants due to reimbursement of these expenses would be included when calculating the NOI. Of course, when the tenant must pay the expenses, we might expect the rent to be lower. It is necessary to consider specific lease terms when estimating NOI. As mentioned before, typical lease terms vary from country to country.

A general calculation of NOI is shown in Exhibit 5.

Exhibit 5   Calculating NOI

Rental income at full occupancy

+ Other income (such as parking)

---

[3] NOI in this real estate property context is similar to earnings before interest, taxes, depreciation, and amortization (EBITDA) in a financial reporting context.

[4] One example is a software package called ARGUS Valuation DCF, which was initially used primarily in the United States. There are now versions in many other languages, including Japanese, Chinese, German, and Spanish. See www.argussoftware.com for further information.

[5] Cash flows may also be affected by capital expenditures for such items as a roof replacement. Sometimes such items are accounted for by including a "reserve allowance" as one of the expenses. The reserve allowance spreads the cost of the capital expenditure over time. At other times, the expenditure may be deducted from NOI in the year it is expected to occur.

Exhibit 5   (Continued)

= *Potential gross income (PGI)*

 − Vacancy and collection loss

= *Effective gross income (EGI)*

 − Operating expenses (OE)

= *Net operating income (NOI)*

EXAMPLE 12

Net Operating Income

A 50-unit apartment building rents for $1,000 per unit per month. It currently has 45 units rented. Operating expenses, including property taxes, insurance, maintenance, and advertising, are typically 40 percent of effective gross income. The property manager is paid 10 percent of effective gross income. Other income from parking and laundry is expected to average $500 per rented unit per year. Calculate the NOI.

Solution:

Rental income at full occupancy	50 × $1,000 × 12 =	$600,000
Other income	50 × $500 =	+25,000
Potential gross income		$625,000
Vacancy loss	5/50 or 10% × $625,000 =	−62,500
Effective gross income		$562,500
Property management	10% of $562,500 =	−56,250
Other operating expenses	40% of $562,500 =	−225,000
Net operating income		$281,250

6.2 The Direct Capitalization Method

The direct capitalization method capitalizes the current NOI at a rate known as the capitalization rate, or cap rate for short. If we think about the inverse of the cap rate as a multiplier, the approach is analogous to an income multiplier. The direct capitalization method differs from the DCF method, in which future operating income (a proxy for cash flow) is discounted at a discount rate to produce a present value.

6.2.1 *The Capitalization Rate and the Discount Rate*

The cap and discount rates are closely linked but are not the same. Briefly, the discount rate is the return required from an investment and comprises the risk-free rate plus a risk premium specific to the investment. The cap rate is lower than the discount rate because it is calculated using the current NOI. So, the cap rate is like a current yield for the property whereas the discount rate is applied to current and future NOI, which may be expected to grow. In general, when income and value are growing at a constant compound growth rate, we have:

Cap rate = Discount rate − Growth rate   (1)

The growth rate is implicit in the cap rate, but we have to make it explicit for a DCF valuation.

6.2.2 *Defining the Capitalization Rate*

The capitalization rate is a very important measure for valuing income-producing real estate property. The cap rate is defined as follows:

Cap rate = NOI/Value   (2)

where the NOI is usually based on what is expected during the current or first year of ownership of the property. Sometimes the term *going-in cap rate* is used to clarify that it is based on the first year of ownership when the investor is *going into* the deal. (Later, we will see that the *terminal cap rate* is based on expected income for the year after the anticipated sale of the property.)

The value used in the above cap rate formula is an estimate of what the property is worth at the time of purchase. If we rearrange the above equation and solve for value we see that:

Value = NOI/Cap rate   (3)

So, if we know the appropriate cap rate, we can estimate the value of the property by dividing its first-year NOI by the cap rate.

Where does the cap rate come from? That will be an important part of our discussion. A simple answer is that it is based on observing what other similar or comparable properties are selling for. Assuming that the sale price for a comparable property is a good indication of the value of the subject property, we have:

Cap rate = NOI/Sale price of comparable   (4)

We would not want to rely on the price for just one sale to indicate what the cap rate is. We want to observe several sales of similar properties before drawing conclusions about what cap rates investors are willing to accept for a property. As we will discuss later, there are also reasons why we would expect the cap rate to differ for different properties, such as what the future income potential is for the property—that is, how it is expected to change after the first year. This is important because the cap rate is only explicitly based on the first-year income. But the cap rate that investors are willing to accept depends on how they expect the income to change in the future and the risk of that income. These expectations are said to be implicit in the cap rate.

The cap rate is like a snapshot at a point in time of the relationship between NOI and value. It is somewhat analogous to the price–earnings multiple for a stock except that it is the reciprocal.[6] The reciprocal of the cap rate is price divided by NOI. Just as stocks with greater earnings growth potential tend to have higher price–earnings multiples, properties with greater income growth potential have higher ratios of price to current NOI and thus lower cap rates.

It is often necessary to make adjustments based on specific lease terms and characteristics of a market. For example, a similar approach is common in the United Kingdom, where the term fully let property is used to refer to a property that is leased at market rent because either it has a new tenant or the rent has just been reviewed. In such cases, the appraisal is undertaken by applying a capitalization rate to this rent rather than to NOI because leases usually require the tenant to pay all costs. The cap rate derived by dividing rent by the recent sales prices of comparables is often called the all risks yield (ARY). Note that the term "yield" in this case is used like a "current yield" based on first-year NOI. It is a cap rate and will differ from the total return that an investor might expect to get from future growth in NOI and value. If it is assumed,

---

6 In the United Kingdom, the reciprocal of the cap rate is called the "years purchase" (YP). It is the number of years that it would take for income at the current level to be equal to the original purchase price.

however, that the rent will be level in the foreseeable future (like a perpetuity), then the cap rate will be the same as the return and the all risks yield will be an internal rate of return (IRR) or yield to maturity.

In simple terms, the valuation is:

Market value = Rent/ARY   (5)

Again, this valuation is essentially the same as dividing NOI by the cap rate as discussed earlier except the occupant is assumed to be responsible for all expenses so the rent is divided by the ARY.[7] ARY is a cap rate and will differ from the required total return (the discount rate) an investor might expect to get by future growth in NOI and value. If rents are expected to increase after every rent review, then the investor's expected return will be higher than the cap rate. If rents are expected to increase at a constant compound rate, then the investor's expected return (discount rate) will equal the cap rate plus the growth rate.

EXAMPLE 13

Capitalizing NOI

A property has just been let at an NOI of £250,000 for the first year, and the capitalization rate on comparable properties is 5 percent. What is the value of the property?

Solution:

Value = NOI/Cap rate = £250,000/0.05 = £5,000,000

Suppose the rent review for the property in Example 13 occurs every year and rents are expected to increase 2 percent each year. An approximation of the IRR would simply be the cap rate plus the growth rate; in this case, a 5 percent cap rate plus 2 percent rent growth results in a 7 percent IRR. Of course, if the rent review were less frequent, as in the United Kingdom where it is typically every five years, then we could not simply add the growth rate to the cap rate to get the IRR. But it would still be higher than the cap rate if rents were expected to increase.

6.2.3 Stabilized NOI

When the cap rate is applied to the forecasted first-year NOI for the property, the implicit assumption is that the first-year NOI is representative of what the typical first-year NOI would be for similar properties. In some cases, the appraiser might project an NOI to be used to estimate value that is different from what might actually be expected for the first year of ownership for the property if what is actually expected is not typical.

An example of this might be when a property is undergoing a renovation and there is a temporarily higher-than-typical amount of vacancy until the renovation is complete. The purpose of the appraisal might be to estimate what the property will be worth once the renovation is complete. A cap rate will be used from properties that are not being renovated because they are more typical. Thus, the appraiser projects what is referred to as a **stabilized NOI**, which is what the NOI would be if the property were not being renovated—in other words, what the NOI will be once the renovation is complete. This NOI is used to estimate the value. Of course, if the

---

7 In practice, management costs should also be considered, although operating costs falling on the landlord are typically much lower than in the United States.

property is being purchased before the renovation is complete, a slightly lower price will be paid because the purchaser has to wait for the renovation to be complete to get the higher NOI. Applying the cap rate to the lower NOI that is occurring during the renovation will understate the value of the property because it implicitly assumes that the lower NOI is expected to continue.[8]

EXAMPLE 14

Value of a Property to be Renovated

A property is being purchased that requires some renovation to be competitive with otherwise comparable properties. Renovations satisfactory to the purchaser will be completed by the seller at the seller's expense. If it were already renovated, it would have NOI of ¥9 million next year, which would be expected to increase by 3 percent per year thereafter. Investors would normally require a 12 percent IRR (discount rate) to purchase the property after it is renovated. Because of the renovation, the NOI will only be ¥4 million next year. But after that, the NOI is expected to be the same as it would be if it had already been renovated at the time of purchase. What is the value of or the price a typical investor is willing to pay for the property?

Solution:

If the property was already renovated (and the NOI stabilized), the value would be:

Value if renovated = ¥9,000,000/(0.12 − 0.03) = ¥100,000,000

But because of the renovation, there is a loss in income of ¥5 million during the first year. If for simplicity we assume that this would have been received at the end of the year, then the present value of the lost income at a 12 percent discount rate is as follows:

Loss in value = ¥5,000,000/(1.12) = ¥4,464,286

Thus, the value of the property is as follows:

Value if renovated	¥100,000,000
Less loss in value	− ¥4,464,286
= Value	¥95,535,714

An alternative approach is to get the present value of the first year's income and the value in a year when renovated.

{¥4,000,000 + [¥9,000,000(1.03)]/(0.12− 0.03)]}/(1.12) = ¥95,535,714

6.2.4 *Other Forms of the Income Approach*

Direct capitalization usually uses NOI and a cap rate. However, there are some alternatives to the use of NOI and a cap rate. For example, a *gross income multiplier* might be used in some situations. The gross income multiplier is the ratio of the sale price to the gross income expected from the property in the first year after sale. It may be obtained from comparable sales in a similar way to what was illustrated for cap rates. The problem with using a gross income multiplier is that it does not explicitly consider vacancy rates and operating expenses. Thus, it implicitly assumes that the ratio

---

[8] Some readers may correctly think that, rather than use a stabilized NOI, a lower cap rate could be used to reflect the fact that the NOI will be higher in the future. The problem is that it is not easy to know how much lower the cap rate should be if there are no sales of comparable properties intended for renovation.

of vacancy and expenses to gross income is similar for the comparable and subject properties. But if, for example, expenses were expected to be lower on one property versus another because it was more energy efficient, an investor would pay more for the same rent. Thus, its gross income multiplier should be higher. Use of a gross rent multiplier is also considered a form of direct capitalization but is generally not considered as reliable as using a capitalization rate.

6.3 The Discounted Cash Flow (DCF) Method

The direct capitalization method typically estimates value by capitalizing the first-year NOI at a cap rate derived from market evidence.[9]

6.3.1 *The Relationship between Discount Rate and Cap Rate*

If the income and value for a property are expected to change over time at the same compound rate—for example, 3 percent per year—then the relationship between the cap rate and discount rate is the same as in Equation 1:

Cap rate = Discount rate – Growth rate

To see the intuition behind this, let us solve for the discount rate, which is the return that is required to invest in the property.

Discount rate = Cap rate + Growth rate

Recall that the cap rate is based on first-year NOI. The growth rate captures how NOI will change in the future along with the property value. Thus, we can say that the investor's return (discount rate) comes from the return on first-year income (cap rate) plus the growth in income and value over time (growth rate). Although income and value may not always change at the same compound rate each year, this formula gives us insight into the relationship between the discount rate and the cap rate. Essentially, the difference between the discount and cap rates has to do with growth in income and value.

Intuitively, given that both methods start from the same NOI in the first year, you would pay more for an income stream that will grow than for one that will be constant. So, the price is higher and the cap rate is lower when the NOI is growing. This is what is meant by the growth being *implicit* in the cap rate. If the growth rate is constant, we can extend Equation 3 using Equation 1 to give:

$$V = NOI/(r - g) \qquad\qquad (6)$$

where:

> r = the discount rate (required return)
> g = the growth rate for income (given constant growth in income, value will grow at the same rate)

This equation is analogous to the dividend growth model applied to stocks. If NOI is not expected to grow at a constant rate, then NOIs are projected into the future and each period's NOI is discounted to arrive at a value of the property. Rather than project NOIs into infinity, typically, NOIs are projected for a specified holding period and a terminal value (estimated sale price) at the end of the holding period is estimated.

---

9 The DCF method (sometimes referred to as a yield capitalization method) involves projecting income beyond the first year and discounting that income at a discount rate (yield rate). The terms *yield rate* and *discount rate* are being used synonymously in this discussion, as are the terms *yield capitalization* and *discounted cash flow* analysis.

EXAMPLE 15

Growth Explicit Appraisal

NOI is expected to be $100,000 the first year, and after that, NOI is expected to increase at 2 percent per year for the foreseeable future. The property value is also expected to increase by 2 percent per year. Investors expect to get a 12 percent IRR given the level of risk, and therefore, the value is estimated using a 12 percent discount rate. What is the value of the property today (beginning of first year)?

Solution:

$$
\begin{aligned}
V = NOI/(r - g) \\
= \$100,000/(0.12 - 0.02) \\
= \$100,000/0.10 \\
= \$1,000,000
\end{aligned}
$$

6.3.2 *The Terminal Capitalization Rate*

When a DCF methodology is used to value a property, generally, one of the important inputs is the estimated sale price of the property at the end of a typical holding period. This input is often referred to as the estimated terminal value. Estimating the terminal value of a property can be quite challenging in practice, especially given that the purpose of the analysis is to estimate the value of the property today. But if we do not know the value of the property today, how can we know what it will be worth in the future when sold to another investor? This means we must also use some method for estimating what the property will be worth when sold in the future.

In theory, this value is based on the present value of income to be received by the *next* investor. But we usually do not try to project NOI for another holding period beyond the initial one. Rather, we rely on the direct capitalization method using the NOI of the first year of ownership for the next investor and a cap rate. The cap rate used to estimate the resale price or terminal value is referred to as a *terminal cap rate* or *residual cap rate*. It is a cap rate that is selected at the time of valuation to be applied to the NOI earned in the first year after the property is expected to be sold to a new buyer.

Selecting a terminal cap rate is challenging. Recall that the cap rate equals the discount rate less the growth rate when income and value are growing constantly at the same rate. Whether constant growth is realistic or not, we know that the cap rate will be higher (lower) if the discount rate is higher (lower). Similarly, the cap rate will be lower if the growth rate is expected to be higher, and vice versa. These relationships also apply to the terminal cap rate as well as the going-in cap rate.

The terminal cap rate could be the same, higher, or lower than the going-in cap rate depending on expected discount and growth rates at the time of sale. If interest rates are expected to be higher in the future, pushing up discount rates, then terminal cap rates might be higher. The growth rate is often assumed to be a little lower because the property is older at the time of sale and may not be as competitive. This situation would result in a slightly higher terminal cap rate. Uncertainty about what the NOI will be in the future may also result in selecting a higher terminal cap rate. The point is that the terminal cap rate is not necessarily the same as the going-in cap rate at the time of the appraisal.

EXAMPLE 16

Appraisal with a Terminal Value

Net operating income (NOI) is expected to be level at $100,000 per year for the next five years because of existing leases. Starting in Year 6, the NOI is expected to increase to $120,000 because of lease rollovers and increase at 2 percent per year thereafter. The property value is also expected to increase at 2 percent per year after Year 5. Investors require a 12 percent return and expect to hold the property for five years. What is the current value of the property?

Solution:

Exhibit 6 shows the projected NOI for this example. Because NOI and property value are expected to grow at the same constant rate after Year 5, we can calculate the cap rate at that time based on the discount rate less the growth rate. That gives us a terminal cap rate that can be used to estimate the value that the property could be sold for at the end of Year 5 (based on the income a buyer would get after that). We can then discount this value along with the income for Years 1–5 to get the present value.

Exhibit 6   Projected Income

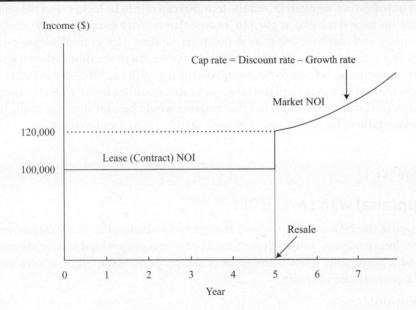

Step 1   Estimate resale price after five years.

Resale (residual) or "terminal" cap rate = 12% − 2% = 10%

Apply this to NOI in Year 6:

Resale = $120,000/0.10 = $1,200,000

Note: The value that can be obtained by selling the property at some point in the future is often referred to as the "*reversion.*"

(continued)

> **Exhibit 6   (Continued)**
>
> Step 2   Discount the level NOI for the first five years and the resale
> price.[10]
>
> PMT = \$100,000
>
> FV = \$1,200,000
>
> n = 5
>
> i = 12%
>
> Solving for PV, the current value of the property is estimated to be
> \$1,041,390.
> Note that the implied going-in cap rate is \$100,000/\$1,041,390 = 9.60%.

In Example 16, the going-in cap rate is lower than the terminal cap rate. An investor is willing to pay a higher price for the current NOI because he or she knows that it will increase when the lease is renewed at market rents in five years. The expected rent jump on lease renewal is implicit in the cap rate.

As noted earlier, we often expect the terminal cap rate to be higher than the going-in cap rate because it is being applied to income that is more uncertain. Also, the property is older and may have less growth potential. Finding a lower implied going-in cap rate in this example is consistent with this. However, there are times when we would expect the terminal cap rate to be lower than the going-in cap rate—for example, if we thought that interest rates and thus discount rates would be lower when the property is sold in the future or we expected that markets would be a lot stronger in the future with expectations for higher rental growth than in the current market.

EXAMPLE 17

Appraisal with Level NOI

Suppose the NOI from a property is expected to be level at \$600,000 per year for a long period of time such that, for all practical purposes, it can be assumed to be a perpetuity. What is the value of the property assuming investors want a 12 percent rate of return?

Solution:

In this case, the growth rate is zero, so we have:

Value = NOI/Discount rate
Value = \$600,000/0.12 = \$5,000,000

Note that in this case the cap rate will be the same as the discount rate. This is true when there is no expected change in income and value over time.

---

10 The solution is shown as if it were obtained with either a financial calculator or Microsoft Excel functions.

6.3.3 *Adapting to Different Lease Structures*

Lease structures vary across locales and can have an effect on the way value is typically estimated in a specific locale. For example, in the United Kingdom, lease structures have influenced the development of specific approaches to appraisal. In the United Kingdom, the term valuation is typically used rather than the term appraisal. A valuation, like an appraisal, is usually an assessment of "the most likely selling price" of a property or its market value (MV). While the cost approach (discussed in Section 7.1) is used in particular circumstances and the sales comparison approach dominates the single-family home market, the most common approach to valuing commercial property combines elements of direct capitalization (often with implicit discounted cash flow analysis) and explicit discounted cash flow analysis. This combination has been developed in response to the typical structure of UK leases.

In Section 6.2.2, we discussed the use of a cap rate called the all risks yield to value a fully let property (a property fully leased at current market rents with the tenant[s] paying all operating expenses) in the United Kingdom. If the appraisal date falls between the initial letting (or the last rent review) and the next rent review, adjustments have to be made because the contract rent (referred to as passing rent) is not equal to the current market rent (referred to as the open market rent). If the current market rent is greater than the contract rent, then the rent is likely to be adjusted upward at the time of the rent review and the property has what is referred to in the United Kingdom as a *"reversionary potential"* because of the higher rent at the next rent review.[11] This expected increase in rent has to be included in the appraisal.

There are several ways of dealing with this expected change in rent, but each should result in a similar valuation. One way, which is referred to as the "term and reversion approach" in the United Kingdom, simply splits the income into two components. The *term rent* is the fixed passing (current contract) rent from the date of appraisal to the next rent review, and the *reversion* is the estimated rental value (ERV). The values of the two components of the income stream are appraised separately by the application of different capitalization rates.

The capitalization rate used for the reversion is derived from sales of comparable fully let properties, on the basis that the reversion is equivalent to a fully let property, because both have potential for income growth every five years due to rent review.[12] However, the capitalized reversionary income is a future value, so it has to be discounted from the time of the rent review to the present. By convention, the rate used to discount this future reversionary value to the present is the same as the capitalization rate used to calculate the reversionary value, although they do not have to be the same.

The discount rate applied to the term rent is typically lower than that for the reversion because the term rent is regarded as less risky because it is secured by existing leases and tenants are less likely to default when they have leases with below-market-rate rents. Example 18 illustrates estimating the value of a property with term rent and reversion.

---

11 The term *reversion* is used in the United States to refer to the proceeds from the sale of a property that may or may not be at the end of a lease. Reversion and reversionary potential are similar in that they both refer to expected future benefits.

12 This assumes capitalization rates will not change significantly between the time of the appraisal and the time of the rent review.

EXAMPLE 18

A Term and Reversion Valuation

A property was let for a five-year term three years ago at £400,000 per year. Rent reviews occur every five years. The estimated rental value (ERV) in the current market is £450,000, and the all risks yield (cap rate) on comparable fully let properties is 5 percent. A lower rate of 4 percent is considered appropriate to discount the term rent because it is less risky than market rent (ERV). Exhibit 7 shows the assumed cash flows for this example. Estimate the value of the property.

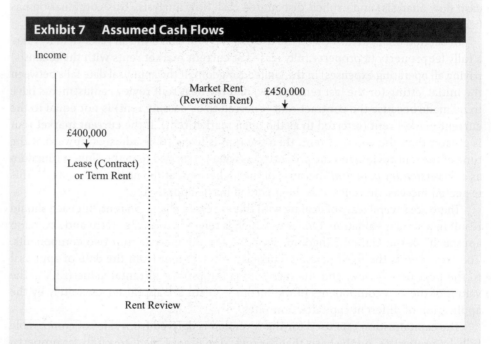

Exhibit 7   Assumed Cash Flows

Solution:

The first step is to find the present value of the term rent of £400,000 per year for two years. At a 4 percent discount rate, the present value of £400,000 per year for two years is £754,438. The second step is to estimate the present value of the £450,000 ERV at the time of the rent review. At a 5 percent capitalization rate, this value is £9,000,000 (= £450,000/0.05). This value is at the time of rent review and must be discounted back for two years to the present. Using a discount rate that is the same as the capitalization rate of 5 percent results in a present value of £8,163,265. Adding this to the value of the term rent of £754,438 results in a total value of £8,917,703. In summary:

Term rent	£400,000	
PV 2 years at 4%	× 1.8860947	
Value of term rent		= £754,438
Reversion to ERV	£450,000	
PV perpetuity at 5%	÷ 0.05	
Value at rent review		= £9,000,000
PV 2 years at 5%	× 0.9070295	

Value of reversion	= £8,163,265
Total capital value	£8,917,703

Note that despite the differences in terminology, this example is similar to Example 16, in which there was level income for five years and an assumed resale at the end of the fifth year. Recall that the value associated with resale of the property in the future is often referred to as the reversion value. It is the same concept as in this example. The value of the property is equal to the value of the income received for a period of time plus the expected value from sale in the future (at the end of the period) regardless of whether the property is actually sold or not. In Example 18, the property could be sold at the time of rent review for £9 million. So the total value is equal to the present value of the income until the rent review plus the present value of what the property could be sold for at rent review.

A variation of the above method that is sometimes used in the United Kingdom is referred to as the "layer method." The only difference is that it deals with the higher income expected from the rent review in a different way mathematically. It assumes that one source of income is the current contract rent as if it would continue indefinitely (perpetuity) and then adds to the value of this income the value from the incremental rent expected to be received after the rent review. A cap rate close to or equal to the all risks yield is normally applied to the contract rent because it is regarded as secure income—rent reviews are upward only in the United Kingdom and rental growth should ensure that the rent from the new lease will be at least as high as the current rent. The additional income expected after the rent review is often capitalized at a higher rate than the all risks yield because it is regarded as more risky although it could increase even more after subsequent rent reviews, and as we have seen, a higher growth rate for income results in a lower cap rate. Example 19 illustrates the use of the layer method.

EXAMPLE 19

The Layer Method

Consider the same property as in Example 18. The cash flow is shown in Exhibit 8. The current contract (term) rent is to be discounted at 5 percent, and the incremental rent is to be discounted at 6 percent. Estimate the value of the property using the layer method.

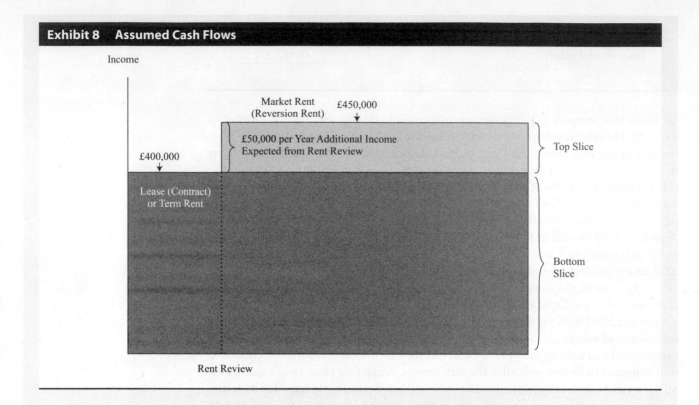

Exhibit 8   Assumed Cash Flows

Solution:

Using the layer method, the valuation is as follows:

Term rent	£400,000	
PV in perpetuity at 5%	÷ 0.05	
Value of bottom slice		= £8,000,000
Reversion to ERV	£450,000	
Less bottom slice	− £400,000	
Top slice rent =	£50,000	
PV perpetuity at 6%	× 16.6666667	
PV 2 years at 6%	× 0.8899964	
Value of top slice		= £741,664
Total capital value		£8,741,664

This method produces a slightly different answer from that shown in Example 18. In theory, the cap rates could have been adjusted to produce the same answer as in Example 18; in practice, adjustments involve both market convention and subjectivity.

6.3.4 *The Equivalent Yield*

In Examples 18 and 19, different cap rates were applied to the two different sources of income (current contract rent versus market rent to be received at rent review). There is a single discount rate that could be applied mathematically to both income streams that would result in the same value. This rate is referred to as the "equivalent yield." Again, we must be careful about terminology because this rate will not be an IRR unless one assumes there will not be any increase in rent after the first rent review. Otherwise, the equivalent yield is simply an average of the two separate cap rates—although not a simple average because of the mathematics of discounting. A concept proposed by Investment Property Databank (IPD) in the United Kingdom is to show the "effective yield" for a property being valued, where the effective yield is an IRR calculation based on reasonable assumptions for future rent reviews beyond the first one. The concept of an effective yield would be the same as the discount rate that would be used to value a property using discounted cash flow analysis, and an effective yield can be calculated regardless of how the value was estimated. That is, based on the value being estimated by the appraiser, what would the investor expect to earn as an IRR based on projected future cash flows either to perpetuity or with a resale at the end of a holding period? In theory, the holding period would not matter because the resale price represents the present value of income beyond the holding period. So having a holding period assumption is more for convenience and being realistic about how far into the future cash flows can be estimated.

6.4 Advanced DCF: Lease-by-Lease Analysis

The use of a DCF approach for real estate income-producing properties, especially when there are lots of tenants and more complex leases, is intuitively appealing. The general steps to a DCF analysis are as follows:

- Project income from existing leases
- Make assumptions about lease renewals
- Make assumptions about operating expenses
- Make assumptions about capital expenditures
- Make assumptions about absorption of any vacant space
- Estimate resale value (reversion)
- Select discount rate to find PV of cash flows

6.4.1 *Project Income from Existing Leases*

This step involves capturing the start and end dates for each lease and the various determinants of rent under the lease, such as the base rent, projected increases in the base rent (steps), and adjustments that may occur because the lease is linked to an index (such as a CPI adjustment). The projected income from existing leases would include income from expense reimbursements on leases that provide for the tenant being billed for some portion of the operating expenses because either it is a net lease or it is a gross lease but has a provision for pass-through of expenses to the tenant if they exceed a certain amount.

6.4.2 *Make Assumptions about Lease Renewals*

Assumptions also have to be made about what will happen when a lease comes up for renewal—often referred to as market leasing assumptions. That is, does the appraiser think it will be renewed or not? These assumptions are usually not as simple as saying it will be renewed or will not be renewed but involve estimating a probability that the lease will be renewed, which is referred to as the renewal probability. For example, for a particular tenant or group of tenants, it might be assumed that there is a 70 percent chance that the lease will be renewed and a 30 percent chance that it will not be renewed. Estimating this probability obviously involves some judgment, but the estimate will be based on historical experience with different types of tenants as well as consideration of economic conditions likely to exist at the time of the lease renewal.

The assumption about lease renewal probabilities affects cash flows in several ways. First, the assumption about the rent that would be received from an existing tenant that renews a lease may be lower than that expected from a new tenant found to lease the space if the existing tenant does not renew. This is because the owner may be willing to accept a lower rent from an existing tenant that is already in place and has been paying rent on time, and the space will not be vacant until a new tenant is found. Second, a new tenant is more likely to ask the owner to spend money to fix up the tenant's space—so-called tenant improvements (TIs). Third, finding a new tenant is likely to involve paying leasing commissions to a broker, whereas the commissions might be avoided or be less if an existing tenant renews.

In conjunction with making assumptions about the lease renewal probability, the analyst would also indicate how many months it will take to lease the space if the lease is not renewed. This is usually done by specifying the number of months vacant if a lease is not renewed. Combining assumptions about the renewal probability, the number of months vacant, and the length for a new lease is one way to estimate a vacancy rate for the property. For example, a 60 percent renewal probability with 10 months vacant if not renewed suggests that there is a 40 percent chance the lease will not be renewed, so on average there would be 40% × 10 months or 4 months vacancy when the lease comes up for renewal. If the typical lease is 3 years or 36 months, then this suggests a vacancy rate due to this lease of 4 months every 40 months (36 + 4) or a 10 percent vacancy rate.

6.4.3 *Make Assumptions about Operating Expenses*

Operating expenses involve items that must be paid by the owner, such as property taxes, insurance, maintenance, management, marketing, and utilities. Even if the tenant is responsible for paying some or all of the expenses, they often must first be paid by the owner, and then the owner is reimbursed by the tenant. So they would be included as an expense, and there would be additional reimbursement income from the tenant for those expenses that are the tenant's responsibility.

Operating expenses are often categorized as fixed, variable, or a hybrid of the two. By variable expenses, we mean that they depend on the level of occupancy, whereas fixed expenses do not depend on the level of occupancy. Fixed expenses can still change over time—for example, they may increase with inflation. Most expenses change over time because of inflation. But some expenses also depend on the occupancy of the property, such as the management fee, which is often a percentage of income collected from tenants. Insurance and property taxes are more likely to be fixed and not vary with occupancy. Utilities may be a hybrid. With more tenants, there will be higher utility expenses, but there is usually some fixed amount of utility expense even for a building that is almost empty; common areas (lobbies, hallways, and so on) must be heated/air conditioned and adequately lit. The temperature of unoccupied spaces may be kept within a certain range to prevent damage. Thus, utilities might be considered to be partially fixed and partially variable.

EXAMPLE 20

Utility Expenses

Utilities are assumed to be 25 percent fixed and 75 percent variable. If a 200,000 square foot building was fully occupied, the utility expense would be $4 per square foot. Assuming that all utility expenses are allocated to occupied space, what is the utility expense per occupied square foot if the building is 80 percent occupied?

Solution:

The fixed portion is ($4 × 0.25 × 200,000)/(0.80 × 200,000) = $1.25 per occupied square foot.

The variable portion is $4 × 0.75 = $3.00 per occupied square foot.

The total utility expense is $4.25 per occupied square foot.

6.4.4 *Make Assumptions about Capital Expenditures*

In addition to the operating expenses discussed above, there may be additional expenditures that have to be paid for items that are not ordinary annual expenses, such as a new heating and air conditioning system or replacing a roof. These items are referred to as capital expenditures (or capex), and they affect cash flows. Funds used to fix up a tenant's space for a new lease are also considered capital expenditures, as are funds spent to renovate the building. These capital expenditures are deducted from the NOI to calculate cash flow that would be discounted when doing a DCF analysis. Note that these expenditures will differ in most years, and in some years there may not be any. They are lumpy by nature. In some cases, analysts estimate on average what the annual amount of capital expenditures will be and have a deduction each year for capital expenditures rather than project exactly in which year(s) they might spend the money. In such cases, capex should still be a deduction from NOI, although some analysts include it along with other operating expenses and call it a "replacement reserve." Regardless of how the capex is handled, the present value of the cash flows should be essentially the same.

6.4.5 *Make Assumptions about Absorption of Any Vacant Space*

The property being valued may also have some space that is currently vacant and needs to be leased up. Accounting for currently vacant space involves making an assumption as to when the space is likely to be leased, which could involve several leases starting at different points in time in the future. Until the space is leased, it will be reflected in the vacancy rate for the property, as will space that is vacant as a result of the lease renewal assumptions discussed above.

6.4.6 *Estimate Resale Value (Reversion)*

When doing a DCF analysis, the usual practice is to make an assumption as to how long the property will be held by the initial investor. For example, it might be assumed that the property will be held for 10 years and then sold to a second investor. An alternative would be to project cash flows for the entire economic life of the property, although there would still normally be value to the land after the building is ready for demolition.

Obviously, it is harder to project cash flows the further we go in the future, so for practical purposes, a holding period of about 10 years is typically used. This allows us to capture the details of existing leases and what will happen when most if not all of them renew if the lease term of the longest lease is 10 years or less. Having a holding period that goes beyond when existing leases expire can make it easier to estimate the resale price at the end of the holding period because all leases will be at market rents and have normal rent growth thereafter. In contrast, if there were unexpired leases that had unusually low (or high) contract rent, they could bias the estimate of the resale price if not properly accounted for when estimating the resale price.

The way the resale price is often estimated is to use the concept of a terminal cap rate that was discussed earlier. The idea is that, although we want to capture the details of the leases for the next 10 years or so of the holding period, to get the resale price we will revert to a more simple direct capitalization approach. If the holding period is 10 years, the expected NOI in Year 11 would be used to estimate the resale price because this is the first year of NOI for the next buyer.

Recall our earlier discussion of the terminal cap rate and the relationship between the cap rate, the discount rate, and expected future growth in NOI and value. The terminal cap rate will capture how income and value is projected to change for a new investor. We could say that the resale price will be the present value of cash flows expected after that. So even though we select a holding period when the property will be sold, we are still implicitly considering all future cash flows for the property. We only try to capture the detail on a year-by-year basis up until the end of the holding period plus one year.

Note that, in theory, the length of the holding period does not matter because the resale price reflects the present value of cash flows expected after the holding period. So the choice of a holding period is somewhat arbitrary, and it is more important to pick one that goes beyond the term of existing leases for the reasons discussed above. To elaborate, if there was a major lease that had significantly below-market rent under the contract terms of the lease, its income would be expected to increase when the lease ends, which should result in higher income from that point forward. The analyst would want to capture this in his or her analysis. But if the income used to estimate the resale price is before the lease expires, applying a cap rate to that income may underestimate the resale price because it would not capture the growth in income and value when this lease renews.

6.4.7 *Select Discount Rate to Find PV of Cash Flows*

Ultimately, the purpose of a DCF analysis is to discount the projected future cash flows, including the resale price, to get a present value. This requires selection of an appropriate discount rate to capture the riskiness of the cash flows. Knowing what the discount rate should be can be a challenge because it is not directly observable. That is, analysts do not know what the investor projected as cash flows in the future and what return was expected at the time a property was purchased—although analysts could ask the buyer, which is one of the ways, analysts try to determine what discount rate to use. That is, analysts can survey buyers of properties in the market to find out what return they expected when they purchased the property. Some companies and organizations publish the results of investor surveys.

The discount rate should be higher than what the mortgage rate would be for a loan on the property—regardless of whether the investor plans to actually get a loan. This is because investing in the property is usually considered riskier than making a loan on the property. The lender gets repaid before the investor receives any cash flow, and thus the lender bears less risk than the investor. So the discount rate should have a risk premium beyond that reflected in the mortgage rate.

Some argue that more than one discount rate is applicable because some cash flows expected from a property are riskier than others. For example, a lower discount rate might be used to find the present value of the income from existing leases, but a higher discount rate might be used for the income from lease renewals and resale. That said, even if a single discount rate is used, it can be thought of as an average of the different rates that might be applied to different components of the cash flow. So, the important thing is to use a discount rate that reflects, on average, how risky the investment is compared with alternatives.

EXAMPLE 21

Direct Capitalization and Discounted Cash Flow

What is the main difference between direct capitalization and discounted cash flow (DCF) analysis?

Solution:

Direct capitalization applies a capitalization rate or an income multiplier to the forecasted first-year NOI. Thus, expected increases (growth) in NOI in the future must be implicit in the multiplier or cap rate. In contrast, when doing a DCF, the future cash flows are projected each year until sale of the property. Then each year's cash flow and the expected resale proceeds are discounted using a discount rate. Thus, the future income pattern, including the effect of growth, is explicit in a DCF. Furthermore, DCF often considers other cash flows that might occur in the future that are not reflected in NOI, such as capital expenditures.

6.5 Advantages and Disadvantages of the Income Approach

We have seen that there are many ways of applying the income approach, ranging from a relatively simple use of a cap rate with direct capitalization to more advanced DCF analysis that involves projecting cash flows over a holding period and capturing the details of the leases for each year of the holding period.

The *advantage* of the more complex DCF approach is that it captures the cash flows that investors actually care about. And this approach does not depend on current transactions from comparable sales as long as we feel that we can select an appropriate discount rate.

The *disadvantage* is the amount of detailed information that is needed and the need to forecast what will happen in the future even if it is just forecasting a growth rate for the NOI and not doing a detailed lease-by-lease analysis. Selecting an appropriate discount rate is critical, as is selecting an appropriate terminal cap rate. Small variations in assumptions can have a significant impact on the value.

Because it can be tedious to capture all the details of existing leases, specialized software is often used to do DCF analysis.

6.6 Common Errors

Discounted cash flow analysis requires a lot of assumptions, and analysts may knowingly or otherwise make assumptions that are not consistent with reality. The following are some of the more common erroneous assumptions:

- The discount rate does not reflect the risk.
- Income growth is greater than expense growth.
- The terminal cap rate is not logical compared with the implied going-in cap rate.
- The terminal cap rate is applied to an income that is not typical.
- The cyclical nature of real estate markets is not recognized.

EXAMPLE 22

Disadvantages of and Errors in Discounted Cash Flow Analysis

A property is being valued using an 8 percent discount rate. A terminal capitalization rate of 5.5 percent was used to estimate the resale price. After solving for value, the appraiser calculates the implied going-in capitalization rate to be 6 percent. Market rents and property values have been increasing about 1 percent per year, and that is expected to continue in the foreseeable future. Current mortgage rates for a loan on the property would be 7.5 percent. Do the assumed discount and terminal capitalization rates seem reasonable?

Solution:

There are several "red flags" or warning signs. First, the discount rate is only 50 basis points above the mortgage rate. Whether this is a sufficient risk premium for an equity investor is questionable. Second, the terminal capitalization rate is less than the going-in capitalization rate, which suggests either interest rates will fall in the future or NOI and property values will increase at an even faster rate in the future. Usually, terminal capitalization rates are the same as or slightly higher than going-in capitalization rates to reflect the fact that the property will be older when sold, and older properties usually have less NOI growth. Finally, the difference between the discount rate of 8 percent and the going-in capitalization rate of 6 percent implies 2 percent per year growth. Yet NOI and property values are expected to increase only about 1 percent per year. Overall, it appears that the appraiser may be overvaluing the property.

7 THE COST AND SALES COMPARISON APPROACHES TO VALUATION

We now turn to two other approaches to valuation: the cost approach and the sales comparison approach. The cost approach is typically used for unusual properties or those with specialized use for which market comparables are difficult to obtain. The sales comparison approach is most commonly used for single-family homes, where income is not relevant and sales data for reasonable comparables is available.

7.1 The Cost Approach

The cost approach involves estimating the value of the building(s) based on adjusted replacement cost. The estimated value of the land (usually from a sales comparison approach) is added to the estimated value of the building to arrive at the estimated total value of the property. To determine the value of the building, the **replacement cost**, assuming it was built today using current construction costs and standards, is first estimated.[13] The replacement cost is adjusted for different types of depreciation (loss in value) to arrive at a **depreciated replacement cost**.[14]

The first type of depreciation is for **physical deterioration**, which is generally related to the age of the property because components of the property wear out over time. There are two types of physical deterioration: curable and incurable. Curable means that fixing the problem will add value that is at least as great as the cost of the cure. For example, replacing a roof might increase the value of the property by at least as much as the cost of doing so and, therefore, is curable. Fixing a structural problem with the foundation of the building may cost more to cure than the amount that it would increase the value of the property if cured and would be considered incurable deterioration.

---

[13] There is sometimes a distinction made between "replacement cost" and "reproduction cost," where reproduction cost refers to the cost of creating an exact replica of the building using the original building materials. In contrast, replacement cost refers to creating a building that provides the same utility to users but is constructed with modern building materials. Reproduction cost may be higher than replacement cost because it is not economical to construct the building using the original materials. Thus, replacement cost is more relevant as a starting point to estimate value using the cost approach.

[14] It should be noted that the depreciation being estimated for the cost approach may have little relationship to the amount of depreciation that would be used on financial statements using a historical cost approach to accounting.

The replacement cost estimate for the property assumes it is a new building that has no obsolescence. That is, it is the value assuming nothing needs cured. Thus, the cost of fixing any curable items would have to be deducted from the replacement cost. A prospective purchaser would not pay as much for a property that had items that need to be fixed and would likely deduct the cost of fixing them from the purchase price.

After deducting the cost of fixing curable items from the replacement cost of the property, a deduction still has to be made for incurable depreciation. A buyer would pay less for a building that is older and has wear and tear. Because incurable depreciation by definition would not be feasible to fix because it does not increase value as much as the cost to fix, we would not deduct the cost of fixing it from the replacement cost. Rather, appraisers try to estimate how a property's age is likely to affect its value. A simple way that is often used to estimate this depreciation is to base it on the effective age of the property relative to its economic life. The effective age can differ from the actual age if it has more or less than the normal amount of wear and tear. For example, if the property has an effective age of 10 years and its economic life is usually 50 years, then the physical depreciation is assumed to be 10/50 or 20 percent. This ratio is applied to the value calculated above, which is after subtracting the curable depreciation from the replacement cost so as to not double count. That is, we have already accounted for the loss in value due to curable depreciation.

The second type of depreciation is referred to as **functional obsolescence**. It is a loss in value due to a design that is different from that of a new building constructed with an appropriate design for the intended use of the property. This could result from changes in design standards since the building was constructed or because the building had a poor design to start, even if it were a relatively new building. Functional obsolescence usually results in the building generating less NOI than it otherwise would because the building may be less efficient and have a higher operating expense or may not command as much rent as a building with the proper design. The amount of functional obsolescence is often estimated by the present value of the income loss due to the obsolescence. For example, suppose an office has a poorly designed elevator system such that there tends to be unusually long waiting times for tenants and visitors to use them. This situation affects the types of tenants that are willing to rent space in the building, and the rent is less than it would be if the elevators had greater capacity. The appraiser determines that this design flaw likely reduces NOI by about $25,000 per year. An 8 percent cap rate is considered appropriate to estimate the value of the property. This cap rate can be applied to the $25,000 loss in NOI due to the poor elevator design to arrive at a $312,500 loss in value due to functional obsolescence. This amount is deducted from the replacement cost.

Finally, there is depreciation that is external to the property. This *external obsolescence* is due to either the location of the property or economic conditions. **Locational obsolescence** results when the location is not optimal for the property. It usually occurs because something happens after the building was constructed that changes the desirability of the location for the existing use; the existing use may no longer be the highest and best use of the site.

For example, a luxury apartment building is on a site where the highest and best use when it was first developed was to construct the luxury apartment. But perhaps after the apartment was constructed, a manufacturing plant that was allowed by the zoning was built on a nearby site, and this made the location much less desirable for a luxury apartment building. That is, a luxury apartment building is no longer the highest and best use of the site. Perhaps now the highest and best use is an apartment building that would have lower rents and appeal to people working at the manufacturing plant.

After the manufacturing plant was built, rents had to be lowered on the apartment building currently on the site. Thus, its value is lower than it would be on a site where the highest and best use is still a luxury apartment building. Suppose the decline in the value of the apartment building (land and building) is $200,000. This amount is the total loss in value due to the manufacturing plant. But some of this loss in value would show up in the land value being lower, which would be reflected in comparable land sales taking place after the manufacturing plant was built being lower than before it was built and lower at better locations. For example, a vacant site near the manufacturing plant would have sold for $100,000 before the manufacturing plant was built but would now sell for $75,000 to be used for low-income housing. Thus, some of the loss in value of the property would already be reflected in the lower land value, and this portion does not have to be deducted from the replacement cost of the building.

The land value for the existing luxury office building near the manufacturing plant would be $75,000 based on its use for lower-income apartments if vacant. Because the land value reflects a $25,000 loss in value, the amount of locational obsolescence attributed to the building would be the $200,000 total decline in value less the $25,000 attributed to the land or $175,000. Thus, $175,000 is deducted from the replacement cost of the building in the cost approach.

Economic obsolescence results when new construction is not feasible under current economic conditions. This usually occurs when rent levels are not sufficiently high to generate a value for a newly constructed property that is at least equal to the development costs (including a profit to the developer). Thus, the replacement cost of the new property exceeds what it would really be worth if it were developed. In this situation, even a new building would have a loss in value.

In Exhibit 9, the cost approach is illustrated for a small office building. The building has a replacement cost of $16 million plus a developer's profit of $750,000. This is what it would cost to build a brand new building that has the same utility as the property being valued. The land value of $4 million is based on comparable sales of other parcels of land. The subject property is not new and has some deferred maintenance that is curable; spending money to fix these items (such as replacing the roof) will add at least as much value as the cost of curing the problem. The cost to cure the building amounts to $1 million. It has to be deducted from replacement cost because the subject property needs these repairs whereas the replacement cost assumes everything is new.

An older building will also have additional physical deterioration (wear and tear) due to age that is not curable but must be accounted for. As discussed previously, a common way of doing this is to use the ratio of the effective age of the property to its economic life. Effective age could be higher or lower than the actual age, depending on how well maintained the property is or whether it has unusually large or small deterioration. In this case, the effective age is 10 years and the economic life is 50 years, which means it is 10/50 or 20 percent worn out. This ratio is applied to the amount we arrived at after deducting the curable depreciation from the replacement cost.[15] This results in a deduction of $3,150,000 [= (16,750,000 − 1,000,000)0.20] for wear and tear that is not curable.

Next, functional obsolescence, which has to do with design problems, is considered. In this case, the property is deemed to have a poor floor plan compared with a modern building. It also has higher-than-average energy consumption. Keep in mind that we are estimating the value of the property "as is" with its existing design flaws. The deduction for this functional obsolescence is estimated at $1.75 million.

Locational obsolescence also has to be considered. The construction of roads in an adjacent park reduced the amenity value compared with a typical office building in this market. In other words, the location is not the most desirable location for this office building. This lowers the market rent for the property, which is estimated to lower the value by $1 million. Finally, there is some economic obsolescence, which

---

15 To not deduct the curable items before applying the 20 percent to account for incurable iveitms would be double-counting. If the curable items were fixed, they would be brand new. We are trying to capture the additional depreciation on the portions of the building that cannot be cured.

is due to recent construction of competing properties that has resulted in a higher vacancy rate than would be typical for a new building. It results in a loss in value of $1 million. Subtracting all of the depreciation discussed above results in a depreciated building value of $8.85 million. Finally, adding the land value of $4 million results in a value estimate of $12.85 million.

Exhibit 9	The Cost Approach			
Market value of the land (from comparables)				$4,000,000
Replacement cost, including constructor's profit				
Building costs (psf)	$200			
Total area (sf)	80,000			
			$16,000,000	
Developer's profit		$750,000		
			$16,750,000	
Reduction for curable deterioration		$1,000,000		
			$15,750,000	
Reduction for incurable deterioration				
Total economic life	50			
Remaining economic life	40			
Effective age	10			
Ratio of effective to total	20%			
Reduction for incurable deterioration		$3,150,000		
			$12,600,000	
Reduction for functional obsolescence (poor floor plan and substandard energy efficiency)		$1,750,000		
			$10,850,000	
Reduction for locational obsolescence (recent construction of roads in park land thus reducing amenity)		$1,000,000		
			$9,850,000	
Reduction for economic obsolescence (recent construction of competing properties thus increasing supply and vacancy rates)		$1,000,000		
Building value			$8,850,000	
Final appraised value (building and land)				**$12,850,000**

EXAMPLE 23

The Cost Approach

A 12-year-old industrial property is being valued using the cost approach. The appraiser feels that it has an effective age of 15 years based on its current condition. For example, there are cracks in the foundation that are not feasible to repair (incurable physical depreciation). That is, it would cost more to try to repair these problems than the value that would be created in the property. The appraiser believes that it has a 60-year remaining economic life (75-year total economic life).

The building was constructed using a greater ceiling height than users require in the current market (super-adequacy). It would cost $27 million to reproduce (reproduction cost) the building with the same ceiling height but $25 million to construct a replacement property (replacement cost) with the same utility but a normal ceiling height.

The higher ceiling results in increased heating and air-conditioning costs of $50,000 per year. A cap rate that would be used to value the property would be 10 percent.

The building was designed to include a cafeteria that is no longer functional (functional obsolescence). This area can be converted to usable space at a conversion cost of $25,000, and it is believed that the value of the property would increase by at least this amount (curable functional obsolescence).

The roof needs to be replaced at a cost of $250,000, and other necessary repairs amount to $50,000. The costs of these repairs will increase the value of the building by at least their $300,000 cost (curable physical depreciation).

The road providing access to the property is a two-lane road, whereas newer industrial properties are accessible by four-lane roads. This has a negative impact on rents (locational obsolescence), which is estimated to reduce NOI by $100,000 per year.

Based on comparable sales of vacant land, the land is estimated to be worth $5 million. Estimate the value using the cost approach.

Solution:

Preliminary Calculations:

Replacement cost (built to current standards)				$25,000,000
Physical depreciation				
Roof		$250,000		
Other		50,000		
Total curable physical depreciation		$300,000		$300,000
Replacement cost after curable physical depreciation				$24,700,000
Ratio of effective age to total economic life	= 15/75 = 20%			
Incurable physical depreciation	20.00%	×	$24,700,000 =	$4,940,000
Curable functional obsolescence				
Conversion of cafeteria				$25,000
Incurable functional obsolescence				
Extra HVAC costs	$50,000	/	10.00% =	$500,000
Locational obsolescence	$100,000	/	10.00% =	$1,000,000

Cost Approach Summary:

Replacement Cost		$25,000,000
Physical deterioration:		
Curable	$300,000	
Incurable	$4,940,000	
Functional obsolescence		
Curable	$25,000	
Incurable	$500,000	
Locational obsolescence	$1,000,000	
Total depreciation	$6,765,000	$6,765,000
Depreciated cost		$18,235,000
Plus: Land value		5,000,000
Estimated value from cost approach		$23,235,000

7.2 The Sales Comparison Approach

The sales comparison approach implicitly assumes that the value of a property depends on what other comparable properties are selling for in the current market. Ideally, the comparables would be exactly the same as the subject property in terms of size, age, location, quality of construction, amenities, view, and so on, and would be sold on the same date as the date of the appraised value. Obviously, this is impossible, so adjustments have to be made to each of the comparables for differences from the "subject" property due to these factors. The idea is to determine what the comparables would have sold for if they were like the subject property.

Exhibit 10 shows the sales comparison approach applied to a subject property. There have been sales of five comparable properties within the last year. They are similar to the subject property, but there are always some differences that need to be accounted for. The idea is to determine how much each of the comparables would have sold for if they were exactly the same as the subject property. Calculating the price per square foot (or square meter) is often a good way to account for differences in size, although other measures of size may be appropriate in some cases, such as cubic feet (or cubic meters) for a warehouse or number of units in an apartment building.

Next, the price per square foot is adjusted for each of the comparables. For example, Comparable 1 is in good condition. The subject property is in only average condition. Thus, we lower the price per square foot of the comparable to determine what it would have sold for if it were in only average condition like the subject property. Each comparable is adjusted to what it would sell for if its location, condition, age, and time of sale were the same as the subject property. Notice that after these adjustments, the range in price per square foot is tighter across the five comparables.

In this example, we average the price per square foot for each of the comparables, although in many cases more weight may be given to comparables that the appraiser feels are more similar to the subject property or where they feel more confident in the adjustments. We multiply this price per square foot by the square feet of the subject property to arrive at our estimate of value using the sales comparison approach.

Exhibit 10	The Sales Comparison Approach					
	Subject	**Comparables**				
Variable	**Property**	**1**	**2**	**3**	**4**	**5**
Size (square feet)	15,000	25,000	20,000	10,000	16,000	12,500
Age (years)	10	1	5	10	15	20
Condition	Average	Good	Good	Good	Average	Poor
Location	Prime	Prime	Secondary	Secondary	Secondary	Prime
Date of sale (months ago)		3	9	6	7	12
Sale price		$5,500,000	$3,000,000	$1,300,000	$1,750,000	$1,300,000
Sale price psf		$220	$150	$130	$109	$104
Adjustments						
Age (years)		−22.5%	−12.5%	0.0%	12.5%	25.0%
Condition		−10.0%	−10.0%	−10.0%	0.0%	10.0%
Location		0.0%	20.0%	20.0%	20.0%	0.0%
Date of sale (months ago)		1.5%	4.5%	3.0%	3.5%	6.0%
Adjusted price psf		$151.80	$153.00	$146.90	$148.24	$146.64
Average price psf	$149.30					
Appraised value	**$2,239,500**					

The following indicates how the adjustments were made to the comparables to reflect the characteristics of the subject property. The adjustments to Comparable 1 are discussed to help clarify the process.

1 Depreciated at 2.5 percent per annum. Because the subject property is nine years older, a depreciation adjustment of −22.5% (= 9 × 2.5%) reduces the value of Comparable 1.

2 Condition adjustment after average depreciation is taken into account: Good, none; Average, 10%; Poor, 20%. Because Comparable 1 is in good condition and the subject property is in only average condition, a condition adjustment of −10 percent reduces the value of Comparable 1.

3 Location adjustment: Prime, none; Secondary, 20%. Comparable 1 and the subject property are both in prime locations, so no location adjustment is made.

4 Market has been rising by 0.5 percent per month. Thus, an adjustment of 1.5 percent is made to the sale price of Comparable 1 because the sale occurred three months ago.

EXAMPLE 24

The Sales Comparison Approach

Referring to Exhibit 10, suppose there is a sixth comparable that sold one month ago for $2.686 million. It is 15,000 square feet, eight years old, in good condition, and in a prime location. What is the adjusted price per square foot based on this comparable?

Solution:

The sale price per square foot is $2,686,000/15,000 = $179. This price must be adjusted downward by 5 percent because it is two years newer than the subject, down by 10 percent because the condition is better than that of the subject property, and up by 1/2 percent because prices have increased since this comparable sold. This results in an adjusted price per square foot of $153.05.

7.3 Advantages and Disadvantages of the Cost and Sales Comparison Approaches

The cost approach to valuation is sometimes said to set an upper limit on the value. It is assumed that an investor would never pay more than the cost to buy land and develop a comparable building. This assumption may be somewhat of an overstatement because it can take time and effort to develop another building and find tenants. Furthermore, there may not be the demand for another building of the same type in the market. That said, one would question a value that is much higher than implied by the cost approach. The main disadvantage of the cost approach is that it can be difficult to estimate the depreciation for a property that is older and/or has much obsolescence. So the cost approach will be most reliable for newer properties that have a relatively modern design in a stable market.

The sales comparison approach relies on a reasonable number of comparable sales to be able to gauge what investors are expected to be willing to pay for the subject property. When the market is active, the sales comparison approach can be quite reliable. But when the market is weak, there tends to be fewer transactions, which makes it difficult to find comparable properties at a location reasonably close to the subject property. Even in an active market, there may be limited comparable sales for some properties, such as regional malls or special purpose properties.

Finally, the sales comparison approach assumes the investors who are buying properties are behaving rationally. That is, it assumes that the prices paid by investors in the current market are representative of market values. However, as mentioned in Section 5.1.1, the investment value to a particular investor may result in that investor being willing to pay a price in excess of market value. Also, there are times when investors in general are overly exuberant and there is a "bubble" in prices being paid for properties. This raises the question of whether these prices still represent "market value" because it seems likely that prices will eventually fall back to a more normal level. It is often argued that the appraiser's job is to measure what investors are willing to pay whether they think it is rational or not because market value is a most probable selling price.

RECONCILIATION   8

We have discussed three different approaches to valuation: the income, cost, and sales comparison approaches. It would be highly unusual to get the same answer from all three approaches. They rely on different sources of data and different assumptions, and although in theory they should produce the same answer, in practice, this would be unlikely because of imperfections in the data and inefficiencies in the market. Thus, the appraiser needs to *reconcile* the differences and arrive at a final conclusion about the value.

Some approaches may be more applicable than others, depending on the property types and market conditions. The purpose of reconciliation is to decide which approach or approaches you have the most confidence in and come up with a final estimate of value. In an active market with lots of transactions, the appraiser may have more confidence in the sales comparison approach. This may be the case for apartment buildings in many markets. When there are fewer transactions, as might be the case during weak markets or for property types that do not transact as frequently, the appraiser may have more confidence in the income approach. For example, there may be only one large regional mall in a smaller town, so there are no comparable sales of regional malls to rely on. But the appraiser may have all the details of the existing leases and be pretty confident in what investors want as a rate of return for regional malls around the country because they have similar kinds of tenants.

EXAMPLE 25

Choosing among the Three Approaches

Suppose it is a weak market with hardly any transactions taking place and no new construction during the past year. Investors indicate that they will purchase properties if they can get an adequate return for the risk. What does this suggest about the reliability of the three approaches?

Solution:

The sales comparison approach relies on having transactions to use as comparables. Therefore, in a weak market with few transactions, it is difficult to apply this approach. The replacement cost of a building could be calculated, but if new construction is not feasible, then there is economic depreciation that can be hard to estimate. There is a loss in value because market rents are not high enough to provide an adequate return on new construction. Assuming the property being appraised is generating income, a value can always be calculated using the income approach as long as the appraiser can determine an appropriate discount rate that reflects what the typical investor would require to invest in the property. Thus, in this kind of market, the income approach is likely to be the most reliable.

---

9   DUE DILIGENCE

The property value is usually estimated as part of the process of a property transaction, whether done by a hired appraiser[16] or by the investor. In addition, investors—both private debt and equity investors—will normally go through a process of "due diligence" to verify other facts and conditions that might affect the value of the property and that might not have been identified by the appraiser. The following is an example of items that are usually part of this process:

- Review the leases for the major tenants and review the history of rental payments and any defaults or late payments.
- Get copies of bills for operating expenses, such as utility expenses.

---

16 Terminology may vary among locales. For example, an appraiser is called a "valuer" in the United Kingdom and other parts of Europe.

- Look at cash flow statements of the previous owner for operating expenses and revenues.

- Have an environmental inspection to be sure there are no issues, such as a contaminant material on the site.

- Have a physical/engineering inspection to be sure there are no structural issues with the property and to check the condition of the building systems, structures, foundation, and adequacy of utilities.

- Have an attorney or appropriate party review the ownership history to be sure there are no issues related to the seller's ability to transfer free and clear title that is not subject to any previously unidentified liens.

- Review service and maintenance agreements to determine whether there are recurring problems.

- Have a property survey to determine whether the physical improvements are in the boundary lines of the site and to find out if there are any easements that would affect the value.

- Verify that the property is compliant with zoning, environmental regulations, parking ratios, and so on.

- Verify that property taxes, insurance, special assessments, and so on, have been paid.

When an investor decides to acquire commercial real estate, they will often sign a contract or "letter of intent" that states the investor's intent to acquire the property at a specified price but subject to due diligence. If problems are found during the due diligence period, the investor is likely to try to renegotiate the price or back out of the deal, which he or she can do because either the contract contains a conditional clause or a letter of intent was used. A contract that contains a conditional clause or a letter of intent is not a binding contract. The prospective buyer may have to forfeit a deposit depending on the terms of the conditional contract or the letter of intent. In some countries, it may not be customary to use a conditional contract or a letter of intent as a first step. In such countries, some due diligence should be done before entering into a contract that will be binding. Conducting due diligence can be costly but lowers the risk of acquiring a property or lending funds on a property with unexpected legal or physical problems.

EXAMPLE 26

Due Diligence

What is the primary purpose of due diligence?

Solution:

Due diligence is done to identify legal, environmental, physical, and other unanticipated problems that have not been disclosed by the seller that could be quite costly to remediate or that could negatively affect value. If identified, an issue or issues could result in negotiating a lower price or allow the investor to walk away from the transaction.

10   VALUATION IN AN INTERNATIONAL CONTEXT

As mentioned earlier in the reading, different lease structures and conventions can result in slightly different approaches to valuation in different countries, but the underlying principles are very similar and tending to converge with increasing amounts of cross-border investment in real estate and the need for standardized ways of analyzing properties. This is especially evident in the increasing use of DCF analysis—especially for properties that are institutionally owned.

We have discussed the different approaches and techniques that are used to value properties, such as the sales comparison, cost, and income approaches. And we have discussed several ways of applying the income approach because variations in its application tend to occur depending on the lease structure of the property and tradition in the country. Differences across countries will mainly be based on which approaches are emphasized and which of the ways of applying the approach is used.

As an example, Germany has a tradition of valuing the land and building separately even when using the income approach. The land is valued using a sales comparison approach because the government has good data on land sales. So when using the income approach, it is simply assumed that the land is being leased. That is, the land is assumed to be owned by an entity other than the entity that owns the building. Thus, an assumed land lease payment is deducted from the NOI. The resulting cash flow represents income to the building and can be discounted or a cap rate can be applied to it in the same way we have illustrated in this reading. The resulting value will be for the building, and this value can then be added to the value of the land from the sales comparison approach to get the total value. This same approach is used in the United States when the land is actually being leased from a third party. The point is that this is just a slight variation in applying the concepts and techniques illustrated in this reading.

We now set out some general international comparisons. In different international markets, professionals operate in different regulatory environments, have different training, may use specific definitions of the key concepts, may apply different interpretations of common concepts, use variations of basic methods, and have differing availability of key data. These issues affect the local practices of appraisal to different extents in different countries.

Although there has been a progressive extension of international standards and common approaches,[17] it is always useful to be aware of local approaches.[18] However, it is important to bear in mind that the general concepts are the same and that value should have the same bases in any market, that is, it is derived from an income stream that has a risk associated with it. Any appraisal method, however much it may appear otherwise, is simply a way to establish an appropriate value for that income.

Some key differences among countries are summarized in Exhibit 11.

---

17 The quest for international standards in valuation has a long history. The RICS in the United Kingdom has for many years produced its valuation standards rules and guidance in the form of the *Red Book* and has been expanding internationally as the main international professional body for appraisers. In Europe, since the early 1980s, the European Group of Valuers' Associations has produced its *Blue Book* of valuation standards. The International Valuation Standards Council (ISVC) produces the "International Valuation Standards."

18 For those interested in the differences within Europe, the European Mortgage Federation in 2009 produced a study titled "EMF Study on the Valuation of Property for Lending Purposes." It analyzes 16 separate European markets according to a number of criteria, including the regulatory framework, methods, and the training of valuers.

Exhibit 11   Summary of International Valuation Methodologies[19]

Country	Valuation Framework	Valuation Approaches	Lease Structure and Rent Reviews	Landlord vs. Tenant Expense Responsibility	Globalization
China	People's Republic of China and Regulations for Urban Land Valuation	Sales Comparison, Cost, and Income Approaches	2- to 3-year terms Upon expiry	Landlord: structure Tenant: interior, maintenance, insurance	DCF methodology gaining popularity
France	La Charte de l'Expertise en Évaluation Immobilière, [Le COB]	Sales Comparison and Cost Approaches, Comparative Implicit Capitalization	3-, 6-, 9-year terms Upon expiry, rental changes tie to INSEE Index	Landlord: structure Tenant: interior, maintenance, insurance	DCF gaining popularity with international investments/ valuations
Germany	WertV, WertR BelWertV	Sales Comparison, Cost, and Income Approaches	5-, 10-year terms Upon expiry, rental changes tie to cost of living index	Landlord: structure 'Dach und Fach' Tenant: interior	DCF gaining popularity with international investments/ valuations
Japan	Ministry of Land, Infrastructure, Transport and Tourism	Sales Comparison, Cost, and Income Approaches	3-, 5-year terms 6 months prior to lease expiration	Landlord: repair Tenant: inside maintenance, insurance	DCF used as an analysis tool and widely used in international investments/ valuations
United Kingdom	Royal Institution of Chartered Surveyors (RICS) *Red Book*	Sales Comparison and Cost Approaches, Implicit Capitalization	Recently changed from 25 years to 10, 15 years 5-year upward only	Landlord: minimal Tenant: all repairs, insurance	DCF used as an analysis tool and widely used in international investments/ valuations
United States	Universal Standards of Professional Appraisal Practice (USPAP)	Sales Comparison and Cost Approaches, Implicit Capitalization, DCF	3-, 5-year terms 10+ years Upon expiry	Depends on lease structure	DCF used extensively by institutional investors

INDICES

11

An investor will find a variety of real estate indices to choose from and may find one that seems representative of the market of interest to them. However, the investor should be aware of how the index is constructed and the inherent limitations resulting

---

19 An excellent reference on differences in appraisal practices across countries can be found in *Real Estate Valuation in Global Markets*, 2nd edition, edited by Howard Gelbtuch, MAI, and published by the Appraisal Institute in 2011.

from the construction method. Investors should also be aware that the apparent low correlation of real estate with other asset classes may be due to limitations in real estate index construction.

11.1 Appraisal-Based Indices

Many indices rely on appraisals to estimate how the value of a portfolio of properties or the real estate market in general is changing over time. Real estate indices often rely on appraisals to estimate values because there usually are not sufficient transactions of the same property to rely on transactions to indicate value. Even though there may be real estate transactions occurring, it is not the same property; differences in sale prices (transaction prices) can be due to changes in the market or differences in the characteristics of the property (size, age, location, and so on). Appraisal-based indices combine valuation information from individual properties and provide a measure of market movements.

A well-known index that measures the change in values of real estate held by institutional investors in the United States is the NCREIF Property Index (NPI).[20] Members of NCREIF, who are investment managers and pension fund plan sponsors, contribute information on the appraised value along with the NOI, capital expenditures, and other information, such as occupancy, to NCREIF every quarter. This information is then used to create an index that measures the performance of these properties quarterly. The return for all the properties is calculated as follows:[21]

$$\text{Return} = \frac{\begin{array}{c} \text{NOI} - \text{Capital expenditures} \\ + \left(\text{Ending market value} - \text{Beginning market value}\right) \end{array}}{\text{Beginning market value}} \qquad (7)$$

In Equation 7, the beginning and ending market values are based on the appraisals of the properties.

The return calculated with this formula is commonly known as the holding period return and is equivalent to a single-period IRR (the IRR if the property were purchased at the beginning of the quarter at its beginning market value and sold at the end of the quarter at its ending market value). A similar equation is used to calculate the returns on stocks and bonds, but in those cases an actual transaction price is typically used. Because this is not possible for real estate, the appraised value is used.

The above return is first calculated for each individual property and then value weighted to get the return for all properties in the index. An alternative would be to equal weight each property, but value weighing gives the return for the portfolio of properties because properties with more value do affect the portfolio more than properties with less value (and less income).

We saw earlier that taking the NOI and dividing by the beginning market value gives the cap rate for the property, which is also referred to as the income return for the property or for the index when it is for all properties. The remaining component in the equation ([Ending market value – Beginning market value – Capital expenditures]/Beginning market value) is referred to as the capital return. It is the change in value net of capital expenditures. To have a positive capital return, the value must increase by more than any funds invested in the property for capital expenditures. That is, replacing the roof may increase the market value but results in a positive rate of return only if the value increases by more than what was spent to replace the roof.

---

20 See www.ncreif.org for further information. NCREIF provides a variety of indices based on different factors, such as property type and location.
21 The actual formula used by NCREIF differs slightly to capture the fact that the NOI and capital expenditures may occur throughout the quarter and not just at the very end. But the differences between the NPI calculation and the simplified formula shown in Equation 7 are not significant.

It should also be noted that the income return is not the same as cash flow because cash flow is calculated after capital expenditures. That is, the amount of cash flow available each quarter is NOI – Capital expenditures. Thus, we can also think of the total return in the above formula as measuring the cash flow (NOI – Capital expenditures) plus the change in value (Ending market value – Beginning market value).

Having an index like the one described above is important because it allows us to compare the performance of real estate with other asset classes, such as stocks and bonds. The quarterly returns are also important for measuring risk, which is often measured as the volatility or standard deviation of the quarterly returns. The index is also a benchmark to which the returns for individual funds can be compared. For example, an investment manager may have a fund of properties that a pension fund or wealthy investor has invested in, and the pension fund or investor may want to know if that investment manager has done better or worse than a benchmark that reflects how the broader market has performed.

Appraisal-based indices, such as the NCREIF Property Index, are also available in many other countries. Many of them are available from Investment Property Databank (IPD), which produces indices for 23 countries.[22] The IPD indices are calculated in a similar manner to the NPI.[23]

EXAMPLE 27

Appraisal-Based Indices

Why are appraisals often used to create real estate performance indices?

Solution:

Because properties do not transact very frequently, it is more difficult to create transaction-based indices as is done for publicly traded securities. Appraisal-based indices can be constructed even when there are no transactions by relying on quarterly or annual appraisals of the property. Of course when there are no transactions, it is also difficult for appraisers to estimate value.

11.2 Transaction-Based Indices

In recent years, indices have been created that are based on actual transactions rather than appraised values. These indices have been made possible by companies that collect information on enough transactions to create an index based only on transactions. In fact, both NCREIF and IPD have transaction information that can be used for this purpose. When creating a transaction-based index, the fact that the same property does not sell very frequently is still an issue. So, to develop an index that measures changes in value quarterly as discussed above for the appraisal index, the fact that there are different properties selling every quarter needs to be controlled for. Some econometric technique, usually involving a regression analysis, is used to address the issue and to create the index. There are two main ways this is done. One is to create what is referred to as a repeat sales index, and the other is to create what is referred to as a hedonic index.

---

22 Australia, Austria, Belgium, Canada, Denmark, Finland, France, Germany, Ireland, Italy, Japan, South Korea, the Netherlands, New Zealand, Norway, Poland, Portugal, South Africa, Spain, Sweden, Switzerland, the United Kingdom, and the United States.

23 See www.ipd.com for further information.

A repeat sales index, as the name implies, relies on repeat sales of the same property. A particular property may sell only twice during the entire period of the index. But if there are at least some properties that have sold each quarter, the repeat sales regression methodology can use this information to create an index. Of course, the more sales, the more reliable is the index. In general, the idea of this type of index is that, because it is the same property that sold twice, the change in value between the two sale dates indicates how market conditions have changed over time. The regression methodology allocates this change in value to each time period—that is, each quarter based on the information from sales that occurred that quarter. The details of how the regression works is beyond the scope of this reading. An example of a repeat sales index for commercial real estate in the United States is the Moody's REAL index.[24]

A hedonic index does not require repeat sales of the same property. It requires only one sale. The way it controls for the fact that different properties are selling each quarter is to include variables in the regression that control for differences in the characteristics of the property, such as size, age, quality of construction, and location. These independent variables in the regression reflect how differences in characteristics cause values to differ so that they can be separated from the differences in value due to changes in market conditions from quarter to quarter. Again, the details of this regression are beyond the scope of this reading. The point is that there are ways of constructing indices that are based only on transactions. But they require a lot of data and are usually most reliable at the national level for the major property types, but sometimes they are reliable at the regional level of a country if sufficient transactions are available.

EXAMPLE 28

Transaction-Based Indices

Describe two main ways of creating transaction-based indices.

Solution:

The two main ways are (1) a repeat sales index and (2) a hedonic index. A repeat sales index requires repeat sales of the same property; because it is the same property, controls for differences in property characteristics, such as its size and location, are not required. A hedonic index requires only one sale of a property and thus can usually include more properties than a repeat sales index, but it must control for "hedonic" characteristics of the property, such as its size and location.

11.3 Advantages and Disadvantages of Appraisal-Based and Transaction-Based Indices

All indices, whether appraisal- or transaction-based, have advantages and disadvantages. Appraisal-based indices are often criticized for having appraisal lag, which results from appraised values tending to lag when there are sudden shifts in the market. In an upward market, transaction prices usually start to rise first, and then as these higher prices are reflected in comparable sales and investor surveys, they are captured in appraised values. Thus, appraisal-based indices may not capture the price increase until a quarter or more after it was reflected in transactions. The same lag would also occur in a down market, with appraised values not falling as soon as transaction prices.

---

24 See www.realindices.com for further information.

Another cause of appraisal lag is that all properties in an appraisal-based index may not be appraised every quarter. A manager may assume the value has stayed the same for several quarters until he or she goes through the appraisal process to estimate a new value. This causes a lag in the index. That being said, if the investment managers are all using appraised values to measure returns and if the index is based on appraised values, then it is an "apples to apples" comparison.

If the purpose of the index is for comparison with other asset classes that are publicly traded, however, appraisal lag is more of an issue. Appraisal lag tends to "smooth" the index, meaning that it has less volatility. It behaves somewhat like a moving average of what an index would look like if it were based on values obtained from transactions rather than appraisals. Thus, appraisal-based indices may underestimate the volatility of real estate returns. Because of the lag in appraisal-based real estate indices, they will also tend to have a lower correlation with other asset classes. This is problematic if the index is used in asset allocation models to determine how much of a portfolio should be allocated to real estate versus other asset classes. The allocation to real estate would likely be overestimated.

There are two general ways of adjusting for the appraisal lag. The first is to "unsmooth" the appraisal-based index. Several techniques have been developed to do this, although they are beyond the scope of this reading. In general, these techniques attempt to adjust for the appraisal lag; the resulting unsmoothed index will have more volatility and more correlation with other asset classes. The second way of adjusting for the appraisal lag is to use a transaction-based index when comparing real estate with other asset classes.

Transaction-based indices tend to lead appraisal-based indices for the reasons discussed above but can be noisy (that is, they include random elements in the observations) because of the need to use statistical techniques to estimate the index. So, there may be upward or downward movements from quarter to quarter that are somewhat random even though in general (viewed over a year or more) the index is capturing the correct movements in the market. The challenge for those creating these indices is to try to keep the noise to a minimum through use of appropriate statistical techniques and collecting as much data as possible.

EXAMPLE 29

Comparing Appraisal-Based and Transaction-Based Indices

What are the main differences between the performance of appraisal-based and transaction-based indices?

Solution:

An appraisal-based index will tend to have less volatility and lag a transaction-based index, resulting in a lower correlation with other asset classes being reported for an appraisal-based index.

PRIVATE MARKET REAL ESTATE DEBT   12

Thus far, our focus has been on analyzing a property without considering whether there would be debt financing on the property or it would be purchased on an all-cash basis. This is because the way a property is financed should not affect the property's value. This does not mean that the overall level of interest rates and availability of debt in the market do not affect values. It means that, for a given property, the investor paying all cash should be paying the same price as one who decides to use some debt financing. Of course, investors who do use debt financing will normally expect to earn a higher rate of return on their equity investment. This is because they expect to earn a greater return on the property than what they will be paying the lender. Thus, there will be positive financial leverage. By borrowing money, the investor is taking on more risk in anticipation of a higher return on equity invested. The risk is higher because with debt there will be more uncertainty as to what return the investor will actually earn on equity because the investor gets what is left over after paying the lender. A small drop in property value can result in a large decrease in the investor's return if a high amount of debt was used to finance the property. When a property is valued without explicitly considering financing, the discount rate can be thought of as a weighted average of the rate of return an equity investor would want and the interest rate on the debt.

The maximum amount of debt that an investor can obtain on commercial real estate is usually limited by either the ratio of the loan to the appraised value of the property (loan to value or LTV) or the debt service coverage ratio (DSCR), depending on which measure results in the lowest loan amount. The debt service coverage ratio is the ratio of the first-year NOI to the loan payment (referred to as debt service for commercial real estate). That is,

$$\text{DSCR} = \text{NOI/Debt service} \tag{8}$$

The debt service includes both interest and principal payments on the mortgage. The principal payments are the portion of the loan payment that amortizes the loan over the loan term. An "interest-only" loan would be one that has no principal payments, so the loan balance would remain constant over time. Interest-only loans typically either revert to amortizing loans at some point or have a specified maturity date. For example, an interest-only loan might be made that requires the entire balance of the loan to be repaid after 7–10 years (referred to as a "balloon payment"). Lenders typically require a DSCR of 1.2 or greater to provide a margin of safety that the NOI from the property can cover the debt service.

EXAMPLE 30

Loans on Real Estate

A property has been appraised for $5 million and is expected to have NOI of $400,000 in the first year. The lender is willing to make an interest-only loan at an 8 percent interest rate as long as the loan-to-value ratio does not exceed 80 percent and the DSCR is at least 1.25. The balance of the loan will be due after seven years. How much of a loan can be obtained?

Solution:

Based on the loan-to-value ratio, the loan would be 80 percent of $5 million or $4 million. With a DSCR of 1.25, the maximum debt service would be $400,000/1.25 = $320,000. This amount is the mortgage payment that would result in a 1.25 DSCR for an interest-only loan.

If the loan is interest only, then we can obtain the loan amount by simply dividing the mortgage payment by the interest rate. Therefore, the loan amount would be $320,000/0.08 = $4,000,000.

In this case, we obtain the same loan amount based on either the LTV or DSCR requirements of the lender. If one ratio had resulted in a lower loan amount, that would normally be the maximum that could be borrowed.

When financing is used on a property, equity investors often look at their first-year return on equity or "equity dividend rate" as a measure of how much cash flow they are getting as a percentage of their equity investment. This is sometimes referred to as a "cash-on-cash" return because it measures how much cash they are receiving as a percentage of the cash equity they put into the investment.

EXAMPLE 31

Equity Dividend Rate

Using the information in Example 30, what is the equity dividend rate or cash-on-cash return assuming the property is purchased at its appraised value?

Solution:

The first-year cash flow is the NOI less the mortgage payment.

NOI	$400,000
DS	$320,000
Cash flow	$80,000

The amount of equity is the purchase price less the loan amount.

Price	$5,000,000
Mortgage	$4,000,000
Equity	$1,000,000

The equity yield rate is the Cash flow/Equity = $80,000/$1,000,000 = 8%. Keep in mind that this is not an IRR that would be earned over a holding period until the property is sold. The equity investor does not share any of the price appreciation in the value of the property with the lender.

For loans called "participation" loans, the lender might receive some of the price appreciation, but it would be in exchange for a lower interest rate on the loan.

EXAMPLE 32

Leveraged IRR

Refer to the previous examples 30 and 31. Suppose the property is sold for $6 million after five years. What IRR will the equity investor receive on his or her investment?

Solution:

The cash flow received by the equity investor from the sale will be the sale price less the mortgage balance, or $6 million − $4 million = $2 million. Using a financial calculator,

$$PV = -\$1,000,000 \text{ (using a calculator, this is input as a negative to indicate the negative cash flow at the beginning of the investment)}$$

$$PMT = \$80,000$$
$$n = 5$$
$$FV = \$2,000,000$$
$$\text{Solve for } i = 21.14\%$$

This is an IRR based on the equity invested in the property.

EXAMPLE 33

Unleveraged IRR

Refer to the previous examples 30, 31, and 32. What would the IRR be if the property were purchased on an all-cash basis (no loan)?

Solution:

Now the equity investor will receive all the cash flow from sale ($6 million) and the NOI ($400,000). The initial investment will be $5 million. Using a financial calculator,

$$PV = -\$5,000,000$$
$$PMT = \$400,000$$
$$n = 5$$
$$FV - \$6,000,000$$
$$\text{Solve for } i = 11.20\%$$

This is an IRR based on an unleveraged (all-cash) investment in the property. The difference between this IRR (11.20 percent) and the IRR the equity investor receives with a loan calculated in Example 32 of 21.14 percent reflects positive financial leverage. The property earns 11.20 percent before adding a loan, and the loan is at 8 percent, so the investor is benefiting from the spread between 11.20 percent and 8 percent.

SUMMARY

Real estate property is an asset class that plays a significant role in many investment portfolios. Because of the unique characteristics of real estate property, it tends to behave differently from other asset classes, such as stocks, bonds, and commodities, and thus has different risks and diversification benefits. Private real estate investments are especially unique because the investments are not publicly traded and require different analytic techniques from publicly traded assets. Because of the lack of transactions, the appraisal process is required to value real estate property. Many of the indices and benchmarks used for private real estate also rely on appraisals, and because of this characteristic, they behave differently from indices for publicly traded assets, such as the S&P 500.

The factors that affect the performance of private real estate investments tend to be similar across countries, and the methods for valuing real estate property tend to be similar. Cross-border investment is facilitated by the development of standardized ways of analyzing real estate and by responses to the demand for transparency and sufficient data to do the necessary due diligence. As the availability of real estate data improves along with the technology to analyze the data, real estate markets are likely to become more efficient.

Key points of the reading include the following:

- Real estate investments make up a significant portion of the portfolios of many investors.

- Real estate investments can occur in four basic forms: private equity (direct ownership), publicly traded equity (indirect ownership claim), private debt (direct mortgage lending), and publicly traded debt (securitized mortgages).

- Each of the basic forms of real estate investment has its own risks, expected returns, regulations, legal structures, and market structures.

- There are many motivations for investing in real estate income property. The key ones are current income, price appreciation, inflation hedge, diversification, and tax benefits.

- Equity investors generally expect a higher rate of return than lenders (debt investors) because they take on more risk. The returns to equity real estate investors have two components: an income stream and a capital appreciation. Adding equity real estate investments to a traditional portfolio will potentially have diversification benefits because of the less-than-perfect correlation of equity real estate returns with returns to stocks and bonds. If the income stream can be adjusted for inflation and real estate prices increase with inflation, then equity real estate investments may provide an inflation hedge.

- Debt investors in real estate expect to receive their return from promised cash flows and typically do not participate in any appreciation in value of the underlying real estate. Thus, debt investments in real estate are similar to other fixed-income investments, such as bonds.

- Regardless of the form of real estate investment, the value of the underlying real estate property can affect the performance of the investment. Location is a critical factor in determining the value of a real estate property.

- Real estate property has some unique characteristics compared with other investment asset classes. These characteristics include heterogeneity and fixed location, high unit value, management intensiveness, high transaction costs, depreciation, sensitivity to the credit market, illiquidity, and difficulty of value and price determination.

- There are many different types of real estate properties in which to invest. The main commercial (income-producing) real estate property types are office, industrial and warehouse, retail, and multi-family. There are other types of commercial properties, which are typically classified by their specific use.

- There are risk factors common to commercial property, but each property type is likely to have a different susceptibility to these factors. The key risk factors that can affect commercial real estate include business conditions, lead time for new development, cost and availability of capital, unexpected inflation, demographics, lack of liquidity, environmental issues, availability of information, management expertise, and leverage.

- Location, lease structures, and economic factors, such as employment growth, economic growth, consumer spending, and population growth, affect the value of each property type.

- An understanding of the lease structure is important when analyzing a real estate investment.

- Appraisals estimate the value of real estate income property. Definitions of value include market value, investment value, value in use, and mortgage lending value.

- Generally, three different approaches are used by appraisers to estimate value: income, cost, and sales comparison.

- The income approach includes direct capitalization and discounted cash flow methods. Both methods focus on net operating income as an input to the value of a property.

- The cost approach estimates the value of a property based on adjusted replacement cost. This approach is typically used for unusual properties for which market comparables are difficult to obtain.

- The sales comparison approach estimates the value of a property based on what comparable properties are selling for in the current market.

- Due diligence investigates factors that might affect the value of a property. These factors include leases and lease history; operating expenses; environmental issues; structural integrity; lien, ownership, and property tax history; and compliance with relevant laws and regulations.

- Appraisal-based and transaction-based indices are used to track the performance of private real estate. Appraisal-based indices tend to lag transaction-based indices and appear to have lower volatility and lower correlation with other asset classes than transaction-based indices.

- When debt financing is used to purchase a property, additional ratios and returns calculated and interpreted by debt and/or equity investors include the loan-to-value ratio, the debt service coverage ratio, the equity dividend rate (cash-on-cash return), and leveraged and unleveraged internal rates of return.

PRACTICE PROBLEMS

The following information relates to Questions 1–12

Amanda Rodriguez is an alternative investments analyst for a US investment management firm, Delphinus Brothers. Delphinus' Chief Investment Officer, Michael Tang, has informed Rodriguez that he wants to reduce the amount invested in traditional asset classes and gain exposure to the real estate sector by acquiring commercial property in the United States. Rodriguez is to analyze potential commercial real estate investments for Delphinus Brothers. Selected data on three commercial real estate properties is presented in Exhibit 1.

Exhibit 1	Selected Property Data		
	Property #1	**Property #2**	**Property #3**
Property Type	**Downtown Office Building**	**Grocery-Anchored Retail Center**	**Multi-Family Building**
Location	New York, NY	Miami, FL	Boston, MA
Occupancy	90.00%	93.00%	95.00%
Square Feet or Number of Units	100,000 sf	205,000 sf	300 units
Gross Potential Rent	$4,250,000	$1,800,000	$3,100,000
Expense Reimbursement Revenue	$330,000	$426,248	$0
Other Income (includes % Rent)	$550,000	$15,000	$45,000
Potential Gross Income	$5,130,000	$2,241,248	$3,145,000
Vacancy Loss	($513,000)	($156,887)	($157,250)
Effective Gross Income	$5,079,000	$2,084,361	$2,987,750
Property Management Fees	($203,160)	($83,374)	($119,510)
Other Operating Expenses	($2,100,000)	($342,874)	($1,175,000)
Net Operating Income (NOI)	$2,775,840	$1,658,113	$1,693,240

Rodriguez reviews the three properties with Tang, who indicates that he would like her to focus on Property #1 because of his prediction of robust job growth in New York City over the next ten years. To complete her analysis, Rodriquez assembles additional data on Property #1, which is presented in Exhibits 2, 3 and 4.

As part of the review, Tang asks Rodriguez to evaluate financing alternatives to determine if it would be better to use debt financing or to make an all cash purchase. Tang directs Rodriguez to inquire about terms with Richmond Life Insurance Company, a publicly traded company, which is an active lender on commercial real estate property. Rodriquez obtains the following information from Richmond Life for a loan on Property #1: loan term of 5 years, interest rate of 5.75% interest-only, maximum loan to value of 75%, and minimum debt service coverage ratio of 1.5x.

Exhibit 2   6-Year Net Operating Income (NOI) and DCF Assumptions for Property #1

	Year 1	Year 2	Year 3	Year 4	Year 5	Year 6
NOI	$2,775,840	$2,859,119	$2,944,889	$3,033,235	$3,124,232	$3,217,959

DCF Assumptions

Investment Hold Period	5 years
Going-in Cap Rate	5.25%
Terminal Cap Rate	6.00%
Discount Rate	7.25%
Income/Value Growth Rate	Constant

Exhibit 3   Sales Comparison Data for Property #1

Variable	Property 1	Sales Comp A	Sales Comp B	Sales Comp C
Age (years)	10	5	12	25
Condition	Good	Excellent	Good	Average
Location	Prime	Secondary	Secondary	Prime
Sale price psf		$415 psf	$395 psf	$400 psf

Adjustments

Age (years)		−10%	2%	10%
Condition		−10%	0%	10%
Location		15%	15%	0%
Total Adjustments		−5%	17%	20%

Exhibit 4   Other Selected Data for Property #1

Land Value	$7,000,000
Replacement Cost	$59,000,000
Total Depreciation	$5,000,000

After reviewing her research materials, Rodriguez formulates the following two conclusions:

Conclusion 1   Benefits of private equity real estate investments include owners' ability to attain diversification benefits, to earn current income, and to achieve tax benefits.

Conclusion 2   Risk factors of private equity real estate investments include business conditions, demographics, the cost of debt and equity capital, and financial leverage.

1   Which of the following is *most likely* accurate regarding Property #2 described in Exhibit 1?

   A   Operating expense risk is borne by the owner.

   B   The lease term for the largest tenant is greater than three years.

   C   There is a significant amount of percentage rent linked to sales levels.

2   Based upon Exhibits 2, 3 and 4, which of the following statements is *most* accurate regarding the valuation of Property #1?

   A   The cost approach valuation is $71,000,000.

   B   The adjusted price psf for Sales Comp B is $423 psf.

   C   The terminal value at the end of year 5 in the income approach is $53,632,650.

3   Based on Exhibit 2, the growth rate of Property #1 is *closest* to:

   A   0.75%

   B   1.25%.

   C   2.00%.

4   Based on Exhibit 2, the value of Property #1 utilizing the discounted cash flow method is *closest* to:

   A $48,650,100.

   B $49,750,900.

   C $55,150,300.

5   Based on Exhibit 2, relative to the estimated value of Property #1 under the discounted cash flow method, the estimated value of Property #1 using the direct capitalization method is:

   A   equal.

   B   lower.

   C   higher.

6   Based upon Exhibits 1 and 3, the estimated value of Property #1 using the sales comparison approach (assigning equal weight to each comparable) is *closest* to:

   A   40,050,000.

   B   40,300,000.

   C   44,500,000.

7   In the event that Delphinus purchases Property #2, the due diligence process would *most likely* require a review of:

   A   all tenant leases.

   B   tenant sales data.

   C   the grocery anchor lease.

8   Compared to an all-cash purchase, a mortgage on Property #1 through Richmond Life would *most likely* result in Delphinus earning:

   A   a lower return on equity.

   B   a higher return on equity.

   C   the same return on equity.

9 Assuming an appraised value of $48,000,000, Richmond Life Insurance Company's maximum loan amount on Property #1 would be *closest* to:

   A $32,000,000.

   B $36,000,000.

   C $45,000,000.

10 Rodriguez's Conclusion 1 is:

   A correct.

   B incorrect, because tax benefits do not apply to tax-exempt entities.

   C incorrect, because private real estate is highly correlated to stocks.

11 Rodriguez's Conclusion 2 is:

   A correct.

   B incorrect, because inflation is not a risk factor.

   C incorrect, because the cost of equity capital is not a risk factor.

12 Richmond Life Insurance Company's potential investment would be *most likely* described as:

   A private real estate debt.

   B private real estate equity.

   C publicly traded real estate debt.

The following information relates to Questions 13–28

First Life Insurance Company, Ltd., a life insurance company located in the United Kingdom, maintains a stock and bond portfolio and also invests in all four quadrants of the real estate market; private equity, public equity, private debt, and public debt. Each of the four real estate quadrants has a manager assigned to it. First Life intends to increase its allocation to real estate. The Chief Investment Officer (CIO) has scheduled a meeting with the four real estate managers to discuss the allocation to real estate and to each real estate quadrant. Leslie Green, who manages the private equity quadrant, believes her quadrant offers the greatest potential and has identified three investment properties to consider for acquisition. Selected information for the three properties is presented in Exhibit 1.

Exhibit 1	**Selected Information on Potential Private Equity Real Estate Investments**		
	Property		
	A	**B**	**C**
Property description	**Single Tenant Office**	**Shopping Center**	**Warehouse**
Size (square meters)	3,000	5,000	9,000
Lease type	Net	Gross	Net
Expected loan to value ratio	70%	75%	80%
Total economic life	50 years	30 years	50 years
Remaining economic life	30 years	23 years	20 years

Exhibit 1 (Continued)

	Property		
	A	**B**	**C**
Property description	**Single Tenant Office**	**Shopping Center**	**Warehouse**
Rental income (at full occupancy)	£575,000	£610,000	£590,000
Other income	£27,000	£183,000	£29,500
Vacancy and collection loss	£0	£61,000	£59,000
Property management fee	£21,500	£35,000	£22,000
Other operating expenses	£0	£234,000	£0
Discount rate	11.5%	9.25%	11.25%
Growth rate	2.0%	See Assumption 2	3.0%
Terminal cap rate		11.00%	
Market value of land	£1,500,000	£1,750,000	£4,000,000
Replacement costs			
▪ Building costs	£8,725,000	£4,500,000	£12,500,000
▪ Developer's profit	£410,000	£210,000	£585,000
Deterioration – curable and incurable	£4,104,000	£1,329,000	£8,021,000
Obsolescence			
▪ Functional	£250,000	£50,000	£750,000
▪ Locational	£500,000	£200,000	£1,000,000
▪ Economic	£500,000	£100,000	£1,000,000
Comparable adjusted price per square meter			
▪ Comparable Property 1	£1,750	£950	£730
▪ Comparable Property 2	£1,825	£1,090	£680
▪ Comparable Property 3	£1,675	£875	£725

To prepare for the upcoming meeting, Green has asked her research analyst, Ian Cook, for a valuation of each of these properties under the income, cost and sales comparison approaches using the information provided in Exhibit 1, and the following two assumptions:

Assumption 1   The holding period for each property is expected to be five years.

Assumption 2   Property B is expected to have the same net operating income for the holding period due to existing leases, and a one-time 20% increase in year 6 due to lease rollovers. No further growth is assumed thereafter.

In reviewing Exhibit 1, Green notes the disproportionate estimated obsolescence charges for Property C relative to the other properties and asks Cook to verify the reasonableness of these estimates. Green also reminds Cook that they will need to conduct proper due diligence. In that regard, Green indicates that she is concerned whether a covered parking lot that was added to Property A encroaches (is partially located) on adjoining properties. Green would like for Cook to identify an expert and present documentation to address her concerns regarding the parking lot.

In addition to discussing the new allocation, the CIO informs Green that she wants to discuss the appropriate real estate index for the private equity real estate quadrant at the upcoming meeting. The CIO believes that the current index may result in over-allocating resources to the private equity real estate quadrant.

13 The *most* effective justification that Green could present for directing the increased allocation to her quadrant would be that, relative to the other quadrants, her quadrant of real estate investments:

    A provides greater liquidity.

    B requires less professional management.

    C enables greater decision-making control.

14 Relative to the expected correlation between First Life's portfolio of public REIT holdings and its stock and bond portfolio, the expected correlation between First Life's private equity real estate portfolio and its stock and bond portfolio is *most likely* to be:

    A lower.

    B higher.

    C the same.

15 Which of the properties in Exhibit 1 exposes the owner to the greatest risk related to operating expenses?

    A Property A

    B Property B

    C Property C

16 Which property in Exhibit 1 is *most likely* to be affected by import and export activity?

    A Property A

    B Property B

    C Property C

17 Which property in Exhibit 1 would *most likely* require the greatest amount of active management?

    A Property A

    B Property B

    C Property C

18 Which property in Exhibit 1 is *most likely* to have a percentage lease?

    A Property A

    B Property B

    C Property C

19 The disproportionate charges for Property C noted by Green are *least likely* to explicitly factor into the estimate of property value using the:

    A cost approach.

    B income approach.

    C sales comparison approach.

20 Based upon Exhibit 1, which of the following statements regarding Property A is *most* accurate?

    A The going-in capitalization rate is 13.5%.

    B It appears the riskiest of the three properties.

    C The net operating income in the first year is £298,000.

21 Based upon Exhibit 1, the value of Property C using the direct capitalization method is *closest* to:

   A £3,778,900.

   B £4,786,700.

   C £6,527,300.

22 Based upon Exhibit 1 and Assumptions 1 and 2, the value of Property B using the discounted cash flow method, assuming a five-year holding period, is *closest* to:

   A £4,708,700.

   B £5,035,600.

   C £5,050,900.

23 Which method under the income approach is *least likely* to provide a realistic valuation for Property B?

   A Layer method

   B Direct capitalization method

   C Discounted cash flow method

24 Based upon Exhibit 1, the value of Property A using the cost approach is *closest* to:

   A £5,281,000.

   B £6,531,000.

   C £9,385,000.

25 Based upon Exhibit 1, the value of Property B using the sales comparison approach is *closest* to:

   A £4,781,000.

   B £4,858,000.

   C £6,110,000.

26 Which due diligence item would be *most* useful in addressing Green's concerns regarding Property A?

   A Property survey

   B Engineering inspection

   C Environmental inspection

27 The real estate index currently being used by First Life to evaluate private equity real estate investments is *most likely:*

   A an appraisal-based index.

   B a transaction-based index.

   C the NCREIF property index.

28 Based upon Exhibit 1, the property expected to be most highly leveraged is:

   A Property A

   B Property B

   C Property C

SOLUTIONS

1 B is correct. The lease term for the anchor tenant is typically longer than the usual 3 to 5 year term for smaller tenants. The data in Exhibit 1 suggest that the operating expenses are passed on to the tenant; the sum of Property Management Fees and Other Operating Expenses equal the Expense Reimbursement Revenue. Also, Other Income is only $15,000 suggesting that there is a minimal amount of percentage rent linked to sales thresholds.

2 C is correct. The terminal value using the income approach is $53,632,650 (= Year 6 NOI/terminal cap rate = $3,217,959 / 0.06). The value of the property using the cost approach is $61,000,000 (= Land Value + Building Replacement Cost − Total Depreciation = $7,000,000 + $59,000,000 − $5,000,000). The adjusted sales price per square foot for Sales Comp B is $462 psf (= $395 × 1.17).

3 C is correct. There is a constant growth rate in income and value; growth rate = discount rate (7.25%) − going-in cap rate (5.25%) = 2.00%.

4 B is correct. The value of Property 1 using the discounted cash flow method is $49,750,931, or $49,750,900 rounded, calculated as follows:

		Discount period	Discounted value*
Year 1 NOI	$2,775,840	1	$2,588,196
Year 2 NOI	$2,859,119	2	$2,485,637
Year 3 NOI	$2,944,889	3	$2,387,135
Year 4 NOI	$3,033,235	4	$2,292,540
Year 5 NOI	$3,124,232	5	$2,201,693
Terminal Value**	$53,632,650	5	$37,795,731
Property #1 DCF value			$49,750,932

* Discount rate = 7.25%
** The terminal value = Year 6 NOI/terminal cap rate = $3,217,959/0.06 = $53,632,650

5 C is correct. The direct capitalization method estimate of value for Property #1 is $52,873,143 (= Year 1 NOI/Going-in Cap Rate = $2,775,840/0.0525), which is greater than the estimated DCF value of $49,750,932.

Value of Property #1 under the discounted cash flow method:

		Discount period	Discounted value*
Year 1 NOI	$2,775,840	1	$2,588,196
Year 2 NOI	$2,859,119	2	$2,485,637
Year 3 NOI	$2,944,889	3	$2,387,135
Year 4 NOI	$3,033,235	4	$2,292,540
Year 5 NOI	$3,124,232	5	$2,201,693
Terminal Value**	$53,632,650	5	$37,795,731
Property #1 DCF value			$49,750,932

* Discount rate = 7.25%
** The terminal value = Year 6 NOI/terminal cap rate = $3,217,959/0.06 = $53,632,650

6 C is correct. The estimate of the value of Property #1 using the sales comparison approach is:

	Unadjusted psf	Adjusted psf
Sales Comp 1	$415	$394 (= $415 × 0.95)
Sales Comp 2	$395	$462 (= $395 × 1.17)
Sales Comp 3	$400	$480 (= $400 × 1.20)
Average	$403	$445

Estimated Value of Property #1 = $44,500,000 (= $445 psf × 100,000 sf)

7 C is correct. The due diligence process includes a review of leases for major tenants which would include the grocery anchor tenant. Typically, only major tenant leases will be reviewed in the due diligence process, and smaller tenant leases will likely not be reviewed. Also, the fact that Other Income is only $15,000 suggests that percentage rent linked to sales levels is minimal and has not been underwritten in the valuation and acquisition process.

8 B is correct. Delphinus will expect to earn a higher return on equity with the use of a mortgage to finance a portion of the purchase. The quoted mortgage interest rate of 5.75% is less than the discount rate of 7.25%.

9 A is correct. The maximum amount of debt that an investor can obtain on commercial real estate is usually limited by either the ratio of the loan to the appraised value of the property (loan to value or LTV) or the debt service coverage ratio (DSCR) depending on which measure results in the lowest loan amount. The maximum LTV is 75% of the appraised value of $48,000,000 or $36,000,000. The loan amount based on the minimum DSCR would be $32,183,652 determined as follows:

Maximum debt service = Year 1 NOI/DSCR = $2,775,840/1.5 = $1,850,560

Loan amount (interest only loan) = maximum debt service/mortgage rate = $1,850,560/0.0575 = $32,183,652 (rounded to $32,000,000).

10 A is correct. Benefits of private equity real estate investments include owners' ability to attain diversification benefits, to earn current income, and to achieve tax benefits.

11 A is correct. Business conditions, demographics, the cost of debt and equity capital, and financial leverage are characteristic sources of risk for real estate investments.

12 A is correct. Richmond Life's investment would be a mortgage which falls under private debt on the four quadrants.

13 C is correct. Private equity investments in real estate enable greater decision-making control relative to real estate investments in the other three quadrants. A private real estate equity investor or direct owner of real estate has responsibility for management of the real estate, including maintaining the properties, negotiating leases and collecting rents. These responsibilities increase the investor's control in the decision-making process. Investors in publicly traded REITs or real estate debt instruments would not typically have significant influence over these decisions.

14 A is correct. Evidence suggests that private equity real estate investments have a lower correlation with stocks and bonds than publicly traded REITs. When real estate is publicly traded it tends to behave more like the rest of the stock market than the real estate market.

15 B is correct. Property B is a gross lease, which requires the owner to pay the operating expenses. Accordingly, the owner, First Life, incurs the risk of Property B's operating expenses, such as utilities, increasing in the future.

16 C is correct. Property C is a warehouse, and is most likely affected by import and export activity in the economy. Property A (office) and Property B (retail) would typically be less dependent on import and export activity when compared to a warehouse property.

17 B is correct. Property B is a shopping center and would most likely require more active management than a single tenant office (Property A) or a warehouse (Property C); the owner would need to maintain the right tenant mix and promote the facility.

18 B is correct. Property B is a shopping center, a type of retail property. A percentage lease is a unique aspect of many retail leases, which requires the tenant to pay additional rent once their sales reach a certain level. The lease will typically specify a "minimum rent" that must be paid regardless of the tenant's sales. Percentage rent may be paid by the tenant once the tenant's sales reach a certain level or breakpoint.

19 B is correct. Obsolescence charges reduce the value of a property using the cost approach and are factored into the sales comparison approach by adjustments, including condition and location, to the price per square foot. The cash flows to the property should reflect obsolescence; less rent is received if the property is not of an appropriate design for the intended use, is in a poor location, or if economic conditions are poor. Therefore, obsolescence is implicitly, not explicitly, factored into the estimate of property value using the income approach.

20 B is correct. Property A has been assigned the highest discount rate (11.5%) and thus is considered to be the riskiest investment of the three alternatives. This may be because of the reliance on a single tenant. The going-in capitalization rate is 9.5% (cap rate = discount rate – growth rate). The net operating income (NOI) is £580,500 (= rental income + other income – property management fee = £575,000 + £27,000 – £21,500).

21 C is correct. Under the direct capitalization method, the value of the property = NOI/(r – g).

Calculate net operating income (NOI):

> NOI = rental income + other income – vacancy and collection loss – property management costs
> NOI = £590,000 + £29,500 – £59,000 – £22,000 = £538,500

Then, value the property using the cap rate:

> Value of property = £538,500/(11.25% – 3.0%) = £6,527,273, rounded to £6,527,300.

22 B is correct. The value of Property B using the discounted cash flow method is £5,035,600.

The value using the discounted cash flow method is based on the present value of the net operating income (NOI) and the estimated property resale price.

Calculate NOI (constant during five-year holding period from Assumption 2)

> NOI = rental income (at full occupancy) + other income − vacancy and collection loss − property management fee − other operating expenses
>
> NOI = £610,000 + £183,000 − £61,000 − £35,000 − £234,000 = £463,000

Estimate property value at end of five years:

> NOI starting in year 6 is 20% higher due to lease rollovers (from Assumption 2)
>
> NOI starting in year 6 = £463,000 × 1.20 = £555,600

Terminal cap rate (given) = 11%

> Applying the terminal cap rate yields a property value of £5,050,909 (= £555,600/0.11)

Find the present value of the expected annual NOI and the estimated property resale value using the given discount rate of 9.25%:

> N = 5
> FV = £5,050,909
> PMT = £463,000
> I = 9.25

Solving for PV, the current value of the property is estimated to be £5,034,643, or £5,034,600 rounded.

23 B is correct. The net operating income for Property B is expected to be level for the next 5 years, due to existing leases, and grow 20% in year 6. A direct capitalization method would not be appropriate due to the multiple growth rates. A discounted cash flow method that assigns a terminal value, or a layer method, should be used.

24 A is correct. The value of Property A using the cost method is equal to the replacement cost, adjusted for the different types of depreciation (loss in value):

> Value of Property A = land value + (replacement building cost + developer's profit) − deterioration − functional obsolescence − locational obsolescence − economic obsolescence
> = £1,500,000 + (£8,725,000 + £410,000) − £4,104,000 − £250,000 − £500,000 − £500,000
> = £5,281,000

25 B is correct. The value of a property using the sales comparison approach equals the adjusted price per square meter using comparable properties times property size. The value of Property B using the sales comparison approach is:

> Average adjusted price per square meter of comparable properties 1, 2, and 3 for Property B = (£950 + £1,090 + £875)/3 = £971.67
>
> Applying the £971.67 average adjusted price per square meter to Property B gives a value of £4,858,300 (= £971.67 × 5,000 square meters = £4,858,350, or £4,858,000 rounded).

26 A is correct. A property survey can determine whether the physical improvements, such as the covered parking lot, are in the boundary lines of the site and if there are any easements that would affect the value of the property.

27 A is correct. An appraisal-based index is most likely to result in the over-allocation mentioned by the CIO due to the appraisal lag. The appraisal lag tends to "smooth" the index meaning that it has less volatility. It behaves

somewhat like a moving average of what an index would look like if based on values obtained from transactions rather than appraisals. Thus, appraisal-based indices may underestimate the volatility of real estate returns. Because of the lag in the index, appraisal-based real estate indices will also tend to have a lower correlation with other asset classes. This is problematic if the index is used in asset allocation models; the amount allocated to the asset class that appears to have lower correlation with other asset classes and less volatility will be greater than it should be.

28 C is correct. Property C has an expected loan to value ratio of 80%, which is higher than the loan to value ratio for Property A (70%) or Property B (75%).

44

Publicly Traded Real Estate Securities

by Anthony Paolone, CFA, Ian Rossa O'Reilly, CFA, and David Kruth, CFA

Anthony Paolone, CFA (USA). Ian Rossa O'Reilly, CFA (Canada). David Kruth, CFA (USA).

LEARNING OUTCOMES

Mastery	The candidate should be able to:
☐	a. describe types of publicly traded real estate securities;
☐	b. explain advantages and disadvantages of investing in real estate through publicly traded securities;
☐	c. explain economic value determinants, investment characteristics, principal risks, and due diligence considerations for real estate investment trust (REIT) shares;
☐	d. describe types of REITs;
☐	e. justify the use of net asset value per share (NAVPS) in REIT valuation and estimate NAVPS based on forecasted cash net operating income;
☐	f. describe the use of funds from operations (FFO) and adjusted funds from operations (AFFO) in REIT valuation;
☐	g. compare the net asset value, relative value (price-to-FFO and price-to-AFFO), and discounted cash flow approaches to REIT valuation;
☐	h. calculate the value of a REIT share using net asset value, price-to-FFO and price-to-AFFO, and discounted cash flow approaches.

INTRODUCTION

1

This reading provides an overview of the publicly traded real estate securities, focusing on equity real estate investment trusts (REITs) and their valuation.

Real estate investments may play several roles in a portfolio. Investment in commercial real estate property—also called income-producing, rental, or investment property—may be either in the form of direct ownership investment or indirect investment by means of equity securities. They can provide an above-average current yield compared with other equity investments and may provide a degree of protection against inflation, especially when rental rates are inflation-indexed, rise periodically by pre-determined amounts, or are easily adjusted. Real estate investment can be an effective means of diversification in many investment portfolios.

REITs are the most widely held type of real estate equity security. The valuation of REITs is similar in some respects to the valuation of other kinds of equity securities, but also takes into account unique aspects of real estate and sometimes uses specialized measures. This reading introduces and describes REIT valuation.

The reading is organized as follows: Section 2 provides an overview of publicly traded real estate securities. Section 3 describes publicly traded equity REITs in detail, including their structure, investment characteristics, and analysis and due diligence considerations. Section 4 presents real estate operating companies (REOCs). Sections 5, 6, and 7 present net asset value, relative valuation, and discounted cash flow valuation for REIT shares, respectively. After a mini case study in Section 8, Section 9 summarizes the reading.

2 TYPES OF PUBLICLY TRADED REAL ESTATE SECURITIES

Publicly traded real estate securities fall into two principal categories: equity (i.e., ownership) investments in properties and debt investments (i.e., primarily mortgages secured by properties). Globally, the principal types of publicly traded real estate securities are real estate investment trusts, real estate operating companies, and mortgage-backed securities.

- **Real estate investment trusts (REITs)** are tax-advantaged entities (companies or trusts) that typically own, operate, and—to a limited extent—develop income-producing real estate property (hereafter, "real estate property" may simply be referred to as "real estate"). Such REITs are called equity REITs. Mortgage REITs make loans secured by real estate. REITs' tax-advantage is a result of being allowed to deduct dividends paid; this deduction effectively makes REITs exempt from corporate income tax.

- **Real estate operating companies** (REOCs) are ordinary taxable real estate ownership companies. Businesses are organized as REOCs, as opposed to REITs, when they are located in countries that do not have a tax-advantaged REIT regime in place or when they engage to a large extent in the development of real estate properties, often with the intent to sell. The primary cash inflows are from sales of developed or improved properties rather than from recurring lease or rental income.

- **Mortgage-backed securities** (MBS) are asset-backed securitized debt obligations that represent rights to receive cash flows from portfolios of mortgage loans—mortgage loans on commercial properties in the case of commercial mortgage-backed securities (CMBS) and mortgage loans on residential properties in the case of residential mortgage-backed securities (RMBS). The market capitalization of publicly traded real estate equity securities is greatly exceeded by the market value of real estate debt securities, in particular mortgage-backed securities. Real estate debt securities are discussed further in fixed-income readings in the CFA program curriculum.

In addition to publicly traded real estate securities, there are privately held real estate securities that include private REITs and REOCs, privately held mortgages, private debt issues, and bank debt. Exhibit 1 shows how real estate securities may be classified in four quadrants.

Exhibit 1	Types of Real Estate Securities	
	Public	**Private**
Equity	Equity REITs, REOCs	Private REITs, Private REOCs
Debt	Mortgage REITs, CMBS, RMBS	Mortgages, Private debt, Bank debt

As of the end of September 2011, the market value of publicly traded real estate investment trusts and real estate operating companies globally was approximately US$800 billion, whereas the total face value of residential and commercial mortgage-related securities was approximately US$9 trillion. Details about relative sizes by geographic areas and/or security types are shown in Exhibit 2.

Exhibit 2   Relative Size and Composition of Publicly Traded Real Estate Equity Securities Markets As of 30 September 2011

Panel A: Percentage of market value of publicly traded real estate equity securities (REITs and REOCs) in developed markets

By Region		By Country	
North America	50	United States	44.4
Asia	35	Hong Kong	11.7
Europe	15	Japan	10.2
		Australia	8.4
		United Kingdom	5.5
		Canada	5.3
		Singapore	4.2
		France	3.9
		Switzerland	1.4
		Netherlands	1.3
		Sweden	1.1
		Others	2.6

Panel B: Percentage of market value of publicly traded equity real estate equity securities in developed markets by type of structure

	Global	North America	Europe	Asia
REITs	74	97	68	43
Non-REITs, REOCs	26	3	32	57

Source: Based on data from FTSE EPRA/NAREIT

Publicly traded real estate securities typically retain some of the characteristics of direct ownership of income-producing real estate. Income-producing real estate usually provides relatively predictable, recurring, contractual rental income under the terms of lease agreements. It also tends to generate capital appreciation over the long term (provided there are no major distortions to rental markets from over-building) because the replacement cost of buildings and prices for land tend to increase. Capital appreciation can result from general price inflation, the scarcity of well-located property, local population increases, and/or growth in economic activity. It should be noted, however, that changes in discount rates (the required rate of return of property investors) can also have significant effects on the value of income-producing real estate.

As an investment asset class, income-producing real estate offers the advantages of stability of income based on its contractual revenue from leases and a measure of long-term inflation protection because, over the long term, rents tend to rise with inflation. In the United States over the past 30 years (1980–2010), the FTSE NAREIT All Equity REITs Index achieved a compounded annual total return of 11.9 percent compared with 10.7 percent for the S&P 500 Index and 8.9 percent for the Barclays Capital Aggregate Bond Index. The US Consumer Price Index increased an average of 3.2 percent annually over the period.

The relative stability of income from income-producing real estate also permits substantial financial leverage to be used, typically in the form of mortgage debt (i.e., debt secured by a lien on real property as collateral). Use of financial leverage can enhance rates of return on equity capital when, on an after-tax basis, the rate of return on assets exceeds the interest rate on the mortgage. The ability, however, to use above-average financial leverage brings greater risk.

3 PUBLICLY TRADED EQUITY REITS

Most REITs are **equity REITs** that invest in ownership positions in income-producing real estate. Equity REITs seek to grow cash flows from their owned real estate, to expand ownership through investing in additional properties, and to selectively develop, improve, or redevelop properties.

Publicly traded equity REITs are the focus of this reading.[1] Other REIT types include mortgage REITs and hybrid REITs. **Mortgage REITs** are REITs that invest the bulk (typically 75 percent or more) of their assets in interest-bearing mortgages, mortgage securities, or short-term loans secured by real estate. The total market value of mortgage REITs is relatively small in comparison with equity REITs. **Hybrid REITs** are REITs that own and operate income-producing real estate, as do equity REITs, but invest in mortgages as well. There are relatively few hybrid REITs.

3.1 Market Background

For many decades, real estate equities have represented significant parts of European (notably the United Kingdom) stock markets, whereas real estate development and ownership has featured prominently in the diversified activities of a large number of Asian companies, notably in Hong Kong and Singapore. Real estate equities, although introduced earlier in the US market, did not gain a large representation in US equity markets until after the severe commercial property collapse of the early 1990s. That collapse left many properties either in financially troubled developer/investor hands or in foreclosure. Many such properties were securitized successfully as REITs, exploiting the conservative operating policies mandated by the REIT structure (especially the reliance on contractual rental income) and the conservative financial policies demanded by REIT investors, as discussed in Section 3.3.

---

1 Besides publicly traded REITs, private REITs exist. Private REITs are similar to equity REITs in their business model but do not trade on active exchanges. Private REITs are generally sponsored by real estate organizations and have limited liquidity. They are bought by institutional investors or are marketed to small investors by financial planners.

HISTORICAL DEVELOPMENT OF REITS

US REITs, which have provided a model for REIT legislation worldwide, can trace their origins to business trusts formed in Boston, Massachusetts, in the mid-nineteenth century, when the wealth created by the industrial revolution led to increasing demand for real estate investments. State laws at the time prevented a corporation from owning real estate other than that required for its business. The so-called "Massachusetts trust" was the first US legal entity created to specifically permit investment in real estate. It provided for the transfer of shares, limited liability for passive investors, elimination of federal taxation at the trust level, and the retention of specialized management. The structure became less desirable because of changes in tax laws in the first half of the twentieth century, but was revived by the US Congress in 1960. By the early 1970s, a substantial portion of US REITs' assets was concentrated in high risk construction and development loans. Banks, thrifts, and insurance companies could not directly engage in such high-yield lending because of regulations and statutory restrictions, but they did so indirectly by sponsoring publicly funded REITs that bore their names. But poor lending practices, high leverage, and conflicts of interest between banks and their REIT subsidiaries, as well as the effects of an economic recession, a real estate downturn, and changes in tax laws combined to generate numerous developer bankruptcies and a major decline in the number of REITs and their assets. Record high interest rates caused a severe contraction in the real estate industry in the early 1980s. It was not until the early 1990s, after another even more severe commercial property collapse, that REITs became the securitization vehicle of choice in moving property ownership from distressed owners into the better capitalized hands of long-term, income-oriented investors.

From 1990 to 1995, the equity market capitalization of US REITs rose from US$8.5 billion to US$56 billion and the number of REITs almost doubled to 223. As of early 2011, the US REIT industry consists of about 150 REITs with an equity capitalization of approximately US$350 billion.

REITs are important in a number of markets outside the United States. Beginning in the early 1990s, Canada had a significant increase in equity REITs. As of 2011, there are approximately 30 REITs in Canada with a market capitalization of C$38 billion. The REIT structure was introduced in Australia in 1971; as of 2011, there are 70 A-REITs with a market capitalization of over A$100 billion. REITs have been introduced in Japan (J-REITs in 2001), Singapore (S-REITs in 2002), Hong Kong (2005), the United Kingdom (2006), and Germany (G-REITs in 2007). In Brazil, REITs (called Fundos de Investimento Imobiliaro, or FIIs) have existed since 1993 but were first accorded exemption from income taxation in 2006 if owned by individual investors and listed on the stock exchange. The first REIT in the United Arab Emirates was formed in Dubai in 2010. As of early 2011, there are about 30 countries with legislation authorizing REITs.

REIT-type legislation is currently being studied in China, India, and Pakistan. In China, the planned large-scale introduction of REITs has been delayed by the financial crisis of 2007–2009 and government controls on the real estate industry. As a result of their strong growth since the early 1990s, REITs now represent the majority of the available publicly traded real estate equity securities in the world by number and market value.

As shown in Exhibit 3, REIT ownership in the United States—the largest market for REITs in the world—is widely diversified by type of investor.

Exhibit 3	Estimated Ownership of US REITs by Type of Investor
Type of Investor	**Percent**
Index funds	25
Individual investors	15
REIT sector dedicated funds	15

(continued)

Exhibit 3	(Continued)	
Type of Investor		**Percent**
Pension funds		10
Insiders (managements, boards)		5
Other institutional investors (e.g., stock funds, income funds, hedge funds)		30

Source: J.P. Morgan estimates.

3.2 REIT Structure

REITs can have simple structures in which they hold and operate their properties directly; however, REITs are generally structured to facilitate the tax-efficient acquisition of properties. Umbrella partnership REITs (UPREITs) and DOWNREITs are examples of structures in which partnerships hold REIT properties; the structures have the purpose of avoiding recognition of taxable income if appreciated property is transferred to the REIT. In the United States, most REITs are structured as **UPREITs**, under which the REIT has a controlling interest in and serves as the general partner (with responsibility for operations) of a partnership that owns and operates all or most of the properties.[2] A **DOWNREIT** structure is a variation of the UPREIT under which the REIT owns more than one partnership and may own properties at both the REIT level and the partnership level. A DOWNREIT can form partnerships for each property acquisition it undertakes.

REITs are subject to the same regulatory, financial reporting, disclosure, and governance requirements as other public companies.

3.3 Investment Characteristics

REITs are typically exempt from income taxation at the corporate (or trust) level if a specified majority of their income and assets relate to income-producing property (75 percent or more, depending on the country) and all or virtually all their potentially taxable income is distributed to shareholders (or unit holders). REITs are a tax-efficient conduit for cash flows from rental income. In the United States, REIT distributions to shareholders are classified for tax purposes into ordinary income (taxed at investors' top marginal tax rates); return of capital (the portion of distributions in excess of a REIT's earnings, treated as a return of capital and deducted from the investor's share cost basis for tax purposes); and capital gains (qualifying for lower capital gains tax rates).

The investment characteristics of both public and private REITs generally include the following:

- Exemption from income taxes at the corporate/trust level: REITs are typically required to distribute most of their potentially taxable income to gain exemption from corporate taxation.

- High income distributions: As a result of the distribution requirement, dividend yields are typically significantly higher than the yields on most other publicly traded equities. Exhibit 4 shows representative historic yields for REITs, stocks, and bonds in the United States.

---

2 An UPREIT offers partnership-limited units (convertible into REIT units) to property sellers who do not pay capital gains taxes on their sale of property until they convert their limited-partnership units into REIT shares. Advantages to a property seller, in addition to tax deferral, include diversification, greater liquidity, and professional management.

Exhibit 4	Historic Yields on S&P US REIT Index, S&P 500 Index, and 10-year US Treasury Bonds

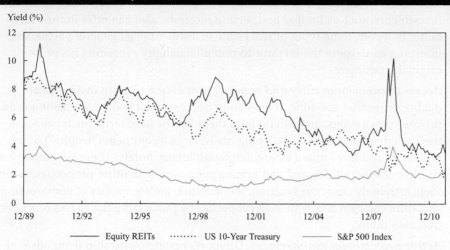

Relatively low volatility of reported income: As a result of REIT regulations that require income to be predominantly from rents and interest, REITs typically use conservative, rental-property-focused business models. The contractual nature of rental income (with the exception of hotel REITs) results in relatively stable revenue streams.

More frequent secondary equity offerings compared with industrial companies: As a result of the distribution requirement, REITs may not be able to retain earnings to finance growth and may need to issue equity to finance property acquisitions. REIT investors should be ready to evaluate the merits of these acquisitions and related financings.

As a result of these features, REITs are relatively stable savings, retirement, and income-producing investments. Compared with direct investments in income-producing property, REITs offer much greater ease of ownership in both small and large amounts, greater liquidity, and opportunities for broader diversification.

3.3.1 *Advantages of Publicly Traded Equity Real Estate Securities*

Compared with owning private real estate assets, publicly traded equity real estate securities, whether equity REITs or REOCs, offer the following advantages:

Greater liquidity: The ability to trade shares on stock exchanges provides greater liquidity than is available in buying and selling real estate in property markets. Thus, such securities permit greater flexibility in timing the realization of cash values and gains/losses. By comparison, direct investments in real estate and in real estate partnerships are generally less immediately liquid and have greater transaction costs even where property markets are quite active and highly sophisticated. These contrasts result from the fact that property transactions are large in relation to average stock market transactions, involve unique properties, and require considerably more time to complete because of the need to negotiate the terms of the transaction and to conduct due diligence (which may include financial, legal, and environmental considerations).

Lower investment requirements: Shares that represent fractional interests in REITs or REOCs can be bought with a much lower investment than a single commercial property.

- *Limited liability*: Similar to shareholders of other public companies, REIT investors have no liability for the debts and obligations of the REITs in which they invest beyond their original capital investment. Other types of real estate investments, such as limited partnership interests, also can offer limited liability; however, some types of real estate investment (e.g., general partnership interests) can expose the investor to potential liability exceeding his or her original investment.

- *Access to superior quality and range of properties*: Certain institutional-quality properties are difficult to acquire because most owners (pension funds, private corporations, and REITs) hold them for the long term. Such properties include super-regional shopping malls, large, prominent ("trophy") office buildings, and to a limited extent, landmark luxury hotels. These properties can command superior demand and pricing compared with other properties, given their extremely attractive location, architecture, and/or quality of construction. Investors can gain access to such properties by purchasing the shares of REITs that own them.

- *Active professional management*: Direct real estate ownership demands real estate expertise or asset/property management skills. Investors in publicly traded real estate equity securities do not require such expertise or skills; investors in REITs and REOCs benefit from having their property interests actively managed on their behalf by professional managers and from having their business interests overseen and guided by boards of directors. The REITs' standards of operating and financial efficiency benefit from the scrutiny and influence of public investors, which encourages best practices on the part of management and boards. Despite the constraint of low-income retention rates, capable managements can still add value by careful specialization by property type and region; by efficient operations focusing on maximizing rental rates and occupancies and minimizing operating costs; by property enhancements, refinancing, sales, and reinvestments; and/or by selected new development activity and property acquisitions financed on attractive terms with debt and/or equity.

- *Diversification*: By investing in REITs, investors can diversify their real estate portfolios by geography and property type. Such diversification is hard to achieve in direct property investing because of the typically large size and value of each property.

In addition, REITs tend to offer additional advantages compared with publicly traded REOCs:

- *Taxation*: REITs are typically exempt from the double taxation of income that comes from taxes being due at the corporate level and again when dividends or distributions are made to shareholders, as is the case in some jurisdictions such as the United States. In most jurisdictions, there are no taxes payable by a REIT if it: (1) meets certain requirements for types of assets held, typically rental property (75 percent of total assets in real estate for US REITs), (2) derives the bulk of its income from rents or mortgage interest on real estate (75 percent for US REITs), (3) has limited non-rental property assets, and (4) pays out in dividends/distributions nearly all of its taxable income (at least 90 percent in the United States). The dividends/distributions that REIT shareholders receive are typically divided into ordinary taxable income, capital gains, and return of capital, and are taxed at their respective rates in the first two cases. REIT shareholders do not have to pay current income tax on the portion of distributions that exceeds the REIT's taxable income (calculated after depreciation charges) because that portion of distributions is treated as a return of capital, which is deducted from the shareholders' cost basis for his/her shares. When the shares are eventually sold, the excess of the amount received over the cost basis of the shares is taxed as capital gains. This treatment of portions of their distributions as return of capital is generally favorable for investors from a tax perspective.

■ *Earnings predictability*: The contractual nature of REITs' rental income tends to give them a greater degree of earnings predictability than that of most industrial and natural resource companies.

■ *High income payout ratios and yields*: The typically high income payout ratios of REITs make them among the most stable and highest yielding of publicly traded equities.

REOCs have the following advantage compared with REITs:

■ *Operating flexibility*: REOCs are free to invest in any kind of real estate or related activity subject only to the limitations that may be imposed by their articles of incorporation and/or the market. This flexibility gives management the opportunity to allocate more resources to development activity, which has the potential of delivering high returns. Compared with REITs, REOCs can retain more of their income for re-investment when they believe attractive opportunities exist to create value for investors. REOCs are free to use a wider range of capital structures and degrees of financial leverage in their activities.

In contrast with REOCs, REITs are constrained in their investments, operations, and distributions; these constraints may prevent REITs from maximizing their returns.

EXAMPLE 1

Advantages of Publicly Traded Real Estate Investments

1 Which of the following assets requires the *most* expertise in real estate on the part of the investor?

    A A REOC share

    B An equity REIT share

    C A direct investment in a single property

2 Which of the following has the *most* operating and financial flexibility?

    A A REOC

    B An equity REIT

    C A direct investment in a single property

Solution to 1:

C is correct. Direct investment in a single property requires a high level of real estate expertise. Investment in publicly traded equity investments (in REITs or REOCs) requires much less expertise because investors benefit from having their property interests actively managed on their behalf by professional managers and from having their business interests overseen and guided by boards of directors, as in the case of all public corporations.

Solution to 2:

A is correct. REOCs are free to invest in any kind of real estate or related activity without limitation. This freedom gives management the opportunity to create more value in development activity and in trading real estate and to retain as much of their income as they believe is appropriate. A wider range of capital structures and degrees of financial leverage may be used in the process. In contrast with REOCs, REITs face restrictions on the amount of income and assets accounted for by activities other than collecting rent and interest payments. Direct investment is less liquid and divisible than REOC and REIT shares, which limits the operational flexibility of such investment.

3.3.2 *Disadvantages of Publicly Traded Equity Real Estate Securities*

Potential disadvantages of publicly traded real estate securities include those related to the following:

■ *Taxation*: Although REITs are typically tax-advantaged compared with generic common share investment, direct property investment has tax advantages compared with both REIT and REOC investing. Unlike direct property ownership and partnership investments in some countries, REITs and REOCs generally cannot pass on tax losses to their investors as deductions from their taxable income. Also, in jurisdictions permitting deferral of tax when a property investment is exchanged or sold and replaced by similar property within a short period of time (e.g., the 180-day "Section 1031 Like-Kind Exchange" rule in the United States), REIT shares do not qualify for such tax-deferred exchanges.

■ *Control*: Minority shareholders in a publicly traded REIT have less control over property-level investment decisions than do direct property owners.

■ *Costs*: The maintenance of a publicly traded REIT structure is costly and may not be recouped by offsetting benefits if the REIT lacks sufficient economies of scale or the value added by management is small.

■ *Stock market determined pricing and returns*: The stock market value of a REIT is more volatile than the appraised **net asset value** of a REIT, suggesting risk is lower for direct property investors. But net asset values based on appraised values rather than actual transaction prices tend to underestimate volatility.[3] Appraised values tend to be backward-looking by nature (because of typically being based on the sales price of comparable property transactions that have already closed) and may not react to changes in market trends. Additionally, there is a psychological tendency to smooth valuations by ignoring outlier transactions.

■ *Structural conflicts and related costs*: The use of UPREIT and DOWNREIT structures can create conflicts of interest between the partnership and REIT shareholders when it comes to making decisions on the disposition of properties or increasing company debt levels and may involve additional administrative costs. For example, the disposition of a particular property or the use of more mortgage debt financing might have tax implications for the limited partners who sold the property to the operating partnership and tax considerations could cause their interests to vary from the best interests of the REIT as a whole.

■ *Relatively moderate income growth potential*: The relatively low rate of income retention by REITs implies a low rate of reinvestment for future growth. This low rate of reinvestment tends to reduce income growth potential. Relatedly, the stock market's tendency to focus on earnings growth can cause REIT shares to underperform in periods during which the market highly values fast-growing companies; such periods tend to coincide with time of high consumer, business, and investor confidence.

---

3 Appraised values are based on a range of considerations including recent market prices for comparable property sales (assuming willing buyers and willing sellers were involved), discounted cash flow analysis, and **depreciated replacement cost**. Property appraisal is discussed in the reading on private real estate investment.

■ *Potential for forced equity issuance at disadvantageous prices*: REITs typically use financial leverage and are regularly in the debt markets to refinance their maturing debt. If a REIT's management of its overall financial leverage and the timing and type of its debt maturities is flawed, these issues can combine with a lack of substantial retained cash flow to force equity issuance at dilutive prices, especially during periods of weak credit availability (e.g., 2008–2009). Note that timely debt and equity financing and share repurchase activity if market prices fall below intrinsic values, using the retained portion of operating cash flows or the proceeds of debt issuance or property sales, can yield benefits to remaining REIT shareholders.

EXAMPLE 2

Publicly Traded Real Estate Investments

1 Which of the following types of real estate investment is *most* appropriate for an investor seeking to maximize control?

   A REIT

   B REOC

   C Direct investment in income-producing property

2 Which of the following best represents an advantage of REITs over a direct investment in an income-producing property?

   A Diversification

   B Operating flexibility

   C Income growth potential

Solution to 1:

C is correct. Control is most characteristic of a direct investment in and ownership of income-producing property.

Solution to 2:

A is correct. REITs provide diversification of property holdings. B is incorrect because REITs do face restrictions on the amount of income and assets accounted for by activities other than collecting rent and interest payments; these restrictions can prevent a REIT from maximizing its returns. C is incorrect because the relatively low rates of income retention that are required to maintain a REIT's tax-free status can detract from income growth potential.

EXAMPLE 3

Investment Objectives

Two real estate investors are each choosing from among the following investment types: REOC, equity REIT, or a direct investment in an income-producing property. Investor A's primary objective is liquidity, and Investor B's primary objective is maximum growth/capital gain potential. State and explain which real estate investment type best suits:

1 Investor A.

2 Investor B.

Solution to 1:

For Investor A, with a liquidity objective, REOC and REIT investments are most appropriate because REOCs and REITs are traded on stock exchanges and are more liquid. Direct investments in income-producing property are generally less liquid.

Solution to 2:

For Investor B, with a maximum growth objective, REOCs and direct property investment are most appropriate because REOCs and direct investors are free to invest in any kind of real estate or related activity without limitation and to reinvest as much of their income as they believe is appropriate for their objectives. This freedom gives them the opportunity to create more value in development activity and in trading real estate. REITs' constraints prevent them from retaining earnings to reinvest, so their growth opportunities are more limited.

3.4 Considerations in Analysis and Due Diligence

For equity REITs as a group, key specific investment characteristics, opportunities, and risks should be assessed when conducting due diligence of their shares for investment purposes.

- *Remaining lease terms.* Short remaining lease terms provide mark-to-market opportunities on rents. They are a positive consideration in an expansionary economy and/or rental rate environment and a negative one in a declining economy and/or rental market. Hotels and multi-family residential properties have the shortest lease terms, whereas shopping centers, offices, and industrial buildings typically have the longest lease terms.

- *Inflation protection.* Leases that have pre-set periodic increases in rent throughout the lease term (or that have minimum or base rents linked to the local inflation rate) provide a degree of inflation protection for investors.

- *Market rent analysis.* Current market rents should be compared with rents paid by existing tenants. Low in-place rents provide upside potential to cash flows upon lease re-negotiation and high in-place rents represent additional risk to maintaining current cash flows.

- *Costs of re-leasing space.* Costs to lease space when a lease matures typically include brokerage commissions, allowances for tenants' improvements to their space, free rent, and downtime between leases. Such costs can be burdensome for landlords.

- *Tenant concentration.* Tenants that rent significant amounts of space and the percentage of rents paid by these significant tenants should be noted. Assessing the financial strength of significant tenants and the risk they pose to the REIT are important parts of necessary due diligence.

- *Availability of new competitive supply.* The potential for new competitive supply to the REIT's existing properties should be analyzed by examining new buildings under construction or planned by other developers and by assessing the likelihood of more projects gaining approval.

- *Balance sheet/leverage analysis.* A detailed review of the REIT's balance sheet, including leverage levels, cost of debt, and debt maturity profile should be completed.

- *Management.* Due diligence should include a review of senior management's background, skill sets, track records, years of experience, and length of time with the REIT.

The next section describes subtypes of equity REITs and any due diligence considerations that apply specifically to the subtypes.

3.5 Equity REITs: Property Subtypes

Equity REITs, the predominant form of REITs, are actively managed enterprises seeking to maximize the returns from their property portfolios by applying management skills in operations and finance. For this reason, most REITs focus on a particular property type, striving to excel in operating efficiency and growth while still being mindful of risk-reducing strategies, including diversification by geography and by the number and quality of properties and tenants. The analysis of equity REITs is conducted along the same lines as that of publicly traded equities in general: commencing with industry analysis, followed by company analysis, and then equity valuation. Certain specific economic value determinants, investment characteristics, risks, and areas for analysis and due diligence, apply to each property subtype of REITs shown in Exhibit 5.

Exhibit 5	Global REITs by Property Type Held
Property Type	**Percentage of Total**
Shopping center/Retail	23.3
Office	14.5
Residential	11.3
Healthcare	6.8
Hotel/Resort	2.7
Industrial	4.2
Industrial/Office	1.0
Self-storage	2.6
Diversified	33.6

The following sections discuss these property types in more detail.

3.5.1 *Shopping Center/Retail REITs*

Shopping center or **retail REITs** invest in such retail properties as regional shopping malls, community/neighborhood shopping centers, and to a lesser degree, premium retail space in leading cities.

Regional shopping malls are large spaces, often enclosed, in which retailing tends to be in higher-priced discretionary goods (e.g., fashionable clothing). Tenants' leases in regional malls usually have terms of 3–10 years and typically require tenants—except for the largest "anchor" retailers—to pay the greater of a fixed-minimum rental rate and a percentage of their sales. "Anchor" retailers, however, have very long-term, fixed-rent leases or own their premises. As part of their total rent under typical **net leases**, tenants pay a **net rent**, all of which goes to the landlord, plus a share of the common area costs of the mall based on their proportionate share of the space leased. Despite the link between tenants' sales and rent, revenue streams are relatively stable because of high levels of minimum rent that often represent well over 90 percent of revenue.

Community shopping centers—consisting of stores linked by open-air walkways or, in the case of so-called "power centers" or "big-box centers," linked by parking lots—generally provide such basic necessity goods and services as food and groceries, home furnishings, hardware, discount merchandise, fast food, and banking, with similar lease maturities but non-participatory rents that are usually subject to periodic increases.

For shopping center REITs, analysts often analyze such factors as rental rates and sales per square foot/meter for the rental property portfolio, dividing them into same portfolio and new space addition components.

3.5.2 Office REITs

Office REITs invest in and manage multi-tenanted office properties in central business districts of cities and suburban markets. Lease terms are typically long (5–25 years) with contractual base rents that are fixed and adjust upward (typically every 5–10 years). In addition to base rents, tenants pay their proportionate share of operating expenses, common area costs, and property taxes. Rental income tends to be stable year-to-year, but over the longer term (5–10 years) it can be affected by changes in office market vacancy and rental rates that characterize the office industry cycle. This cycle arises because of long office tower construction and interior finishing periods (three or more years) and the willingness of developers to build large buildings in which only a portion of the space has been preleased. These factors result in the commencement of construction of new space during periods of strong economic growth and the completion of new space potentially during economic downturns when tenant demand is low.

Analysts of office REITs pay particular attention to new space under construction in a REIT's local market, to site locations and access to public transportation and highways, and to business conditions for a REIT's principal tenants. Analysts also focus on the quality of a REIT's office space, focusing on such factor as location, convenience, utilitarian and architectural appeal, and the age and durability of the building.

3.5.3 Industrial REITs

Industrial REITs hold portfolios of single-tenant or multi-tenant industrial properties that are used as warehouses, distribution centers, light manufacturing facilities, and small office or "flex" space for sales, administrative, or related functions.

Industrial property and industrial REITs are less cyclical than some other property/REIT types including hotel, health care, and storage. The long-term net leases (5–25 years) that pertain to industrial space, the short time required to build industrial buildings (usually well under a year), and the tendency to build and prelease and/or build space to suit particular tenants dampen any rapid change of rental income and values.

Analysts pay particular attention to trends in tenants' requirements and the impact these can have on the obsolescence of existing space and the need for new types of space. Strategic property locations—such as near a port, airport, or highway—are important positive considerations. Shifts in the composition of national and local industrial bases and trade play important roles in this regard and can sometimes be difficult to detect and forecast. Trends in new supply and demand in the local market are closely scrutinized.

3.5.4 Multi-family/Residential REITs

Multi-family/residential REITs invest in and manage rental apartments for lease to individual tenants, typically using one-year leases. Rental apartment demand tends to be relatively stable, but fluctuations in rental income can occur as a result of competition from condominium construction, tenant (move-in) inducements, regional economic strengths and weaknesses, the effects of inflation on such operating costs as energy and other utility costs, and taxes and maintenance costs (because apartment leases often tend to be **gross leases** under which many or all of such costs are paid for by the landlord).

Analysts pay particular attention to local demographics and income trends, age and competitive appeal, cost and availability of homeownership in local markets, and the degree of government control of local residential rents. Fuel and energy costs receive particular attention because properties are usually leased under gross leases that require landlords to pay for part or all of the building operating costs.

3.5.5 *Storage REITs*

Storage REITs own and operate self-storage properties, sometimes referred to as mini-warehouse facilities. Space in these facilities is rented under gross leases (i.e., no additional payments are due for operating costs or property taxes), usually on a monthly basis by individuals for storing personal items and by small businesses. Ease of entry into this growing field has led to periods of overbuilding.

Analysts pay special attention to the rate of construction of new competitive facilities, trends in housing sales activity that can affect the demand for temporary storage, local demographic trends, new business start-up activity, and seasonal trends in demand for storage facilities that can be significant in some markets.

3.5.6 *Health Care REITs*

Health care REITs invest in skilled nursing facilities (nursing homes), assisted living and independent residential facilities for retired persons, hospitals, medical office buildings, and rehabilitation centers. In many countries, REITs are not permitted to operate these facilities themselves if they wish to maintain their REIT status and must lease them to health care providers; these leases are usually net leases. REITs may jeopardize their tax status (no tax at trust level) if they are found to be operating a business in violation of their passive investment restriction. Although largely resistant to the effects of economic recessions, health care REITs are exposed to the effects of population demographics, government funding programs for health care, construction cycles, the financial condition of health care facilities operators/lessees, and any costs arising from litigation by residents.

Analysts scrutinize operating trends in facilities, in government funding, in litigation settlements, and insurance costs. Amounts of competitors' new facilities under construction in relation to prospective demand and prospects for acquisitions are also key points of focus.

3.5.7 *Hotel REITs*

Hotel REITs own hotel properties but, similar to health care REITs, in many countries they must refrain from operating their properties themselves to maintain their tax-advantaged REIT status. Hotel REITs typically lease all their properties to taxable REIT subsidiaries (or to third-party lessees) who operate them ensuring the hotel REIT parent receives passive rental income. This rental income typically accounts for the major portion of a hotel's net operating cash flow. Management of the hotel is usually turned over to hotel management companies, many of which own widely recognized hotel brands. The net effect of this structure is that although the hotel REIT is tax exempt to the extent that it meets its income distribution and other REIT requirements, a minor portion of net operating cash flow from hotel properties may be subject to income taxation. The hotel sector is cyclical because it is not protected by long-term leases and is thus exposed to business-cycle driven short-term changes in regional, national, and international business and leisure travel. Exposure to travel disruptions also increases revenue volatility.

Analysts examine trends in occupancies, average room rates, and operating profit margins by hotel type and geographic location; statistics are compared with industry averages published by government and private-sector hotel industry statistics providers. Revenue per available room (RevPAR), the product of average room rate by average occupancy, is a widely monitored barometer of the hotel business. Attention is also paid to trends in hotel room forward bookings by category (individual, corporate, group, and convention), in food and beverage and banqueting sales, and in margins. Expenditures on maintaining and improving property, plant, and equipment are scrutinized, and the rates of new room construction and completion in local markets are watched very closely in view of the cyclicality of demand and the long duration of hotel construction (typically 1.5 to 3 years). Because income is so variable in this sector, analysts need to be wary of hotel REITs that use high financial leverage.

3.5.8 Diversified REITs

Diversified REITs own and operate in more than one type of property and are more common in Europe and Asia than in the United States. Some investors favor the reduced risk and wider opportunities that come from diversification. An analysis of management's experience with each property type and degree of local market presence are obviously important in reviewing diversified REITs.

3.6 Economic Drivers

Exhibit 6 shows major economic factors affecting REITs and their relative importance for different types of equity REITs. The measures of relative importance should be viewed as an approximate guide only because the relative importance can vary especially for extreme changes in the economic factors. Over the course of a full business cycle, however, the measures of relative importance shown tend to apply.

Risks tend to be greatest for those REITs in property-type sectors where tenant/occupant demand for space can fluctuate most widely in the short-term (notably hotels) and in which dislocations between supply and demand are most likely to occur (notably office, hotel, and health care). However, the quality and locations of properties held by a REIT, their leasing, and financing status are also extremely important factors in determining a REIT's risk profile.

Exhibit 6	Importance of Factors Affecting Economic Value for Various Property Types				
	National GDP Growth	Job Creation	Retail Sales Growth	Population Growth	New Space Supply vs. Demand
Retail	1	3	2	4	4
Office	1	2	5	4	3
Industrial	1	5	2	3	4
Multi-family	1	2	5	2	4
Storage	1	3	5	2	4
Health care	1	4	5	2	3
Hotels	1	2	5	4	3

Note: 1 = most important, 5 = least important
Source: Based on data from the authors' research

Growth in the economy or national GDP is generally the most important single economic factor affecting the outlook for all types of property and REITs. Retail sales growth is reflected in the sales growth of shopping center tenants and influences directly (through rental rates based on a percentage of sales) and indirectly (through tenants' ability to pay more rent and landlords' efforts to take advantage of this increase) the rental rates and occupancies in shopping centers.

Job creation tends to be reflected in increased demand for office space to accommodate white collar workers and in requirements for more retail space to cater to related increases in spending. Job creation also tends to be reflected in (1) increased demand for multi-family accommodation as newly employed people gain the financial means to rent their own accommodation, (2) greater hotel room demand as leisure and business travel increase in response to an expanded workforce, and (3) increased use of storage space as personal and small business needs for space rise.

Office, hotel, and health care properties and the REITs that invest in those property types are more prone to supply–demand dislocations because of (1) the long time taken to construct new space (space on which construction commences in a booming economy may be completed two or three years later, potentially during a recession) and (2) the large size of many facilities, which can contribute to excess supply on completion. Population growth tends to be reflected in increased demand for multi-family accommodations, storage, and health care facilities.

EXAMPLE 4

REITs and Due Diligence

1 Which of the following statistics is similarly relevant for a shopping center, office, or hotel REIT?

   A Occupancy

   B Forward bookings

   C Sales per square foot

2 Which of the following types of REITs is *least* directly sensitive to population growth?

   A Office

   B Health care

   C Multi-family residential

3 In addition to the analysis of occupancy, rental rate, lease expiry, and financing statistics, analysts of office REITs are *most likely* to pay particular attention to trends in:

   A job creation.

   B population growth.

   C retail sales growth.

4 Which of the following types of REITs would be expected to experience the *greatest* cash flow volatility?

   A Hotel

   B Industrial

   C Shopping center

Solution to 1:

A is correct. Occupancy is a critical variable for all three types of REITs. Forward bookings would be relevant for only hotel REITs; sales per square foot for shopping center REITs.

Solution to 2:

A is correct. Population growth ranks as a less significant factor for office REITs and a more significant factor for health care and multi-family residential REITs. Different economic factors affect different property types to a varying degree, given their lease structures and competitive environment.

Solution to 3:

A is correct. Job creation is most significant for office REITs. Population growth is more significant for multi-family, storage, and health care REITs than for office REITs, as shown in Exhibit 6, whereas retail sales growth is more significant for shopping center/retail and industrial REITs than for office REITs.

Solution to 4:

A is correct. Hotel room demand fluctuates with economic activity; there are no long-term leases on hotel rooms to protect hotel REITs' revenue streams from changes in demand. Industrial and shopping center REITs benefit from long-term leases on their properties and from the relatively mild dislocations between supply and demand caused by the construction of new space in these sub-sectors.

4

REAL ESTATE OPERATING COMPANIES

Publicly traded real estate equities exist in forms other than REITs. **Real estate operating companies** (REOCs) are ordinary taxable corporations that operate in the real estate industry in countries that do not have a tax-advantaged REIT regime in place or are engaged in real estate activities of a kind and to an extent that do not fit within their country's REIT framework. Such ineligible activity generally takes the form of development or land investment in which the cash flows are not recurring income from lease revenues. Examples of such REOCs are

- Hongkong Land, a leading office investor and residential developer listed in Singapore (registered in Bermuda, part of Singapore Straits Times Index; this company left Hong Kong prior to the 1997 transfer to China),

- Brookfield Office Properties, an international office investor and property manager listed in Toronto and New York with a low income payout ratio, and

- China Vanke, China's largest residential property developer.

REOCs offer essentially the same advantages and disadvantages as REITs with respect to investing in real estate directly, but with some differences.

REITs and REOCs face similar operating and financial risks as private real estate investments, including leasing, operating, financing, and market risks as well as exposure to general economic risk. Despite certain advantages of REOCs, such as operating flexibility, the equity markets of most countries show a preference for the tax advantages, high-income distributions, and rigorous operating and financial mandates that come with REIT status. Consequently, in many markets there is a tendency for REOCs to experience less access to equity capital and lower market valuations (and higher cost of equity) than REITs. REOCs are usually able to elect to convert to

REIT status if they meet the general requirements of REITs but, depending on their countries of domicile, must consider potential local tax consequences for themselves and their shareholders that may be triggered by the change.[4]

EXAMPLE 5

REOCs

1 Which of the following statements is *most* accurate?

   A REOCs are subject to the same tax rules as trusts.

   B REOCs are subject to the same tax rules as ordinary corporations.

   C REITs usually cannot elect to convert to REOCs without changing their income payout rates and sources of income.

2 Which of the following statements is *most* accurate? REOCs:

   A can invest in any type of real estate without losing their tax status.

   B are a more prevalent and popular investment asset class than REITs globally.

   C do not pay any income taxes if they pay out all their taxable income to their shareholders.

Solution to 1:

B is correct. REOCs are taxed in the same way as ordinary corporations. A is not correct because REOCs are taxed as corporations; C is not correct because REITs do not need to change their income payout rates or sources of income to become REOCs.

Solution to 2:

A is correct. REOCs, unlike REITs, can generally invest in any type of real estate without losing their tax status. C is incorrect because REOCs do not enjoy such a tax advantage. B is incorrect because, as shown in Exhibit 2, REOCs globally represent less invested capital than REITs.

VALUATION: NET ASSET VALUE APPROACH

5

Approaches analysts take to valuing equity include those based on asset value estimates, price multiple comparisons, and discounted cash flow. These general approaches are used to value shares of REITs and REOCs and will be addressed in Sections 5, 6, and 7, respectively.

   Two possible measures of value that analysts might use are book value per share (BVPS) and net asset value per share (NAVPS) based on reported accounting values and market values for assets, respectively. NAVPS is the relevant valuation measure for valuing REITs and REOCs.

   NAVPS is often used as a fundamental benchmark for the value of a REIT or REOC. Discounts in the REIT share price from NAVPS are interpreted as indications of potential undervaluation, and premiums in the REIT share price to NAVPS, in the

---

4 Because their leverage is high and they can use accelerated depreciation, REOCs' cash tax liabilities are frequently relatively low.

absence of indications of positive future events, such as a successful property development completion or expected high value creation by a management team, suggest potential overvaluation. By way of qualification, however, these assessments must be made in the context of the stock market's tendency to be forward looking in its valuations and at times to have different investment criteria from property markets.

The net asset value may be viewed as the largest component of the intrinsic value of a REIT or REOC, the balance being investors' assessments of the value of any non-asset-based income streams (e.g., fee or management income), the value added by management of the REIT or REOC, and the value of any contingent liabilities.[5]

Section 5.1 explains why BVPS can diverge from NAVPS; analysts need to understand in detail the accounting for REITs' investment properties in order to evaluate the relevance of accounting information. Section 5.2 then illustrates the estimation of NAVPS.

5.1 Accounting for Investment Properties

The value of the investment property portfolio of a REIT or REOC is a very important element in the valuation of its shares. Analysts should take care to understand the basis on which a REIT's investment properties are valued. If accounting is on a fair value basis, accounting values may be relevant for asset-based valuation. If historical cost values are used, however, accounting values are generally not relevant.

Investment property is defined under International Financial Reporting Standards (IFRS) as property that is owned (or, in some cases, leased under a finance lease) for the purpose of earning rentals or capital appreciation or both. Buildings owned by a company and leased to tenants are investment properties. In contrast, other long-lived tangible assets (i.e., property considered to be property, plant, and equipment) are owner-occupied properties used for producing the company's goods and services or for housing the company's administrative activities. Investment properties do not include long-lived tangible assets held for sale in the ordinary course of business. For example, the houses and property owned by a housing construction company are considered to be its inventory.

Under IFRS, companies are allowed to value investment properties using either a cost model or a fair value model. The cost model is identical to the cost model used for property, plant, and equipment. Under the fair value model, all changes in the fair value of the asset affect net income. To use the fair value model, a company must be able to reliably determine the property's fair value on a continuing basis. In general, a company must apply its chosen model (cost or fair value) to all of its investment property. If a company chooses the fair value model for its investment property, it must continue to use the fair value model until it disposes of the property or changes its use such that it is no longer considered investment property (e.g., it becomes owner-occupied property or part of inventory). The company must continue to use the fair value model for that property even if transactions on comparable properties, used to estimate fair value, become less frequent.

Investment property appears as a separate line item on the balance sheet. Companies are required to disclose whether they use the fair value model or the cost model for their investment property. If the company uses the fair value model, it must make additional disclosures about how it determines fair value and must provide reconciliation between the beginning and ending carrying amounts of investment property. If

---

5 The intrinsic value of an investment, as discussed in other parts of the CFA curriculum, is the value ascribed to an investment on the basis of a hypothetically complete understanding of its characteristics. It is generally estimated on a going-concern basis.

the company uses the cost model, it must make additional disclosures—for example, the depreciation method and useful lives must be disclosed. In addition, if the company uses the cost model, it must also disclose the fair value of investment property.

In contrast to IFRS, under US generally accepted accounting principles (US GAAP), there is no specific definition of investment property. Most operating companies and real estate companies in the United States that hold investment-type property use the historical cost accounting model. This model does not accurately represent the economic values of assets and liabilities or the current economic return or income to a business in environments of significant price and cost changes. This issue is especially evident in companies whose businesses involve the purchase and long-term retention of assets, notably real estate, because under historical cost accounting, assets including buildings are generally carried at depreciated historical cost. These figures can be written down when they undergo a permanent impairment in economic value, but they can only be written up under exceptional circumstances, such as mergers, acquisitions, or reorganizations. The historical cost accounting practices that prevail in regard to investment property assets in the United States, the largest market for REITs in the world, tend to distort the measure of economic income and asset value by understating carrying values on long-held property assets and overstating depreciation on assets that are often appreciating in value because of general price inflation or other property-specific reasons.

5.2 Net Asset Value Per Share: Calculation

As a result of shortcomings in accounting reported values, investment analysts and investors use estimates of **net asset value per share**. NAVPS is the difference between a real estate company's assets and its liabilities, *all taken at current market values instead of accounting book values*, divided by the number of shares outstanding. NAVPS is a superior measure of the net worth of a company compared with book value per share.

In valuing a REIT's or REOC's real estate portfolio, analysts will look for the results of existing appraisals if they are available (such as those provided by companies reporting under IFRS). If they are not available or if they disagree with the assumptions or methodology of the appraisals, analysts will often capitalize the rental streams—represented by net operating income (NOI)—produced by a REIT's or REOC's properties, using a market required rate of return. The market required rate of return, usually referred to as the **capitalization rate** or "**cap rate**," is the rate used in the marketplace in recent transactions to capitalize similar-risk future income streams into a present value. It is calculated as the NOI of a comparable property or portfolio of comparable properties divided by the total value of the comparable(s) as represented by transaction prices. Analysts will often seek to corroborate the property valuations obtained with price per square foot information on transactions involving similar types of properties, as well as replacement cost information (adjusted for depreciation and the age and condition of the buildings). These estimated asset values will be substituted for the book values of the properties on the balance sheet and adjustments made to any related accounting assets, such as capitalized leases, to avoid double counting.

Generally, goodwill, deferred financing expenses, and deferred tax assets will be excluded to arrive at a "hard" economic value for total assets. Liabilities will be similarly adjusted to replace the face value of debt with market values if these are significantly different (e.g., as a result of changes in interest rates) and any such "soft" liabilities as deferred tax liabilities will be removed. The revised net worth of the company divided by the number of shares outstanding is the NAV. Although this figure is calculated before provision for any income or capital gains taxes that might be payable on liquidation, the inability to predict how the company or its assets might be sold and the prospect that it might be kept intact in an acquisition cause investors to look to the pre-tax asset value as their primary net worth benchmark. If a company has held its assets for many years and has a very low remaining depreciable value for its assets for tax purposes, this can color investors' perspectives on valuation. Quantifying the effects of a low adjusted cost base, however, is impeded by lack of knowledge of the tax circumstances and strategies of a would-be acquirer.

Exhibit 7 provides an example of the calculations involved in estimating NAV based on capitalizing rental streams. Because the book values of assets are based on historical costs, the analyst estimates NAVPS. First, by capitalizing NOI with certain adjustments, the analyst obtains an estimate of the value of rental properties, then the value of other tangible assets is added and the total netted of liabilities. This net amount, NAV, is then divided by the number of shares outstanding to obtain NAVPS.

The second line in Exhibit 7 shows the adjustment to remove **non-cash rents**; these are the result of the accounting practice of "straight lining" the rental revenue from long-term leases. (The amount of this deduction is the difference between the average contractual rent over the leases' terms and the cash rent actually paid.) NOI is also increased to reflect a full year's rent for properties acquired during the course of the year, resulting in pro forma "cash NOI" for the previous 12 months of $267,299,000. This figure is then increased to include expected growth for the next 12 months at 1.5 percent, resulting in expected next 12-months cash NOI of $271,308,000.

An appropriate capitalization rate is then estimated based on recent transactions for comparable properties in the property market. An estimated value for the REIT's operating real estate is obtained by dividing expected next 12-months cash NOI by the decimalized capitalization rate (in this case, 0.07). The book values of the REIT's other tangible assets including cash, accounts receivable, land for future development, and prepaid expenses are added to obtain estimated gross asset value. (Land is sometimes taken at market value if this can be determined reliably; but because land is often difficult to value and of low liquidity, analysts tend to use book values.) From this figure, debt and other liabilities (but not deferred taxes because this item is an accounting provision rather than an economic liability) are subtracted to obtain net asset value. Division by the number of shares outstanding produces NAVPS.

Exhibit 7	Analyst Adjustments to REIT financials to obtain NAVPS

Office Equity REIT Inc.
Net Asset Value Per Share Estimate
(In Thousands, Except Per Share Data)

Last 12-months real estate NOI	$270,432
Less: Non-cash rents	7,667
Plus: Adjustment for full impact of acquisitions (1)	4,534
Pro forma cash NOI for last 12 months	$267,299
Plus: Next 12 months growth in NOI (2)	$4,009
Estimated next 12 months cash NOI	$271,308
Assumed cap rate (3)	7.00%
Estimated value of operating real estate	$3,875,829
Plus: Cash and equivalents	$65,554
Plus: Land held for future development	34,566
Plus: Accounts receivable	45,667
Plus: Prepaid/Other assets (4)	23,456
Estimated gross asset value	$4,045,072
Less: Total debt	$1,010,988

Exhibit 7   (Continued)

Office Equity REIT Inc.
Net Asset Value Per Share Estimate
(In Thousands, Except Per Share Data)

Less: Other liabilities	119,886
Net asset value	$2,914,198
Shares outstanding	55,689

1 50 percent of the expected return on acquisitions was made in the middle of 2010.

2 Growth is estimated at 1.5 percent.

3 Cap rate is based on recent comparable transactions in the property market.

4 This figure does not include intangible assets.

NAVPS is calculated to be $2,914,198 divided by 55,689 shares, which equals $52.33 per share.

5.3 Net Asset Value Per Share: Application

REITs have a relatively active private investment market for their business assets; namely, the direct investment property market. This market facilitates the estimation of a REIT's or REOC's net asset value: an estimate of the value of their underlying real estate if it were sold in the private market, debt obligations were satisfied, and the remaining capital—the net asset value—was distributed to shareholders. This approach is unique to REITs and REOCs because commercial real estate assets transact relatively frequently in the private market, and as a result an investor can make observations about how such properties trade on the basis of the capitalization rate (the rate obtained by dividing net operating income by total value) or on the basis of price per square foot, and apply these valuations to the assets of a public company. In fact, in the United States, it is estimated that only 10–15 percent of commercial real estate is held by publicly traded REITs, thus making the private market far larger than the public market, although less active. To draw a parallel, using a NAV approach to value REITs is much like using the sum-of-the-parts approach to valuing a company with multiple business lines.

The NAV approach to valuation is most often used by sector-focused real estate investors that view REITs and REOCs primarily as liquid forms of commercial real estate ownership. Value-oriented investors also tend to focus on NAV when stocks are trading at significant discounts to the underlying value of the assets. In addition, NAV analysis becomes particularly important when there is significant leveraged buyout (LBO) activity in the broader market. At such times, LBO sponsors attempt to buy REITs trading at large discounts to NAV to realize their underlying real estate value. Conversely, when REIT stocks trade at large premiums to NAV, IPO activity and stock issuance activity increases because the public markets are essentially ascribing more value to the real estate than the private markets are. Over time, REITs and REOCs in the United States and globally have at times traded at premiums-to-NAV of more than 25 percent and at other times at discounts from NAV exceeding 25 percent. Thus, if the NAV of a REIT were $20/share, the stock might trade as low as $15/share or as high as $25/share, depending on a range of factors.

5.3.1 *Important Considerations in a NAV-Based Approach to Valuing REITs*

Although NAV estimates provide investors with a specific value, there are a number of important considerations that should be taken into account when using this approach to value REITs and REOCs. First, investors must understand the implications of using a private market valuation tool on a publicly traded security. In this context, it is useful to examine how NAVs are calculated.

The methods most commonly used to calculate NAV are (1) using a capitalization rate or "cap rate" approach to valuing the NOI of a property or portfolio of properties; (2) applying value per square foot (or unit) to a property or portfolio of properties; and/or (3) using appraised values disclosed in the company's financial statements (permitted under IFRS but not hitherto or currently under US GAAP).[6] An analyst may adjust these appraised values reported by the company if he or she does not agree with the underlying assumptions and if there is sufficient information to do so. In the first two instances, the cap rates and values per square foot are derived from observing transactions that have occurred in the marketplace. In contrast, most sophisticated direct purchasers of commercial real estate arrive at a purchase price after doing detailed forecasting of the cash flows they expect to achieve from owning and operating a specific property over their investment time horizon. These cash flows are then discounted to a present value or purchase price. Whatever that present value or purchase price is, an analyst can estimate value by dividing an estimate of NOI by the cap rate, essentially the required rate of current return for income streams of that risk. In addition, an analyst can take the present value or purchase price and divide by the property's rentable area for a value per square foot. The point is that cap rates and values per square foot result from a more detailed analysis and discounted cash flow process. The discount rate used by a private owner/operator of commercial real estate could be different from the discount rate used by investors purchasing shares of REITs.

NAV reflects the value of a REIT's assets to a private market buyer, which may or may not be the same as the value that public equity investors ascribe to the business. This fact is one of the reasons for the wide historical premium/discount range stocks trade at relative to NAV estimates. Another reason is that the stock market tends to focus more on the outlook for short-term future changes in income and asset value than the property market, which is more focused on long term valuation. As alluded to earlier, it is possible that REITs and REOCs can trade at some premium or discount to NAV until the premium/discount becomes wide enough for market forces to close the arbitrage gap.

Another factor to consider when using a NAV approach to REIT/REOC valuation is that NAV implicitly treats a company as an individual asset or static pool of assets. In reality, such treatment is not consistent with a going concern assumption. Management teams have different track records and abilities to produce value over time, assets can be purchased and sold, and capital market decisions can add or subtract value. An investor must thus consider how much value a management team can add to (or subtract from) current NAV. For instance, an investor may be willing to purchase REIT A trading at a 10 percent premium to NAV versus REIT B trading at a small discount to NAV because the management team of REIT A has a stronger track record and better opportunities to grow the NAV compared with REIT B, therefore justifying the premium at which REIT A trades relative to REIT B.

NAV estimates can also become quite subjective when property markets become illiquid and few transactions are observable, or when REITs and REOCs own hundreds of properties, making it difficult for an investor to estimate exactly how much the portfolio would be worth if the assets were sold individually. There may also be a

---

6 At the time of this writing, US GAAP requires property assets to be carried in financial statements at depreciated cost.

large-portfolio premium in good economic environments when prospective strategic purchasers may be willing to pay a premium to acquire a large amount of desired property at once, or a large-portfolio discount when there are few buyers for the kind of property in question. In addition, such assets as undeveloped land, very large properties with few comparable assets, properties with specific uses, service businesses, and joint ventures complicate the process of estimating NAV with accuracy and confidence.

5.3.2 Further Observations on NAV

Among institutional investors, the most common view is that if REIT management is performing well in the sense of creating value, REITs and REOCs should trade at premiums to underlying NAVPS. The rationale is based on the following:

1 Investors in the stocks have liquidity on a day-to-day basis, whereas a private investor in real estate does not, thus warranting a lower required return rate (higher value) in the public market than the private market for the same assets.

2 The competitive nature of the public markets and size of the organizations should attract above-average management teams, which should produce better real estate operating performance and lead to better investment decisions than the average private real estate concern.

In conclusion, although NAV is by its nature an absolute valuation metric, in practice it is often more useful as a relative valuation tool. If all REITs are trading above NAV or below NAV, selecting individual REITs could become a relative exercise—that is, purchasing the REIT stock trading at the smallest premium to NAV when REITs are trading above NAV, or selling the REIT trading at the smallest discount to NAV when REITs are all trading at a discount to NAV. In practice, NAV is also used as a relative metric by investors looking at implied cap rates. To calculate the implied cap rate of a REIT or REOC, the current price is used in an NAV model to work backward and solve for the cap rate. By doing so, an investor looking at two similar portfolios of real estate could ascertain if the market is valuing these portfolios differently based on the implied cap rates.

VALUATION: RELATIVE VALUE (PRICE MULTIPLE) APPROACH

6

Conventional equity valuation approaches, including "market-based" or relative value approaches, are used with some adaptations to value REITs and REOCs. Such multiples as price-to-funds from operations (P/FFO), price-to-adjusted funds from operations (P/AFFO), and enterprise value-to-earnings before interest, taxes, depreciation, and amortization (EV/EBITDA) are used for valuing shares of REITs and REOCs in much the same way as for valuing shares in other industries. Funds from operations and adjusted funds from operations are defined and discussed in detail in Section 6.2.

6.1 Relative Value Approach to Valuing REIT Stocks

The relative value measures most frequently used in valuing REIT shares are P/FFO and P/AFFO. The ratio EV/EBITDA is used to a lesser extent. Like the P/E and P/CF multiples used for valuing equities in industrial sectors, P/FFO and P/AFFO multiples allow investors to quickly ascertain the value of a given REIT's shares compared with other REIT shares, or to compare the current valuation level of a REIT's shares with historical levels.[7] Within the REIT sector, P/FFO and P/AFFO multiples are also often compared with the average multiple of companies owning similar properties; for example, comparing the P/FFO multiple of a REIT that owns office properties with the average P/FFO multiple for all REITs owning office properties. These multiples are typically calculated using current stock prices and year-ahead estimated FFO or AFFO.

There are three main drivers behind the P/FFO, P/AFFO, and EV/EBITDA multiples of most REITs and REOCs:

1 *Expectation for growth in FFO/AFFO*: The higher the expected growth, the higher the multiple or relative valuation. Growth can be driven by business model (e.g., REITs and REOCs successful in real estate development often generate above-average FFO/AFFO growth over time), geography (e.g., having a concentration of properties in primary, supply-constrained markets, such as New York City or London, can give landlords more pricing power and higher cash flow growth than can be obtained in secondary markets), and other factors (e.g., management skill or lease structure).

2 *Risk associated with the underlying real estate*: For example, owning apartments is viewed as having less cash flow variability than owning hotels. As such, apartment-focused REITs have tended to trade at relatively high multiples compared with hotel REITs.

3 *Risks associated with company's capital structures and access to capital*: As financial leverage increases, equities' FFO and AFFO multiples decrease because required return increases as risk increases.

Financial disclosure and transparency can also have material effects on multiples. As discussed in Section 6.2, FFO has some shortcomings; but because it is the most standardized measure of a REIT or REOC's earning power, P/FFO is the most frequently used multiple in analyzing the sector. It is, in essence, the REIT sector equivalent of P/E. Investors can derive a quick "cash flow" multiple by looking at P/AFFO because AFFO makes a variety of adjustments to FFO that result in an approximation of cash earnings.

6.2 Funds from Operations and Adjusted Funds from Operations

REIT analysts and investors make extensive use of two cash flow measures that are particularly relevant to real estate.[8] The objective of both is to improve on net earnings as a measure of profit. **Funds from operations** (FFO) is a widely accepted and reported supplemental measure of the operating income of a REIT or real estate operating company. FFO is defined as accounting net earnings excluding (1) depreciation charges (depreciation expense) on real estate, (2) deferred tax charges (the deferred portion of tax expenses), and (3) gains or losses from sales of property and debt restructuring.

Why is depreciation excluded? Investors believe that real estate maintains its value to a greater extent than other business assets, often appreciating in value over the long-term, and that depreciation deductions under IFRS and US GAAP do not represent economic reality. A taxable REOC that uses a moderate degree of leverage and regularly chooses to reinvest most of its income in its business usually will be able to defer a large part of its annual tax liability; that is, its cash income taxes will be low as a result of the accelerated depreciation rates for tax purposes permitted in most countries. Analysts tend to exclude the deferred tax liability and the related

---

7 Comparisons with the overall market are not generally made.
8 Note that "cash flow" is used in an approximate sense. FFO is closer to a cash number than net earnings, but it is not exactly a cash number.

periodic deferred tax charges because they regard them as economically questionable. The deferred tax liability may not be paid for many years, if at all, or may change in amount depending on future tax rates, laws, and corporate tax planning. Gains and losses from sales of property and debt restructuring are excluded on the grounds that they do not represent sustainable, normal income. Accordingly, depreciation and deferred tax charges are added back to net earnings, and gains and losses from sales of property and debt restructuring are excluded in computing FFO.

Adjusted funds from operations (AFFO), also known as **funds available for distribution** (FAD) or **cash available for distribution** (CAD), is a refinement of FFO that is designed to be a more accurate measure of current economic income. AFFO is most often defined as FFO adjusted to remove any non-cash rent and to subtract maintenance-type capital expenditures and leasing costs (including leasing agents' commissions and tenants' improvement allowances). So-called **straight-line rent** is the average contractual rent over a lease term and this figure is recognized as revenue under IFRS and US GAAP. The difference between this figure and the cash rent paid during the period is the amount of the non-cash rent or **straight-line rent adjustment**. Because most long-term leases contain escalating rental rates, this difference in rental revenue recognition can be significant. Also, deductions from FFO for capital expenditures related to maintenance and for leasing the space in properties reflect costs that need to be incurred to maintain the value of properties. The purpose of the adjustments to net earnings made in computing FFO and AFFO is to obtain a more tangible, cash-focused measure of sustainable economic income that reduces reliance on non-cash accounting estimates and excludes non-economic, non-cash charges.

AFFO is superior to FFO as a measure of economic income because it takes into account the capital expenditures necessary to maintain the economic income of a property portfolio. It is open, however, to more variation and error in estimation than FFO. The precise annual provision required to maintain and lease the space in a property is difficult to predict, and the actual expense in any single year may be significantly more or less than the norm because of the timing of capital expenditure programs and the uneven expiration schedule of leases. Consequently, estimates of FFO are more frequently cited measures, although analysts and investors will tend to base their investment judgments to a significant degree on their AFFO estimates. Although many REITs and REOCs compute and refer to AFFO in their disclosures, their methods of computation and their assumptions vary. Firms that compile statistics and estimates of publicly traded enterprises for publications, such as Bloomberg and Thomson Reuters, tend not to gather AFFO estimates because of the absence of a universally accepted methodology for computing AFFO and inconsistent corporate reporting of actual AFFO figures, which hinders corroboration of analysts' estimates.

Net operating income was previously mentioned in relation to checking NAV estimates. It is an important income measure that analysts use as a starting point in making their adjustments to income and book value of assets. **Net operating income** (NOI) is defined as gross rental revenue minus operating costs (which include estimated vacancy and collection losses, insurance costs, taxes, utilities, and repairs and maintenance expenses) but before deducting depreciation, corporate overhead, and interest expense. After deduction from NOI of general and administrative (G&A) expenses, the figure obtained is earnings before interest, depreciation, and amortization (EBITDA). Subtracting interest expense from EBITDA results in FFO, and the further deduction of non-cash rent, maintenance type capital expenditures, and leasing commissions gives AFFO. Exhibit 8 illustrates the most straightforward, convenient way of calculating FFO and AFFO for hypothetical Office Equity REIT Inc.

Exhibit 8	Calculation of FFO and AFFO Office Equity REIT Inc (in thousands, except per share data)

Panel A: Calculation of funds from operations

Net income available to common	$160,638
Add: Depreciation and amortization	$101,100
Funds from operations	$261,738
FFO per share (55,689 shares outstanding)	**$4.70**

Panel B: Calculation of adjusted funds from operations

Funds from operations	$261,738
Less: Non-cash (straight-line) rent adjustment	$21,103
Less: Recurring maintenance-type capital expenditures and leasing commissions	$55,765
Adjusted funds from operations	$184,870
AFFO per share (55,689 shares outstanding)	**$3.32**

EXAMPLE 6

Analyst Adjustments (I)

1 Which of the following is the *best* measure of a REIT's current economic return to shareholders?

   A NOI

   B FFO

   C AFFO

2 An analyst gathers the following information for a REIT:

NOI	$115 million
Book value of properties	$1,005 million
Market value of debt outstanding	$505 million
Market cap rate	7%
Shares outstanding	100 million
Book value per share	$5.00

The REITs NAV per share is *closest* to:

   A $10.05.

   B $11.38.

   C $16.42.

3 All else equal, estimated NAV per share will decrease with an increase in/to the:

   A capitalization rate.

   B estimated growth rate.

   C deferred tax liabilities.

Solution to 1:

C is correct. AFFO is calculated from FFO by deducting non-cash rent, capital expenditures for maintenance, and leasing costs.

B is incorrect because it does not account for non-cash rent, capital expenditures for maintenance, and leasing costs. A is incorrect because it does not account for interest expense, general and administrative expense, non-cash rent, capital expenditures for maintenance, and leasing costs, which are appropriate deductions in calculating current economic return.

Solution to 2:

B is correct. The NAVPS estimates real estate values by capitalizing NOI. Valuing $115 million of NOI with a capitalization rate of 7 percent yields a value for the properties of $1,642,857,000. After deducting $505 million of debt at market value, NAV is $1,137,857,000; NAVPS equals NAV divided by 100 million shares outstanding, or $11.38.

A is incorrect because it is the book value of the assets (not the net assets) per share: $1,005 million divided by 100 million shares = $10.05 per share. It does not take into account the market value of the assets and does not deduct debt. C is incorrect because it is the market value of the real estate; that is, NOI capitalized at 7 percent, divided by 100 million shares: $1,642,857,000/100,000,000 = $16.42. This calculation excludes other assets and liabilities of the entity.

Solution to 3:

A is correct. The capitalization rate is used to calculate the estimated value of operating real estate because it is the NOI as a percentage of the value of operating real estate: NOI/Capitalization rate = Estimated value. As the capitalization rate increases, the estimated value of operating real estate and thus the NAV will decrease.

B is incorrect because an increase in the estimated growth rate would increase the estimated NOI, and the estimated value of operating income. C is incorrect because deferred liabilities are not counted as "hard" liabilities and subtracted from the NAV.

EXAMPLE 7

Analyst Adjustments (II)

1 An increase in the capitalization rate will *most likely* decrease a REIT's:

A cost of debt.

B estimated NOI.

C estimated NAV.

2 An analyst gathers the following information for a REIT:

Non-cash (straight-line) rent	£207,430
Depreciation	£611,900
Recurring maintenance-type capital expenditures and leasing commissions	£550,750
Adjusted funds from operations	£3,320,000
AFFO per share	£3.32

The REIT's funds from operations (FFO) per share is *closest* to:

A £3.93.

B £4.08.

C £4.48.

3 Which of the following estimates is *least likely* to be compiled by firms that publish REIT analysts' estimates?

A FFO

B AFFO

C Revenues

Solution to 1:

C is correct. The capitalization rate is used to estimate the market value of real estate, which is then used to calculate NAV.

A is incorrect because a higher capitalization rate does not decrease the REIT's cost of debt. B is incorrect because the estimated NOI is based on income growth, not the capitalization rate.

Solution to 2:

B is correct. FFO = AFFO + Non-cash (straight-line) rent + Recurring maintenance-type capital expenditures and leasing commissions = 3,320,000 + 550,750 + 207,430 = £4,078,180. The number of shares outstanding = 3,320,000/3.32 = 1,000,000. FFO/share = 4,078,180/1,000,000 ≈ £4.08.

A is incorrect because it adds depreciation to AFFO (3,320,000 + 611,900 = £3,931,900. 3,931,900/1,000,000 ≈ £3.93 per share.) Depreciation is added to NOI (not AFFO) to find FFO. C is incorrect because it also adds depreciation to AFFO + Non-cash (straight-line) rent + Recurring maintenance-type capital expenditures and leasing commissions. That is incorrect because depreciation is not part of the difference between FFO and AFFO.

Solution to 3:

B is correct. Firms that compile statistics and estimates of REITs tend not to gather AFFO estimates because of the absence of a universally accepted methodology for computing AFFO and inconsistent corporate reporting of actual AFFO figures.

6.3 P/FFO and P/AFFO Multiples: Advantages and Drawbacks

The US REIT industry began to expand rapidly in the 1990s. Exhibit 9 presents some evidence on the US REIT market for 1995–2011 (essentially, two complete commercial real estate cycles). REITs' trading multiples were lowest in late 1999 and early 2000, at about 7 to 8 times (denoted 8x) for P/FFO and about 9 to 10x for P/AFFO. Multiples for REITs and REOCs were at their highest in early 2007, when P/FFO multiples approached 20x and P/AFFO multiples were about 24x.

Exhibit 9   Historic P/FFO and P/AFFO Multiples for US REITs

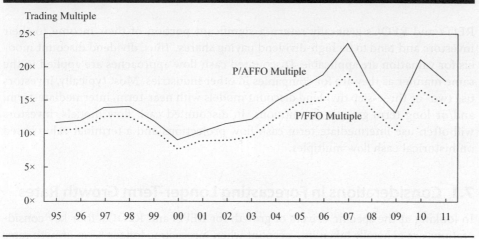

The key benefits of using P/FFO and P/AFFO multiples in the valuation of REITs and REOCs are as follows:

1 Multiples of earnings measures of this kind are widely accepted in evaluating shares across global stock markets and industries.

2 In light of this acceptance, portfolio managers can put the valuation of REITs and REOCs into context with other investment alternatives.

3 FFO estimates are readily available through market data providers, such as Bloomberg and Thomson Reuters, which facilitates calculating P/FFO multiples.

4 Multiples can be used in conjunction with such items as expected growth and leverage levels to deepen the relative analysis among REITs and REOCs.[9]

There are also drawbacks. Multiples are not a perfect basis for valuation because of the following:

1 Applying a multiple to FFO or AFFO may not capture the intrinsic value of all real estate assets held by the REIT or REOC; for example, land parcels and empty buildings may not currently produce income and hence do not contribute to FFO but have value.

2 P/FFO does not adjust for the impact of recurring capital expenditures needed to keep properties operating smoothly; and although P/AFFO should do so, wide variations in estimates and assumptions are incorporated into the calculation of AFFO.

3 In recent years, an increased level of such one-time items as gains and accounting charges, as well as new revenue recognition rules, have affected the income statement, thus making P/FFO and P/AFFO more difficult to compute and complicating comparisons between companies.

---

9 Neither FFO nor AFFO take into account differences in leverage; leverage ratios can be used to adjust for differences in leverage among REITs when comparing valuations based on FFO and AFFO multiples.

7   VALUATION: DISCOUNTED CASH FLOW APPROACH

REITs and REOCs generally return a significant portion of their income to their investors and tend to be high-dividend paying shares. Thus, dividend discount models for valuation are applicable. Discounted cash flow approaches are applied in the same manner as they are for companies in other industries. Most typically, investors use two- or three-step dividend discount models with near-term, intermediate-term, and/or long-term growth assumptions. In discounted cash flow models, investors will often use intermediate-term cash flow projections and a terminal value based on historical cash flow multiples.

7.1 Considerations in Forecasting Longer-Term Growth Rates

In looking at the specific drivers of growth for REITs and REOCs, four key considerations are generally taken into account when forecasting longer-term growth rates in these models.

1 *Internal growth potential* that stem from rent increases over time. In general, companies with portfolios of real estate located in supply-constrained markets with robust demand have a better ability to raise rents and increase cash flow. The opposite is true for portfolios in more supply-saturated markets or markets with tepid tenant demand conditions and prospects. Over the long term, well-managed property portfolios in good markets tend to generate cash flow growth at a level slightly above inflation.

2 *Investment activities*, such as acquisitions, new development, re-development, or dispositions of assets, have an impact on long-term growth. Successful development-oriented companies have shown better growth over time because returns on invested capital are generally higher on development than on acquisitions. Somewhat counter-intuitively, dispositions of weaker assets with below-average growth prospects are often dilutive to earnings because the cap rates at which such properties are sold are higher than the yields at which proceeds are re-invested, which reflects lower risk premiums. Thus, a REIT or REOC that undergoes a repositioning of a material portion of its portfolio into higher-quality properties could face cash flow growth pressure in the near term.

3 *Capital structure* can have an impact on growth, particularly in the short term as companies raise or lower their leverage. This is because of the positive leverage spread enjoyed by most REITs and REOCs; that is, going-in cap rates on property investments exceed the cost of debt. These benefits, however, can be reversed by adverse changes in the capital markets or missteps by management on acquisitions or operations. In general, REIT investors tend to be conservative and oriented toward stable, recurring income and to be averse to high leverage in REITs.

4 *Retaining and reinvesting a portion of free cash flow* can make a contribution to the growth rate. Although REITs often pay out the majority of cash flow to investors in the form of dividends, the high rates of depreciation allowed under most countries' tax laws allow companies, including REITs, to retain enough cash flow without incurring current income taxes to add 1 to 3 percentage points to annual growth.

7.2 Some Perspective on Long-Term Growth Rates

If the previously mentioned components of growth are added together, an analyst can derive a long-run growth rate. For successfully managed REITs and REOCs with good portfolios, the resulting growth rate should be in the high-single-digit percentage range. Given core cash flow growth of about 3–4 percent, 1–2 percent growth from investment activity over time, 2–3 percent growth from the financial leverage that magnifies the two growth drivers, and another 0–1 percent from reinvesting free cash flow, the long-run growth rate estimate ranges from 6 to 10 percent and the averages of the components would add up to an 8 percent long-run growth rate. The long-run growth for the average US REIT from the mid-1990s through 2010, however, was barely more than 0 percent per year, with only the top companies achieving 4–7 percent average annual cash flow growth. So, although in theory REITs and REOCs should show higher growth rates, in reality the impact of the business cycle, operational and investment missteps, and a highly dilutive process of balance sheet strengthening through equity issuance after the credit crisis of 2008 and 2009 all have had a negative effect on growth.

The other key component in discounted cash flow models and dividend discount models is required returns. Although a detailed discussion about deriving required returns is beyond the scope of this reading, most rates used in practice have ranged widely from 7 percent to 13 percent. The conventional argument is that the risk premium—and thus the discount rate—associated with REITs and REOCs should be lower than the average stock in the broader market because the underlying business of owning income-producing real estate should be less volatile because of contractual revenue streams from leases. A long-term look at the betas of REIT shares suggests values tend to be less than 1.0, which supports this view.

Considering the points just outlined, the key drawback to using dividend discount models and discounted cash flow models for valuing REITs and REOCs is the high sensitivity of these valuation models to the key inputs of growth and discount rates.

EXAMPLE 8

Valuation (I)

1 When using a relative P/AFFO or P/FFO multiple approach in the valuation of a REIT or REOC, which of the following considerations is the *most* important to take into account?

   A The discount rate

   B The NOI capitalization rate

   C Relative AFFO or FFO growth rates and different leverage levels

2 Which of the following is the *most* significant contributor to P/FFO and P/AFFO valuation multiples for REITs and REOCs?

   A The average age of the management team

   B The exchange on which the REIT stock is listed

   C The geographic location of properties in a REIT's portfolio

3 Which of the following is *not* a challenge in accurately estimating net asset value (NAV)?

   A Estimating the value of goodwill and intangible assets

   B Identifying the capitalization rates on comparable properties trading in the property market

   C   Ascribing an accurate value to a REIT's land holdings, projects under development, and joint ventures

4 Which of the following is *least likely* to cause persistent differences between estimated NAVs and stock prices?

   A   A surplus of takeover arbitrage capital in the markets

   B   Different discount rates being applied to privately held assets versus a liquid security

   C   A strong history of growth that prompts stock investors to pay a premium to the real estate value for a good management team

5 Which of the following are important in using a discounted cash flow model to value REITs?

   A   The capitalization rate

   B   The net asset value discount

   C   The payout ratio and the amount of financial leverage used by the REIT

Solution to 1:

C is correct. The main drivers of a relative multiple approach to valuation are risks associated with capital structure (leverage) and underlying real estate as well as expectations for growth (relative AFFO or FFO growth rates), so both should be considered.

A and B are incorrect because they relate to the dividend discount model and NAV approaches to valuation, respectively.

Solution to 2:

C is correct. Geography determines expectations for growth and risks, two main drivers of a relative multiple approach to valuation.

A is incorrect because although management skill may contribute to expected growth, management age does not. B is incorrect because the REIT's listing exchange is largely irrelevant to its investment value.

Solution to 3:

A is correct. These "soft" assets are ascribed no value by analysts in a net asset value calculation.

B is incorrect because estimating cap rates is a challenge in that they can be somewhat subjective when the properties sold differ significantly and/or few transactions are observable. C is incorrect because such assets as undeveloped land, buildings under construction, large properties with few comparable assets, service businesses, and joint ventures complicate the process of estimating NAV with accuracy and confidence.

Solution to 4:

A is correct. A surplus of takeover arbitrage capital in the markets is likely to close the gap between share prices and net asset values by generating takeovers.

B is incorrect because different discount rates may be used to reflect differences in liquidity, which persist until both securities are either publicly or privately traded. C is incorrect because the management's reputation and its effect on security value persist as long as the management remains.

Solution to 5:

C is correct. The payout ratio or level of retained cash flow affects long-term growth rates and the REIT's financial leverage is a determinant of its overall risk exposure and thus discount rate. Both growth and discount rates are key components of the discounted cash flow model.

A and B are incorrect because they both relate to the net asset value approach to REIT valuation.

REIT VALUATION: MINI CASE STUDY

8

In this section, we undertake the valuation of a REIT by using the previously outlined approaches for valuation. The REIT in our example is Capitol Shopping Center REIT Inc (CRE), a fictitious company that owns and operates retail shopping centers primarily in the Washington DC metropolitan area. The following are CRE's income statements, balance sheets, and cash flow statements for 2009 and 2010.

Exhibit 10 Capitol Shopping Center REIT Inc. (in thousands, except per share data)

Panel A: Income statements

	Three Months Ending 31 December		Year Ending 31 December	
	2010	**2009**	**2010**	**2009**
Rental revenue	$133,700	$130,300	$517,546	$501,600
Other property income	3,600	2,100	14,850	13,450
Total property revenue	$137,300	$132,400	$532,396	$515,050
Rental expenses	$29,813	$28,725	$112,571	$109,775
Property taxes	15,050	14,850	57,418	55,375
Total property expenses	$44,863	$43,575	$169,989	$165,150
Property net operating income	$92,437	$88,825	$362,407	$349,900
Other income	$450	$385	$1,840	$1,675
General & Administrative expenses	$6,150	$7,280	$23,860	$26,415
EBITDA	$86,737	$81,930	$340,387	$325,160
Depreciation & amortization	$28,460	$27,316	$115,110	$111,020
Net interest expense	$25,867	$25,015	$100,823	$99,173
Net income available to common	$32,410	$29,599	$124,454	$114,967
Weighted average common shares	61,100	60,100	60,600	60,100
Earnings per share	$0.53	$0.49	$2.05	$1.91

Panel B: Balance sheets

	Year Ending 31 December	
	2010	**2009**
Assets		
Real estate, at cost		
Operating real estate	$3,627,576	$3,496,370
Land held for future development	$133,785	$133,785

(continued)

Exhibit 10   (Continued)

Panel B: Balance sheets

	Year Ending 31 December	
	2010	**2009**
	$3,761,361	$3,630,155
Less accumulated depreciation	($938,097)	($822,987)
Net real estate	$2,823,264	$2,807,168
Cash and equivalents	$85,736	$23,856
Accounts receivable, net	$72,191	$73,699
Deferred rent receivable, net	$38,165	$33,053
Prepaid expenses and other assets	$106,913	$101,604
Total Assets	$3,126,269	$3,039,380
Liabilities and Shareholders' Equity		
Liabilities		
Mortgages payable	$701,884	$647,253
Notes payable	$1,090,745	$1,090,745
Accounts payable and other liabilities	$219,498	$200,439
Total liabilities	$2,012,127	$1,938,437
Common shares and equity	$1,114,142	$1,100,943
Total Liabilities and Shareholders' Equity	$3,126,269	$3,039,380

Panel C: Cash Flow Statements

	Year Ending 31 December	
	2010	**2009**
Operating Activities		
Net income	$124,454	$114,967
Depreciation and amortization	$115,110	$111,020
Change in accounts receivable	$1,508	$452
Change in deferred rents	($5,112)	($4,981)
Change in prepaid expenses and other assets	($5,309)	$1,237
Change in accounts payable and other liabilities	$19,059	($11,584)
Net cash provided by operating activities	$249,710	$211,111
Investing Activities		
Acquisition of real estate	($111,200)	($22,846)
Capital expenditures on operating real estate	($20,006)	($18,965)
Net cash used in investing activities	($131,206)	($41,811)
Financing Activities		
Issuance of mortgages	$54,631	$14,213
Issuance of common shares	$58,425	$0
Dividends paid to common shareholders	($169,680)	($165,275)
Net cash used in financing activities	($56,624)	($151,062)
Increase (decrease) in cash and equivalents	$61,880	$18,238

Exhibit 10   (Continued)

Panel C: Cash Flow Statements

	Year Ending 31 December	
	2010	**2009**
Cash and cash equivalents, beginning of year	$23,856	$5,618
Cash and cash equivalents, end of year	$85,736	$23,856

CRE also publishes a supplemental investor packet that provides further disclosures used by the investment community to analyze the company. The following shows its adjustments to arrive at FFO and AFFO, and its calculation of dividend payouts based on dividends paid.

Exhibit 11   Capitol Shopping Center REIT Inc. FFO, AFFO, and Dividend Payouts (in thousands, except per share data)

	Three Months Ending 31 December		Year Ending 31 December	
	2010	**2009**	**2010**	**2009**
Funds from operations				
Net income available to common	$32,410	$29,599	$124,454	$114,967
Depreciation & amortization	$28,460	$27,316	$115,110	$111,020
Funds from operations	$60,870	$56,915	$239,564	$225,987
FFO/Share	$1.00	$0.95	$3.95	$3.76
Adjusted funds from operations				
Funds from operations	$60,870	$56,915	$239,564	$225,987
Less Non-cash rents (1)	($1,469)	($1,325)	($5,112)	($4,981)
Less Recurring capital expenditures (2)	($5,638)	($5,101)	($20,006)	($18,965)
Adjusted funds from operations	$53,763	$50,489	$214,446	$202,041
AFFO/Share	$0.88	$0.84	$3.54	$3.36
Dividends/Share	$0.70	$0.69	$2.80	$2.75
Dividend Payout Ratios				
On FFO	70.0%	72.6%	70.9%	73.1%
On AFFO	79.6%	82.1%	79.1%	81.8%
Weighted average common shares	61,100	60,100	60,600	60,100

1   Non-cash rents include the impact of straight-lining contractual rent increases in leases, per accounting rules. The change in deferred rents can often provide the impact of this accounting on rental revenues.

2   Recurring capital expenditures include those costs needed to maintain the revenue-producing ability of existing assets, such as leasing commissions to keep or attract new tenants, maintenance items such as roofs and parking lot repairs, and basic build-outs of space as an inducement to attract tenants.

The historical stock price and company's financial statements, including disclosures, are used to complete a simple analysis of the balance sheet, as follows.

Exhibit 12	Capitol Shopping Center REIT Inc. Balance Sheet Analysis (in thousands, except per-share data)	

	Year Ending 31 December	
	2010	2009
Ending debt	$1,792,629	$1,737,998
Ending stock price	$72.36	$61.50
Ending shares	61,100	60,100
Ending market capitalization	$4,421,196	$3,696,150
Debt/Total market capitalization	*40.5%*	*47.0%*
Peer group debt/Total market capitalization	47.1%	56.7%
All REITs debt/Total market capitalization	42.8%	49.6%
EBITDA	$340,387	$325,160
Interest expense	$100,823	$99,173
Interest coverage	*3.38x*	*3.28x*
Peer group interest coverage	2.35x	2.16x
All REITs interest coverage	2.58x	2.27x
Ending net debt	$1,706,893	$1,714,142
EBITDA	$340,387	$325,160
Net debt-to-EBITDA	*5.01x*	*5.27x*
Peer group net debt-to-EBITDA	7.10x	8.60x
All REITs net debt-to-EBITDA	6.70x	7.80x
Ending net debt	$1,706,893	$1,714,142
Ending gross real estate	$3,761,361	$3,630,155
Net debt/Gross real estate (Book)	*45.4%*	*47.2%*
Peer group net debt/Gross real estate (Book)	52.8%	55.1%
All REITs net debt/Gross real estate (Book)	49.6%	52.6%

The exhibits provide a recent historical picture of CRE's financial performance and balance sheet. Some key points about the company's properties operations, dividend policy, recent business activity, and historical trading attributes follow.

■ CRE owns properties that are generally considered defensive in the commercial real estate sector. This is because many of its properties are tenanted by basic necessity goods retailers such as grocery stores, drug stores, dry cleaners, etc.

■ CRE's location in the Washington, DC metropolitan area is generally viewed as favorable for two key reasons: (1) Washington, DC is the capital of the United States, and the government is the largest driver of employment, which has historically provided more stability compared with the private sector; and (2) the city is a fairly dense area with strict zoning restrictions and new construction of shopping centers is difficult, which limits competing new supply.

■ CRE has been able to increase its rents and net operating income by 2–3 percent each year, on average, in the past decade.

■ The past two reported years (2009 and 2010) were difficult for the broader commercial real estate markets. CRE was able to achieve positive growth while many of its REIT peers saw FFO and AFFO decline. As forecasts call for improving fundamental property-level conditions, CRE's portfolio may not have as much "upside" because it did not experience the decline in occupancy and rents that other REITs did.

■ In the middle of 2010, the company purchased a portfolio of three shopping centers from a local developer for a total price of $111.2 million. The return on these assets in the first year is an estimated 6.75 percent. The company was able to achieve a better going-in cap rate on this acquisition than the market averages of 6.0–6.25 percent because of its strong relationships and reputation with tenants, commercial property brokers, and competitors as well as its ability to act quickly because of its strong balance sheet. In addition, the property is not fully leased, leaving potential to increase net operating income if CRE can attract additional tenants. CRE funded the purchase with a $54.6 million mortgage at a 6 percent interest rate and cash from a common stock offering of 1 million shares and from cash on hand.

■ The company intends to make additional acquisitions in the future as part of its growth plan. It intends to use a combination of debt, common equity, and internally generated cash to make these purchases. It typically requires the properties it acquires to generate an unleveraged internal rate of return of 9.5 percent in the form of current yield and capital appreciation over time.

■ CRE's balance sheet strategy is to operate at less than 50 percent debt/market capitalization, with a preference for leverage to be closer to 40 percent. At year-end 2010, CRE's debt/market capitalization was 40.5 percent and its interest coverage was 3.38x. The company's current in-place average debt cost is 5.7 percent. By comparison, CRE's peers operate at an average leverage level of 47.1 percent and have an interest coverage ratio of 2.35x.

■ CRE's board has chosen a dividend policy that provides an approximate 80 percent payout of cash flow, or AFFO. This level allows the company to pay an attractive dividend to shareholders, retain some cash flow, provide a cushion in the event of a downturn, and remain in compliance with REIT payout requirements in the United States. It is easily able to meet these REIT payout requirements because the requirements are based on taxable net income, which is calculated after deducting depreciation. In fact, CRE's dividend level has run well in excess of taxable net income, according to comments made by its management.

■ Over the last decade, CRE has traded between 9 and19x FFO, while its peers have traded between 8 and 18x, and all REITs have traded between 7 and 20x. On an AFFO basis, CRE's historical multiple has been 10–21x, with its peers trading between 9–19x, and all REITs being in the 9–24x range.

■ Currently, shopping center REITs are estimated to be trading at 7.6 percent above analyst estimates of net asset value (NAV). The overall REIT sector is estimated to be trading at a 14.8 percent premium to estimate NAV.

■ CRE's historical beta to the broader equity market is 0.80. The current risk-free rate of return is 4.0 percent, and the market risk premium is estimated at 5.0 percent.

Investors and analysts that cover CRE have published estimates for its FFO/share, AFFO/share, and dividends/share for the next three years. Putting the average, or "consensus," of these estimates together with the company's reported results reveals the following FFO/AFFO and dividend snapshot.

| Exhibit 13 | Capitol Shopping Center REIT Inc. Historical and Forecast Earnings and Dividends (all amounts are per-share) | | | | |

	Year Ending 31 December				
	2009A	**2010A**	**2011E**	**2012E**	**2013E**
CRE's FFO/Share	$3.76	$3.95	$4.23	$4.59	$4.80
Growth	—	5.1%	7.1%	8.5%	4.6%
Peer group FFO/Share growth	—	3.4%	6.8%	8.2%	4.2%
All REITs FFO/Share growth	—	1.2%	7.9%	9.8%	10.2%
CRE's AFFO/Share	$3.36	$3.54	$3.76	$4.09	$4.31
Growth	—	5.4%	6.2%	8.8%	5.4%
Peer group AFFO/Share growth	—	−1.0%	6.2%	9.1%	4.8%
All REITs AFFO/Share growth	—	−3.0%	8.1%	9.7%	10.8%
CRE's dividends/Share	$2.75	$2.80	$2.98	$3.25	$3.40
Growth	—	1.8%	6.4%	9.1%	4.6%
Peer group dividends/Share growth	—	−2.0%	5.6%	7.9%	5.1%
All REITs dividends/Share growth	—	−5.0%	7.8%	8.9%	6.0%
CRE's dividend payout on AFFO	81.8%	79.1%	79.3%	79.5%	78.9%

Taking the recent stock price of $69.85/share and focusing on the next two years (as most analysts looking at multiples do), comparative FFO/AFFO multiples for CRE can be determined. A look at the multiples of its direct peers and the entire REIT industry trade is also included.

| Exhibit 14 | Comparative Multiple Analysis | | | |

	P/FFO		P/AFFO	
	2011E	**2012E**	**2011E**	**2012E**
Capitol Shopping Center REIT, Inc (CRE) (1)	16.5x	15.2x	18.6x	17.1x
Shopping center oriented REITs	14.5x	13.3x	16.1x	14.5x
All REITs	14.2x	12.8x	16.5x	14.6x
CRE's Premium/(Discount) To...				
Shopping center REITs	13.8%	14.3%	15.5%	17.9%
All REITs	16.2%	18.8%	12.7%	17.1%

1   Based on a current stock price of $69.85.

8.1 Checking the Valuation: Analysis Based on Relative Valuation

In analyzing CRE's FFO/AFFO multiples, we find that at the current stock price of $69.85, CRE trades at a premium valuation level compared with its direct peers (other shopping center REITs) as well as the overall REIT industry. When considering whether this level is warranted or not, the following items should be considered:

1 Is CRE's expected FFO and AFFO growth likely to be better or worse than those of its peers and the overall REIT industry in the next two years?

2 What is the historical FFO/AFFO multiple range for CRE, shopping center REITs, and the overall REIT industry?

3 Are there any company-specific considerations that justify a higher or lower relative multiple?

For the first consideration, we estimate that CRE's FFO and AFFO growth in 2011 should be approximately 6–7 percent and move up to 8–9 percent in 2012. As shown in Exhibit 13, this estimate is roughly in-line with that of its shopping center–focused peers but is lower than the growth expected from all REITs, which should average about 8 percent in 2011 and move up to nearly 10 percent in 2012. On its own, this estimate would suggest that CRE is expensive relative to its peers because its FFO and AFFO multiples are at premiums but its growth is largely in-line with its peers. CRE also appears expensive relative to all REITs because expected FFO and AFFO growth is lower than what is expected from REITs as a whole, yet CRE's multiples are higher than the REIT group average.

Regarding the second consideration, the company's FFO multiple has ranged from 9–19x over the last 10 years, compared with 8–18x for its peers and 7–20x for the overall REIT industry. Regarding historical AFFO trading multiples, CRE's range in the last 10 years has been 10–21x, with its shopping center REIT peers in the 9–19x range and the overall REIT industry in the 9–24x range. Based on these figures, it appears CRE has historically traded at some premium to its peers, but the current premium is larger than usual. Similarly, CRE appears to be trading at a larger premium to the overall REIT group than it has historically. In addition, it is noteworthy that for CRE's stock and the REIT sector, P/FFO and P/AFFO valuations are at the upper end of the historical range, suggesting that REITs in general are not cheap based on historical multiples.

Addressing the third consideration, it is notable that the company's geographic exposure is considered lower risk. In addition, the company has demonstrated positive AFFO growth during times when its peers saw declining AFFO, such as in 2010. It was also able to increase its dividend when other REITs made dividend cuts. An analyst might also note that CRE's leverage of 40.5 percent on the basis of debt to total market cap and interest coverage level of 3.38x is more conservative than its peers, as are virtually all of its other balance sheet leverage metrics. These points suggest that some premium valuation is warranted because of lower financial risk.

In total, the above analysis points to CRE being overvalued when using a relative multiple approach to valuation, or P/FFO and P/AFFO multiples. To derive a specific current value estimate for CRE, an investor might ascribe overall REIT group P/FFO and P/AFFO multiples to CRE in the near-term because of the company's expected growth being lower than the average REIT, offset by the company's historical premium for its geography and track record. In doing so, an investor would arrive at a share value of $60.07 using P/FFO of 14.2x for 2011 for the overall REIT group multiplied by CRE's expected FFO in 2011 of $4.23/share. Using the same methodology for AFFO equates to a $62.04 share value. These values imply that the share would need to decline by 11–14 percent to become more attractive to an investor using P/FFO and P/AFFO multiples.

8.2 Further Analysis Based on Net Asset Value Per Share

We now use NAVPS to value the shares of Capitol Shopping Center REIT Inc. To find the value, we use the previously detailed financial statements and commentary about where assets trade that are similar to those owned by CRE. By finding this information, we can estimate a value for the company if its properties were sold, debt was paid off, and capital was returned to shareholders. Our calculation to arrive at NAVPS is shown in Exhibit 15.

Exhibit 15	Capitol Shopping Center REIT Inc. Net Asset Value (NAV) Estimate (in thousands, except per-share data)
Last 12-Months real estate NOI	$362,407
Less: Non-cash rents	(5,112)
Plus: Adjustment for full impact of acquisitions (1)	3,753
Pro forma cash NOI for last 12 months	$361,048
Plus: Next 12-months growth (2)	$9,026
Estimated next 12-months cash NOI	$370,074
Assumed cap rate (3)	6.125%
Estimated value of operating real estate	$6,042,024
Plus: Cash and equivalents	$85,736
Plus: Land held for future development	133,785
Plus: Accounts receivable	72,191
Plus: Prepaid/Other assets (4)	53,457
Estimated gross asset value	$6,387,193
Less: Total debt	$1,792,629
Less: Other liabilities	219,498
Net asset value	$4,375,066
Shares outstanding	61,100
NAV/Share	**$71.61**

1   Calculated as half of the 6.75% return on the company's $111.2 million investment made in the middle of 2010.

2   Assuming the 2.5% midpoint of the company's historical 2-3% growth.

3   At the midpoint of recent transactions in the market of 6-6.25%.

4   We cut this to half of book to account for any non-tangible assets that could be included in the accounting figure.

Note: Due to rounding to nearest thousand, figures may not sum precisely.

As shown in Exhibit 15, CRE's NAV is estimated at $71.61/share. This NAV is higher than the current stock price of $69.85, implying that CRE is trading at a 2.5 percent *discount* to NAV. Although this value alone does not show that the shares are significantly undervalued compared with its real estate, an investor should also consider that (1) CRE's direct peers are trading at NAV *premiums* of 7–8 percent, (2) the overall REIT industry is trading at an average NAV premium of almost 15 percent, and (3) Capitol Shopping Center REIT's management team has been able to earn more from its properties and grow its cash flow faster than its competitors in the marketplace. Considering these factors, an investor could conclude that CRE should at least trade at a NAV premium in line with its direct peers, implying a value of about $77 for the shares. If it trades at a NAV premium in line with the overall REIT group, the share value is $82.

Whether the analyst takes a pure NAV valuation approach to valuing shares of CRE or uses NAV as a relative metric, the conclusion is that the shares of Capitol Shopping Center REIT are undervalued using this valuation method.

8.3 Further Analysis Based on a Dividend Discount Model Approach to Valuation

The final approach we take to valuing shares of Capitol Shopping Center REIT is to use a two-step dividend discount model (DDM). In the first step, we use the published estimates for the company's dividend in 2011, 2012, and 2013. In the second step, we assume a long-run dividend growth rate of 5 percent, essentially using Gordon's constant growth model. We arrive at this growth rate after considering the company's historical NOI growth of 2–3 percent, roughly 40–50 percent financial leverage, and future acquisitions that help drive growth. In addition, we assume CRE's board maintains an 80 percent dividend payout ratio. To arrive at a discount rate, we observe that CRE's historical beta to the broader equity market is 0.80, the assumed risk-free rate is 4 percent, and the assumed equity risk premium is 5 percent. Using the capital asset pricing model (CAPM), we calculate a cost of equity capital of 4% + 0.8(5%) = 8 percent for the stock. The next table combines our assumptions to derive a net present value of the projected dividends.

Exhibits 16 and 17 provide a summary of the dividends we use for steps one and two in the model.

Exhibit 16	Capitol Shopping Center REIT Inc. Dividends for Use in a Two-Step DDM (all amounts are per-share)			
	Year Ending 31 December			
	Step One		**Step Two**	
	2011E	**2012E**	**2013E**	**In Perpetuity**
AFFO/Share	$3.76	$4.09	$4.31	...
Growth	—	*8.8%*	*5.4%*	*5.0%*
Dividends/Share	$2.98	$3.25	$3.40	...
Growth	—	*9.1%*	*4.6%*	*5.0%*
Dividend payout on AFFO	79.3%	79.5%	78.9%	80.0%

Exhibit 17	Capitol Shopping Center REIT Inc. Valuation Using Two-Step DDM (all amounts are per-share)			
	Year Ending 31 December			
	Step One			**Step Two**
	2011E	**2012E**	**2013E**	**2014E**
Dividends/Share	$2.98	$3.25	$3.40	$3.57
Value of stock at end of 2013 (1)	—	—	$119.00	
Cash flow to investors	$2.98	$3.25	$122.40	

(continued)

Exhibit 17	(Continued)			

	Year Ending 31 December			
	Step One			Step Two
	2011E	**2012E**	**2013E**	**2014E**

Net Present Value of Cash Flow (Dividends) = \$102.71

1   Calculated as \$3.57/(0.08 − 0.05).

Using a two-step dividend discount model approach to valuation, we calculate a share value of \$102.71 for Capitol Shopping Center REIT Inc. This value is about 47 percent higher than the current price of \$69.85 and suggests that the shares are currently undervalued. Compared with the relative valuation approaches, this approach indicates that CRE is undervalued, not overvalued. This result is consistent with the NAV approach, which also indicated that CRE is undervalued. The discrepancy between estimated value and price is largest using the dividend discount model. This result is not particularly surprising in light of the sensitivity of results when using this valuation approach to small differences in valuation assumptions that we referred to earlier.

8.4 Selection of Valuation Methods

As this discussion demonstrates, different valuation methods can yield different results. Under such circumstances, an analyst should re-examine the assumptions made to investigate why the approaches are generating such different results. The method(s) selected by an analyst may depend on which one(s) the analyst believes use(s) the most reliable assumptions, which one(s) the analyst believes will be used by other investors, or which one(s) best reflect the analyst's own investment philosophy or view of value. The analyst may choose to take a single valuation approach, a mid-point in the range of values obtained by using several approaches, or elect to use a weighted average of the values obtained based on the analyst's view of the relative reliability of the models used to arrive at the values.

EXAMPLE 9

Valuation (II)

1   If the outlook for economic growth turns negative and property market transaction volumes decline, it is *least likely* that CRE's:

   A   P/FFO and P/AFFO would be lower.

   B   relative P/FFO and P/AFFO multiples would be higher.

   C   NAV becomes the most useful valuation method.

2   If other REITs have no land on their balance sheets, how is CRE's "Land held for future development" *best* factored into a relative P/FFO or P/AFFO multiple valuation?

   A   There should be no impact on multiples as a result of land value.

   B   CRE would warrant lower multiples to account for land value.

   C   CRE would warrant higher multiples to account for land value.

3 An analyst speaks with private market real estate investors and learns that because interest rates have just increased 200 bps, buyers will require future property acquisitions to have going-in cap rates that are 100–200 bps higher than those on recent property market transactions. The analyst's estimate of NAV for CRE *most likely*:

   A increases as cap rates are higher.

   B decreases as cap rates are higher.

   C remain the same unless CRE has debt maturing in the near term.

4 An analyst determines that CRE purchased its "Land held for future development" 15 years ago, and that on average land values at that time were one-third of what they are today. Which of the following *best* adjusts NAV to reflect this consideration?

   A The cap rate on operating assets should be changed.

   B Land value, and thus NAV, should be adjusted higher to reflect today's valuations.

   C NAV is still mainly a representation of book values, thus there should be no adjustments.

5 Zoning in CRE's real estate markets is changed to allow more new space in the future, dampening CRE's long-term FFO growth by about 0.5 percent. The effect on CRE's valuation using a dividend discount model is *most likely* that the present value of the dividend stream:

   A decreases because of lower growth.

   B remains the same.

   C increases because of the new supply.

Solution to 1:

C is correct. NAV becomes more subjective in a negative and less liquid market with fewer observable transactions, and thus this basis of valuation becomes less useful and reliable.

A and B are incorrect because P/FFO and P/AFFO are likely to fall in a negative economic environment, but investors may be willing to pay a relative premium for CRE's stock based on its superior stability in economically challenging times.

Solution to 2:

C is correct. Although it may not produce income that contributes to FFO or AFFO, the land has value and represents a source of greater internal growth potential. For that reason, A and B are incorrect.

Solution to 3:

B is correct. Estimated real estate value decreases as the cap rate increases. Because NAV is derived directly from estimated real estate value, it also decreases. For this reason, A is incorrect. C is incorrect because an increase in cap rates decreases asset values. The fact that CRE has debt maturing in the near term is not a key factor influencing NAV.

Solution to 4:

B is correct. An analyst tries to attribute market values to real property owned.

A is incorrect because the cap rate used by analysts in calculating NAVs represents the return on only the income-producing asset portfolio and does not relate to land holdings that are not currently producing any income. C is incorrect because NAV is not a representation of book values, which rely on accounting methodology rather than market values.

Solution to 5:

A is correct. Lower growth affects the projected dividend stream, decreasing its present value. For that reason, B and C are incorrect.

EXAMPLE 10

Valuation (III)

1   An analyst gathers the following information for two REITs:

	Price/NAV	Capitalization rate used in NAV
REIT A	100%	6%
REIT B	99%	8%

If the REITs have similar property portfolio values, interest expense, and corporate overhead, which REIT *most likely* has the higher Price/FFO?

A   REIT A

B   REIT B

C   They will have similar P/FFOs because their ratios of price to NAV are almost identical.

2   An analyst gathers the following information for two REITs:

	P/NAV	P/AFFO	AFFO Payout Ratio	Est. annual AFFO growth
REIT A	98%	12.8 X	50%	4.0%
REIT B	101%	13.0 X	90%	3.5%

All else being equal, if both REITs have a 10 percent rate of return on retained and reinvested cash flows, which of the REITs is *most* attractively priced?

A   REIT A

B   REIT B

C   Neither REIT is more attractively priced than the other

Solution to 1:

A is correct. A lower capitalization rate (i.e., a lower NOI with such other parameters as interest costs and corporate expenses being the same) implies a lower FFO and hence a higher P/FFO ratio if P/NAV ratios are similar, as is the case here.

B is incorrect because A has a lower capitalization rate, implying a lower FFO and hence a higher P/FFO ratio if P/NAV ratios are similar, as is the case here. C is incorrect because it neglects the effect of the lower capitalization rate of REIT A.

> **Solution to 2:**
>
> B is correct. REIT B is cheaper because it is able to generate almost the same growth in AFFO as REIT A while retaining only 10 percent of AFFO compared with a 50 percent retention rate in the case of REIT A. Because both REITS are achieving a 10 percent return on retained AFFO, it suggests that REIT B has much more growth in returns coming from its existing portfolio of properties. Given very similar P/AFFO multiples for the two REITs, REIT B is more attractively priced. Also for these reasons, A and C are incorrect.

SUMMARY

This reading has presented publicly traded real estate securities, including their structure, economic drivers, investment characteristics, and valuation. Among the important points made by the reading are the following:

- The principal types of publicly traded real estate securities available globally are real estate investment trusts, real estate operating companies, and residential and commercial mortgage-backed securities.

- Publicly traded equity real estate securities offer investors participation in the returns from investment real estate with the advantages of superior liquidity in small and large amounts; greater potential for diversification by property, geography, and property type; access to a superior quality and range of properties; the benefit of management services; limited liability; the ability to use shares as tax-advantaged currency in making acquisitions; protection accorded by corporate governance, disclosure, and other securities regulations; and, in the case of REITs, exemption from income taxation within the REIT if prescribed requirements are met.

- Disadvantages include the costs of maintaining a publicly traded corporate structure, pricing determined by the stock market and returns that can be volatile, potential for structural conflicts of interest, and tax differences compared with direct ownership of property that can be disadvantageous under some circumstances.

- Compared with other publicly traded shares, REITs offer higher than average yields and greater stability of income and returns. They are amenable to a net asset value approach to valuation because of the existence of active private markets for their real estate assets. Compared with REOCs, REITs offer higher yields and income tax exemption but have less operating flexibility to invest in a broad range of real estate activities as well as less potential for growth from reinvesting their operating cash flows because of their high income-to-payout ratios.

- In assessing the investment merits of REITs, investors analyze the effects of trends in general economic activity, retail sales, job creation, population growth, and new supply and demand for specific types of space. They also pay particular attention to occupancies, leasing activity, rental rates, remaining lease terms, in-place rents compared with market rents, costs to maintain space and re-lease space, tenants' financial health and tenant concentration in the portfolio, financial leverage, debt maturities and costs, and the quality of management.

■ Analysts make adjustments to the historic cost-based financial statements of REITs and REOCs to obtain better measures of current income and net worth. The three principal figures they calculate and use are (1) funds from operations or accounting net earnings excluding depreciation, deferred tax charges, and gains or losses on sales of property and debt restructuring; (2) adjusted funds from operations, or funds from operations adjusted to remove straight-line rent and to provide for maintenance-type capital expenditures and leasing costs, including leasing agents' commissions and tenants' improvement allowances; and (3) net asset value or the difference between a real estate companies' assets and liabilities ranking prior to shareholders' equity, all valued at market values instead of accounting book values.

■ REITs and REOCs are valued using a net asset value per share, price-to-FFO, price-to-AFFO, price-to-NAV, or a discounted cash flow approach, or combinations of these approaches. Three important factors influencing the P/FFO and P/AFFO of REITs and REOCs are expectations for growth in FFO/AFFO, risks associated with the underlying real estate, and risks associated with companies' capital structure and access to capital. The P/NAV approach to valuation can be used as either an absolute basis of valuation or a relative valuation approach. NAV reflects, however, the estimated value of a REIT's assets to a private market buyer, which may or may not be the same as the value that public equity investors ascribe to the business; this fact is one of the reasons for the wide historical premium/discount range at which REITs trade relative to NAV estimates.

■ REITs and REOCs generally return a significant portion of their income to their investors and as a result tend to pay high dividends. Thus, dividend discount or discounted cash flow models for valuation are also applicable. These valuation approaches are applied in the same manner as they are for shares in other industries. Most typically, investors utilize two- or three-step dividend discount models with near-term, intermediate-term, and/or long-term growth assumptions. In discounted cash flow models, investors will often use intermediate-term cash flow projections and a terminal value based on historical cash flow multiples.

PRACTICE PROBLEMS

The following information relates to Questions 1–6

Hui Lin, CFA is an investment manager looking to diversify his portfolio by adding equity real estate investments. Lin and his investment analyst, Maria Nowak, are discussing whether they should invest in publicly traded real estate investment trusts (REITs) or public real estate operating companies (REOCs). Nowak expresses a strong preference for investing in public REITs in taxable accounts.

Lin schedules a meeting to discuss this matter, and for the meeting, Lin asks Nowak to gather data on three specific REITs and come prepared to explain her preference for public REITs over public REOCs. At the meeting, Lin asks Nowak:

> "Why do you prefer to invest in public REITs over public REOCs for taxable accounts?"

Nowak provides Lin with an explanation for her preference of public REITs and provides Lin with data on the three REITs shown in Exhibits 1 and 2.

The meeting concludes with Lin directing Nowak to identify the key investment characteristics along with the principal risks of each REIT and to investigate the valuation of the three REITs. Specifically, Lin asks Nowak to value each REIT using four different methodologies:

Method 1   Net asset value

Method 2   Discounted cash flow valuation using a two-step dividend model

Method 3   Relative valuation using property subsector average P/FFO multiple

Method 4   Relative valuation using property subsector average P/AFFO multiple

Exhibit 1 Select REIT Financial Information			
	REIT A	**REIT B**	**REIT C**
Property subsector	**Office**	**Storage**	**Health Care**
Estimated 12 months cash net operating income (NOI)	$350,000	$267,000	$425,000
Funds from operations (FFO)	$316,965	$290,612	$368,007
Cash and equivalents	$308,700	$230,850	$341,000
Accounts receivable	$205,800	$282,150	$279,000
Debt and other liabilities	$2,014,000	$2,013,500	$2,010,000
Non-cash rents	$25,991	$24,702	$29,808
Recurring maintenance-type capital expenditures	$63,769	$60,852	$80,961
Shares outstanding	56,100	67,900	72,300

Exhibit 2	REIT Dividend Forecasts and Average Price Multiples		
	REIT A	**REIT B**	**REIT C**
Expected annual dividend next year	$3.80	$2.25	$4.00
Dividend growth rate in years 2 and 3	4.0%	5.0%	4.5%
Dividend growth rate (after year 3 into perpetuity)	3.5%	4.5%	4.0%
Assumed cap rate	7.0%	6.25%	6.5%
Property subsector average P/FFO multiple	14.4x	13.5x	15.1x
Property subsector average P/AFFO multiple	18.3x	17.1x	18.9x

Note: Nowak estimates an 8% cost of equity capital for all REITs and a risk-free rate of 4.0%.

1 Nowak's *most likely* response to Lin's question is that the type of real estate security she prefers:

  A offers a high degree of operating flexibility.

  B provides dividend income that is exempt from double taxation.

  C has below-average correlations with overall stock market returns.

2 Based upon Exhibits 1 and 2, the value per share for REIT A using valuation Method 1 is *closest* to:

  A $51.26.

  B $62.40.

  C $98.30.

3 Based upon Exhibits 1 and 2, the value per share of REIT B using valuation Method 3 is *closest* to:

  A $40.77.

  B $57.78.

  C $73.19.

4 Based on Exhibit 2, the value per share of REIT C using valuation Method 2 is *closest* to:

  A $55.83.

  B $97.57.

  C $100.91.

5 Based upon Exhibits 1 and 2, the value per share of REIT A using valuation Method 4 is *closest* to:

  A $58.32.

  B $74.12.

  C $103.40.

6 The risk factor *most likely* to adversely impact an investment in REIT B is:

  A new competitive facilities.

  B tenants' sales per square foot.

  C obsolescence of existing space.

The following information relates to Questions 7–12

Tim Wang is a financial advisor specializing in commercial real estate investing. He is meeting with Mark Caudill, a new client who is looking to diversify his investment portfolio by adding real estate investments. Caudill has heard about various investment vehicles related to real estate from his friends and is seeking a more in-depth understanding of these investments from Wang.

Wang begins the meeting by advising Caudill of the many options that are available when investing in real estate, including:

Option 1   Direct ownership in real estate

Option 2   Publicly traded real estate investment trusts (REITs)

Option 3   Publicly traded real estate operating companies (REOCs)

Option 4   Publicly-traded residential mortgage-backed securities (RMBSs)

Wang next asks Caudill about his investment preferences. Caudill responds by telling Wang that he prefers to invest in equity securities that are highly liquid, provide high income, and are not subject to double taxation.

Caudill asks Wang how the economic performance of REITs and REOCs is evaluated, and how their shares are valued. Wang advises Caudill there are multiple measures of economic performance for REITs and REOCs, including:

Measure 1   Net operating income (NOI)

Measure 2   Funds from operations (FFO)

Measure 3   Adjusted funds from operations (AFFO)

In response, Caudill asks Wang:

"Which of the three measures is the best measure of a REIT's current economic return to shareholders?"

To help Caudill's understanding of valuation, Wang presents Caudill with data on Baldwin, a health care REIT that primarily invests in independent and assisted senior housing communities in large cities across the United States. Select financial data on Baldwin for the past two years are provided in Exhibit 1.

Before the meeting, Wang had put together some valuation assumptions for Baldwin in anticipation of discussing valuation with Caudill. Wang explains the process of valuing a REIT share using discounted cash flow analysis, and proceeds to estimate the value of Baldwin on a per share basis using a two-step dividend discount model using the data provided in Exhibit 2.

Exhibit 1	Baldwin REIT Summarized Income Statement (in thousands of dollars, except per share data)	
	Year Ending December 31	
	2011	**2010**
Rental income	339,009	296,777
Other property income	6,112	4,033
Total income	345,121	300,810
Rental expenses		
Property operating expenses	19,195	14,273
Property taxes	3,610	3,327

(continued)

Exhibit 1	**(Continued)**	

	Year Ending December 31	
	2011	**2010**
Total property expenses	22,805	17,600
Net operating income	322,316	283,210
Other income (gains on sale of properties)	2,162	1,003
General and administrative expenses	21,865	19,899
Depreciation and amortization	90,409	78,583
Net interest expenses	70,017	56,404
Net income	142,187	129,327
Weighted average shares outstanding	121,944	121,863
Earnings per share	1.17	1.06
Dividend per share	0.93	0.85
Price/FFO, based upon year-end stock price	11.5x	12.7x

Exhibit 2	**Baldwin Valuation Projections and Assumptions**
Current risk-free rate	4.0%
Baldwin beta	0.90
Market risk premium	5.0%
Appropriate discount rate (CAPM)	8.5%
Expected dividend per share, 1 year from today	$1.00
Expected dividend per share, 2 years from today	$1.06
Long-term growth rate in dividends, starting in year 3	5.0%

7   Based on Caudill's investment preferences, the type of real estate investment Wang is *most likely* to recommend to Caudill is:

  A   Option 2.

  B   Option 3.

  C   Option 4.

8   Relative to Option 2 and Option 3, an advantage of investing in Option 1 is:

  A   greater liquidity.

  B   lower investment requirements.

  C   greater control over property level investment decisions.

9   The Baldwin REIT is *least likely* to experience long-run negative effects from a/ an:

  A   economic recession.

  B   unfavorable change in population demographics.

  C   major reduction in government funding of health care.

10   The *most appropriate* response to Caudill's question is:

    A   Measure 1

    B   Measure 2

    C   Measure 3

11 Based on Exhibit 1, the 2011 year-end share price of Baldwin was *closest* to:

    A $13.23.

    B $21.73.

    C $30.36.

12 Based upon Exhibit 2, the intrinsic value of the Baldwin REIT on a per share basis using the two-step dividend discount model is *closest* to:

    A $26.72.

    B $27.59.

    C $28.83.

SOLUTIONS

1   B is correct. REITs are tax-advantaged entities whereas REOC securities are not typically tax-advantaged entities. More specifically, REITs are typically exempted from the double taxation of income that comes from taxes being due at the corporate level and again when dividends or distributions are made to shareholders in some jurisdictions such at the United States.

2   B is correct. The NAV is $62.40.

Estimated Cash NOI	350,000
Assumed cap rate	0.07
Estimated value of operating real estate (350,000/.07)	5,000,000
Plus: cash + accounts receivable	514,500
Less: Debt and other liabilities	2,014,000
Net Asset Value	3,500,500
Shares outstanding	56,100
NAV/share	**$62.40**

3   B is correct. The value per share is $57.78, calculated as:

Funds from operations (FFO) = $290,612

Shares outstanding = 67,900 shares

FFO/share = $290,612/67,900 shares = $4.28

Applying the property subsector average P/FFO multiple of 13.5x yields a value per share of:

$4.28 × 13.5 = $57.78.

4   C is correct. The value per share for REIT C is $100.91.

	Step One			Step Two
	Year 1	Year 2	Year 3	Year 4
Dividends per share:	$4.00	$4.18	$4.37	$4.54
Value of stock at end of 2013[a]:			$113.57	
			$117.94	
Discount rate: 8.00%				
Net present value of all dividends[b]: $100.91				

[a] Calculated as $4.54 / (0.08 − 0.04) = $113.57
[b] Calculated as: $4.00 / (1.08) + $4.18 / (1.08)^2 + $117.94 / (1.08)^3 = $100.91

5   B is correct. The value per share is $74.11, calculated as:

Funds from operations (FFO) = $316,965

Less: Non-cash rents: $25,991

Less: Recurring maintenance-type capital expenditures: $63,769

Equals: AFFO: $227,205

Shares outstanding = 56,100 shares

AFFO/share = $227,205/56,100 shares = $4.05.

Applying the property subsector average P/AFFO multiple of 18.3x yields a value per share of:

$4.05 × 18.3 = $74.12.

6   A is correct. As a storage REIT, this investment faces competitive pressures because of the ease of entry into the field of self-storage properties can lead to periods of overbuilding.

7   A is correct. Option 2, publicly traded REITs, best satisfy Caudill's investment preferences. REITs are equity investments that, in general, are income tax exempt at the corporate/trust level, so there is no double income taxation. To qualify for the income tax exemption, REITs are legally obligated to pay out a high percentage of income to their shareholders, and this typically results in relatively high income for investors. Lastly, public REITs are generally liquid as they are traded in stock exchanges.

8   C is correct. Direct property ownership offers greater control over property level investment decisions in comparison to the level of control exhibited by shareholders in REITs and REOCs.

9   A is correct. Baldwin, a health care REIT, is largely resistant to economic recessions but is exposed to changes in population demographics and changes in government funding for health care.

10   C is correct. Measure 3, adjusted funds from operations (AFFO), is a refinement of FFO that is designed to be a more accurate measure of current economic income. In essence, FFO is adjusted to remove any non-cash rent and to include a provision for maintenance-type capital expenditures and leasing costs. Maintenance expenses are required for a business to continue as a going concern.

11   B is correct. Baldwin's FFO per share in 2011 was $1.89, and the resulting share price was $21.73. First, calculate FFO per share in 2011, and then apply the year-end P/FFO multiple of 11.5x.

FFO = accounting net earnings, excluding: (a) depreciation charges on real estate, (b) deferred tax charges, and (c) gains or losses from sales of property and debt restructuring.

2011 accounting net income: $142,187

2011 depreciation charges: $90,409

2011 deferred tax charges: N/A

2011 gains on sale of properties (other income): $2,162

2011 shares outstanding = 121,944

2011 year-end price/FFO = 11.5x

2011 Baldwin's FFO per share = ($142,187 + $90,409 − $2,162)/121,944 shares = $1.89. At the given 2011 year-end price/FFO multiple of 11.5x, this results in a share price for Baldwin of $1.89 × 11.5 = $21.73.

12   C is correct. The estimated value per share for the Baldwin REIT using a two-step dividend discount model is $28.83, calculated as:

	Step One		Step Two
	Year 1	Year 2	Year 3
Dividends per share:	$1.00	$1.06	$1.11
Value of stock at end of Year 2[1]:		$31.80	
		$32.86	

Discount rate: 8.50%

Net present value of all dividends[2]: $28.83

[1] Calculated as $1.11/(0.085 − 0.05) = $31.80
[2] Calculated as: $1.00/(1.085) + $32.86/(1.085)² = $28.83

READING
45

Private Equity Valuation

by Yves Courtois, CMT, CFA, and Tim Jenkinson, PhD

Yves Courtois, CMT, CFA, is at KPMG (Luxembourg). Tim Jenkinson, PhD, is at Said Business School, Oxford University (United Kingdom).

LEARNING OUTCOMES

Mastery	The candidate should be able to:
☐	a. explain sources of value creation in private equity;
☐	b. explain how private equity firms align their interests with those of the managers of portfolio companies;
☐	c. distinguish between the characteristics of buyout and venture capital investments;
☐	d. describe valuation issues in buyout and venture capital transactions;
☐	e. explain alternative exit routes in private equity and their impact on value;
☐	f. explain private equity fund structures, terms, valuation, and due diligence in the context of an analysis of private equity fund returns;
☐	g. explain risks and costs of investing in private equity;
☐	h. interpret and compare financial performance of private equity funds from the perspective of an investor;
☐	i. calculate management fees, carried interest, net asset value, distributed to paid in (DPI), residual value to paid in (RVPI), and total value to paid in (TVPI) of a private equity fund;

A Note on Valuation of Venture Capital Deals: (Appendix 45)

☐	j. calculate pre-money valuation, post-money valuation, ownership fraction, and price per share applying the venture capital method 1) with single and multiple financing rounds and 2) in terms of IRR;
☐	k. demonstrate alternative methods to account for risk in venture capital.

1 INTRODUCTION

Private equity is playing an increasing role in the global economy. In the last decade, private equity has grown from a small, niche activity to a critical component of the financial system. One manifestation of this has been the huge amount of money that investors have committed to private equity, estimated at around $1.5 trillion globally between 1998 and 2006. And this is just the equity portion of total financing. As will be explained later, many private equity deals employ significant amounts of debt, and so the value of the transactions involving private equity funds is often 2 or 3 times the actual equity raised. Until recently, few people even knew the names of the main private equity players. But now such organizations as Blackstone, Carlyle, KKR, Texas Pacific Group, and Permira are recognized as major forces in the global financial system. Fund sizes have grown—to over $20 billion at their largest—as have the size and complexity of the transactions that private equity funds are able to undertake, such as the $45 billion acquisition of the US energy company TXU. In 2006, it was estimated that private equity funds were involved in approximately one-quarter of all merger and acquisition activities.

There can be two perspectives on private equity valuation. In Section 2, we primarily take the perspective of the private equity firm that is evaluating potential investments. When a private equity firm is performing valuations of potential acquisitions, this effort is particularly complex because in most cases, except for public-to-private transactions, there will be no market prices to refer to. Private equity firms can face considerable challenges in valuing these companies, and this reading discusses the main ways in which valuation is approached. In Section 3, we take the perspective of an outside investor who is looking at the costs and risks of investing in a fund sponsored by the private equity firm.

Definitions of private equity differ, but in this reading we include the entire asset class of equity investments that are not quoted on stock markets. The private equity class stretches from venture capital (VC)—working with early stage companies that in many cases have no revenues but have potentially good ideas or technology—all the way through to large buyouts (leveraged buyout, or LBO) in which the private equity firm buys the entire company. In some cases, these companies might themselves be quoted on the stock market, and the private equity fund performs a public-to-private transaction thereby removing the entire company from the stock market. But in the majority of cases, buyout transactions will involve privately owned companies and, very often, a particular division of an existing company. There are many other forms of later-stage financing, such as providing capital to back the expansion of existing businesses, but for this reading we will refer simply to *venture capital* and *buyouts* as the two main forms of private equity.

Many classifications of private equity are available. Exhibit 1 provides a set of classifications proposed by the European Venture Capital Association (EVCA).

Exhibit 1	Classification of Private Equity in Terms of Stage and Type of Financing of Portfolio Companies	
Broad Category	**Subcategory**	**Brief Description**
Venture capital	Seed stage	Financing provided to research business ideas, develop prototype products, or conduct market research.
	Start-up stage	Financing to recently created companies with well articulated business and marketing plans.
	Expansion stage	Financing to companies that have started their selling effort and may be already breaking even. Financing may serve to expand production capacity, product development, or provide working capital.
	Replacement capital	Financing provided to purchase shares from other existing venture capital investors or to reduce financial leverage.
Buyout	Acquisition capital	Financing in the form of debt, equity, or quasi-equity provided to a company to acquire another company.
	Leverage buyout	Financing provided by a LBO firm to acquire a company.
	Management buyout	Financing provided to the management to acquire a company, specific product line, or division (carve-out).
Special situations	Mezzanine finance	Financing generally provided in the form of subordinated debt and an equity kicker (warrants, equity, etc.) frequently in the context of LBO transactions.
	Distressed securities	Financing of companies in need of restructuring or facing financial distress.
	One-time opportunities	Financing in relation to changing industry trends and new government regulations.
	Others	Other forms of private equity financing are also possible (i.e., activist investing, etc.).

Source: www.evca.com.

These classifications are not exhaustive. Private equity funds may also be classified depending on their geographical (national, regional, or global) and/or sector focus (e.g., diversified industrials, telecommunications, biotechnologies, healthcare, industrials, etc.).

How is the invested money split between venture capital and buyout deals? In broad terms, around four-fifths of the money has been flowing into buyouts in recent years in both the United States and Europe. In part this is because of the sheer scale of buyouts in which an individual deal can absorb several billion dollars of capital. In contrast, venture capital deals tend to drip feed money into companies as they develop. But investors also have been increasingly focusing on buyout funds, in which, in recent years at least, the average returns earned have tended to be higher.

Where does the money come from and how are the private equity funds organized? Most of the money comes from institutional investors, such as pension funds, endowments, and insurance companies, although many high-net-worth individuals also invest directly or through fund-of-funds intermediaries who provide their investors with a more diversified portfolio of investments. At present, the proportion of assets allocated by investors to private equity is considerably higher in the United States than in Europe, although surveys of European investors find that the fund managers plan to increase their allocation to private equity. So the flow of money into private equity is likely to continue and indeed grow, depending, of course, on market conditions.

One distinctive characteristic of private equity investment is a buy-to-sell orientation. Private equity fund investors typically expect their money returned, with a handsome profit, within 10 years of committing their funds. The economic incentives of the funds are aligned with this goal, as is explained later. In the next section we discuss this buy-to-sell approach and how funds are typically organized.

2   INTRODUCTION TO VALUATION TECHNIQUES IN PRIVATE EQUITY TRANSACTIONS

This reading is not intended to be a comprehensive review of valuation techniques applicable to private equity transactions. Instead, we highlight some essential considerations specific to private equity. As you might expect, private equity firms are a rich laboratory for applying the principles of asset and equity valuation. The case study on venture capital valuation that follows this reading demonstrates how a specific valuation technique can be applied.

First and foremost, we must distinguish between the price paid for a private equity stake and the valuation of such private equity stake. The price paid for a private equity stake is the outcome of a negotiation process between two or more parties with each possibly assigning a different value to that same private equity stake. Unlike shares of public companies that are traded regularly on a regulated market, buyers and sellers of private equity interests generally employ more efforts to uncover their value. Private equity valuation is thus time bound and dependent on the respective motives and interests of buyers and sellers.

The selection of the appropriate valuation methodologies depends largely on the stage of development of a private equity portfolio company. Exhibit 2 provides an overview of some of the main methodologies employed in private equity valuation and an indication of the stage of company development for which they may apply.

Exhibit 2 Overview of Selected Valuation Methodologies and Their Possible Application in Private Equity		
Valuation Technique	**Brief Description**	**Application**
Income approach: Discounted cash flows (DCF)	Value is obtained by discounting expected future cash flows at an appropriate cost of capital.	Generally applies across the broad spectrum of company stages. Given the emphasis on expected cash flows, this methodology provides the most relevant results when applied to companies with a sufficient operating history. Therefore, most applicable to companies operating from the expansion up to the maturity phase.
Relative value: Earnings multiples	Application of an earnings multiple to the earnings of a portfolio company. The earnings multiple is frequently obtained from the average of a group of public companies operating in a similar business and of comparable size. Commonly used multiples include: Price/Earnings (P/E), Enterprise Value/EBITDA, Enterprise Value/Sales.	Generally applies to companies with a significant operating history and predictable stream of cash flows. May also apply with caution to companies operating at the expansion stage. Rarely applies to early stage or start-up companies.

Exhibit 2	(Continued)	

Valuation Technique	Brief Description	Application
Real option	The right to undertake a business decision (call or put option). Requires judgmental assumptions about key option parameters.	Generally applies to situations in which the management or shareholders have significant flexibility in making radically different strategic decisions (i.e., option to undertake or abandon a high risk, high return project). Therefore, generally applies to some companies operating at the seed or start-up phase.
Replacement cost	Estimated cost to recreate the business as it stands as of the valuation date.	Generally applies to early (seed and start-up) stage companies or companies operating at the development stage and generating negative cash flows. Rarely applies to mature companies as it is difficult to estimate the cost to recreate a company with a long operating history. For example, it would be difficult to estimate the cost to recreate a long established brand like Coca-Cola, whereas the replacement cost methodology may be used to estimate the brand value for a recently launched beverage (R&D expenses, marketing costs, etc.).

One other methodology, the venture capital method, is discussed more fully as part of the case study that follows this reading.

Note that in a vibrant and booming private equity market, there is a natural tendency among participants to focus primarily on the earnings approach to determine value. This approach is perceived as providing a benchmark value corresponding best to the state of the current private equity market. Because of the lack of liquidity of private equity investments, the concurrent use of other valuation metrics is strongly recommended.

Thus, valuation does not involve simply performing a net present value calculation on a static set of future profit projections. The forecasts of the existing management or vendors are, of course, a natural place to start, but one of the key ways private equity firms add value is by challenging the way businesses are run. The business would have additional value if the private equity firm improves the business's financing, operations, management, and marketing.

In most transactions, private equity investors are faced with a set of investment decisions that are based on an assessment of prospective returns and associated probabilities. Private equity firms are confronted generally with a large flow of information arising from detailed due diligence investigations and from complex financial models. It is essential to understand the extent of the upside and downside potential of internal and external factors affecting the business and their resulting effect on net income and free cash flows. Any possible scenario must pass the judgmental test of how realistic it is. The defined scenarios should be based not only on the analysis of past events, but on what future events may realistically happen, given knowledge of the present. The interplay between exogenous factors (such as favorable and unfavorable macroeconomic conditions, interest rates, and exchange rates) and value drivers for the business (such as sales margins and required investments) should also be considered carefully. For example, what will be the sales growth if competition increases or if competing new technologies are introduced?

When building the financial forecasts, all variables in the financial projections should be linked to key fundamental factors influencing the business with assigned subjective probabilities. The use of Monte Carlo simulation, often using a spreadsheet add-in such as Crystal Ball™ or @RISK, further enhances the quality of the analysis and may be instrumental in identifying significant financial upsides and downsides to the business. In a Monte Carlo simulation, the analyst must model the fundamental value drivers of the portfolio company, which are in turn linked to a valuation model. Base case, worst case, and best case scenarios (sometimes called a triangular approach) and associated probabilities should be discussed with line managers for each value driver with the objective being to ensure that the simulation is as close as possible to the realities of the business and encompasses the range of possible outcomes.

Other key considerations when evaluating a private equity transaction include the value of control, the impact of illiquidity, and the extent of any country risk. Estimating the discount for illiquidity and marketability and a premium for control are among the most subjective decisions in private equity valuation. The control premium is an incremental value associated with a bloc of shares that will be instrumental in gaining control of a company. In most buyouts, the entire equity capital is acquired by the private equity purchasers. But in venture capital deals, investors often acquire minority positions. In this case the control premium (if any) largely depends on the relative strength and alignment of interest of shareholders willing to gain control. For example, in a situation with only a limited number of investors able to acquire control, the control premium is likely to be much more significant relative to a situation with a dominant controlling shareholder invested along with a large number of much smaller shareholders.

The distinction between marketability and liquidity is more subtle. The cost of illiquidity may be defined as the cost of finding prospective buyers and represents the speed of conversion of the assets to cash, whereas the cost of marketability is closely related to the right to sell the assets. In practice, the marketability and liquidity discounts are frequently lumped together.

The cost for illiquidity and premium for control may be closely related because illiquidity may be more acute when there is a fierce battle for control. But there are many dimensions to illiquidity. The size of the illiquidity discount may be influenced by such factors as the shareholding structure, the level of profitability and its expected sustainability, the possibility of an initial public offering (IPO) in the near future, and the size of the private company. Because determining the relative importance of each factor may be difficult, the illiquidity discount is frequently assessed overall on a judgmental basis. In practice, the discount for illiquidity and premium for control are both adjustments to the preliminary value estimate instead of being factored into the cost of capital.

When valuing private equity portfolio companies in emerging markets, country risk may also represent a significant additional source of risk frequently added to a modified version of the standard CAPM. Estimating the appropriate country risk premium represents another significant challenge in emerging markets private equity valuation. These technical hurdles relate not only to private equity investments in emerging markets but also increasingly to global private equity transactions conducted "en-bloc" in multiple countries. More than 15 approaches exist for the estimation of the country risk premium.[1]

Valuation in private equity transactions is, therefore, very challenging. Whereas traditional valuation methodologies, such as discounted cash flow analysis, adjusted present value, and techniques based on comparisons from the public market of precedent transactions, are used frequently by investment and valuation professionals, they are applied to private equity situations with care, taking into consideration stress

---

1 The modified country spread model, also called the modified Goldman model, is frequently used in practice. The Erb, Harvey, and Viskanta model, also called the country risk rating model, is gaining increasing popularity among valuation practitioners, partly because of its ease of use and theoretical appeal. For a comprehensive analysis of this topic, see *Estimating Cost of Capital in Emerging Markets*, Yves Courtois, CFA Institute webcasts, www.cfainstitute.org.

tests and a range of possible future scenarios for the business. Given the challenges of private equity valuation, value estimates based on a combination of several valuation methodologies will provide the strongest support for the estimated value. Private equity valuation is a process that starts as a support for decision making at the transaction phase but should also serve as a monitoring tool to capture new opportunities, or protect from losses, with the objective to continuously create value until the investment is exited. It also serves as a performance reporting tool to investors while the company remains in the fund portfolio. These ongoing valuation and reporting issues are discussed in Section 3.

2.1 How Is Value Created in Private Equity?

The question of how private equity funds actually create value has been much debated inside and outside the private equity industry. The survival of the private equity governance model depends on some economic advantages it may have over the public equity governance model. These potential advantages, described more fully below, include 1) the ability to re-engineer the private firm to generate superior returns, 2) the ability to access credit markets on favorable terms, and 3) a better alignment of interests between private equity firm owners and the managers of the firms they control.

Do private equity houses have superior ability to re-engineer companies and, therefore, generate superior returns? Some of the largest private equity organizations, such as Kohlberg Kravis Roberts (KKR), The Carlyle Group, Texas Pacific Group (TPG), or Blackstone Group, have developed in-house high-end consulting capabilities supported frequently by seasoned industry veterans (former CEOs, CFOs, senior advisers), and have a proven ability to execute deals on a global basis. Irrespective of their size, some of the very best private equity firms have developed effective re-engineering capabilities to add value to their investments. But it is hard to believe that this factor, all else being equal, is the main driver of value added in private equity. Assuming that private equity houses have a superior ability to re-engineer companies, this would mean that public companies have inherently less ability to conduct re-engineering or organizational changes relative to corporations held by private equity organizations. Many public companies, like General Electric or Toyota, have established a long track record of creating value. Thus, only a part of value added created by private equity houses may be explained by superior reorganization and re-engineering capabilities. The answer must also come from other factors.

Is financial leverage the main driver of private equity returns in buyouts? Ample availability of credit at favorable terms (such as low credit spreads and few covenants) led in 2006 and the first half of 2007 to a significant increase in leverage available to buyout transactions. Borrowing 6 to 8 times EBITDA (earnings before interest, taxes, depreciation, and amortization) has been frequent for large transactions conducted during this period. Note that in private equity, leverage is typically measured as a multiple of EBITDA instead of equity. Relative to comparable publicly quoted companies, there is a much greater use of debt in a typical buyout transaction.

When considering the impact of leverage on value, we should naturally turn to one of the foundations of modern finance: the Modigliani–Miller theorem.[2] This theorem, in its basic form, states that, in the absence of taxes, asymmetric information, bankruptcy costs, and assuming efficient markets, the value of a firm is not affected by how the firm is financed. In other words, it should not matter if the firm is financed by equity or debt. The relaxing of the "no taxes assumption" raises interesting questions in leveraged buyouts as the tax shield on the acquisition debt creates value as a

---

2 F. Modigliani and M. Miller, "The Cost of Capital, Corporation Finance and the Theory of Investment." *American Economic Review* (June 1958).

result of tax deductibility of interest. One would also expect that the financial leverage of a firm would be set at a level where bankruptcy costs do not outweigh these tax benefits. Unlike public companies, private equity firms may have a better ability to raise higher levels of debt as a result of a better control over management but also as a result of their reputation for having raised, and repaid, such high levels of debt in previous transactions.

Such debt financing is raised initially from the syndicated loan market, but then is frequently repackaged via sophisticated structured products, such as collateralized loan obligations (CLOs), which consist of a portfolio of leveraged loans. In some cases the private equity funds issue high-yield bonds as a way of financing the portfolio company, and these often are sold to funds that create collateralized debt obligations (CDOs). This raises the question of whether a massive transfer of risks to the credit markets is taking place in private equity. If the answer to this last question is positive, then one would expect that it will self-correct during the next economic downturn. Note that at the time of this writing (early 2008), the CDO and CLO markets were undergoing a significant slowdown as a result of the credit market turmoil that started in the summer of 2007, triggered by the subprime mortgage crisis. The CDO and CLO markets are (at this time) inactive. As a result, the LBO market for very large transactions ("mega buyouts") was affected by a lack of financing. Additional leverage is also gained by means of equity-like instruments at the acquisition vehicle level, which are frequently located in a favorable jurisdiction such as Luxembourg, the Channel Islands, Cayman Islands, or the British Virgin Islands. Note that acquisitions by large buyout private equity firms are generally held by a top holding company in a favorable tax jurisdiction. The top holding company's share capital and equity-like instruments are held in turn by investment funds run by a general partner who is controlled by the private equity buyout firm. These instruments are treated as debt for tax purposes within the limits of thin capitalization rules in certain jurisdictions. In Luxembourg, such equity-like instruments are called convertible preferred equity certificates, or CPECs.

The effect of leverage may also be analyzed through Jensen's free cash flow hypothesis.[3] According to Jensen, low growth companies generating high free cash flows tend to invest in projects destroying value (i.e., with a negative net present value) instead of distributing excess cash to shareholders. This argument is a possible explanation[4] as to why a LBO transaction may generate value as excess cash is used to repay the senior debt tranche, effectively removing the management's discretionary use of cash. Part of the value added in private equity may thus be explained by the level of financial leverage.

What other factors may then significantly explain the returns earned by private equity funds? One important factor is the alignment of economic interests between private equity owners and the managers of the companies they control, which can crystallize management efforts to achieve ambitious milestones set by the private equity owners. Results-driven management pay packages, along with various contractual clauses, ensure that managers receive proper incentives to reach their targets, and that they will not be left behind after the private equity house exits their investment. Examples of such contract terms include tag-along, drag-along rights, which are contractual provisions in share purchase agreements that ensure any potential future acquirer of the company may not acquire control without extending an acquisition offer to all shareholders, including the management of the company.

---

3 Jensen, M., "Agency Costs of Free Cash Flow, Corporate Finance and Takeovers," *American Economic Review*, vol. 76 no. 2 (1986).
4 Jensen, M., "Eclipse of the Public Corporation," *Harvard Business Review*, 67 (1989).

Empirical evidence also shows that managers from public companies subsequently acquired by private equity groups tend to acknowledge an increased level of directness and intensity of input enabling them to conduct higher value-added projects over a longer time frame after the buyout, as opposed to the "short-termism" prevailing during their public market period. This short-termism is mostly driven by shareholders' expectations, the analyst community, and the broad market participants who place a significant emphasis on management to meet quarterly earnings targets. As private equity firms have a longer time horizon in managing their equity investments, they are able to attract talented managers having the ability to implement sometimes profound restructuring plans in isolation of short-term market consequences. Note however, that private equity firms are not the sole catalysts of change at large companies. Some large organizations, for example General Electric, have a proven ability to stir entrepreneurship at all levels within the company and generate substantial value over a long time horizon.

Effective structuring of investments terms (called the "term sheet") results in a balance of rights and obligations between the private equity firm and the management team. In addition to the clauses discussed above, the following contractual clauses are important illustrations of how private equity firms ensure that the management team is focused on achieving the business plan and that if the objectives are not met, the control and equity allocation held by the private equity firm will increase:

- *Corporate board seats*: ensures private equity control in case of major corporate events such as company sale, takeover, restructuring, IPO, bankruptcy, or liquidation.
- *Noncompete clause*: generally imposed on founders and prevents them from restarting the same activity during a predefined period of time.
- *Preferred dividends and liquidation preference*: private equity firms generally come first when distributions take place, and may be guaranteed a minimum multiple of their original investment before other shareholders receive their returns.
- *Reserved matters*: some domains of strategic importance (such as changes in the business plan, acquisitions, or divestitures) are subject to approval or veto by the private equity firm.
- *Earn-outs (mostly in venture capital)*: mechanism linking the acquisition price paid by the private equity firm to the company's future financial performance over a predetermined time horizon, generally not exceeding 2 to 3 years.

Effective contractual structuring of the investment can thus be a significant source of return to private equity firms. In particular, it may allow venture capital firms, which invest in companies with considerable uncertainties over their future, to significantly increase their level of control over time and even seize control in case the company fails to achieve the agreed goals.

2.2 Using Market Data in Valuation

In most private equity transactions—with the exception of public-to-privates—there is no direct market evidence on the valuation of the company being acquired. But virtually all valuation techniques employ evidence from the market at differing stages in the calculation, rather than relying entirely on accounting data and management forecasts.

The two most important ways in which market data are used to infer the value of the entity being acquired are by analyzing comparison companies that are quoted on public markets and valuations implied by recent transactions involving similar entities. Typically, these techniques focus on the trading or acquisition multiples that exist in the public markets or in recent transactions. For instance, suppose a valuation is sought in the food sector for a retail chain, which is currently a privately owned company. The comparison company approach would look at the trading multiples—such as enterprise value to EBITDA—of comparable public companies, and use this multiple to value the target. Similarly, if there are recent M&A transactions in the food retail sector, the transactions multiples paid could be used to inform the current market value of the target. Of course, it is very important to make sure that the comparisons are appropriate, and this is not always possible, especially for certain businesses that operate in niche sectors or that are pioneering in terms of their products or services.

The use of market data is also important in the DCF approaches, in particular in estimating an appropriate discount rate. Cost of capital for private companies is estimated generally using the same weighted average cost of capital (WACC) formula[5] used for public companies. A serious challenge, however, in assessing the cost of equity in private equity settings is the lack of public historical data on share prices and returns. Therefore, beta (β), which represents the relative exposure of company shares to the market, must be estimated by means of a proxy. This is performed typically by estimating the beta for comparable companies, and then adjusting for financial and operating leverage. When conducting this benchmark exercise, several issues that may depend on analyst judgment should be considered: To what extent are the selected comparable public firms genuinely comparable to the target firm? Should outlying companies be excluded? What is the target debt-to-equity ratio of the target firm vs. industry average? What group of comparable public companies should be selected if the target firm operates in several business segments?

Finally, in DCF valuation techniques, forecasts of future financial performance usually are only available for a few years ahead. Therefore, it is almost always necessary to estimate the terminal value of the company beyond this forecasting horizon. In order to do this, it is possible to apply a perpetual growth rate assumption, although small changes in the assumed growth rate, which are very difficult to predict, can have a significant impact on the resulting valuation. An alternative is to use an assumption about the trading multiple that exists (or is predicted to exist) in public markets, and apply this to the last years' forecast values. For instance, if over the economic cycle the average enterprise value to EBITDA ratio for the publicly quoted companies in an industry is 10, then this might be applied to the final forecast value for EBITDA for the private target as a way of estimating the terminal value.

2.3 Contrasting Valuation in Venture Capital and Buyout Settings

Buyout and venture capital funds are the two main categories of private equity investments both in terms of number of funds and invested amounts. Whereas a venture capital firm may have a specialized industry focus—looking for the next rising star in technology, in life sciences, or another industry—LBO firms generally invest in a portfolio of firms with more predictable cash flow patterns. Venture capital firms (investing in new firms and new technologies) seek revenue growth, whereas buyout firms (investing in larger, established firms) focus more on EBIT or EBITDA growth. The approach to company valuation is thus fundamentally different, and Exhibit 3 presents some of the key distinctions.

---

5 WACC = $[E/(E + D)] \times$ (Cost of equity) + $[D/(E + D)] \times$ (Cost of debt) $(1 - $ Tax rate), where E is the market value of equity and D is the market value of debt.

Exhibit 3	Characteristics of Buyout and Venture Capital Investments

Buyout Investments:	Venture Capital Investments:
▪ Steady and predictable cash flows	▪ Low cash flow predictability, cash flow projections may not be realistic
▪ Excellent market position (can be a niche player)	▪ Lack of market history, new market and possibly unproven future market (early stage venture)
▪ Significant asset base (may serve as basis for collateral lending)	▪ Weak asset base
▪ Strong and experienced management team	▪ Newly formed management team with strong individual track record as entrepreneurs
▪ Extensive use of leverage consisting of a large proportion of senior debt and significant layer of junior and/or mezzanine debt	▪ Primarily equity funded. Use of leverage is rare and very limited
▪ Risk is measurable (mature businesses, long operating history)	▪ Assessment of risk is difficult because of new technologies, new markets, lack of operating history
▪ Predictable exit (secondary buyout, sale to a strategic buyer, IPO)	▪ Exit difficult to anticipate (IPO, trade sale, secondary venture sale)
▪ Established products	▪ Technological breakthrough but route to market yet to be proven
▪ Potential for restructuring and cost reduction	▪ Significant cash burn rate required to ensure company development and commercial viability
▪ Low working capital requirement	▪ Expanding capital requirement if in the growth phase
▪ Buyout firm typically conducts full blown due diligence approach before investing in the target firm (financial, strategic, commercial, legal, tax, environmental)	▪ Venture capital firm tends to conduct primarily a technology and commercial due diligence before investing; financial due diligence is limited as portfolio companies have no or very little operating history
▪ Buyout firm monitors cash flow management, strategic, and business planning	▪ Venture capital firm monitors achievement of milestones defined in business plan and growth management
▪ Returns of investment portfolios are generally characterized by lower variance across returns from underlying investments; bankruptcies are rare events	▪ Returns of investment portfolios are generally characterized by very high returns from a limited number of highly successful investments and a significant number of write-offs from low performing investments or failures
▪ Large buyout firms are generally significant players in capital markets	▪ Venture capital firms tend to be much less active in capital markets
▪ Most transactions are auctions, involving multiple potential acquirers	▪ Many transactions are "proprietary," being the result of relationships between venture capitalists and entrepreneurs
▪ Strong performing buyout firms tend to have a better ability to raise larger funds after they have successfully raised their first funds[a]	▪ Venture capital firms tend to be less scalable relative to buyout firms; the increase in size of subsequent funds tend to be less significant[b]
▪ Variable revenue to the general partner (GP) at buyout firms generally comprise the following three sources: carried interest, transaction fees, and monitoring fees[c]	▪ Carried interest (participation in profits) is generally the main source of variable revenue to the general partner at venture capital firms; transaction and monitoring fees are rare in practice[d]

[a] Andrew Metrick and Ayako Yasuda, "The Economics of Private Equity Funds." University of Pennsylvania, The Wharton School (September 9, 2007).
[b] Ibid.
[c] Ibid.
[d] Ibid.

2.4 Valuation Issues in Buyout Transactions

A buyout is a form of private equity transaction in which the buyer acquires from the seller a controlling stake in the equity capital of a target company. The generic term "buyout" thus refers explicitly to the notion of acquiring control. It comprises a wide range of techniques, including but not limited to, management buyouts (MBOs), leveraged buyouts (LBOs), or takeovers. Our focus in this reading will be on LBOs, which consist in the acquisition of a company using borrowed money to finance a significant portion of the acquisition price.

Typically, the structuring of LBO transactions involves a negotiation between the providers of equity capital, senior debt, high yield bonds, and mezzanine finance. Mezzanine finance[6] is a hybrid form of financing that may be perceived as a bridge between equity and debt. It is generally structured flexibly and tailored to fit the specific requirements of every transaction.

2.4.1 The LBO Model

The LBO model is not a separate valuation technique, but rather a way of determining the impact of the capital structure, purchase price, and various other parameters on the returns expected by the private equity fund from the deal.

The LBO model has three main input parameters: the cash flow forecasts of the target company, the expected return from the providers of financing (equity, senior debt, high yield bonds, mezzanine), and the amount of financing available for the transaction. The free cash flow forecasts of the target company are generally prepared by the management of the target company and are subject to an extensive due diligence process (strategic, commercial, financial, legal, and environmental) to determine the reliability of such forecasts. These forecasts are prepared on the basis of an explicit forecast horizon that generally corresponds to the expected holding horizon of the private equity firm in the equity capital of the target company.

The exit year is typically considered as a variable with the objective to determine the expected IRR sensitivity on the equity capital around the anticipated exit date. The exit value is determined most frequently by reference to an expected range of exit multiples determined on the basis of a peer group of comparable companies (Enterprise Value-to-EBITDA).

On the basis of the input parameters, the LBO model provides the maximum price that can be paid to the seller while satisfying the target returns for the providers of financing. This is why the LBO model is not a valuation methodology per se. It is a negotiation tool that helps develop a range of acceptable prices to conclude the transaction.

Exhibit 4 is a "value creation chart," summarizing the sources of the additional value between the exit value and the original cost. Value creation comes from a combination of factors: earnings growth arising from operational improvements and enhanced corporate governance; multiple expansion depending on pre-identified potential exits; and optimal financial leverage and repayment of part of the debt with operational cash flows before the exit. Each component of the value creation chart should be carefully considered and backed by supporting analyses, frequently coming from the lengthy due diligence process (especially commercial, tax, and financial) and also from a strategic review with the objective to quantify the range of plausible value creation.

---

6 For a more comprehensive discussion of mezzanine finance, refer to "Mezzanine Finance—A Hybrid Instrument with a Future," *Economic Briefing No 42*, Credit Suisse (2006).

Exhibit 4   Typical Leveraged Buyout Value Creation Chart

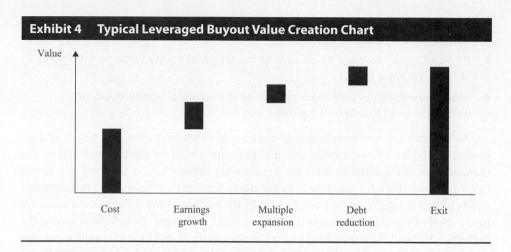

Exhibit 5 provides an example of a €5,000 (amounts in millions) investment in a private equity transaction. The transaction is financed with 50 percent debt and 50 percent equity. The €2,500 equity investment is further broken into €2,400 of preference shares owned by the private equity fund, €95 of equity owned by the private equity fund, and €5 of management equity. The preference shares are promised a 12 percent annual return (paid at exit). The private equity firm equity is promised 95 percent of the residual value of the firm after creditors and preference shares are paid, and management equity holders are promised the remaining 5 percent.

Exhibit 5   Stakeholder Payoffs

	Invested	Proceeds	Multiple	IRR
Management	€5m	€109m	21.8x	85%
PE fund	€2,495m	€6,291m	2.5x	20%

€5,000m enterprise value
12% rolled up dividend to preference shares
Management contribute €5m of equity
PE fund €95m equity and all the preference shares
Lenders fund the debt

€5,000m

Management Equity 5
PE Equity 95

Preference
Shares
2,400

Debt
2,500

2008

€8,000m

Management 109

PE Fund's
Equity
2,061

Preference
Shares
4,230

Debt 1,600

2013

Assume that the exit value, five years after investment, is 1.6 times the original cost. The initial investment of €5,000 has an exit value of €8,000. The specific payoffs for the four claimants are as follows:

- Senior debt has been partially retired with operational cash flows, reducing debt from €2,500 to €1,600. So debtholders get €1,600.

- Preference shares are paid a 12 percent return for 5 years, so they receive €2,400(1.12)^5 = €4,230.
- PE Fund equity receives 95 percent of the terminal equity value, or 0.95[8000 – (4230 + 1600)] = €2,061.
- Management equity receives 5 percent of the terminal equity value, or 0.05[8000 – (4230 + 1600)] = €109.

As you can see, preference shares increase in value over time as a result of their preferred dividend being capitalized, and the equity held by the PE fund and by the management is expected to increase significantly depending on the total enterprise value upon exit. Both the equity sold to managers, frequently known as the management equity program (MEP), and the equity held by the private equity firm are most sensitive to the level of the exit. The larger the exit multiple, the larger the upside potential for both the MEP and the equity held by the private equity firm. In the example, assuming that an exit of 1.6 times cash may be achieved at the anticipated exit date (2013), the management would realize an IRR of 85 percent per annum on its investment and the private equity fund equity holders an IRR of 20 percent per annum. The private equity firm also earns 12 percent per annum on its preference shares.

This chart also demonstrates the critical importance of leverage in buyout transactions. A reduction in financial leverage over time is instrumental in magnifying returns available to shareholders. Note that the bulk of financial leverage in LBOs consists of senior debt, much of which will be amortizing. Therefore, the reduction in financial leverage gradually increases over time as a proportion of principal is paid back to senior lenders on an annual or semi-annual basis depending on the terms of senior debt. As a result of senior debt gradual repayment over time, a larger proportion of operating cash flows becomes available to equity holders. Of course, this mechanism works well as long as no significant adverse economic factors negatively impact the business of the target LBO company and also provided that a successful exit can be handled in the foreseeable future. It should be remembered, however, that these high levels of debt increase significantly the risks borne by the equity investors, and such increased risk should be taken into account when comparing the realized returns with alternative investment classes (such as investments in the stock market).

Typically, a series of scenarios with varying levels of cash exits, growth assumptions, and debt levels are engineered with the use of an LBO model, using as inputs the required rate of return from each stakeholder (equity, mezzanine, senior debt holders), to gain a sound understanding of the buyout firm's flexibility in conducting the deal.

2.5 Valuation Issues in Venture Capital Transactions

In venture capital, pre-money valuation and post-money valuation are two fundamental concepts. Pre-money valuation (PRE) refers to the agreed value of a company prior to a round of financing or investment (I). Post-money valuation (POST) is the value of a company after the financing or investing round. Therefore:

POST = PRE + I

The proportionate ownership of the venture capital investor is determined by I/POST.

EXAMPLE 1

Investment and Ownership Interest of a VC Firm

A venture capital firm invests £1 million on a £1.5 million pre-money valuation and the VC firm obtains 40 percent of shares. In this case, PRE is £1.5 million, POST is £2.5 million, and the proportion financed by venture capital is £1 million/£2.5 million. The parties agreed that the VC firm would retain 40 percent of the shares and have that proportion of the rights of shareholders should dividends be paid or the firm sold.

Typically, both pre-money valuation and the level of the venture capital investment are subject to intense negotiations between the founders and the venture capital firm, bearing in mind the fundamental issue of dilution of ownership. Dilution of ownership is the reduction in the proportional ownership of a shareholder in the capital of a company resulting from the issuance of additional shares and/or of securities convertible into shares at some stage in the future. Additional financing rounds and the issuance of stock options to the management of a company are examples of dilution of ownership.

In VC transactions, there is typically significant uncertainty surrounding the projected future cash flows. Consequently, the discounted cash flow methodology is rarely used as the first method to determine value. Similarly, there are challenges applying the comparable companies approach as start-ups generally have unique features and it may be extremely difficult to find comparable quoted companies operating in the same field. Alternative valuation methodologies including the venture capital approach[7] or the real option methodology are also used to determine value. Traditional valuation methodologies typically comprise the income approach (discounted cash flow valuation), the relative value or market approach (information relative to a group of comparable companies is gathered and normalized relative to the EBITDA, EBIT, and revenue of the company being valued), and the cost approach (cost to recreate or replace the asset or company). Generally speaking, the appraisal of intangible assets, comprising the founder's know-how, experience, licenses, patents, and in progress research and development (IPRD), along with an assessment of the expected market potential of the company's product or products in development form the basis for assessing a pre-money valuation. Because of the significant level of uncertainty surrounding the business, it is not infrequent to observe a cap on the pre-money valuation (i.e., €3 million, €5 million, etc.).

In buyouts, given the significant predictability of cash flows, the income-based approach (discounted cash flows, adjusted present value, LBO model, target IRR) is frequently used as a primary method to determine the value of equity, considering the expected change in leverage until the time of exit of the investment. The initial high and declining financial leverage is the main technical valuation issue that needs to be adequately factored into the income approach when applied to a buyout valuation. The value is also frequently corroborated by an analysis of the peer group of comparable publicly traded companies.

2.6 Exit Routes: Returning Cash to Investors

The exit is among the most critical mechanisms to unlock value in private equity. Most private equity firms consider their exit options prior to investing and factor their assessment of the exit outcome into their analysis of target and expected internal rate of return.

Private equity investors generally have access to the following four exit routes for their investments:

- *Initial Public Offering (IPO)*: going public offers significant advantages including higher valuation multiples as a result of an enhanced liquidity, access to large amounts of capital, and the possibility to attract higher caliber managers. But an

---

7 Discussed in "A Note on Valuation of Venture Capital Deals."

IPO comes at the expense of a cumbersome process, less flexibility, and significant costs. Therefore, an IPO is an appropriate exit route for private companies with an established operating history, excellent growth prospects, and having a sufficient size. Timing of the IPO is also an important consideration. After the internet bubble collapse in March 2000, the number of successful IPOs plummeted in the subsequent years, forcing venture capital firms to change their exit plans for many of their investments.

▪ *Secondary Market*: sale of stake held by a financial investor to other financial investors or to strategic investors (companies operating or willing to establish in the same sector or market of the portfolio company). With the increased segmentation of private equity, secondary market transactions tend to occur within each segment, i.e., buyout firms tend to sell to other buyout firms (secondary buyouts) and venture firms to other venture firms (secondary venture capital transactions). These secondary market transactions are very common in practice and currently account for a significant proportion of exits, especially in the buyout segment. Venture capital exits by means of a buyout are also possible but rare in practice as buyout firms are reluctant to finance development stage companies with a significant amount of leverage. The two main advantages of secondary market transactions are 1) the possibility to achieve the highest valuation multiples in the absence of an IPO, and 2) with the segmentation of private equity firms, specialized firms have the skill to bring their portfolio companies to the next level (restructuring, merger, new market) and sell either to a strategic investor seeking to exploit synergies or to another private equity firm having another set of skills and the ability to further add value to the portfolio company.

▪ *Management Buyout (MBO)*: takeover by the management group using significant amounts of leverage to finance the acquisition of the company. Alignment of interest is optimal under this exit scenario but may come at the expense of an excessive leverage that may significantly reduce the company's flexibility.

▪ *Liquidation*: controlling shareholders have the power to liquidate the company if the company is no longer viable. This exit mechanism generally results in a floor value for the portfolio company but may come at a cost of very negative publicity for the private equity firm if the portfolio company is large and the employee count is significant.

Timing the exit and determining the optimal exit route are important investment management decisions to be made by private equity firms. Although the exit may be carefully planned, the unexpected can cause changes to the exit plan. This may mean that the exit could be delayed or accelerated depending on the market or purely opportunistic circumstances. Suppose, for example, that an LBO firm is planning an exit of one of its portfolio companies but the public market and economic conditions have collapsed, rendering any exit via a trade sale or an IPO unprofitable. The LBO firm may instead conduct another acquisition at depressed prices, merge this acquisition with the portfolio company with the objective to strengthen its market position or product range, and wait for better market conditions before conducting the sale. Flexibility is thus critical in private equity during harder times and underlines the importance for a private equity firm to have sufficient financial strength.

There seems to be no boundaries to the size of the largest buyout transactions as expectations have been consistently exceeded over the past few years and the $50 billion threshold appears now to be in sight for the largest buyout firms. The three largest buyout transactions in history, HCA Inc., Equity Office, and TXU Corporation, were all undertaken over the eighteen months before this reading was written. Private equity firms appear to be moving into uncharted territory in regards to managing exits at that level. The central question about these mega buyout transactions is how the exit will take place given that the extent of the exit possibilities is much more limited relative to smaller deals. IPOs, for example, raise significantly more challenges, such as the need for a gradual exit over time because only a single block of shares can be sold initially, and may prove excessively risky if market conditions are suboptimal. Some large companies may be viewed as holding companies of a portfolio of real assets. Such companies may be sold in tranches to prospective buyers. The real challenge will be for unified companies for which an exit will need to take place for the entire entity.

Understanding the anticipated exit provides clues as to what valuation methodologies or IRR models to employ. Timing of the exit will influence the way stress testing is conducted on the expected exit multiple. When the exit is anticipated in the near future (one to two years), the prevailing valuation multiples extracted from comparable quoted firms provide good guidance on the expected exit multiple. Stress tests on that value may be conducted for small incremental changes and on the basis of market knowledge. If the exit is anticipated in a much longer time horizon, the current valuation multiples are less relevant and stress tests may need to be conducted on a wider range of values to determine the anticipated exit multiple. Stress testing in this context consists of simulating incremental changes in the input variables of the valuation model (such as components of the discount factor, terminal growth rates, etc.) and to financial forecasts (sales growth, assumed future operating margins, etc.) in order to determine the range of value outcomes and to assess the stability of the valuation methodology.

2.7 Summary

Valuation is the most critical aspect of private equity transactions. The investment decision-making process typically flows from the screening of investment opportunities to preparing a proposal, appraising the investment, structuring the deal, and finally to the negotiating phase. Because of the difficulties in valuing private companies, a variety of alternative valuation methods are typically used to provide guidance on the appropriate range. Along with the various due diligence investigations (commercial or strategic, financial, legal, tax, environmental) generally conducted on private equity investment opportunities, valuation serves a dual purpose: assessing a company's ability to generate superior cash flows from a distinctive competitive advantage and serving as a benchmark for negotiations with the seller. After all, although seeing opportunities for adding value is important, it is also essential—for the investors in the private equity fund—that the seller does not appropriate all the potential gains by extracting a high price during the transaction.

Post-investment, valuation of private equity investments is also very important, as investors expect to be fully informed about the performance of the portfolio companies. This raises a separate set of issues, which are considered in the next section.

PRIVATE EQUITY FUND STRUCTURES AND VALUATION

3

When analyzing and evaluating financial performance of a private equity fund from the perspective of an investor, a solid grasp of private equity fund structures, terms of investment, private equity fund valuation, and due diligence are an absolute prerequisite. The distinctive characteristics of private equity relative to public equities raise many more challenges when interpreting financial performance. Two of the main differentiating characteristics of private equity, in addition to the structure and terms, relate to the nature of subscriptions made by investors in private equity structures and to the "J" curve effect. Investors commit initially a certain amount to the private equity fund that is subsequently drawn by the fund as the fund's capital is deployed in target portfolio companies. This contrasts with public market investing in which investment orders typically are disbursed fully at the time the orders are settled on the markets. The "J-curve" effect refers to the typical time profile of reported returns by private equity funds, whereby low or negative returns are reported in the early years of a private equity fund (in large part as a result of the fees' impact on net returns), followed by increased returns thereafter as the private equity firm manages portfolio companies toward the exit.

3.1 Understanding Private Equity Fund Structures

The limited partnership has emerged as the dominant form for private equity structures in most jurisdictions. Funds that are structured as limited partnerships are governed by a limited partnership agreement between the fund manager, called the general partner (GP), and the fund's investors, called limited partners (LPs). Whereas the GP has management control over the fund and is jointly liable for all debts, LPs have limited liability, i.e., they do not risk more than the amount of their investment in the fund. The other main alternative to the limited partnership is a corporate structure, called company limited by shares, which mirrors in its functioning the limited partnership but offers a better legal protection to the GP and to some extent the LPs, depending on the jurisdictions. Some fund structures, especially the Luxembourg-based private equity fund vehicle SICAR (société d'investissement en capital à risque), are subject to a light regulatory oversight offering enhanced protection to LPs. The vast majority of these private equity fund structures are "closed end," which restricts existing investors from redeeming their shares over the lifetime of the fund and limiting new investors to entering the fund only at predefined time periods, at the discretion of the GP.

Private equity firms operate effectively in two businesses: the business of managing private equity investments and the business of raising funds. Therefore, private equity firms tend to plan their marketing efforts well in advance of the launch of their funds to ensure that the announced target fund size will be met successfully once the fund is effectively started. The premarketing phase of a private equity fund, depending on whether it is a first fund or a following fund, may take between one to two years. Once investors effectively commit their investments in the fund, private equity managers draw on investors' commitments as the fund is being deployed and invested in portfolio companies. Private equity funds tend to have a duration of 10–12 years, generally extendable to an additional 2–3 years. Exhibit 6 illustrates the funding stages for a private equity fund.

Exhibit 6 Funding Stages for a Private Equity Fund

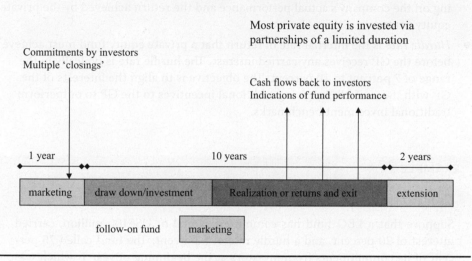

Fund terms are contractually defined in a fund prospectus or limited partnership agreement available to qualified prospective investors. The definition of qualified investors depends on the jurisdiction. Typically, wealth criteria (exceeding US$1 million, for example) and/or a minimum subscription threshold (minimum €125,000, for example) apply. The nature of the terms are frequently the result of the balance of negotiation power between GPs and LPs. Although the balance of negotiation power used to be in favor of LPs, it has now turned in favor of GPs, at least among the oversubscribed funds. Any significant downturn in private equity may change the balance of power in favor of LPs. Negotiation of terms has the objective to ensure alignment of interests between the GP and LPs and defining the GP's incentives (transaction fees, profit shares, etc.) The most significant terms may be categorized into economic and corporate governance terms.

Economic Terms

- *Management fees* represent a percentage of committed capital paid annually to the GP during the lifetime of the fund. Fees in the region of 1.5 percent to 2.5 percent are fairly common. Although less frequent, management fees may also be calculated on the basis of the net asset value or on invested capital.

- *Transaction fees* are fees paid to GPs in their advisory capacity when they provide investment banking services for a transaction (mergers and acquisitions, IPOs) benefiting the fund. These fees may be subject to sharing agreements with LPs, typically according to a 50/50 split between the GP and LPs. When such fee-sharing agreements apply, they generally come as a deduction to the management fees.

- *Carried interest* represents the general partner's share of profits generated by a private equity fund. Carried interest is frequently in the region of 20 percent of the fund's profits (after management fees).

- *Ratchet* is a mechanism that determines the allocation of equity between shareholders and the management team of the private equity controlled company. A ratchet enables the management team to increase its equity allocation depending on the company's actual performance and the return achieved by the private equity firm.

- *Hurdle rate* is the internal rate of return that a private equity fund must achieve before the GP receives any carried interest. The hurdle rate is typically in the range of 7 percent to 10 percent. The objective is to align the interests of the GP with those of LPs by giving additional incentives to the GP to outperform traditional investment benchmarks.

EXAMPLE 2

Calculation of Carried Interest

Suppose that a LBO fund has committed capital of US$100 million, carried interest of 20 percent, and a hurdle rate of 8 percent. The fund called 75 percent of its commitments from investors at the beginning of year 1, which was invested at the beginning of year 1 in target company A for $40 million and target company B for $35 million. Suppose that at the end of year 2, a profit of $5 million has been realized by the GP upon exit of the investment in company A, and the value of the investment in company B has remained unchanged. Suppose also that the GP is entitled to carried interest on a deal-by-deal basis, i.e., the IRR used to calculate carried interest is calculated for each investment upon exit. A theoretical carried interest of $1 million (20 percent of $5 million) could be granted to the GP, but the IRR upon exit of investment in company A is only 6.1 percent. Until the IRR exceeds the hurdle rate, no carried interest may be paid to the GP.

- *Target fund size* is expressed as an absolute amount in the fund prospectus or information memorandum. This information is critical as it provides a signal both about the GP's capacity to manage a portfolio of a predefined size and also in terms of fund raising. A fund that closed with a significantly lower size relative to the target size would raise questions about the GP's ability to raise funds on the market and would be perceived as a negative signal.

- *Vintage year* is the year the private equity fund was launched. Reference to vintage year allows performance comparison of funds of the same stage and industry focus.

- *Term of the fund* is typically 10 years, extendable for additional shorter periods (by agreement with the investors). Although infrequently observed, funds can also be of unlimited duration, and in this case are often quoted on stock markets (such as investment trusts).

Corporate Governance Terms

- *Key man clause.* Under the key man clause, a certain number of key named executives are expected to play an active role in the management of the fund. In case of the departure of such a key executive or insufficient time spent in the management of the fund, the "key man" clause provides that the GP may be prohibited from making any new investments until a new key executive is appointed.

- *Disclosure and confidentiality.* Private equity firms have no obligations to disclose publicly their financial performance. A court ruling[8] requiring California Public Employees Retirement System (CalPERS) to report publicly its returns on private equity investments, the Freedom of Information Act (FOIA) in the United States, and similar legislation in other European countries have led public pension funds to report information about their private equity investments. Disclosable information relates to financial performance of the underlying funds but does not extend to information on the companies in which the funds invest. This latter information is not typically disclosed. The reporting by CalPERS is a prominent example of the application of this clause.[9] Some private equity fund terms may be more restrictive on confidentiality and information disclosure and effectively limit information available to investors subject to FOIA.

- *Clawback provision.* A clawback provision requires the GP to return capital to LPs in excess of the agreed profit split between the GP and LPs. This provision ensures that, when a private equity firm exits from a highly profitable investment early in the fund's life but subsequent exits are less profitable, the GP pays back capital contributions, fees, and expenses to LPs to ensure that the profit split is in line with the fund's prospectus. The clawback is normally due on termination of the fund but may be subject to an annual reconciliation (or "true-up").

- *Distribution waterfall.* A distribution waterfall is a mechanism providing an order of distributions to LPs first before the GP receives carried interest. Two distinct distribution mechanisms are predominant: deal-by-deal waterfalls allowing earlier distribution of carried interest to the GP after each individual deal (mostly employed in the United States) and total return waterfalls resulting in earlier distributions to LPs because carried interest is calculated on the profits of the entire portfolio (mostly employed in Europe and for funds-of-funds). Under the total return method, two alternatives are possible to calculate carried interest. In the first alternative, the GP receives carried interest only after the fund has returned the entire committed capital to LPs. In the second alternative, the GP receives carried interest on any distribution as long as the value of the investment portfolio exceeds a certain threshold (usually 20 percent) above invested capital.

EXAMPLE 3

Distribution Waterfalls

Suppose a private equity fund has a committed capital totaling £300 million and a carried interest of 20 percent. After a first investment of £30 million, the fund exits the investment 9 months later with a £15 million profit. Under the deal-by-deal method, the GP would be entitled to 20 percent of the deal profit, i.e., £3 million. In the first alternative of the total return method, the entire proceeds of the sale, i.e., £45 million, are entitled to the LPs and nothing (yet) to the GP. In the second alternative, the exit value of £45 million exceeds by more than 20 percent the invested value of £30 million. The GP would thus be entitled to £3 million.

---

8 S. Chaplinsky and S. Perry, "CalPERS vs. Mercury News: Disclosure comes to private equity," Darden Business Publishing.

9 Information about CalPERS' private equity holdings is available from the company's website, www.calpers.ca.gov.

> Continuing the above example with a clawback provision with an annual true-up, suppose that the deal-by-deal method applies and that a second investment of £25 million is concluded with a loss of £5 million 1 year later. Therefore, at the annual true-up, the GP would have to pay back £1 million to LPs. In practice, an escrow account is used to regulate these fluctuations until termination of the fund.

- *Tag-along, drag along rights* are contractual provisions in share purchase agreements that ensure any potential future acquirer of the company may not acquire control without extending an acquisition offer to all shareholders, including the management of the company.

- *No-fault divorce*. A GP may be removed without cause, provided that a super majority (generally above 75 percent) of LPs approve that removal.

- *Removal for "cause"* is a clause that allows either a removal of the GP or an earlier termination of the fund for "cause." Such "cause" may include gross negligence of the GP, a "key person" event, a felony conviction of a key management person, bankruptcy of the GP, or a material breach of the fund prospectus.

- *Investment restrictions* generally impose a minimum level of diversification of the fund's investments, a geographic and/or sector focus, or limits on borrowing.

- *Co-investment*. LPs generally have a first right of co-investing along with the GP. This can be advantageous for the LPs as fees and profit share are likely to be lower (or zero) on co-invested capital. The GP and affiliated parties are also typically restricted in their co-investments to prevent conflicts of interest with their LPs. Crossover co-investments are a classic example of a conflict of interest. A crossover co-investment occurs when a subsequent fund launched by the same GP invests in a portfolio company that has received funding from a previous fund.

3.2 What Are the Risks and Costs of Investing in Private Equity?

Private equity investing is typically restricted by laws and regulations in most jurisdictions to "qualified investors" comprising institutions and high-net-worth individuals meeting certain wealth criteria. These restrictions are motivated by the high levels of risks incurred in private equity investing, and are generally subject to disclosure in the private equity fund prospectus. Such risks may be categorized as general private equity risk factors, investment strategy specific risk factors (buyout, venture capital, mezzanine), industry specific risk factors, risk factors specific to the investment vehicle, and sometimes regional or emerging market risks when applicable.

Following are some general private equity risk factors:

- *Illiquidity of investments*: Because private equity investments are generally not traded on any securities market, the exit of investments may not be conducted on a timely basis.

- *Unquoted investments*: Investing in unquoted securities may be risky relative to investing in securities quoted on a regulated securities exchange.

- *Competition for attractive investment opportunities*: Competition for finding investment opportunities on attractive terms may be high.

- *Reliance on the management of investee companies (agency risk)*: There is no assurance that the management of the investee companies will run the company in the best interests of the private equity firm, particularly in earlier stage deals in which the management may retain a controlling stake in the company and enjoy certain private benefits of control.

- *Loss of capital*: High business and financial risks may result in substantial loss of capital.

- *Government regulations*: Investee companies' product and services may be subject to changes in government regulations that adversely impact their business model.

- *Taxation risk*: Tax treatment of capital gains, dividends, or limited partnerships may change over time.

- *Valuation of investments*: Valuation of private equity investments is subject to significant judgment. When valuations are not conducted by an independent party, they may be subject to biases.

- *Lack of investment capital*: Investee companies may require additional future financing that may not be available.

- *Lack of diversification*: Investment portfolios may be highly concentrated and may, therefore, be exposed to significant losses. Investors generally want to invest in a mix of private equity funds of different vintages, different stages of developments for underlying investments in portfolio companies, and achieve a certain level of diversification across various private equity strategies (large and mid-market buyout, venture capital, mezzanine, restructuring).

- *Market risk*: Changes in general market conditions (interest rates, currency exchange rates) may adversely affect private equity investments. The impact of market risk is, however, long term in nature given the long-term horizon of private equity firms. Temporary short-term market fluctuations are generally irrelevant.

Costs associated with private equity investing are substantially more significant relative to public market investing. These costs may be broken down as follows:

- *Transaction fees*: Corresponding to due diligence, bank financing costs, legal fees for arranging acquisition, and sale transactions in investee companies.

- *Investment vehicle fund setup costs*: Comprises mainly legal costs for the setup of the investment vehicle. Such costs are typically amortized over the life of the investment vehicle.

- *Administrative costs*: Custodian, transfer agent, and accounting costs generally charged yearly as a fraction of the investment vehicle's net asset value.

- *Audit costs*: A fixed annual fee.

- *Management and performance fees*: These are generally more significant relative to plain investment funds. A 2 percent management fee and a 20 percent performance fee are common in the private equity industry.

- *Dilution*: A more subtle source of cost, dilution may come from stock option plans granted to the management and to the private equity firm and from additional rounds of financing.

- *Placement fees*: Fundraising fees may be charged up front or by means of a trailer fee by the fund raiser. A trailer fee is generally charged annually, corresponding to a fraction of the amount invested by limited partners as long as these amounts remain invested in the investment vehicle. An up front placement fee of 2 percent is not uncommon in private equity.

3.3 Due Diligence Investigations by Potential Investors

Prior to investing in a private equity fund, prospective investors generally conduct a thorough due diligence on the fund. Several fundamental characteristics of private equity funds underline the importance of the due diligence process.

■ Private equity funds tend to exhibit a strong persistence of returns over time. This means that top performing funds tend to continue to outperform and poor performing funds also tend to continue to perform poorly or disappear.

■ The performance range between funds is extremely large. For example, the difference between top quartile and third quartile fund IRRs can be about 20 percentage points.

■ Liquidity in private equity is typically very limited and thus LPs are locked for the long term. On the other hand, when private equity funds exit an investment, they return the cash to the investors immediately. Therefore, the "duration" of an investment in private equity is typically shorter than the maximum life of the fund.

The European Venture Capital association (EVCA) has issued an "Illustrative due diligence questionnaire—Venture capital funds," that may serve as a guide, but not as a substitute, for the due diligence process conducted by LPs before investing in a venture capital or private equity fund.

3.4 Private Equity Fund Valuation

The description of private equity valuation[10] in a fund prospectus is generally associated with the fund's calculation of net asset value (NAV). The NAV is generally defined as the value of the fund assets less liabilities corresponding to the accrued fund expenses. The fund's assets are frequently valued by GPs, depending on their valuation policies, in the following ways:[11]

1 at cost with significant adjustments for subsequent financing events or deterioration

2 at lower of cost or market value

3 by a revaluation of a portfolio company whenever a new financing round involving new investors takes place

4 at cost with no interim adjustment until the exit

5 with a discount for restricted securities[12]

6 more rarely, marked to market by reference to a peer group of public comparables and applying illiquidity discounts.

Private equity industry valuation standards, such as those originally produced by the British, French, and European industry associations (latest revisions can be found at www.privateequityvaluation.com), have increasingly been adopted by funds operating in many jurisdictions.

Industry practices suggest that because a valuation is adjusted with a new round of financing, the NAV may be more stale in down markets when there is a long gap between funding rounds. This mechanism is similar to the valuation of investment funds of publicly quoted securities. There is thus a fundamental implicit break-up

---

10 For a comprehensive discussion of this topic, refer to Thomas Meyer and Pierre-Yves Mathonet, *Beyond the J Curve: Managing a Portfolio of Venture Capital and Private Equity Funds*, Wiley, (2004).

11 Foster Center for Entrepreneurship and Private Equity, Dartmouth College.

12 Example: Reg. 144 securities.

assumption whereby the fund may be broken up at any time, the funds underlying investments may be liquidated individually and immediately, and the proceeds returned to LPs. Whereas this fundamental break-up assumption may hold for publicly traded securities, which are marked to market, this assumption may be more questionable for private equity investment portfolios typically held over a long period of time. The fundamental question facing investors is: At what value should investments in portfolio companies be reported, prior to the private equity fund exiting the investment and returning the proceeds to the LPs? There is no straight answer to that question as there is no market for securities issued by private equity companies.

Undrawn LP commitments raise additional challenges for private equity fund valuation. Although undrawn commitments represent a LP's legal obligations to meet capital calls in the future, they are not accounted for in the NAV calculation. The value of such undrawn commitments largely depends on the expected cash flows that will be generated by future investments made by the GP. Although undrawn commitments are not part of the NAV, they should be viewed as unfunded liabilities. McGrady[13] suggested to "gauge the reaction to the unfunded portion, a seller may consider the ease with which a general partnership could raise another fund in the current market."

Comparisons between private equity funds following different investment strategies require a careful analysis of their respective valuation policies in order to avoid biases. Whereas, for example, an early stage venture capital fund may keep its investments at cost, a late stage development capital fund may mark its portfolio companies by reference to public market comparables. At times when a market bubble is forming in certain sectors, such as the technology bubble in 2000, such reference to public market comparables may distort the valuation of portfolio companies and thus reported fund returns.

Another important aspect of private equity valuations is that they are mostly performed by GPs. Under the pressure from LPs, an increasing number of annual or semi-annual valuations are performed by independent valuers that are mandated by GPs.

The above discussion on private equity valuation emphasizes both the qualitative and quantitative issues that need to be taken into consideration.

3.5 Evaluating Fund Performance

Because each private equity fund is unique, the assessment of financial performance needs to be made with a good knowledge of the specific fund structure, terms, valuation policies, and the outcome of the due diligence. Typically, an analysis of a private equity fund's financial performance includes the following.

3.5.1 *Analysis of IRR and Multiples Gross and Net of Fees since Inception*

Here, net of fees means net of management fees, carried interest, or of any other financial arrangements that accrue to the GP. The IRR, a cash-flow-weighted rate of return, is deemed the most appropriate measure of private equity performance by the Global Investment Performance Standards (GIPS), Venture Capital and Private Equity Valuation Principles, and by other venture capital and private equity standards. The interpretation of IRR in private equity should, however, be subject to caution because an implicit assumption behind the IRR calculation is that the fund is fully liquid, whereas a significant portion of the NAV is illiquid during a substantial part of a private equity fund's life. Therefore, valuation of portfolio companies according to industry standards is important to ensure the quality of the IRR figures.

---

13 C. McGrady, Pricing private equity secondary transactions, Dallas, TX, Cogent Partners (2002).

The distinction between gross and net IRR is also important. Gross IRR relates cash flows between the private equity fund and its portfolio companies and is often considered a good measure of the investment management team's track record in creating value. Net IRR relates cash flows between the private equity fund and LPs, and so captures the returns enjoyed by investors. Fees and profit shares create significant deviations between gross and net IRRs. IRR analysis is often combined with a benchmark IRR analysis, i.e., the median IRR for the relevant peer group of comparable private equity funds operating with a similar investment strategy and vintage year. This is particularly important because there are clear trends over time in private equity returns, with some vintage years producing much higher returns than others.

In addition to IRR, multiples are used frequently as a measure of performance. Multiples simply measure the total return to investors relative to the total sum invested. Although multiples ignore the time value of money, their ease of calculation and their ability to differentiate between "realized" actual proceeds from divestments and "unrealized" portfolio subject to GP valuation make these ratios very popular among LPs. The multiples used most frequently by LPs and also defined by GIPS that provide additional information about private equity funds performance are as follows:

- PIC (paid in capital): the ratio of paid in capital to date divided by committed capital. This ratio provides information about the proportion of capital called by a GP.

- DPI (distributed to paid in): cumulative distributions paid out to LPs as a proportion of the cumulative invested capital. This ratio is often called "cash-on-cash return." It provides an indication of the private equity fund's realized return on investment. DPI is presented net of management fees and carried interest.

- RVPI (residual value to paid in): value of LPs' shareholding held with the private equity fund as a proportion of the cumulative invested capital. The numerator is measured as the remaining portfolio companies as valued by the GP. This ratio is a measure of the private equity fund's unrealized return on investment. RVPI is presented net of management fees and carried interest.

- TVPI (total value to paid in): the portfolio companies' distributed and undistributed value as a proportion of the cumulative invested capital. TVPI is the sum of DPI and RVPI. TVPI is presented net of management fees and carried interest.

In addition to quantitative measures of return, an analysis of a private equity fund financial performance also includes:

- an analysis of realized investments since inception, commenting on all successes and failures;

- an analysis of unrealized investments, highlighting all red flags in the portfolio and the expected time to exit per portfolio company;

- a cash flow forecast at the portfolio company level and for the aggregate portfolio; and

- an analysis of portfolio valuation, audited financial statements, and the NAV.

EXAMPLE 4

Calculating and Interpreting a Private Equity Fund Performance

Suppose that a private equity fund has a DPI of 0.07 and a RVPI of 0.62 after 5 years. IRR is –17 percent. The fund follows a venture capital strategy in high technology, has a vintage year of 1999, and a term of 10 years. A DPI of 7 percent indicates that few successful exits were made. A RVPI of 62 percent points to an extended J-curve effect for the fund as TVPI amounts to 69 percent at the midlife of the fund. A vintage year of 1999 provides hints that the fund was actually started before the technology market crash of 2000 and that the routes to exit for portfolio companies have been dramatically changed. During the technology market crash, the investment portfolio probably suffered a number of complete write-offs. In this situation, an LP should thus consider the state of the existing portfolio to examine the number of write-offs and other signals of ailing companies in the fund portfolio. The risk of not recovering the invested amount at termination of the fund is significant. Compliance with valuation policies by the GP should also be closely monitored by LPs to ensure that the GP's expectations are not excessive given the current state of the portfolio.

Note that with the increased allocations to private equity, performance comparisons across asset classes are often misinterpreted. IRR, the standard measure of private equity returns, is cash-flow-weighted, whereas performance of most other asset classes is measured in terms of time-weighted rate of return. In an attempt to solve these performance comparison issues, new performance measurement techniques have been developed. One of them, called the Public Market Equivalent (PME), was proposed by Austin Long and Craig Nickles in the mid-1990s. It provides a solution to this benchmarking issue, but its reliability poses, at times, serious problems.[14] Put simply, PME is the cash-flow-weighted rate of return of an index (S&P 500 or any other index) assuming the same cash flow pattern as a private equity fund. It is thus an index return measure.

CONCEPT IN ACTION: EVALUATING A PRIVATE EQUITY FUND

4

This section illustrates the use of many of the concepts above to evaluate the performance of a private equity fund.

Michael Hornsby, CFA, is a Senior Investment Officer at Icarus, a UK-based institutional investor in private equity. He is contemplating an investment in Europa Venture Partners III, a new late stage technology venture capital fund, after a thorough due diligence performed on the fund and an updated due diligence on the GP. Icarus has been an investor in Europa Venture Partners' (EVP) previous two funds, EVP I and EVP II. Icarus has been satisfied with the performance of EVP so far and is seeking to further expand its relationship with this GP because Icarus considers it a niche venture capital firm operating in a less crowded segment of the pan-European technology markets. As a result of its success, EVP decided to increase its carried interest for the third fund to 25 percent from 20 percent for the previous two funds.

---

14 Christophe Rouvinez, "Private Equity Benchmarking with PME +," *Venture Capital Journal* (August 2003).

Hornsby has received the information about the fund's financial performance and is seeking assistance in calculating and interpreting financial performance for a number of specific queries as outlined below.

Europa Venture Partners (EVP)

General Partner   Europa Venture Partners (EVP) was established to provide equity financing to later stage technology companies in need of development capital across Europe. The GP seeks to provide strategic support to seasoned entrepreneurial teams and bring proven new technologies to the market. The GP targets investment in portfolio companies between €2 million and €10 million.

Fund	Vintage	**Established in 1999** Actual Fund Size (€ Millions)	Capital Called (%)	Mgmt Fees (%)	**Type: Development Capital** Carried Interest (%)	Hurdle Rate (%)	Term	Report Date
EVP I	2001	125	92	2	20	8	2009	31 Dec 2006
EVP II	2003	360	48	2	20	8	2012	31 Dec 2006

Financial performance for investments by Icarus in EVP funds

Fund	Committed Capital (€ Millions)	Capital Called Down	Gross IRR (%)	Net IRR (%)	DPI (X)	RVPI (X)	TVPI (X)	Quartile
EVP I	10	9.2	16.1	11.3	1.26	1.29	2.55	1
EVP II	25	12.0	1.6	(0.4)	0.35	1.13	1.48	2

Hornsby also is interested in verifying management fees, carried interest, and the NAV of EVP I. He has the following information about yearly capital calls, operating results, and distributions.

Calls, Operating Results, and Distributions (€ Million)

	2001	2002	2003	2004	2005	2006
Called-down	50	15	10	25	10	5
Realized results	0	0	10	35	40	80
Unrealized results	−5	−15	15	10	15	25
Distributions	—	—	—	25	45	75

Operating results correspond to the sum of realized results from exits of portfolio companies and of unrealized results from the revaluation of investments held in portfolio companies. In addition to the information available on EVP I, Hornsby also knows from the fund prospectus that the distribution waterfall is calculated according to the total return method following the first alternative, i.e., the GP receives carried interest only after the fund has returned the entire committed capital to LPs. Management fees are calculated on the basis of the paid-in capital. Hornsby also wants to calculate DPI, RVPI, and TVPI of EVP I for 2006 and is interested in understanding how to calculate gross and net IRRs.

1   Interpret and compare the financial performance of EVP I and EVP II.

2   Based on the information given, calculate the management fees, carried interest, and the NAV of EVP I. Also calculate DPI, RVPI, and TVPI of EVP I for 2006. Explain on the basis of EVP I how gross and net IRRs are calculated, and calculate the gross and net IRRs.

Solution to 1:

In the table above, the first venture capital fund (EVP I) made its first capital call in 2001 and returned €1.26 (all amounts in millions) for every €1 that had been drawn down to LPs two years ahead of the termination of the fund. EVP I residual value remains high at 1.29 times capital drawn down, which is a good signal about the profitability of the fund at termination. The fund ranks in the first quartile, which means that it belongs to the best performing funds of that category and vintage year. Gross IRR of 16.1 percent after 6 years of operations, and 11.3 percent net of fees represents a good performance.

The second fund exhibits, to date, very modest performance in terms of gross and net IRR, which indicates that the fund is still experiencing the J-curve effect. EVP II has returned 35 percent of capital drawn down to LPs and a residual value of 113 percent of capital drawn down, which indicates that despite the fund being in its early years, the GP has already managed a number of profitable exits and increased the value of the investment portfolio half way through the termination of the fund. Actual fund size significantly exceeds previous fund size and is an indication that the GP is gaining momentum in terms of fund raising, probably partly attributable to the strong performance of the first fund.

Solution to 2:

Cash Flows and Distributions (€ Million)

Year	Called-down (1)	Paid-in Capital (2)	Mgmt Fees (3)	Operating Results (4)	NAV before Distributions (5)	Carried Interest (6)	Distributions (7)	NAV after Distributions (8)
2001	50	50	1.0	−5	44.0			44.0
2002	15	65	1.3	−15	42.7			42.7
2003	10	75	1.5	25	76.2			76.2
2004	25	100	2.0	45	144.2	3.8	25	115.4
2005	10	110	2.2	55	178.2	6.8	45	126.4
2006	5	115	2.3	105	234.1	11.2	75	147.9

Based on this table, the calculations of DPI, RVPI, and TVPI can be derived as follows:

- Paid-in capital = Cumulative capital called-down (shown in Column 2)
- Management fees = (2 Percent) × (Column 2)

- Carried interest: The first year that NAV is higher than committed capital (€125m), carried interest is 20 percent of the excess, or (20 Percent) ([NAV in Column 5] − €125m). Thereafter, provided that NAV before distribution exceeds committed capital, carried interest is (20 Percent)(increase in NAV before distributions). For example, carried interest in 2006 is calculated as follows: (20 Percent)(234.1 − 178.2)

- NAV before distributions = NAV after distributions$_{t-1}$ + (Column 1) − (Column 3) + (Column 4)

- NAV after distributions = (Column 5) − (Column 6) − (Column 7)

- DPI = (25 + 45 + 75)/115 or 1.26x

- RVPI = 147.9/115 or 1.29x

- TVPI = 1.26 + 1.29 = 2.55x

The IRRs may be developed as follows:

- Gross IRRs are estimated by calculating the internal rate of return between the following cash flows: called down capital at the beginning of period (Column 1) and the previous year's operating results (Column 4).

- Net IRRs are estimated by calculating the internal rate of return between the following cash flows: called down capital at the beginning of period (Column 1) and the previous year's operating results (Column 4) net of management fees (Column 3) and carried interest (Column 6). The calculated IRRs are in the bottom row of the following table.

Year End	Cash Flows for Gross IRR	Cash Flows for Net IRR
2000	−50	−50.0
2001	−20	−21.0
2002	−25	−26.3
2003	0	−1.5
2004	35	29.2
2005	50	41.0
2006	105	91.5
IRR	16.1%	11.3%

5   PREFATORY COMMENTS ON THE CASE STUDY

The case study that follows is a complement to this private equity valuation reading and is included to show the reader how to apply in context valuation methodologies in a private equity setting.

A Note on Valuation of Venture Capital Deals

This technical note on the valuation of venture capital deals is meant to explain the foundations of the venture capital method for valuing venture capital investments, the specific issues and diligences that must be addressed, and illustrate the concept in action with a case study.

SUMMARY

This reading focuses on valuation issues confronting investors in a private equity fund and the methods that the funds use to make investment decisions.

- Private equity funds seek to add value by various means, including optimizing financial structures, incentivizing management, and creating operational improvements.

- Private equity can be thought of as an alternative system of governance for corporations: rather than ownership and control being separated as in most publicly quoted companies, private equity concentrates ownership and control. Many view this governance arbitrage as a fundamental source of the returns earned by the best private equity funds.

- A critical role for the GP is valuation of potential investments. But because these investments are usually privately owned, valuation encounters a myriad of challenges, some of which have been discussed in this reading.

- Valuation techniques differ according to the nature of the investment. Early stage ventures require very different techniques than leveraged buyouts. Private equity professionals tend to use multiple techniques when performing a valuation, and they explore many different scenarios for the future development of the business.

- In buyouts the availability of debt financing can have a big impact on the scale of private equity activity and also seems to impact the valuations observed in the market.

- Because private equity funds have incentives to acquire, add value, and then exit within the lifetime of the fund, they are considered buy-to-sell investors. Planning the exit route for the investment is a critical role for the GP, and a well-timed and executed investment can be a significant source of realized value.

- In addition to the problems encountered by the private equity funds in valuing potential portfolio investments, many challenges exist in valuing the investment portfolio on an ongoing basis. This is because the investments have no easily observed market value, and there is a high element of judgment involved in valuing each of the portfolio companies prior to their sale by the fund.

- The two main metrics for measuring the ongoing and ultimate performance of private equity funds are IRR and multiples. Comparisons of the observed returns from private equity across funds and with other assets are demanding because it is important to control for the timing of cash flows, differences in risk, portfolio composition, and vintage year effects.

APPENDIX: A NOTE ON VALUATION OF VENTURE CAPITAL DEALS

When times are mysterious serious numbers are eager to please.

—Musician, Paul Simon, in the lyrics to his song *When Numbers Get Serious*

In this note, I discuss some of the fundamental issues of valuation in venture capital deals. The topics discussed are not necessarily limited to venture capital-backed companies, but they frequently surface in entrepreneurial companies that are financed either by venture capitalists or other private equity investors.

In Section 1, I introduce the so-called venture capital method. This is really a simple net present value (NPV) method that takes the perspective of the investor instead of the firm. This method has the advantage of extreme simplicity, but it makes many strong assumptions that limit its usefulness. I focus on three main issues in the remaining sections. In Section 2, I examine the problem of determining the terminal value. In Section 3, I examine the treatment of risk. In Section 4, I examine how to determine the funding requirements and I examine a number of ways of dealing with multiple financing rounds. In Section 5, I briefly cover the use of these methods in actual negotiations.

1 The Basic Venture Capital Method

1.1 An Example

There exists a simple approach to valuation that is sometimes referred to as the venture capital method. The method is sometimes explained in the language of internal rates of return (IRR) and sometimes in terms of NPV. Since most of you have been more exposed to the NPV framework, I will use that language. I will then show that it is in fact *identical* to the IRR framework.

To illustrate my method I will use a fictional start-up company called "SpiffyCalc," which is seeking financing from a venture capital fund by the name of "Vulture Ventures." Studying their crystal ball, the founders of SpiffyCalc expect to be able to sell the company for $25 million in four years.[15] At this point they need to raise $3 million. Vulture Ventures considers this a risky business and wants to apply a discount rate of 50 percent to be adequately compensated for the risk they will bear.[16] The entrepreneurs also decided that whatever valuation they would get, they wanted to own 1 million shares, which they thought would be a cool number to brag about.

---

15 In Section 2, I discuss how one might replace the crystal ball by a liquid crystal display screen, as a slight improvement in the art of future telling.
16 In Section 3, I discuss discount rates in more detail.

It is useful to define variables for the key assumptions we have made.

V = terminal value (at time of exit) = $25 million (in four years)

t = time to exit event = 4 years

I = amount of investment = $3 million

r = discount return used by investors = 50 percent

x = number of existing shares (owned by the entrepreneurs) = 1 million

Step 1   *Determine the Post-Money Valuation*

The only positive cash flow in this model occurs at the time of exit (typically an IPO or an acquisition), where we measure the terminal value of the company, denoted by V = $25 million. This means that after receiving the required $3 million, the initial value of the company is simply the discounted terminal value in 4 years' time. If Vulture Ventures is using a discount rate of 50 percent, the NPV of the terminal value in four years is $V/(1 + r)^t$ = $25 million/$(1.5)^4$ = $4,938,272 = POST. This is called the post-money valuation, i.e., the value of the company once the initial investment has been made. Intuitively, this is the value that is being placed on the entire company. This value is obviously not realized at the time of financing, as it depends on the belief that there will be great financial returns in the future.

Step 2   *Determine the Pre-Money Valuation*

Subtracting the cost of the investment of $3 million from the post-money valuation yields PRE = $1,938,272. This is called the pre-money valuation.

Step 3   *Determine the Ownership Fraction*

Vulture Ventures is investing $3 million in a venture valued at $4,938,272. In order to get back its money it therefore needs to own a sufficient fraction of the company. If they own a fraction F = $3 million/$4,938,272 = 60.75 percent, they get their required rate of return on their investment.

Step 4   *Obtain the Number of Shares*

The founders want to hold 1 million shares. When Vulture Ventures makes its investment it needs to calculate the number of shares required to achieve its desired ownership fraction. In order to obtain a 60.75 percent ownership share, Vulture Venture makes the following calculation: let x be the number of shares owned by the founders (x = 1 million) and y be the number of shares that Vulture Ventures requires, then $y/(1,000,000 + y)$ = F = 60.75 percent. After some algebraic transformation we get y = 1,000,000 [0.6075/(1−0.6075)] = 1,547,771. Vulture Ventures thus needs 1,547,771 shares to obtain their desired 60.75 percent of the company.

Step 5   *Obtain the Price of Shares*

The price of shares is thus given by $3 million/1,547,771 = $1.94.

1.2 The General Case

We can calculate all important variables of a deal in a simple five step procedure:

Step 1   POST = $V/(1 + r)^t$

POST is the post-money valuation.

Step 2   PRE = POST − I

PRE is the pre-money valuation.

Step 3 $F = I/POST$

F is the required ownership fraction for the investor.

Step 4 $y = x\,[F/(1 - F)]$

y is the number of shares the investors require to achieve their desired ownership fraction.

Step 5 $p_1 = I/y$

p_1 is the price per share.

1.3 Sensitivity Analysis with the Basic Venture Capital Method

It is interesting to do some sensitivity analysis. How will the value of the company change if we change our assumptions? We will examine the effect of changing the following assumptions:

Variation 1   reduce the terminal value by 10 percent

Variation 2   increase the discount rate by an absolute 10 percent

Variation 3   increase investment by 10 percent

Variation 4   increase time to exit by 10 percent

Variation 5   increase the number of exiting shares: this has no effect on any real values!

Single Period NPV Method		Base Model	Variation 1	Variation 2
Exit Value	V	$25,000,000	**$22,500,000**	$25,000,000
Time to exit	t	4	4	4
Discount rate	r	50.00%	50.00%	**60.00%**
Investment amount	I	$3,000,000	$3,000,000	$3,000,000
Number of existing shares	x	1,000,000	1,000,000	1,000,000
Post-Money	POST	$4,938,272	$4,444,444	$3,814,697
Pre-Money	PRE	$1,938,272	$1,444,444	$814,697
Ownership fraction of investors	F	60.75%	67.50%	78.64%
Ownership fraction of entrepreneurs	1 – F	39.25%	32.50%	21.36%
Number of new shares	y	1,547,771	2,076,923	3,682,349
Price per share	p	$1.94	$1.44	$0.81
Final wealth of investors		$15,187,500	$15,187,500	$19,660,800
Final wealth of entrepreneurs		$9,812,500	$7,312,500	$5,339,200
NPV of investors' wealth		$3,000,000	$3,000,000	$3,000,000
NPV of entrepreneurs' wealth		$1,938,272	$1,444,444	$814,697

Single Period NPV Method		Variation 3	Variation 4	Variation 5
Exit Value	V	$25,000,000	$25,000,000	$25,000,000
Time to exit	t	4	**4.4**	4
Discount rate	r	50.00%	50.00%	50.00%
Investment amount	I	**$3,300,000**	$3,000,000	$3,000,000
Number of existing shares	x	1,000,000	1,000,000	**2,000,000**
Post-Money	POST	$4,938,272	$4,198,928	$4,938,272

Single Period NPV Method		Variation 3	Variation 4	Variation 5
Pre-Money	PRE	$1,638,272	$1,198,928	$1,938,272
Ownership fraction of investors	F	66.83%	71.45%	60.75%
Ownership fraction of entrepreneurs	$1 - F$	33.18%	28.55%	39.25%
Number of new shares	y	2,014,318	2,502,235	3,095,541
Price per share	p	$1.64	$1.20	$0.97
Final wealth of investors		$16,706,250	$17,861,700	$15,187,500
Final wealth of entrepreneurs		$8,293,750	$7,138,300	$9,812,500
NPV of investors' wealth		$3,300,000	$3,000,000	$3,000,000
NPV of entrepreneurs' wealth		$1,638,272	$1,198,928	$1,938,272

1.4 The Treatment of Option Pools

One subtle point in this calculation is the treatment of an employee option pool. Most venture capital deals include a nontrivial amount of shares for the option pool. This option pool will be depleted over time as the company hires executives and other employees. How do we account for the option pool in these calculations? The norm is that the entrepreneurs' shares and the option pool are lumped into one. Consider an example where the entrepreneurs receive 2 million shares, the investors receive 2 million shares, and there is an option pool of 1 million shares. Investors are investing $2 million at $1 per share. We then say that the post-money valuation is $5 million and the pre-money valuation is $3 million. Note, however, that from the entrepreneurs' perspective they are getting only $2 million of the pre-money valuation. The other $1 million is reserved for the option pool.

1.5 An Alternative Phrasing of the Venture Capital Method in Terms of IRR

The so-called venture capital method is often explained in the language of IRRs. While the IRR is often a problematic method in finance, our venture capital method is sufficiently simple that the IRR and the NPV method give *exactly the same answer*. Below I use the above example to walk you through the logic of the IRR calculation in the way it is sometimes presented as the venture capital method.

Step 1 *Determine the future wealth that Vulture Ventures needs to obtain in order to achieve their desired IRR.*

When Vulture Ventures decides to invest in a company, it formulates a "desired rate of return." Suppose that Vulture Ventures is asking for 50 percent IRR. Also, SpiffyCalc needs an investment of $3 million. We can then determine how much money Vulture Ventures needs to accumulate in order to achieve its desired return. Vulture Ventures would want to make $3 million $\times (1.5)^4 = \$15,187,500$ in four years.

Step 2 *Determine the fraction of shares that Vulture Ventures needs to hold in order to achieve the desired IRR.*

To find out the required percentage of shares that Vulture Ventures needs to achieve a 50 percent IRR, we simply divide its required wealth by the estimated value of the company, i.e., $15,187,500/$25 million = 0.6075. Vulture Ventures would thus need 60.75 percent of the shares.

Step 3 *Determine the number of shares.*

When Vulture Ventures makes its investment it needs to calculate the number of shares required to achieve its desired ownership fraction. We assume that the founders of SpiffyCalc issued themselves 1,000,000 shares, and nobody else owns any other shares. We then calculate how many shares Vulture Ventures needs to obtain a 60.75 percent ownership share in the company. Using the same reasoning as before let x be the number of shares owned by the founders ($x = 1,000,000$) and y be the number of shares that Vulture Ventures requires, then $y/(1,000,000 + y) = 0.6075$. After some algebraic transformation we have $y = 1,000,000 [0.6075/(1 - 0.6075)] = 1,547,771$. Vulture Ventures thus needs 1,547,771 shares to obtain their desired 60.75 percent of the company.

Step 4   *Determine the price of shares.*

Given that Vulture Ventures is investing $3 million, the price of a share is $3 million/1,547,771 = $1.94.

Step 5   *Determine post-money valuation.*

The post-money valuation can actually be calculated in a number of ways. First, if an investment of $3 million buys 60.75 percent of the company, then it must be that 60.75 percent × post-money valuation = $3 million. It follows that the post-money valuation is given by $3 million/0.6075 = $4,938,272. Another way to obtain the post-money valuation is to note that there are 2,547,771 shares in the company that are valued at $1.94, so the post-money valuation is 2,547,771 × $1.94 ≈ $4.94 million (allowing for rounding error).

Step 6   *Determine pre-money valuation.*

To calculate the pre-money valuation we simply subtract the value of the VC's investment from the post-money valuation. This is $4,938,272 − $3 million = $1,938,272. Another way of calculating the pre-money valuation is to evaluate the existing shares at the new price, i.e., 1,000,000 × $1.94 ≈ $1.94 million (again allowing for rounding error).

We note that all the values are exactly the same as for the NPV method. The only difference is that one additional step was needed in the IRR method, namely to calculate the required wealth of the investors at a future point in time.[17]

Again, we can write down the general case:

Step 1 $W = I (1 + r)^t$

W is the amount of wealth investors expect to accumulate.

Step 2 $F = W/V$

F is the fraction of share ownership required by investors.

Step 3 $y = x [F/(1 - F)]$

y is the number of shares the investors require to achieve their desired ownership fraction.

Step 4 $p_1 = I/y$

p_1 is the price per share.

Step 5 $POST = I/F$ or $POST = p_1 \times (x + y)$

POST is the post-money valuation.

Step 6 $PRE = POST - I$ or $PRE = p_1 \times x$

---

17 In the spreadsheet that accompanies the case, future wealth is also discounted back into the present to obtain the NPV of the stakes for the entrepreneurs and investors.

PRE is the pre-money valuation.

2 Estimating the Terminal Value

Conceptually the terminal value represents the value of the company at the time of an exit event, be it an IPO or an acquisition.[18] Probably the most frequently used method to determine the terminal value is to take a multiple of earnings at the time of exit. Typically an estimate is taken of what the earnings are before tax, and then an industry multiple is taken. The difficulty is obviously to come up with a good estimate of the earnings and to find an appropriate industry multiple. This is particularly difficult for highly innovative ventures that operate in new or emerging industries.

Instead of taking a multiple of earnings, one might also consider taking multiples of sales or assets, or indeed of whatever other accounting measure is meaningful in that specific industry. The common methodology of all these multiples calculations is to look at comparable firms in the industry. One problem is that it is often difficult to find truly comparable companies. Another problem is that one typically looks at recent comparable deals. If a company is financed at a time when the stock market peaks and it uses recent IPOs as a basis of comparison, it will obtain large multiples. But these multiples may not reflect the multiples that it will be able to obtain when it plans to go public several years later.[19]

In principle, better methods of estimating terminal value would be to use NPV, CAPM, APT, or whatever equilibrium valuation model we think fits the data best. The problem, however, is that it is exceedingly difficult to come up with reasonable cash flow projections. And indeed, again one would look at comparable firms in the industry to come up with these estimates. These calculations may therefore not be much more accurate than the rough estimates using the multiples method.

Note that the implicit assumption for these estimates of the terminal value is typically that they measure the value of the company in case of success. This leads us to examine the issue of risk more carefully.

3 Accounting for Risk

In the venture capital method of valuation, the estimate of the terminal value is typically based on some kind of success scenario. Because there is considerable risk involved in a typical venture capital deal, venture capitalists usually apply a very high discount risk "to compensate for the risk." It is not hard to see why they use this method. Venture capitalists are negotiating with entrepreneurs who are often overconfident and have a strong tendency to overstate the prospects of their new ventures. Venture capitalists can argue with them for some time, but rather than having a long and aggravating debate about these estimates, the VCs can simply deflate them by applying a higher discount rate. I therefore suspect that the venture capital method is simply a victim of bargaining dynamics. The method, however, is rather confusing, as it combines two distinct reasons for discounting. One of the reasons is that VCs need to be compensated for holding significant (and typically nondiversifiable) risk. The second is that VCs do not believe that the venture will necessarily succeed. The problem here is that the earnings estimate does not represent the *expected* earnings, but the earnings in case of success.[20] There are two closely related ways of dealing with this.

---

18 To be precise, the relevant value is the pre-money valuation at the exit event.

19 While one would think that venture capitalists take this effect into account (and indeed they typically use that argument to talk multiples down) it is still true that venture capital valuations appreciate in times of rising stock markets.

20 Technically speaking, the first aspect is true risk as measured in terms of the variance (or covariance) of returns. The second aspect does not concern the variance, but the overestimation of the mean.

The first method is to simply recognize the fact that the discount rate incorporates a "risk of failure" component, as well as a true risk–diversification component. Since venture capitalists are not diversified, they may use a high discount rate to account for the variability of returns around their expected value.[21] Suppose, for example, that the risk–aversion of the VC fund implies an approximate risk-adjusted discount rate of 20 percent. If it was certain that this company would succeed, then the post-money valuation would simply be given by $25 million/ $(1.2)^4$ = \$12,056,327. But suppose now that the investors actually believe that the company might simply falter (with no value left) and that the probability of that event happening is 20 percent each year. The probability of getting the terminal valuation is only $(80 \text{ percent})^4$ = 40.96 percent, so that that the expected postmoney valuation is only $0.4096 \times \$12,056,327$ = \$4,938,272. We chose those numbers such that we get the same post-money valuation as before. This can be seen from the following: Let π be the probability of failure in any one year, then

$$\text{POST} = \frac{(1-\pi)^t X}{(1+r)^t} = \left(\frac{1-\pi}{1+r}\right)^t X = \frac{X}{(1+\tilde{r})^t} \text{ where } \tilde{r} = \frac{1+r}{1-\pi} - 1$$

$$= \frac{r+\pi}{1-\pi}$$

In our case $\tilde{r} = \frac{1+0.2}{1-0.2} - 1 = 0.5$: a 20 percent failure rate, combined with a 20 percent discount rate, have the combined effect of a 50 percent discount rate. Note that these numbers do not simply add up, so we need to go through the above formulas.

The second method is to allow for a variety of scenarios to generate a less biased estimate of expected returns. Typically we would try to adjust the terminal value to better reflect our true expectations. For example, SpiffyCalc's estimate of $25 million may have been based on an estimated earnings of $2.5 million and a multiple of 10. Suppose now that $2.5 million earnings is in fact an optimistic estimate. Suppose that there is a possibility that SpiffyCalc's product won't work, in which case the company will have no earnings. Or it may work, but the opportunity is smaller than originally hoped for, so that earnings in year 3 are only $1 million and the multiple is only 5, reflecting a lower growth potential. Suppose now that each of these three scenarios are equally likely. The expected terminal value is not $25 million but only 1/3 × $0 + 1/3 × 5 × $1 million + 1/3 × 10 × $2.5 million = $10 million.

When valuing the company, the VC may now use a lower discount rate that reflects only the true amount of risk in the venture. Using the corrected estimate of $10 million and applying a 20 percent discount rate as before leads to a post-money valuation of $4,822,531. The VC would need to own 62.21 percent of the company.

4 Investment Amounts and Multiple Rounds of Finance

How do we determine the amount of money that needs to be raised? Again, there are a variety of methods. A simple and powerful method is to go to the entrepreneurs' financial projections and look at their cash flow statement, which tracks the expected cash balances of the company over time. An important insight that comes out of this method is that it is often better to raise money in several rounds. We illustrate this with our hypothetical example of SpiffyCalc.

---

21 The limited partners of the VC funds, however, tend to be very diversified. This can lead to some conflicts of interest, which we will not dwell on here.

4.1 An Example

Starting with a cash balance of $0, the company projects the following cash balances:

End of Year 1	End of Year 2	End of Year 3	End of Year 4	End of Year 5
$(1,600,000)	$(2,700,000)	$(4,600,000)	$(2,600,000)	$1,200,000

Looking at these numbers, SpiffyCalc realized that raising $3 million would get the company through its first two years. But after two years the company would need some additional money to survive. Indeed, SpiffyCalc estimated that the lowest cash balance would occur at the end of year 3, and that it would generate positive cash flows thereafter. The company therefore recognized that it needed to raise a total of $4.6 million. It also thought that it was more prudent to leave itself with some safety cushion, so it decided to raise a total of $5 million dollars. When it put those numbers into its spreadsheet, however, the numbers demonstrated that investors needed to receive 101.25 percent of the company and that its pre-money valuation was –$61,728. This obviously means that at $5 million, the project was a negative NPV project.

But SpiffyCalc also noticed that it didn't need to raise the entire $5 million right from the start. For example, it could initially raise $3 million, and then raise the remaining $2 million after two years. In this case, the valuation method needs to take into account that the equity that first-round investors put into the business will be diluted in future rounds. This is a difficult problem, as it requires that we make assumptions about the terms of financing of these future rounds. While these assumptions may be difficult to get by, ignoring them will almost certainly lead to an inaccurate valuation. Indeed, ignoring future dilution will lead the venture capitalist to pay too much. The NPV framework is the most flexible and powerful method to account for future dilution.[22]

Suppose now that SpiffyCalc has already identified "Slowtrain Investors" as a potential investor for that second round. Suppose also that all investors apply a 50 percent discount rate through the four years before SpiffyCalc expects to be acquired. At the end of the second year, when "Slowtrain Investors" makes the second round investment, it would be doing the same calculation as we did above. It would use $POST_2$ = $25 million/$(1.5)^2$ = $11,111,111 as the postmoney valuation. It would ask for a 2,000,000/11,111,111 = 18.00 percent ownership stake. This means that the existing owners of the firm (the founders) and the first round investors (Vulture Ventures) would jointly only retain 82 percent of the company, or $0.82 \times \$11,111,111 = \$9,111,111$. This is also the pre-money valuation at the time of this second round of financing, and no coincidence, since the pre-money valuation measures precisely the value for the existing owners of the firm.

For the first round investment, Vulture Ventures can then expect the company to be worth $9,111,111 at the time of the second round, i.e., in two years' time. It then uses the same method as above to calculate the post-money valuation at the time of the first round, i.e., $POST_1$ = $9,111,111/$(1.5)^2$ = $4,049,383. This implies that it will ask for 3,000,000/$4,049,383 = 74.09 percent of the shares of the company. Note, however, that Vulture Ventures will not own 74.09 percent after four years. Instead, it expects a future dilution that will bring its ownership down to $f_1 = 0.82 \times 0.7409 =$

---

22 It is sometimes argued that future dilution does not matter in efficient markets, but we have to be careful with this argument. In a typical venture capital situation the company can only meet its financial projections if it manages to raise additional capital. In that sense the future dilution applies not to new investment opportunities of the company, but to the realization of the current investment opportunity. As an early round investor we therefore want to take account of the future dilution. This is different from the scenario in which future dilution relates to raising money for future investment opportunities that are additively separable from the current investment.

60.75 percent (the lower case notation indicates final ownership, after dilution). This is obviously a familiar number, as we have seen before that Vulture Ventures needs exactly 60.75 percent to get their required return on their investment of $3 million.

So far we haven't said anything about the number of shares and the price of shares for either the first or second round. In fact, we cannot calculate the price and number of shares for the second round before we calculate the price and number of shares for the first round. For this first round, we use the usual method, i.e., $y_1 = x_1 F_1/(1 - F_1) = 1,000,000 \times 0.7409/(1 - 0.7409) = 2,858,824$ and thus $p_1 = 3,000,000/2,858,824 = \$1.05$. For the second round we repeat the exercise. The important step, however, is to use the correct number of shares, namely the total number of existing shares (irrespective of whether they are owned by the entrepreneur or the investor). We have $x_2 = (x_1 + y_1) = 1,000,000 + 2,858,824 = 3,858,824$ as the number of existing shares at the time of the second round. The new number of shares required is thus $y_2 = x_2 F_2/(1 - F_2) = 3,858,824(0.18)/(1 - 0.18) = 847,059$. The price of the second round shares is then given by $\$2,000,000/847,059 = \$2.36$.

The following table summarizes these assumptions and results.

NPV Method with Two Rounds of Financing	Time of Exit	Second Round	First Round
Exit Value	$25,000,000		
Compound discount rate		2.25	2.25
Investment amount		2,000,000	3,000,000
Number of existing shares		3,858,824	1,000,000
Post-Money		$11,111,111	$4,049,383
Pre-Money		$9,111,111	$1,049,383
Ownership Fraction		18.00%	74.09%
Number of new shares		847,059	2,858,824
Price per share		$2.36	$1.05
Ownership shares of entrepreneurs	21.25%		
Wealth of entrepreneurs	$5,312,500	$2,361,111	$1,049,383
Ownership shares of first round investors	60.75%		
Wealth of first round investors	$15,187,500	$6,750,000	$3,000,000
Ownership shares of second round investors	18.00%		
Wealth of second round investors	$4,500,000	$2,000,000	

4.2 The General Case with Multiple Rounds of Financing

We are now in a position to examine the general case. We show the formulas for the case where there are two rounds of financing. All variables pertaining to round 1 (2) will have the subscript $_{1\,(2)}$. The case with an arbitrary number of rounds is a straightforward extension discussed at the end of the section.

Step 1   *Define appropriate compound interest rates.*

Suppose that the terminal value is expected to occur at some date T_3, the second round at some date T_2, and the first round is happening at date T_1. Define $(1 + R_2)$ as the compound discount rate between time T_2 and T_3. If, for example, there are three years between the second round and the exit time, and if the discount rate for these three years is 40 percent, 35 percent, and 30 percent, respectively, then $(1 + R_2) = 1.4 \times 1.35 \times 1.3$. The compound discount rate $(1 + R_1)$ is defined similarly for the time between dates T_1 and T_2 (not T_3!!!).

Step 2 $POST_2 = V/(1 + R_2)$

Where $POST_2$ is the post-money valuation at the time of the second round, V is the terminal value and R_2 is the compound discount rate between the time of the second round and the time of exit.

Step 3 $PRE_2 = POST_2 - I_2$

PRE_2 is the pre-money valuation at the time of the second round of financing and I_2 is the amount raised in the second round.

Step 4 $POST_1 = PRE_2/(1 + R_1)$

Where $POST_1$ is the post-money valuation at the time of the first round and R_1 is the compound discount rate between the time of the first and second rounds.

Step 5 $PRE_1 = POST_1 - I_1$

PRE_1 is the pre-money valuation at the time of the first round of financing, and I_1 is the amount raised in the first round.

Step 6 $F_2 = I_2/POST_2$

F_2 is the required ownership fraction for the investors in the second round.

Step 7 $F_1 = I_1/POST_1$

F_1 is the required ownership fraction for the investors in the first round (this is not their final ownership share, as they will get diluted by a factor of $(1 - F_2)$ in the second round).

Step 8 $y_1 = x_1 [F_1/(1 - F_1)]$

y_1 is the number of new shares that the investors in the first round require to achieve their desired ownership fraction, and x_1 is the number of existing shares.[23]

Step 9 $p_1 = I_1/y_1$

p_1 is the price per share in the first round.

Step 10 $x_2 = x_1 + y_1$

x_2 is the number of existing shares at the time of the second round.

Step 11 $y_2 = x_2 [F_2/(1 - F_2)]$

y_2 is the number of new shares that the investors in the second round require to achieve their desired ownership fraction.

Step 12 $p_2 = I_2/y_2$

p_2 is the price per share in the second round.

The general case is a straightforward extension of the case with two rounds. First we need to define the compound discount rates between all the rounds. Then we find the post- and pre-money valuations working backwards from the terminal value to each round of financing, all the way back to the first round of financing. For each round we discount the pre-money valuation of the subsequent round to get the post-money valuation of the round. Once we have the post-money valuations for all rounds we can calculate all the required ownership shares. To get the number and prices of shares we begin with the usual formula for the first round and then count up for each round.

---

23 If there are no pre-existing shares, one may also fix a total number of shares and then simply allocate them according to the fractions F_1 and $(1 - F_1)$.

4.3 Some Further Examples

Consider a first variation of the model. Suppose that the discount rate is highest in the early years and becomes lower after a while. For example, assume that the discount rate is 60 percent in the first year, stays at 50 percent in years two and three, and falls to 40 percent in the fourth year. This changes our compound discount rates: we have $(1 + R_2) = 1.5 \times 1.4 = 2.1$ and $(1 + R_1) = 1.6 \times 1.5 = 2.4$

Variation 1	Time of Exit	Second Round	First Round
Exit Value	$25,000,000		
Compound discount rate		2.1	2.4
Investment amount		2,000,000	3,000,000
Number of existing shares		3,661,972	1,000,000
Post-Money		$11,904,762	$4,126,984
Pre-Money		$9,904,762	$1,126,984
Ownership Fraction		16.80%	72.69%
Number of new shares		739,437	2,661,972
Price per share		$2.70	$1.13
Ownership shares of entrepreneurs	22.72%		
Wealth of entrepreneurs	$5,680,000	$2,704,762	$1,126,984
Ownership shares of first round investors	60.48%		
Wealth of first round investors	$15,120,000	$7,200,000	$3,000,000
Ownership shares of second round investors	16.80%		
Wealth of second round investors	$4,200,000	$2,000,000	

There are many other variations that we can examine in this model. A second variation of particular interest is to examine the role of the timing of the second round. Suppose, for example, that SpiffyCalc might be able to delay the timing of the second round by one year. In this case the compound discount rates are given by $(1 + R_2) = 1.4$ and $(1 + R_1) = 1.6 \times 1.5 \times 1.5 = 3.6$. Delaying the second round of financing would improve the valuation of the company.

Variation 2	Time of Exit	Second Round	First Round
Exit Value	$25,000,000		
Compound discount rate		1.4	3.6
Investment amount		2,000,000	3,000,000
Number of existing shares		3,135,593	1,000,000
Post-Money		$17,857,143	$4,404,762
Pre-Money		$15,857,143	$1,404,762
Ownership Fraction		11.20%	68.11%
Number of new shares		395,480	2,135,593
Price per share		$5.06	$1.40
Ownership shares of entrepreneurs	28.32%		
Wealth of entrepreneurs	$7,080,000	$5,057,143	$1,404,762
Ownership shares of first round investors	60.48%		
Wealth of first round investors	$15,120,000	$10,800,000	$3,000,000
Ownership shares of second round investors	11.20%		
Wealth of second round investors	$2,800,000	$2,000,000	

5 The Determinants of Valuation: Looking beyond the Numbers

To put things in perspective, it should be said that any method of valuation depends critically on the assumptions we make. Indeed, any valuation number can be justified by an appropriate choice of the discount rates and the terminal value. There is a more fundamental point here. A valuation method is a sophisticated tool for determining how entrepreneurs and venture capitalists should split the returns of the new venture. But the actual split, i.e., the actual deal, is not really driven by the valuation method, but rather by the outcome of the bargaining between the entrepreneurs and the venture capitalists. The relative bargaining power is thus the true economic determinant of the valuation that entrepreneurs will obtain for their companies. The valuation method, however, is an important tool to master for all parties involved, as it often provides the quantitative basis for the negotiation.

PRACTICE PROBLEMS

1   Jo Ann Ng is a senior analyst at SING INVEST, a large regional mid-market buyout manager in Singapore. She is considering the exit possibilities for an existing investment in a mature automotive parts manufacturer that was acquired 3 years ago at a multiple of 7.5 times EBITDA. SING INVEST originally anticipated exiting its investment in China Auto Parts, Inc. within 3 to 6 years. Ng noted that current market conditions have deteriorated and that companies operating in a similar business trade at an average multiple of 5.5 times EBITDA. She deemed, however, based on analyst reports and industry knowledge that the market is expected to recover strongly within the next two years because of the fast increasing demand for cars in emerging markets. Upon review of market opportunities, Ng also noted that China Gear Box, Inc., a smaller Chinese auto parts manufacturer presenting potential strong synergies with China Auto Parts, Inc., is available for sale at an EBITDA multiple of 4.5. Exits by means of an IPO or a trade sale to a financial or strategic (company) buyer are possible in China. How would you advise Ng to enhance value upon exit of China Auto Parts?

2   Wenda Lee, CFA, is a portfolio manager at a UK-based private equity institutional investor. She is considering an investment in a mid-market European buyout fund to achieve a better diversification of her firm's existing private equity portfolio. She short listed two funds that she deemed to have a similar risk return profile. Before deciding which one to invest in, she is carefully reviewing and comparing the terms of each fund.

	Mid-Market Fund A	**Mid-Market Fund B**
Management fees	2.5%	1.5%
Transaction fees	100% to the GP	50–50% split
Carried interest	15%	20%
Hurdle rate	6%	9%
Clawback provision	No	Yes
Distribution waterfall	Deal-by-deal	Total return

Based on the analysis of terms, which fund would you recommend to Lee?

3   Jean Pierre Dupont is the CIO of a French pension fund allocating a substantial portion of its assets to private equity. The existing private equity portfolio comprises mainly large buyout funds, mezzanine funds, and a limited allocation to a special situations fund. The pension fund decided to further increase its allocation to European venture capital. The investment committee of the pension fund requested Dupont present an analysis of five key investment characteristics specific to venture capital relative to buyout investing. Can you assist Dupont in this request?

4   Discuss the ways that private equity funds can create value.

5 What problems are encountered when using comparable publicly traded companies to value private acquisition targets?

6 What are the main ways in which the performance of private equity limited partnerships can be measured A) during the life of the fund, and B) once all investments have been exited?

The following information relates to Questions 7–12

Martha Brady is the chief investment officer (CIO) of the Upper Darby County (UDC) public employees' pension system. Brady is considering an allocation of a portion of the pension system's assets to private equity. She has asked two of her analysts, Jennifer Chau, CFA, and Matthew Hermansky, to provide more information about the workings of the private equity market.

Brady recognizes that the private equity asset class covers a broad spectrum of equity investments that are not traded in public markets. She asks Chau to describe the major differences between assets that constitute this asset class. Chau notes that the private equity class ranges from venture capital financing of early stage companies to complete buyouts of large publicly traded or even privately held companies. Chau describes some of the characteristics of venture capital and buyout investments.

Chau mentions that private equity firms take care to align the economic interests of the managers of the investments they control with the interests of the private equity firms. Various contractual clauses are inserted in the compensation contracts of the management team in order to reward or punish managers who do not meet agreed on target objectives.

One concern is the illiquidity of private equity investments over time. But some funds are returned to investors over the life of the fund because a number of investment opportunities are exited early. A number of provisions describe the distribution of returns to investors, some of which favor the limited partners. One such provision is the distribution waterfall mechanism that provides distributions to limited partners (LP) before the general partner (GP) receives the carried interest. This distribution mechanism is called the total return waterfall.

Chau prepares the following data to illustrate the distribution waterfall mechanism and the funds provided to limited partners when a private equity fund with a zero hurdle rate exits from its first three projects during a three-year period.

Exhibit 1	Investment Returns and Distribution Waterfalls
Private equity committed capital	$400 million
Carried interest	20%
First project investment capital	$20 million
Second project investment capital	$45 million
Third project investment capital	$50 million
Proceeds from first project	$25 million
Proceeds from second project	$35 million
Proceeds from third project	$65 million

Chau cautions that investors must understand the terminology used to describe the performance of private equity funds. Interpretation of performance numbers should be made with the awareness that much of the fund assets are illiquid during a substantial part of the fund's life. She provides the latest data in Exhibit 2 for Alpha, Beta, and Gamma Funds—diversified high-technology venture capital funds formed five years ago and each with five years remaining to termination.

Chau studies the data and comments: "Of the three funds, the Alpha Fund has the best chance to outperform over the remaining life. First, because the management has earned such a relatively high residual value on capital and will be able to earn a high return on the remaining funds called down. At termination, the RVPI will earn double the '0.65' value when the rest of the funds are called down. Second, its 'cash on cash' return as measured by DPI is already as high as that of the Beta Fund. PIC, or paid-in capital, provides information about the proportion of capital called by the GP. The PIC of Alpha is relatively low relative to Beta and Gamma."

Exhibit 2 Financial Performance of Alpha, Beta, and Gamma Funds

Fund	PIC	DPI	RVPI
Alpha	0.30	0.10	0.65
Beta	0.85	0.10	1.25
Gamma	0.85	1.25	0.75

Hermansky notes that a private equity fund's ability to properly plan and execute its exit from an investment is vital for the fund's success. Venture funds such as Alpha, Beta, and Gamma take special care to plan for exiting from investments. Venture funds tend to focus on certain types of exits, especially when equity markets are strong.

Brady then asks the analysts what procedures private equity firms would use to value investments in their portfolios as well as any other investments that might be added to the portfolio. She is concerned about buying into a fund with existing assets that do not have public market prices to ascertain value. In such cases, the GP may overvalue the assets and new investors in the fund will pay a higher NAV for the fund assets than they are worth.

Hermansky makes three statements regarding the valuation methods used in private equity transactions during the early stages of selling a fund to investors.

Statement 1 For venture capital investment in the early stages of analysis, emphasis is placed on the discounted cash flow approach to valuation.

Statement 2 For buyout investments, income-based approaches are used frequently as a primary method of valuation.

Statement 3 If a comparable group of companies exist, multiples of revenues or earnings are used frequently to derive a value for venture capital investments.

7 The characteristic that is *most likely* common to both the venture capital and buyout private equity investment is:

A measurable and assessable risk.

B the extensive use of financial leverage.

C the strength of the individual track record and ability of members of management.

8 The contractual term enabling management of the private equity controlled company to be rewarded with increased equity ownership as a result of meeting performance targets is called:

  A a ratchet.

  B the tag-along right.

  C the clawback provision.

9 For the projects described in Exhibit 1, under a deal-by-deal method with a clawback provision and true-up every three years, the cumulative dollar amount the GP receives by the end of the three years is equal to:

  A one million.

  B two million.

  C three million.

10 Are Chau's two reasons for interpreting Alpha Fund as the best performing fund over the remaining life correct?

  A No.

  B Yes.

  C The first reason is correct, but the second reason is incorrect.

11 The exit route for a venture capital investment is *least likely* to be in the form of a(n):

  A initial public offering (IPO).

  B sale to other venture funds targeting the same sector.

  C buyout by the management of the venture investment.

12 Which statement by Hermansky is the *least* valid?

  A Statement 1.

  B Statement 2.

  C Statement 3.

SOLUTIONS

1 The exit strategies available to SING INVEST to divest their holding in China Auto Parts, Inc. will largely depend on the following two factors:

● Time remaining until the fund's term expires. If the time remaining is sufficiently long, the fund's manager has more flexibility to work out an exit at more favorable market circumstances and terms.

● Amount of undrawn commitments from LPs in the fund. If sufficient LP commitments can be drawn, the fund manager may take advantage of current market investment opportunities at depressed market prices with the objective to enhance returns upon exit in an expected more favorable market environment.

In the case of China Auto Parts Inc., depending on an analysis of the above, Ng could advise the acquisition of China Gear Box, Inc. subject to an indepth analysis of potential synergies with China Auto Parts, Inc. The objective here may thus be twofold: benefit from short-term market conditions and enhance the value of existing investments by reinforcing their market potential with a strategic merger.

2 Assuming that both funds have similar risk return characteristics, a closer analysis of economic and corporate governance terms should be instrumental in determining which fund to select.

In economic terms, Mid-Market Fund B has a higher carried interest relative to Mid-Market Fund A, but Mid-Market Fund B has a fee structure that is better aligned with the interests of LPs. A larger proportion of Mid-Market Fund B's fees will be on achieving successful exits (through the carried interest), whereas Mid-Market Fund A will earn relatively larger fees on running the fund (management fees and transaction fees) without necessarily achieving high performance. In addition, the 9 percent hurdle rate of Mid-Market Fund B is indicative of a stronger confidence of the fund manager to achieve a minimum compounded 9 percent return to LPs under which no carried interest will be paid.

In corporate governance terms, Mid-Market Fund B is far better aligned with the interests of LPs as a result of a clawback provision and a more favorable distribution waterfall to LPs that will allow payment of carried interest on a total return basis instead of deal-by-deal.

The conclusion is that Mid-Market Fund B appears better aligned with the interests of LPs.

3

Venture Capital	Buyout
Primarily equity funded. Use of leverage is rare and very limited.	Extensive use of leverage consisting of a large proportion of senior debt and a significant layer of junior and/or mezzanine debt.
Returns of investment portfolios are generally characterized by very high returns from a limited number of highly successful investments and a significant number of write-offs from low performing investments or failures.	Returns of investment portfolios are generally characterized by lower variance across returns from underlying investments. Bankruptcies are rare events.

Venture Capital	Buyout
Venture capital firm monitors achievement of milestones defined in business plan and growth management.	Buyout firm monitors cash flow management and strategic and business planning.
Expanding capital requirement if in the growth phase.	Low working capital requirement.
Assessment of risk is difficult because of new technologies, new markets, and lack of operating history.	Risk is measurable (e.g., mature businesses, long operating history, etc.).

4 The main ways that private equity funds can create value include the following:

- Operational improvements and clearly defined strategies. In the case of later stage companies and buyouts, private equity owners can often create value by focusing the business on its most profitable opportunities and providing new strategic direction for the business. In the case of venture capital deals, the private equity funds can provide valuable business experience, mentor management, and offer access to their network of contacts and other portfolio companies.

- Creating incentives for managers and aligning their goals with the investors. This is often achieved by providing significant monetary rewards to management if the private equity fund secures a profitable exit. In the case of buyouts, the free cash flow available to management is minimized by taking on significant amounts of debt financing.

- Optimizing the financial structure of the company. In the case of buyouts, the use of debt can reduce the tax payments made by the company and reduce the cost of capital. There may also be opportunities in certain market conditions to take advantage of any mispricing of risk by lenders, which can allow the private equity funds to take advantage of interest rates that do not fully reflect the risks being carried by the lenders. Many would point to the period from mid-2006 to mid-2007 as a period when such conditions prevailed.

5 There are many complexities in using comparable companies to value private targets, including the following:

- The lack of public comparison companies operating in the same business, facing the same risks, and at the same stage of development. It is often possible to identify "approximate" comparisons but very rare to find an exact match. It is essential, therefore, to use judgment when using comparison company information, rather than just taking the average multiples derived from a sample of disparate companies.

- Comparison companies may have different capital structures, so estimated beta coefficients and some financial ratios should be adjusted accordingly.

- Reported accounting numbers for earnings must be chosen carefully and adjusted for any exceptional items, atypical revenues, and costs in the reference year. Care must also be taken to decide which earnings figures to compare—the main choices are trailing earnings (the last 12 months), earnings from the last audited accounts, or prospective year-ahead earnings.

6 In the early years of a fund, all measures of returns are of little relevance because fees drag down the reported returns and investments are initially valued at cost. This produces the J-curve effect. After a few years (longer in the case of venture capital investments), performance measures become more meaningful and the two main measures used by investors are IRR and return

multiples (of the initial sum invested). During the life of the fund it is necessary to value the non-exited investments and add them to the realized returns. The former inevitably involves an element of judgment on the part of the General Partner, especially when it is difficult to estimate the likely market value of the investment. Once all the investments have been exited, the multiples and IRR can be estimated easily, taking account of the exact timing of the cash flows into and out of the fund. The most relevant measures for investors are computed net of management fees and any carried interest earned by the General Partner.

7   C is correct. Members of both the firm being bought out and the venture capital investment usually have strong individual management track records. Extensive financial leverage is common in buyouts but not venture capital investments, whereas measurable risk is more common in buyouts than in venture capital situations.

8   A is correct.

9   B is correct. On a cumulative basis for three years, the fund earns $10 million, of which $2 million goes to the GP. The $2 million earned by the GP corresponds to 20 percent of the difference between total three-year proceeds and three-year invested capital, or $0.2[(25 + 35 + 65) - (20 + 45 + 50)]$.

10 A is correct. Chau misinterprets DPI, RVPI, and PIC. The returns earned to date are for each dollar of invested capital, that which has been drawn down, not total returns. Chau mistakenly believes (assuming the same management skill) the result for Alpha Fund at termination will be on the order of $3 \times 0.65 = 1.95$ instead of 0.65. In both cases, Alpha Fund has underperformed relative to the other two funds.

11 C is correct. Leverage needed to finance a management buyout is not readily available to firms with limited history.

12 A is correct. Statement 1 is the least likely to be valid.

READING
46

Commodities and Commodity Derivatives: An Introduction

by David Burkart, CFA, and James Alan Finnegan, RMA, CFA

David Burkart, CFA, is at Coloma Capital Futures, LLC (USA). James Alan Finnegan, RMA, CFA (USA).

LEARNING OUTCOMES

Mastery	The candidate should be able to
☐	**a.** compare characteristics of commodity sectors;
☐	**b.** compare the life cycle of commodity sectors from production through trading or consumption;
☐	**c.** contrast the valuation of commodities with the valuation of equities and bonds;
☐	**d.** describe types of participants in commodity futures markets;
☐	**e.** analyze the relationship between spot prices and expected future prices in markets in contango and markets in backwardation;
☐	**f.** compare theories of commodity futures returns;
☐	**g.** describe, calculate, and interpret the components of total return for a fully collateralized commodity futures contract;
☐	**h.** contrast roll return in markets in contango and markets in backwardation;
☐	**i.** describe how commodity swaps are used to obtain or modify exposure to commodities;
☐	**j.** describe how the construction of commodity indexes affects index returns.

1   INTRODUCTION

This reading presents the characteristics and valuation of commodities and commodity derivatives. Given that investment in commodities is conducted primarily through futures markets, the concepts and theories behind commodity futures is a primary focus of the reading. In particular, the relationship between spot and futures prices, as well as the underlying components of futures returns, are key analytical considerations.

What do we mean when we talk about investing in commodities? A basic economic definition is that a commodity is a physical good attributable to a natural resource that is tradable and supplied without substantial differentiation by the general public.

Commodities trade in physical (spot) markets and in futures and forward markets. Spot markets involve the physical transfer of goods between buyers and sellers; prices in these markets reflect current (or very near term) supply and demand conditions. Global commodity futures markets constitute financial exchanges of standardized futures contracts in which a price is established in the market today for the sale of some defined quantity and quality of a commodity at a future date of delivery; execution of the contract may be focused on cash settlement or physical delivery.

Commodity futures exchanges allow for risk transfer and provide a valuable price discovery mechanism that reflects the collective views of all market participants with regard to the future supply and demand prospects of a commodity. Given the financial (versus physical) nature of their contract execution, commodity exchanges allow important parties beyond traditional suppliers and buyers—speculators, arbitrageurs, private equity, endowments, and other institutional investors—to participate in these price discovery and risk transfer processes. Standardized contracts and organized exchanges also offer liquidity (i.e., trading volumes) to facilitate closing, reducing, expanding, or opening new hedges or exposures as circumstances change on a daily basis.

Forward markets exist alongside futures markets in certain commodities for use by entities that require customization in contract terms. Forwards are largely outside the scope of this reading and discussed only briefly. Exposure to commodities is also traded in the swap markets for both speculative and hedging purposes. Investment managers may want to establish swap positions to match certain portfolio needs, whereas producers may want to adjust their commodity risk (e.g., the origin of their cattle or the chemical specifications of their crude oil).

Commodities offer the potential for diversification benefits in a multi-asset class portfolio because of historically low average return correlation with stocks and bonds. In addition, certain academic studies (e.g., Gorton and Rouwenhorst 2006; Erb and Harvey 2006) demonstrate that some commodities have historically had inflation hedging qualities.

This reading is organized as follows: Section 2 provides an overview of physical commodity markets, including the major sectors, their life cycles, and their valuation. Section 3 describes futures market participants, commodity futures pricing, and the analysis of commodity returns, including the concepts of contango and backwardation. Section 4 reviews the use of swap instruments rather than futures to gain exposure to commodities. Section 5 reviews the various commodity indexes given their importance as benchmarks for the asset class and investment vehicles. Finally, Section 6 concludes with a summary of the major points of the reading.

COMMODITIES OVERVIEW

2

Commodities are an asset class inherently different from traditional financial assets, such as equities and bonds. These latter assets are securities that are claims on either productive capital assets and/or financial assets and thus are expected to generate cash flows for their owners. The intrinsic value of these securities is the present discounted value of their expected future cash flows. Commodities are valued differently. Commodities' value derives from either their use as consumables or as inputs to the production of goods and services. Because a number of commodities need to be processed or have a limited life before spoiling or decaying, an astute analyst will take into account the growth and extraction patterns of the various commodities as well as the logistics associated with transporting these physical goods. Therefore, commodities, while seemingly familiar, offer distinct sets of risk exposures for investors.

2.1 Commodity Sectors

The world of commodities is relatively broad but can be defined and separated in a reasonable manner. Although there are several ways to segment the asset class by sector, in this reading we use the approach that is the basis for the Thomson Reuters/CoreCommodity CRB Index developed by the well-recognized Commodities Research Bureau: energy, grains, industrial (base) metals, livestock, precious metals, and softs (cash crops). This segmentation is more granular than most others used in practice and is reasonably consistent with the activities of most market participants. Each of these sectors has a number of individual characteristics that are important in determining the supply and demand for each commodity. A key concept is how easily and cost-effectively the commodity can be stored, as well as such related issues as frequency/timing of consumption, spoilage, insurance, and ease of transportation to consumers. Other important aspects that affect supply and demand are weather and geo-political and geo-economic events. The perceptive analyst will note that many of these influences are macro in nature. By understanding how these events impact each sector, one can have a view of the asset class as a whole. The following sections review several of the more important commodities in detail.

2.1.1 *Energy*

Although there are many forms of energy in the world, only a few are actively and broadly traded. Coal, for example, has very deep markets in China, but they are effectively non-accessible to non-commercial, non-Chinese entities at this time. In practice, there are typically three distinct products and value chains in the energy sector: (1) crude oil, (2) natural gas, and (3) refined products. The energy sector is the most economically valuable of all the commodities, with entire countries and regions dependent on extraction, production, refining, and trading of particular energy commodity products. Refined products have fueled the global industrial (and post-industrial) economy for more than 100 years. They are strategic to the national interest of all countries. Without oil and natural gas (or viable alternatives for low-cost, widespread transportation and electricity), modern society would degrade rapidly as trade disappears and the availability of food and other necessities collapses. Harvests would rot in the fields, imports and exports would halt, and metals would not be refined. The accessibility and exchange of energy, therefore, affects society and its health.

Crude Oil Crude oil (or petroleum) is a combustible liquid created by large quantities of dead organisms (typically algae and plants) trapped in rock formations that were buried and then subjected to a high degree of heat and pressure over tens of thousands of years. Therefore, the ultimate storage for crude oil is to leave it in the ground itself.

Unlike other commodities that require special storage facilities, crude oil can be left on its own for another 10 thousand years. Furthermore, it has limited use by itself. It must be extracted, transported, and refined into useful products.

There are important differences in the quality of crude oil that are reflected in the varied prices of oil depending on its source. Crude oil from the North Sea (represented by Brent Crude), Middle East (typically represented by a price benchmark, such as "Abu Dhabi Light"), Nigeria (Bonny Light), or the southern United States (represented by the West Texas Intermediate or Louisiana Light price benchmarks) can all sell at a substantial premium to heavier oils, such as benchmark Mayan Crude (from Mexico). Crude oil that is relatively low in density and flows freely at room temperature is called light, making for easier processing (and less environmental impact) as well as often yielding more valuable gasoline and diesel fuel. The term "sweet" refers to low sulfur content, a contaminant that destroys metal piping because of its form as sulfuric acid.

With oil effectively stored underground, weather has had only a temporary impact historically—for example, a hurricane or typhoon would "shut in" production of offshore oil as crews abandoned rigs or moved their ships. More important is the interaction between oil and overall economic growth. As economies grow, they use more oil (or more specifically, the products derived from oil) for transportation, chemicals, and synthetic materials such as plastics and fibers. Therefore, the availability and affordability of oil facilitates economic activity by lowering the costs of trade. Higher oil prices are often described as increasing taxes on the consumer because more of a person's income is used to receive the same amount of goods and services. Hence, the drivers of global oil supply and demand (which, in turn, determine price), including technology, politics, and the business cycle (generally via the availability of credit), are key considerations. Technology affects oil usage in three forms: the level of technology for extraction, the level of technology and efficiency in which oil is transformed into useful products, and the efficiency with which these products are used by the engines that burn them.

The production of shale oil—oil that is trapped in tight rock formations—has recently undergone a technological revolution. New processes in drilling, pressurization, and extraction make oil more available at a reasonable cost by accessing this new source of supply in rock formations where oil has existed but could not be removed economically on a mass scale. Oil refineries use different technologies to break down oil into its components and to address the generated pollution. About 20% of the energy content of oil is used by refineries themselves in the refining process, so a more energy efficient refinery means more energy for automobiles, manufacturing, and so on. Efficiency by the end users of refined products also affects the supply and demand balance for oil. For example, as mileage efficiency has improved in automobile engines, the amount of gasoline (and hence oil) demand in the United States has stagnated. Technologies for energy production that do not use any form of oil (e.g., solar, wind, nuclear) have an impact on the demand for oil as the costs of those substitutes become more affordable.

Geopolitical conflict—particularly in the Middle East—is the most dramatic risk factor in the supply of oil given that over half of economically viable reserves exist in that region. If there is conflict in a major oil-producing country, then its oil supplies are either reserved for that conflict or simply unavailable for extraction because of the destruction of infrastructure. There are also critical logistical "pinch points," such as the Straits of Hormuz, which provides for the passage of more than 70% of Asia's oil from the Middle East to Asian countries, such as Japan, China, India, and South Korea, that have high energy demand but limited indigenous oil reserves. A war or conflict prohibiting movement of oil through this strait would be a major blow to the global economy. Less extreme but just as relevant examples would be environmental limits on the extraction and/or transportation of oil. Politics can thus overwhelm the technological effects, at least in the short term.

The impact and interaction of the business cycle with oil can be seen in the opposite direction—the destruction of credit in a recession lowers the consumer's demand for oil. The disruption of business by bankruptcy or civil disorder also lowers demand as does uncertainty or diminished business confidence. Conversely, the opposite of these forces can spur the need for petroleum products.

Natural Gas   Natural gas is formed similarly to crude oil but is in vapor form and thus can be used directly. It may be found in shale formations as well as more traditional wells both on-shore and off-shore. Natural gas is typically categorized by its source as either "associated gas" (coming up from an oil well) or "unassociated gas" (coming from a gas field or shale rock where oil is not present). Because associated gas is a co-product of oil production, its supply is not directly driven by the demand for gas, but rather oil demand. In some cases, this gas is collected and re-injected into the oil field to maintain pressure and keep oil production costs low. Unlike crude oil, natural gas can be used cost-effectively and directly for transportation and electrical generation after it is processed to clean out impurities, the most common of which is carbon dioxide. Heavier compounds (called natural gas liquids or NGLs) are also extracted and are extremely valuable in chemical production.

Storage and transportation costs are relatively high for natural gas because of the need to keep the gas under pressure. Transportation via ship is in a liquefied form (i.e., liquefied natural gas or LNG), which requires special terminals that cryogenically cool the gas to −260 degrees Fahrenheit, the point at which it becomes a liquid. The terminals that handle LNG typically can either process exports or imports but not both. LNG costs may be four to five times cash costs from a producing site. Liquid crude oil is comparatively easily transported via ship. The global drivers of natural gas supply and demand are similar to crude oil, but the focus is on electrical generation (lower greenhouse gas and pollutant emissions). Weather is also a key driver of demand, with heating needs during the winter and cooling requirements in summer. A colder winter drives up natural gas demand whereas a hotter summer does the same via the use of air conditioning. Therefore, seasonality and available supplies can radically change natural gas prices.

Refined Products   Refined products are end-use fuels, such as heating oil, gas oil, jet fuel, propane, gasoline, and bunker fuel. For all the importance of crude oil, it is basically useless until it is refined into more pure forms of energy. The refined product is what powers our cars, trucks, planes, and ships and provides raw materials for chemical production. It also coats our roads in the form of asphalt (the most recycled product in the world). Typically refined products have a short shelf life, with availability measured in days. Therefore, refineries must run continuously and coordinate scheduled maintenance to ensure adequate supplies.

Many refineries are located on major coastlines and ports so that they can easily access ocean-borne supplies of crude oil. For example, the US Gulf Coast from Texas to Alabama has approximately 45% of the country's total refining capacity and 50% of the country's natural gas plant processing capacity. This concentration makes refineries in the region more susceptible to bad weather, with hurricanes or typhoons able to disrupt supply if refineries are damaged and halt demand if the population experiences flooding. Gasoline has winter and summer blends and is in greater demand during better weather because of leisure travel. Heating oil or natural gas is used in home heating in the winter, depending on the location. Environmental mandates have tightened the allowed pollution standards for refined products, increasing processing costs and thus hurting demand.

2.1.2 Grains

The development and advancement of agriculture is intrinsically tied to the rise of civilization. Low-cost and available food allows a society to focus its time and energy on technology, construction, and other activities. Row crops, in particular corn, soy, wheat, and rice, have become the staple of diets throughout the world. Corn (i.e., maize), which originated in the Americas, is now grown globally. The largest producers are the United States, Brazil, and China. Although consumed directly by humans, the primary uses for corn are actually for fuel (ethanol) and animal feed (the leftovers of ethanol production as well as direct corn consumption).

As an inert form of life, grains generally have a long enough storage period to last season over season, and sometimes multiple seasons. Practically, they are grown in defined seasons and stored until the next season comes around. Some crops can be grown multiple times per year—North American farmers can sometimes "double-crop" soy and Brazilian farmers can sometimes "triple-crop" soy. Alternatively, sometimes corn and soy can be planted on the same land consecutively in the same season. Weather is extremely important, with the levels of heat and precipitation determining yields and acreage. Drought conditions can kill off plants and flooding can drown them. Disease and pests are also factors. Weather can change the course of nations, such as drought causing the Soviet Union to buy US wheat in the 1980s as well as contributing to the Arab Spring political upheaval in the 2010s. As with energy, technology and politics play a key role in food supply and demand, with genetic modification, biofuel substitution, and social stress all affected by these core foods.

2.1.3 Industrial (Base) Metals

This sector largely represents mined ore that is processed (usually via smelters) into copper, aluminum (or aluminium), nickel, zinc, lead, tin, and iron. These commodities are used in industrial production, including construction, infrastructure development, and durable goods (cars, planes, ships, household goods, and military products) manufacturing. Industrial product demand is associated directly with GDP growth. In fact, copper is sometimes referred to as "Dr. Copper" (with a PhD in economics) because its price reasonably indicates the direction of industrial production and GDP growth. Most industrial metals can be stored for years, if not decades, making it less susceptible to weather issues. But demand may be affected by weather and seasonal factors (e.g., building construction requires cooperative conditions). Beyond the business cycle, politics have a sizable impact on metals pricing, with labor action (strikes) limiting supply while imposing costs on society, development decisions (mines and smelters have high fixed investment requirements), and environmental concerns related to air and water pollution.

2.1.4 Livestock

This sector includes hogs, cattle, sheep, and poultry. Livestock depends on low-cost inputs for mass production as well as the development cycle in emerging markets for growth. As emerging market countries develop a growing middle class population, their diets move away from sustenance foods (rice, maize) to animal products (chicken, beef, pork) and processed foods. Therefore, the livestock sector is tied to events in grain markets and GDP per capita. Livestock is storable in the sense that all one has to do is keep the animal alive; hence its "storage" costs are tied to grain prices. If grain prices increase dramatically (such as during a drought), then animals are slaughtered more quickly to avoid the higher cost of maintaining (i.e., feeding) them. This effectively pulls supply forward in the near term, temporarily lowering prices. However, assuming grain prices fall and the herds are allowed to rebuild, there may be a supply lag for a few years as the animals mature, and thus prices may increase.

Slaughtered animal meat is generally frozen (directly or after being processed into meat products, such as sausage, bacon, etc.), so storage of the final product can be for extended periods of time. Weather has perhaps a surprising impact on animal health and weights. In winter, cattle tend to suffer more than hogs and chickens because of their height. In summer, heat and humidity limit the weight gain in hogs. Disease also plays an outsized role in this sector, with avian flu, bovine spongiform encephalopathy (i.e., mad cow disease), and porcine epidemic diarrhea virus (PEDv) all having caused sharp price volatility in the past. Some of these diseases drive the price down because of fears about transmission to humans, but others send prices higher because the animals have to be slaughtered, driving down supply. Another influence on the supply of livestock is the government-permitted use of drugs and growth hormones. Substitute proteins (poultry, fish, soy) may be used depending on their maturation cycle and consumer preferences. Finally, the livestock sector is becoming more global in nature as the rise of emerging market wealth has led to not only greater import/export trade but also cross-border mergers and acquisitions (e.g., Brazilian-based JBS acquiring American-based Swift and Chinese-based Shuanghui buying American-based Smithfield Foods).

2.1.5 Precious Metals

This set of metals is unique because they straddle the monetary and industrial worlds. Gold, silver, and platinum have acted as stores of value (i.e., similar to currencies) as well as consumed inputs in electronics, auto parts, and jewelry. Storability is measured not in years but in decades, centuries, and even millennia. All the gold that has ever been found basically still exists and equals about 174,100 tonnes or a cube 21 meters per side. Weather has effectively no impact on the availability of precious metals given their long storability. More important are global supply and demand effects, such as inflation expectations, fund flows, and industrial production. Inflation and fund flows are related to the currency aspect of gold and, to a certain extent, other metals. If fiat currencies (paper currencies) are inflated, then the price of other forms of money, such as gold, gain in relative value. In this way, gold acts as a hedge to the value of paper currencies. A similar aspect occurs during wartime when deficit government spending is commonplace, physical goods are generally in short supply, and the fungibility and lack of traceability of assets is at a premium. Industrial needs for silver, platinum, and palladium—platinum and palladium being used in catalytic converters for automobiles—make up about half the demand for these precious metals. Thus, for these metals, technology plays a part in shaping the demand curve. Production also has shifted dramatically: historically South Africa was the leading mining country for gold, but since 2007, China has taken over as the global leader. Jewelry production is also an important use of both gold and silver. In developing countries, such as China and India, jewelry demand has soared with growing wealth because it is a status symbol and outward sign of success.

2.1.6 Softs (Cash Crops)

This sector includes cotton, coffee, sugar, and cocoa and originates from the idea that soft commodities are grown, as opposed to hard commodities that are mined. Currently, softs are generally cash crops (i.e., sold for income as opposed to consumed for subsistence, such as grains). The largest soft crops are grown in countries that are close to the equator in South America, Africa, and Asia. Storability is an issue because freshness determines the quality and weight of the commodity. Some countries have maintained strategic stockpiles (e.g., China for cotton) to try to control domestic prices. Weather is an important factor because many of these softs are dependent on high levels of properly timed rainfall. A freeze can severely damage crops and disease can also take its toll. As with livestock, the nature of softs as a cash crop means that the demand for softs is related to global (notably emerging market) wealth given the worldwide popularity of coffee, sugar, and cocoa.

As noted in this section, each commodity sector is quite unique in terms of its fundamental drivers. With this context in mind, we will now examine the life cycle of the sectors from production to consumption—and their interaction—in more detail.

EXAMPLE 1

Commodity Sector Demand

Industrial activity *most likely* affects the demand for which of the following commodities?

A Copper

B Natural gas

C Softs (e.g., cotton, coffee, sugar and cocoa)

Solution:

A is correct. Copper is used for construction, infrastructure development, and the manufacture of durable goods, all of which are economically sensitive. B is incorrect because demand for natural gas is primarily driven by weather conditions (heating or cooling). C is incorrect because demand for softs is driven primarily by global wealth.

EXAMPLE 2

Commodity Sector Risks

Which of the following commodity sectors are *least* affected in the short-term by weather-related risks?

A Energy

B Livestock

C Precious metals

Solution:

C is correct. Weather has very little impact on the availability of precious metals given their significant storability. Inflation expectations, fund flows, and industrial production are more important factors. A is incorrect because energy production is often located in coastal zones that are vulnerable to severe weather. B is incorrect because the health of livestock is vulnerable to weather conditions because of the risks of death and disease by extreme cold, wet, and heat.

2.2 Life Cycle of Commodities

The life cycle of commodities varies considerably depending on the economic, technical, and structural (i.e., industry, value chain) profile of each commodity, as well as the sector. Conceptually, the commodity production life cycle reflects and amplifies the changes in storage, weather, and political/economic events that shift supply and demand. A short life cycle allows for relatively rapid adjustment to outside events, whereas a long life cycle generally limits the ability of the market to react. These shifts, in turn, feed into the economics for the valuation and shape of the commodity supply and demand curves, plus their respective price elasticities of demand and supply. Understanding the life cycle builds understanding of, and ideally ability to forecast, what drives market actions and commodity returns.

Among the food commodities, agriculture and livestock have well-defined seasons and growth cycles that are specific to geographic regions. For example, by March of each year, corn planting may be finished in the southern US but not yet started in Canada. Meanwhile, the corn harvest may be underway in Brazil and Argentina given their reverse seasonal cycle in the southern hemisphere. Each geographic location also represents local markets that have different domestic and export demand. These differences affect the nature (level and reliability) of demand and the power of buyers to extend or contract the life cycle.

In comparison, commodities in the energy and metals sectors are extracted all year around. Their life cycle changes are generally at the margin of a continuous process, as opposed to being centered at a discrete time or season. But the products from crude oil and metal ore have seasonal demands depending on weather (e.g., gasoline demand in the summer and heating oil demand in the winter) that affect the life cycle and usage of the underlying commodity. And, with all the differences between the varieties even within the same sector, the life cycles depicted have to be representative and selective. The life cycles of several key commodity sectors follows.

Energy

For an example of the differences within a sector, one need look no further than the energy sector. Natural gas can be consumed nearly after extraction from the ground. Crude oil, on the other hand, has to be transformed into something else; crude is useless in its innate form. The refined products in turn (e.g., gasoline and heating oil) have a number of potential processing steps depending on the quality of crude oil input and the relative demand for the various products. The steps for the energy complex may be thought of as shown in Exhibit 1.

Exhibit 1	Steps for the Energy Complex		
Step	**Title**	**Timing**	**Description**
1.	Extraction	50–100 days to begin	A drilling location is selected after surveys, and the well is dug. With the well in place, the siphoning of the crude oil or natural gas begins. There may be enough underground pressure for the hydrocarbons to come out naturally or water or other processes may be used to create such pressure. The fracturing process (also known as "fracking") for shale is applied at this step as well.
2.	Transportation	1–10 days	Once the energy is out of the ground, it is centralized locally and shipped via pipe, ship, train, or truck to a storage facility, refinery, or consumer. Historically, only crude oil and refined products were transported by ship, but with liquefaction technology, natural gas (LNG) is also sent by ship.
3.	Storage	Days to a few months	Crude oil is commercially stored for a few months on average in the United States, Singapore, and Northern Europe, as well as strategically by many countries. In addition, oil may be stored on tanker ships. Natural gas may be delivered directly to the end consumer. A large portion of natural gas is injected into storage for the winter months, or transferred to peak-shaving gas storage facilities during especially cold periods when pipeline capacity is insufficient to meet demand.

(continued)

Exhibit 1   (Continued)

Step	Title	Timing	Description
4.	Trading	N/A	Only natural gas is consumed at this stage, hence trading in futures contracts reflects pricing just prior to consumption because it does not need to be refined. But crude oil requires further processing to be consumed.
5.	Refining	3–5 days	Crude oil is distilled into its component parts via a process generally called cracking. Heat is used to successively boil off the components that are in turn cooled down and collected (e.g., gasoline), until only the remnants (e.g., asphalt) are left.
6.	Transportation and Trading	5–20 days	The distilled products are separated and shipped to their various locations—by ship, pipe, train, or truck—for use by the end consumer. Consumption of crude oil products occurs at this point, such as gasoline, heating oil, and jet fuel, along with commodity futures trading in these products.

Sources: Based on information from www.chevron.ca/operations/refining/refineryworks.asp (accessed 23 November 2015) and authors' research.

Refineries are extraordinarily expensive to build—typically several billion in US dollar terms—depending on the processes required to purify and distill the oil. Part of the cost depends on the expected specifications of the crude oil input. Generally speaking, a low-grade, high sulfur source would require more investment than one with an assured lighter, "sweeter" source. Pipelines are also very costly: For example, the Keystone XL pipeline expansion between Canada and the United States was originally estimated to cost $5 billion in 2010 but was doubled to $10 billion in 2014. Even in countries dealing with violent insurrections (e.g., Libya, Iraq, Nigeria), damage to refineries has been generally modest because of their value to all parties. Pipelines, however, are often destroyed or cut off. Although these costs may appear staggering, they actually pale in comparison with the costs (and risks) of oil exploration, especially in deep offshore locations or geographically remote (or geo-politically risky) regions. In addition, national oil companies (those owned by governments) that produce crude oil have a powerful incentive to invest in large (and costly) refining operations, especially if their type of crude oil is difficult and expensive to refine. Otherwise, they are left with only crude oil (no direct market) and little power to convert this raw material into useful products.

The crude oil market has a number of futures contracts and indexes that follow local grades and origins but the two most commonly traded set of contracts follow the US-based crude oil (West Texas Intermediate, or WTI, crude oil) and the UK-located Brent crude oil from the North Sea. Likewise there are futures for natural gas, gasoil, gasoline, and heating oil. Each has different delivery locations and standards, but the WTI and Brent contracts represent a high-quality refinery input that exploration and production companies can use as a hedging device.

EXAMPLE 3

Energy Life Cycle

Which of the following is a primary difference in the production life cycle between crude oil and natural gas?

A   Only crude oil needs to be stored.

B Natural gas is not transported via ships.

C Natural gas requires very little additional processing after extraction compared with crude oil.

Solution:

C is correct. Natural gas can be used within a short time frame after it is extracted from the ground, but crude oil must first be processed for later use. A is incorrect because both oil and natural gas are stored before usage. B is incorrect because both oil and natural gas are transported using ships.

Industrial/Precious Metals

The life cycle of both precious and industrial metals is probably the most flexible because the ore, as well as the finished products, can be stored for months (if not years) given the relative resistance to spoilage by metals (assuming proper storage). Exposed ore and metals can oxidize (e.g., iron rusts) and take up a substantial amount of space. Using copper as an example, the many steps in the purification process are shown in Exhibit 2.

	Step Name	Description
Exhibit 2	**Copper Purification Process**	
1.	Extracting	Ore (raw earth with ~2% metal content) is removed via a mine or open pit.
2.	Grinding	Ore is then ground into powder to facilitate purification processes.
3.	Concentrating	Ore is enriched via froth flotation with unwanted material (gangue) sinking to the bottom and removed. Metal content reaches 25%.
4.	Roasting	The powdered, enriched ore is heated to 500 degrees Celsius to 700 degrees Celsius to remove sulfur and dry the ore, which is still a solid called calcine.
5.	Smelting	The solid calcine is heated to 1200 degrees Celsius and melts. More impurities are removed as slag, increasing the metal content to 60%.
6.	Converting	Air is blown into the liquid forming blister copper, which is 99% pure.
7.	Electro-refining	The blister is reshaped into anodes and purified to 99.99% metal by electrolysis.
8.	Storage/Logistics	The purified metal is held typically in a bonded warehouse until shipped to an end user.

Sources: Based on information from http://resources.schoolscience.co.uk/CDA/14-16/cumining/copch2pg1.html (accessed 23 November 2015), http://www.madehow.com/Volume-4/Copper.html (accessed 23 November 2015), and authors' research.

A key consideration regarding the supply of most metals is the economies of scale involved in the smelter and processing plants built to convert ore into useful metals. These are huge facilities for which marginal costs (i.e., the cost to convert the last pound or kilogram of processed ore into a useful metal) decline substantially with both the scale of the facility and its utilization (output as a percentage of capacity). As a result, when supply exceeds demand for a given industrial metal, it is difficult for suppliers to either cut back production or halt it entirely. Overproduction often continues until smaller or financially weaker competitors are forced to shut down. Because demand for industrial metals fluctuates with overall economic growth, as was discussed previously, there are substantial incentives for metals producers to invest in new capacity when their utilization (and profit) is high, but huge economic and financial penalties for operating these facilities when demand falls off during an economic downturn. Ironically, given the typical economic cycle and the time lag involved between deciding to expand capacity, new supply often arrives just as demand is declining—which exacerbates pricing and profit declines. This tendency has been further amplified by national governments seeking to "move down" the value chain (i.e., capture more added value) from simply being a producer and exporter of ore to investing in smelting and processing capacity to provide the commodity. Government motives are often not entirely economic (profit seeking) but based on national goals of economic development and creating and maintaining employment. Although this motivation also is true in other commodity sectors, such as the crude oil refining industry, the relative stability of demand for various energy needs (regardless of macroeconomic conditions) makes this effect of supply and demand instability seen in industrial metals less of a key factor.

With the lack of seasonality in much of the metals complex (apart from construction), buyers and sellers can match their needs with contracts that come due every month of the year.

EXAMPLE 4

Industrial Metals Life Cycle

Because of large economies of scale for processing industrial metals, producers:

A   immediately shut down new capacity when supply exceeds demand.

B   have an incentive to maintain operating production levels when demand declines.

C   find it difficult to cut back production or capacity even when supply exceeds demand or demand slows.

Solution:

C is correct. Given the sizable facilities in which metals are produced, reducing capacity is difficult when demand slows. A is incorrect because of the time lag involved in responding to reduced demand conditions. B is incorrect because producers would face financial losses if they maintained production levels when there is a decline in demand.

Livestock

Livestock grows year-round but good weather and access to high-quality pasture and feed accelerates weight gain. As a result, there is fluctuation in the availability of animals ready for slaughter. The timing to maturity typically increases with size, with poultry maturing in a matter of weeks, hogs in months, and cattle in a few years. Taking the example of a hog, the life cycle begins with a sow (female hog) giving birth, with the optimal timing after the summer heat. Normally it takes about six months to raise a piglet to slaughter weight, and during that time it can be fed almost anything to get it up to weight. In mass-scale production, soymeal and cornmeal are the most common foods. In contrast, cattle take longer to raise. For mass-scale breeding, the first one to two years are spent as "feeder cattle" and eat a grass diet in pasture. The next phase covers an additional 6–12 months whereby cattle are in a feed lot being fattened to slaughter weight, generally on a corn-based diet.

The livestock industry in the US has historically been among the least export-oriented of all the commodities because of the high risk of spoilage once an animal is slaughtered. However, advances in cryogenics (freezing) technologies with regard to chicken, beef, and pork mean that increasingly these products are moving from one part of the world to another in response to differences in production costs and demand. And as emerging and frontier market countries develop middle class consumers capable of purchasing meat protein as a regular part of their diet, there has been increased interest and investment in the livestock and meatpacking industries in such countries as the United States and Brazil. These industries combine low cost sources of animal feed, large grazing acreage and strong domestic demand (leading to facilities with substantial economies of scale) as key export points to supply global demand.

Ranchers and slaughterhouses trade hog and cattle futures to hedge against their processed meat commitments. Ranchers can hedge both young cattle that are still on pasture (called feeder cattle) and animals being fattened for butchering (called live cattle).

EXAMPLE 5

Livestock Life Cycle

The US livestock sector is among the least export-oriented commodity sectors because of:

A low technological innovation in the sector.

B high risk of spoilage once animals are slaughtered.

C little or no demand for US livestock from outside the United States.

Solution:

B is correct. Livestock incur a high risk of spoilage once they are slaughtered unless the meat is frozen. A is incorrect because advances in cryogenics have improved the ability to export from the United States. C is incorrect because demand for US livestock has expanded internationally, particularly in emerging market countries that are experiencing economic growth.

Grains

Grains in the northern hemisphere follow a similar growth cycle with an analogous but opposite growth cycle in the southern hemisphere. Plants similarly mature according to the following process of steps: (1) planting (placing the seeds in the ground after preparation/fertilization work); (2) growth (the emerging of the seedling to plant maturity); (3) pod/ear/head formation (the food grain is created); and (4) harvest (the collection of the grain by the farmer). The timing in North America is shown in Exhibit 3.

Exhibit 3   Timing for Grain Production in North America

	Corn	Soybeans	Wheat*
Planting	April–May	May–June	Sept–Oct
Growth	June–Aug	July–Aug	Nov–Mar
Pod/Ear/Head Formation	Aug–Sept	Sept	April–May
Harvest	Sept–Nov	Sept–Oct	June–July

* The hard winter wheat variety, which has a higher protein content, is used here.

Because demand for grains is year round, they are regularly stored in silos and warehouses globally. Some countries have a central purchasing bureau and others depend on local or international trading companies to maintain stockpiles. To maintain hygienic standards, specialized port facilities, packing houses, and vehicles are used. Poor standards and logistics can result in a substantial loss of value to grains.

Farmers and consumers can trade futures to hedge their exposure to the crop in question, and the contract delivery months reflect the different times of the growing cycle outlined earlier. Ranchers also can use grain futures to hedge against the cost of feeding an animal.

Softs

Coffee, cocoa, cotton, and sugar are very different soft commodities in this sector, so we will focus on one that is grown broadly—coffee. Coffee is harvested somewhere all year around, but the best quality coffees are from high-altitude plantations and are picked in the middle of the harvest periods. Exhibit 4 shows the timetable for harvesting coffee in various countries. Newly planted coffee trees take about three to four years to bear a fruit, called a cherry. Harvesting takes place in the same field in multiple sweeps because cherries ripen at different times. After the coffee cherries are picked (by hand, to ensure that only ripe ones are taken), the husk and fruit are removed and the remaining bean dried. More than half of coffee uses the dry method in which the harvested cherries are laid out in the sun for two to three weeks. The wet method uses fresh water to soak the cherries, the soft pulp is removed, the bean is fermented for 12–48 hours, and then the bean is dried either in the sun or by a dryer for 24–36 hours. The "green" beans are then hulled, sorted, and bagged for their final markets. With most of the consumption in faraway foreign markets, ships are commonly used to transport the beans to their buyer, which may store them in a bonded warehouse. After delivery, typically by truck, the local buyer roasts the beans and ships them to the retail location (e.g., coffee house or supermarket) for purchase or brewing.

Exhibit 4	Timetable for Coffee Harvesting											
Month	Jan	Feb	Mar	Apr	May	Jun	Jul	Aug	Sep	Oct	Nov	Dec
Brazil							Harvest	Harvest	Harvest	Harvest	Harvest	
Central America	Harvest	Harvest	Harvest							Harvest	Harvest	Harvest
Vietnam	Harvest	Harvest	Harvest								Harvest	Harvest
Java						Harvest	Harvest	Harvest	Harvest	Harvest		
Kenya	Harvest	Harvest	Harvest			Harvest	Harvest			Harvest	Harvest	Harvest
Jamaica	Harvest	Harvest	Harvest									Harvest

Sources: Based on information from www.sweetmarias.com (accessed 23 November 2015) and authors' research.

Coffee comes in two main varieties, robusta and arabica, although there are many others. Generally speaking, robusta beans are lower quality with less flavor than the arabica. Brazil is the world's largest coffee producer and produces a mix of both beans, whereas Vietnam, the second largest producer, predominantly produces robusta. There are two futures contracts associated with coffee: the robusta variety is traded in London and the arabica variety is traded in New York. The physical delivery aspect of these contracts allows for sellers to deliver the beans to an authorized bonded warehouse as fulfillment of the contract at expiration. Therefore, farmers and distributors can sell futures contracts to hedge the sales price of production, and coffee roasters can buy futures contracts to hedge coffee bean purchase costs; contract maturities can be selected by each to match their product delivery schedules.

Although the number and variety of commodities are too large to cover in this limited space, we illustrated the key life cycle types: (1) straight-through consumption with natural gas; (2) input–output production life cycle with crude oil and gasoline, heating oil, and other products; (3) seasonal planting production with grains; and (4) year-round production with coffee.

2.3 Valuation of Commodities

The valuation of commodities compared with that of equities and bonds can be summarized by the fact that stocks and bonds represent financial assets, whereas commodities are almost always physical assets.[1] More specifically, stocks and bonds are claims on the economic output (profits) of a business, usually a corporation.

In contrast, commodities are tangible items with an intrinsic (but variable) economic value (e.g., a lump of gold, a pile of coal, a bushel of corn). They do not generate future cash flows beyond what can be realized through their purchase and sale. In addition, the standard financial instruments that are based on commodities are not financial assets (like a stock or bond) but derivative contracts with finite lifetimes, such as futures contracts. As with other types of derivatives, commodity derivative contracts can and do have value—but they are contingent on some other factors, such as the price of the underlying commodity. Hence, the valuation of commodities is not based on the estimation of future profitability and cash flows but a discounted forecast of future possible prices based on such factors as the supply and demand of the physical item or the expected volatility of future prices. On the one hand, this forecast may be quite formal and elaborately estimated by a producer or consumer. One can imagine the detailed inputs available to an oil company based on the labor and capital expenses needed to extract oil, refine it, and transport it to final sale as gasoline in your automobile. On the other hand, this forecast may be instinctively done by a floor trader with little fundamental analysis but instead professional judgment based on years of experience and perhaps some technical analysis.

As opposed to a stock or bond that receives periodic income, owning a commodity incurs transportation and storage costs. These ongoing expenditures affect the shape of the forward price curve of the commodity derivative contracts with different expiration dates. If storage and transportation costs are substantial, the prices for a commodity futures contract will likely be incrementally higher as one looks farther into the future. However, sometimes the demand for the commodity can move the spot price higher than the futures price. The price reflects the fact that, instead of going long a futures contract, one could buy the commodity today and store it until a future date for use. The expenditure would be the outlay/investment at today's spot price for the commodity along with (or net of) the future costs one would incur to store and hold it. This time element to commodity storage and supply and demand can generate "roll return" and affect investment returns. These and other factors figure into the assessment of futures pricing, which we will cover later.

Some commodity contracts require actual delivery of the physical commodity at the end of the contract versus settlement in a cash payment (based on the difference between the contract future price and the spot price prevailing at the time of contract expiration). The force of arbitrage—which reflects the law of one price—may not be entirely enforced by arbitrageurs because some participants do not have the ability to

---

1 We say "almost always" because some new classes of commodities, such as electricity or weather, are not physical assets in the sense that you can touch or store them.

make or take delivery of the physical commodity. In these situations, the relationships that link spot and futures prices are not an equality but a range that only indicates the limit or boundary of value differences that can occur.

There is an important additional consideration concerning the link between spot and futures prices in commodities. Some of the largest users of commodity futures are businesses seeking to hedge price risk when that price is either a critical source of revenue or cost in their business operations. For example, the airline industry is very dependent on the cost of jet fuel for operating their planes. The highly competitive nature of the industry results in tremendous price pressure on airfares, with a need for airlines to fill each flight with as many passengers as possible. The futures and swaps markets for jet fuel allow airlines to hedge the price of future fuel purchases (particularly against future shocks in oil prices that cannot be foreseen or anticipated).

In addition, the price discovery process of the commodity futures markets provides airlines with insights about future fuel prices that help determine what prices to offer their customers for future flights while still making a profit. In fact, airline ticket sales are—in effect—selling a contract at a price set today for future delivery of a service, namely a plane flight. In this case, the airlines will typically hedge their price risk and uncertainty about future fuel costs by purchasing ("going long") futures contracts.

EXAMPLE 6

Commodities versus Stocks and Bonds

In contrast to financial assets, such as stocks and bonds:

A   commodities are always physical goods.

B   commodities generate periodic cash flows.

C   commodity investment is primarily via derivatives.

Solution:

C is correct. The most common way to invest in commodities is via derivatives. A is incorrect because although most commodities are physical goods, certain new classes, such as electricity or weather, are not tangible. B is incorrect because commodities may incur, rather than generate, periodic cash flow through transportation and storage costs (when the commodities are physically owned).

EXAMPLE 7

Spot Commodity Valuation

What is a key distinction between the valuation of commodities compared with the valuation of stocks and bonds?

A   Valuation of commodities cannot be conducted using technical analysis.

B   Valuation of commodities focuses on supply and demand, whereas valuation of stocks and bonds focuses on discounted cash flows.

C   Valuation of stocks and bonds focuses on future supply and demand, whereas commodity valuation focuses on future profit margins and cash flow.

Solution:

B is correct. The valuation of commodities is based on a forecast of future prices based on supply and demand factors, as well as expected price volatility. In contrast, the valuation of stocks and bonds is based on estimating future profitability and/or cash flow. A is incorrect because technical analysis is sometimes applied to valuing commodities. C is incorrect for the reasons stated for choice B.

COMMODITY FUTURES MARKETS

3

Public commodity markets are structured as futures markets—that is, as a central exchange where participants trade standardized contracts to make and take delivery at a specified place at a specified future timeframe. As mentioned, futures contracts are derivatives because the value of the contract is derived from another asset. Both futures and forward contracts are binding agreements that establish a price today for delivery of a commodity in the future (or settlement of the contract in cash at expiration). As mentioned at the beginning of the reading, the focus of this reading is on futures, with forwards discussed only briefly.

3.1 Futures Market Participants

The key difference between futures and forward contracts is that futures contracts are standardized agreements traded on public exchanges, such as the Chicago Mercantile Exchange (CME), Intercontinental Exchange (ICE), and Shanghai Commodities Exchange. Standardization allows a participant to enter into a contract without ever knowing who the counterparty is. In addition, the exchange oversees trading and margin requirements and provides some degree of self-imposed regulatory oversight. In contrast, forward contracts are bilateral agreements between a known party that wants to go long and one that wants to go short. Because of their bilateral nature, forwards are considered to be OTC (or over the counter) contracts with less regulatory oversight and much more customization to the specific needs of the hedging (or speculating) party. Often, the counterparty for a forward contract is a financial institution that is providing liquidity or customization in exchange for a fee. Although futures markets require that daily cash movements in the futures price be paid from the losing positions to the winning positions, forward contracts are usually only settled upon expiration or with some custom frequency dictated by the contract.

Early commodity exchanges operated as forward markets, but too often participants would go bankrupt when unrealized losses became realized at the end of the contract. The futures process was introduced to minimize this risk because the exchange acts as guarantor of the payments. The first modern organized futures exchange was the Dojima Rice Exchange in Osaka, Japan, which was founded in 1710. The structure of futures markets is important to understand as a way of understanding the goals and roles of the various participants. When we consider any commodity, for every producer of that commodity there is a consumer. Thus, for participants who are long the physical commodity and want to sell it, there are also participants who are short the physical commodity and want to buy it. Therefore, for fairness between the two sets of participants, longs and shorts need to operate on an equal basis. As a coincident observation, the commodity markets are net zero in terms of aggregate futures positions (futures contract longs equals futures contract shorts). In contrast, with markets for stocks and bonds, there is a net long position because the issued stocks' and bonds' market value are equal to the net aggregate positions at the end of each day. Shorting an equity is constrained by the short seller's need to locate shares to short, the requirement to reimburse dividends on borrowed shares, and requirements to post and pay interest on margin that generally exceeds the margin required for long equity positions (as in the US under Regulation T). By contrast, shorting commodity futures is much simpler and short investors need to post only the same margin that long investors post.

There are a number of participants in commodity futures markets. First are *hedgers*, who trade in the markets to hedge their exposures related to the commodity. The second are long-term and short-term *traders* and *investors* (including index investors), who speculate on market direction or volatility and provide liquidity and price discovery for the markets in exchange for the expectation of making a profit. Third are the *exchanges* (or clearing houses), which set trading rules and provide the infrastructure of transmitting prices and payments. Fourth are *analysts* who use the exchange information for non-trading purposes, such as evaluating commodity businesses, creating products that are based on commodity futures (e.g., exchange-traded funds, swaps, and notes), and making public policy decisions. Analysts also include brokers and other financial intermediaries who participate in the markets but do not take a position. Finally, *regulators* of both the exchange and traders exist to monitor and police the markets, investigate malfeasance, and provide a venue for complaints.

3.1.1 *Commodity Hedgers*

Hedgers tend to be knowledgeable market participants—one would expect that a company that drills for oil knows something about the supply and demand for oil and related forms of energy (at least in the long run). However, hedgers may not be accurate predictors of the future supply and demand for their product. Consider a baker who buys wheat for future delivery and benefits from a surprise drought (has locked in a low price in a supply-constrained market). However, the baker is hurt if the weather is beneficial (has effectively overpaid during a bumper crop). Given that a hedger can make delivery (if short the futures contract) or take delivery (if long the futures contract), he or she is generally motivated by risk mitigation with regards to cash flow, so the risk is more of an opportunity cost rather than an actual one.

It is important to keep in mind that hedging and speculating are not synonymous with (respectively) being long or short. As Exhibit 5 illustrates with some examples, both long and short positions can be associated with either hedging or speculating.

Exhibit 5	Examples of Hedging and Speculating Positions	
	Long Position	**Short Position**
Hedging	Food manufacturer seeking to hedge the price of corn needed for snack chips	Gold mining company seeking to hedge the future price of gold against potential declines
Speculating	Integrated oil company seeking to capitalize on its knowledge of physical oil markets by making bets on future price movements	Commodity trading adviser (CTA) seeking to earn a profit for clients via a macro-commodity investment fund

Note also that hedgers tend to speculate based on their perceived unique insight into market conditions and determine the amount of hedging that is appropriate. From a regulatory standpoint in the United States, the difficulty in clearly distinguishing between hedging and speculating, therefore, has resulted in the separation of commodity producers and consumers from other trading participants regardless of whether commercial participants are actually speculating.

3.1.2 *Commodity Traders and Investors*

The commodity trading community, like other groups of traders, consists of three primary types: (1) informed investors, (2) liquidity providers, and (3) arbitrageurs. Informed investors largely represent the aforementioned hedgers and speculators, including index and institutional investors. With regard to the hedger, as mentioned previously, a company that drills for oil clearly is familiar with the supply and demand for oil and related forms of energy (at least in the long run). But hedgers may not be accurate predictors of the *future* supply and demand for their product.

Speculators, who believe that they have an information advantage, seek to out-perform the hedger by buying or selling futures contracts in conjunction with—or opposite from—the hedger. This trading may be on a micro-second time scale or a multi-month perspective. For example, if a speculator has a weather prediction process that is superior, he or she has an information advantage and will trade accordingly. Alternatively, a speculator may be willing to act as a liquidity provider, knowing that producers and consumers may not be in the market at the same time. By buying when the producer wants to sell and selling when the consumer is ready to buy, speculators may be able to make a profit. In this sense, speculators are willing to step in, under the right pricing circumstances, to provide insurance to hedgers in return for an expected (albeit not guaranteed) profit.

Finally, arbitrageurs who have the ability to inventory physical commodities can attempt to capitalize on mispricing between the commodity (along with related storage and financing cost) versus the futures price. They may own the storage facilities (bonded warehouses, grain silos, feedlots) and work to manage that inventory in conjunction with the futures prices to attempt to make arbitrage-style profits.

3.1.3 *Commodity Exchanges*

Commodity futures markets are found throughout the world. The CME and ICE are the primary US markets, having consolidated the bulk of the various specialist exchanges. Elsewhere in the Americas, the primary commodity exchange is in Brazil where BM&FBOVESPA trades grains and livestock. In Europe, the London Metals Exchange (currently owned by Hong Kong-based HKex Group) is the main industrial metals location globally. Energy and shipping are also traded out of London. In Asia, Japan's Osaka Dojima Commodity Exchange and the Tokyo Commodity Exchange compete with China's Dalian Commodity Exchange. Finally, Indonesia (Palm Oil), Singapore (rubber), and Australia (energy, grains, wool) have supplementary commodity futures markets. Given that people all over the world need food, energy, and materials, exchanges have formed globally to meet those needs.

3.1.4 *Commodity Market Analysts*

Non-market participants use the exchange information to perform research and conduct policy as well as to facilitate market participation. Their activities affect market behavior, albeit in an indirect manner. Research may be commercially based. For example, a manufacturer may want to project and forecast the energy cost of a new process or product as part of an academic study comparing one market structure with another. Commodity prices are a key component in understanding sources of inflation and are used in other indexes that indicate quality of life for consumers and households. Governments that control natural resource extraction (e.g., nationalized oil companies) or tax commodity extraction by private entities are also interested in understanding futures markets to promote or discourage investment and/or raise revenue.

3.1.5 *Commodity Regulators*

Finally, various regulatory bodies monitor the global commodity markets. In the United States, commodity and futures regulation fall under the Commodity Futures Trading Commission (CFTC), which has very limited overlap with other financial regulatory bodies, such as the Securities and Exchange Commission. The CFTC delegates much of the direct monitoring to the National Futures Association (NFA)—a self-regulatory body—whose members are the authorized direct participants in the markets with customer responsibilities (e.g., clearing firms, brokers, advisers).

Outside the United States, most other countries have a unified regulatory structure. For example, the China Securities Regulatory Commission regulates both futures and securities (i.e., stocks and bonds). In Europe, most legislation in the area of financial services is initiated at the European Union (EU) level primarily through the European Securities and Markets Authority (ESMA). The Markets in Financial Instruments Directive (MiFID) that came into force in 2007 was a key element of EU financial market integration that focused largely on deregulation. Since 2009, existing legislative instruments, particularly for commodity derivative markets, have been revised and new regulations have been introduced with the aim to strengthen oversight and regulation, and are subject to G–20 commitments. Overseeing these different regulatory bodies is the International Organization of Securities Commissions (IOSCO), which is the international association of the world's securities and futures markets.

In all regions, the interests of the financial sector strongly influence debates and legislation on financial market regulation, including that of commodities. For example, the International Swaps and Derivatives Association (ISDA) publishes its positions and comments on draft regulatory proposals.

EXAMPLE 8

Commodity Market Participants

Commodity traders that often provide insurance to hedgers are *best* described as:

A   arbitrageurs.

B   liquidity providers.

C   informed investors.

Solution:

B is correct. Liquidity providers often play the role of providing an insurance service to hedgers who need to unload and transfer price risk by entering into futures contracts. A is incorrect because arbitrageurs typically seek to capitalize and profit on mispricing due to a lack of information in the marketplace. C is incorrect because informed investors predominantly keep commodity futures markets efficient by capitalizing on mispricing attributable to a lack of information in the marketplace.

3.2 Spot and Futures Pricing

Commodity prices are typically represented by (1) spot prices in the physical markets and (2) futures prices for later delivery. The **spot price** is simply the current price to deliver a physical commodity to a specific location or purchase and transport it away from a designated location. Examples of a spot price may be the price quoted at a grain silo, a natural gas pipeline, an oil storage tank, or a sugar refinery.

A **futures price** is a price agreed on to deliver or receive a defined quantity (and often quality) of a commodity at a future date. Although a producer and a consumer can enter into a bilateral contract to exchange a commodity for money in the future, there are (conveniently) many standardized contracts that trade on exchanges for buyers and sellers to use. Recall that a bilateral agreement is a forward contract, compared with a futures contract that is standardized and trades on a futures exchange. One benefit of futures markets is that information regarding contracts (number, price, etc.) is publicly available. In this way, the price discovery process that brings buyers and sellers into agreement is shared broadly and efficiently (in real time) with a global marketplace among the aforementioned market participants. Futures contracts have maturities extending up to about a year (e.g., livestock) to several years (e.g., crude oil).

The difference between spot and futures prices is generally called the **basis**. Depending on the specified commodity and its current circumstances (e.g., supply and demand outlook), the spot price may be higher or lower than the futures price. When the spot price exceeds the futures price, the situation is called **backwardation**, and the opposite case is called **contango**. The origin of the word "contango" is a bit murky, but one theory is that it came from the word "continuation" used in the context of the London Stock Exchange in the mid-1800s. During this period, contango was a fee paid by the buyer to the seller to defer settlement of a trade (hence the near-term price would be less expensive than the longer-term price). The term backwardation describes the same arrangement if it was "backward," or reversed (i.e., payment to defer settlement was made by the seller to the buyer).

Backwardation and contango are also used to describe the relationship between two futures contracts of the same commodity. When the near-term (i.e., closer to expiration) futures contract price is higher than the longer-term futures contract price, the futures market for the commodity is in backwardation. In contrast, when the near-term futures contract price is lower than the longer-term futures contract price, the futures market for the commodity is in contango. The price difference (whether in backwardation or contango) is called the calendar spread. Generally speaking and assuming stable spot prices, the producer is willing to take a price in the future that is lower than the current spot price because it provides a level of certainty for the producer's business. The seller of that insurance on the other side of the trade profits because the lower futures price converges to the higher spot price over time. This relationship occurs when future commodity prices are expected to be higher because of a variety of reasons related to economic growth, weather, geo-political risks, supply disruptions, and so on. As a long owner of a futures contract in contango, value will erode over time as the contract pricing moves closer to the spot price. This relationship can be very costly for long holders of contracts if they roll futures positions over time. Although backwardation is conceptually "normal," there are certain commodities that often trade in contango.

Exhibit 6 is a graphic representation of backwardation in West Texas Intermediate crude oil on the close of 31 May 2014 on the CME's New York Mercantile Exchange (NYMEX).

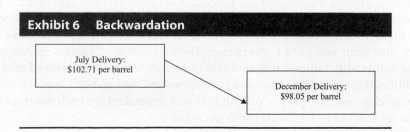

Exhibit 6   Backwardation

July Delivery:
$102.71 per barrel

December Delivery:
$98.05 per barrel

For contracts in a single (common) commodity, such as lean hogs or crude oil, the price differences may be traded as a spread rather than individually.

Exhibit 7 is a graphic representation of contango in lean hogs on the close of 31 May 2014 on the CME.

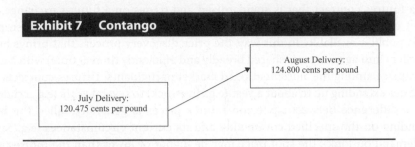

Exhibit 7   Contango

July Delivery:
120.475 cents per pound

August Delivery:
124.800 cents per pound

From these examples, the lean hogs July–August calendar spread is –4.325 cents per pound (120.475 – 124.800) and crude oil July–December calendar spread is $4.66 per barrel (102.71 – 98.05).

A positive calendar spread is associated with futures markets that are in backwardation, whereas a negative calendar spread in commodities is associated with futures markets that are in contango. These calendar spreads are traded with their own bid–ask prices, trading range, and order book, similar to the single-month (i.e., nearest to expiration) future contracts. Note that from this one trade, two contracts (one for each side—or "leg"—of the spread) appear on an exchange's trading account and use their respective closing prices to determine profit or loss. Therefore, in the end, all trades and positions are valued at the close-of-day prices.

Commodity futures are settled by either cash or physical delivery. Cash-settled contracts, such as feeder cattle traded on the CME, have no value after the maturity date. Cash-settlement is an important innovation in the evolution and development of commodity futures markets. To a certain extent, cash settlement enabled higher involvement of two key participants in today's futures markets: speculators and arbitrageurs. It also introduced an entirely new way that hedgers (long or short) could participate in the market to transfer the future price risk of having to sell or buy a commodity without the complications associated with requiring physical delivery. Physical-settled commodity futures contracts require that the title of the actual commodity be transferred by the seller of the futures contract to the buyer at a particular place, on or by a particular date, and of a particular quality specification. For example, under a futures contract with West Texas Intermediate crude oil as the underlying physical commodity, crude oil meeting minimum specifications must be delivered to Cushing, Oklahoma, in the United States. Meanwhile, a similar futures contract with Brent crude oil as the underlying physical commodity has delivery points in the North Sea off the coast of the United Kingdom. Supply and demand differences at these two faraway geographical locations can cause price divergences despite otherwise similar specifications.

Physical delivery also ensures a convergence of the futures and spot market, which may not necessarily occur in a cash-settled market. Note that this statement does not imply market manipulation in cash-settled markets because trading costs or other factors may limit complete convergence. The emergence of central exchanges for trading commodity futures facilitated this convergence with standardized contracts. In addition, these exchanges provided centrally established, publicly available pricing, which quickly replaced private pricing that was dependent on both contract terms and the location of where transactions occurred.

Physical delivery can become complicated by such factors as quality or variety differences in the commodity. For example, robusta coffee (traded in the United Kingdom) cannot be delivered for arabica coffee (traded in the United States) because it is a different variety of coffee and a different venue for delivery. Likewise, raw (or unprocessed) sugar that is traded in the United States cannot be delivered for white processed sugar that is traded in the United Kingdom. Futures markets can address some of these peculiarities involving quality or differences in supply. When physical delivery is required, some futures contracts require a premium or discount associated with specifications. For example, arabica coffee prices are automatically adjusted based on the country of origin and the location of the warehouse where delivery is made.

In summary, spot prices are highly localized and associated with physical delivery, limiting the degree to which interested participants can seek to hedge or speculate on their future direction. In contrast, futures prices can be global (and if not, at least regional or national in scope). They also are standardized for trading on exchanges to promote liquidity; act as a reference price point for customized (i.e., forward) contracts; and generate widely available, minimally biased data for market participants and governments to judge supply and demand and to make planning decisions.

In this manner, futures can be used to allocate risk and generate returns for market participants. On the surface, futures trading may seem muddled and chaotic on a micro level, but serves as an overall social benefit by sending signals to producers and consumers for hedging and inventory-sizing purposes and to governments for the potential impact of policy decisions.

EXAMPLE 9

Spot and Futures Pricing (1)

The current spot price of the futures contract nearest to expiration for West Texas Intermediate (WTI) crude oil is $95.20 per barrel, whereas the six-month futures contract for WTI is priced at $84.75 per barrel. Based on this information:

A   the futures market for WTI crude oil is currently in a state of contango.

B   the futures market for WTI crude oil is currently in a state of backwardation.

C   the shipping and delivery cost of WTI crude oil for a futures contract expiring in six months with physical delivery to Cushing, Texas, is $10.45 per barrel.

Solution:

B is correct. Commodity futures markets are in a state of backwardation when the spot price is greater than the price of near-term (i.e., nearest to expiration) futures contracts, and correspondingly, the price of near-term futures contracts is greater than longer-term contracts. A is incorrect because the market would be in contango only if the futures price exceeded that of the spot price. C is incorrect because the shipping and delivery costs associated with physical delivery of a commodity are only one component in determining a commodity futures contract price.

EXAMPLE 10

Spot and Futures Pricing (2)

An important distinction between spot and futures prices for commodities is that:

A spot prices are universal across regions, but futures prices vary by location.

B futures prices do not reflect differences in quality or composition for a commodity.

C spot prices vary across region based on quality/composition and local supply and demand factors.

Solution:

C is correct. Spot prices of commodities vary across regions, reflecting logistical constraints and supply and demand imbalances that prevent the movement of materials. A is incorrect because spot prices tend to vary by region, as noted earlier. B is incorrect because futures contracts are based on standardized specifications for the composition and quality.

EXAMPLE 11

Spot and Futures Pricing (3)

An arbitrageur has two active positions in the commodity futures markets—one for lean hogs and the other for natural gas. The calendar spread on the lean hogs contract is −$0.452 per pound and the calendar spread on the natural gas contract is +$1.10 per million BTU (British Thermal Units). Based on this information, we can say that:

A only the spreads of these commodities, and not the individual prices, can be traded in commodity markets.

B the lean hogs futures market is in a state of backwardation and the natural gas futures market is in a state of contango.

C the lean hogs futures market is in a state of contango and the natural gas futures market is in a state of backwardation.

Solution:

C is correct. The spread is the difference between the current spot price for a commodity and the futures contract price. Because futures markets in a state of contango will have futures prices that exceed the spot price, the spread for these markets is negative. Conversely, in a state of backwardation, the spread is positive. A is incorrect because either the individual prices or spreads can be traded. B is incorrect because, as mentioned earlier, the negative spread of lean hogs futures indicates a state of contango, whereas the positive spread of natural gas futures indicates a state of backwardation.

EXAMPLE 12

Spot and Futures Pricing (4)

A futures price curve for commodities in backwardation:

A always remains in backwardation in the long term.

B can fluctuate between contango and backwardation in the long term.

C reflects structural long-term industry factors, as opposed to dynamic market supply and demand pressures.

Solution:

B is correct. During periods of market stress or fundamental structural change in market conditions, some commodity futures price curves can rapidly shift from contango to backwardation or vice versa. A is incorrect because futures price curves can vacillate between contango and backwardation. C is incorrect because the shape of a commodity futures price curve reflects both long-term industry factors as well as market expectations of future supply and demand of the underlying commodity(ies).

3.3 Futures Returns

Commodity futures markets have a reputation for volatility, but similar to other asset classes, there are theoretical bases for their long-run behavior. The original purpose of futures markets is for producers and consumers to hedge physical raw materials. In this section, we will discuss the underpinning theories of commodity futures returns, deconstruct the components of futures returns (i.e., at an index level), and close with thoughts on term structure (i.e., contango versus backwardation and implications of rolling futures contracts).

3.3.1 Theories of Futures Returns

Several theories have been proposed to explain the shape of the futures price curve, which has a dramatic impact on commodity futures returns. This reading covers three of the most important theories: (1) Insurance Theory, (2) Hedging Pressure Hypothesis, and (3) Theory of Storage.

3.3.1.1 Insurance Theory   Keynes (1930), the noted economist and market speculator, proposed one of the earliest known theories on the shape of a commodity futures price curve. Also known as his theory of "normal backwardation," Keynes, in his 1930 tome *A Treatise on Money*, proposed that producers use commodity futures markets for insurance by locking in prices and thus make their revenues more predictable. A commodity producer is long the physical good and thus would be motivated to sell the commodity for future delivery to hedge its sales price. Imagine a farmer who thinks that next year she will grow a certain amount of soybeans on her land. She can sell a portion of her crop today that will be harvested months later to lock in those prices. She can then spend money on fertilizer and seed with more confidence about her budget. She may not be locking in a profit, but she would better understand her financial condition. Keynes' theory assumes that the futures curve is in backwardation "normally" because our farmer would persistently sell forward, pushing down prices in the future. Alternatively, this theory posits that the futures price has to be lower than the current spot price as a form of payment or remuneration to the speculator who takes on the price risk and provides price insurance to the commodity seller. The concept of normal backwardation is illustrated in Exhibit 8, using soybean prices pre- and post-harvest.

Exhibit 8   Normal Backwardation

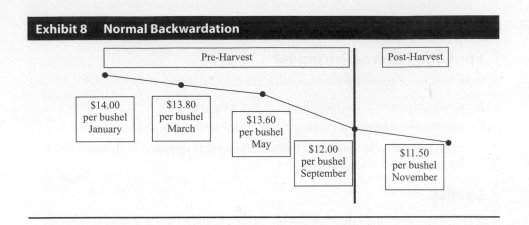

In terms of returns, if the front price is stable (in our example, $14.00), then an investor can buy a further-dated contract (e.g., September) at $12.00 and wait for that contract to become the current contract. As September approaches (and assuming no change in front prices) the September contract will reach $14.00 at maturity, and the speculator will make a profit of $2 per contract. Even if the contract does not fully converge, this theory holds that there should be positive excess returns (sometimes referred to as the risk premium) via this process to induce buying. As noted earlier, this process acts as a type of insurance for the farmer as well as a return for the investor providing such insurance.

Looking at the evidence, however, markets failed to match Keynes' hypothesis. Kolb (1992) looked at 29 futures contracts and concluded (with some humor) that "normal backwardation is not normal." That is, the presence of backwardation does not necessarily generate positive returns in a statistically significant fashion for the investor (or that contango leads to negative returns, for that matter). This result confirmed other studies, including one by Fama and French (1987). Therefore, a more sophisticated view developed to explain futures markets in contango (i.e., when the shape of the futures price curve is upward sloping with more distant contract dates), recognizing that certain commodity futures markets often show persistently higher prices in the future as opposed to the backwardation outlined by Keynes. This view is called the Hedging Pressure Hypothesis.

3.3.1.2 Hedging Pressure Hypothesis   This perspective stemmed from multiple works, most notably outlined by De Roon, Nijman, and Veld (2000) who drew from Cootner (1960). Their research analyzed 20 futures markets from 1986 to 1994 and concluded that hedging pressure plays an important role in explaining futures returns. Hedging pressure occurs when both producers and consumers seek to protect themselves from commodity market price volatility by entering into price hedges to stabilize their projected profits and cash flow. Producers of commodities will tend or want to sell commodities forward and thus sell commodity futures. On the other side, consumers of commodities want to lock in prices of their commodity purchases and buy commodity futures. This theory applies to the aforementioned farmer selling a portion of next year's crop today. It can also apply to a central bank that wants to buy gold during each of the next 12 months as part of its monetary operations; or a refinery that may want to lock in the price of its oil purchases and, conversely, the prices of its gasoline and heating oil production.

If the two forces of producers and consumers both seeking price protection are equal in weight, then one can envision a flat commodity curve, such as Exhibit 9 illustrates. In this idealized situation, the natural needs for price insurance by commodity buyers and sellers offset each other. There is no discount on the commodity futures price required to induce speculators to accept the commodity price risk because the hedging needs of both the buyer and seller complement and offset each other.

Exhibit 9   Balanced Hedging Between Producers and Consumers

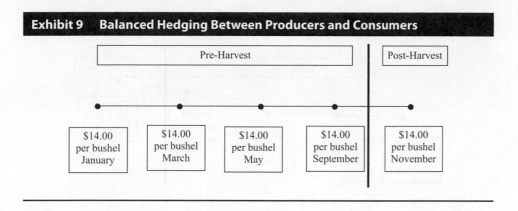

To use a different example, consider the problem of snowfall in the New England region of the United States. On one hand, small municipalities in Vermont, New Hampshire, or Maine may experience high levels of annual snowfall that are a risk to their snow removal budgets. On the other hand, ski resorts in New England have an opposite risk challenge: low snowfall creates skiing revenue shortfalls (or adds to costs because of the need for man-made snow), whereas high snowfall winters are a potential bonanza for both higher revenue and lower operating costs. This situation is another example of when the hedging needs of two parties can offset each other and create mutually beneficial outcome.

If commodity producers as a group are more interested in selling forward (seeking price insurance) than commodity consumers (as per the concept of normal backwardation), then the relative imbalance in demand for price protection will lead to the need for speculators to complete the market. But speculators will only do so when futures prices trade at a sufficient discount to compensate for the price risk they will take on. In this case, the shape and structure of the futures price curve can be illustrated as backwardation, as shown in Exhibit 10, which is consistent with Keynes' Insurance Theory.

Exhibit 10   Commodity Producers Exceed Consumers (Backwardation)

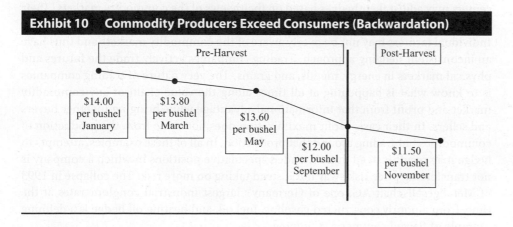

Finally, if the buyers (as a group) of soybeans are especially worried about the availability of the crop in the next harvest but producers of soybeans are less concerned about crop prices, there would be an imbalance in the demand for price insurance away from producers and to buyers. This situation would lead to a futures price curve that represents a market in contango, as illustrated in Exhibit 11. In this case, the additional demand for price insurance among buyers (versus sellers) of the commodity will lead them to bid up the futures price to induce speculators to take on this price uncertainty risk.

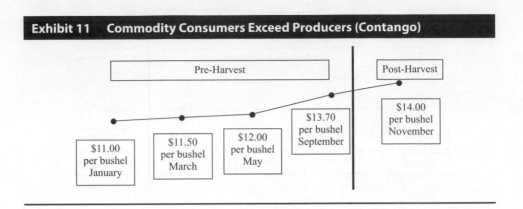

Exhibit 11   Commodity Consumers Exceed Producers (Contango)

Pre-Harvest

Post-Harvest

$11.00 per bushel January

$11.50 per bushel March

$12.00 per bushel May

$13.70 per bushel September

$14.00 per bushel November

Although this theory is more robust than the Keynes' Insurance Theory, it is still incomplete. One issue is that producers generally have greater exposure to commodity price risk than consumers do (Hicks 1939). There are companies (as well as countries) that are almost entirely dependent on commodity production and thus are very concentrated in one sector, such as energy (e.g., British Petroleum, ExxonMobil), grains (e.g., Cargill, Louis Dreyfus), and metals (e.g., BHP Billiton, Vale, Rio Tinto, Shenhua).

Commodity consumers on the other hand are very diffuse and often have other priorities (i.e., few if any individual people hedge their meat consumption or gasoline spending). Companies that purchase and use commodities in their products have a mixed record of price hedging, depending on the importance of the commodities in their cost structure. Clothing companies (e.g., Gap) generally do not hedge cotton because the spending is only a few percentage points of their expense base. Marketing and store experience (seen in rent, occupancy, and depreciation expenses) are much more important. But fast food companies hedge a wide variety of commodity inputs (e.g., livestock, grains, energy) because of the high degree of competition for prepared food at a low price point (e.g., McDonald's, Burger King, Wendy's).

In addition, both producers and consumers speculate on commodity prices, whether it is intended or unintended. Corporate treasury departments that serve as profit centers may adjust their hedges based on their views of the commodity markets. Their primary function may be to hedge, but a profit incentive can lead them to speculate. Individual farmers may not be overly aware of the commodity markets and thus have an inconsistent hedging approach. Trading companies actively trade the futures and physical markets in energy, metals, and grains. The very nature of trading companies is to know what is happening at all times along the value chain of any commodity market and profit from that informational advantage while bringing together buyers and sellers. In their case, profit maximization does not come from the production of commodities but trading around that production. In all of these examples, attempts to hedge may result instead in unintended speculative positions in which a company is not transferring price risk away but instead taking on more risk. The collapse in 1993 of Metallgesellschaft AG, one of Germany's largest industrial conglomerates at the time, from a poorly constructed gasoline, fuel oil, and heating oil hedge is a defining example of flawed commercial hedging.

In summary, despite its intuitive logic, applying the Hedging Pressure Hypothesis remains a challenge because measuring the asymmetry in hedging pressure between buyers and sellers of a commodity is very difficult.

3.3.1.3 Theory of Storage This theory, originally postulated by Kaldor (1939), focuses on how the level of commodity inventories helps shape commodity futures price curves. The key issue this theory attempts to address is whether supply or demand of the commodity dominates in terms of its price economics. Recall that commodities are physical assets, not virtual assets like stocks and bonds. Physical assets have to be stored, and storage incurs costs (rent, insurance, inspections, spoilage, etc.). Therefore, a commodity that is regularly stored should have a higher price in the future (contango) to account for those storage costs. In other words, supply dominates demand. In contrast, a commodity that is consumed along a value chain that allows for just-in-time delivery and use (i.e., minimal inventories and storage) can avoid these costs. In this situation, demand dominates supply and current prices are higher than futures prices (i.e., backwardation).

In theoretical terms, available inventory generates a benefit called a convenience yield. Having a physical supply of the commodity available is convenient for consumers of the commodity (e.g., individuals, bread companies, meat processors, refiners) because it acts as a buffer to a potential supply disruption that could otherwise force a shutdown of their operations. Because this type of risk/concern is inversely related to the inventory size and the general availability of the commodity (and confidence in its continued availability), the convenience yield is low when stock is abundant. However, the yield rises as inventories diminish and concerns regarding future availability of the commodity increase.

As a result, Theory of Storage states that futures prices can be written this way:

Futures price = Spot price of the physical commodity + Direct storage costs
(such as rent and insurance) − Convenience yield

This equation indicates that price returns and the shape of the curve can move in conjunction with the changes in the available inventory as well as actual and expected supply and demand. For example, when civil war broke out in Libya in 2011, the production of that country's high-quality crude oil was placed in jeopardy, constricting supply. In reaction, the spot price for high-quality crude oil increased. At the same time, the convenience yield decreased in the futures contracts closer to expiration because there was a scramble to tap into alternative oil supplies for European refiners. The high quality of Libyan crude oil also restricted which substitute crude oil supplies could be used to replace production from the blocked oil fields and how soon these replacements could be available. The real-world constraints and complications imposed by geography and the logistics of the oil industry resulted in a multi-month delay on replacement supplies. As a result, in the further-out (i.e., longer time to expiration) futures contracts, the reaction was muted as traders assumed that such replacement supplies would be available. Thus the convenience yield remained lower in the deferred months. For this and other reasons, crude oil was pressured to trade in backwardation during 2011.

Unfortunately, while all these theories are reasonable and attractive, they have components that are unobservable or highly volatile and, therefore, not reliably calculable. Commodity producers and consumers regard storage costs as proprietary information. Events (weather, war, technology) can radically adjust convenience yield in a short time with unknown magnitude. Corn suitable for feed may not be suitable for human consumption so defining inventories is tricky. In the end, we have frameworks and theories but they are not easily applied and require judgment and analysis by a trader or a valuation system.

EXAMPLE 13

Theories of Commodity Futures Returns (1)

Which of the following *best* describes the Insurance Theory of futures returns?

A Speculators will not provide insurance unless the futures price exceeds the spot price.

> **B** Producers of a commodity will accept a lower future price (versus the spot price) in exchange for the certainty of locking in that price.
>
> **C** Commodity futures markets result in a state of contango because of speculators insisting on a risk premium in exchange for accepting price risk.

Solution:

B is correct. Under the Insurance Theory of futures returns, Keynes stated that producers of a commodity would prefer to accept a discount on the potential future spot price in return for the certainty of knowing the future selling price in advance. A is incorrect because the futures price must be below the spot price (normal backwardation) under the Insurance Theory of futures returns. C is incorrect because the Insurance Theory of futures returns implies markets are in backwardation, not contango.

EXAMPLE 14

Theories of Commodity Futures Returns (2)

Under the Hedging Pressure Hypothesis, when hedging activity of commodity futures buyers exceeds that of commodity futures sellers, that futures market is *most likely*:

A flat.

B in contango.

C in backwardation.

Solution:

B is correct. Under the Hedging Pressure Hypothesis, a market in contango typically results when excess demand for price insurance among commodity futures buyers drives up the futures price to induce speculators to take on price uncertainty risk. A is incorrect because a flat market would likely occur if futures demand activity largely equaled that of supply. C is incorrect because under this scenario, the futures market would be in contango, not backwardation.

EXAMPLE 15

Theories of Commodity Futures Returns (3)

Under the Theory of Storage, the convenience yield is:

A not affected by the supply of a commodity.

B typically low when the supply of a commodity is scarce.

C typically high when the supply of a commodity is scarce.

Solution:

C is correct. Under the Theory of Storage, the convenience yield of a commodity increases as supply (inventories) diminish and concerns about the future availability increase. A is incorrect because supply levels have a discernible effect on the convenience yield, as mentioned. B is incorrect because the convenience yield would likely be high, as opposed to low, when supply is limited.

EXAMPLE 16

Theories of Commodity Futures Returns (4)

Which of the following represents the formula for a futures price according to the Theory of Storage?

A Futures price = Spot price of the physical commodity + Direct storage costs – Convenience yield

B Futures price = Spot price of the physical commodity + Direct storage costs + Convenience yield

C Futures price = Spot price of the physical commodity – Direct storage costs + Convenience yield.

Solution:

A is correct. According to the Theory of Storage, the futures price reflects the current spot price as well as costs incurred in actually holding the commodity until its delivery. Such costs include direct storage, such as inventory and insurance costs. Finally, because there is a convenience yield (or benefit) to owning a commodity as a form of insurance against potential supply disruptions), this term is subtracted from the current price of the commodity.

3.3.2 *Components of Futures Returns*

The total return on a commodity investment in futures is different from a total return on the physical assets. So, why do investors tend to use futures to gain their exposure to commodities? Building on the previous section, one can see that physical commodities need to be stored, fed, or perhaps treated against spoilage. Each commodity can be very different in its maintenance requirements; sustaining a hog in Mexico would be very different from storing crude oil in Nigeria.

The total return on commodity futures is traditionally analyzed into three components: the price return (or spot yield), the roll return (or roll yield) and the collateral return (or collateral yield).

The **price return** is the change in commodity futures prices, generally the front month contract. Note that this change is different from the change in the price of the physical commodity because lack of standardization of the physical markets makes that a difficult task. Calculating the price return is straightforward, as shown in the following equation:

Price return = (Current price – Previous price)/Previous price

In addition, as investors move from futures contract to contract, they must "roll" that exposure by selling the current contract as it approaches expiration and buying the next contract (assuming a long position). Depending on the shape of the futures curve, there is likely a difference between the two prices. Thus, a portfolio may require buying more far contracts than the near contracts being sold. Investors can observe this scenario if backwardation is driving the shape of the commodity futures price curve.

Example: Assume an investor has £110 of exposure in wheat futures and the near contract is worth £10 of exposure (so, the investor has £110 exposure divided by £10 per contract, or 11 contracts), but the far (i.e., longer expiration date) contract is worth only £9 of exposure. Therefore, for the investor to roll forward his contracts and maintain a constant level of exposure, he needs to roll the 11 contracts forward and also buy an additional 1 contract to keep the post-roll exposure close to the pre-roll exposure (£110 exposure divided by £9 per contract equals 12.2, or 12 contracts rounded).

In the opposite case, if the futures price curve shape is being driven by contango—with a higher futures price in the far contract—this scenario will require the purchase of fewer commodity contracts than in the near position.

Example: Assume an investor has £108 of exposure in regular unleaded gasoline (or petrol) futures and the near contract is worth £9 of exposure (so, the investor has £108 exposure divided by £9 per contract, or 12 contracts), but the far contract is worth £10 of exposure. Therefore, for the investor to roll forward her contracts and maintain a constant level of exposure, she needs to roll only 11 contracts and sell the extra 1 near contract to keep the post-roll exposure close to the pre-roll exposure (£108 exposure divided by £10 per contract equals 10.8, or 11 contracts rounded).

Note that this roll return is not a return in the sense that it can be independently captured; investors cannot construct a portfolio consisting of only roll returns. Instead, **roll return** is an accounting calculation used to replicate a portion of the total return for a fully collateralized (i.e., with no leverage) commodity index. As defined, the roll return is effectively the accounting difference (in percentage terms) between the near-term commodity futures contract price and the farther-term commodity futures contract price:[2]

Roll return = [(Near-term futures contract closing price – Farther-term futures contract closing price)/Near-term futures contract closing price] × Percentage of the position in the futures contract being rolled

As an example, consider the roll from the March contract to the April contract for WTI Crude Oil on 7 February 2014 using the S&P GSCI (formerly the Goldman Sachs Commodity Index) methodology, which rolls its positions over a five-day period (so 1/5 = 20% per day):

March contract closing price: $99.88/barrel

April contract closing price: $99.35/barrel

($99.88 – $99.35)/$99.88 = 0.53% gross roll return × 20% rollover portion
= 0.11% net roll return

Note that different indices use different periods and/or weights in their "rolling methodology." In Section 5, we will further discuss the rolling methodology of various indices.

In his book *Expected Returns*, Ilmanen (2011) raises the argument that roll return is approximately equal to a risk premium. This concept harkens back to Keynes and his theory of "normal backwardation." Keynes proposed that speculators take the other side of the transaction from commodity producers—who sell forward to lock in their cash flows—in an attempt to earn an excess return as compensation for providing price insurance to producers. Ilmanen attempts to demonstrate that positive long-run average returns are associated with positive roll return (i.e., in commodities

---

2 Roll return is sometimes defined in monetary terms rather than as a percent as here.

for which futures prices are in backwardation) and negative long-run average returns are associated with negative roll return. However, because 40% of the commodities examined (p. 255) had negative roll returns but positive total returns, one cannot directly conclude that backwardation earns a positive total return.

The **collateral return** is the yield (e.g., interest rate) for the bonds or cash used to maintain the investor's futures position(s). The minimum amount of funds is called the initial margin. If an investor has less cash than required by the exchange to maintain the position, the broker who acts as custodian will require more funds (a margin call) or close the position (buying to cover a short position or selling to eliminate a long position). Collateral thus acts as insurance for the exchange that the investor can pay for losses.

For return calculations on indexed investments, the amount of cash would be considered equal to the notional value of the futures. This approach means no leverage. For expected returns, commonly, investors should use a risk-free government bond that most closely matches the term projected. Most commodity indexes use short-term US Treasury bills, but if one is forecasting 10-year returns then, for collateral return purposes, a 10-year constant maturity government bond would have a more appropriate term.

Although indexes will be discussed more fully later in the reading, to illustrate the commodity return elements just discussed, one can use an index—in this case, the aforementioned S&P GSCI, which has the longest back tested and live history of the investable commodity indexes. Exhibit 12 shows the disaggregation of its return components.

Exhibit 12	**Average Annual Return Components of the S&P GSCI, January 1970–December 2014**			
S&P GSCI Return	**Total Return**	**Spot Return**	**Roll Return[1]**	**Collateral Return[1]**
Return[2]	8.1%	3.2%	−0.7%	5.5%
Risk[3]	19.9%	19.9%	4.7%	1.0%
Correlation[4]		0.97	0.11	0.13

[1] Roll return is defined as the excess return on the S&P GSCI minus the spot of the S&P GSCI. Collateral return is defined as the total return on the S&P GSCI minus the excess return of the S&P GSCI. The excess return measures the returns accrued from investing in uncollateralized nearby commodity futures.
[2] Monthly returns are used.
[3] Risk is defined as annualized standard deviation.
[4] Correlation with the S&P GSCI Total Return.
Source: Based on data from S&P Dow Jones indexes.

As can be seen in the table, over the past 40+ years, the S&P GSCI generated 8.1% in geometrically compounded annualized returns, with about two-thirds derived from interest rates (collateral return). The commodity price spot return component of the index (which has varied over time) contributed to approximately 40% of the total return (3.2% out of 8.1%), whereas the roll return subtracted from the overall return by −0.7% (or 70 bps) on an annualized basis. Investors can see the effect of commodities on inflation via the price return.

The volatility and correlations of the components of index returns are driven by the changes in the spot price return (effectively the same annualized standard deviation of 19.9% as the S&P GSCI with a 97% correlation). The roll return and collateral return do not drive, in general, the monthly returns historically. This link between commodity futures prices and commodity indexes helps to distinguish commodities as a separate and investable asset class.

In summary, the total return on a fully collateralized commodity futures contract can be described as the spot price return plus the roll return plus collateral return (risk free rate return). With an index, a return from rebalancing the index's component weights—a **rebalance return**—would also be added. Using historical data (at the risk of it becoming outdated over time), one can demonstratively use the total return deconstruction to analyze commodities.

EXAMPLE 17

Total Returns for Futures Contracts (1)

A commodity futures market with pricing in backwardation will exhibit which of the following characteristics?

A The roll return is usually negative.

B Rolling an expiring futures contract forward will require buying more contracts in order to maintain the same dollar position in the futures markets.

C Rolling an expiring futures contract forward will require buying fewer contracts in order to maintain the same dollar position in the futures markets.

Solution:

B is correct. Commodity futures markets in backwardation exhibit price curves in which longer-dated futures prices are priced lower than near-dated contracts, and the nearest dated contract is priced less than the current spot price. With a lower futures price on the futures curve, rolling contracts forward in backwardation would require purchasing more contracts to maintain the same dollar position. A is incorrect because the roll return is usually positive, not negative, in markets in backwardation. C is incorrect because an investor would need to purchase more, not fewer, contracts in markets in backwardation to maintain his or her total dollar position.

EXAMPLE 18

Total Returns for Futures Contracts (2)

An investor has realized a 5% price return on a commodity futures contract position and a 2.5% roll return after all her contracts were rolled forward. She had held this position for one year with required initial collateral of 10% of the position at a risk-free rate of 2% per year. Her total return on this position (annualized excluding leverage) was:

A 2.7%.

B 7.3%.

C 7.7%.

Solution:

C is correct. Total return on a commodity futures position is expressed as:

Total return = Price return + Roll return + Collateral return

In this case, she held the contracts for one year, so the price return of 5% is an annualized figure. In addition, the roll return is also an annual 2.5%. Her collateral return equals 2% per year × 10% initial collateral investment = 0.2%.

So, her total return (annualized) is

Total return = 5% + 2.5% + 0.2% = 7.7%

EXAMPLE 19

Total Returns for Futures Contracts (3)

An investor has a $10,000 position in long futures contracts for soybeans that he wants to roll forward. The current contracts, which are close to expiration, are priced at $4.00 per bushel whereas the longer term contract he wants to roll into is priced at $2.50 per bushel. What are the transactions—in terms of buying and selling new contracts—he needs to execute in order to maintain his current exposure?

A Close out (sell) 2,500 near-term contracts and initiate (buy) 4,000 of the longer-term contracts.

B Close out (buy) 2,500 near-term contracts and initiate (sell) 4,000 of the longer term contracts.

C Let the 2,500 near-term contracts expire and use any proceeds to purchase an additional 2,500 of the longer-term contracts.

Solution:

A is correct. To roll over the same level of total exposure ($10,000), he will need to do the following:
Sell:

$10,000/$4.00 per contract = 2,500 existing contracts

And replace this position by purchasing:

$10,000/$2.50 per contract = 4,000 existing contracts

3.3.3 Contango, Backwardation, and the Roll Return

To reiterate, contango and backwardation—and the resulting roll return—fundamentally reflect underlying supply and demand expectations and are accounting mechanisms for the commodity term structure. We can gain a sense of these patterns by again examining the history of an index. Recall that from January 1970 to March 2014, the historical roll return of the S&P GSCI subtracted 0.7% from the average annual total return, with a standard deviation of 4.7%. That historical roll return varied over this time period, as depicted in Exhibit 13.

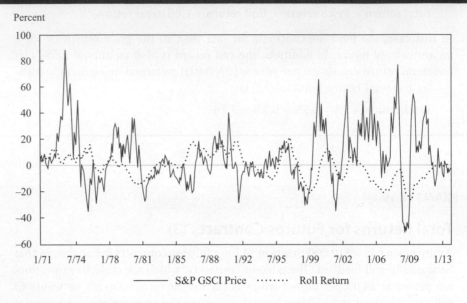

Exhibit 13   Historical One-Year S&P GSCI Price and Roll Return (Monthly Returns, January 1970–December 2014)

Note: The roll return is rolling monthly

As the graph shows, periods of either backwardation or contango do not persist indefinitely. A simple review of the Exhibit 13 history demonstrates as much. Furthermore, with a correlation of 3%, roll return is not very indicative of price return, also contrary to popular belief. Positive price returns are associated with negative roll returns as well as positive roll returns. In some cases, certain sectors are indeed associated with contango, as can be seen in Exhibit 14.

Exhibit 14   Average Annual Sector Roll Return and Standard Deviation[a]

	S&P GSCI Total	Energy	Industrial Metals	Agriculture	Livestock	Precious Metals	Softs
Mean roll return (annual)[b]	−0.7%	−0.4%	−1.3%	−4.1%	−1.4%	−5.4%	−5.5%
Standard deviation of the mean (annual)[b]	0.4%	0.8%	0.5%	0.4%	0.5%	0.2%	0.7%
Maximum roll return (annual)[b]	18.9%	31.5%	45.9%	29.3%	35.5%	−0.4%	25.6%
Minimum roll return (annual)[b]	−29.6%	−39.5%	−16.6%	−18.6%	−31.2%	−15.4%	−24.9%

[a] The periods covered vary by sector:

- S&P GSCI Total: December 1969–December 2014
- Energy: December 1982–December 2014
- Industrial Metals: December 1976–December 2014
- Agriculture: December 1969–December 2014
- Livestock: December 1969–December 2014
- Precious Metals: December 1972–December 2014
- Softs: December 1994–December 2014

Exhibit 14   (Continued)

[b] Calculated using rolling 12-month periods of monthly data.

Source: Based on data from Bloomberg and Coloma Capital Futures.

Exhibit 14 highlights a few important factors. First, industrial metals, agriculture, livestock, precious metals, and softs have statistically strong negative mean roll returns. As such, only energy has a reasonable statistical possibility of a positive mean roll return. Note from our comparison of the commodity sectors that industrial metals, agriculture, livestock, precious metals, and softs are stored for extended periods in warehouses, silos, and feedlots. In fact, precious metals historically have had negative roll returns because of gold's perpetual storage as an alternative currency. Energy is consumed on a real-time basis apart from various strategic reserves, with the minimal storage buffer thus creating a lower or negative convenience yield. One can also conclude that indexes and long-only strategies that overweight agriculture, livestock, precious metals, and softs should expect to see negative roll returns (or roll yields). Energy commodities (apart from natural gas) have the opportunity for more positive roll return. However, an index or strategy that focuses on price return has the possibility to overcome roll return (at least historically).

In conclusion, roll return can have an important impact on any single period return but overall has been relatively modest compared with price return. Furthermore, roll return is very sector dependent, which leads to a conclusion that sector diversification or concentration will have a profound impact on an investor's overall roll return based on a diversified portfolio of commodity futures.

EXAMPLE 20

Roll Return

When measuring its contribution to the total return of a commodity futures position, the roll return:

A typically has a significant contribution to total return over both single and multiple periods.

B typically has a modest contribution to total return in any single period, but can be significant over multiple periods.

C is always close to zero.

Solution:

B is correct. Historically, the roll return has had a relatively modest impact on overall commodity futures return in the short term, but can be meaningful over longer time periods. A is incorrect because the roll return is typically modest over shorter periods of time, as noted earlier. C is incorrect because futures contracts generate positive or negative roll returns, depending on the commodity and prevailing market conditions.

4   COMMODITY SWAPS

Instead of futures, some investors can gain market exposure to or hedge risk of commodities via swaps. A **commodity swap** is a legal contract involving the exchange of payments over multiple dates as determined by specified reference prices or indexes relating to commodities. In the world of commodities, a series of futures contracts often form the basis of the reference prices. For example, an independent oil refiner may want to hedge its oil purchases over an extended period. The refiner may not want to manage a large number of futures contracts, but maintain flexibility with regard to its oil supply source. By entering into a swap contract—particularly one that is cash settled instead of physically settled—the refiner can be protected from a price spike and yet maintain flexibility of delivery.

Based on this example, one can see why commercial participants use swaps: the instrument provides both risk management and risk transfer while eliminating the need to set up and manage multiple futures contracts. Swaps also provide a degree of customization not possible with standardized futures contracts. The refiner in the example may negotiate a swap for a specific quality of crude oil (e.g., Heavy Louisiana Sweet instead of West Texas Intermediate or WTI) as its reference price, or a blend of crudes that shifts throughout the year depending on the season. Customization through the use of a swap may also have value by changing the quantity of crude oil hedged over time, such as lowering the exposure during the planned shutdown and maintenance periods at the refinery.

On the other side of the transaction from the refiner (or other hedging or speculating entity) would be a swap dealer, typically a financial intermediary, such as a bank or trading company.[3] The dealer, in turn, may hedge its price risk exposure assumed in the swap through the futures market or, alternatively, negotiate its own swap with another party or arrange an oil purchase contract with a crude oil producer. The dealer may also choose to keep the price risk exposure, seeking to profit from its market information. A diagram demonstrating this swap transaction is shown in Exhibit 15.

Exhibit 15   Swap Market Participant Structure

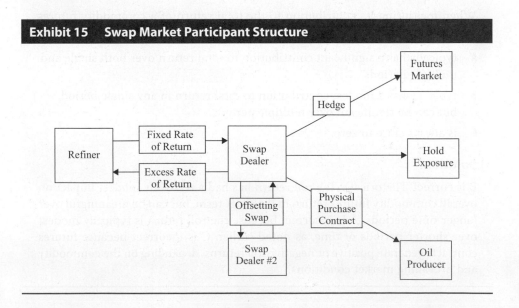

To further understand the diagram in Exhibit 15, assume we had the following scenario:

1 An oil refiner goes long a swap that pays the amount exceeding $100 per barrel every month.

2 The oil refiner would pay a swap counterparty a premium (in this example, $25) for this privilege because it is effectively long a series of call options.

The flow of funds in the swap transaction would be as shown in Exhibit 16.

Exhibit 16   Flow of Funds for Swap Transaction Example

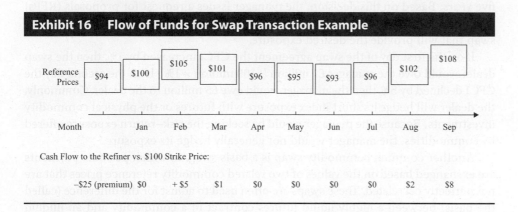

Total gain/loss on this swap to the refiner is −$9 (found by summing the cash flows and ignoring present value calculations or other considerations).

Although this example of a swap lost money and effectively increased the refiner's cost of a barrel of oil by $1 for this time period (given that the net loss on the swap was $9 over nine months), the swap protected the company against the risk of a cash squeeze during those months when an oil price spike could have impaired the liquidity of the company. The swap also defined the cost up front, giving a measure of cash flow predictability. Accounting standards and practice for swaps may also have an impact on the attractiveness of swaps. Given that oil prices are subject to many events beyond a company's control, a company looking to protect itself from financing risk may find that a swap can be a valuable tool.

There are many types of swaps available in the marketplace because they are not standardized, exchange-traded contracts like futures. The previous example of the refiner is an example of an excess return swap. In this arrangement, payments are made or received by either party based on a return calculated by changes in the level of the index relative to a benchmark or fixed level. As such, this change would be defined as the "excess" return and multiplied by some notional amount (versus the absolute level of change in the index).

Another common swap in commodities is a total return swap, in which one party receives payment based on the change in the level of an index (over consecutive valuation dates) multiplied by the notional amount of the swap. The difference between an excess return swap and a total return swap is that the latter includes the funding (i.e., collateral) portion of an index value. If the level of the index increases, the swap buyer receives payment net of the fee paid to the seller; if the level of the index decreases between two valuation dates, the swap seller receives payment (plus the fee charged to the buyer). This type of swap is generally used by large institutional investors (e.g., pension plans) as opposed to commodity producers or buyers. With a total return swap, the investor seeks exposure to commodity returns, often because of the low return correlation of commodities with other asset classes (e.g., stocks or bonds) or as a reflection of the view that commodities provide a valuable inflation hedge for asset/

liability matching (or ALM). Therefore, such investors would engage in a total return swap that provides them with long exposure to the future returns from a commodity index that is used as the reference price.

As an example of a total return swap, assume an investor who manages a defined benefit retirement plan desires commodity exposure for the reasons noted earlier. Given the size of the portfolio manager's plan assets (assume £2 billion), the manager is seeking approximately 5% exposure of plan assets to commodities. More specifically, the manager has decided that this £100 million exposure (5% of £2 billion) should be to the (hypothetical) China Futures Commodity Index (CFCI) and should remain for five years. Based on this decision, the manager issues a request for proposals (RFPs) and, after evaluating the various bidders, contracts with a Swiss bank for a total return swap that will provide the desired exposure.

If on the first day of the swap agreement the CFCI increased by 1%, then the swap dealer would owe the manager £1 million (£100 million × 1%). If on the second day the CFCI declined by 5%, then the manager would owe £5 million to the dealer. Commonly, the dealer will hedge its short index exposure with futures or the physical commodity investments. Because the manager would be seeking the risk–return exposure offered by commodities, the manager would not generally hedge its exposure.

Another common commodity swap is a basis swap, in which periodic payments are exchanged based on the values of two related commodity reference prices that are not perfectly correlated. These swaps are often used to adjust for the difference (called the basis) between a highly liquid futures contract in a commodity and an illiquid but related material. For example, a swap may pay the difference between the average daily prices of Brent Crude Oil (very liquid) and heavy crude oil available for delivery in the Gulf of Mexico (very illiquid). This can be a very valuable arrangement for, in this example, refineries on the US Gulf Coast that have heavily invested in processing cheaper heavy crudes that come from such countries as Mexico or Venezuela. Because prices of these crudes do not always move in tandem with more common crudes like Brent, they derive a price basis between the two. It should be noted that "basis" has other meanings as well depending on the commodity in question. For example, in grains, the basis may refer to the difference between the soybean contract and physical soybeans available for delivery at the Mississippi River.

Two final types of relatively common commodity swaps are variance swaps and volatility swaps. Variance swaps of commodities are similar in concept to variance swaps of equities in that there is a variance buyer and a variance seller. Two parties agree to periodically exchange payments based on the proportional difference between an observed/actual variance in the price levels of a commodity (over consecutive time periods), and some fixed amount of variance established at the outset of the contract. If this difference is positive, the variance swap buyer receives a payment; if it is negative, the variance swap seller receives payment. Often the variance differences (observed versus fixed) are capped to limit upside and losses.

Volatility commodity swaps are very similar to variance swaps, with the exception that the direction and amount of payments are determined relative to the observed versus expected volatility for a reference price commodity. In this arrangement, the two sides are not speculating on the level or direction of prices but instead on how volatile prices will be versus expectations. A volatility seller will profit if realized volatility is lower than expectations, whereas the counterparty volatility buyer anticipates higher than expected volatility.

EXAMPLE 21

Commodity Swaps (1)

A portfolio manager enters into a $100 million (notional) total return commodity swap to obtain a long position in commodity exposure. The position is reset monthly against a broad-based commodity index. At the end of the first month, the index is up 3% and at the end of the second month, the index declines 2%. What are two payments that would occur between the portfolio manager and the swap dealer on the other side of the swap transaction?

A No payments are exchanged because a net cash flow only occurs when the swap agreement expires.

B $3 million would be paid by the swap dealer to the portfolio manager (after Month 1) and $2 million would be paid by the portfolio manager to the swap dealer (after Month 2).

C $3 million would be paid by the portfolio manager to the swap dealer (after Month 1) and $2 million would be paid by the swap dealer to the portfolio manager (after Month 2).

Solution:

B is correct. Because the portfolio manager has a long position in the total return commodity swap, he or she will receive payments when the commodity index rises and make payments when the commodity index declines. The payment calculations after the first two months are as follows:

Month 1: $100 million × 3% = $3 million

Month 2: $100 million × −2% = −$2 million

A is incorrect because swap payments are made periodically (in this case monthly) and not withheld to the end of the contract. C is incorrect because the payments would be in the opposite direction for each month.

EXAMPLE 22

Commodity Swaps (2)

In a commodity volatility swap, the direction and amount of payments are determined relative to the observed versus reference:

A direction in the price of a commodity.

B variance for the price of a commodity.

C volatility for the price of a commodity.

Solution:

C is correct. In a commodity volatility swap, the two sides of the transaction are speculating on expected volatility. A volatility seller will profit if realized volatility is lower than expectations, whereas the volatility buyer benefits from higher than expected volatility. A is incorrect because a volatility swap is based on price volatility, not direction. B is incorrect because a volatility swap is based on price volatility as opposed to price variance (price volatility squared).

5   COMMODITY INDEXES

As in other parts of the investment universe, indexes have been created to portray the aggregate movement of commodity prices, investment vehicles, and investing approaches. In fact, one could say that an asset class does not exist without the presence of at least one representative index. From a practical perspective, indexes allow reference pricing for financial contracts, such as for the swaps mentioned previously.

Commodity indexes play three primary roles in commodity sector investments. First, an index can be used as a benchmark to evaluate broader moves in commodity pricing. Second, as a broad indicator, an index can be used for macroeconomic or forecasting purposes by examining statistically significant relationships between movements in the commodity index and other macroeconomic variables. Finally, an index can act as the basis for an investment vehicle or contract providing the information needed to record, monitor, and evaluate price changes that affect contract value.

Although there are a number of commodity indexes, the following are used most frequently for the purposes just mentioned: (1) the S&P GSCI; (2) the Bloomberg Commodity Index (BCOM), formerly known as the Dow Jones–UBS Commodity Index (DJ–UBS); (3) the Deutsche Bank Liquid Commodity Index (DBLCI); (4) the Thomson Reuters/CoreCommodity CRB Index (TR/CC CRB); and (5) the Rogers International Commodities Index (RICI). The following are key characteristics that differentiate each of these indexes:

- The *breadth* of coverage (number of commodities and sectors) included in each index, noting that some commodities have multiple reference contracts (e.g., for crude oil, the common contracts are for West Texas Intermediate in the United States and Brent Crude for Europe).

- The relative *weightings* assigned to each component/commodity, and the related methodology for how these weights are determined.

- The *rolling methodology* for determining how those contracts that are about to expire are rolled over into future months. This decision has a direct impact on the roll return (or yield) of the overall commodity. Recall that roll return is one of the three key components of overall commodity returns.

- The methodology and frequency for *rebalancing* the weights of the individual commodities, sectors, and contracts in the index to maintain the relative weightings assigned to each investment. As with stocks and bonds within a portfolio, the opportunity to earn positive rebalance returns for commodities depends on the correlation of the underlying components of the index and the propensity of underperforming components to revert back to the mean. For example, a drought may cause cotton prices to increase, but a strong crop the following year will cause prices to collapse. A rebalance sale of the overvalued cotton exposure into an undervalued exposure should "lock in" some of that gain. The rebalance return will likely vary depending on the methodology used by the index.

- The *governance* of indexes is important because it is the process by which all the aforementioned rules are implemented. For example, some indexes are rules-based, whereas others are selection-based. The rules-based indexes follow a quantitative methodology, whereas selection-based indexes are more qualitative in that an index committee picks the commodities. Also, governance oversees the independence of index providers so that, according to best practices of the Index Industry Association, the asset price should be independent from the index provider, which, in turn, should be independent from the product provider (e.g., the exchange-traded fund or swap provider).

For the index to be a viable and useful construct, it should be investable—that is, investors or their agents should be able to replicate the methodology outlined to translate the index concept into a representation of the asset class. For this reason, index providers and investors must be mindful of the venues (physical or electronic) for trading each commodity index, the liquidity and turnover of contracts based on each commodity index, and the term structure of each index (i.e., how far into the future the index extends and which months it covers). The weighting method for components in an index is key to diversification and—combined with rebalancing frequency—influences the opportunity to earn positive rebalance returns.

An index that requires investments in exchanges all over the world is more difficult and expensive for an investor to replicate. An emphasis on illiquid contracts has a negative impact on transaction costs. Contracts without a full yield curve may be a challenge to analyze and trade. In other words, seemingly small execution concerns are magnified when constructing a benchmark that represents an entire asset class like commodities. And indexes that choose (perhaps inadvertently) contracts that more commonly trade in backwardation may appear to improve forward-looking performance (because this generates a positive roll return), whereas those that more commonly trade in contango may hurt performance. Exhibit 17 summarizes the various elements of the main indexes discussed.

Exhibit 17　Overview of Major Commodity Indexes

			Index		
Element	S&P GSCI	BCOM	DBLCI	TR/CC CRB	RICI
Adoption date	1991	1998	2003	2005 (current version)	1998
Number of commodities	24	22	14	19	37
Weighting method	Production weighted	Production and liquidity weighted	Fixed weight	Fixed weight	Fixed weight
Rolling methodology	Nearby most liquid contract, monthly	Front month to next or second month	Optimized on roll return	Front month to next month	Front month to next month
Rebalancing frequency	Annual	Annual	Annual	Monthly	Monthly
Individual investor funds available?	Yes	Yes	Yes	No (although there is an exchange-traded fund on a related index)	No

Note: Information is as of 1 August 2014.
Source: Information from respective sponsor websites, Bloomberg, and authors' research.

Exhibit 17 helps distinguish the key characteristics that differentiate these five commercially important commodity indexes. In terms of coverage (the number of commodities and sectors included in the index), all five of these indexes have broad sector coverage, including energy, grains, livestock, precious metals, industrial metals, and softs. The only exception is the DBLCI, which does not have any softs or livestock exposure. At the other extreme, the RICI includes relatively exotic (and thus illiquid) commodities, such as lumber, oats, and rubber. As a further example of its unique nature, the RICI once included adzuki beans (the red beans found in many Asian cuisines) and palm oil.[4]

5.1 S&P GSCI

The S&P GSCI is the oldest of the selected commodity indexes. The index is based on 24 commodities and applies liquidity screens to include only those contracts with an established minimum level of trading volume and available historical pricing. It uses a world production value-weighting scheme that gives the largest weight to the most valuable commodity on the basis of physical trade value. It should be no surprise that crude oil has the highest single weight and energy has the highest sector weight (historically as high as 80%) in this index. This approach is most similar to a market-capitalization weighted index of nearly all major bond and stock market indexes. Like some market-capitalization indexes (particularly in emerging or frontier markets), the resulting weights of the S&P GSCI can be highly concentrated. The rolling methodology focuses on owning the front (i.e., near-term) contracts to address the highest liquidity and where supply and demand shocks are most likely to have an impact.

5.2 Bloomberg Commodity Index

The BCOM (formerly the DJ–UBS) is based on 22 commodities. It includes liquidity as both a weighting factor and screening factor, although the index is selection-based, meaning a committee uses judgment to pick the included commodities. The rules of index construction also place caps on the size of the sectors (33% maximum) and floors on individual commodities (2% minimum). These differences mean that very different index composition and weights can occur. For example, the energy sector currently dominates the S&P GSCI (as high as 80% weight), whereas the BCOM's exposure is much lower (approximately 30%). However, exposure to natural gas as a single component of energy is higher in the BCOM (approximately 9%) than in the S&P GSCI (approximately 3%). Given that natural gas had an annualized roll cost of about 19% (often the highest roll cost of all the commodities), the higher weighting of natural gas in the BCOM implies that the index has to find other sources of return (e.g., price return and rebalance return) to overcome the drag that natural gas inventory storage creates through negative roll return. The rolling methodology focuses on owning the front (i.e., near-term) contracts.

5.3 Deutsche Bank Liquid Commodity Index

The DBLCI uses a fixed-weighting scheme to allocate exposure. The most notable/unique feature of this index is its rolling methodology. Instead of focusing on near-term contracts, it is optimized based on the time value of maximized backwardation/minimized contango for the contracts that fall within the next 12 calendar months. As an example, a June 2014 copper futures contract may be at 1% backwardation versus May 2014 copper contract. But if the July 2014 copper contract is at a 3% backwardation (1.5% per month, or 3% divided by two months) versus the 1% backwardation per month on the June 2014 contract, then the DBLCI will roll to the July 2014 contract in preference to the June 2014 contract. Therefore, one could argue the DBLCI takes an active decision with regards to roll return positioning as compared with the other indexes.

---

4 Perhaps this uniqueness is not so unusual given that the sponsor is Jim Rogers, known for his unique investment style.

5.4 Thomson Reuters/CoreCommodity CRB Index

The TR/CC CRB consists of 19 commodities and is a continuation of the first investable commodities index published by the Commodities Research Bureau in 1978 (although an earlier iteration started in 1957). It uses a fixed-weighting scheme to allocate exposure. An index management committee decides the weights based on a number of factors, including diversification, sector representation, liquidity, and economic importance. It also clusters the fixed weights into a number of tiers. As a result, constituents are moved from tier to tier. The rolling methodology focuses on owning the front (i.e., near-term) contracts that mechanically focus on the front month or second front month and do not require a particular calculation.

5.5 Rogers International Commodity Index

The RICI uses a fixed-weighting scheme to allocate exposure among 37 different commodities and was designed by investor Jim Rogers in the late 1990s. An index management committee decides the weights based on a number of factors, including diversification, sector representation, liquidity, and economic importance. Like the TR/CC CRB index, it also clusters the fixed weights into a number of tiers. As a result, constituents are moved from tier to tier as they gain or lose relative importance as seen by the committee. Energy is the largest weight but still a highly diversified basket. Some energy constituents are denominated in non-US dollar terms—such as rubber (traded in Japan in Japanese yen) and cocoa (traded in London in British pounds)—which potentially adds a foreign exchange exposure element to the index returns.

5.6 Rebalancing Frequency

Rebalancing frequency plays a role in index returns, especially for those indexes that rebalance more frequently, such as the TR/CC CRB and RICI. Theoretically, from portfolio management theory, rebalancing is more important if a market is frequently mean reverting because there are more peaks to sell and valleys to buy. However, frequent rebalancing can lead to underperformance in a trending market because the outperforming assets are sold but continue up in price, whereas the underperforming assets are purchased but still drift lower.

The relative performance of the monthly rebalanced indexes (TR/CC CRB and RICI) versus the annual rebalance of the other indexes will depend on the length of time of price trends: more frequent mean reversions should favor the former two indexes, but a longer-term trend will more likely favor the annually rebalancing indexes. If an index uses a floating weighting scheme, such as production value (fully or partially), then the higher (lower) futures prices usually coincide with higher (lower) physical prices. Therefore, with this kind of approach, the magnitude of rebalancing weights are generally lower than a fixed-weight scheme because the post-rebalance weights will generally drift in line with the current portfolio weights. As a result, the S&P GSCI and BCOM indexes typically have lower rebalancing costs and—in a trending market—have an opportunity to outperform their fixed-weight index counterparts, particularly those that have a relatively frequent rebalance period.

5.7 Commodity Index Summary

There is no dominant index based on a particular methodology. Relative performance will occur based on the circumstances of the markets and the time period examined. Evaluating which index is superior for a *long-term* investment generates modest if any value. Per the authors' research, these indexes have been all both highly correlated (well above 70%) with each other, and have had low (roughly 0%) correlations with traditional asset classes (e.g., US large-cap stocks, US bonds, international stocks). As with equities, for which there are many different index providers, commodity indexes act in parallel even when their returns (and Sharpe ratios) frequently differ dramatically over time.

EXAMPLE 23

Commodity Indexes (1)

All else being equal, compared with an equally weighted commodity index, a production value-weighted index (such as the S&P GSCI) will be:

A   less sensitive to energy sector returns.

B   more sensitive to energy sector returns.

C   equally sensitive to energy sector returns.

Solution:

B is correct. The energy sector will comprise a sizable portion of a production value-weighted index, and thus will be a meaningful driver of returns for such an index. A is incorrect because a production value-weighted index will be more, not less, sensitive to the energy sector. C is incorrect because a production value-weighted index will be more, not equally, sensitive to the energy sector.

EXAMPLE 24

Commodity Indexes (2)

Which of the following statements is **not** correct regarding commodity futures indexes?

A   Commodity sectors in backwardation typically improve index returns.

B   An index that invests in several futures exchanges provides a high degree of diversification.

C   Total returns of the major commodity indexes have low correlation with traditional asset classes, such as equities and bonds.

Solution:

B is correct. Commodity futures exchanges throughout the world are highly correlated and thus provide little diversification benefits. A is incorrect because markets in backwardation typically have positive roll yields, and thus will likely improve index returns (although the price return may still not be positive and thus the total return may still be negative). C is incorrect because commodity index returns do indeed have historically low correlation with equities and bonds.

SUMMARY

- Commodities are a diverse asset class comprised of various sectors: energy, grains, industrial (base) metals, livestock, precious metals, and softs (cash crops). Each of these sectors has a number of characteristics that are important in determining the supply and demand for each commodity, including ease of storage, geo-politics, and weather.

- The life cycle of commodities varies considerably depending on the economic, technical and structural (i.e., industry, value chain) profile of each commodity as well as the sector. A short life cycle allows for relatively rapid adjustment to outside events, whereas a long life cycle generally limits the ability of the market to react.

- The valuation of commodities relative to that of equities and bonds can be summarized by noting that equities and bonds represent financial assets whereas commodities are physical assets. The valuation of commodities is not based on the estimation of future profitability and cash flows but rather on a discounted forecast of future possible prices based on such factors as the supply and demand of the physical item.

- The commodity trading environment is similar to other asset classes, with three types of trading participants: (1) informed investors/hedgers, (2) speculators, and (3) arbitrageurs.

- Commodities have two general pricing forms: spot prices in the physical markets and futures prices for later delivery. The spot price is the current price to deliver or purchase a physical commodity at a specific location. A futures price is an exchange-based price agreed on to deliver or receive a defined quantity and often quality of a commodity at a future date.

- The difference between spot and futures prices is generally called the basis. When the spot price is higher than the futures price, it is called backwardation, and when it is lower it is called contango. Backwardation and contango are also used to describe the relationship between two futures contracts of the same commodity.

- Commodity contracts can be settled by either cash or physical delivery.

- There are three primary theories of futures returns.

  - In Insurance Theory, commodity producers who are long the physical good are motived to sell the commodity for future delivery to hedge their production price risk exposure.

  - The Hedging Pressure Hypothesis describes when producers along with consumers seek to protect themselves from commodity market price volatility by entering into price hedges to stabilize their projected profits and cash flow.

  - The Theory of Storage focuses on supply and demand dynamics of commodity inventories, including the concept of "convenience yield."

- The total return of a fully collateralized commodity futures contract can be quantified as the spot price return plus the roll return plus the collateral return (risk-free rate return).

- The roll return is effectively the weighted accounting difference (in percentage terms) between the near-term commodity futures contract price and the farther-term commodity futures contract price.

- ▪ A commodity swap is a legal contract calling for the exchange of payments over multiple dates as determined by several reference prices or indexes.

- ▪ The most relevant commodity swaps include excess return swaps, total return swaps, basis swaps, and variance/volatility swaps.

- ▪ The five primary commodity indexes based on assets are (1) the S&P GSCI; (2) the Bloomberg Commodity Index, formerly the Dow Jones–UBS Commodity Index; (3) the Deutsche Bank Liquid Commodity Index; (4) the Thomson Reuters/CoreCommodity CRB Index; and (5) the Rogers International Commodities Index.

- ▪ The key differentiating characteristics of commodity indexes are

  - ● the breadth and selection methodology of coverage (number of commodities and sectors) included in each index, noting that some commodities have multiple reference contracts.

  - ● the relative weightings assigned to each component/commodity, and the related methodology for how these weights are determined.

  - ● the methodology and frequency for rolling the individual futures contracts.

  - ● the methodology and frequency for rebalancing the weights of the individual commodities and sectors.

  - ● the governance that determines which commodities are selected.

REFERENCES:

Cootner, Paul H. 1960. "Returns to Speculators: Telser versus Keynes." *Journal of Political Economy*, vol. 68, no. 4 (August): 396–404.

De Roon, Frans A., Theo E. Nijman, and Chris Veld. 2000. "Hedging Pressure Effects in Futures Markets." *Journal of Finance*, vol. 55, no. 3 (June): 1437–1456.

Erb, Claude B., and Campbell R. Harvey. 2006. "The Strategic and Tactical Value of Commodity Futures." *Financial Analysts Journal*, vol. 62, no. 2 (March/April): 69–97.

Fama, Eugene F., and Kenneth R. French. 1987. "Commodity Futures Prices: Some Evidence on Forecast Power, Premiums and the Theory of Storage." *Journal of Business*, vol. 60, no. 1 (January): 55–73.

Gorton, Gary, and K. Geert Rouwenhorst. 2006. "Facts and Fantasies about Commodity Futures." *Financial Analysts Journal*, vol. 62, no. 2 (March/April): 47–68.

Hicks, John R. 1939. *Value and Capital: An Inquiry Into Some Fundamental Principles of Economic Theory*. London: Oxford University Press.

Ilmanen, Antti. 2011. *Expected Returns: An Investor's Guide to Harvesting Market Rewards*. Hoboken, NJ: John Wiley & Sons.

Kaldor, Nicholas. 1939. "Speculation and Economic Stability." *Review of Economic Studies*, vol. 7, no. 1 (October): 1–27.

Keynes, John M. 1930. *A Treatise on Money, Volume 2: The Applied Theory of Money*. London: Macmillan.

Kolb, Robert W. 1992. "Is Normal Backwardation Normal?" *Journal of Futures Markets*, vol. 12, no. 1 (February): 75–91.

Portfolio Management

TOPIC LEVEL LEARNING OUTCOME

The candidate should be able to explain and demonstrate the use of portfolio theory in risk and return estimation, security selection, and other practical applications. The candidate should also be able to explain the portfolio management process.

16

Portfolio Management

Process, Asset Allocation, and Risk Management

The first reading in this study session explains the portfolio management process. The second reading describes multifactor models of asset returns and selected applications of such models. The final reading introduces investment risk measurement and management.

READING ASSIGNMENTS

READING

47

The Portfolio Management Process and the Investment Policy Statement

by John L. Maginn, CFA, Donald L. Tuttle, PhD, CFA,
Dennis W. McLeavey, CFA, and Jerald E. Pinto, PhD, CFA

John L. Maginn, CFA (USA). Donald L. Tuttle, PhD, CFA (USA). Dennis W. McLeavey, CFA, is at the University of Rhode Island (USA). Jerald E. Pinto, PhD, CFA, is at CFA Institute (USA).

LEARNING OUTCOMES

Mastery	The candidate should be able to:
☐	a. explain the importance of the portfolio perspective;
☐	b. describe the steps of the portfolio management process and the components of those steps;
☐	c. explain the role of the investment policy statement in the portfolio management process and describe the elements of an investment policy statement;
☐	d. explain how capital market expectations and the investment policy statement help influence the strategic asset allocation decision and how an investor's investment time horizon may influence the investor's strategic asset allocation;
☐	e. define investment objectives and constraints and explain and distinguish among the types of investment objectives and constraints;
☐	f. contrast the types of investment time horizons, determine the time horizon for a particular investor, and evaluate the effects of this time horizon on portfolio choice;
☐	g. justify ethical conduct as a requirement for managing investment portfolios.

1   INTRODUCTION

In setting out to master the concepts and tools of portfolio management, we first need a coherent description of the portfolio management process. The portfolio management process is an integrated set of steps undertaken in a consistent manner to create and maintain an appropriate portfolio (combination of assets) to meet clients' stated goals. The process we present in this reading is a distillation of the shared elements of current practice.

Because it serves as the foundation for the process, we also introduce the investment policy statement through a discussion of its main components. An investment policy statement (IPS) is a written document that clearly sets out a client's return objectives and risk tolerance over that client's relevant time horizon, along with applicable constraints such as liquidity needs, tax considerations, regulatory requirements, and unique circumstances.

The portfolio management process moves from planning, through execution, and then to feedback. In the planning step, investment objectives and policies are formulated, capital market expectations are formed, and strategic asset allocations are established. In the execution step, the portfolio manager constructs the portfolio. In the feedback step, the manager monitors and evaluates the portfolio compared with the plan. Any changes suggested by the feedback must be examined carefully to ensure that they represent long-run considerations.

The investment policy statement provides the foundation of the portfolio management process. In creating an IPS, the manager writes down the client's special characteristics and needs. The IPS must clearly communicate the client's objectives and constraints. The IPS thereby becomes a plan that can be executed by any advisor or portfolio manager the client might subsequently hire. A properly developed IPS disciplines the portfolio management process and helps ensure against ad hoc revisions in strategy.

When combined with capital market expectations, the IPS forms the basis for a strategic asset allocation. Capital market expectations concern the risk and return characteristics of capital market instruments such as stocks and bonds. The strategic asset allocation establishes acceptable exposures to IPS-permissible asset classes to achieve the client's long-run objectives and constraints.

The portfolio perspective underlies the portfolio management process and IPS. The next sections illustrate this perspective.

2   INVESTMENT MANAGEMENT

Investment management is the service of professionally investing money. As a profession, investment management has its roots in the activities of European investment bankers in managing the fortunes created by the Industrial Revolution. By the beginning of the 21st century, investment management had become an important part of the financial services sector of all developed economies. By the end of 2003, the United States alone had approximately 15,000 money managers (registered investment advisors) responsible for investing more than $23 trillion, according to the *Directory of Registered Investment Advisors* (Standard & Poor's, 2004). No worldwide count of investment advisors is available, but looking at another familiar professionally managed investment, the number of mutual funds stood at about 54,000 at year-end 2003; of these funds only 15 percent were US based.[1]

The economics of investment management are relatively simple. An investment manager's revenue is fee driven; primarily, fees are based on a percentage of the average amount of assets under management and the type of investment program run for the client, as spelled out in detail in the investment management contract or other governing document. Consequently, an investment management firm's size is judged by the amount of assets under management, which is thus directly related to manager's revenue, another measure of size. Traditionally, the value of an investment management business (or a first estimate of value) is determined as a multiple of its annual fee income.

To understand an investment management firm or product beyond its size, we need to know not only its investment disciplines but also the type or types of investor it primarily serves. Broadly speaking, investors can be described as institutional or individual. Institutional investors are entities such as pension funds, foundations and endowments, insurance companies, and banks that ultimately serve as financial intermediaries between individuals and financial markets. The investment policy decisions of institutional investors are typically made by investment committees or trustees, with at least some members having a professional background in finance. The committee members or trustees frequently also bear a fiduciary relationship to the funds for which they have investment responsibility. Such a relationship, if it is present, imposes some legal standards regarding processes and decisions, which is reflected in the processes of the investment managers who serve that market segment.

Beginning in the second half of the 20th century, the tremendous growth of institutional investors, especially defined benefit pension plans, spurred a tremendous expansion in investment management firms or investment units of other entities (such as bank trust divisions) to service their needs.[2] As the potentially onerous financial responsibilities imposed on the sponsors by such plans became more evident, however, the 1980s and 1990s saw trends to other types of retirement schemes focused on participant responsibility for investment decisions and results. In addition, a long-lasting worldwide economic expansion created a great amount of individual wealth. As a result, investment advisors oriented to serving high-net-worth individuals as well as mutual funds (which serve the individual and, to a lesser extent, the smaller institutional market) gained in relative importance.

Such individual-investor-oriented advisors may incorporate a heavy personal financial planning emphasis in their services. Many wealthy families establish family offices to serve as trusted managers of their finances. Family offices are entities, typically organized and owned by a family, that assume responsibility for services such as financial planning, estate planning, and asset management, as well as a range of practical matters from tax return preparation to bill paying. Some family offices evolve such depth in professional staff that they open access to their services to other families (multi-family offices). In contrast to family offices, some investment management businesses service both individual and institutional markets, sometimes in separate divisions or corporate units, sometimes worldwide, and sometimes as part of a financial giant (American Express and Citigroup are examples of such financial supermarkets). In such cases, wrap-fee accounts packaging the services of outside

---

1 These facts are based on statistics produced by the Investment Company Institute and the International Investment Funds Association.

2 A defined benefit pension plan specifies the plan sponsor's obligations in terms of benefit to plan participants. The plan sponsor bears the investment risk of such plans.

investment managers may vie for the client's business with in-house, separately managed accounts, as well as in-house mutual funds, external mutual funds, and other offerings marketed by a brokerage arm of the business.

Investment management companies employ portfolio managers, analysts, and traders, as well as marketing and support personnel. Portfolio managers may use both outside research produced by **sell-side analysts** (analysts employed by brokerages) and research generated by in-house analysts—so-called **buy-side analysts** (analysts employed by an investment manager or institutional investor). The staffing of in-house research departments depends on the size of the investment management firm, the variety of investment offerings, and the investment disciplines employed. An example may illustrate the variety of talent employed: The research department of one money manager with $30 billion in assets under management employs 34 equity analysts, 23 credit analysts, 3 hedge fund analysts, 12 quantitative analysts, 4 risk management professionals, 1 economist, and 1 economic analyst. That same company has a trading department with 8 equity and 8 bond traders and many support personnel. CFA charterholders can be found in all of these functions.

3   THE PORTFOLIO PERSPECTIVE

The portfolio perspective is our focus on the aggregate of all the investor's holdings: the portfolio. Because economic fundamentals influence the average returns of many assets, the risk associated with one asset's returns is generally related to the risk associated with other assets' returns. If we evaluate the prospects of each asset in isolation and ignore their interrelationships, we will likely misunderstand the risk and return prospects of the investor's total investment position—our most basic concern.

The historical roots of this portfolio perspective date to the work of Nobel laureate Harry Markowitz (1952). Markowitz and subsequent researchers, such as Jack Treynor and Nobel laureate William Sharpe, established the field of modern portfolio theory (MPT)—the analysis of rational portfolio choices based on the efficient use of risk. Modern portfolio theory revolutionized investment management. First, professional investment practice began to recognize the importance of the portfolio perspective in achieving investment objectives. Second, MPT helped spread the knowledge and use of quantitative methods in portfolio management. Today, quantitative and qualitative concepts complement each other in investment management practice.

In developing his theory of portfolio choice, Markowitz began with the perspective of investing for a single period. Others, including Nobel laureate Robert Merton, explored the dynamics of portfolio choice in a multiperiod setting. These subsequent contributions have greatly enriched the content of MPT.

If Markowitz, Merton, and other researchers created the supply, three developments in the investment community created demand for the portfolio perspective. First, institutional investing emerged worldwide to play an increasingly dominant role in financial markets. Measuring and controlling the risk of large pools of money became imperative. The second development was the increasing availability of ever-cheaper computer processing power and communications possibilities. As a result, a broader range of techniques for implementing MPT portfolio concepts became feasible. The third related development was the professionalization of the investment management field. This professionalization has been reflected in the worldwide growth of the professional accreditation program leading to the Chartered Financial Analyst (CFA®) designation.

PORTFOLIO MANAGEMENT AS A PROCESS

4

The unified presentation of portfolio management as a process represented an important advance in the investment management literature. Prior to the introduction of this concept in the first edition of this book, much of the traditional literature reflected an approach of selecting individual securities without an overall plan. Through the eyes of the professional, however, portfolio management is a *process*, an integrated set of activities that combine in a logical, orderly manner to produce a desired product. The process view is a *dynamic* and *flexible* concept that applies to all types of portfolio investments—bonds, stocks, real estate, gold, collectibles; to various organizational types—trust company, investment counsel firm, insurance company, mutual fund; to a full range of investors—individuals, pension plans, endowments, foundations, insurance companies, banks; and is independent of manager, location, investment philosophy, style, or approach. Portfolio management is a continuous and systematic process complete with feedback loops for monitoring and rebalancing. The process can be as loose or as disciplined, as quantitative or as qualitative, and as simple or as complex as its operators desire.

The portfolio management process is the same in every application: an integrated set of steps undertaken in a consistent manner to create and maintain appropriate combinations of investment assets. In the next sections, we explore the main features of this process.

THE PORTFOLIO MANAGEMENT PROCESS LOGIC

5

Three elements in managing any business process are planning, execution, and feedback. These same elements form the basis for the portfolio management process as depicted in Figure 1.

5.1 The Planning Step

The planning step is described in the four leftmost boxes in Figure 1. The top two boxes represent investor-related input factors, while the bottom two factors represent economic and market input.

5.1.1 *Identifying and Specifying the Investor's Objectives and Constraints*

The first task in investment planning is to identify and specify the investor's objectives and constraints. **Investment objectives** are desired investment outcomes. In investments, objectives chiefly pertain to return and risk. Constraints are limitations on the investor's ability to take full or partial advantage of particular investments. For example, an investor may face constraints related to the concentration of holdings as a result of government regulation, or restrictions in a governing legal document. Constraints are either internal, such as a client's specific liquidity needs, time horizon, and unique circumstances, or external, such as tax issues and legal and regulatory requirements. In Section 6, we examine the objective and constraint specification process.

5.1.2 *Creating the Investment Policy Statement*

Once a client has specified a set of objectives and constraints, the manager's next task is to formulate the investment policy statement. The IPS serves as the governing document for all investment decision-making. In addition to objectives and constraints, the IPS may also cover a variety of other issues. For example, the IPS generally details

Figure 1   The Portfolio Construction, Monitoring, and Revision Process

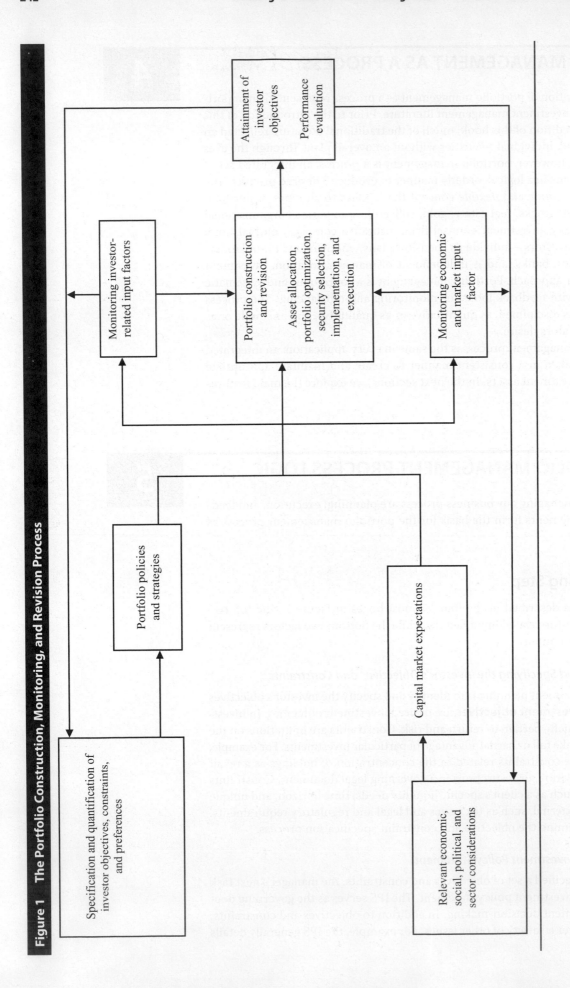

reporting requirements, rebalancing guidelines, frequency and format of investment communication, manager fees, investment strategy, and the desired investment style or styles of investment managers. A typical IPS includes the following elements:

- a brief client description;

- the purpose of establishing policies and guidelines;

- the duties and investment responsibilities of parties involved, particularly those relating to fiduciary duties, communication, operational efficiency, and accountability. Parties involved include the client, any investment committee, the investment manager, and the bank custodian;

- the statement of investment goals, objectives, and constraints;

- the schedule for review of investment performance as well as the IPS itself;

- performance measures and benchmarks to be used in performance evaluation;

- any considerations to be taken into account in developing the strategic asset allocation;

- investment strategies and investment style(s); and

- guidelines for rebalancing the portfolio based on feedback.

The IPS forms the basis for the strategic asset allocation, which reflects the interaction of objectives and constraints with the investor's long-run capital market expectations. When experienced professionals include the policy allocation as part of the IPS, they are implicitly forming capital market expectations and also examining the interaction of objectives and constraints with long-run capital market expectations. In practice, one may see IPSs that include strategic asset allocations, but we will maintain a distinction between the two types.

The planning process involves the concrete elaboration of an **investment strategy**—that is, the manager's approach to investment analysis and security selection. A clearly formulated investment strategy organizes and clarifies the basis for investment decisions. It also guides those decisions toward achieving investment objectives. In the broadest sense, investment strategies are passive, active, or semiactive.

- In a passive investment approach, portfolio composition does not react to changes in capital market expectations (*passive* means *not reacting*). For example, a portfolio indexed to the MSCI-Europe Index, an index representing European equity markets, might add or drop a holding in response to a change in the index composition but not in response to changes in capital market expectations concerning the security's investment value. **Indexing**, a common passive approach to investing, refers to holding a portfolio of securities designed to replicate the returns on a specified index of securities. A second type of passive investing is a strict buy-and-hold strategy, such as a fixed, but non-indexed, portfolio of bonds to be held to maturity.

- In contrast, with an active investment approach, a portfolio manager will respond to changing capital market expectations. Active management of a portfolio means that its holdings differ from the portfolio's **benchmark** or comparison portfolio in an attempt to produce positive excess risk-adjusted returns, also known as positive **alpha**. Securities held in different-from-benchmark weights reflect expectations of the portfolio manager that differ from consensus expectations. If the portfolio manager's differential expectations are also on average correct, active portfolio management may add value.

- A third category, the semiactive, risk-controlled active, or enhanced index approach, seeks positive alpha while keeping tight control over risk relative to the portfolio's benchmark. As an example, an index-tilt strategy seeks to track closely the risk of a securities index while adding a targeted amount of incremental value by tilting portfolio weightings in some direction that the manager expects to be profitable.

Active investment approaches encompass a very wide range of disciplines. To organize this diversity, investment analysts appeal to the concept of investment style. Following Brown and Goetzmann (1997), we can define an investment style (such as an emphasis on growth stocks or value stocks) as a natural grouping of investment disciplines that has some predictive power in explaining the future dispersion in returns across portfolios.

5.1.3 *Forming Capital Market Expectations*

The manager's third task in the planning process is to form capital market expectations. Long-run forecasts of risk and return characteristics for various asset classes form the basis for choosing portfolios that maximize expected return for given levels of risk, or minimize risk for given levels of expected return.

5.1.4 *Creating the Strategic Asset Allocation*

The fourth and final task in the planning process is determining the strategic asset allocation. Here the manager combines the IPS and capital market expectations to determine target asset class weights; maximum and minimum permissible asset class weights are often also specified as a risk-control mechanism. The investor may seek both single-period and multiperiod perspectives in the return and risk characteristics of asset allocations under consideration. A single-period perspective has the advantage of simplicity. A multiperiod perspective can address the liquidity and tax considerations that arise from rebalancing portfolios over time, as well as serial correlation (long- and short-term dependencies) in returns, but is more costly to implement.

This reading focuses on the creation of an IPS in the planning step and thereby lays the groundwork for the discussion in other readings of tailoring the IPS to individual and institutional investors' needs. The execution and feedback steps in the portfolio management process are as important as the planning step. For now, we merely outline how these steps fit in the portfolio management process.

5.2 The Execution Step

The execution step is represented by the "portfolio construction and revision" box in Figure 1. In the execution step, the manager integrates investment strategies with capital market expectations to select the specific assets for the portfolio (the portfolio selection/composition decision). Portfolio managers initiate portfolio decisions based on analysts' inputs, and trading desks then implement these decisions (portfolio implementation decision). Subsequently, the portfolio is revised as investor circumstances or capital market expectations change; thus the execution step interacts constantly with the feedback step.

In making the portfolio selection/composition decision, portfolio managers may use the techniques of portfolio optimization. Portfolio optimization—quantitative tools for combining assets efficiently to achieve a set of return and risk objectives—plays a key role in the integration of strategies with expectations and appears in Figure 1 in the portfolio construction and revision box.

At times, a portfolio's actual asset allocation may purposefully and temporarily differ from the strategic asset allocation. For example, the asset allocation might change to reflect an investor's current circumstances that are different from normal. The temporary allocation may remain in place until circumstances return to those described in the IPS and reflected in the strategic asset allocation. If the changed circumstances become permanent, the manager must update the investor's IPS and the temporary asset allocation plan will effectively become the new strategic asset allocation. A strategy known as tactical asset allocation also results in differences from the strategic asset allocation. Tactical asset allocation responds to changes in short-term capital market expectations rather than to investor circumstances.

The portfolio implementation decision is as important as the portfolio selection/composition decision. Poorly managed executions result in transaction costs that reduce performance. Transaction costs include all costs of trading, including explicit transaction costs, implicit transaction costs, and missed trade opportunity costs. Explicit transaction costs include commissions paid to brokers, fees paid to exchanges, and taxes. Implicit transaction costs include bid–ask spreads and market price impacts of large trades. Missed trade opportunity costs can arise due to price changes that prevent trades from being filled.

In sum, in the execution step, plans are turned into reality—with all the attendant real-world challenges.

5.3 The Feedback Step

In any business endeavor, feedback and control are essential elements in reaching a goal. In portfolio management, this step has two components: monitoring and rebalancing, and performance evaluation.

5.3.1 *Monitoring and Rebalancing*

Monitoring and rebalancing involve the use of feedback to manage ongoing exposures to available investment opportunities so that the client's current objectives and constraints continue to be satisfied. Two types of factors are monitored: investor-related factors such as the investor's circumstances, and economic and market input factors.

One impetus for portfolio revision is a change in investment objectives or constraints because of changes in investor circumstances. Portfolio managers need a process in place to stay informed of changes in clients' circumstances. The termination of a pension plan or death of a spouse may trigger an abrupt change in a client's time horizon and tax concerns, and the IPS should list the occurrence of such changes as a basis for appropriate portfolio revision.

More predictably, changes in economic and market input factors give rise to the regular need for portfolio revision. Again, portfolio managers need to systematically review the risk attributes of assets as well as economic and capital market factors. A change in expectations may trigger portfolio revision. When asset price changes occur, however, revisions can be required even without changes in expectations. The actual timing and magnitude of rebalancing may be triggered by review periods or by specific rules governing the management of the portfolio and deviation from the tolerances or ranges specified in the strategic asset allocation, or the timing and magnitude may be at the discretion of the manager. For example, suppose the policy allocation calls for an initial portfolio with a 70 percent weighting to stocks and a 30 percent weighting to bonds. Suppose the value of the stock holdings then grows by 40 percent, while the value of the bond holdings grows by 10 percent. The new weighting is roughly 75 percent in stocks and 25 percent in bonds. To bring the portfolio back into compliance with investment policy, it must be rebalanced back to the long-term policy weights. In any event, the rebalancing decision is a crucial one that must take into account many factors, such as transaction costs and taxes (for taxable investors). Disciplined rebalancing will have a major impact on the attainment of investment objectives. Rebalancing takes us back to the issues of execution, as is appropriate in a feedback process.

5.3.2 *Performance Evaluation*

Investment performance must periodically be evaluated by the investor to assess progress toward the achievement of investment objectives as well as to assess portfolio management skill.

The assessment of portfolio management skill has three components. Performance measurement involves the calculation of the portfolio's rate of return. Performance attribution examines why the portfolio performed as it did and involves determining the sources of a portfolio's performance. **Performance appraisal** is the evaluation of whether or not the manager is doing a good job based on how the portfolio did relative to a benchmark (a comparison portfolio).

Often, we can examine a portfolio's performance, in terms of absolute returns, through three sources: decisions regarding the strategic asset allocation, **market timing** (returns attributable to shorter-term tactical deviations from the strategic asset allocation), and security selection (skill in selecting individual securities within an asset class). However, portfolio management is frequently conducted with reference to a benchmark, or for some entities, with reference to a stream of projected liabilities or a specified target rate of return. As a result, relative portfolio performance evaluation, in addition to absolute performance measurement, is often of key importance.

With respect to relative performance we may ask questions such as, "Relative to the investment manager's benchmark, what economic sectors were underweighted or overweighted?" or "What was the manager's rationale for these decisions and how successful were they?" Portfolio evaluation may also be conducted with respect to specific risk models, such as multifactor models, which attempt to explain asset returns in terms of exposures to a set of risk factors.

Concurrent with evaluation of the manager is the ongoing review of the benchmark to establish its continuing suitability. For some benchmarks, this review would include a thorough understanding of how economic sectors and subsectors are determined in the benchmark, the classification of securities within them, and how frequently the classifications change. For any benchmark, one would review whether the benchmark continues to be a fair measuring stick given the manager's mandate.

As with other parts of the portfolio management process, performance evaluation and performance presentation are critical. These topics play a central role in the portfolio management process.

5.4 A Definition of Portfolio Management

In sum, the process logic is incorporated in the following definition, which is the cornerstone for this book. Portfolio management is an ongoing process in which

- investment objectives and constraints are identified and specified;
- investment strategies are developed;
- portfolio composition is decided in detail;
- portfolio decisions are initiated by portfolio managers and implemented by traders;
- portfolio performance is measured and evaluated;
- investor and market conditions are monitored; and
- any necessary rebalancing is implemented.

Although we have provided general insights into the portfolio management process, we make no judgments and voice no opinions about how the process should be organized, who should make which decisions, or any other process-operating matter. How well the process works is a critical component of investment success. In a survey of pension fund chief operating officers, Ambachtsheer, Capelle, and Scheibelhut (1998) found that 98 percent of the respondents cited a poor portfolio management process as a barrier to achieving excellence in organizational performance. The organization of the portfolio management process of any investment management company should be the result of careful planning.

INVESTMENT OBJECTIVES AND CONSTRAINTS

6

As previously discussed, the IPS is the cornerstone of the portfolio management process. Because of the IPS's fundamental importance, we introduce its main components in this reading. In this section, we return to the tasks of identifying and specifying the investor's objectives and constraints that initiate the planning step.

Although we discuss objectives first and then constraints, the actual process of delineating these for any investor may appropriately start with an examination of investor constraints. For example, a short time horizon affects the investor's ability to take risk.

6.1 Objectives

The two objectives in this framework, risk and return, are interdependent—one cannot be discussed without reference to the other. The risk objective limits how high the investor can set the return objective.

6.1.1 Risk Objective

The first element of the risk–return framework is the risk objective because it will largely determine the return objective. A 10 percent standard deviation risk objective, for example, implies a different asset allocation than a 15 percent standard deviation risk objective, because expected asset risk is generally positively correlated with expected asset return. In formulating a risk objective, the investor must address the following questions:

1 *How do I measure risk?* Risk measurement is a key issue in investments, and several approaches exist for measuring risk. In practice, risk may be measured in absolute terms or in relative terms with reference to various risk concepts. Examples of absolute risk objectives are a specified level of standard deviation or variance of total return. The **variance** of a random variable is the expected value of squared deviations from the random variable's mean. Variance is often referred to as volatility. **Standard deviation** is the positive square root of variance. An example of a relative risk objective is a specified level of tracking risk. Tracking risk is the standard deviation of the differences between a portfolio's and the benchmark's total returns.

Downside risk concepts, such as **value at risk (VaR)**, may also be important to an investor. Value at risk is a probability-based measure of the loss that one anticipates will be exceeded only a specified small fraction of the time over a given horizon—for example, in 5 percent of all monthly holding periods. Besides statistical measures of risk, other risk exposures, such as exposures to specific economic sectors, or risk with respect to a factor model of returns, may be relevant as well.

2 *What is the investor's willingness to take risk?* The investor's stated willingness to take risk is often very different for institutional versus individual investors. Managers should try to understand the behavioral and, for individuals, the

personality factors behind an investor's willingness to take risk. In the reading on individual investors, we explore behavioral issues in reference to the investor's willingness to take risk.

3 *What is the investor's ability to take risk?* Even if an investor is eager to bear risk, practical or financial limitations often limit the amount of risk that can be prudently assumed. For the sake of illustration, in the following discussion we talk about risk in terms of the volatility of asset values.

● In terms of spending needs, how much volatility would inconvenience an investor who depends on investments (such as a university in relationship to its endowment fund)? Or, how much volatility would inconvenience an investor who otherwise cannot afford to incur substantial short-term losses? Investors with high levels of wealth relative to probable worst-case short-term loss scenarios can take more risk.

● In terms of long-term wealth targets or obligations, how much volatility might prevent the investor from reaching these goals? Investors with high levels of wealth relative to long-term wealth targets or obligations can take more risk.

● What are the investor's liabilities or pseudo liabilities? An institution may face legally promised future payments to beneficiaries (liabilities) and an individual may face future retirement spending needs (pseudo liabilities).

● What is the investor's financial strength—that is, the ability to increase the savings/contribution level if the portfolio cannot support the planned spending? More financial strength means more risk can be taken.

4 *How much risk is the investor both willing and able to bear?* The answer to this question defines the investor's risk tolerance. Risk tolerance, the capacity to accept risk, is a function of both an investor's willingness and ability to do so. Risk tolerance can also be described in terms of risk aversion, the degree of an investor's inability and unwillingness to take risk. The investor's specific risk objectives are formulated with that investor's level of risk tolerance in mind. Importantly, any assessment of risk tolerance must consider both an investor's willingness and that investor's ability to take risk. When a mismatch exists between the two, determining risk tolerance requires educating the client on the dangers of excess risk taking or of ignoring inflation risk, depending on the case. In our presentation in this book, we assume that such education has taken place and that we are providing an appropriate risk objective in the IPS proposed to the client. When an investor's willingness to accept risk exceeds ability to do so, ability prudently places a limit on the amount of risk the investor should assume. When ability exceeds willingness, the investor may fall short of the return objective because willingness would be the limiting factor. These interactions are shown in Table 1.

An investor with an above-average ability to assume risk may have legitimate reasons for choosing a lower risk strategy. As well, an investor may face the pleasant situation of having an excess of wealth to meet financial needs for a long period of time. In these cases, the investor needs to have a clear understanding of the eventual consequences of the decision to effectively spend down excess wealth over time. As with any strategy, such a decision must be reevaluated periodically. In the case of a high-net-worth investor who has earned substantial wealth from entrepreneurial risk taking, such an investor may now simply not want to lose wealth and may desire only liquidity to spend in order to maintain her current lifestyle.

5 *What are the specific risk objective(s)?* Just as risk may be measured either absolutely or relatively, we may specify both absolute risk and relative risk objectives. In practice, investors often find that quantitative risk objectives are easier to specify in relative than in absolute terms. Possibly as a consequence, absolute risk objectives in particular are frequently specified in qualitative rather than quantitative terms.

What distinguishes the risk objective from risk tolerance is the level of specificity. For example, the statement that a person has a "lower than average risk tolerance" might be converted operationally into "the loss in any one year is not to exceed *x* percent of portfolio value" or "annual volatility of the portfolio is not to exceed *y* percent." Often, clients—particularly individual investors—do not understand or appreciate this level of specificity, and more-general risk-tolerance statements substitute for a quantitative risk objective.

6 *How should the investor allocate risk?* This is how some investors frame capital allocation decisions today, particularly when active strategies will play a role in the portfolio. The question may concern the portfolio as a whole or some part of it. Risk budgeting disciplines address the above question most directly. After the investor has determined the *measure* of risk of concern to him (e.g., VaR or tracking risk) and the *desired total quantity of risk* (the overall risk budget), an investor using risk budgeting would allocate the overall risk budget to specific investments so as to maximize expected overall risk-adjusted return. The resulting optimal risk budgets for the investments would translate to specific allocations of capital to them.

Table 1   Risk Tolerance

Willingness to Take Risk	Ability to Take Risk	
	Below Average	**Above Average**
Below Average	Below-average risk tolerance	Resolution needed
Above Average	Resolution needed	Above-average risk tolerance

6.1.2 *Return Objective*

The second element of the investment policy framework is the return objective, which must be consistent with the risk objective. Just as tension may exist between willingness and ability in setting the risk objective, so the return objective requires a resolution of return desires versus the risk objective. In formulating a return objective, the investor must address the following four questions:

1 *How is return measured?* The usual measure is total return, the sum of the return from price appreciation and the return from investment income. Return may be stated as an absolute amount, such as 10 percent a year, or as a return relative to the benchmark's return, such as benchmark return plus 2 percent a year. Nominal returns must be distinguished from real returns. Nominal returns are unadjusted for inflation. Real returns are adjusted for inflation and sometimes simply called inflation-adjusted returns. Also, pretax returns must be distinguished from post-tax returns. Pretax returns are returns before taxes, and post-tax returns are returns after taxes are paid on investment income and realized capital gains.

2 *How much return does the investor say she wants?* This amount is the stated return desire. These wants or desires may be realistic or unrealistic. For example, an investor may have higher than average return desires to meet high consumption desires or a high ending wealth target: for instance, "I want a 20 percent annual return." The advisor or portfolio manager must continually evaluate the desire for high returns in light of the investor's ability to assume risk and the reasonableness of the stated return desire, especially relative to capital market expectations.

3 *How much return does the investor need to achieve, on average?* This amount is the required return or return requirement. Requirements are more stringent than desires because investors with requirements typically must achieve those returns, at least on average. An example of a return requirement is the average return a pension fund projects it must earn to fund liabilities to current and future pensioners, based on actuarial calculations. The compound rate of return that an individual investor must earn to attain the asset base needed for retirement is another example of a return requirement. A third example would be the return that a retired investor must earn on his investment portfolio to cover his annual living expenses. We illustrate these last two cases.

Suppose that a married couple needs £2 million in 18 years to fund retirement. Their current investable assets total £1,200,000. The projected future need (£2 million) incorporates expected inflation. The couple would need to earn $(£2,000,000/£1,200,000)^{1/18} - 1.0 = 2.88$ percent per year after-tax to achieve their goal. Every cash flow needs to be accounted for in such calculations. If the couple needed to liquidate £25,000 from the portfolio at the end of each year (keeping all other facts unchanged), they would need to earn 4.55 percent per year on an after-tax basis to have £2 million in 18 years (a financial calculator is needed to confirm this result). If all investment returns were taxed at 35 percent, 4.55 percent after tax would correspond to a 7 percent pretax required return $[4.55/(1 - 0.35) = 7\%]$.

A retiree may depend on his investment portfolio for some or all of his living expenses. That need defines a return requirement. Suppose that a retiree must achieve a 4 percent after-tax return on his current investment portfolio to meet his current annual living expenses. Thus, his return requirement on a real, after-tax basis is 4 percent per year. If he expects inflation to be 2 percent per year and a 40 percent tax rate applies to investment returns from any source, we could estimate his pretax nominal return requirement as (After-tax real return requirement + Expected inflation rate)/(1 − Tax rate) = (4% + 2%)/(1 − 0.40) = 10 percent.

In contrast to desired returns, which can be reduced if incongruent with risk objectives, large required returns are an important source of potential conflict between return and risk objectives. Other required return issues that are relevant to specific situations include the following:

● What are the needs and desires for current spending versus ending wealth?

● How do nominal total return requirements relate to expected rates of price inflation? If assets fund obligations subject to inflation, the return requirements should reflect expected rates of inflation.

4 *What are the specific return objectives?* The return objective incorporates the required return, the stated return desire, and the risk objective into a measurable annual total return specification. For example, an investor with a 5 percent after-tax, required, inflation-adjusted annual rate of return but above-average risk tolerance might reasonably set a higher than 5 percent after-tax, inflation-adjusted annual rate of return objective to maximize expected wealth.

An investor's return objective should be consistent with that investor's risk objective. A high return objective may suggest an asset allocation with an expected level of risk that is too great in relation to the risk objective, for example. In addition, the anticipated return from the portfolio should be sufficient to meet wealth objectives or liabilities that the portfolio must fund.

For investors with current investment income needs, the return objective should be sufficient to meet spending needs from capital appreciation and investment income: When a well-considered return objective is not consistent with risk tolerance, other adjustments may need to take place, such as increasing savings or modifying wealth objectives.

An investor delegating portfolio management to an investment manager will communicate a mandate—a set of instructions detailing the investment manager's task and how his performance will be evaluated—that includes a specification of the manager's benchmark. Because the manager's performance will be evaluated against the benchmark, the benchmark's total return is an effective return objective for the investment manager. These instructions may be part of the investment policy statement or, in the case of a portfolio with multiple managers, outlined in separate instructions for each mandate to each manager.

Although an absolute return objective is sometimes set (e.g., 8 percent), the reality of the markets suggests that a relative return objective may be more plausible. A relative return objective is stated as a return relative to the portfolio benchmark's total return (e.g., 1 percent higher than the benchmark).

Table 2 illustrates the variation in return requirement and risk tolerance among various categories of investors.

Table 2	Return Requirements and Risk Tolerances of Various Investors	
Type of Investor	**Return Requirement**	**Risk Tolerance**
Individual	Depends on stage of life, circumstances, and obligations	Varies
Pension Plans (Defined Benefit)	The return that will adequately fund liabilities on an inflation-adjusted basis	Depends on plan and sponsor characteristics, plan features, funding status, and workforce characteristics
Pension Plans (Defined Contribution)	Depends on stage of life of individual participants	Varies with the risk tolerance of individual participants
Foundations and Endowments	The return that will cover annual spending, investment expenses, and expected inflation	Determined by amount of assets relative to needs, but generally above-average or average
Life Insurance Companies	Determined by rates used to determine policyholder reserves	Below average due to factors such as regulatory constraints
Non-Life-Insurance Companies	Determined by the need to price policies competitively and by financial needs	Below average due to factors such as regulatory constraints
Banks	Determined by cost of funds	Varies

6.2 Constraints

The investor's risk and return objectives are set within the context of several constraints: liquidity, time horizon, tax concerns, legal and regulatory factors, and unique circumstances. Although all of these factors influence portfolio choice, the first two constraints bear directly on the investor's ability to take risk and thus constrain both risk and return objectives.

6.2.1 *Liquidity*

A liquidity requirement is a need for cash *in excess of new contributions* (for pension plans and endowments, for example) or *savings* (for individuals) at a specified point in time. Such needs may be anticipated or unanticipated, but either way they stem from liquidity events. An example of a liquidity event is planned construction of a building in one year.

The liquidity requirement may reflect nonrecurring needs or the desire to hold cash against unanticipated needs (a safety or reserve fund). This requirement may be met by holding cash or cash equivalents in the portfolio or by converting other assets into cash equivalents. Any risk of economic loss because of the need to sell relatively less liquid assets to meet liquidity requirements is **liquidity risk**. (An asset that can be converted into cash only at relatively high total cost is said to be relatively less liquid.) Liquidity risk, therefore, arises for two reasons: an asset-side reason (asset liquidity) and a liability-side reason (liquidity requirements). Portfolio managers control asset selection but not liquidity requirements; as a result, in practice, managers use asset selection to manage liquidity risk. If the portfolio's asset and income base are large relative to its potential liquidity requirements, relatively less liquid assets can be held. A distinct consideration is liquidity requirements in relation to price risk of the asset—the risk of fluctuations in market price. Assets with high price risk are frequently less liquid, especially during market downturns. If the timing of an investor's liquidity requirements is significantly correlated with market downturns, these requirements can influence asset selection in favor of less risky assets. In many cases, therefore, consideration of both liquidity risk and price risk means that an investor will choose to hold some part of the portfolio in highly liquid and low-price-risk assets in anticipation of future liquidity requirements. Investors may also modify the payoff structure of a risky portfolio to address liquidity requirements using derivative strategies, although such modifications often incur costs. (**Derivatives** are contracts whose payoffs depend on the value of another asset, often called the underlying asset.)

6.2.2 *Time Horizon*

Time horizon most often refers to the time period associated with an investment objective. Investment objectives and associated time horizons may be short term, long term, or a combination of the two. (A time horizon of 10 years or more is often considered to be long term. Investment performance over the long term should average results over several market and business cycles.) A multistage horizon is a combination of shorter term and longer term horizons. An example of a multistage horizon is the case of funding children's education shorter term and the investor's retirement longer term.

Other constraints, such as a unique circumstance or a specific liquidity requirement, can also affect an investor's time horizon. For example, an individual investor's temporary family living arrangement can dictate that his time horizon constraint be stated in multistage terms. Similarly, an institutional investor's need to make an imminent substantial disbursement of funds for a capital project can necessitate a multistage approach to the time horizon constraint.

In general, relevant time horizon questions include the following:

■ *How does the length of the time horizon modify the investor's ability to take risk?* The longer the time horizon the more risk the investor can take. The longer the time horizon, the greater the investor's ability to replenish investment resources by increasing savings. A long-term investor's labor income may also be an asset sufficiently stable to support a higher level of portfolio risk.[3] Cash may be safe for a short-term investor but risky for a long-term investor who will be faced with continuously reinvesting.

■ *How does the length of the time horizon modify the investor's asset allocation?* Many investors allocate a greater proportion of funds to risky assets when they address long-term as opposed to short-term investment objectives. Decreased risk-taking ability with shorter horizons can thus constrain portfolio choice.

■ *How does the investor's willingness and ability to bear fluctuations in portfolio value modify the asset allocation?* With a focus on risk, even an investor with a long-term objective may limit risk taking because of sensitivity to the possibility of substantial interim losses. The chance of unanticipated liquidity needs may increase during market downturns, for instance, because a market downturn may be linked to a decline in economic activity affecting income or other sources of wealth. An investor that often faces unanticipated short-term liquidity needs will usually favor investments with a shorter time horizon so as to limit the risk of loss of value.

■ *How does a multistage time horizon constrain the investor's asset allocation?* The investment policy must be designed to accommodate all time horizons in a multistage horizon case. Such design will probably entail some compromise in the setting of objectives to attain short-, medium-, and long-term goals.

6.2.3 *Tax Concerns*

A country's tax policy can affect important aspects of investment decision-making for investors who reside there. Tax concerns arise for taxable investors because tax payments reduce the amount of the total return that can be used for current needs or reinvested for future growth. Differences between the tax rates applying to investment income and capital gains will influence taxable investors' choice of investments and their timing of sales. Estate taxes on wealth triggered by the investor's death can also affect investment decisions. Finally, tax policy changes that affect security prices affect both taxable and tax-exempt investors.

6.2.4 *Legal and Regulatory Factors*

Legal and regulatory factors are external factors imposed by governmental, regulatory, or oversight authorities, which may constrain investment decision-making. For example, some countries limit the use of certain assets or asset classes in retirement accounts. In the United States, the Employee Retirement Income Security Act (ERISA) of 1974, as interpreted by regulatory agencies and the courts, limits the acquisition and holding of employer securities by certain pension plans. In another example, insurance companies may face regulatory constraints on their investment portfolio holdings.

6.2.5 *Unique Circumstances*

Unique circumstances are internal factors (other than a liquidity requirement, time horizon, or tax concern) that may constrain portfolio choices. For example, a university endowment may be constrained to avoid certain investments against which there may be ethical objections or social responsibility considerations. Similarly, an individual investor's portfolio choices may be constrained by circumstances focusing on health needs, support of dependents, and other circumstances unique to the particular individual. Investors may specify avoidance of nondomestic shares or

---

3 See Campbell and Viceira (2002) for a discussion of this and the following point.

derivatives. Portfolio choices may also be constrained by investor capability in terms of both human resources and financial resources such as time, interest, background, and technical expertise.

7   THE DYNAMICS OF THE PROCESS

One of the truly satisfying aspects of portfolio management as a professional activity is the underlying logic and the dynamism of the portfolio process concept. In a broad sense, the work of analysts, economists, and market strategists is all a matter of "getting ready." The work of portfolio management is the action: taking the inputs and moving step by step through the orderly process of converting this raw material into a portfolio that maximizes expected return relative to the investor's ability to bear risk, that meets the investor's constraints and preferences, and that integrates portfolio policies with expectational factors and market uncertainties. Portfolio management is where the payoff is, because this is where it all comes together. Of course, it is the end result of this process that is judged: the performance of the portfolio relative to expectations and comparison standards.

Professionalism is enhanced and practice improved by managing portfolios as a process that

- consists of the steps outlined in this volume;
- flows logically and systematically through an orderly sequence of decision-making; and
- is continuous once put into motion with respect to a given investor.

This view approaches portfolio management not as a set of separate elements operating by fits and starts as intuition or inspiration dictates but rather as an integrated whole in which every decision moves the portfolio down the process path and in which no decision can be skipped without sacrificing functional integrity.

8   THE FUTURE OF PORTFOLIO MANAGEMENT

In the last few decades, portfolio management has become a more science-based discipline somewhat analogous to engineering and medicine. As in these other fields, advances in basic theory, technology, and market structure constantly translate into improvements in products and professional practices.

Among the most significant recent theoretical advances in investments is the recognition that the risk characteristics of the nontradable assets owned by an individual client, such as future earnings from a job, a business, or an expected inheritance, should be included in the definition of that client's portfolio. In the institutional area also, there is an increasing awareness and use of multifactor risk models and methods of managing risk.

Among the most significant market developments is the emergence of a broad range of new standardized derivative contracts—swaps, futures, and options. As active trading in these standardized products continues to develop, they make possible the creation of an infinite variety of customized investment products tailored to the needs of specific clients. As analysts continue to develop a more comprehensive view of risk, they also command a wider set of tools with which to manage it.[4]

THE ETHICAL RESPONSIBILITIES OF PORTFOLIO MANAGERS

9

In this reading, we have initiated a course of study that we hope will further the reader in his or her career as an investment professional. We select the term investment *professional* advisedly. Dictionaries define professional as "conforming to the standards of a profession." Every thoughtful person who has explored the subject has concluded that professional standards are of two types: standards of competence and standards of conduct. Merely drawing a livelihood from managing or advising on the investment of client monies is insufficient in itself to make an investment professional.

But verbal distinctions are not the most important point. The conduct of a portfolio manager affects the well-being of clients and many other people. The connection to individuals and their welfare is always present; it is no less important in those institutional contexts in which the portfolio manager may never meet the client. In the first years of the 21st century press attention focused on abuses in the US mutual fund industry such as late trading, abusive market timing, selective disclosure of information on portfolio holdings, and undisclosed payments for "shelf space" to gain placement on brokers' preferred lists.[5] Certain fund executives facilitated or participated in these activities for personal enrichment, at the expense of the well-being of their clients, mutual fund shareholders. In truth, the docket of cases of professional misconduct is never empty, but the profession can and must work towards minimizing it. The portfolio manager must keep foremost in mind that he or she is in a position of trust, requiring ethical conduct towards the public, client, prospects, employers, employees, and fellow workers. For CFA Institute members, this position of trust is reflected in the Code of Ethics and Standards of Professional Conduct to which members subscribe, as well as in the Professional Conduct Statement they submit annually. Ethical conduct is the foundation requirement for managing investment portfolios.

SUMMARY

In this reading, we have presented the portfolio management process and the elements of the investment policy statement.

- According to the portfolio perspective, individual investments should be judged in the context of how much risk they add to a portfolio rather than on how risky they are on a stand-alone basis.

- The three steps in the portfolio management process are the planning step (objectives and constraint determination, investment policy statement creation, capital market expectation formation, and strategic asset allocation creation);

---

4 This section on the future of portfolio management was contributed by Dr. Zvi Bodie.
5 The listing follows the enumeration of William H. Donaldson, CFA, chair of the US Securities and Exchange Commission, in a speech to the Mutual Fund Directors Forum on 7 January 2004.

the execution step (portfolio selection/composition and portfolio implementation); and the feedback step (performance evaluation and portfolio monitoring and rebalancing).

■ Investment objectives are specific and measurable desired performance outcomes, and constraints are limitations on the ability to make use of particular investments. The two types of objectives are risk and return. The two types of constraints are internal (posed by the characteristics of the investor) and external (imposed by outside agencies).

■ An investment policy statement is a written planning document that governs all investment decisions for the client. This document integrates a client's needs, preferences, and circumstances into a statement of that client's objectives and constraints.

■ A policy or strategic asset allocation establishes exposures to IPS-permissible asset classes in a manner designed to satisfy the client's long-run objectives and constraints. The plan reflects the interaction of objectives and constraints with long-run capital market expectations.

■ In a passive investment strategy approach, portfolio composition does not react to changes in expectations; an example is indexing, which involves a fixed portfolio designed to replicate the returns on an index. An active approach involves holding a portfolio different from a benchmark or comparison portfolio for the purpose of producing positive excess risk-adjusted returns. A semiactive approach refers to an indexing approach with controlled use of weights different from the benchmark.

■ The portfolio selection/composition decision concerns portfolio construction and often uses portfolio optimization to combine assets efficiently to achieve return and risk objectives. The portfolio implementation decision concerns the trading desk function of implementing portfolio decisions and involves explicit and implicit transaction costs.

■ The elements of performance evaluation are performance measurement, attribution, and appraisal. Performance measurement is the calculation of portfolio rates of return. Performance attribution is the analysis of those rates of return to determine the factors that explain how the return was achieved. Performance appraisal assesses how well the portfolio manager performed on a risk-adjusted basis, whether absolute or relative to a benchmark.

■ Portfolio monitoring and rebalancing use feedback to manage ongoing exposures to available investment opportunities in order to continually satisfy the client's current objectives and constraints.

■ Portfolio management is an ongoing process in which the investment objectives and constraints are identified and specified, investment policies and strategies are developed, the portfolio composition is decided in detail, portfolio decisions are initiated by portfolio managers and implemented by traders, portfolio performance is evaluated, investor and market conditions are monitored, and any necessary rebalancing is implemented.

■ To determine a risk objective, there are several steps: specify a risk measure (or measures) such as standard deviation, determine the investor's willingness to take risk, determine the investor's ability to take risk, synthesize the investor's willingness and ability into the investor's risk tolerance, and specify an objective using the measure(s) in the first step above.

■ To determine a return objective, there are several steps: specify a return measure such as total nominal return, determine the investor's stated return desire, determine the investor's required rate of return, and specify an objective in terms of the return measure in the first step above.

- A liquidity requirement is a need for cash in excess of the contribution rate or the savings rate at a specified point in time. This need may be either anticipated or unanticipated.

- A time horizon is the time period associated with an investment objective. Investment objectives and associated time horizons may be short term, long term, or a combination of these two. A multistage horizon is a combination of shorter term and longer term horizons. A time horizon can be considered a constraint because shorter time horizons generally indicate lower risk tolerance and hence constrain portfolio choice, making it more conservative.

- A tax concern is any issue arising from a tax structure that reduces the amount of the total return that can be used for current needs or reinvested for future growth. Tax concerns constrain portfolio choice. If differences exist between the tax rates applying to investment income and capital gains, tax considerations will influence the choice of investment.

- Legal and regulatory factors are external considerations that may constrain investment decision making. For example, a government agency may limit the use of certain asset classes in retirement portfolios.

- Unique circumstances are internal factors (other than a liquidity requirement, time horizon, or tax concerns) that may constrain portfolio choices. For example, an investor seeking to avoid investments in tobacco companies will place an internal constraint on portfolio choice.

REFERENCES

Ambachtsheer, Keith, Ronald Capelle, and Tom Scheibelhut. 1998. "Improving Pension Fund Performance." *Financial Analysts Journal*, vol. 54, no. 6: 15–21.

Brown, Stephen, and William Goetzmann. 1997. "Mutual Fund Styles." *Journal of Financial Economics*, vol. 43, no. 3: 373–399.

Campbell, John, and Luis Viceira. 2002. *Strategic Asset Allocation: Portfolio Choice for Long-Term Investors*. Oxford University Press.

Markowitz, Harry. 1952. "Portfolio Selection." *Journal of Finance*, vol. 7, no. 1: 77–91.

Standard & Poor's. 2004. *Directory of Registered Investment Advisors*. Charlottesville, VA: Money Market Directories.

PRACTICE PROBLEMS

1 A An individual expects to save €50,000 during the coming year from income from non-portfolio sources, such as salary. She will need €95,000 within the year to make a down payment for a house purchase. What is her liquidity requirement for the coming year?

B Endowments are funds that are typically owned by non-profit institutions involved in educational, medical, cultural, and other charitable activities. Classified as institutional investors, endowments are almost always established with the intent of lasting into perpetuity.

The Wilson-Fowler Endowment was established in the United States to provide financial support to Wilson-Fowler College. An endowment's spending rate defines the fraction of endowment assets distributed to the supported institution. The Wilson-Fowler Endowment has established a spending rate of 4 percent a year; the endowment follows the simple rule of spending, in a given year, an amount equal to 4% × (Market value of the endowment at the end of the prior year). This amount is committed to the budgetary support of the college for the coming year. At the end of the prior year, the market value of the Wilson-Fowler Endowment's assets stood at $75,000,000. In addition, the Wilson-Fowler Endowment has committed to contribute $1,000,000 in the coming year to the construction of a new student dormitory. Planners at the endowment expect the endowment to receive contributions or gifts (from alumni and other sources) of $400,000 over the coming year. What is the anticipated liquidity requirement of the Wilson-Fowler Endowment for the coming year?

2 The Executive Director of the Judd University Endowment estimates that the capital markets will provide a 9 percent expected return for an endowment portfolio taking above-average risk, and a 7 percent expected return for an endowment portfolio taking average risk. The Judd Endowment provides tuition scholarships for Judd University students. The spending rate has been 4 percent, and the expected tuition inflation rate is 3 percent. Recently university officials have pressured the endowment to increase the spending rate to 6 percent. The endowment has an average to below-average ability to accept risk and only an average willingness to take risk, but a university official claims that the risk tolerance should be raised because higher returns are needed. Discuss an appropriate return objective and risk tolerance for the Judd Endowment.

3 Stux (1994) describes a country allocation strategy across five major equity markets: the United States, the United Kingdom, Germany, France, and Japan. In this strategy, a measure of relative attractiveness among the five equity markets is used as a factor in determining the weights of the five equity markets in the overall portfolio. The investment in each country, however, whatever the country's weight, is an indexed investment in the equity market of that country. The weights of the five equity markets in the overall portfolio generally are expected to differ from benchmark weights (the weights of the countries in an appropriate benchmark for the international equity market), within limits.

Practice Problems and Solutions: 1–4 taken from *Managing Investment Portfolios: A Dynamic Process*, Third Edition, John L. Maginn, CFA, Donald L. Tuttle, PhD, CFA, Jerald E. Pinto, PhD, CFA, and Dennis W. McLeavey, CFA, editors. © 2006 CFA Institute. All other problems and solutions © CFA Institute. All rights reserved.

A Characterize the two components (portfolio weights and within-country investments) of the country allocation strategy using the text's framework for classifying investment strategies.

B Characterize the country allocation strategy overall.

4 Characterize each of the investment objectives given below as one of the following: an absolute risk objective, a relative risk objective, an absolute return objective, or a relative return objective.

A Achieve a rate of return of 8 percent a year.

B Limit the standard deviation of portfolio returns to 20 percent a year or less.

C Achieve returns in the top quartile of the portfolio's peer universe (the set of portfolios with similar investment objectives and characteristics).

D Maintain a 10 percent or smaller probability that the portfolio's return falls below the threshold level of 5 percent per annum over a one-year time horizon.

E Achieve a tracking risk of no more than 4 percent per annum with respect to the portfolio's benchmark.

The following information relates to Questions 5–10

James Stephenson, age 55 and single, is a surgeon who has accumulated a substantial investment portfolio without a clear long-term strategy in mind. Two of his patients who work in financial markets comment as follows:

James Hrdina: "My investment firm, based on its experience with investors, has standard investment policy statements in five categories. You would be better served to adopt one of these standard policy statements instead of spending time developing a policy based on your individual circumstances."

Charles Gionta: "Developing a long-term policy can be unwise given the fluctuations of the market. You want your investment advisor to react continuously to changing conditions and not be limited by a set policy."

Stephenson hires a financial advisor, Caroline Coppa. At their initial meeting, Coppa compiles the following notes:

Stephenson currently has a $2.0 million portfolio that has a large concentration in small-capitalization US equities. Over the past five years, the portfolio has averaged 20 percent annual total return on investment. Stephenson hopes that, over the long term, his portfolio will continue to earn 20 percent annually. When asked about his risk tolerance, he described it as "average." He was surprised when informed that US small-cap portfolios have experienced extremely high volatility.

He does not expect to retire before age 70. His current income is more than sufficient to meet his expenses. Upon retirement, he plans to sell his surgical practice and use the proceeds to purchase an annuity to cover his post-retirement cash flow needs.

Both his income and realized capital gains are taxed at a 30 percent rate. No pertinent legal or regulatory issues apply. He has no pension or retirement plan but does have sufficient health insurance for post-retirement needs.

5 The comments about investment policy statements made by Stephenson's patients are *best* characterized as:

	Hrdina	Gionta
A	Correct	Correct
B	Incorrect	Correct
C	Incorrect	Incorrect

6 In formulating the return objective for Stephenson's investment policy statement, the *most* appropriate determining factor for Coppa to focus on is:

A return desires.

B ability to take risk.

C return requirement.

7 Stephenson's willingness and ability to accept risk can be *best* characterized as:

	Willingness to accept risk	Ability to accept risk
A	Below average	Above average
B	Above average	Below average
C	Above average	Above average

8 Stephenson's tax and liquidity constraints can be *best* characterized as:

	Tax constraint	Liquidity constraint
A	Significant	Significant
B	Significant	Insignificant
C	Insignificant	Insignificant

9 Stephenson's time horizon is *best* characterized as:

A short-term and single-stage.

B long-term and single-stage.

C long-term and multistage.

10 Stephenson's return objective and risk tolerance are *most* appropriately described as:

	Return Objective	Risk Tolerance
A	Below average	Above average
B	Above average	Below average
C	Above average	Above average

The following information relates to Questions 11–16

Gina Benedetti, a trust officer at an Italian bank, interviewed Alessandro Santalucia, a new client. A summary of her interview appears in Exhibit 1.

Exhibit 1	Interview Summary for Client Alessandro Santalucia
Age	45
Family	Married but divorce is pending; three children ages 16, 17, and 18
Hobbies	Speed boat racing, mountain climbing
Business	Real estate speculation, buying firms with turn-around potential
Assets	€1 million in his private business and real estate and €500,000 in a nondiversified investment portfolio
Retirement plans	None; wishes to continue working until physically unable to do so
Current income	Spending modestly exceeds income
Spending plans/ Requirements	Children's college education (estimated at €30,000/year per child); divorce settlement may be up to one-half of his assets

Benedetti develops an investment policy statement and recommended asset allocation for Santalucia and puts the following notes in Santalucia's file:

1   I met with our staff economist to review his thinking on short-term trends in the economy and financial markets. I relied greatly on his forecast to draft an investment policy statement for Santalucia.

2   Santalucia's situation is very similar to that of another client from several years ago. I used that client's asset allocation as a basis for my portfolio recommendations for Santalucia.

Benedetti next meets with her firm's research analyst, Kurt Westerlund, to discuss changes to the firm's recommended list. One company of interest is an upcoming initial public offering (IPO) for Palladio Corp. To analyze this IPO, Westerlund used data from 20 publicly traded peer companies with business lines similar to Palladio's. He combined them into an equally weighted portfolio to approximate the anticipated behavior of Palladio's stock once it becomes publicly traded. Some of this information is presented in Exhibit 2.

During their conversation, Westerlund makes several statements about Palladio and the capital markets:

Statement #1   "I estimated the Palladio proxy portfolio's beta over several different time periods, and this portfolio beta has always been stable, with the high and low estimates within 5 percent of each other. However, Palladio's estimated beta will be more volatile over time than that of the proxy portfolio."

Statement #2   "The estimation of beta is affected by several factors, including regression to the mean, volume of trading, and the market proxy used."

Statement #3   "The capital market line (CML) uses a measure of total risk, and the SML uses a standardized measure of systematic risk."

Statement #4   "The SML is the equation that specifies the required/expected return for a security that is implied by the CML when the market is in equilibrium."

Exhibit 2	Data for Palladio Peer Firms Monthly Data, May 2000–May 2006 (Returns Measured as Decimal; 1% = 0.01)	
	Palladio Proxy Portfolio	**Market**
Average monthly return	0.0051	0.0025
Variance of returns	0.0033	0.0021
Covariance with market return	0.0015	0.0021
Correlation with market return	0.5697	1.000

Benedetti notes that the current short-term government bill rate offers 2.5 percent annually and her firm's economist anticipates a market risk premium of 7.0 percent on stock market investments.

In addition to her consideration of Palladio, Benedetti wants to review Borgonovo, Inc., and decide whether it should remain on the bank's recommended list or be removed. Borgonovo has a beta of 1.2, and a forecasted return of 9.0 percent.

11 Which of the following *best* describes Santalucia's current risk tolerance and liquidity constraint? Santalucia's risk tolerance is:

A   below average, and his liquidity constraint is significant.

B   above average, and his liquidity constraint is significant.

C   above average, and his liquidity constraint is insignificant.

12 Do Benedetti's two notes for Santalucia's file describe the correct process for constructing an investment policy statement and for developing portfolio recommendations?

	Note #1 on investment policy statement process	Note #2 on developing portfolio recommendations
A	No	No
B	Yes	No
C	Yes	Yes

13 Are Westerlund's statements #1 and #2 correct regarding the:

	Palladio systematic risk?	factors affecting beta estimation?
A	No	Yes
B	Yes	No
C	Yes	Yes

14 Are Westerlund's statements #3 and #4 correct regarding:

	types of risk measures?	equilibrium?
A	No	No
B	Yes	No
C	Yes	Yes

15 Based on Exhibit 2, the estimated beta for Palladio is *closest* to:

A 0.40.

B 0.57.

C 0.71.

16 Based on the relationship of Borgonovo's stock to the SML, what is the *most* appropriate decision Benedetti should make regarding the Borgonovo stock?

   A Keep Borgonovo on the recommended list because it plots below the SML.

   B Keep Borgonovo on the recommended list because it plots above the SML.

   C Remove Borgonovo from the recommended list because it plots below the SML.

SOLUTIONS

1 **A** The liquidity requirement for this individual is her need for cash in excess of her savings during the coming year. Therefore, her liquidity requirement is €95,000 – €50,000 = €45,000.

   B The Wilson-Fowler Endowment's anticipated liquidity requirement is $600,000, calculated as $1,000,000 (the planned contribution to the construction of the new dormitory) minus $400,000 (the anticipated amount of new contributions to the endowment). Note that the amount of 4% × $75,000,000 = $3,000,000, as provided for in the spending rule, is fully committed to budgetary support; thus this amount is not available to help meet the endowment's planned contribution to the building project.

2 The Judd Endowment's risk tolerance is limited by its ability and willingness to accept risk. Risk tolerance is *not* a function of a need for higher returns. The return objective should be consistent with risk tolerance, so an appropriate return objective for the Judd Endowment is 7 percent. A spending rate of 6 percent is too high for this endowment; raising the return objective to 9 percent would only compound the problem created by a 6 percent spending rate, which is inappropriately high for this endowment.

3 **A** The country allocation strategy as described mixes elements of active and passive investment approaches. The portfolio weights are actively determined and differ from benchmark weights, within limits. However, the investments in individual countries are passive, indexed investments.

   B Overall, we can classify the country allocation strategy as a semiactive or controlled-active investment approach.

4 **A** This is an absolute return objective because it does not reference a comparison to the performance of another portfolio but rather is stated in terms of a fixed number (an 8 percent annual return).

   B This is an absolute risk objective because it does not reference a comparison to the performance of another portfolio but rather is stated in terms of a fixed number (a standard deviation of return of 20 percent a year).

   C This is a relative return objective because it references a comparison to the performance of other portfolios.

   D This is an absolute risk objective because it addresses the risk that a portfolio's return will fall below a minimum acceptable level over a stated time horizon.

   E This is a relative risk objective because it references a comparison to the performance of another portfolio, the benchmark.

5 C is correct. The comments about investment policy statements made by Stephenson's patients are incorrect. The IPS should identify pertinent investment objectives and constraints for a *particular* investor. Clearly identified objectives and constraints ensure that the policy statement is accurate and relevant to the investor's specific situation and desires. The result should be an optimal balance between return and risk for that investor. The IPS provides a long-term plan for an investor and a basis for making disciplined investment decisions over time. The absence of an investment policy statement reduces decision making to an individual-event basis and often leads to pursuing short-term opportunities that may not contribute to, or may even detract from, reaching long-term goals.

6 B is correct. An investor's ability to take risk puts an upper limit on a reasonable return objective.

7 C is correct. Even though Stephenson describes his risk tolerance as "average," his present investment portfolio and his desire for large returns indicate an above-average willingness to take risk. His financial situation (large asset base, ample income to cover expenses, lack of need for liquidity, and long time horizon) indicates an above-average ability to accept risk.

8 B is correct. Stephenson has adequate income to cover his living expenses and has no major outlays for which he needs cash, so his liquidity needs are minimal. He is not a tax-exempt investor (both income and capital gains are taxed at 30%), so taxes should play a considerable role in his investment decisions.

9 C is correct. Stephenson's time horizon is long—he is currently only 55 years old. The time horizon consists of two stages: the first stage extends to his retirement in 15 years; the second stage may last for 20 years or more and extends from retirement until his death.

10 C is correct.

Risk: Stephenson has an above-average risk tolerance based on both his ability and willingness to assume risk. His large asset base, long time horizon, ample income to cover expenses, and lack of need for liquidity or cash flow indicate an above-average ability to assume risk. His concentration in US small-capitalization stocks and his desire for high returns indicate substantial willingness to assume risk.

Return: Stephenson's financial circumstances (long time horizon, sizable asset base, ample income, and low liquidity needs) and his risk tolerance warrant an above-average total return objective. His expressed desire for a continued return of 20 percent, however, is unrealistic. Coppa should counsel Stephenson on what level of returns to reasonably expect from the financial markets over long periods of time and to define an achievable return objective.

11 A is correct. Santalucia's lifestyle and business career (speedboats, mountain climbing, real estate speculation, turnarounds) show a *willingness* to take risks. His current *ability* to take risks is diminished, given his total assets and his expected divorce settlement, his current income/spending situation, and upcoming college bills. When an investor's willingness to accept risk exceeds the ability to do so, ability prudently places a limit on the amount of risk the investor should assume. Santalucia's pending divorce and college education bills create a significant liquidity constraint.

12 A is correct. Neither note describes the correct process. The IPS process requires that members first identify and specify the investor's objectives and constraints and then create the investment policy statement. Incorporating short-term economic trends into the policy statement is inappropriate. Only after the IPS has been created should members form capital market expectations and then create the strategic asset allocation. Using another client's asset allocation from several years earlier is inappropriate because it does not include current capital market expectations.

13 C is correct. Westerlund's first statement is correct: Beta is more stable for portfolios than for individual stocks. The second statement is also correct: Beta estimation is affected by all the listed items.

14 C is correct. The first statement is correct: Variance, or total risk, is the relevant risk measure for the CML; the SML uses beta, the asset's risk standardized by the market's risk. The second statement is also correct: The SML is based on the CML and both are equilibrium relationships.

15 C is correct. The estimated beta is the covariance of Palladio's returns with the market's returns divided by the variance of the market's returns, or 0.0015/0.0021 = 0.714.

16 C is correct. The SML required return for Borgonovo is 2.5% + 1.2(7%) = 10.9%. With a forecasted return of 9.0%, Borgonovo lies below the SML (indicating it is overvalued) and should be removed from the bank's recommended list.

READING

48

An Introduction to Multifactor Models

by Jerald E. Pinto, PhD, CFA, and Eugene L. Podkaminer, CFA

Jerald E. Pinto, PhD, CFA, is at CFA Institute (USA). Eugene L. Podkaminer, CFA, is at Callan Associates (USA).

LEARNING OUTCOMES

Mastery	The candidate should be able to:
☐	**a.** describe arbitrage pricing theory (APT), including its underlying assumptions and its relation to multifactor models;
☐	**b.** define arbitrage opportunity and determine whether an arbitrage opportunity exists;
☐	**c.** calculate the expected return on an asset given an asset's factor sensitivities and the factor risk premiums;
☐	**d.** describe and compare macroeconomic factor models, fundamental factor models, and statistical factor models;
☐	**e.** explain sources of active risk and interpret tracking risk and the information ratio;
☐	**f.** describe uses of multifactor models and interpret the output of analyses based on multifactor models;
☐	**g.** describe the potential benefits for investors in considering multiple risk dimensions when modeling asset returns.

INTRODUCTION   1

As used in investments, a **factor** is a variable or a characteristic with which individual asset returns are correlated. Models using multiple factors are used by asset owners, asset managers, investment consultants, and risk managers for a variety of portfolio construction, portfolio management, risk management, and general analytical purposes. In comparison to single-factor models (typically based on a market risk factor), multifactor models offer increased explanatory power and flexibility. These comparative strengths of multifactor models allow practitioners to

■ build portfolios that replicate or modify in a desired way the characteristics of a particular index;

- establish desired exposures to one or more risk factors, including those that express specific macro expectations (such as views on inflation or economic growth), in portfolios;

- perform granular risk and return attribution on actively managed portfolios;

- understand the comparative risk exposures of equity, fixed-income, and other asset class returns;

- identify active decisions relative to a benchmark and measure the sizing of those decisions; and

- ensure that an investor's aggregate portfolio is meeting active risk and return objectives commensurate with active fees.

Multifactor models have come to dominate investment practice, having demonstrated their value in helping asset managers and asset owners address practical tasks in measuring and controlling risk. This reading explains and illustrates the various practical uses of multifactor models.

The reading is organized as follows. Section 2 describes the modern portfolio theory background of multifactor models. Section 3 describes arbitrage pricing theory and provides a general expression for multifactor models. Section 4 describes the types of multifactor models, and Section 5 describes selected applications. Section 6 summarizes major points.

2 ▪ MULTIFACTOR MODELS AND MODERN PORTFOLIO THEORY

In 1952, Markowitz introduced a framework for constructing portfolios of securities by quantitatively considering each investment in the context of a portfolio rather than in isolation; that framework is widely known today as modern portfolio theory (MPT). Markowitz simplified modeling asset returns using a multivariate normal distribution, which completely defines the distribution of returns in terms of mean returns, return variances, and return correlations. One of the key insights of MPT is that any value of correlation among asset returns of less than one offers the potential for risk reduction by means of diversification. In 1964, Sharpe introduced the capital asset pricing model (CAPM), a model for the expected return of assets in equilibrium based on a mean–variance foundation. The CAPM and the literature that developed around it has provided investors with useful and influential concepts—such as alpha, beta, and systematic risk—for thinking about investing. The concept of systematic risk, for example, is critical to understanding multifactor models. There are potentially many different types of risks to which an investment may be subject, but they are generally not equally important so far as investment valuation is concerned. Risk that can be avoided by holding an asset in a portfolio, where the risk might be offset by the various risks of other assets, should not be compensated by higher expected return, according to theory. By contrast, investors would expect compensation for bearing an asset's non-diversifiable risk—**systematic risk**; only this risk, theory indicates, should be **priced risk**. In the CAPM, an asset's systematic risk is a positive function of its beta, which measures the sensitivity of an asset's return to the market's return.[1] According

---

[1] Beta can be analyzed as the correlation of the asset's returns with the market return multiplied by a constant that increases with the asset's return standard deviation.

to the CAPM, differences in mean return are explained by a single factor, the market portfolio return. Greater risk with respect to the market factor—represented by higher beta—is expected to be associated with higher return.

The accumulation of evidence from the equity markets during the decades following the CAPM's development have provided clear indications that the CAPM provides an incomplete description of risk and that models incorporating multiple sources of systematic risk more effectively model asset returns.[2] There are, however, various perspectives in practice on how to model risk in the context of multifactor models. This reading will examine some of these, focusing on macroeconomic factor models and fundamental factor models, in subsequent sections.

ARBITRAGE PRICING THEORY

3

In the 1970s, Ross (1976) developed the arbitrage pricing theory (APT) as an alternative to the CAPM. APT introduced a framework that explains the expected return of an asset (or portfolio) in equilibrium as a linear function of the risk of the asset (or portfolio) with respect to a set of factors capturing systematic risk. Unlike the CAPM, the APT does not indicate the identity or even the number of risk factors. Rather, for any multifactor model assumed to generate returns ("return-generating process"), the theory gives the associated expression for the asset's expected return.

Suppose that K factors are assumed to generate returns. Then the simplest expression for a multifactor model for the return of asset i is given by

$$R_i = a_i + b_{i1}I_1 + b_{i2}I_2 + \ldots + b_{iK}I_K + \varepsilon_i, \tag{1}$$

where

R_i = the return to asset i

a_i = an intercept term

I_k = the return to factor k, $k = 1, 2, \ldots, K$

b_{ik} = the sensitivity of the return on asset i to the return to factor k, $k = 1, 2, \ldots, K$

ε_i = an error term with a zero mean that represents the portion of the return to asset i not explained by the factor model

The intercept term a_i is the expected return of asset i, given that all the factors take on a value of zero. Equation 1 presents a multifactor return-generating process (a time-series model for returns). In any given period, the model may not account fully for the asset's return, as indicated by the error term. But error is assumed to average to zero. Another common formulation subtracts the risk-free rate from both sides of Equation 1 so that the dependent variable is the return in excess of the risk-free rate and one of the explanatory variables is a factor return in excess of the risk-free rate. (The Carhart model described below is an example.)

Based on Equation 1, the APT provides an expression for the expected return of asset i assuming that financial markets are in equilibrium. The APT is similar to the CAPM, but the APT makes less strong assumptions than the CAPM.[3] The APT makes just three key assumptions:

1 A factor model describes asset returns.

---

2 See Bodie, Kane, and Marcus (2014) for an introduction to the empirical evidence.
3 The CAPM can be viewed as a special case of the APT that results from making a set of strong additional assumptions about investors and markets.

2 There are many assets, so investors can form well-diversified portfolios that eliminate asset-specific risk.

3 No arbitrage opportunities exist among well-diversified portfolios.

Arbitrage is a risk-free operation that requires no net investment of money but earns an expected positive net profit.[4] An **arbitrage opportunity** is an opportunity to conduct an arbitrage—an opportunity to earn an expected positive net profit without risk and with no net investment of money.

In the first assumption, the number of factors is not specified. The second assumption allows investors to form portfolios with factor risk but without asset-specific risk. The third assumption is the condition of financial market equilibrium.

Empirical evidence indicates that Assumption 2 is reasonable. When a portfolio contains many stocks, the asset-specific or non-systematic risk of individual stocks makes almost no contribution to the variance of portfolio returns. Roll and Ross (2001) found that only 1%–3% of a well-diversified portfolio's variance comes from the non-systematic variance of the individual stocks in the portfolio, as Exhibit 1 shows.

Exhibit 1   Sources of Volatility: The Case of a Well-Diversified Portfolio

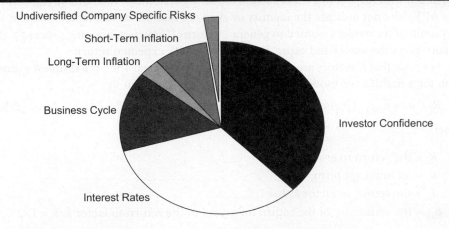

Source: What Is the Arbitrage Pricing Theory. Retrieved May 25, 2001, from the World Wide Web: www.rollross.com/apt.html. Reprinted with permission of Richard Roll.

According to the APT, if the above three assumptions hold, the following equation holds:[5]

$$E(R_p) = R_F + \lambda_1\beta_{p,1} + \dots + \lambda_K\beta_{p,K} \tag{2}$$

where

$E(R_p)$ = the expected return to portfolio p

R_F = the risk-free rate

λ_j = the expected reward for bearing the risk of factor j

$\beta_{p,j}$ = the sensitivity of the portfolio to factor j

K = the number of factors

---

4 The word "arbitrage" or the phrase "risk arbitrage" is also sometimes used in practice to describe investment operations in which significant risk is present.

5 A risk-free asset is assumed. If no risk-free asset exists, in place of R_F we write λ_0 to represent the expected return on a risky portfolio with zero sensitivity to all the factors. The number of factors is not specified but must be much lower than the number of assets, a condition fulfilled in practice.

The APT equation, Equation 2, says that the expected return on any well-diversified portfolio is linearly related to the factor sensitivities of that portfolio.

The **factor risk premium** (or **factor price**), λ_j, represents the expected reward for bearing the risk of a portfolio with a sensitivity of 1 to factor j and a sensitivity of 0 to all other factors. The exact interpretation of "expected reward" depends on the multifactor model that is the basis for Equation 2. For example, in the Carhart four-factor model shown later as Equation 3, the risk premium for the market factor is the expected return of the market in excess of the risk-free rate; the factor risk premiums for the other three factors are the mean returns of the specific portfolios held long (e.g., the portfolio of small-cap stocks for the "small minus big" factor) minus the mean return for a related but opposite portfolio (e.g., a portfolio of large-cap stocks, in the case of that factor). A portfolio with a sensitivity of 1 to factor j and a sensitivity of 0 to all other factors is called a **pure factor portfolio** for factor j (or simply the **factor portfolio** for factor j).

For example, suppose we have a portfolio with a sensitivity of 1 with respect to Factor 1 and a sensitivity of 0 to all other factors. Using Equation 2, the expected return on this portfolio is $E_1 = R_F + \lambda_1 \times 1$. If $E_1 = 0.12$ and $R_F = 0.04$, then the risk premium for Factor 1 is

$$0.12 = 0.04 + \lambda_1 \times 1$$

$$\lambda_1 = 0.12 - 0.04 = 0.08 \text{ or } 8\%$$

EXAMPLE 1

Determining the Parameters in a One-Factor APT Model

Suppose we have three well-diversified portfolios that are each sensitive to the same single factor. Exhibit 2 shows the expected returns and factor sensitivities of these portfolios. Assume that the expected returns reflect a one-year investment horizon. To keep the analysis simple, all investors are assumed to agree upon the expected returns of the three portfolios as shown in the exhibit.

Exhibit 2	Sample Portfolios for a One-Factor Model	
Portfolio	**Expected Return**	**Factor Sensitivity**
A	0.075	0.5
B	0.150	2.0
C	0.070	0.4

We can use these data to determine the parameters of the APT equation. According to Equation 2, for any well-diversified portfolio and assuming a single factor explains returns, we have $E(R_p) = R_F + \lambda_1 \beta_{p,1}$. The factor sensitivities and expected returns are known; thus there are two unknowns, the parameters R_F and λ_1. Because two points define a straight line, we need to set up only two equations. Selecting Portfolios A and B, we have

$$E(R_A) = 0.075 = R_F + 0.5\lambda_1$$

and

$$E(R_B) = 0.150 = R_F + 2\lambda_1$$

From the equation for Portfolio A, we have $R_F = 0.075 - 0.5\lambda_1$. Substituting this expression for the risk-free rate into the equation for Portfolio B gives

$$0.15 = 0.075 - 0.5\lambda_1 + 2\lambda_1$$

$$0.15 = 0.075 + 1.5\lambda_1$$

So we have $\lambda_1 = (0.15 - 0.075)/1.5 = 0.05$. Substituting this value for λ_1 back into the equation for the expected return to Portfolio A yields

$$0.075 = R_F + 0.05 \times 0.5$$

$$R_F = 0.05$$

So the risk-free rate is 0.05 or 5%, and the factor premium for the common factor is also 0.05 or 5%. The APT equation is

$$E(R_p) = 0.05 + 0.05\beta_{p,1}$$

From Exhibit 2, Portfolio C has a factor sensitivity of 0.4. Therefore, according to the APT, the expected return of Portfolio C should be

$$E(R_B) = 0.05 + (0.05 \times 0.4) = 0.07$$

which is consistent with the expected return for Portfolio C given in Exhibit 2.

EXAMPLE 2

Checking Whether Portfolio Returns Are Consistent with No Arbitrage

In this example, we examine how to tell whether expected returns and factor sensitivities for a set of well-diversified portfolios may indicate the presence of an arbitrage opportunity. Exhibit 3 provides data on four hypothetical portfolios. The data for Portfolios A, B, and C are repeated from Exhibit 2. Portfolio D is a new portfolio. The factor sensitivities given relate to the one-factor APT model $E(R_p) = 0.05 + 0.05\beta_{p,1}$ derived in Example 1. As in Example 1, all investors are assumed to agree upon the expected returns of the portfolios. The question raised by the addition of this new Portfolio D is, Has the addition of this portfolio created an arbitrage opportunity? If there exists a portfolio that can be formed from Portfolios A, B, and C that has the same factor sensitivity as Portfolio D but a different expected return, then an arbitrage opportunity exists: Portfolio D would be either undervalued (if it offers a relatively high expected return) or overvalued (if it offers a relatively low expected return).

Exhibit 3	Sample Portfolios for a One-Factor Model	
Portfolio	Expected Return	Factor Sensitivity
A	0.0750	0.50
B	0.1500	2.00
C	0.0700	0.40
D	0.0800	0.45
0.5A + 0.5C	0.0725	0.45

Exhibit 3 gives data for an equally weighted portfolio of A and C. The expected return and factor sensitivity of this new portfolio are calculated as weighted averages of the expected returns and factor sensitivities of A and C. Expected return is thus $(0.50)(0.0750) + (0.50)(0.07) = 0.0725$, or 7.25%. The factor sensitivity is $(0.50)(0.50) + (0.50)(0.40) = 0.45$. Note that the factor sensitivity of 0.45 matches the factor sensitivity of Portfolio D. In this case, the configuration of expected returns in relation to factor risk presents an arbitrage opportunity involving Portfolios A, C, and D. Portfolio D offers, at 8%, an expected return that is too high given its factor sensitivity. According to the assumed APT model, the expected return on Portfolio D should be $E(R_D) = 0.05 + 0.05\beta_{D,1} = 0.05 + (0.05 \times 0.45) = 0.0725$, or 7.25%. Portfolio D is undervalued relative to its factor risk. We will buy D (hold it long) in the portfolio that exploits the arbitrage opportunity (the **arbitrage portfolio**). We purchase D using the proceeds from selling short an equally weighted portfolio of A and C with exactly the same 0.45 factor sensitivity as D.

The arbitrage thus involves the following strategy: Invest $10,000 in Portfolio D and fund that investment by selling short an equally weighted portfolio of Portfolios A and C; then close out the investment position at the end of one year (the investment horizon for expected returns). Exhibit 4 demonstrates the arbitrage profits to the arbitrage strategy. The final row of the exhibit shows the net cash flow to the arbitrage portfolio.

Exhibit 4   Arbitrage Opportunity within Sample Portfolios

	Initial Cash Flow	Final Cash Flow	Factor Sensitivity
Portfolio D	−$10,000.00	$10,800.00	0.45
Portfolios A and C	$10,000.00	−$10,725.00	−0.45
Sum	$0.00	$75.00	0.00

As Exhibit 4 shows, if we buy $10,000 of Portfolio D and sell $10,000 of an equally weighted portfolio of Portfolios A and C, we have an initial net cash flow of $0. The expected value of our investment in Portfolio D at the end of one year is $10,000(1 + 0.08) = $10,800. The expected value of our short position in Portfolios A and C at the end of one year is −$10,000(1.0725) = −$10,725. So, the combined expected cash flow from our investment position in one year is $75.

What about the risk? Exhibit 4 shows that the factor risk has been eliminated: Purchasing D and selling short an equally weighted portfolio of A and C creates a portfolio with a factor sensitivity of $0.45 − 0.45 = 0$. The portfolios are well diversified, and we assume any asset-specific risk is negligible.

Because an arbitrage is possible, Portfolios A, C, and D cannot all be consistent with the same equilibrium. If Portfolio D actually had an expected return of 8%, investors would bid up its price until the expected return fell and the arbitrage opportunity vanished. Thus, arbitrage restores equilibrium relationships among expected returns.

The Carhart four-factor model, also known as the four-factor model or simply the Carhart model, is a frequently referenced multifactor model in current equity portfolio management practice. Presented in Carhart (1997), it is an extension of the three-factor model developed by Fama and French (1992) to include a momentum factor. According to the model, there are three groups of stocks that tend to have higher returns than those predicted solely by their sensitivity to the market return:

- Small-capitalization stocks
- Low price-to-book-ratio stocks, commonly referred to as "value" stocks
- Stocks whose prices have been rising, commonly referred to as "momentum" stocks

On the basis of that evidence, the Carhart model posits the existence of three systematic risk factors beyond the market risk factor. They are named, in the same order as above, the following:

- Small minus big (SMB)
- High minus low (HML)
- Winners minus losers (WML)

Equation 3a is the Carhart model, in which the excess return on the portfolio is explained as a function of the portfolio's sensitivity to a market index (RMRF), a market capitalization factor (SMB), a book-value-to-price factor (HML), and a momentum factor (WML).

$$R_p - R_F = a_p + b_{p1}\text{RMRF} + b_{p2}\text{SMB} + b_{p3}\text{HML} + b_{p4}\text{WML} + \varepsilon_p \qquad \text{(3a)}$$

where

R_p and R_F = the return on the portfolio and the risk-free rate of return, respectively

a_p = "alpha" or return in excess of that expected given the portfolio's level of systematic risk (assuming the four factors capture all systematic risk)

b_p = the sensitivity of the portfolio to the given factor

RMRF = the return on a value-weighted equity index in excess of the one-month T-bill rate

SMB = small minus big, a size (market capitalization) factor; SMB is the average return on three small-cap portfolios minus the average return on three large-cap portfolios

HML = high minus low, the average return on two high book-to-market portfolios minus the average return on two low book-to-market portfolios

WML = winners minus losers, a momentum factor; WML is the return on a portfolio of the past year's winners minus the return on a portfolio of the past year's losers[6]

ε_p = an error term that represents the portion of the return to the portfolio, p, not explained by the model

Following Equation 2, the Carhart model can be stated as giving equilibrium expected return as

$$E(R_p) = R_F + \beta_{p,1}\text{RMRF} + \beta_{p,2}\text{SMB} + \beta_{p,3}\text{HML} + \beta_{p,4}\text{WML} \qquad \text{(3b)}$$

because the expected value of alpha is zero.

---

6 WML is an equally weighted average of the stocks with the highest 30% month returns lagged 1 month minus the equally weighted average of the stocks with the lowest 30% 11-month returns lagged 1 month. WML has the label PR1YR in the original paper by Carhart.

The Carhart model can be viewed as a multifactor extension of the CAPM that explicitly incorporates drivers of differences in expected returns among assets variables that are viewed as anomalies from a pure CAPM perspective. (The term "anomaly" in this context refers to an observed capital market regularity that is not explained by, or contradicts, a theory of asset pricing.) From the perspective of the CAPM, there are size, value, and momentum anomalies. From the perspective of the Carhart model, however, size, value, and momentum represent systematic risk factors; exposure to them is expected to be compensated in the marketplace in the form of differences in mean return.

Size, value, and momentum are common themes in equity portfolio construction, and all three factors continue to have robust uses in active management risk decomposition and return attribution.

MULTIFACTOR MODELS: TYPES

4

Having introduced the APT, it is appropriate to examine the diversity of multifactor models in current use.

In the following sections, we explain the basic principles of multifactor models and discuss various types of models and their application. We also expand on the APT, which relates the expected return of investments to their risk with respect to a set of factors.

4.1 Factors and Types of Multifactor Models

Many varieties of multifactor models have been proposed and researched. We can categorize most of them into three main groups according to the type of factor used:

- In a **macroeconomic factor model**, the factors are surprises in macroeconomic variables that significantly explain returns. In the example of equities, the factors can be understood as affecting either the expected future cash flows of companies or the interest rate used to discount these cash flows back to the present. Among macroeconomic factors that have been used are interest rates, inflation risk, business cycle risk, and credit spreads.

- In a **fundamental factor model**, the factors are attributes of stocks or companies that are important in explaining cross-sectional differences in stock prices. Among the fundamental factors that have been used are the book-value-to-price ratio, market capitalization, the price-to-earnings ratio, and financial leverage.

- In a **statistical factor model**, statistical methods are applied to historical returns of a group of securities to extract factors that can explain the observed returns of securities in the group. In statistical factor models, the factors are actually portfolios of the securities in the group under study and are therefore defined by portfolio weights. Two major types of factor models are factor analysis models and principal components models. In factor analysis models, the factors are the portfolios of securities that best explain (reproduce) historical *return covariances*. In principal components models, the factors are portfolios of securities that best explain (reproduce) the historical *return variances*.

A potential advantage of statistical factor models is that they make minimal assumptions. But the interpretation of statistical factors is generally difficult, in contrast to macroeconomic and fundamental factors. A statistical factor that is a portfolio with weights that are similar to market index weights might be interpreted as "the market factor," for example. But in general, associating a statistical factor with economic meaning may not be possible. Because understanding statistical factor models requires substantial preparation in quantitative methods, a detailed discussion of statistical factor models is outside the scope of this reading.

Our discussion concentrates on macroeconomic factor models and fundamental factor models. Industry use has generally favored fundamental and macroeconomic models, perhaps because such models are much more easily interpreted and rely less on data-mining approaches; nevertheless, statistical factor models have proponents and are also used in practical applications.

4.2 The Structure of Macroeconomic Factor Models

The representation of returns in macroeconomic factor models assumes that the returns to each asset are correlated with only the surprises in some factors related to the aggregate economy, such as inflation or real output.[7] We can define *surprise* in general as the actual value minus predicted (or expected) value. A factor's surprise is the component of the factor's return that was unexpected, and the factor surprises constitute the model's independent variables. This idea contrasts with the representation of independent variables as returns in Equation 2, reflecting the fact that how the independent variables are represented varies across different types of models.

Suppose that K macro factors explain asset returns. Then in a macroeconomic factor model, Equation 4 expresses the return of asset i:

$$R_i = a_i + b_{i1}F_1 + b_{i2}F_2 + \ldots + b_{iK}F_K + \varepsilon_i \qquad (4)$$

where

R_i = the return to asset i

a_i = the expected return to asset i

b_{ik} = the sensitivity of the return on asset i to a surprise in factor k, $k = 1, 2, \ldots, K$

F_k = the surprise in the factor k, $k = 1, 2, \ldots, K$

ε_i = an error term with a zero mean that represents the portion of the return to asset i not explained by the factor model

Surprise in a macroeconomic factor can be illustrated as follows: Suppose we are analyzing monthly returns for stocks. At the beginning of each month, we have a prediction of inflation for the month. The prediction may come from an econometric model or a professional economic forecaster, for example. Suppose our forecast at the beginning of the month is that inflation will be 0.4% during the month. At the end of the month, we find that inflation was actually 0.5% during the month. During any month,

Actual inflation = Predicted inflation + Surprise inflation

In this case, actual inflation was 0.5% and predicted inflation was 0.4%. Therefore, the surprise in inflation was 0.5% − 0.4% = 0.1%.

What is the effect of defining the factors in terms of surprises? Suppose we believe that inflation and gross domestic product (GDP) growth are two factors that carry risk premiums; that is, inflation and GDP represent priced risk. (GDP is a money measure of the goods and services produced within a country's borders.) We do not use the predicted values of these variables because the predicted values should already be reflected in stock prices and thus in their expected returns. The intercept a_i, the expected return to asset i, reflects the effect of the predicted values of the macroeconomic variables on expected stock returns. The surprise in the macroeconomic

---

[7] See, for example, Burmeister, Roll, and Ross (1994).

variables during the month, however, contains new information about the variable. As a result, this model structure analyzes the return to an asset in three components: the asset's expected return, its unexpected return resulting from new information about the factors, and an error term.

Consider a factor model in which the returns to each asset are correlated with two factors. For example, we might assume that the returns for a particular stock are correlated with surprises in inflation rates and surprises in GDP growth. For stock i, the return to the stock can be modeled as

$$R_i = a_i + b_{i1}F_{INFL} + b_{i2}F_{GDP} + \varepsilon_i$$

where

R_i = the return to stock i

a_i = the expected return to stock i

b_{i1} = the sensitivity of the return to stock i to inflation rate surprises

F_{INFL} = the surprise in inflation rates

b_{i2} = the sensitivity of the return to stock i to GDP growth surprises

F_{GDP} = the surprise in GDP growth (assumed to be uncorrelated with F_{INT})

ε_i = an error term with a zero mean that represents the portion of the return to asset i not explained by the factor model

Consider first how to interpret b_{i1}. The factor model predicts that a 1 percentage point surprise in inflation rates will contribute b_{i1} percentage points to the return to stock i. The slope coefficient b_{i2} has a similar interpretation relative to the GDP growth factor. Thus, slope coefficients are naturally interpreted as the factor sensitivities of the asset. A *factor sensitivity* is a measure of the response of return to each unit of increase in a factor, holding all other factors constant. (Factor sensitivities are sometimes called *factor betas* or *factor loadings*.)

Now consider how to interpret the intercept a_i. Recall that the error term has a mean or average value of zero. If the surprises in both inflation rates and GDP growth are zero, the factor model predicts that the return to asset i will be a_i. Thus, a_i is the expected value of the return to stock i.

Finally, consider the error term, ε_i. The intercept a_i represents the asset's expected return. The term $(b_{i1}F_{INT} + b_{i2}F_{GDP})$ represents the return resulting from factor surprises, and we have interpreted these as the sources of risk shared with other assets. The term ε_i is the part of return that is unexplained by expected return or the factor surprises. If we have adequately represented the sources of common risk (the factors), then ε_i must represent an asset-specific risk. For a stock, it might represent the return from an unanticipated company-specific event.

The risk premium for the GDP growth factor is typically positive. The risk premium for the inflation factor, however, is typically negative. Thus, an asset with a positive sensitivity to the inflation factor—an asset with returns that tend to be positive in response to unexpectedly high inflation—would have a lower required return than if its inflation sensitivity were negative; an asset with positive sensitivity to inflation would be in demand for its inflation-hedging ability.

This discussion has broader applications: It can be used for various asset classes, including fixed income and commodities, and can also be used in asset allocation where asset classes can be examined in relation to inflation and GDP growth, as illustrated below. In Exhibit 5, each quadrant reflects a unique mix of inflation and economic growth expectations. Certain asset classes or securities can be expected to perform differently in various inflation and GDP growth regimes and can be plotted in the appropriate quadrant, thus forming a concrete illustration of a two-factor model, as shown below.

Exhibit 5	Growth and Inflation Factor Matrix	
	Inflation	
	Low Inflation/Low Growth	**High Inflation/Low Growth**
	■ Cash	■ Inflation-linked bonds
	■ Government bonds	■ Commodities
		■ Infrastructure
Growth	**Low Inflation/High Growth**	**High Inflation/High Growth**
	■ Equity	■ Real assets (real estate, timber-land, farmland, energy)
	■ Corporate debt	

Note: Entries are assets likely to benefit from the specified combination of growth and inflation.

In macroeconomic factor models, the time series of factor surprises are constructed first. Regression analysis is then used to estimate assets' sensitivities to the factors. In practice, estimated sensitivities and intercepts are often acquired from one of the many consulting companies that specialize in factor models. When we have the parameters for the individual assets in a portfolio, we can calculate the portfolio's parameters as a weighted average of the parameters of individual assets. An individual asset's weight in that calculation is the proportion of the total market value of the portfolio that the individual asset represents.

EXAMPLE 3

Estimating Returns for a Two-Stock Portfolio Given Factor Sensitivities

Suppose that stock returns are affected by two common factors: surprises in inflation and surprises in GDP growth. A portfolio manager is analyzing the returns on a portfolio of two stocks, Manumatic (MANM) and Nextech (NXT). The following equations describe the returns for those stocks, where the factors F_{INFL} and F_{GDP} represent the surprise in inflation and GDP growth, respectively:

$$R_{MANM} = 0.09 - 1F_{INFL} + 1F_{GDP} + \varepsilon_{MANM}$$

$$R_{NXT} = 0.12 + 2F_{INFL} + 4F_{GDP} + \varepsilon_{NXT}$$

One-third of the portfolio is invested in Manumatic stock, and two-thirds is invested in Nextech stock.

1 Formulate an expression for the return on the portfolio.

2 State the expected return on the portfolio.

3 Calculate the return on the portfolio given that the surprises in inflation and GDP growth are 1% and 0%, respectively, assuming that the error terms for MANM and NXT both equal 0.5%.

In evaluating the equations for surprises in inflation and GDP, amounts stated in percentage terms need to be converted to decimal form.

Solution to 1:

The portfolio's return is the following weighted average of the returns to the two stocks:

$$R_P = (1/3)(0.09) + (2/3)(0.12) + [(1/3)(-1) + (2/3)(2)]F_{INFL} + [(1/3)(1) +$$
$$(2/3)(4)]F_{GDP} + (1/3)\varepsilon_{MANM} + (2/3)\varepsilon_{NXT}$$
$$= 0.11 + 1F_{INFL} + 3F_{GDP} + (1/3)\varepsilon_{MANM} + (2/3)\varepsilon_{NXT}$$

Solution to 2:

The expected return on the portfolio is 11%, the value of the intercept in the expression obtained in the solution to 1.

Solution to 3:

$$R_P = 0.11 + 1F_{INFL} + 3F_{GDP} + (1/3)\varepsilon_{MANM} + (2/3)\varepsilon_{NXT}$$
$$= 0.11 + 1(0.01) + 3(0) + (1/3)(0.005) + (2/3)(0.005)$$
$$= 0.125, \text{ or } 12.5\%$$

4.3 The Structure of Fundamental Factor Models

We earlier gave the equation of a macroeconomic factor model as

$$R_i = a_i + b_{i1}F_1 + b_{i2}F_2 + \dots + b_{iK}F_K + \varepsilon_i$$

We can also represent the structure of fundamental factor models with this equation, but we need to interpret the terms differently.

In fundamental factor models, the factors are stated as *returns* rather than return *surprises* in relation to predicted values, so they do not generally have expected values of zero. This approach changes the meaning of the intercept, which is no longer interpreted as the expected return.[8]

Factor sensitivities are also interpreted differently in most fundamental factor models. In fundamental factor models, the factor sensitivities are attributes of the security. An asset's sensitivity to a factor is expressed using a **standardized beta**, the value of the attribute for the asset minus the average value of the attribute across all stocks divided by the standard deviation of the attribute's values across all stocks.

$$b_{ik} = \frac{\text{Value of attribute } k \text{ for asset } i - \text{Average value of attribute } k}{\sigma(\text{Values of attribute } k)} \qquad (5)$$

Consider a fundamental model for equities that uses a dividend yield factor. After standardization, a stock with an average dividend yield will have a factor sensitivity of 0, a stock with a dividend yield one standard deviation above the average will have a factor sensitivity of 1, and a stock with a dividend yield one standard deviation below the average will have a factor sensitivity of −1. Suppose, for example, that an investment has a dividend yield of 3.5% and that the average dividend yield across all stocks being considered is 2.5%. Further, suppose that the standard deviation of dividend yields across all stocks is 2%. The investment's sensitivity to dividend yield is (3.5% − 2.5%)/2% = 0.50, or one-half standard deviation above average. The scaling permits all factor sensitivities to be interpreted similarly, despite differences in units of measure and scale in the variables. The exception to this interpretation is factors for

---

8 If the coefficients were not standardized as described in the following paragraph, the intercept could be interpreted as the risk-free rate, because it would be the return to an asset with no factor risk (zero factor betas) and no asset-specific risk. With standardized coefficients, the intercept is not interpreted beyond being an intercept in a regression included so that the expected asset-specific risk equals zero.

binary variables, such as industry membership. A company either participates in an industry or does not. Industry factor sensitivities are typically modeled by 0–1 dummy variables.[9] The sensitivity is 1 if the stock belongs to the industry and 0 if it does not.

A second distinction between macroeconomic multifactor models and fundamental factor models is that with the former, we develop the factor (surprise) series first and then estimate the factor sensitivities through regressions; with the latter, we generally specify the factor sensitivities (attributes) first and then estimate the factor returns through regressions.

Financial analysts use fundamental factor models for a variety of purposes, including portfolio performance attribution and risk analysis. (*Performance attribution* consists of return attribution and risk attribution. *Return attribution* is a set of techniques used to identify the sources of the excess return of a portfolio against its benchmark. *Risk attribution* addresses the sources of risk, identifying the sources of portfolio volatility for absolute mandates and the sources of tracking risk for relative mandates.) Fundamental factor models focus on explaining the returns to individual stocks using observable fundamental factors that describe either attributes of the securities themselves or attributes of the securities' issuers. Industry membership, price-to-earnings ratio, book-value-to-price ratio, size, and financial leverage are examples of fundamental factors.

Example 4 discusses a study that examined macroeconomic, fundamental, and statistical factor models.

EXAMPLE 4

Comparing Types of Factor Models

Connor (1995) contrasted a macroeconomic factor model with a fundamental factor model to compare how well the models explain stock returns.

Connor reported the results of applying a macroeconomic factor model to the returns for 779 large-cap US stocks based on monthly data from January 1985 through December 1993. Using five macroeconomic factors, Connor was able to explain approximately 11% of the variance of return on these stocks.[10] Exhibit 6 shows his results.

Exhibit 6	The Explanatory Power of the Macroeconomic Factors	
Factor	**Explanatory Power from Using Each Factor Alone**	**Increase in Explanatory Power from Adding Each Factor to All the Others**
Inflation	1.3%	0.0%
Term structure	1.1%	7.7%

---

9 To further explain 0–1 variables, industry membership is measured on a nominal scale because measurement consists only in identifying the industry to which a company belongs. A nominal variable can be represented in a regression by a dummy variable (a variable that takes on the value of 0 or 1). For more on dummy variables, see the reading on multiple regression.

10 The explanatory power of a given model was computed as 1 − [(Average asset-specific variance of return across stocks)/(Average total variance of return across stocks)]. The variance estimates were corrected for degrees of freedom, so the marginal contribution of a factor to explanatory power can be zero or negative. Explanatory power captures the proportion of the total variance of return that a given model explains for the average stock.

Exhibit 6   (Continued)

Factor	Explanatory Power from Using Each Factor Alone	Increase in Explanatory Power from Adding Each Factor to All the Others
Industrial production	0.5%	0.3%
Default premium	2.4%	8.1%
Unemployment	−0.3%	0.1%
All factors (total explanatory power)		10.9%

Source: Connor (1995).

Connor also reported a fundamental factor analysis of the same companies. The factor model employed was the BARRA US-E2 model (as of 2015, the current version is E4). Exhibit 7 shows these results. In the exhibit, "variability in markets" represents the stock's volatility, "success" is a price momentum variable, "trade activity" distinguishes stocks by how often their shares trade, and "growth" distinguishes stocks by past and anticipated earnings growth.[11]

Exhibit 7   The Explanatory Power of the Fundamental Factors

Factor	Explanatory Power from Using Each Factor Alone	Increase in Explanatory Power from Adding Each Factor to All the Others
Industries	16.3%	18.0%
Variability in markets	4.3%	0.9%
Success	2.8%	0.8%
Size	1.4%	0.6%
Trade activity	1.4%	0.5%
Growth	3.0%	0.4%
Earnings to price	2.2%	0.6%
Book to price	1.5%	0.6%
Earnings variability	2.5%	0.4%
Financial leverage	0.9%	0.5%
Foreign investment	0.7%	0.4%
Labor intensity	2.2%	0.5%
Dividend yield	2.9%	0.4%
All factors (total explanatory power)		42.6%

Source: Connor (1995).

---

11 The explanations of the variables are from Grinold and Kahn (1994); Connor did not supply definitions.

As Exhibit 7 shows, the most important fundamental factor is "industries," represented by 55 industry dummy variables. The fundamental factor model explained approximately 43% of the variation in stock returns, compared with approximately 11% for the macroeconomic factor model. Because "industries" must sum to the market and the market portfolio is not incorporated in the macroeconomic factor model, some advantage to the explanatory power of the fundamental factor may be built into the specific models being compared. Connor's article also does not provide tests of the statistical significance of the various factors in either model; however, Connor's research is strong evidence for the usefulness of fundamental factor models, and this evidence is mirrored by the wide use of those models in the investment community. Fundamental factor models are frequently used in portfolio performance attribution, for example. Typically, fundamental factor models employ many more factors than macroeconomic factor models, giving a more detailed picture of the sources of an investment manager's returns.

We cannot conclude from this study, however, that fundamental factor models are inherently superior to macroeconomic factor models. Each major type of model has its uses. The factors in various macroeconomic factor models are individually backed by statistical evidence that they represent systematic risk (i.e., risk that cannot be diversified away). The same may not be true of each factor in a fundamental factor model; for example, a portfolio manager can easily construct a portfolio that excludes a particular industry, so exposure to a particular industry is not systematic risk. The two types of factors, macroeconomic and fundamental, have different implications for measuring and managing risk, in general. The macroeconomic factor set is parsimonious (five variables in the model studied) and allows a portfolio manager to incorporate economic views into portfolio construction by adjustments to portfolio exposures to macro factors. The fundamental factor set examined by Connor is large (67 variables, including the 55 industry dummy variables), and at the expense of greater complexity, it can give a more detailed picture of risk in terms that are easily related to company and security characteristics. Connor found that the macroeconomic factor model had no marginal explanatory power when added to the fundamental factor model, implying that the fundamental risk attributes capture all the risk characteristics represented by the macroeconomic factor betas. Because the fundamental factors supply such a detailed description of the characteristics of a stock and its issuer, however, this finding is not necessarily surprising.

We encounter a range of distinct representations of risk in the fundamental models that are currently used in practical applications. Diversity exists in both the identity and exact definition of factors as well as in the underlying functional form and estimation procedures. Despite the diversity, we can place the factors of most fundamental factor models for equities into three broad groups:

- **Company fundamental factors.** These are factors related to the company's internal performance. Examples are factors relating to earnings growth, earnings variability, earnings momentum, and financial leverage.

- **Company share-related factors.** These factors include valuation measures and other factors related to share price or the trading characteristics of the shares. In contrast to the previous category, these factors directly incorporate investors' expectations concerning the company. Examples include price multiples such as earnings yield, dividend yield, and book to market. Market capitalization falls under this heading. Various models incorporate variables relating to share price momentum, share price volatility, and trading activity that fall in this category.

- **Macroeconomic factors.** Sector or industry membership factors fall under this heading. Various models include factors such as CAPM beta, other similar measures of systematic risk, and yield curve level sensitivity, all of which can be placed in this category.

For global factor models in particular, a classification of country, industry, and style factors is often used. In that classification, country and industry factors are dummy variables for country and industry membership, respectively. Style factors include those related to earnings, risk, and valuation that define types of securities typical of various styles of investing.

MULTIFACTOR MODELS: SELECTED APPLICATIONS

5

The following sections present selected applications of multifactor models in investment practice. The applications discussed are return attribution, risk attribution, portfolio construction, and strategic portfolio decisions.

We begin by discussing portfolio return attribution and risk attribution, focusing on the analysis of benchmark-relative returns.

After discussing performance attribution and risk analysis, we explain the use of multifactor models in creating a portfolio with a desired set of risk exposures.

Additionally, multifactor models can be used for asset allocation purposes. Some large, sophisticated asset owners have chosen to define their asset allocation opportunity sets in terms of macroeconomic or thematic factors and aggregate factor exposures (represented by pure factor portfolios as defined earlier). Many others are examining their traditionally derived asset allocation policies using factor models to map asset class exposure to factor sensitivities. The trend toward factor-based asset allocation has two chief causes: first is the increasing availability of sophisticated factor models (like the BARRA models used in the examples below), and second is the more intense focus by asset owners on the many dimensions of risk.

5.1 Factor Models in Return Attribution

Multifactor models can help us understand in detail the sources of a manager's returns relative to a benchmark. For simplicity, in this section we analyze the sources of the returns of a portfolio fully invested in the equities of a single national equity market,[12] though the same methodology can be applied across asset classes and geographies.

Analysts often favor fundamental multifactor models in decomposing (separating into basic elements) the sources of returns. In contrast to statistical factor models, fundamental factor models allow the sources of portfolio performance to be described using commonly understood terms. Fundamental factors are also thematically understandable and can be incorporated into simple narratives for clients concerning return or risk attribution.

---

12 This assumption allows us to ignore the roles of country selection, asset allocation, market timing, and currency hedging, greatly simplifying the analysis. However, we can perform similar analyses using multifactor models in a more general context.

Also, in contrast to macroeconomic factor models, fundamental models express investment style choices and security characteristics more directly and often in greater detail.

We first need to understand the objectives of active managers. As mentioned previously, managers are commonly evaluated relative to a specified benchmark. Active portfolio managers hold securities in different-from-benchmark weights in an attempt to add value to their portfolios relative to a passive investment approach. Securities held in different-from-benchmark weights reflect portfolio manager expectations that differ from consensus expectations. For an equity manager, those expectations may relate to common factors driving equity returns or to considerations unique to a company. Thus, when we evaluate an active manager, we want to ask questions such as, Did the manager have insights that were effectively translated into returns in excess of those that were available from a passive alternative? Analyzing the sources of returns using multifactor models can help answer these questions.

The return on a portfolio, R_p, can be viewed as the sum of the benchmark's return, R_B, and the **active return** (portfolio return minus benchmark return):

$$\text{Active return} = R_p - R_B \tag{6}$$

With the help of a factor model, we can analyze a portfolio manager's active return as the sum of two components. The first component is the product of the portfolio manager's factor tilts (over- or underweights relative to the benchmark factor sensitivities) and the factor returns; we call that component the return from factor tilts. The second component of active return reflects the manager's skill in individual asset selection (ability to overweight securities that outperform the benchmark or underweight securities that underperform the benchmark); we call that component security selection. Equation 7 shows the decomposition of active return into those two components, where k represents the factor or factors represented in the benchmark portfolio:

$$\text{Active return} = \sum_{k=1}^{K}\Big[(\text{Portfolio sensitivity})_k - (\text{Benchmark sensitivity})_k\Big] \\ \times (\text{Factor return})_k + \text{Security selection} \tag{7}$$

In Equation 7, the portfolio's and benchmark's sensitivities to each factor are calculated as of the beginning of the evaluation period.

EXAMPLE 5

Four-Factor Model Active Return Decomposition

As an equity analyst at a pension fund sponsor, Ronald Service uses the Carhart four-factor multifactor model of Equation 3a to evaluate US equity portfolios:

$$R_p - R_F = a_p + b_{p1}\text{RMRF} + b_{p2}\text{SMB} + b_{p3}\text{HML} + b_{p4}\text{WML} + \varepsilon_p$$

Service's current task is to evaluate the performance of the most recently hired US equity manager. That manager's benchmark is an index representing the performance of the 1,000 largest US stocks by market value. The manager describes himself as a "stock picker" and points to his performance in beating the benchmark as evidence that he is successful. Exhibit 8 presents an analysis based on the Carhart model of the sources of that manager's active return during the year, given an assumed set of factor returns. In Exhibit 8, the entry titled "A. Return from Factor Tilts," equal to 2.1241%, is the sum of the four numbers above it. The exhibit ("B. Security Selection") gives security selection as equal to −0.05%. Active return is found as the sum of these two components: 2.1241% + (−0.05%) = 2.0741%.

Exhibit 8	Active Return Decomposition					
	Factor Sensitivity				**Contribution to Active Return**	
Factor	**Portfolio (1)**	**Benchmark (2)**	**Difference (3) = (1) − (2)**	**Factor Return (4)**	**Absolute (3) × (4)**	**Proportion of Total Active**
RMRF	0.95	1.00	−0.05	5.52%	−0.2760%	−13.3%
SMB	−1.05	−1.00	−0.05	−3.35%	0.1675%	8.1%
HML	0.40	0.00	0.40	5.10%	2.0400%	98.4%
WML	0.05	0.03	0.02	9.63%	0.1926%	9.3%
			A. Return from Factor Tilts =		2.1241%	102.4%
			B. Security Selection =		−0.0500%	−2.4%
			C. Active Return (A + B) =		2.0741%	100.0%

From his previous work, Service knows that the returns to growth-style portfolios often have a positive sensitivity to the momentum factor (WML). By contrast, the returns to certain value-style portfolios, in particular those following a contrarian strategy, often have a negative sensitivity to the momentum factor. Using the information given, address the following questions (assume the benchmark chosen for the manager is appropriate):

1   Determine the manager's investment mandate and his actual investment style.

2   Evaluate the sources of the manager's active return for the year.

3   What concerns might Service discuss with the manager as a result of the return decomposition?

Solution to 1:

The benchmarks chosen for the manager should reflect the baseline risk characteristics of the manager's investment opportunity set and his mandate. We can ascertain whether the manager's actual style follows the mandate by examining the portfolio's actual factor exposures:

▪ The sensitivities of the benchmark are consistent with the description in the text. The sensitivity to RMRF of 1 indicates that the assigned benchmark has average market risk, consistent with it being a broad-based index; the negative sensitivity to SMB indicates a large-cap orientation. The mandate might be described as large-cap without a value/growth bias (HML is zero) or a momentum bias (WML is close to zero).

▪ Stocks with high book-to-market ratios are generally viewed as value stocks. Because the equity manager has a positive sensitivity to HML (0.40), it appears that the manager has a value orientation. The manager is approximately neutral to the momentum factor, so the equity manager is not a momentum investor and probably not a contrarian value investor. In summary, the above considerations suggest that the manager has a large-cap value orientation.

Solution to 2:

The dominant source of the manager's positive active return was his positive active exposure to the HML factor. The bet contributed approximately 98% of the realized active return of about 2.07%. The manager's active exposure to the overall market (RMRF) was unprofitable, but his active exposures to small stocks

(SMB) and to momentum (WML) were profitable; however, the magnitudes of the manager's active exposures to RMRF, SMB, and WML were relatively small, so the effects of those bets on active return were minor compared with his large and successful bet on HML.

Solution to 3:

Although the manager is a self-described "stock picker," his active return from security selection in this period was actually negative. His positive active return resulted from the concurrence of a large active bet on HML and a high return to that factor during the period. If the market had favored growth rather than value without the manager doing better in individual security selection, the manager's performance would have been unsatisfactory. Service's conversations with the manager should focus on evidence that he can predict changes in returns to the HML factor and on the manager's stock selection discipline.

5.2 Factor Models in Risk Attribution

Building on the discussion of active returns, this section explores the analysis of active risk. A few key terms are important to the understanding of how factor models are used to build an understanding of a portfolio manager's risk exposures. We will describe them briefly before moving on to the detailed discussion of risk attribution.

Active risk can be represented by the standard deviation of active returns. A traditional term for that standard deviation is **tracking error** (TE). **Tracking risk** is a synonym for tracking error that is often used in the CFA Program curriculum. We will use the abbreviation TE for the concept of active risk and refer to it usually as tracking error:

$$TE = s(R_p - R_B) \tag{8}$$

In Equation 8, $s(R_p - R_B)$ indicates that we take the sample standard deviation (indicated by s) of the time series of differences between the portfolio return, R_p, and the benchmark return, R_B. We should be careful that active return and tracking error are stated on the same time basis.[13]

As a broad indication of the range for tracking error, in US equity markets a well-executed passive investment strategy can often achieve a tracking error on the order of 0.10% or less per annum. A low-risk active or enhanced index investment strategy, which makes tightly controlled use of managers' expectations, often has a tracking error goal of 2% per annum. A diversified active large-cap equity strategy that might be benchmarked to the S&P 500 Index would commonly have a tracking error in the range of 2%–6% per annum. An aggressive active equity manager might have a tracking error in the range of 6%–10% or more.

Somewhat analogous to the use of the traditional Sharpe measure in evaluating absolute returns, the **information ratio** (IR) is a tool for evaluating mean active returns per unit of active risk. The historical or *ex post* IR is expressed as follows:

$$IR = \frac{\overline{R}_p - \overline{R}_B}{s(R_p - R_B)} \tag{9}$$

---

13 As an approximation assuming returns are serially uncorrelated, to annualize a daily TE based on daily returns, we multiply daily TE by $(250)^{1/2}$ based on 250 trading days in a year; to annualize a monthly TE based on monthly returns, we multiply monthly TE by $(12)^{1/2}$.

In the numerator of Equation 9, $\bar{R}_p$ and $\bar{R}_B$ stand for the sample mean return on the portfolio and the sample mean return on the benchmark, respectively.[14] To illustrate the calculation, if a portfolio achieved a mean return of 9% during the same period that its benchmark earned a mean return of 7.5% and the portfolio's tracking error (the denominator) was 6%, we would calculate an information ratio of (9% − 7.5%)/6% = 0.25. Setting guidelines for acceptable active risk or tracking error is one of the methods that some investors use to ensure that the overall risk and style characteristics of their investments are in line with their chosen benchmark.

Note that in addition to focusing exclusively on *active* risk, multifactor models can also be used to decompose and attribute sources of *total* risk. For instance, a multi-asset class multi-strategy long/short fund can be evaluated with an appropriate multifactor model to reveal insights on sources of total risk.

EXAMPLE 6

Creating Active Manager Guidelines

The framework of active return and active risk is appealing to investors who want to manage the risk of investments. The benchmark serves as a known and continuously observable reference standard in relation to which quantitative risk and return objectives may be stated and communicated. For example, a US public employee retirement system invited investment managers to submit proposals to manage a "low-active-risk US large-cap equity fund" that would be subject to the following constraints:

- Shares must be components of the S&P 500.

- The portfolio should have a minimum of 200 issues. At time of purchase, the maximum amount that may be invested in any one issuer is 5% of the portfolio at market value or 150% of the issuers' weight within the S&P 500, whichever is greater.

- The portfolio must have a minimum information ratio of 0.30 either since inception or over the last seven years.

- The portfolio must also have tracking risk of less than 3% with respect to the S&P 500 either since inception or over the last seven years.

Once a suitable active manager is found and hired, these requirements can be written into the manager's guidelines. The retirement system's individual mandates would be set such that the sum of mandates across managers would equal the desired risk exposures.

---

14 The expression for IR given here assumes that the portfolio being evaluated has the same systematic risk as its benchmark. There is also a more precise form of the information ratio that corrects for any differences in systematic risk relative to the benchmark. This form has alpha, rather than active return, in the numerator and the portfolio's residual (non-systematic) risk in the denominator. See Fischer and Wermers (2013, pp. 75–80) for a detailed treatment of the IR. The IR, especially in the more precise form, is also known as the Treynor–Black appraisal ratio.

Analysts use multifactor models to understand a portfolio manager's risk exposures in detail. By decomposing active risk, the analyst's objective is to measure the portfolio's active exposure along each dimension of risk—in other words, to understand the sources of tracking error.[15] Among the questions analysts will want to answer are the following:

- What active exposures contributed most to the manager's tracking error?

- Was the portfolio manager aware of the nature of his active exposures, and if so, can he articulate a rationale for assuming them?

- Are the portfolio's active risk exposures consistent with the manager's stated investment philosophy?

- Which active bets earned adequate returns for the level of active risk taken?

In addressing these questions, analysts often choose fundamental factor models because they can be used to relate active risk exposures to a manager's portfolio decisions in a fairly direct and intuitive way. In this section, we explain how to decompose or explain a portfolio's active risk using a multifactor model.

We previously addressed the decomposition of active return; now we address the decomposition of active risk. In analyzing risk, it is more convenient to use variances rather than standard deviations because the variances of uncorrelated variables are additive. We refer to the variance of active risk as **active risk squared**:

$$\text{Active risk squared} = s^2(R_p - R_B) \tag{10}$$

We can separate a portfolio's active risk squared into two components:

- **Active factor risk** is the contribution to active risk squared resulting from the portfolio's different-from-benchmark exposures relative to factors specified in the risk model.

- **Active specific risk** or **security selection risk** measures the active non-factor or residual risk assumed by the manager. Portfolio managers attempt to provide a positive average return from security selection as compensation for assuming active specific risk.

As we use the terms, "active specific risk" and "active factor risk" refer to variances rather than standard deviations. When applied to an investment in a single asset class, active risk squared has two components:

$$\text{Active risk squared} = \text{Active factor risk} + \text{Active specific risk} \tag{11}$$

Active factor risk represents the part of active risk squared explained by the portfolio's active factor exposures. Active factor risk can be found indirectly as the risk remaining after active specific risk is deducted from active risk squared. Active specific risk can be expressed as[16]

$$\text{Active specific risk} = \sum_{i=1}^{n} \left(w_i^a \right)^2 \sigma_{\varepsilon_i}^2$$

---

15 The portfolio's active risks are weighted averages of the component securities' active risk. Therefore, we may also perform the analysis at the level of individual holdings. A portfolio manager may find this approach useful in making adjustments to his active risk profile.

16 The direct procedure for calculating active factor risk is as follows. A portfolio's active factor exposure to a given factor j, b_j^a, is found by weighting each asset's sensitivity to factor j by its active weight and summing the terms: $b_j^a = \sum_{i=1}^{n} w_i^a b_{ji}$. Then active factor risk equals $\sum_{i=1}^{K} \sum_{j=1}^{K} b_i^a b_j^a \, \text{cov}\left(F_i, F_j\right)$.

where w_i^a is the ith asset's active weight in the portfolio (that is, the difference between the asset's weight in the portfolio and its weight in the benchmark) and $\sigma_{\varepsilon_i}^2$ is the residual risk of the ith asset (the variance of the ith asset's returns left unexplained by the factors).

EXAMPLE 7

A Comparison of Active Risk

Richard Gray is comparing the risk of four US equity managers who share the same benchmark. He uses a fundamental factor model, the BARRA US-E4 model, which incorporates 12 style factors and a set of 60 industry factors. The style factors measure various fundamental aspects of companies and their shares, such as size, liquidity, leverage, and dividend yield. In the model, companies have non-zero exposures to all industries in which the company operates. Exhibit 9 presents Gray's analysis of the active risk squared of the four managers, based on Equation 11.[17] In Exhibit 9, the column labeled "Industry" gives the portfolio's active factor risk associated with the industry exposures of its holdings; the "Style Factor" column gives the portfolio's active factor risk associated with the exposures of its holdings to the 12 style factors.

Exhibit 9	Active Risk Squared Decomposition				
	Active Factor				
Portfolio	Industry	Style Factor	Total Factor	Active Specific	Active Risk Squared
A	12.25	17.15	29.40	19.60	49
B	1.25	13.75	15.00	10.00	25
C	1.25	17.50	18.75	6.25	25
D	0.03	0.47	0.50	0.50	1

Note: Entries are in % squared.

Using the information in Exhibit 9, address the following:

1 Contrast the active risk decomposition of Portfolios A and B.
2 Contrast the active risk decomposition of Portfolios B and C.
3 Characterize the investment approach of Portfolio D.

Solution to 1:

Exhibit 10 restates the information in Exhibit 9 to show the proportional contributions of the various sources of active risk. (e.g., Portfolio A's active risk related to industry exposures is 25% of active risk squared, calculated as 12.25/49 = 0.25, or 25%).

The last column of Exhibit 10 now shows the square root of active risk squared—that is, active risk or tracking error.

---

17 There is a covariance term in active factor risk, reflecting the correlation of industry membership and the risk indexes, which we assume is negligible in this example.

Exhibit 10	Active Risk Decomposition (re-stated)				
	Active Factor (% of total active)			**Active Specific (% of total active)**	
Portfolio	**Industry**	**Style Factor**	**Total Factor**		**Active Risk**
A	25%	35%	60%	40%	7%
B	5%	55%	60%	40%	5%
C	5%	70%	75%	25%	5%
D	3%	47%	50%	50%	1%

Portfolio A has assumed a higher level of active risk than B (7% versus 5%). Portfolios A and B assumed the same proportions of active factor and active specific risk, but a sharp contrast exists between the two in the types of active factor risk exposure. Portfolio A assumed substantial active industry risk, whereas Portfolio B was approximately industry neutral relative to the benchmark. By contrast, Portfolio B had higher active bets on the style factors representing company and share characteristics.

Solution to 2:

Portfolios B and C were similar in their absolute amounts of active risk. Furthermore, both Portfolios B and C were both approximately industry neutral relative to the benchmark. Portfolio C assumed more active factor risk related to the style factors, but B assumed more active specific risk. It is also possible to infer from the greater level of B's active specific risk that B is somewhat less diversified than C.

Solution to 3:

Portfolio D appears to be a passively managed portfolio, judging by its negligible level of active risk. Referring to Exhibit 10, Portfolio D's active factor risk of 0.50, equal to 0.707% expressed as a standard deviation, indicates that the portfolio's risk exposures very closely match the benchmark.

The discussion of performance attribution and risk analysis has used examples related to common stock portfolios. Multifactor models have also been effectively used in similar roles for portfolios of bonds and other asset classes. For example, factors such as duration and spread can be used to decompose the risk and return of a fixed-income manager.

5.3 Factor Models in Portfolio Construction

Equally as important to the use of multifactor models in analyzing a portfolio's active returns and active risk is the use of such multifactor models in portfolio construction. At this stage of the portfolio management process, multifactor models permit the portfolio manager to make focused bets or to control portfolio risk relative to the benchmark's risk. This greater level of detail in modeling risk that multifactor models afford is useful in both passive and active management.

■ *Passive management.* In managing a fund that seeks to track an index with many component securities, portfolio managers may need to select a sample of securities from the index. Analysts can use multifactor models to replicate an index fund's factor exposures, mirroring those of the index tracked.

- *Active management.* Many quantitative investment managers rely on multifactor models in predicting alpha (excess risk-adjusted returns) or relative return (the return on one asset or asset class relative to that of another) as part of a variety of active investment strategies. In constructing portfolios, analysts use multifactor models to establish desired risk profiles.

- *Rules-based active management (alternative indexes).* These strategies routinely tilt toward factors such as size, value, quality, or momentum when constructing portfolios. As such, alternative index approaches aim to capture some systematic exposure traditionally attributed to manager skill, or "alpha," in a transparent, mechanical, rules-based manner at low cost. Alternative index strategies rely heavily on factor models to introduce intentional factor and style biases versus capitalization-weighted indexes.

In the following, we explore some of these uses in more detail. As indicated, an important use of multifactor models is to establish a specific desired risk profile for a portfolio. In the simplest instance, the portfolio manager may want to create a portfolio with sensitivity to a single factor. This particular (pure) factor portfolio would have a sensitivity of 1 for that factor and a sensitivity (or weight) of 0 for all other factors. It is thus a portfolio with exposure to only one risk factor and exactly represents the risk of that factor. As a pure bet on a source of risk, factor portfolios are of interest to a portfolio manager who wants to hedge that risk (offset it) or speculate on it. This simple case can be expanded to multiple factors where a factor replication portfolio can be built based either on an existing target portfolio or on a set of desired exposures. Example 8 illustrates the use of factor portfolios.

EXAMPLE 8

Factor Portfolios

Analyst Wanda Smithfield has constructed six portfolios for possible use by portfolio managers in her firm. The portfolios are labeled A, B, C, D, E, and F in Exhibit 11. Smithfield adapts a macroeconomic factor model based on research presented in Burmeister, Roll, and Ross (1994). The model includes five factors:

- Confidence risk, based on the yield spread between corporate bonds and government bonds. A positive surprise in the spread suggests that investors are willing to accept a smaller reward for bearing default risk and so that confidence is high.

- Time horizon risk, based on the yield spread between 20-year government bonds and 30-day Treasury bills. A positive surprise indicates increased investor willingness to invest for the long term.

- Inflation risk, measured by the unanticipated change in the inflation rate.

- Business cycle risk, measured by the unexpected change in the level of real business activity.

- Market timing risk, measured as the portion of the return on a broad-based equity index that is unexplained by the first four risk factors.

Exhibit 11	Factor Portfolios					
	Portfolios					
Risk Factor	**A**	**B**	**C**	**D**	**E**	**F**
Confidence risk	0.50	0.00	1.00	0.00	0.00	0.80
Time horizon risk	1.92	0.00	1.00	1.00	1.00	1.00
Inflation risk	0.00	0.00	1.00	0.00	0.00	−1.05
Business cycle risk	1.00	1.00	0.00	0.00	1.00	0.30
Market timing risk	0.90	0.00	1.00	0.00	0.00	0.75

Note: Entries are factor sensitivities.

1 A portfolio manager wants to place a bet that real business activity will increase.

　A Determine and justify the portfolio among the six given that would be most useful to the manager.

　B Would the manager take a long or short position in the portfolio chosen in Part A?

2 A portfolio manager wants to hedge an existing positive (long) exposure to time horizon risk.

　A Determine and justify the portfolio among the six given that would be most useful to the manager.

　B What type of position would the manager take in the portfolio chosen in Part A?

Solution to 1A:

Portfolio B is the most appropriate choice. Portfolio B is the factor portfolio for business cycle risk because it has a sensitivity of 1 to business cycle risk and a sensitivity of 0 to all other risk factors. Portfolio B is thus efficient for placing a pure bet on an increase in real business activity.

Solution to 1B:

The manager would take a long position in Portfolio B to place a bet on an increase in real business activity.

Solution to 2A:

Portfolio D is the appropriate choice. Portfolio D is the factor portfolio for time horizon risk because it has a sensitivity of 1 to time horizon risk and a sensitivity of 0 to all other risk factors. Portfolio D is thus efficient for hedging an existing positive exposure to time horizon risk.

Solution to 2B:

The manager would take a short position in Portfolio D to hedge the positive exposure to time horizon risk.

5.4 How Factor Considerations Can Be Useful in Strategic Portfolio Decisions

Multifactor models can help investors recognize considerations that are relevant in making various strategic decisions. For example, given a sound model of the systematic risk factors that affect assets' mean returns, the investor can ask, relative to other investors,[18]

- What types of risk do I have a comparative advantage in bearing?
- What types of risk am I at a comparative disadvantage in bearing?

For example, university endowments, because they typically have very long investment horizons, may have a comparative advantage in bearing business cycle risk of traded equities or the liquidity risk associated with many private equity investments. They may tilt their strategic asset allocation or investments within an asset class to capture the associated risk premiums for risks that do not much affect them. However, such investors may be at a comparative disadvantage in bearing inflation risk to the extent that the activities they support have historically been subject to cost increases running above the average rate of inflation.

This is a richer framework than that afforded by the CAPM, according to which all investors optimally should invest in two funds: the market portfolio and a risk-free asset. Practically speaking, a CAPM-oriented investor might hold a money market fund and a portfolio of capitalization-weighted broad market indexes across many asset classes, varying the weights in these two in accordance with risk tolerance. These types of considerations are also relevant to individual investors. An individual investor who depends on income from salary or self-employment is sensitive to business cycle risk, in particular to the effects of recessions. If this investor compared two stocks with the same CAPM beta, given his concern about recessions, he might be very sensitive to receiving an adequate premium for investing in procyclical assets. In contrast, an investor with independent wealth and no job-loss concerns would have a comparative advantage in bearing business cycle risk; his optimal risky asset portfolio might be quite different from that of the investor with job-loss concerns in tilting toward greater-than-average exposure to the business cycle factor, all else being equal. Investors should be aware of which priced risks they face and analyze the extent of their exposure.

A multifactor approach can help investors achieve better-diversified and possibly more efficient portfolios. For example, the characteristics of a portfolio can be better explained by a combination of SMB, HML, and WML factors in addition to the market factor than by using the market factor alone.

Thus, compared with single-factor models, multifactor models offer a richer context for investors to search for ways to improve portfolio selection.

---

18 Passive management is a distinct issue from holding a single portfolio. There are efficient-markets arguments for holding indexed investments that are separate from the CAPM. However, an index fund is reasonable for this investor.

SUMMARY

In this reading, we have presented a set of concepts, models, and tools that are key ingredients to quantitative portfolio management and are used to both construct portfolios as well as to attribute sources of risk and return.

- Multifactor models permit a nuanced view of risk that is more granular than the single-factor approach allows.

- Multifactor models describe the return on an asset in terms of the risk of the asset with respect to a set of factors. Such models generally include systematic factors, which explain the average returns of a large number of risky assets. Such factors represent priced risk—risk for which investors require an additional return for bearing.

- The arbitrage pricing theory (APT) describes the expected return on an asset (or portfolio) as a linear function of the risk of the asset with respect to a set of factors. Like the CAPM, the APT describes a financial market equilibrium, but the APT makes less strong assumptions.

- The major assumptions of the APT are as follows:
  - Asset returns are described by a factor model.
  - There are many assets, so asset-specific risk can be eliminated.
  - Assets are priced such that there are no arbitrage opportunities.

- Multifactor models are broadly categorized according to the type of factor used as follows:
  - Macroeconomic factor models
  - Fundamental factor models
  - Statistical factor models

- In *macroeconomic* factor models, the factors are surprises in macroeconomic variables that significantly explain asset class (equity in our examples) returns. Surprise is defined as actual minus forecasted value and has an expected value of zero. The factors can be understood as affecting either the expected future cash flows of companies or the interest rate used to discount these cash flows back to the present and are meant to be uncorrelated.

- In *fundamental* factor models, the factors are attributes of stocks or companies that are important in explaining cross-sectional differences in stock prices. Among the fundamental factors are book-value-to-price ratio, market capitalization, price-to-earnings ratio, and financial leverage.

- In contrast to macroeconomic factor models, in fundamental models the factors are calculated as returns rather than surprises. In fundamental factor models, we generally specify the factor sensitivities (attributes) first and then estimate the factor returns through regressions, in contrast to macroeconomic factor models, in which we first develop the factor (surprise) series and then estimate the factor sensitivities through regressions. The factors of most fundamental factor models may be classified as company fundamental factors, company share-related factors, or macroeconomic factors.

- In *statistical* factor models, statistical methods are applied to a set of historical returns to determine portfolios that explain historical returns in one of two senses. In factor analysis models, the factors are the portfolios that best explain (reproduce) historical return covariances. In principal-components models, the factors are portfolios that best explain (reproduce) the historical return variances.

- Multifactor models have applications to return attribution, risk attribution, portfolio construction, and strategic investment decisions.

- A factor portfolio is a portfolio with unit sensitivity to a factor and zero sensitivity to other factors.

- Active return is the return in excess of the return on the benchmark.

- Active risk is the standard deviation of active returns. Active risk is also called tracking error or tracking risk. Active risk squared can be decomposed as the sum of active factor risk and active specific risk.

- The information ratio (IR) is mean active return divided by active risk (tracking error). The IR measures the increment in mean active return per unit of active risk.

- Factor models have uses in constructing portfolios that track market indexes and in alternative index construction.

- Traditionally, the CAPM approach would allocate assets between the risk-free asset and a broadly diversified index fund. Considering multiple sources of systematic risk may allow investors to improve on that result by tilting away from the market portfolio. Generally, investors would gain from accepting above average (below average) exposures to risks that they have a comparative advantage (comparative disadvantage) in bearing.

REFERENCES

Bodie, Zvi, Alex Kane, and Alan J. Marcus. 2014. *Investments*, 10th ed. Boston: Irwin/McGraw-Hill.

Burmeister, Edwin, Richard Roll, and Stephen A. Ross. 1994. "A Practitioner's Guide to Arbitrage Pricing Theory." In *A Practitioner's Guide to Factor Models*. Charlottesville, VA: Research Foundation of the Institute of Chartered Financial Analysts.

Carhart, Mark M. 1997. "On Persistence in Mutual Fund Performance." *Journal of Finance*, vol. 52, no. 1: 57–82.

Connor, Gregory. 1995. "The Three Types of Factor Models: A Comparison of Their Explanatory Power." *Financial Analysts Journal*, vol. 51, no. 3: 42–46.

Fama, Eugene F., and Kenneth R. French. 1992. "The Cross-Section of Expected Stock Returns." *Journal of Finance*, vol. 47, no. 2: 427–465.

Fischer, B., and R. Wermers. 2013. *Performance Evaluation and Attribution of Security Portfolios*. Oxford, UK: Elsevier.

Grinold, Richard, and Ronald N. Kahn. 1994. "Multi-Factor Models for Portfolio Risk." In *A Practitioner's Guide to Factor Models*. Charlottesville, VA: Research Foundation of the Institute of Chartered Financial Analysts.

Roll, Richard, and Stephen A. Ross. 2001. "What Is the Arbitrage Pricing Theory?" Retrieved 25 May 2001 from www.rollross.com/apt.html.

Ross, S. A. 1976. "The Arbitrage Theory of Capital Asset Pricing." *Journal of Economic Theory*, vol. 13, no. 3: 341–360.

PRACTICE PROBLEMS

1 Compare the assumptions of the arbitrage pricing theory (APT) with those of the capital asset pricing model (CAPM).

2 Last year the return on Harry Company stock was 5 percent. The portion of the return on the stock not explained by a two-factor macroeconomic factor model was 3 percent. Using the data given below, calculate Harry Company stock's expected return.

Macroeconomic Factor Model for Harry Company Stock

Variable	Actual Value (%)	Expected Value (%)	Stock's Factor Sensitivity
Change in interest rate	2.0	0.0	−1.5
Growth in GDP	1.0	4.0	2.0

3 Assume that the following one-factor model describes the expected return for portfolios:

$$E(R_p) = 0.10 + 0.12\beta_{p,1}$$

Also assume that all investors agree on the expected returns and factor sensitivity of the three highly diversified Portfolios A, B, and C given in the following table:

Portfolio	Expected Return	Factor Sensitivity
A	0.20	0.80
B	0.15	1.00
C	0.24	1.20

Assuming the one-factor model is correct and based on the data provided for Portfolios A, B, and C, determine if an arbitrage opportunity exists and explain how it might be exploited.

4 Which type of factor model is most directly applicable to an analysis of the style orientation (for example, growth vs. value) of an active equity investment manager? Justify your answer.

5 Suppose an active equity manager has earned an active return of 110 basis points, of which 80 basis points is the result of security selection ability. Explain the likely source of the remaining 30 basis points of active return.

6 Address the following questions about the information ratio.

A What is the information ratio of an index fund that effectively meets its investment objective?

B   What are the two types of risk an active investment manager can assume in seeking to increase his information ratio?

7   A wealthy investor has no other source of income beyond her investments and that income is expected to reliably meet all her needs. Her investment advisor recommends that she tilt her portfolio to cyclical stocks and high-yield bonds. Explain the advisor's advice in terms of comparative advantage in bearing risk.

SOLUTIONS

1   APT and the CAPM are both models that describe what the expected return on a risky asset should be in equilibrium given its risk. The CAPM is based on a set of assumptions including the assumption that investors' portfolio decisions can be made considering just returns' means, variances, and correlations. The APT makes three assumptions:

1   A factor model describes asset returns.

2   There are many assets, so investors can form well-diversified portfolios that eliminate asset-specific risk.

3   No arbitrage opportunities exist among well-diversified portfolios.

2   In a macroeconomic factor model, the surprise in a factor equals actual value minus expected value. For the interest rate factor, the surprise was 2 percent; for the GDP factor, the surprise was −3 percent. The intercept represents expected return in this type of model. The portion of the stock's return not explained by the factor model is the model's error term.

> 5% = Expected return − 1.5(Interest rate surprise) + 2(GDP surprise) + Error term
> = Expected return − 1.5(2%) + 2(−3%) + 3%
> = Expected return − 6%

Rearranging terms, the expected return for Harry Company stock equals 5% + 6% = 11%.

3   According to the one-factor model for expected returns, the portfolio should have these expected returns if they are correctly priced in terms of their risk:

Portfolio A $E(R_A) = 0.10 + 0.12\beta_{A,1} = 0.10 + (0.12)(0.80) = 0.10 + 0.10 = 0.20$

Portfolio B $E(R_B) = 0.10 + 0.12\beta_{B,1} = 0.10 + (0.12)(1.00) = 0.10 + 0.12 = 0.22$

Portfolio C $E(R_C) = 0.10 + 0.12\beta_{C,1} = 0.10 + (0.12)(1.20) = 0.10 + 0.14 = 0.24$

In the table below, the column for expected return shows that Portfolios A and C are correctly priced but Portfolio B offers too little expected return for its risk, 0.15 or 15%. By shorting Portfolio B (selling an overvalued portfolio) and using the proceeds to buy a portfolio 50% invested in A and 50% invested in C with a sensitivity of 1 that matches the sensitivity of B, for each monetary unit shorted (say each euro), an arbitrage profit of €0.22 − €0.15 = €0.07 is earned.

Portfolio	Expected Return	Factor Sensitivity
A	0.20	0.80
B	0.15	1.00
C	0.24	1.20
0.5A + 0.5C	0.22	1.00

4   A fundamental factor model. Such models typically include many factors related to the company (e.g., earnings) and to valuation that are commonly used indicators of a growth orientation. A macroeconomic factor model may provide relevant information as well, but typically indirectly and in less detail.

5 This remainder of 30 basis points would be attributable to the return from factor tilts. A portfolio manager's active return is the sum of two components, factor tilts and security selection. Factor tilt is the product of the portfolio manager's higher or lower factor sensitivities relative to the benchmark's factor sensitivities and the factor returns. Security selection reflects the manager's ability to overweight securities that outperform or underweight securities that underperform.

6 **A** An index fund that effectively meets its investment objective is expected to have an information ratio of zero, because its active return should be zero.

   B The active manager may assume active factor risk and active specific risk (security selection risk) in seeking a higher information ratio.

7 This wealthy investor has a comparative advantage in bearing business cycle risk compared with the average investor who depends on income from employment. Because the average investor is sensitive to the business cycle and in particular the risk of recession, we would expect there to be a risk premium to hold recession-sensitive securities. Cyclical stocks and high-yield bonds are both very sensitive to the risk of recessions. Because the welfare of the wealthy investor is not affected by recessions, she can tilt her portfolio to include cyclical stocks and high yield bonds to attempt to capture the associated risk premiums.

READING

49

Measuring and Managing Market Risk

by Don M. Chance, PhD, CFA, and Michelle McCarthy

Don M. Chance, PhD, CFA, is at Louisiana State University (USA). Michelle McCarthy is at Nuveen Investments (USA).

LEARNING OUTCOMES

Mastery	The candidate should be able to:
☐	**a.** explain the use of value at risk (VaR) in measuring portfolio risk;
☐	**b.** compare the parametric (variance–covariance), historical simulation, and Monte Carlo simulation methods for estimating VaR;
☐	**c.** estimate and interpret VaR under the parametric, historical simulation, and Monte Carlo simulation methods;
☐	**d.** describe advantages and limitations of VaR;
☐	**e.** describe extensions of VaR;
☐	**f.** describe sensitivity risk measures and scenario risk measures and compare these measures to VaR;
☐	**g.** demonstrate how equity, fixed-income, and options exposure measures may be used in measuring and managing market risk and volatility risk;
☐	**h.** describe the use of sensitivity risk measures and scenario risk measures;
☐	**i.** describe advantages and limitations of sensitivity risk measures and scenario risk measures;
☐	**j.** describe risk measures used by banks, asset managers, pension funds, and insurers;
☐	**k.** explain constraints used in managing market risks, including risk budgeting, position limits, scenario limits, and stop-loss limits;
☐	**l.** explain how risk measures may be used in capital allocation decisions.

1

INTRODUCTION

This reading is an introduction to the process of measuring and managing market risk. Market risk is the risk that arises from movements in stock prices, interest rates, exchange rates, and commodity prices. Market risk is distinguished from credit risk, which is the risk of loss from the failure of a counterparty to make a promised payment, and also from a number of other risks that organizations face, such as breakdowns in their operational procedures. In essence, market risk is the risk arising from changes in the markets to which an organization has exposure.

Risk management is the process of identifying and measuring risk and ensuring that the risks being taken are consistent with the desired risks. The process of managing market risk relies heavily on the use of models. A model is a simplified representation of a real world phenomenon. Financial models attempt to capture the important elements that determine prices and sensitivities in financial markets. In doing so, they provide critical information necessary to manage investment risk. For example, investment risk models help a portfolio manager understand how much the value of the portfolio is likely to change given a change in a certain risk factor. They also provide insight into the gains and losses the portfolio might reasonably be expected to experience and the frequency with which large losses might occur.

Effective risk management, though, is much more than just applying financial models; it requires the application of judgment and experience not only to know how to use the models appropriately, but also to appreciate the strengths and limitations of the models and to know when to supplement or substitute one model with another model or approach.

Financial markets operate more or less continuously and new prices are constantly being generated. As a result, there is a large amount of data on market risk and a lot of collective experience dealing with this risk, making market risk one of the easier financial risks to analyze. Still, market risk is not an easy risk to capture. Although a portfolio's exposures can be identified with some certainty, the potential losses that could arise from those exposures are unknown. The data used to estimate potential losses are generated from past prices and rates, not the ones to come. Risk management models allow the experienced risk manager to blend that historical data with their own forward-looking judgment and they provide a framework within which to test that judgment.

This reading is organized as follows: Section 2 lays a foundation for understanding value at risk, discusses three primary approaches to estimating value at risk, and covers the primary advantages and limitations as well as extensions of value at risk. Section 3 addresses the sensitivity measures used for equities, fixed-income securities, and options and also covers historical and hypothetical scenario risk measures. Section 4 describes various applications and limitations of risk measures as used by different types of market participants. Section 5 discusses the use of constraints in risk management, such as risk budgeting, position limits, scenario limits, stop-loss limits, and capital allocation as risk management tools. Section 6 provides a summary of the reading.

UNDERSTANDING VALUE AT RISK

2

In the late 1980s, **value at risk (VaR)**[1] was developed and, over the next decade, it emerged as one of the most important risk measures in global financial markets. Despite its widespread use, VaR has been the source of much controversy. Critics often express the fear that VaR is used unwisely and unsafely. We will explore the limitations of VaR later, but first, let us establish a definition of this important concept.

2.1 Value at Risk: Formal Definition

Value at risk is the minimum loss that would be expected a certain percentage of the time over a certain period of time given the assumed market conditions. It can be expressed in either currency units or as a percentage of portfolio value. Although this statement is an accurate definition of VaR, it does not provide sufficient clarity to fully comprehend the concept. To better understand what VaR means, let us work with an example. Consider the statement:

> *The 5% VaR of a portfolio is €2.2 million over a one-day period.*

The following three points are important in understanding the concept of VaR:

- VaR can be measured in either currency units (in this example, the euro) or in percentage terms. In this example, if the portfolio value is €400 million, the VaR expressed in percentage terms would be 0.55% (€2.2 million/€400 million = 0.0055).

- VaR is a *minimum* loss. This point cannot be emphasized enough. VaR is often mistakenly assumed to represent *how much one can lose*. If the question is, "how much can one lose?" there is only one answer: *the entire portfolio*. In a €400 million portfolio, assuming no leverage, the most one can lose is €400 million.

- A VaR statement references a time horizon: losses that would be expected to occur over a given period of time. In this example, that period of time is one day. (If VaR is measured on a daily basis, and a typical month has 20–22 business days, then 5% of the days equates to about one day per month.)

These are the three explicit elements of a VaR statement—the *frequency* of losses of a given *minimum magnitude* expressed either in *currency* or *percentage* terms. Thus, the VaR statement can be rephrased as follows: A loss of at least €2.2 million would be expected to occur about once every month.

A 5% VaR is often expressed as its complement—a 95% level of confidence.[2] In this reading, we will typically refer to the notion as a 5% VaR, but we should be mindful that it does imply a 95% level of confidence.

---

1 The term "value at risk" is expressed a number of ways. It is sometimes capitalized and sometimes put in all lower case. It is sometimes hyphenated and sometimes not. It is usually abbreviated as "VaR" and sometimes as "VAR." In this reading, we will express it as either "value at risk" or "VaR."
2 Using the example given in the text, it is correct to say
   - €2.2 million is the minimum loss we would expect 5% of the time; or
   - 5% of the time, losses would be at least €2.2 million; or
   - we would expect a loss of no more than €2.2 million 95% of the time.

The last sentence is sometimes mistakenly phrased as "95% of the time we would expect to lose less than €2.2 million," but this statement could be taken to mean that 95% of the time we would incur losses, although those losses would be less than €2.2 million. In fact, a large percentage of the time we will *make* money.

Exhibit 1 illustrates the concept of VaR, using the 5% case. It depicts a probability distribution of returns from a hypothetical portfolio. The distribution chosen is the familiar normal distribution, known sometimes as the bell curve, but that distribution is only one curve that might be used. In fact, there are compelling arguments that the normal distribution is not the right one to use for financial market returns, and we will take up these arguments later.

Exhibit 1   Illustration of 5% VaR in the Context of a Probability Distribution

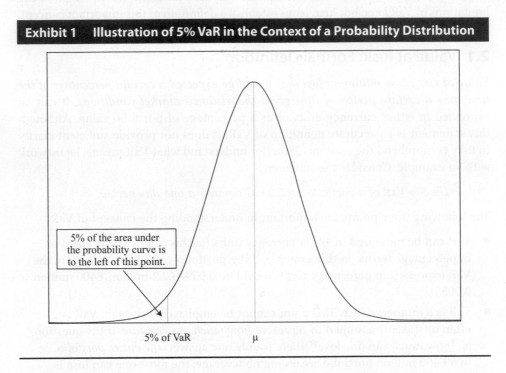

Note that the distribution in Exhibit 1 is centered on the value μ. [The symbol μ (Greek: *mu*) is a common symbol used to represent an expected value.] Near the left tail of the distribution there is the notation "5% VaR" with an indication that 5% of the area under the curve is to the left of the point of the VaR, meaning that the probability of observing a value less than the VaR is 5%.

Thus, it is apparent that VaR is simply a point on the probability distribution of profits or returns from a portfolio. Given the characteristics of the normal distribution, a 5% VaR is equivalent to the point on the distribution that is 1.65 standard deviations below the expected value. Although the concept of VaR can be easily visualized in this manner, actually measuring the VaR is a challenge.

Before we take on that challenge, however, note that there is no formal requirement that VaR be measured at a 5% threshold. It is also common to use a 1% threshold, which is 2.33 standard deviations from the expected value, and some investment managers use a one standard deviation movement (equal to a 16% VaR), both assuming a normal distribution.[3] There is no definitive rule for what VaR cutoff should be used. A specification with a higher confidence level will produce a higher VaR. It is up to the decision maker to choose an appropriate level.

Just as there is no formal requirement that VaR be measured at a 5% cutoff, there is also no formal requirement that VaR be measured using a daily loss estimate. One could reasonably measure VaR on a weekly, bi-weekly, monthly, quarterly, semiannually, or annual basis. Choosing the VaR threshold and the time horizon are examples of why VaR is not a precise measure but in fact entails considerable judgment.

We should also reiterate that VaR can be expressed as a rate of return or in monetary terms. It is typically easier to process the data necessary to estimate VaR in terms of returns, but VaR is most frequently expressed in terms of profits or losses. This point will become clearer as we work through examples.

EXAMPLE 1

Definition of VaR

1 Given a VaR of $12.5 million at 5% for one month, which of the following statements is correct?

A There is a 5% chance of losing $12.5 million over one month.

B There is a 95% chance that the expected loss over the next month is less than $12.5 million.

C The minimum loss that would be expected to occur over one month 5% of the time is $12.5 million.

2 Which of the following statements is **not** correct?

A A 1% VaR implies a downward move of 1%.

B A one standard deviation downward move is equivalent to a 16% VaR.

C A 5% VaR implies a move of 1.65 standard deviations less than the expected value.

Solution to 1:

C is correct because it is the only statement that accurately expresses the VaR. A is incorrect because VaR does not give the likelihood of losing a specific amount. B is incorrect because VaR is not an expected loss—it is a minimum loss.

Solution to 2:

A is correct. A 1% VaR (99% confidence) is the point on the distribution 2.33 standard deviations below the expected value. Answers B and C correctly describe a 16% and 5% VaR, respectively.

To this point, we have given only the conceptual definition of VaR. Defining something is one thing, measuring it can be quite challenging. Such is the case for VaR.

---

3 The 16% VaR relates to a one standard deviation move as follows: In a normal distribution, 50% of the outcomes are to the right of the expected value and 50% are to the left. A one standard deviation interval implies that 68% of the outcomes lie within one standard deviation of the expected value; thus, 34% of the outcomes lie one standard deviation to the left of the expected value, and 34% of the outcomes lie one standard deviation to the right. Adding the 50% of the outcomes that lie to the right of the expect value to the 34% of the outcomes that lie one standard deviation below the expected value means that 84% of all outcomes lie to the right of the point that is one standard deviation to the left of the expected value. Therefore, 16% of all outcomes lie below this point. Thus, a one standard deviation VaR is equivalent to a 16% confidence VaR.

2.2 Estimating VaR

There are typically three methods to estimate VaR: the parametric (variance–covariance) method, the historical simulation method, and the Monte Carlo simulation method. Each of these will be discussed in turn.

The first step of every VaR calculation, regardless of the VaR method used, is to convert the set of holdings in the portfolio into a set of exposures to **risk factors**, a process called **risk decomposition**. In some instances, this process can be very simple—an equity security can be the risk factor itself. In other instances, the process can be highly complex. For example, a convertible bond issued by a foreign entity has both currency and equity risk factors as well as exposures to multiple points on a yield curve of a given credit quality. Fixed-income instruments and derivative products often contain distinct risk exposures that require decomposition in order to accurately capture their loss potential.

The second step of VaR estimation requires gathering a data history for each of the risk factors in the VaR model. The three methods use different approaches to specifying these inputs, which will be discussed in the following sections.[4]

The third step of each method is where the differences between the three VaR methods are most apparent: how each method uses the data to make an estimate of the VaR.

Although most portfolios contain a large number of individual securities and other assets, we will use a two-asset portfolio to illustrate the three VaR methods. Using a limited number of assets permits us to closely observe the essential elements of the VaR estimation procedure without getting mired in the complex mathematics required to accommodate a large number of assets. The objective is to understand the concept of VaR, be aware of how it is estimated, know how it is used, appreciate the benefits of VaR, and be attentive to its limitations. We can achieve these objectives by keeping the portfolio fairly simple.

Our example portfolio has a market value of $150 million and consists of two ETFs—SPDR S&P 500 ETF, representing the US equity exposure, and SPDR Barclay's Long-Term Corporate Bond ETF, representing a corporate bond exposure. Their respective ticker symbols are SPY and LWC; going forward, we will refer to each ETF using its ticker symbol. We will allocate 80% of the portfolio to SPY and 20% of the portfolio to LWC. For the sake of simplicity, the two securities will represent the risk factors, and the return history of each ETF will serve as the risk factor history used in the VaR model. We have collected a set of two years of daily total return data, reflecting both capital appreciation and dividends on each ETF. The period used for this historical data set is called the **lookback period**.[5]

Exhibit 2 provides statistical summary information based on the two years of daily data in the lookback period, covering the period of 2 July 2012 through 30 June 2014.

---

4 The parametric and Monte Carlo methods do not formally require a data history. They require only that the user enter estimates of certain parameters into the computational procedure (expected return, standard deviation, and for some models, skewness and kurtosis). One of the most common sources for estimating parameter inputs for any financial model is historical data, but the user could substitute estimates based on judgement or alternative forecasting models. Indeed, shortly we will override some historical estimates with our own judgement. Nonetheless, the collection of a data history is typically used at least as a starting point in the parametric and Monte Carlo methods and absolutely required for the historical simulation method.

5 Exactly how much data are required to be a representative data set is a complex question that is common to all estimation problems in economics and finance. We will discuss some of the issues on this matter later in this reading.

Exhibit 2	Statistical Estimates from Daily Return Data, 2 July 2012–30 June 2014			
	Daily		**Annualized**	
	Average Return	**Standard Deviation**	**Average Return**	**Standard Deviation**
SPY	0.08%	0.70%	20.72%	11.14%
LWC	0.02%	0.55%	4.21%	8.68%

Correlation of LWC and SPY = −0.1902

SPY produced an annualized average return of almost 21% with a standard deviation of about 11%, significantly different from the long-term historical performance of the S&P 500 Index of approximately 10.5% average return and 20% standard deviation. LWC produced an annualized average return of 4.2% with a standard deviation of about 8.7%. These numbers compare with an average annual return for long-term corporate bonds of slightly more than 6% and a standard deviation of about 8.5%.[6] Although the average return of LWC in the last two years was lower than that of the overall long-term corporate bond sector, the standard deviations were similar.

The risk and return parameters for each risk factor in Exhibit 2 illustrate how one might collect historical data. It is necessary, however, to critically assess the data and apply judgment to modify the inputs if the lookback period is not representative of the expected performance of the securities (or risk factors) going forward. Exercising our judgment, and believing that we have no information to suggest that future performance will deviate from the long-run historical performance, we adjust our inputs and use returns of 10.5% for SPY and 6% for LWC, with standard deviations of 20% for SPY and 8.5% for LWC. These adjustments align the inputs more closely with the long-run historical performance of each sector.[7]

Although the returns and standard deviations experienced over the lookback period have been adjusted to more closely align with long-run historical experience, we will use a correlation estimate approximately equal to the observed correlation over our lookback period. We are assuming that the recent historical relationship of equity and fixed-income returns is a reasonable assumption moving forward. To keep the numbers simple, we round the observed correlation of −0.1902 to −0.20.

Exhibit 3 illustrates our input assumptions for the VaR estimations.

Exhibit 3	Input Assumptions, 2 July 2012–30 June 2014		
		Annualized	
	Allocation	**Return**	**Standard Deviation**
SPY	80%	10.5%	20.0%
LWC	20%	6.0%	8.5%

Correlation of LWC and SPY = −0.20

---

6 Historical data are drawn from Burton Malkiel's *A Random Walk Down Wall Street* (New York: W.W. Norton, 2007).

7 In practice, users will want to use estimates they believe are reflective of current expectations, though clearly one user's estimates could differ widely from another's.

2.2.1 The Parametric Method of VaR Estimation

The **parametric method** of estimating VaR is sometimes referred to as the analytical method and sometimes the variance–covariance method. The parametric method begins, as does each method, with a risk decomposition of the portfolio holdings. It typically assumes that the return distributions for the risk factors in the portfolio are normal. It then uses the expected return and standard deviation of return for each risk factor to estimate the VaR.

Note that we said that this method *typically* uses the normal distribution. Indeed, that is the common case in practice, but there is no formal requirement that the normal distribution be used. The normal distribution conveniently requires only two parameters—the expected value and standard deviation—to encompass everything there is to know about it. If other distributions are used, additional parameters of the distribution, such as skewness and kurtosis, would be required. We will limit the presentation here to the normal distribution, but be aware that other, more accurately representative distributions could be used but would add complexity to the VaR estimation process.

Recall that in defining VaR, we identified a VaR threshold—a point in the left tail of the distribution, typically either the 5% left tail, the 1% left tail, or a one standard deviation move (16%). If the portfolio is characterized by normally distributed returns and the expected value and standard deviation are known, it is a simple matter to identify any point on the distribution. A normal distribution with expected value μ and standard deviation σ can be converted to a standard normal distribution, which is a special case of the normal distribution in which the expected value is zero and the standard deviation is one. A standard normal distribution is also known as a z-distribution. If we have observed a return R from a normal distribution, we can convert to its equivalent z-distribution value by the transformation:

$$z = \frac{R - \mu}{\sigma}$$

In a standard normal (z) distribution, a 5% VaR is 1.65 standard deviations below the expected value of zero. A 1% VaR is 2.33 standard deviations below the expected value of zero. A 16% VaR is one standard deviation below the expected value of zero. Thus, in our example, for a 5% VaR, we wish to know the return that is 1.65 standard deviations to the left of the expected return.

To estimate this VaR, we need the expected return and volatility of the portfolio. The expected return is estimated from the following equation:

$$E(R_p) = w_{SPY}E(R_{SPY}) + w_{LWC}E(R_{LWC}) \tag{1}$$

where the expected return of the portfolio, $E(R_p)$, is equal to the portfolio weights of SPY (w_{SPY}) and LWC (w_{LWC}) multiplied by the expected return of each asset, $E(R_{SPY})$ and $E(R_{LWC})$.

The volatility of the portfolio, σ_p, is estimated from the following equation:

$$\sigma_p = \sqrt{w_{SPY}^2\sigma_{SPY}^2 + w_{LWC}^2\sigma_{LWC}^2 + 2w_{SPY}w_{LWC}\rho_{SPY,LWC}\sigma_{SPY}\sigma_{LWC}} \tag{2}$$

where σ_{SPY} and σ_{LWC} are the standard deviations (volatilities) of SPY and LWC, respectively; $\rho_{SPY,LWC}$ is the correlation between the returns on SPY and LWC, respectively; and $\rho_{SPY,LWC}\sigma_{SPY}\sigma_{LWC}$ is the covariance between SPY and LWC.

Recall that we estimated these parameters from the historical data, with some modifications to make them more consistent with long-run values. The formal calculations for our portfolio based on these adjusted estimates are as follows:

$$E(R_p) = 0.8(0.105) + 0.2(0.06) = 0.096000$$
$$\sigma_p = \sqrt{(0.8)^2(0.2)^2 + (0.2)^2(0.085)^2 + 2(0.8)(0.2)(-0.20)(0.2)(0.085)} = 0.157483$$

Thus, our portfolio, consisting of an 80% position in SPY and a 20% position in LWC, is estimated to have an expected return of 9.6% and a volatility of approximately 15.75%.

But these inputs are based on annual returns. If we want a one-day VaR, we should adjust the expected returns and volatilities to their daily counterparts. Assuming 250 trading days in a year, the expected return is adjusted by dividing by 250 and the standard deviation is adjusted by dividing by the square root of 250.[8] Thus, the daily expected return and volatility are

$$E\left(R_p\right) = \frac{0.096}{250} = 0.000384 \text{ and} \tag{3}$$

$$\sigma_p = \frac{0.157483}{\sqrt{250}} = 0.009960 \tag{4}$$

It is important to note that we have assumed that the statistical properties of the return distribution are constant across the year. Earlier, we annualized the daily data in Exhibit 2 in order to see how our estimates compared with long-term estimates. We made some modest adjustments to the annualized data and then, in Equations 3 and 4, returned to using daily data. To estimate an annual VaR, we would need to use annual data, but we would need a longer lookback period in order to have sufficient data points.[9]

The parametric VaR is now easily obtained. With the distribution centered at the expected return of 0.0384%, and a one standard deviation move equal to 0.996%, a 5% VaR is obtained by identifying the point on the distribution that lies 1.65 standard deviations to the left of the mean. It is now easy to see why parametric VaR is so named—the expected values, standard deviations, and covariances are the *parameters* of the distributions.

The following step-by-step procedure shows how the VaR is derived:

$$[(E(Rp) - 1.65\sigma_p)(-1)](\$150,000,000)$$

Step 1   Multiply the portfolio standard deviation by 1.65.

     $0.009960 \times 1.65 = 0.016434$

Step 2   Subtract the answer obtained in Step 1 from the expected return.

     $0.000384 - 0.016434 = -0.016050$

Step 3   Because VaR is expressed as an absolute number (despite representing an expected loss), change the sign of the value obtained in Step 2.

     Change -0.016050 to 0.016050

Step 4   Multiply the result in Step 3 by the value of the portfolio.[10]

     $\$150,000,000 \times 0.016050 = \$2,407,500$

---

8 If this adjustment sounds confusing, just note that the variance is converted by dividing by time (250 days). Thus, the standard deviation must be adjusted by using the square root of time (250 days).

9 It is important to note that we cannot estimate a daily VaR and annualize it to arrive at an annual VaR estimate. First, to assume that a daily distribution of returns can be extrapolated to an annual distribution is a bold assumption. Second, annualizing the daily VaR is not the same as adjusting the expected return and the standard deviation to annual numbers and then calculating the annual VaR. The expected return is annualized by multiplying the daily return by 250 and the standard deviation is annualized by multiplying the daily standard deviation by the square root of 250. Thus, we can annualize the data and estimate an annual VaR, but we cannot estimate a daily VaR and annualize it without assuming a zero expected return.

10 Asset managers may stop at Step 3 because at that point the measure is expressed as a percentage of the value of the portfolio, which is the unit this group more commonly uses.

Thus, using the parametric method, our estimate of VaR is $2,407,500, meaning that on 5% of trading days the portfolio would be expected to incur a loss of at least $2,407,500.

EXAMPLE 2

Parametric VaR

1   The parameters of normal distribution required to estimate parametric VaR are:

    A   expected value and standard deviation.

    B   skewness and kurtosis.

    C   standard deviation and skewness.

2   Assuming a daily expected return of 0.0384% and daily standard deviation of 0.9960% (as in the example in the text), which of the following is *closest* to the 1% VaR for a $150 million portfolio? Express your answer in dollars.

    A $3.4 million

    B $2.4 million

    C $1.4 million

3   Assuming a daily expected return of 0.0384% and daily standard deviation of 0.9960% (as in the example in the text), the daily 5% parametric VaR is $2,407,530. Rounding the VaR to $2.4 million, which of the following values is *closest* to the annual 5% parametric VaR? Express your answer in dollars.

    A $38 million

    B $25 million

    C $600 million

Solution to 1:

A is correct. The parameters of a normal distribution are the expected value and standard deviation. Skewness, as mentioned in B and C, and kurtosis as mentioned in B, are characteristics used to describe a *non*-normal distribution.

Solution to 2:

A is correct and is obtained as follows:

    Step 1 $2.33 \times 0.009960 = 0.023207$

    Step 2 $0.000384 - 0.023207 = -0.022823$

    Step 3   Convert -0.022823 to 0.022823

    Step 4 $0.022823 \times \$150$ million $= \$3,423,450$.

B is the estimated VaR at a 5% threshold, and C is the estimated VaR using a one-standard deviation threshold.

Solution to 3:

B is correct. It is found by annualizing the daily return and standard deviation and using these figures in the calculation. The annual return and standard deviation are, respectively, 0.096000 (0.000384 × 250) and 0.157483 (0.009960 × $\sqrt{250}$).

    Step 1 $0.157483 \times 1.65 = 0.259847$

    Step 2 $0.096000 - 0.259847 = -0.163847$

    Step 3   Convert -0.163847 to 0.163847

Step 4 $0.163847 \times \$150$ million = $\$24,577,050$.

A incorrectly multiplies the daily VaR by the square root of the number of trading days in a year ($\sqrt{250}$), and C incorrectly multiplies the daily VaR by the approximate number of trading days in a year (250). Neither A nor C make the appropriate adjustment to annualize the standard deviation.

To recap, we see that the parametric VaR method generally makes the assumption that the distribution of returns on the risk factors is normal. Under that assumption, all of the information about a normal distribution is contained in the expected value and standard deviation. Therefore, finding the 5% VaR requires only that we locate the point in the distribution beyond which 5% of the outcomes occur. Although normality is the general assumption of the parametric method, it is not an absolute requirement. Other distributions could be accommodated by incorporating skewness and kurtosis, the third and fourth parameters of the distribution, but that added complexity is not needed to demonstrate the general approach to parametric VaR and is rarely done in practice.

The major advantage of the parametric method is its simplicity and straightforwardness. The assumption of the normal distribution allows us to easily estimate the parameters using historical data, although judgment is required to adjust the parameters when the historical data may be misleading. The parametric method is best used in situations in which one is confident that the normal distribution can be applied as a reasonable approximation of the true distribution, and the parameter estimates are reliable or can be turned into reliable estimates by suitable adjustments. It is important to understand that VaR under the parametric method is very sensitive to the parameter estimates, especially the covariances.

One of the major weaknesses of the parametric method is that it can be difficult to use when the investment portfolio contains options. When options are exercised, they pay off linearly with the underlying, but if never exercised, an option loses 100% of its value. This characteristic leads to a truncated, non-normal distribution that does not lend itself well to the parametric method. But there are some adjustments that can render options more responsive to the parametric method. These adjustments are helpful but not perfect, limiting the usefulness of the parametric method when there are options in the portfolio. Additionally, although the expected return and volatility of the underlying fixed income or equity security may be stable over the life of the option, the distribution of the option changes continuously as the value of the underlying, the volatility of the underlying, and the time to expiration all change.

2.2.2 The Historical Simulation Method of VaR Estimation

The **historical simulation method** of VaR uses the *current* portfolio and reprices it using the actual *historical* changes in the key factors experienced during the lookback period. We begin, as with the parametric method, by decomposing the portfolio into risk factors and gathering the historical returns of each risk factor from the chosen lookback period. Unlike the parametric method, however, we do not characterize the distribution using estimates of the mean return, the standard deviation, or the correlations among the risk factors in the portfolio. Instead, we reprice the current portfolio given the returns that occurred on each day of the historical lookback period and sort the results from largest loss to greatest gain. To estimate a one-day VaR at a 5% confidence interval, we choose the point on the resulting distribution beyond which 5% of the outcomes result in larger losses.

Illustrating this point using a full two years of daily observations would be tedious and consume a great deal of space, so we will condense the process quite a bit and then extrapolate the methodology. Exhibit 4 shows the daily returns on the SPY, the LWC, and our 80% SPY/20% LWC portfolio over the first five days of our historical data set.[11]

Exhibit 4	First Five Days of Historical Returns on the SPY/LWC Portfolio Using the 2 July 2012–30 June 2014 Data		
Day	SPY Return	LWC Return	Portfolio Return[a]
1	0.66%	−0.54%	0.42%
2	−0.45%	−0.05%	−0.37%
3	−0.95%	0.78%	−0.60%
4	−0.13%	0.32%	−0.04%
5	−0.87%	0.49%	−0.60%

[a] The Day 1 portfolio return is obtained by multiplying each holding (SPY, LWC) by its respective weight in the portfolio (80%/20%) and adding the two results together: 0.80(0.0066) + 0.20(−0.0054). Although Exhibit 4 shows only five days of returns, we would, of course, use all of the data at our disposal that is reasonably representative of possible future outcomes.

The historical simulation VaR extracts the portfolio return that lies at the appropriate confidence interval along the distribution. Using Excel's "=percentile(x,y)" function, we calculated the following historical simulation VaRs for our sample portfolio:

- 1% VaR (99% confidence) $2,314,998
- 5% VaR (95% confidence) $1,205,127
- 16% VaR (84% confidence) $618,287

Now, it will be interesting to compare this result with the parametric VaR estimates. Exhibit 5 shows the results side-by-side with the parameters used. The historical simulation method does not directly use these parameters, but it uses the data itself, and these numbers are the parameters implied by the data itself.

Exhibit 5	Comparison of Historical and Parametric VaR Estimates Using 2 July 2012–30 June 2014 Data			
	Historical Simulation Method		Parametric Method	
1% VaR	$2,314,998		$3,423,462	
5% VaR	$1,205,127		$2,407,998	
16% VaR	$618,287		$1,441,800	
	Average Return	Standard Deviation	Average Return	Standard Deviation
SPY	20.72%	11.14%	10.50%	20.00%
LWC	4.21%	8.68%	6.00%	8.50%
Correlation of SPY and LWC	−0.1902		−0.2000	

---

[11] Fixed weights are assumed for all days. Neither historical simulation nor Monte Carlo simulation is intended to be a replication of sequences of prices. They are intended to create a sample of one-day returns for a portfolio of given weights.

The historical simulation VaRs are much smaller, and the differences stem primarily from the adjustments we made to the historical parameters. We adjusted the volatility and the average return estimates of SPY to more closely reflect the historical norms and slightly raised the average return of LWC. Recall, in particular, that our factor history for the S&P 500 exhibited abnormally low volatility relative to the long run experience.

Additionally, our calculations using the historical simulation method were not constrained by the assumption of a normal distribution as was the case with the parametric method. Exhibit 6 is a histogram of the portfolio returns used in the historical simulation results, overlaid with a normal distribution.

Exhibit 6   Histogram of Historical Portfolio Returns (80% SPY and 20% LWC) Using 2 July 2012–30 June 2014 Data

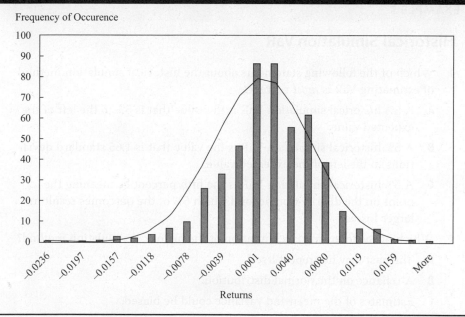

As can be seen, the resulting distribution under the historical simulation method is a departure from a normal distribution. This point again highlights the importance of understanding the underlying assumptions of any VaR model.

There is *no single right way* of estimating VaR. Each method provides an estimate of VaR and is highly sensitive to the input parameters, and similar to many estimation models, they will disagree.

Both the parametric and historical simulation methods in their most basic forms have the limitation that, as with most samples, all observations are weighted equally. The historical simulation method can adjust for this problem, however, by using a weighting methodology that gives more weight to more recent observations and less weight to more distant observations.

The primary advantage of the historical simulation method compared with the parametric method is that the historical simulation method estimates VaR based on what actually happened, so it cannot be dismissed as introducing impossible outcomes. Yet, therein also lies the primary weakness of the historical simulation method: There can be no certainty that a historical event will re-occur, or that it would occur in the same manner or with the same likelihood as represented by the historical data. If one uses a relatively short historical data set, such as from January 1987 through December 1988 (a period encompassing the "Black Monday" of 19 October 1987, when stock markets around the world collapsed in a very short time), an occurrence of this magnitude might be projected to occur once every two years, surely an overstatement of its probability. Thus, the historical simulation method is best used when the distribution of returns during the lookback period are expected to be representative of the future.

The historical method is capable of handling the adjustment of one time horizon to another; that is, the information derived from daily data can be extrapolated to estimate an annual VaR, provided the distribution can be assumed to be stationary. In other words, one can convert each daily return to an annual return and then estimate the annual VaR. Although using annual data to estimate an annual VaR is always preferred, that would require a much longer lookback period.

We noted earlier that the parametric method is not well suited for options. Because the historical simulation method captures the returns that actually occurred, regardless of the type of financial instrument used, it can accommodate options.

EXAMPLE 3

Historical Simulation VaR

1 Which of the following statements about the historical simulation method of estimating VaR is *most* correct?

   A A 5% historical simulation VaR is the value that is 5% to the left of the expected value.

   B A 5% historical simulation VaR is the value that is 1.65 standard deviations to the left of the expected value.

   C A 5% historical simulation VaR is the fifth percentile, meaning the point on the distribution beyond which 5% of the outcomes result in larger losses.

2 Which of the following is a limitation of the historical simulation method?

   A The past may not repeat itself.

   B A reliance on the normal distribution.

   C Estimates of the mean and variance could be biased.

Solution to 1:

C is correct. In the historical method, the portfolio returns are arrayed lowest to highest and the observation at the fifth percentile (95% of the outcomes are better than this outcome) is the VaR. A is not correct because it draws a point on the distribution relative to the expected value rather than the using the 5% of the outcomes that are in the left-most of the distribution. B confuses the parametric and historical methods. In the parametric method, the 5% VaR lies 1.65 standard deviations below the mean.

Solution to 2:

A is correct. The historical simulation method estimates VaR based on the historical distribution of the risk factors. B is not correct; the historical simulation method does not rely on any particular distribution because it simply uses whatever distribution applied in the past. C is not correct because the historical distribution does not formally estimate the mean and variance.

2.2.3 *The Monte Carlo Simulation Method of VaR Estimation*

Monte Carlo simulation is a method of estimating VaR in which the user develops his own assumptions about the statistical characteristics of the distribution and uses those characteristics to generate random outcomes that represent hypothetical returns to a portfolio with the specified characteristics. This method is widely used in the sciences to estimate the statistical distribution of scientific phenomena and has many applications in business and finance.[12] The reference to the famous Mediterranean casino city allegedly came from an observation made by a scientist that the method is similar to tossing dice at a casino.

Monte Carlo simulation avoids the complexity inherent in the parametric method when the portfolio has a large number of assets. (A large number of assets makes the parameters of the distribution difficult to extract.) There can be many risk factors, and the interactions among these risk factors can be too complex to specify. Moreover, Monte Carlo simulation does not need to be constrained by the assumption of normal distributions. Rather than attempt to determine the expected return and volatility of a combination of multiple statistical processes, one would simply simulate these processes, tabulate the statistical results of the simulations, and thereby gain a measure of the combined effects of these complex component processes on the overall risk.

Monte Carlo simulation requires the generation of random values of the underlying unknowns. In our example, the unknowns are the returns on the two risk factors, represented by the SPY and LWC ETFs. We can, of course, assume that the statistical properties of the historical returns—their averages, volatilities, and correlation—are appropriate for use in a simulation or we can modify those values to conform to what we expect to be relevant for the future. For illustrative purposes here, we will simply use the inputs we used in the parametric method.

Recall that we previously assumed for the sake of simplicity that the two securities represent the risk factors. We now decompose the portfolio holdings into these risk factors. First we simulate the returns of these two risk factors, and then we re-price our exposures to the risk factors under the range of simulated returns, recording the results much as we do in the historical simulation method. We then sort the results in order from worst to best. A 5% Monte Carlo VaR would simply be the fifth percentile of the simulated values instead of the historical values.

Yet, it is not quite that simple. We must first decide how many random values to generate. There is no industry standard; the more values we use, the more reliable our answers are, but the more time-consuming the procedure becomes. In addition, we cannot just simulate values of two random variables without accounting for the correlation between the two. For example, if you spin two roulette wheels, you can assume they are independent of each other in much the same manner as are two uncorrelated assets. But most assets have at least a small degree of correlation. In our example, we used the historical correlation of about −0.20. Monte Carlo simulation must take that relationship into account.

For simplicity, this reading will not go into detail on either the mathematical techniques that can account for the correlations among risk factor returns, or the specific method used to simulate outcomes given average values and volatilities for each risk factor; both are beyond the scope of this reading.

For this example, we will use 10,000 simulated returns on SPY and LWC drawn from a normal distribution. Of course, non-normal distributions can be used and they commonly are in practice, but we want to keep the illustration simple to facilitate comparisons between methods. Each set of simulated returns combines to produce a sample with the expected returns and volatilities as we specified. In addition, the returns will have the pre-specified correlation of −0.20. Each pair of returns is weighted 80/20 as desired. We generate the 10,000 outcomes, sort them from worst to best,

---

12 For example, a corporation considering the investment of a large amount of capital in a new project with many uncertain variables could simulate the possible values of these variables and thus gain an understanding of the distribution of the possible returns from this investment. Complex options can often be priced by simulating outcomes of the underlying, determining the payoffs of the option, and then averaging the option payoffs and discounting that value back to the present.

and select the outcome at the 5th percentile for a 5% VaR, or the outcome at the 1st percentile for a 1% VaR, or the outcome at the 16th percentile if we want to evaluate the impact of a one standard deviation move. Using the parameters specified in our example, the simulation returns a distribution from which we can draw the following VaR numbers:

1% VaR = $3,426,424

5% VaR = $2,422,533

16% VaR = $1,429,011

Note that these results are fairly close to VaR under the parametric VaR method, where the 5% VaR was $2,407,530. The slight difference arises from the fact that Monte Carlo simulation only *samples* from a population with certain parameters, and the parametric method *assumes* those parameters. A sample of a distribution will not produce statistics that match the parameters precisely except in extremely large sample sizes, much larger than the 10,000 used here. Exhibit 7 displays a histogram of the simulated returns overlaid with a bell curve representing a normal distribution. Note how the simulated returns appear more normally distributed than do the historical values as illustrated in Exhibit 6. This is because we explicitly assumed a normal distribution when running the simulation to generate the values in our example.

Exhibit 7   Monte Carlo Simulated Returns 80/20 Portfolio of SPY and LWC

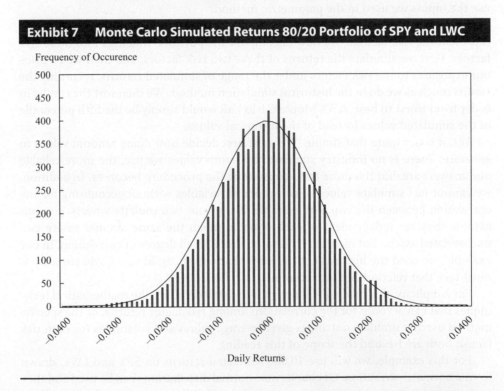

Although we conveniently assumed a normal distribution, one of the advantages of the Monte Carlo method is that it can accommodate virtually *any* distribution. In fact, the flexibility of the Monte Carlo method to handle more complex distributions is its primary attraction. The Monte Carlo and historical simulation methods are much more capable than the parametric method of accurately incorporating the effects of option positions or bond positions with embedded options.

Similar to the historical simulation method, you can scale daily returns to annual returns and extrapolate an estimate of the annual VaR by running a Monte Carlo simulation on these annual returns.

At one time, calculating VaR using the Monte Carlo simulation method was slow, but with the speed of today's computers, it is relatively easy and fast to simulate extremely complex processes for portfolios with thousands of exposures.

EXAMPLE 4

Monte Carlo Simulation VaR

1   When will the Monte Carlo method of estimating VaR produce virtually the same results as the parametric method?

   A   When the Monte Carlo method assumes a non-normal distribution.

   B   When the Monte Carlo method uses the historical return and distribution parameters.

   C   When the parameters and the distribution used in the parametric method are the same as those used in the Monte Carlo method, and the Monte Carlo method uses a sufficiently large sample.

2   Which of the following is an advantage of the Monte Carlo method?

   A   The VaR is easy to calculate with a simple formula.

   B   It is flexible enough to accommodate many types of distributions.

   C   The number of necessary simulations is determined by the parameters.

Solution to 1:

C is correct. The Monte Carlo method simulates outcomes using whatever distribution is specified by the user. *If* a normal distribution is used *and* a sufficiently large number of simulations are run, the parameters of the Monte Carlo sample will converge with those used in the parametric method, and the overall VaR should be very close to that of the parametric method. A is incorrect because the parametric method is not well-adapted to a non-normal distribution. B is not correct because neither the Monte Carlo method nor the parametric method focus on historical outcomes.

Solution to 2:

B is correct. The method can handle any distribution. A is incorrect because Monte Carlo simulation is not a simple formula. C is incorrect; there is no industry-wide agreement as to the necessary number of simulations.

2.3 Advantages and Limitations of VaR

The concept of VaR is solidly grounded in modern portfolio analysis. Nonetheless, the implementation of VaR, both in the estimation procedure and in the application of the concept, presents a number of advantages and limitations.

2.3.1 *Advantages of VaR*

The use of VaR as a risk measure has the following advantages:

■   *Simple concept.* VaR is relatively easy to understand. Although the methodology is fairly technical, the concept itself is not very difficult, so decision makers without technical backgrounds should be able to grasp the likelihood of possible losses that might endanger the organization. Reporting that a daily 5% VaR is, for example, €2.2 million allows the user to assess the risk in the context of the capital deployed. If a portfolio is expected to incur losses of a minimum of €2.2 million on 5% of the trading days, about once a month, this information is valuable in the context of the size of the portfolio.

■ *Easily communicated concept.* VaR captures a considerable amount of information into a single number. If the recipient of the information fully understands the meaning and limitations of VaR, it can be a very significant and practical piece of information.

■ *Provides a basis for risk comparison.* VaR can be useful in comparing risks across asset classes, portfolios, and trading units, giving the risk manager a better picture of which constituents are contributing the least and the most to the overall risk. As such, the risk manager can be better informed as he looks for potential hot spots in the organization. This point will be discussed further in Section 2.4.

■ *Facilitates capital allocation decisions.* The ability to compare VaR across trading units or portfolio positions provides management with a benchmark that can be used in capital allocation decisions. A proprietary trading firm, for example, can find that its VaR in equity trading is $20 million, and its VaR in fixed-income trading is $10 million. If its equity trading portfolio is not expected to take more risk than its fixed-income trading portfolio, then the equity trading activities are taking too much risk or there is too much capital allocated to equity trading. The firm should either make adjustments to realign its VaR or allocate capital in proportion to the relative risks. If a firm is looking to add a position to a portfolio or change the weights of existing portfolio positions, certain extensions of VaR allow the manager to assess the risk of these changes. This topic will be covered in more detail in Section 2.4.

■ *Can be used for performance evaluation.* Risk-adjusted performance measurement requires that return or profit be adjusted by the level of risk taken. VaR can serve as the basis for risk adjustment. Without this adjustment, more profitable units could be perceived as more successful but, when adjusted by VaR, a less profitable unit that poses less risk of loss may be judged more desirable.

■ *Reliability can be verified.* VaR is easily capable of being verified, a process known as backtesting. For example, if the daily VaR is $5 million at 5%, we would expect that on 5% of trading days, a loss of at least $5 million would be incurred. To determine whether a VaR estimate is reliable, one can determine over a historical period of time whether losses of at least $5 million were incurred on 5% of trading days, subject to reasonable statistical variation.

■ *Widely accepted by regulators.* In the United States, the SEC requires that the risk of derivatives positions be disclosed either in the form of a summary table, by sensitivity analysis (a topic we cover later), or by VaR. Thus, VaRs are frequently found in annual reports of financial firms. Global banking regulators also encourage banks to use VaR. These regulations require or encourage the use of VaR, but they do not prescribe how it is implemented, which estimation method is used, or the maximum acceptable VaR.

2.3.2 *Limitations of VaR*

Despite its many advantages, users of VaR must also understand its limitations. The primary limitations of VaR are the following:

■ *Subjectivity.* In spite of the apparent scientific objectivity on which it is based, VaR is actually a rather subjective method. As we saw in the descriptions of the three methods of estimating VaR, there are many decisions to make. At the fundamental level, a decision must be made as to the desired VaR cutoff (5%, 1%, or some other cutoff); over what time horizon the VaR will be measured; and finally, which estimation method will be used. As we have seen here, for each estimation method, there are numerous other discretionary choices to make about inputs, source of data, and so on.

- *Underestimating the frequency of extreme events.* In particular, use of the normal distribution in the parametric method and sometimes in the Monte Carlo method commonly underestimates the likelihood of extreme events that occur in the left tail of the distribution. In other words, there are often more extreme adverse events, called "left tail events," than would be expected under a normal distribution. As mentioned previously, there is no particular requirement that one use the normal distribution. Although the historical simulation method uses whatever distribution the data produce, we chose to illustrate the Monte Carlo method with a normal distribution, and it is virtually always used in the parametric method. Nonetheless, the tendency to favor the normal distribution and other simple and symmetrical distributions often leads to an understatement of the frequency of left tail events.

- *Failure to take into account liquidity.* If some assets in a portfolio are relatively illiquid, VaR could be understated, even under normal market conditions. Additionally, liquidity squeezes are frequently associated with tail events and major market downturns, thereby exacerbating the risk. Although illiquidity in times of stress is a very general problem that affects virtually all of the financial decisions of a firm, reliance on VaR in non-normal market conditions will lead the user to underestimate the magnitude of potential losses.

- *Sensitivity to correlation risk.* Correlation risk is the risk that during times of extreme market stress, correlations among all assets tend to rise significantly. Thus, markets that provide a reasonable degree of diversification under normal conditions tend to decline together under stressed market conditions, thereby no longer providing diversification.

- *Vulnerability to trending or volatility regimes.* A portfolio might remain under its VaR limit every day but lose an amount approaching this limit each day. Under such circumstances, the portfolio could accumulate substantial losses without technically breaching the VaR constraint. Also, during periods of low volatility, VaR will appear quite low, underestimating the losses that could occur when the environment returns to a normal level of volatility.

- *Misunderstanding the meaning of VaR.* VaR is not a worst-case scenario. Losses can and will exceed VaR.

- *Oversimplification.* Although we noted that VaR is an easily communicated concept, it can also oversimplify the picture. And although VaR does indeed consolidate a considerable amount of information into a single number, that number should be interpreted with caution, with an awareness of the other limitations, and supported by additional risk measures.

- *Disregard of right-tail events.* VaR focuses so heavily on the left tail (the losses) that the right tail (potential gains) are often ignored. By examining both tails of the distribution, the user can get a better appreciation of the overall risk–reward trade-off, which is often missed by concentrating only on VaR.

These limitations are not unique to VaR; they apply equally to any technique or measure used to quantify the expected rewards and risks of investing.

EXAMPLE 5

Advantages and Limitations of VaR

1 Which of the following is **not** an advantage of VaR?

  A It is a simple concept to communicate.

  B There is widespread agreement on how to calculate it.

  C It can be used to compare risk across portfolios or trading units.

2 Which of the following is a limitation of VaR?

  A It requires the use of the normal distribution.

  B The maximum VaR is prescribed by federal securities regulators.

  C It focuses exclusively on potential losses, without considering potential gains.

Solution to 1:

B is correct. There is no consensus on how to calculate VaR. A and C are both advantages of VaR, as we noted that VaR is fairly simple to communicate and it can show the contribution of each unit to the overall VaR.

Solution to 2:

C is correct. VaR deals exclusively with left-tail or adverse events. A is wrong because although parametric VaR does generally use the normal distribution, the historical simulation method uses whatever distribution occurred in the past and Monte Carlo simulation uses whatever distribution the user chooses. B is incorrect because regulators do not specify maximum VaRs, although they may encourage and require that the measure be used.

2.4 Extensions of VaR

Clearly no single risk model can answer all of the relevant questions a risk manager may have. As a result, VaR has laid a foundation for a number of variations, each of which provides additional information.

As discussed previously, VaR is a minimum loss, typically expressed as the minimum loss that can be expected to occur 5% of the time. An important and related question is to determine the average loss that would be incurred if the VaR cutoff is exceeded. This measure is sometimes referred to as the **conditional VaR (CVaR)**, although it is not technically a VaR measure. It is the average loss conditional on exceeding the VaR cutoff. So, although VaR answers the question of "what is the minimum loss I can expect at a certain confidence," CVaR answers the question of "how much can I expect to lose if VaR is exceeded." CVaR is also sometimes referred to as the **expected tail loss** or **expected shortfall**. CVaR is best derived using the historical simulation or Monte Carlo methods, in which one can observe all of the returns throughout the distribution and calculate the average of the losses beyond the VaR cutoff. The parametric method uses a continuous distribution and obtaining the average loss beyond the VaR cutoff would require a level of mathematics beyond the scope of this reading.

Using our earlier example, in the historical simulation method, our sample of 500 historical returns was sorted from lowest to highest and the 5% VaR was $1,205,127. With 500 returns in the sample, there are 25 observations (5% of 500) that lie below the VaR estimate. The average of these losses is $1,867,681. Thus, when the VaR is exceeded, we would expect an average loss of about $1.9 million.

For the Monte Carlo method, we generated 10,000 random values and obtained a 5% VaR of $2,422,533. Given 10,000 random values, there are 500 observations in the lowest 5% of the VaR distribution. The CVaR using the Monte Carlo method would be the average of the 500 lowest values, which is $3,058,381.

Note that once again, the CVaR derived using the historical simulation method is lower than the CVaR derived using the Monte Carlo method. As explained earlier, this result can largely be attributed to the lower volatility of the S&P 500 component in the historical data series.

Beyond assessing tail loss, a risk manager often wants to know how the portfolio VaR will change if a position size is changed relative to the remaining positions. This effect can be captured by a concept called **incremental VaR (IVaR)**. Using our example, suppose the portfolio manager is contemplating increasing the risk by increasing the investment in SPY to 90% of the portfolio. We recalculate the VaR under the proposed allocation, and the incremental VaR is the difference between the "before" and "after" VaR. As an example, using the parametric method, the VaR would be expected to increase from $2,407,530 to $2,733,722, thus the IVaR for the 5% case would be $326,192. Or the portfolio manager might wish to add a new asset, thereby reducing the exposure to the existing assets. The risk manager would calculate the VaR under the assumption that the change is made, and the difference between the new VaR and the old VaR is the IVaR. This measure is useful in that it reflects the effect of an anticipated change on the VaR. The risk manager could find that the new VaR will be unacceptably high or that it has possibly even decreased.

A related concept is called **marginal VaR (MVaR)**. It is conceptually similar to incremental VaR in that it reflects the effect of an anticipated change in the portfolio, but it uses formulas derived from calculus to reflect the effect of a very small change in the position. Some people interpret MVaR as a change in the VaR for a $1 or 1% change in the position, although that is not strictly correct. Nonetheless, this interpretation is a reasonable approximation of the concept behind marginal VaR, which is to reflect the impact of a small change. In a diversified portfolio, marginal VaR may be used to determine the contribution of each asset to the overall VaR; the marginal VaRs for all positions may be proportionately weighted to sum to the total VaR.

Both incremental and marginal VaR address the question of what impact a change in the portfolio holdings might have on the total VaR of the portfolio. Both take into account the potential diversifying effects of various positions or subportfolios, and thus they both can be useful in evaluating the potential effect of a trade before the trade is done.

Another related measure is *ex ante* **tracking error**, also known as **relative VaR**, which is a measure of the degree to which the performance of a given investment portfolio might deviate from its benchmark. It is computed using any of the standard VaR models, described earlier, but the portfolio to which VaR is applied contains the portfolio's holdings *minus* the holdings in the specified benchmark. In other words, the benchmark's holdings, weighted in proportion to the value of the subject portfolio, are entered into the VaR modeling process as short positions. VaR for this measure is typically expressed as a one standard deviation annualized measure. If the portfolio is a perfect match to the benchmark, *ex ante* tracking error will be at or near zero. The more the portfolio differs from the benchmark, the larger the *ex ante* tracking error will be.

EXAMPLE 6

Extensions of VaR

1 Conditional VaR measures the:

    A VaR over all possible losses.

    B VaR under normal market conditions.

    C average loss, given that VaR is exceeded.

2 Which of the following correctly identifies incremental VaR?

    A The change in VaR from increasing a position in an asset.

    B The increase in VaR that might occur during extremely volatile markets.

    C The difference between the asset with the highest VaR and the asset with the second highest VaR.

3 Which of the following statements is correct about marginal VaR?

    A The marginal VaR is the same as the incremental VaR.

    B The marginal VaR is the VaR required to meet margin calls.

    C Marginal VaR estimates the change in VaR for a small change in a given portfolio holding.

Solution to 1:

C is correct. Conditional VaR is the average loss conditional on exceeding the VaR. A is not correct because CVaR is not concerned with losses that do not exceed the VaR threshold, and B is incorrect as because VaR does not distinguish between normal and non-normal markets.

Solution to 2:

A correctly defines incremental VaR. Incremental VaR is not a change in VaR from an increase in volatility. B is not correct because incremental volatility reflects the results of intentional changes in exposure, not from uncontrollable market volatility. C is not correct because incremental VaR is not the difference in the VaRs of the assets with the greatest and second greatest VaRs.

Solution to 3:

C is correct. In A, marginal VaR is a similar concept to incremental VaR in that they both deal with the effect of changes in VaR, but they are not the same concept. B is incorrect because marginal VaR has nothing to do with margin calls.

3   OTHER KEY RISK MEASURES—SENSITIVITY AND SCENARIO MEASURES

Just as no single measure of a person's health gives a complete picture of that person's physical condition, no single risk measure gives a full picture of a portfolio's risk profile. As we saw, although VaR has many advantages, it also has many limitations. Therefore, good risk managers will use a comprehensive set of risk tools. In this section, we will look at two additional classes of risk measures, one based on sensitivity analysis and the other based on the use of hypothetical or historical scenarios. The former enables us to estimate how our estimated gains and losses change with changes in the underlying risk factors, whereas the latter are based on situations involving considerable market stress, from which we estimate how our portfolio will perform.

3.1 Sensitivity Risk Measures

Equity, fixed-income, and options positions can be characterized by a number of exposure measures that reflect the sensitivities of these positions to movements in underlying risk factors. Sensitivity measures examine how performance responds to a single change in an underlying risk factor. Understanding and measuring how portfolio positions respond to the underlying sources of risk is a primary objective in managing risk.

3.1.1 *Equity Exposure Measures*

The primary equity exposure measure is the beta. In a simple world, a single market factor drives equity returns; the return on a stock is given by the familiar capital asset pricing model (CAPM):

$$E(R_i) = R_F + \beta_i[E(R_M) - R_F]$$

where $E(R_i)$ is the expected return on the asset or portfolio i, R_F is the risk-free rate, $E(R_m)$ is the expected return on the market portfolio, and β_i is the beta, which is the risk measure. The expression $E(R_m) - R_F$ is the equity risk premium, which is the return investors demand for investing in equities rather than risk-free instruments. It should be apparent from this often-used equation that beta measures the sensitivity of the security's expected return to the equity risk premium. The beta is defined as the covariance of the asset return with the market return divided by the variance of the market return. The broad market beta, which is an average of all individual betas is 1.0. Assets with betas more (less) than 1 are considered more (less) volatile than the market as a whole. The CAPM has a number of extensions, including multifactor models, and risk measures derived from those models can also provide more nuanced information on equity risk exposures.

3.1.2 *Fixed-Income Exposure Measures*

The primary sensitivity exposure measures for fixed-income investments are duration and convexity.[13] **Duration** is sometimes described as the weighted-average time to maturity of a bond, in which the bond is treated as partially maturing on each coupon payment date. Duration is a sensitivity measure. Under the assumption that all interest rates that affect a bond change by the same percentage, the duration is a measure of the sensitivity of the bond price to the interest rate change that characterizes all rates.[14] This single rate can be viewed as the bond's yield, y. Given a bond priced at B and yield change of Δy, the rate of return or percentage price change for the bond is approximately given as follows:

$$\frac{\Delta B}{B} \approx -D\frac{\Delta y}{1 + y}$$

---

13 Obviously, credit is a major factor driving non-government fixed-income markets, but this reading is devoted to market risk, which in the fixed-income market is determined by interest rates. Credit risk is covered extensively in other readings and articles.

14 What we mean by *all* rates changing in an additive manner can be seen as follows. Consider a two-year bond that pays coupon interest in one year and again at the maturity date. The price of the bond is found by discounting the first coupon at the one-year rate and the second coupon and face value at the two-year rate. Duration assumes that the one- and two-year rates change by the same additive amount. To accommodate the assumption that all rates do not always change by the same amount, another concept called key rate duration is sometimes used. It captures the effects of varying rate changes along the term structure.

where D is the duration.[15] (The $\approx$ sign stands for the phrase "approximately equal," and reflects the fact that the relationship is not exact.) In this expression, it is easy to see that duration does reflect the sensitivity of a bond's price to its yield, although under the restrictive assumption of a single change to all rates.[16] As previously mentioned, duration is a time measure, the weighted-average maturity of a bond, in which the bond is viewed as maturing progressively as it makes its coupon payments.

The relationship shown here is approximate. The formula is derived under the assumption that the yield change is infinitesimally small, and duration fails to accurately capture bond price movements when yield changes are relatively large. Thus, in the above expression, Δy is for small yield changes. It is not possible, however, to say how small a yield change must be before it is small enough for the expression to hold true. In addition, the expression holds only at any instant in time and only for that instant. Over longer periods, the relationship will be less accurate because of the passage of time and because Δy is likely to be larger. To accommodate longer periods of time and larger yield changes, we can incorporate a second factor called **convexity**, which is denoted C. Convexity describes the sensitivity of a bond's duration to changes in interest rates. Adding convexity to the expression, we obtain the following formula:

$$\frac{\Delta B}{B} \approx -D\frac{\Delta y}{1+y} + \frac{1}{2}C\frac{\Delta y^2}{(1+y)^2}$$

Convexity can play an important role as a risk measure for large yield changes and long holding periods.

Duration and convexity are essential tools in fixed-income risk management. They allow the risk manager to assess the potential losses to a fixed-income portfolio or position under a given change in interest rates.

3.1.3 *Options Risk Measures*

Derivatives have their own unique exposure measures. Because forwards, futures, and swaps have payoffs that are linear in relation to their underlying, they can often be evaluated using the same exposure measures as their underlying. Options, however, have non-linear payoffs, which result in them having their own family of exposure measures that incorporate this non-linear behavior.

Although options can be very risky instruments in and of themselves, they are a critical tool for effective risk management and are often used to create an exposure to offset an existing risk in the portfolio. The relative riskiness of an option arises from the high degree of leverage embedded in most options. An additional and very important risk can also arise from the sensitivity of an option to the volatility of the underlying security. We will expand on these points in the next few paragraphs.

The most fundamental risk of an option is its sensitivity to the price of the underlying. This sensitivity is called the option's **delta**. Although delta is derived by using mathematics beyond the scope of this reading, we can provide a simple and reasonably effective definition as follows:

$$\Delta \text{ (delta)} \approx \frac{\text{Change in value of option}}{\text{Change in value of underlying}}$$

---

15 Occasionally, the equation is adjusted so that duration is expressed in the form of modified duration, defined as $D_m = D/(1+y)$, and the equation then becomes $\frac{\Delta B}{B} \approx -D_m\Delta y$.

16 Although the assumption of a single change to all rates seems fairly restrictive, ultimately the assumption is encapsulated by assuming that a single discount rate, the yield, drives the bond price. Duration is considered to be a fairly good sensitivity measure.

Call option deltas range from a value of 0 to a value of 1, whereas put option deltas range from a value of 0 to a value of −1. A value of 0 means that the option value does not change when the value of underlying changes, a condition that is never absolutely true but can be roughly true for a very deep out-of-the-money option. A call delta of 1 means that the price of the call option changes in unison with the underlying, a condition that is also never absolutely true but is *approximately* true for very deep in-the-money calls. A put delta of −1 means that the price of the put option changes in unison with the underlying but in the opposite direction, a condition that is also never absolutely true but is *approximately* true for very deep in-the-money puts. As expiration approaches, an in-the-money call (put) delta approaches 1 (−1) and an out-of-the-money call (put) delta approaches 0.

Delta can be used to approximate the new price of an option as the underlying changes. For a call option, we can use the following formula:

$$c + \Delta c \approx c + \Delta_c \Delta S$$

Here, c is the original price of the option and Δc is the change in the price. We approximate the change in the price as the product of the call's delta, Δ_c, and the change in the value of the underlying, ΔS. The same relationship would hold for puts, simply changing the c's to p's.

The delta of an option is somewhat analogous to the duration of a fixed-income security. It is a first-order effect, reflecting the direct change in the value of the option or fixed-income security when the underlying price or yield, respectively, changes. Just as duration captures the effect of only small changes in the yield over a short period of time, delta captures the effect of only small changes in the value of the underlying security over a short period of time. Similar to duration, which has the second-order effect of convexity, we can add a second-order effect for options called **gamma**. Gamma is a measure of how sensitive an option's delta is to a change in the underlying. It is a second-order effect in that it is measuring the sensitivity of the first-order effect, delta. There are several ways to interpret gamma. The delta reflects the direct change in the value of the underlying position, whereas gamma reflects the indirect change, meaning the change in the change. Technically it reflects the change in the delta, as indicated by the following:

$$\Gamma \text{ (gamma)} \approx \frac{\text{Change in delta}}{\text{Change in value of underlying}}$$

As with convexity, gamma itself is not simple to interpret. For example, a call option might have a delta of 0.6 and a gamma of 0.02. It is not easy to determine whether the gamma is large or small. Using the equation just given, if the value of the underlying increases by 0.10 and the gamma is 0.02, then the delta would increase by 0.002 (0.10 × 0.02), from 0.6 to 0.602. Gammas get larger as the option approaches at-the-money and they are large when options approach expiration, unless the option is deeply in or out of the money. Gamma reflects the uncertainty of whether the option will expire in or out of the money. When an option is close to expiration and roughly at the money, a small change in the price of the underlying will determine whether the option expires worthless or in the money. The uncertainty associated with this win-or-lose situation over a very short time frame leads to a large gamma.

Using delta and gamma, the estimated change in the call price is

$$c + \Delta c \approx c + \Delta_c \Delta S + \frac{1}{2}\Gamma_c (\Delta S)^2$$

where Γ_c is the gamma of the call. This equation is similar to the corresponding expression that relates yield changes to bond price changes through duration and convexity. Indeed, as we said, gamma is a second-order effect, like convexity.

A third important sensitivity measure for options is **vega** and it reflects the effect of volatility.[17] Vega is a first-order effect reflecting the relationship between the option price and the volatility of the underlying. Vega is expressed by the following relationship:

$$\text{Vega} \approx \frac{\text{Change in value of option}}{\text{Change in volatility of underlying}}$$

Most options are very sensitive to the volatility of the underlying security. The effect of changing volatility can have a material impact on the value of the option, even when the value of the underlying is not changing.

Using delta, gamma, and vega, the new value of an option given an old value, a change in the value of the underlying, and a change in the volatility can be estimated as follows:

$$c + \Delta c \approx c + \Delta_c \Delta S + \frac{1}{2}\Gamma_c(\Delta S)^2 + \text{vega}(\Delta \sigma)$$

where $\Delta \sigma$ is the change in volatility.

The expression represents a composite sensitivity relationship for options. It reflects the expected response of an option value to changes in the value and volatility of the underlying, the two primary factors that change in an unpredictable manner and influence the option value. For portfolios that contain options, understanding these relationships and using them to assess the portfolio's response to market movements is an essential element of effective risk management.

These option measures are applicable not only to options but also to portfolios that contain options. For example, the delta of a portfolio consisting of a long position in an S&P 500 ETF and a short position in a call option on the ETF has a delta that is determined by both the ETF and the option. The ETF has a delta of 1; it changes one-for-one with the S&P 500. The option delta, as noted, has a delta between 0 and 1, though technically 0 and −1 because the option position is short. The ETF has no gamma or vega, so the portfolio gamma and vega are determined by the option. The overall deltas, gammas, and vegas are sums of the deltas, gammas, and vegas of the component positions, taking into account the relative amounts of money invested in each position. Risk managers need to know the overall deltas, gammas, vegas, durations, convexities, and betas to get a comprehensive picture of the sensitivity of the entire portfolio to the prices and volatilities of the underlying.

EXAMPLE 7

Sensitivity Risk Measures

1   Which of the following *most* accurately characterizes duration and convexity?

   A   Sensitivity of bond prices to interest rates

   B   First- and second-order effects of yield changes on bond prices

   C   Weighted-average time to maturity based on the coupon payments and principal

---

17 You may have noticed a pattern in that the option sensitivity measures with respect to the underlying are called delta and gamma, both Greek words. Vega is not a Greek word, but is often considered one of the so-called *option Greeks*. There are other Greeks—rho, the effect of interest rates, and theta, the effect of time—but we do not cover these here. Other than options in which the underlying is an interest rate or bond price, the effect of interest rates on options is fairly minor. In addition, theta, which measures the rate at which options lose their value (referred to as the time–value decay) does not present a risk management issue because changes in the market environment do not affect the rate of decay.

2 Which of the following statements about the delta of a call option is **not** correct?

A It ranges between 0 and 1.

B It precisely captures the change in the call value when the underlying changes.

C It approaches 1 for an in-the-money option and 0 for an out-of-the-money option.

3 Which of the following statements about gamma and vega are correct?

A Gamma is a second-order effect and vega is a first-order effect.

B Gamma is the effect of volatility and vega is the effect of changes in volatility.

C Gamma is a second-order effect arising from changes in the sensitivity of volatility to the underlying price.

Solution to 1:

B is correct. Duration is the first-order effect and convexity is the second-order effect of a change in interest rates on the value of a bond. A and C are correct with respect to duration, but not for convexity.

Solution to 2:

B is correct. A and C correctly characterize delta, whereas B states that delta is precise, which is incorrect because it gives an approximate relationship.

Solution to 3:

A is correct. B is not correct because Gamma does not capture the effect of volatility. Vega is the effect of volatility, but it relates to the level and not the change in volatility. C is incorrect because, although gamma is a second-order effect on the option value, it is not related to the sensitivity of volatility to the underlying price.

3.2 Scenario Risk Measures

A scenario risk measure estimates the portfolio return that would result from a hypothetical change in markets (a hypothetical scenario) or a repeat of an historical event (a historical scenario). As an example, the risk manager might want to understand how her current portfolio would perform if an event such as the Black Monday of October 1987 were to reoccur. The factor movements that characterized the historical event would be applied to the factor exposures of the current portfolio. Alternatively, the risk manager may develop a hypothetical scenario to describe a market event that has not occurred in the past, but which he or she believes has some probability of occurring in the future. The two elements of scenario risk measures that set them apart from sensitivity risk measures are (1) the use of multiple factor movements used in the scenario measures versus the single factors movements typically used in risk sensitivity measures and (2) the typically larger size of the factor movement used in the scenario measures. Scenario risk measures are related to VaR in that they focus on extreme outcomes, but they are not bound by either recent historical events or assumptions about parameters or probability distributions. **Stress tests**, which apply extreme negative stress to a particular portfolio exposure, are closely related to scenario risk measures. Scenario analysis is an open-ended exercise that could look at positive or negative events, although its most common application is to assess the negative outcomes. Stress tests intentionally focus on extreme negative events to assess the impact of such an event on the portfolio.

The two types of scenario risk measures—historical scenarios and hypothetical scenarios—are discussed in the following sections.

3.2.1 *Historical Scenarios*

Historical scenarios are scenarios that measure the hypothetical portfolio return that would result from a repeat of a particular period of financial market history. Historical scenarios used in risk management include such events as the currency crisis of 1997–1998, the market dislocation surrounding the failure of Long Term Capital Management, the market rout of October 1987, the bursting of the technology bubble in 2001, and the financial crisis of 2008–2009. In order to create an historical scenario, the current set of portfolio holdings is placed into the appropriate valuation models.

Equity positions can often be modeled using their price histories as proxies for their expected behavior, although some practitioners model equities using factor analysis. Valuation models are needed for fixed-income and derivative products because they have a maturity or an expiration feature that must be accommodated when modeling the portfolio. Historical prices for the fixed-income and derivatives positions currently held in the portfolio may not exist, as in the case of a bond that was issued after the historical period being modeled. Even when historical prices for specific instruments do exist, they may not be relevant to the current characteristics of the instrument. Take the case of a 5-year historical price series for a 10-year bond with 1 year remaining to maturity; the historical price series reflects the price volatility of what used to be a longer bond (e.g., five years ago, the bond had six years remaining to maturity; three years ago, the bond had four years remaining to maturity). The volatility of the bond when it had six years remaining to maturity would be higher than it is today, with only one year remaining to maturity. Using its historical price history would mis-characterize the risk of the current portfolio holding. For this reason, the historical yields, spreads, implied volatilities, prices of the underlying assets in derivative contracts, and the other input parameters that drive the pricing of these instruments are more important in explaining the risks of these instruments than the price history of the instrument itself.

Some examples may help to show how fixed-income or derivative valuation models are used in a historical scenario. In the case of a convertible bond, the bond's terms and conditions (e.g., coupon, conversion ratio, maturity) are entered into a convertible bond pricing model. In the case of standard bonds, the terms and conditions of these instruments (e.g., coupon, call features, put features, any amortization or sinking fund features, maturity) are entered into fixed-income pricing models. These modeled fixed-income or derivative holdings, together with the equity holdings, are then re-priced under the conditions that prevailed during the "scenario period"—a given set of dates in the past. Changes in interest rates, credit spreads, implied volatility levels and any asset underlying a derivative product, as well as the historical price changes in the equity portfolio, would all be reflected in the re-priced portfolio. The value of each position is recorded before and after these changes in order to arrive at the gain or loss that would occur under the chosen scenario. Historical scenario events are specifically chosen to represent extreme market dislocations and often exhibit abnormally high correlations among asset classes. It is most common to run the scenario or stress test as if the total price action movement across the period occurs instantaneously, before any rebalancing or management action is possible. The output of the scenario can include

- the total return of the portfolio;
- for long-only asset managers, the total return of the portfolio relative to its benchmark;

- for pensions, insurers, and others whose liabilities are not already incorporated into the portfolio, the total return of the portfolio relative to the change in liabilities under the scenario; and

- any collateral requirements and other cash needs that will be driven by the changes specified in the scenario.

One variation of the historical scenario approach includes running the scenario over multiple days and incorporating actions that the manager might be expected to take during the period. Instead of assuming the shock is a single instant event, this approach assumes it takes place over a number of days, and on each day the portfolio manager can take such actions as selling assets or rebalancing hedges.

Many risk managers are skeptical of this approach because they produce smaller potential loss measures (by design) and do not answer important questions that have been relevant in real crises, such as, "What if the severe price action happens so quickly that the portfolio manager cannot take remedial actions?" Generally, risk managers prefer that a stress testing exercise be tailored to the *initial outcome of a large shock* to ensure that the event is survivable by a portfolio that uses leverage, and that there will not be any unacceptable counterparty exposures or portfolio concentrations before action can be taken to improve the situation. This method also helps to simulate the possibility that liquidity may be unavailable.

Risk managers seeking to measure the impact of a historical scenario need to ensure all relevant risk factors are included. For instance, foreign equities will need to be decomposed into foreign exchange exposure and equity exposure in the analysis. Stress tests typically take the explicit currency approach, which measures the currency exposure of each foreign equity. Alternatively, the risk manager may use an approach that incorporates implicit currency risks, such as companies that may be registered in one country but have earnings flowing in from other countries, and may hedge some of those revenues back to their base currency.

When the historical simulation fully revalues securities under rate and price changes that occurred during the scenario period, the results should be highly accurate. Sometimes, however, scenarios are applied to risk sensitivities rather than the securities themselves. This approach is a simpler form of analysis, but should not be used for options or option-embedded securities. Although it may be tempting to use delta and gamma or duration and convexity to estimate the impact of a scenario on options or option-embedded securities, these measures are not suited for handling the kinds of extreme movements analyzed in scenario analysis. Although gamma and convexity are second-order adjustments that work with delta and duration to estimate extreme movements, they are inadequate for scenario analysis.

Even in simpler fixed-income cases in which there are no options present, care needs to be taken to ensure the analysis does not oversimplify. Duration sensitivities can be used as the inputs to a scenario analysis for straightforward fixed-income instruments, but these sensitivities need to be mapped to the most relevant sectors, credit curves, and yield curve segments before beginning the analysis. If assets are mapped too broadly, the analysis will miss the important differences that could drive the most meaningful outcomes in a given scenario.

It is also important to pay careful attention to how securities or markets that did not yet exist at the time of the scenario are modeled. If, for instance, an analyst is measuring a current portfolio's sensitivity to a recurrence of the 1987 US stock market crash, the analyst needs to determine how to treat stocks in the portfolio that had an initial public offering after 1987. They may need to be mapped to a relevant index or to a similar company, or decomposed into the relevant statistical factors (such as growth, value, volatility, or momentum) by using a factor model before beginning the analysis. Similarly, because credit default swaps did not come into widespread use until 2002, historical scenarios for dates preceding this time would need to be adapted to appropriately reflect the impact of a repeat of that scenario on these new securities.

3.2.2 *Hypothetical Scenarios*

Scenarios have a number of benefits—they can reflect the impact of extreme market movements and they make no specific assumptions regarding normality or correlation. Historical scenarios also have the benefit of being uncontroversial; no one can claim it is impossible for such events to occur, because they did. One problem with scenario analysis lies in ascribing the probability of a given scenario. Most would agree that it is improbable to assume that the exact historical scenario specified will actually occur in precisely the same way in the future. Another potential problem is that, because it has happened (particularly when it has happened recently), risk managers or portfolio managers are inclined to take precautions that make their portfolios safer for a replay of that historical crisis—and, in the process, make their portfolios more vulnerable to a crisis that has not yet happened.

For that reason, risk managers also use hypothetical scenarios—extreme movements and co-movements in different markets that have not necessarily previously occurred. The scenarios used are somewhat difficult to believe, and it is difficult to assess their probability, but they represent the only real method to assess portfolio outcomes under market movements that might be imagined but that have not yet been experienced.

To design an effective hypothetical scenario, it is necessary to identify the portfolio's most significant exposures. Targeting these material exposures and assessing their behavior in various environments is a process called **reverse stress testing**. The risk manager is seeking answers to such questions as the following: What are the top 10 exposures or risk drivers in my portfolio? What would make them risky? What are the top 10 benchmark-relative exposures? Under what scenario would hedges not hedge? Under what scenario would my securities lending activity, ordinarily thought to be riskless, be risky? This is an ideal use of hypothetical scenarios; not to model every possible future state of every market variable, but rather to target those that are highly significant to the portfolio in order to assess, and potentially address, vulnerabilities.

Reverse stress testing is particularly helpful in estimating potential losses if more than one important exposure is affected in a market crisis, as often happens when participants "crowd" into the same exposures; sometimes, apparently unrelated markets experience stress at the same time.

The risk manager might also choose to design a hypothetical geopolitical event, estimating its potential effect on markets and the resulting impact on the portfolio. To develop these scenarios, individuals with varying areas of expertise posit an event such as earthquake in Country Y, or Country X invades Country Z, or banking system implodes in Region A. The group conducting the analysis identifies which markets are most likely to be affected, as well as any identifiable secondary effects. The next step is to establish a potential range of movement for the affected markets. The final scenario is intended to meet the standard of "rare, but not impossible." The exercise is unlikely to be truly accurate in the face of the real event, but it will often help to identify unexpected portfolio vulnerabilities and outcomes and to think through counterparty credit and operational considerations that could exacerbate or accelerate the scenario.

Hypothetical scenarios are particularly beneficial in being able to stress correlation parameters. The scenario is not constrained to assume that assets will co-move as they have done in the past, which can help identify dangers that other forms of risk analysis may miss. Scenarios can be designed to highlight that, in times of stress, correlations often increase; this is often achieved by subjecting markets that typically have little or no correlation with one another to the same or similar movements, thereby simulating a temporarily higher correlation. Scenarios can also be devised to pinpoint times when hedging might work poorly—when assets, such as a bond and the credit default swap used to hedge it, that normally have a high correlation, might temporarily decouple and move by different percentages or even in different directions. This often occurs when markets experience a "flight to quality"—the swap rate may move down as a result of their relative credit strength, whereas the bond yield might increase given its perceived credit risk.

Once a risk manager has completed a scenario analysis, a common question may be, "What do you do with a scenario analysis; what are the action steps?" If the portfolios are within all other rules and guidelines, their exposures have been kept within desired limits and their VaR or *ex ante* tracking error is within the desired range, scenario analysis provides one final opportunity to assess the potential for negative surprises during a given stress event. The action steps might be to trim back positions that are otherwise within all limits and that appear to present comfortable risk exposures under the current environment but would perform unacceptably during a plausible stress environment. In the case of asset management, where clients have elected to be in a given asset class and the asset manager is constrained by that investment mandate, action steps may include adjusting benchmark-relative risk, disclosing to clients the manager's concerns regarding the risks in the portfolio, or changing counterparty or operational procedures to avoid an unwanted event.

But a caution is in order: A portfolio that has no sensitivity to any stress event is unlikely to earn more than the risk-free rate, or in the case of long-only asset managers, outperform the benchmark index. Stress tests and scenarios analyses are best used in the effort to *understand* a portfolio's risk exposures, not to eliminate them. Effective risk management sets a tolerance range for a stress test or scenario that reflects a higher loss possibility than the investment manager would normally find acceptable. Scenarios should be periodically run again, and action should be taken only if the portfolio exceeds this relatively high tolerance level. It is also important to continually evaluate new threats and new market developments and to periodically refresh the set of scenarios, removing scenarios that are no longer meaningful for the portfolio.

Note also that scenario risk measures and stress tests are best used as the final screen in a series of position constraints that include position size limits, exposure limits, and VaR or *ex ante* tracking error limits. They do not serve well as the initial or primary screen, for reasons that will be discussed shortly.

Parties that use leverage, such as banks and hedge funds, are more likely to use single-factor stress tests rather than multifactor scenario analyses. The focus on a single factor helps in assessing whether a given exposure is likely to impair their capital under a given stress movement; these are pass/fail tests. If capital falls below an acceptable level, it could set off a chain reaction of margin calls, withdrawal of financing, and other actions that threaten the viability of the business.

EXAMPLE 8

Scenario Analysis

1 Which of the following is an example of a reverse stress test?

A Identify the top 10 exposures in the portfolio and then generate a hypothetical stress that could adversely affect all 10 simultaneously.

B Find the worst single day's performance that could have occurred for the current portfolio had it been held throughout the past five years.

C Find the returns that occurred in all risk factors in the 2008 global financial crisis, reverse the sign on these, and apply them to today's portfolio.

2   Which kind of market participant is *least likely* to use scenario analysis as a pass/fail stress test?

   A   Bank

   B   Long-only asset manager

   C   Hedge fund using leverage

3   What is the *most* accurate approach to scenario analysis for a portfolio that uses options?

   A   Apply the scenario to option delta.

   B   Apply the scenario to option delta + gamma.

   C   Fully reprice the options using the market returns specified under the scenario.

Solution to 1:

A is correct. B is not a reverse stress test because reverse stress tests focus more narrowly on trouble spots for a specific portfolio. C would illustrate how the portfolio would have performed in an extremely strong market, quite unlike what occurred in 2008.

Solution to 2:

B is correct. Long-only asset managers do not typically use leverage and are thus less likely to become insolvent, making a pass/fail test for solvency less relevant to them. A and C are not correct because parties that use leverage, such as hedge funds and banks, are likely to use stress tests to determine what market movements could impair their capital and lead to insolvency.

Solution to 3:

C is correct. Both A and B risk misestimating the actual results of the scenario because both delta and gamma estimate how an option's value might change for a small move in the underlying asset, not the large movements typically used in a scenario analysis.

3.3 Sensitivity and Scenario Risk Measures and VaR

Although both VaR and sensitivity risk measures deal with related concepts, they have their own distinctions. VaR is a measure of losses and the probability of large losses. Sensitivity risk measures capture changes in the value of an asset in response to a change in something else, such as a market index, an interest rate, or an exchange rate; they do not, however, tell us anything about the probability of a given change in value occurring. For example, we could use duration to measure the change in a bond price for an instantaneous 1 bps change in the yield, but duration does not tell us anything about the likelihood of such a change occurring. Similar statements could be made about equities and the various option measures: Betas and deltas do not tell us how likely a change might be in the underlying risk factors, but given a change, they tell us how responsive the asset or derivative would be.

VaR gives us a broader picture of the risk in the sense that it accounts for the probability of losses of certain amounts. In this sense, it incorporates what we know about the probability of movements in the risk factors. Nonetheless, these sensitivity measures are still very useful in that they allow us to take a much more detailed look at the relationships driving the risk. It is one thing to say that a VaR is $2 million for one day at 5%. We know what that means. But it is equally important to understand what is driving the risk. Is it coming from high beta stocks, high duration bonds, or high delta options? If we find our VaR unacceptable, we have to know where to look to modify it. If we simply use VaR by itself, we will blindly rely on a single number without understanding what factors are driving the number.

VaR has much in common with scenario risk measures in that both types of measures estimate potential loss. VaR tends to do so using a model for which input parameters are created based on market returns from a particular time in history, and thus the VaR estimate is vulnerable if correlation relationships and market volatility during the period in question are not representative of the conditions the portfolio may face in the future. VaR does, however, allow a disciplined method for stressing all factors in the portfolio. Scenario analysis allows the risk assessment to be fully hypothetical, or to be linked to a different and more extreme period of history, helping reduce some of the biases imposed by the VaR model. But there is no guarantee that the scenario chosen will be the "right" one to estimate risk for future markets, and it is particularly difficult to stress all possible risk factors in a hypothetical scenario in a way that does not embed biases similar to those that occur in VaR modeling.

Each of these measures—sensitivity risk measures, scenario risk measures, and VaR—has distinct limitations, but distinct benefits. They are best used in combination because no one measure has the answer, but all provide valuable information that can help risk managers understand the portfolio and avoid unwanted outcomes and surprises.

3.3.1 *Advantages and Limitations of Sensitivity Risk Measures and Scenario Risk Measures*

Before portfolios began using risk measures based on modern portfolio theory, the very first risk measure was "position size"—the value invested in a given type of asset. Position size is a very effective risk measure for homogeneous, long-only portfolios, particularly for those familiar with the homogenous asset class in question; an experienced person can assess what the loss potential of such a portfolio is just by knowing its size. But position size is less useful for assessing interest rate risk, even less useful for summarizing the risk of a multi-asset class portfolio, and less useful still at assessing net risk in a portfolio that uses hedging instruments, short positions, and liabilities.

Sensitivity measures address some of the shortcomings of position size measures. Duration, for example, addresses the difference between a 1-year note and a 30-year note; it measures the level of interest rate risk. Option delta and duration (for fixed income) helps to display net risk in a portfolio that has hedging or short positions with optionality or interest rate risk.

Sensitivities typically do not often distinguish assets by volatility, though. When measured as the sensitivity to a 1 bp or 1% move, they do not tell the user which portfolio has greater loss potential any more than position size measures do; a high-yield bond portfolio might have the same sensitivity to a 0.01% credit spread movement as an investment-grade portfolio, but they do not have the same risk because the credit spreads of the high-yield portfolio are more likely to move 0.01%, or more, than are the credit spreads of the investment-grade bonds. Sensitivity measures do not distinguish by standard deviation/volatility or other higher confidence loss measures. Measuring sensitivity to a one standard deviation movement in an asset's price or yield, however, is one way to overcome this shortcoming of sensitivity.

Granularity: Too Much or Too Little?

Sensitivity measures are aggregated in categories or "buckets." (A bucket is a risk factor description such as "one- to five-year French sovereign debt.") When a number of fixed-income positions are assigned to the same bucket, the effect is an assumption of perfect correlation across the risks encompassed by that bucket. For the "one- to five-year French sovereign debt" risk factor, a short duration position in four-year French sovereign debt will be assumed to fully offset a long duration position in two-year French sovereign debt. However, this may not be true in the case of a non-parallel interest rate change; these points on the yield curve do not have a correlation coefficient of 1 to one another. The broader the buckets used, the more they can hide this kind of correlation risk; but the narrower the buckets used, the greater the complexity, and the more difficult to portray portfolios in simple, accessible ways. The width or the narrowness of the risk-factor buckets used to portray sensitivity measures is referred to as granularity.

Scenario analysis and stress testing have well-deserved popularity, and they address many of the shortcomings of VaR described earlier. Sensitivity and scenario risk measures can complement VaR in the following ways:

■ They do not need to rely on history. Sensitivity and scenario risk measures can be constructed to test the portfolio's vulnerability to a truly never-before-seen market movement. In this way, they can be free of the volatility and correlation behavior of recent market history, which may simply not be representative of stress conditions. In a scenario analysis, assets that typically have a low correlation with one another can be modeled under an assumption of perfect positive correlation simply by simulating an identical price movement for these assets. Alternatively, they can be modeled under an assumption of perfect negative correlation by simulating identical price movements, but in the opposite direction. A scenario might be designed in which a market that typically exhibits an annual standard deviation of 15% moves by 20% in a single day.

■ Scenarios can be designed to overcome any assumption of normal distributions; the shock used could be the equivalent of 1, 10, or 1,000 standard deviations, at the choice of the analyst—or as provided by an actual moment in history.

■ Scenarios can be tailored to expose a portfolio's most concentrated positions to even worse movement than its other exposures, allowing liquidity to be taken into account.

But scenario measures are not without their own limitations:

■ Historical scenarios are interesting, and illuminating, but are not going to happen in exactly the same way again, making hypothetical scenarios necessary to truly fill the gaps identified with the other risk measures listed.

■ Hypothetical scenarios may incorrectly specify how assets will co-move, they may get the magnitude of movements wrong, and they may attempt to adjust for the effects of liquidity and concentration, but might do so incorrectly.

■ Hypothetical scenarios can be very difficult to create and maintain—getting all factors and their relationships accurately represented in the suite of scenarios is a painstaking and possibly never-ending exercise. Accordingly, it is necessary to draw a line of "reasonableness" at which to curtail the scenario analysis, and by the very act of being curtailed, the scenario might miss the real risk.

■ It is very difficult to know how to establish the appropriate limits on a scenario analysis or stress test. Because we are proposing hypothetical movements in markets and risk factors, we cannot use history to assign a probability of such a move occurring. What if rates rise instantaneously 0.50%, 1.00%, or 3.00%? How should the short end of the yield curve move versus the long end? How much should credit spreads of different qualities move? It is difficult to choose.

The more extreme the scenario, and the farther from historical experience, the less likely it is to be found believable or actionable by management of a company or a portfolio. This issue tends to lead scenario constructors to underestimate movement in order to appear credible. As an example, prior to the very large drop in real estate values that prevailed in the United States from 2008 to 2010, no similar nationwide price decline had occurred in history. Risk measurement teams at a number of firms did prepare scenarios that estimated the potential outcome if real estate prices declined meaningfully, but their scenarios in many cases were only half as large as the movements that subsequently occurred. Because these large market movements had never before occurred, there was no historical basis for estimating them, and to do so appeared irresponsible. This is an additional risk of scenario analysis: The need to keep the scenario plausible may lead to it being incorrect.

In sum, scenario analyses and stress tests have the opportunity to correct the failings of probabilistic risk measures, such as VaR and *ex ante* tracking error; but because the version of the future they suggest may be no more accurate than that used in VaR, they may also fail to predict potential loss accurately.

As we can see, each risk measure has elements that are better than the others—and each has important failings. No one measure is the "solution" to risk management; each is useful and necessary to answer certain questions, but not sufficient to answer all possible questions, or to prevent all forms of unexpected loss. Using the measures in combination, to correct each other's failings, is as close to a solution as we come. Designing constraints by using multiple measures is the key practice used by successful risk managers. Viewing a portfolio through these multiple lenses provides a more solid framework for a risk manager or an investor to exercise judgment and can help reduce conceptual bias in portfolio management.

EXAMPLE 9

Limitations of Risk Measures

1   Which of the following is **not** a limitation of VaR?

    A   It does not adjust for bonds of different durations.

    B   It largely relies on recent historical correlations and volatilities.

    C   It can be inaccurate if the size of positions held is large relative to available liquidity.

2   Which of the following statements about sensitivities is true?

    A   When duration is measured as the sensitivity to a 1 bp change in interest rates, it can be biased by choice of the historical period preceding this measure.

    B   Sensitivity measures are the best way to determine how an option can behave under extreme market movements.

    C   Duration effectively assumes that the correlation between a fixed-income exposure and the risk-free rate is 1, whereas beta takes into account the historical correlation between an equity and its comparison index.

3   Which of the following is **not** a limitation of scenario measures?

    A   It is difficult to ascribe probability to a given scenario.

    B   Scenario measures assume a normal distribution, and market returns are not necessarily normal.

    C   They risk being an infinite task; one cannot possibly measure all of the possible future scenarios.

4   Which measures are based on market returns during a particular historical period?

A Hypothetical scenario analysis and duration sensitivity

B Historical scenario analysis and VaR

C Option delta and vega

Solution to 1:

A is correct. Well-executed VaR measures do adjust for bonds of differing duration, and therefore it is not a limitation of VaR. B is incorrect because VaR ordinarily uses some period of recent history as part of the calculation, and this reliance on history is one of its limitations. C is incorrect because VaR can be inaccurate and underestimate risk if portfolio positions are too large relative to the available market liquidity, and this inability to account for the illiquidity of an individual investor's position is an additional limitation of VaR.

Solution to 2:

C is correct. Duration assumes that all interest rates that affect a bond change by the same percentage (an effective correlation of 1). A is incorrect because the 1 bp change in rates is applied to current rates, not historical rates. B is incorrect because sensitivity measures are often too small to reveal the most extreme movements for option positions; the larger shocks used in scenario measures are preferable to reveal option characteristics.

Solution to 3:

B is correct. Scenario measures do not assume any given distribution, and thus this is not a limitation of scenario analysis. A is incorrect because it is in fact difficult to ascribe probability to many scenarios, and thus this is a limitation of scenario analysis. C is also incorrect because it is in fact impossible to measure all possible future scenarios, and this is a limitation of scenario analysis.

Solution to 4:

B is correct. Historical scenarios apply market returns from a particular period to the portfolio, and virtually all VaR methodologies use a historical period to underpin the VaR model, although certain methods may make adjustments if this historical period is seen to be anomalous in some way. A is incorrect because a hypothetical scenario is not based on an actual historical period, and duration sensitivity measures change in value for a given small change in rates, not for a given historical period. C is incorrect because option delta and vega measure how much an option's value will change for a given change in the price of the underlying (delta) or implied volatility (vega), and these are sensitivity measures, not measures based on a particular historical period.

4 APPLICATIONS OF RISK MEASURES

In this section, we examine the practical applications of risk measures. First, we will look at how different types of market participants use risk measures. An understanding of how various market participants use these measures will help as we move to a discussion of their limitations.

4.1 Market Participants and the Different Risk Measures They Use

Three factors tend to greatly influence the types of risk measures used by different market participants:

- The degree to which the market participant is leveraged and the resulting need to assess minimum capitalization/maximum leverage ratios;
- The mix of risk factors to which their business is exposed (e.g., the degree of equity or fixed-income concentration in their portfolios);
- The accounting or regulatory requirements that govern their reporting.

Market participants who use a high degree of leverage typically need to assess their sensitivity to shocks to ensure that they will remain a going concern under very severe, but foreseeable, stresses. This leads them to focus on potential loss measures with a high confidence interval or to focus on rare events that might occur in a short period of time, such as two weeks. Those who use minimal (or no) leverage, such as long-only asset managers, are interested in shock sensitivity as well, but are likely less concerned with trying to discern the difference between a 99.99% (0.01% VaR) worst case and a 99.95% (0.05% VaR) worst case; their focus is more likely on avoiding underperformance; for example, failing to keep pace with their market benchmark when markets are doing well. For this reason, they are often more interested in lower confidence intervals—events that are more likely to occur and lead to underperformance for a given strategy. Unleveraged asset managers may also prefer to measure potential underperformance over longer periods of time, such as a quarter or a year, rather than shorter periods.

For portfolios dominated by fixed-income investments, risk managers focus on how sensitive the portfolios are to instantaneous price and yield changes in a variety of categories and typically emphasize duration, credit spread duration, and key rate duration measures.[18] Risk measurement for fixed-income portfolios is conducted using bond pricing models, and by shifting each market rate assumption in the model and aggregating their portfolio's sensitivity to these market rates. Often, these factors are combined into scenarios representing expected central bank policies, inflation expectations, and/or anticipated fiscal policy changes. When portfolios are dominated by equities, risk managers typically categorize the equities by broad country markets, industries, and market capitalization levels, and they may additionally regress the returns of their portfolios against fundamental factor histories (such as those for growth, value, momentum, and capitalization size) to understand their exposure to such factors.

Portfolios with full fair value accounting,[19] such as US mutual funds, European UCITS funds, and the held-for-sale portfolios of banks, are very well suited to such risk measures as VaR, economic capital (the amount of capital a firm needs to hold if it is to survive severe losses from the risks in its businesses), duration, and beta, all of which rely on measuring the changes in the fair values of assets. Asset/liability gap models are more meaningful when portfolios are subject to book value accounting in whole or in part.

---

18 Credit spread duration measures the impact on an instrument's value if credit spreads move while risk-free rates remain unchanged, and key rate duration (also sometimes called partial duration) measures the sensitivity of a bond's price to changes in specific maturities on the benchmark yield curve.

19 Entities that use fair value accounting, also called mark-to-market accounting, recognize changes in the market value of their holdings each time they prepare a balance sheet and profit and loss statement. Entities that use book value accounting do not recognize these changes, carrying assets at their original value and recording the income provided by that holding on the profit and loss statement; but from time to time, they may have to recognize impairment in an asset and boost reserves if impairments are more likely.

4.1.1 Banks

Banks need to balance a number of sometimes competing aspects of risk to manage their business and meet the expectations of equity investors/equity analysts, bond investors, credit rating agencies, depositors, and regulatory entities. Some banks apply risk measures differently depending on whether the portfolio being assessed is designated as a "held-to-maturity" portfolio, which requires book value accounting, or a "held-for-sale" or "trading book" portfolio, which requires fair value accounting. Other banks will use fair value measures for all risk assessments regardless of the designation used for accounting purposes. In the following list are some of the factors that banks seek to address through their use of risk tools. In compiling this list, we have assumed that banks may treat measures differently depending on accounting treatment.

- *Liquidity gap:* The extent of any liquidity and asset/liability mis-match. The ability to raise sufficient cash for foreseeable payment needs; a view of the liquidity of assets, as well as the expected repayment date of debt.

- *VaR:* The value at risk for the held-for-sale or trading (fair value) portion of the balance sheet.

- *Leverage:* A leverage ratio is typically computed, sometimes according to a regulatory requirement as well as to an internally determined measure. Leverage ratios will weight risk assets using a variety of methods and rules and divide this weighted asset figure by equity. The result is that riskier assets will be assigned a greater weighting, and less risky assets a lower weighting, so that more equity is required to support riskier assets.

- *Sensitivities:* For the held-for-sale portion of their balance sheet, banks measure duration, key rate duration or partial duration, and credit spread duration for interest rate risk positions. Banks will also measure foreign exchange exposure and any equity or commodity exposures. All these exposure measures will include the delta sensitivities of options with any other exposures to the same underlying asset and will also monitor gamma and vega exposures of options. Gamma and vega exposures can be broken out by term to identify how much of these risks come from long-dated versus short-dated options.

- *Economic capital:* This is measured by blending the company's market, credit, and operational risk measures to estimate the total loss the company could suffer at a very high level of confidence (e.g., 99% to 99.99%), usually in one year's time. Economic capital measures are applied to the full balance sheet, including both the held-for-sale and held-for-investment portfolios, and include market, credit, and operational risk capital.

- *Scenario analysis:* Stress tests are applied to the full balance sheet and augment economic capital and liquidity; they are used to identify whether capital is sufficient for targeted, strong negative shocks. Outside of stress testing, significant scenario analysis takes places. Scenario analysis is used to examine how the full balance sheet might be affected by different interest rate, inflation, and credit environments, such as unemployment levels for credit card lenders, home price appreciation/depreciation for mortgage lenders, and business cycle stresses for corporate lenders.

It is common for banks to compute risk measures in distinct business units and geographies and then to aggregate these measures to the parent company entity.

4.1.2 Asset Managers

Asset managers are not typically regulated with regard to sufficient capital or liquidity; they are more commonly regulated for fair treatment of investors—that disclosures are full and accurate, that marketing is not misleading, that one client is not favored over the other. In some jurisdictions, certain market risk measures may be used to define risk limits for different fund types.

In asset management portfolios, risk management efforts are focused primarily on volatility, probability of loss, or probability of underperforming a benchmark rather than insolvency. A diversified, unleveraged, long-only fund is unlikely to see asset values decline below zero in the absence of a wholesale withdrawal of assets by the firm's clients. Although service costs and other items make insolvency a technical possibility, in practice, insolvency is a much higher threat for leveraged portfolios. Although derivative use by asset managers can create effective leverage, these positions are often balanced by an amount of cash in the portfolio equal to the notional exposure created by the derivative mitigating, if not fully eliminating, the impact of leverage.

Asset managers typically measure and view each portfolio separately with respect to its own constraints and limits. However, there are a few exceptions:

- Long-only asset managers: If the adviser has invested its own capital in any of the funds that it manages, these investments may need to be aggregated for the firm to assess its risk exposures across portfolios.

- Hedge funds: A hedge fund manager needs to aggregate the adviser's side-by-side investment in the various funds it advises.

- Funds of funds: Risk measures for these portfolios typically aggregate the risks of the underlying hedge funds to the master fund level.

An asset manager may choose to aggregate exposures across all funds and strategies to determine if it has any unusual concentrations in individual securities or counterparties that would make management actions across all portfolios difficult to carry out (e.g., a single portfolio's holdings in a given security may not pose a liquidity risk, but if the firm were to aggregate all of its holdings in that security, it may find that the portfolio fails to meet the desired liquidity target).

It is important when observing risk measures for asset managers to determine whether they represent the backward-looking variability of realized returns in the portfolio as it was then constituted, or use the current portfolio and measure its potential loss. Backward-looking returns-based measures (typically including standard deviation, *ex post* tracking error, Sharpe ratio, information ratio, and historical beta) have the value of showing the fund's behavior over time and help assess the skill of the manager. Only an analysis of the current holdings, however, will reveal current risk exposures. Measures that use current holdings typically include VaR, *ex ante* tracking error, duration and forward-looking beta, stress tests, and scenario analyses. All risk and performance measures can be conducted on past portfolio holdings or current portfolio holdings; it is important for the user of any measure to determine which ingredients (which set of portfolio holdings, and for market history, what length and smoothing techniques) have been used, in order to use it correctly. Assessing the trends in risk exposures, including whether risk has recently risen or if other important changes have taken place in the strategy, can be accomplished by tracking the risk measures through time.

4.1.2.1 Traditional Asset Managers   Asset managers that use little leverage typically find relative risk measures most meaningful and actionable; the decision to invest in a given asset class is normally the client's, not the adviser's; the adviser seeks to outperform the benchmark representative of the asset class. Exceptions include absolute return funds and asset allocation strategies, but even these can be measured relative to a benchmark. For absolute return strategies, the benchmark is typically cash or a

cash-like hurdle rate; when cash is the benchmark, VaR and *ex ante* tracking error, if measured using the same holding period and confidence interval, will be effectively the same.[20] Asset allocation funds can use an asset allocation index as the benchmark for a relative risk measure, or they can use a custom combination of market benchmarks.

Although banks, insurers, and other market participants favor measuring VaR in currency terms relevant for the institution (e.g., dollars for a US-based insurer, yen for a Japanese bank) and measure duration and similar statistics as the value change for a 1 bps interest rate change, long-only asset managers generally prefer to express VaR in percentage terms and will divide VaR and duration by the net assets of the portfolio being analyzed.[21]

A typical sample of risk measures used by asset managers includes the following:

▪ *Position limits:* Asset managers use position limits as the most frequent form of risk control for the portfolios they manage, particularly in fund offering documents that need to be understandable to a broad range of investors. Position limits include restrictions on country, currency, sector, and asset class; they may measure them in absolute terms or relative to a benchmark, and they are almost always expressed as a percentage of the portfolio's value.

▪ *Sensitivities:* Asset managers use the full range of sensitivity measures, including option adjusted duration, key rate duration, and credit spread duration, and they will typically include the delta exposure of options in these measures. Measures can be expressed in absolute terms as well as relative to a benchmark.

▪ *Beta sensitivity:* Beta is frequently used for equity-only accounts.

▪ *Liquidity:* Asset managers often look at the liquidity characteristics of the assets in their portfolios; it is common to measure, for equity portfolios, what percentage of daily average trading volume the portfolio holds of each equity security and how many days it would take to liquidate a security if the manager did not want it to be too large a portion of trading volume to avoid taking a price concession.

▪ *Scenario analysis:* When long-only asset managers use stress tests or scenario analyses, they typically do so to verify that the risks in the portfolio are as they have been disclosed to investors and to identify any unusual behavior that could arise in stressed markets.

▪ *Active share:* **Active share** is the measure of that percentage of the portfolio that differs from the benchmark index.

▪ *Redemption risk:* Open-end fund managers often assess what percentage of the portfolio could be redeemed at peak times and track this behavior across the funds and asset classes they manage.

▪ *Ex post versus ex ante tracking error:* Limits on *ex ante* tracking error are often used by traditional asset managers as a key risk metric for the portfolios they manage. It provides an estimate of the degree to which the current portfolio could underperform its benchmark. It is worth noting the distinction between *ex post* tracking error[22] and *ex ante* tracking error. Although asset managers use *ex post* tracking error to identify sources of performance and manager skill, they use *ex ante* tracking error to identify whether today's positions could give

---

20 The reason is because cash has no volatility; adding a cash benchmark into a relative VaR calculation does not affect the calculation because its zero volatility cancels out its impact, and the resulting calculation is the same as the VaR of the portfolio.

21 When using returns as the fundamental source of data, it removes the last step in calculating VaR: multiplying by the size of the portfolio.

22 *Ex post* tracking error is the annual standard deviation of a portfolio's historical benchmark-relative returns.

rise to unexpected potential performance. *Ex post* tracking error measures the historical deviation between portfolio returns and benchmark returns, and thus both the portfolio holdings and market returns are historical in this measure. *Ex ante* tracking error takes today's benchmark-relative position and exposes it to the variability of past markets to estimate what kind of benchmark relative performance could arise from the current portfolio. *Ex post* tracking error is a useful tool for assessing manager skill and behavior. But the day after a large change in portfolio strategy, *ex ante* tracking will immediately reflect the portfolio's new return profile, whereas *ex post* tracking error will not do so until the new strategy has been in place long enough to dominate the data history. (If *ex post* tracking error is computed using 200 days of history, the day after a large strategy change, only 1 of the 200 data points will reflect the current risk positioning.) Some asset managers focus on maintaining *ex ante* tracking error boundaries for the portfolios they manage to monitor and balance the potential performance impact of the active risks they are taking.

- *VaR:* VaR is less commonly used as a risk measure than *ex ante* tracking error by traditional asset managers, but it is used by some, particularly for portfolios that are characterized as "absolute return" strategies, for which a given market benchmark may not serve as the portfolio objective.

4.1.2.2 Hedge Funds
Similar to banks, hedge funds that use leverage need to observe sources and uses of cash through time, including when credit lines could be withdrawn, and need to simulate the interplay between market movements, margin calls, and the redemption rights of investors in order to understand worst-case needs for cash. A sample of the typical range of hedge fund market risk measures includes the following:

- *Sensitivities:* All hedge fund strategies will display some form of sensitivity or exposure, so the full range of sensitivity measures are useful for hedge fund risk management.

- *Gross exposure:* Long–short, market neutral, and arbitrage strategies will typically measure long exposure, short exposure, and gross exposure (the sum of the absolute value of long plus short positions) separately; gross position risk is an important guide to the importance of correlation risk for the portfolio.

- *Leverage:* Leverage measures are common for hedge funds; it is important to understand how the measure is treating derivatives and what elements appear in the numerator versus the denominator because there are many different ways to execute the measure.

- *VaR:* Hedge funds that use VaR measures tend to focus on high confidence intervals (more than 90%) and short holding periods, and they rarely use a benchmark-relative measure.

- *Scenarios:* Hedge funds commonly use scenario/stress tests that are well tuned to the specific risks of their strategy, such as for merger arbitrage strategies, the chance that the merger will not take place.

- *Drawdown:* In the case of the following types of hedge fund strategies, standard deviation and historical beta measures can be particularly misleading when seeking to understand what the more extreme risks can be. This is because the strategies listed frequently display decidedly non-normal return distributions and, when this is true, standard deviation is not a good guide to worse-case outcomes. For the following strategies, any historical standard deviation or historical beta measures should be supplemented by a measure of what has been the **maximum drawdown**, often defined as the worst-returning month or quarter for the portfolio or the worst peak-to-trough decline in a portfolio's returns:

- Strategies that focus on credit risk taking, such as long–short credit, credit arbitrage, or bankruptcy investing
- Strategies that focus on events, such as merger arbitrage
- Strategies that make meaningful investments in non-publicly issued assets or other assets that do not reliably have a daily, independent fair value determination
- Strategies that invest in illiquid asset classes or take large positions relative to market size in any asset class
- Strategies that sell options or purchase bonds with embedded options
- Strategies that are highly reliant on correlation relationships, such as equity market neutral

In addition, it is not uncommon for those investing in hedge funds to look at the returns of the hedge fund during a relevant historical period, such as the 2008 financial crisis.

4.1.3 *Pension Funds*

A defined benefit pension plan is required to make payments to its pensioners in the future that are typically determined as a function of a retiree's final salary. This differs from a defined contribution plan, in which the plan's sponsor may be required to make contributions currently, but is not responsible to ensure that they grow to a particular future amount. To meet the required payouts, defined benefit plans have significant market risk management responsibilities; this section describes the practices of defined benefit pension plans only, and all mentions in this section of "pension funds" or "pension plans" refer to defined benefit pensions.

The risk management goal for pension funds is to be sufficiently funded to make future payments to pensioners. The requirements for sufficient funding vary from country to country. Different jurisdictions will have regulations concerning such items as how to compute the present value of pension liabilities, including which interest rates are permitted to be used as a discount rate, and what the sponsor of the pension plan is required to contribute when the assets in the pension fund are lower than the present value of the liabilities. In addition, some jurisdictions impose taxes when surplus—the value of the assets less the value of the liabilities—is withdrawn for other use by the plan sponsor. Although these regional differences will shape the practice of pension plan risk management in different countries, it is typically an exercise in ensuring that the plan is not likely to become significantly under- or overfunded. Overfunding occurs when the funding ratio (the assets divided by the present value of the liabilities) is greater than 100%; underfunding occurs when the funding ratio is under 100%. Overfunding may be cured over time by the plan sponsor not needing to make regular contributions to the plan while the number of employees and their salary levels, which drive the pension benefit, may be growing. Underfunding, if not cured by growth in the assets in the fund over a suitable time horizon as permitted by regulation, is cured by the plan sponsor contributing to the fund. The pension plan's actions will also vary depending on its age (whether it is a new or established plan) and whether it is currently meaningfully under- or overfunded. Important market risk measures or methods for pension funds often include the following:

- *Interest rate and curve risk:* The first step of risk measurement for pension funds is the analysis of expected payments to pensioners in the future. The expected future cash flows are grouped by maturity and, in the case of an international pension fund that must make future payouts in multiple currencies, they may also be grouped by currency. In cases in which the jurisdiction requires a particular fixed-income instrument or curve be used to provide the discount rate for arriving at the present value of the pension liability (such as corporate bonds in the United States, inflation-linked gilts in the United Kingdom, or government bonds in the Netherlands), the liability cash flows will be expressed as a short position at the relevant points on the curve.

- *Surplus at risk:* This measure is an application of VaR. It is computed by entering the assets in the portfolio into a VaR model as long positions and the pension liabilities as short fixed-income positions. It estimates how much the assets might underperform the liabilities, usually over one year, and pension plan sponsors may vary with respect to how high a level of confidence they choose to use (e.g., 84%, 95%, 99%). If the assets in the portfolio were invested precisely in the same fixed-income instruments to which the liabilities have been apportioned, in the same amounts, it would result in zero surplus at risk. In practice, however, it may be impossible to invest in the sizes required in the particular fixed-income instruments specified in the liability analysis, so the pension will invest in other, non-fixed-income investments, such as equities or real assets. The more volatile the investments in the pension fund, and the less well correlated these assets are with the liabilities, the higher the surplus at risk will be. The pension fund may set a threshold level or limit on surplus at risk; when the pension fund's surplus at risk exceeds this limit, pension staff will change the fund's asset allocation to make the assets in the fund better match the liabilities. This liability-focused form of pension investing is commonly referred to as "liability driven investing."

- *Glide path:* In cases in which a pension fund is meaningfully under- or overfunded, or has a high surplus at risk, it may be difficult to make all the changes needed to improve the funded status or to allocate assets to better match liabilities in a short period of time. A glide path, as a tool for managing surplus at risk, charts multi-year stages to change the portfolio from its current state to its target state.

- *Liability hedging exposures versus return generating exposures:* Although matching liabilities is an important goal of pension fund management, it is not the only goal. Pension staff may separate their investment portfolio into investments designed to match the pension liability versus those meant to generate excess returns. The precise instruments linked to the liability cannot always be directly invested in, so a separate portion of the portfolio may be necessary and should perform the function of earning returns that can minimize the chance of having an over- or underfunded status greater than the pension fund's risk tolerance. The return-generating portion of the portfolio also helps to hedge the potential for future changes in the size of the liability that could be caused by longevity risk or by wage growth that exceeds the forecasts currently used to compute the liability.

4.1.4 *Insurers*

Insurers in the largest global economies are subject to significant regulation and accounting oversight regarding how they must retain reserves and reflect their liabilities. Regulation may also affect the pricing permitted by product line. It is common for insurers to aggregate risk from underlying business units to arrive at a firm-wide view of risk.

Insurance liabilities vary in their correlation with financial markets. The risk metrics of property and casualty insurance differ significantly from those used for life insurance and annuity products. Property and casualty insurance, including home, auto, corporate liability insurance, and health insurance, are typically not highly correlated with financial asset markets.

Insurers focus on managing a number of forms of insurance risk, for which they may use such tools as reinsurance and geographic dispersion. The market risk management measures in the property and casualty lines of business include the following:

- *Sensitivities and exposures:* Insurers often design an asset allocation for these portfolios and monitor current exposures to remain within the target ranges set forth in the target asset allocation.

- *Economic capital and VaR:* The risk measurement focus for these lines of business is capital at risk and VaR. The premiums earned in these areas are typically set to compensate for the expected payouts (usually defined as a range of possible payouts), so it is only in cases of greater-than-expected payouts that capital is tapped. The risk modeling effort is to estimate what that catastrophic loss amount could be at a given level of probability. Assessment of the risk to economic capital will include the market risks in the portfolio, as well as characteristics of the insurance exposures and reinsurance coverage.

- *Scenario analysis:* Insurers use scenario analysis like other market participants that have capital at risk, such as banks and hedge funds. For the property and casualty lines, these scenarios may stress the market risks and the insurance risks in the same scenario.

Insurers do not focus on matching assets with liabilities in their property and casualty lines of business. Investment portfolios are not designed to pay out insurance claims in property and casualty insurance businesses—the premium income is primarily used for that purpose. These investments are designed to achieve a good absolute return within the constraints imposed under regulatory reserve requirements; riskier assets are discounted relative to safer, fixed-income assets in measuring required reserves.

Life insurance and annuities have stronger ties to the financial markets, even while retaining distinct mortality-based risk profiles. Life liabilities are very long and the reserves that insurers are required to maintain by insurance regulators are highly dependent on discount rate assumptions. Non-financial inputs include assumptions about mortality and which policyholders will either tap into options in their policy to add coverage at a given level or cancel their policy. Annuities produce returns based on financial assets, with some extra optionality driven by any life insurance elements embedded in the policy. These activities are paired with long-term investment portfolios in a variety of assets that are designed to help the insurer meet future claims.

For life portfolios, market risk measures include the following:

- *Sensitivities:* The exposures of the investment portfolio and the annuity liability are measured and monitored.

- *Asset and liability matching:* The investment portfolio is not designed to be a perfect match to the liabilities; but it is more closely matched to liabilities than is the case in property and casualty insurance.

- *Scenario analysis:* The main focus of risk measurement for the life lines of insurance are measures of potential stress losses based on the differences between the assets in which the insurance company has invested and the liabilities driven by the insurance contracts it has written to its customers. Scenario analyses need to stress both market and non-market sources of cash flow change (in which non-market changes can include changes in longevity).

EXAMPLE 10

Uses of Risk Measures by Market Participants

1   Which type of market participant is *most likely* to consistently express risk measures as a percentage of assets and relative to a benchmark?

   A   Banks

   B   Corporations

   C   Long-only asset managers

2   How does *ex ante* tracking error differ from *ex post* tracking error?

   A   *Ex ante* tracking error takes into account the behavior of options whereas *ex post* tracking error does not.

   B   *Ex post* tracking error uses a more accurate forecast of future markets than the forecast used for *ex ante* tracking error.

   C   *Ex ante* tracking error uses *current* portfolio holdings exposed to the variability of historical markets, whereas *ex post* tracking error measures the variability of *historical* portfolio holdings in historical markets.

Solution to 1:

C is correct. Long-only asset managers most commonly express risk measures in percentage terms and relative to a benchmark, whereas the entities in answers A and B measure risk more commonly in currency units and in absolute terms (not relative to a benchmark). Banks occasionally express risk measures, such as economic capital, as a percentage of assets or other balance sheet measures, but bank risk measures are typically expressed in currency units.

Solution to 2:

C is correct. A is incorrect because although *ex post* tracking error accounts for the options that were in the portfolio in the past, *ex ante* tracking error might actually misstate the risk of options if it is computed using the parametric method. B is incorrect because *ex post* tracking error is not aiming to forecast the future, it is only measuring the variability of past results.

USING CONSTRAINTS IN MARKET RISK MANAGEMENT

5

Designing suitable constraints to be used in market risk management is essential to managing risk effectively. Risk *measurements* in and of themselves cannot be said to be restrictive or unrestrictive—it is the *limits* placed on the measures that drive action. VaR can be measured to a very high confidence level (for example, 99%) or to a low level (for example, 84%); but placing a loose limit on a 99% confidence VaR measure could be less of a constraint than placing a tight limit on an 84% confidence measure. It is not the confidence interval that drives conservatism as much as the limit that is placed on it.

   If constraints are too tight, they may limit the pursuit of perceived opportunities and might shrink returns or profitability to a sub-optimal level. If constraints are too loose, outsized losses can occur, threatening the viability of the portfolio or business. The concept of "restrictive" or "unrestrictive" relates to the risk appetite of the firm or portfolio and the sizes of losses it can tolerate. Unrestrictive limits are typically set far from current risk levels and permit larger losses than restrictive limits. As an example, for a leveraged portfolio in which insolvency could occur if cumulative daily losses exceed $10 million, and the portfolio's current two week, 1% VaR measure is $3 million, an unrestrictive limit might be one set at $10 million. If the portfolio increased positions and went right up to its limit, a mis-estimation of VaR could result in insolvency; and the fact that losses are expected to exceed the measure at least 1% of the time could mean disaster. But if the limit were set at $4 million, the portfolio might under-allocate the capital it has to invest and fail to make a high enough return on equity to thrive in a competitive environment.

Before applying constraints, particularly those involving potential loss measures such as VaR or a scenario analysis, it is worth considering how far down in the organizational hierarchy to impose them. If applied exclusively to lower level business units, the firm's aggregate risk exposure fails to take advantage of offsetting risks that may occur at higher levels of the organization. As a result, the overall company may never be able to invest according to its risk tolerance because it is "stopped out" by rules lower in the organization. For example, imagine a bank with five trading desks: It might have an overall VaR tolerance of €10 million and might set each trading desk's limit for its standalone VaR at €2 million, which seems reasonable. If there is anything lower than perfect correlation across these desks' positions, however, and particularly if one desk has a short position that to some degree serves as an offset to another desk's long position, the firm will never be able to use its €10 million risk appetite in full. The cure for this problem is over-allocation, but with the caveat that a given desk might need to be cut back to its pro rata share in the event that correlations among trading desks are higher than, or the short positions across the different portfolios are not as offsetting as, the over-allocation assumes. Alternatively, some firms might use marginal VaR for each trading desk, allocating each desk a VaR budget such that the total VaR is the sum of each individual desk's marginal VaR. This approach permits each trading desk to "reinvest" the diversification benefits obtained at the aggregate level.

Among the constraints most often used in risk management are risk budgeting, position limits, scenario limits, and stop-loss limits. As is the case in risk measurement, for which multiple measures work better than any one measure alone does, so it is in risk constraints: No one approach on its own works perfectly; they are most effective in combination.

5.1 Risk Budgeting

In **risk budgeting**, the total risk appetite of the firm or portfolio is agreed on at the highest level of the entity and then allocated to sub-activities. Risk budgeting typically rests on a foundation of VaR or *ex ante* tracking error.

A bank might establish limit on total economic capital or VaR, and describe this limit as its risk appetite. Next, it might allocate this risk appetite among the basic risk types (market, credit, and operational) and different business units, geographies, and activities. It allocates to the business unit and/or risk type by specifying a limit, using its chosen measure, for that given activity. For example, it might allow its European business to use 20% of its market risk capital (the portion of its economic capital expected to be used to support market risk taking) and 40% of its credit risk capital, whereas its Asian business might have a different limit. It will set these limits based on the expected long-term profitability of the opportunity set and the demonstrated skill of a business at delivering profitable results, taking into consideration shareholders' expectations regarding the activities the bank is engaged in.[23]

A pension fund sponsor might begin with its tolerance for how much of a mismatch it is willing to tolerate overall between the total value of assets and its liabilities—its surplus at risk. Surplus at risk can be the starting point for its asset allocation decision making. Once the broad asset allocation is established, usually expressed via a set of benchmarks, the pension fund sponsor might further establish its tolerance for underperformance in a given asset class and allocate that tolerance to the asset managers selected to manage the assets by assigning each an *ex ante* tracking error budget.

A portfolio manager might have an *ex ante* tracking error budget explicitly provided by the client, or if none is provided by the client, it might instead develop a tracking error budget based on her investment philosophy and market practice. Given this budget, she will seek to optimize the portfolio's exposures relative to the benchmark to ensure that the strategies that generate the most tracking error for the portfolio are those for which she expects the greatest reward.

5.2 Position Limits

Risk budgeting follows a clear logic; but as we have noted, VaR-based measures have a number of drawbacks. One of them is that they perform poorly if portfolios are unusually concentrated, particularly with respect to market liquidity.

Position limits are limits on the market value of any given investment, or the notional principal amount for a derivative contract. They can be expressed in currency units or as a percentage of some other value, such as net assets. Position limits do not take into account duration, volatility, and correlation, as VaR does, but they are excellent controls on overconcentration. Like risk budgeting, position limits need to be used carefully; if every asset type that a portfolio manager could invest in is constrained, he will have no room to succeed in outperforming the benchmark or generating absolute returns, assuming that is the mandate. Position limits should not be overly prescriptive but should address the event risk and single name risk that VaR handles so poorly, such as

- limits per issuer;
- limits per currency or country;
- limits on categories expected to be minimized in a given strategy, such as high-yield credit or emerging market equities;
- limits on gross size of long–short positions or derivative activity; and
- limits on asset ownership that correspond to market liquidity measures, such as daily average trading volume.

5.3 Scenario Limits

A scenario limit is a limit on the estimated loss for a given scenario, which if exceeded, would require corrective action in the portfolio.

---

23 As an example of potential shareholder expectations, consider a case in which a firm's shareholder disclosure suggests that the firm's predominant market risk-taking activities are in the Asian markets and that there is less risk-taking activity in Europe. Shareholders will be surprised if greater losses are incurred from its European business than its Asian business. Market risk capital limits for the European business should be lower than for the Asian business to be consistent with shareholder disclosures.

As discussed in Section 3.3, scenarios also address shortcomings of VaR, such as the potential for changes in correlation or for extreme movements that might not be predicted using a normal distribution or the historical lookback period used for the VaR measure. Just producing scenario analysis, however, without having any related action steps is not a very valuable exercise.

The action steps that generally follow a scenario analysis are to examine (1) whether the results are within risk tolerance and, in the case of asset managers, (2) whether the results are well incorporated into investor disclosures. To determine whether results are within the established risk tolerance, a tolerance level for each scenario must be developed. It is better to establish a higher tolerance for potential loss under the most extreme scenarios. If the same limit is applied to all scenarios, even extremely unlikely scenarios (e.g., "interest rates rise 1,000,000%"), then the portfolio will simply not be able to take any risk. The risk manager then observes over time whether the portfolio's sensitivity to the scenario is increasing, or crosses, this high-tolerance bound.

5.4 Stop-Loss Limits

A **stop-loss limit** requires a reduction in the size of a portfolio, or its complete liquidation, when a loss of a particular size occurs in a specified period.

One of the limitations of VaR described in Section 2.3.2 was "trending," in which a portfolio remains under its VaR limit each day but cumulatively loses more than expected. This trending can be managed by imposing and monitoring stop-loss limits in addition to the VaR constraints. In one form of a stop-loss limit, the portfolio's positions are unwound if its losses over a pre-specified period exceed a pre-specified level. (Those levels are typically defined to align with the overall risk tolerance.) As an example, a portfolio might have a 10 day, 1% VaR limit of $5 million, but it will be liquidated if its cumulative monthly loss ever exceeds $8 million. The relationship between the stop-loss and the VaR measure can vary, depending on management preferences as well as the differing time periods with which the measures are specified.

An alternative approach to a stop-loss limit might instead be to impose a requirement to undertake hedging activity, which may include purchases of protective options, after losses of a given magnitude, with the magnitude of the hedge increasing as losses increase. This approach, called drawdown control or portfolio insurance, is more dynamic and more sophisticated than the simpler stop-loss limit.

5.5 Risk Measures and Capital Allocation

In market risk management, capital allocation is the practice of placing limits on each of a company's activities in order to ensure that the areas in which it expects the greatest reward and has the greatest expertise are given the resources needed to accomplish their goals. Allocating capital wisely ensures that an unproven strategy does not use up all of the firm's risk appetite and, in so doing, deprive the areas most likely to be successful of the capital they need to execute on their strategy.

Economic capital is often used to estimate how much of shareholders' equity could be lost by the portfolio under very unfavorable circumstances. Capital allocation may start with a measurement of economic capital (the amount of capital a firm needs to hold if it is to survive severe losses from the risks in its businesses). The company's actual, physical on-balance-sheet capital must exceed the measure of economic capital, and a minimum level of economic capital must be established to ensure that the company does not take on a risk of loss that will exceed its available capital. The company first establishes its overall risk appetite in economic capital terms, and then subdivides this appetite among its units. This exercise is similar to risk budgeting, but in the case of corporations, banks, insurers, or hedge funds, it is more likely to be called "capital allocation." Capital allocation is often used in cases in which leverage is used by the portfolio or in which the strategy has meaningful **tail risk**, meaning that losses in extreme events could be far greater than would be expected for a portfolio of assets with a normal distribution. Economic capital is designed to measure how much shareholders' equity could be required to meet tail risk losses. Strategies that have greater-than-expected tail risk include those that sell options, sell insurance, take substantial credit risk, or have unique liquidity or exposure concentration risks. Although risk budgeting more commonly focuses on losses at the one standard deviation level, capital allocation focuses on losses at a very high confidence level in order to capture the magnitude of capital that is placed at risk by the strategy. Capital allocation seeks to understand how much of an investor's scarce resources are, or could be, used by a given portfolio, thereby making it unavailable to other portfolios.

Because a company's capital is a scarce resource and relatively expensive, it should be deployed in activities that have the best chance of earning a superior rate of return. It also should be deployed in a way that investors expect, in activities in which the company has expertise, and in strategies that investors believe the company can successfully execute.

To optimize the use of capital, the "owner" of the capital will typically establish a hurdle rate over a given time horizon; this is often expressed as the expected rate of return per unit of capital allocated. Two potential activities, Portfolio A and Portfolio B, might require different amounts of capital. Portfolio A might require €325,000, and its expected return might be €50,000 per year (15.4%). Portfolio B might have a reasonable expectation of earning €100,000 per year, but it might require €1,000,000 in capital (a 10% return). If the investor has an annualized hurdle rate of 15%, Portfolio A will exceed the hurdle rate and appear a better user of capital than Portfolio B, even though the absolute income for Portfolio B is higher.

Beyond measuring and limiting economic capital, capital allocation is sometimes used as a broad term for allocating costly resources. In some cases, the costly resource is cash; if, for instance, the portfolio has invested in options and futures trading strategies that require heavy use of margin and overcollateralization, its use of economic capital could be low and available cash may be the constraining factor. For other types of investors, such as banks or insurance companies, the capital required by regulatory bodies could be relatively large and these capital measures may be the most onerous constraint and thus the basis of capital allocation.

When the current measure of economic capital is a smaller number than the portfolio's cash or regulatory capital needs, it may not be the binding constraint. But when it is higher than other measures, it can become the binding constraint, and the one to which hurdle rates should be applied.

EXAMPLE 11

Creating Constraints with Risk Measures

1   Which of the following is **not** an example of risk budgeting?
    A   Giving a foreign exchange trading desk a VaR limit of $10 million
    B   Allowing a portfolio manager to have an *ex ante* tracking error up to 5% in a given portfolio
    C   Reducing the positions in a portfolio after a loss of a 5% of capital has occurred in a single month
2   Which statement is true regarding risk budgeting in cases in which marginal VaR is used?
    A   The total risk budget is never equal to the sum of the individual subportfolios' risk budgets.

    B The total risk budget is always equal to the sum of the individual sub-portfolios' risk budgets.

    C If the total risk budget is equal to the sum of the individual sub-portfolios' risk budgets, there is a risk that this approach may cause capital to be underutilized.

Solution to 1:

C is correct. This is an example of a stop-loss limit, not risk budgeting. The other choices are both examples of risk budgeting.

Solution to 2:

B is correct. When using marginal VaR, the total risk budget will be equal to the sum of the individual risk budgets. Choice A is not correct. C is also incorrect; it would be correct if each sub-portfolio's individual VaR measure, not adjusted for its marginal contribution, were used, which could lead to underutilization of capital.

SUMMARY

This reading on market risk management models covers various techniques used to manage the risk arising from market fluctuations in prices and rates. The key points are summarized as follows.

- Value at risk (VaR) is the minimum loss in either currency units or as a percentage of portfolio value that would be expected to be incurred a certain percentage of the time over a certain period of time given assumed market conditions.

- VaR requires the decomposition of portfolio performance into risk factors.

- The three methods of estimating VaR are the parametric method, the historical simulation method, and the Monte Carlo simulation method.

- The parametric method of VaR estimation typically provides a VaR estimate from the left tail of a normal distribution, incorporating the expected returns, variances, and covariances of the components of the portfolio.

- The parametric method exploits the simplicity of the normal distribution but provides a poor estimate of VaR when returns are not normally distributed, as might occur when a portfolio contains options.

- The historical simulation method of VaR estimation uses historical return data on the portfolio's current holdings and allocation.

- The historical simulation method has the advantage of incorporating events that actually occurred and does not require the specification of a distribution or the estimation of parameters, but it is only useful to the extent that the future resembles the past.

- The Monte Carlo simulation method of VaR estimation requires the specification of a statistical distribution of returns and the generation of random outcomes from that distribution.

- The Monte Carlo simulation method is extremely flexible but can be complex and time consuming to use.

- There is no single right way of estimating VaR.

- The advantages of VaR include the following: It is a simple concept; it is relatively easy to understand; it is easily communicated, capturing much information in a single number; it can be useful in comparing risks across asset classes, portfolios, and trading units and, as such, it facilitates capital allocation decisions; it can be used for performance evaluation; it can be verified by using backtesting; it is widely accepted by regulators.

- The primary limitations of VaR are that it is a subjective measure and highly sensitive to numerous discretionary choices made in the course of computation; it can underestimate the frequency of extreme events; it fails to account for the lack of liquidity; it is sensitive to correlation risk; it is vulnerable to trending or volatility regimes; it is often misunderstood as a worst-case scenario; it can oversimplify the picture of risk; it focuses heavily on the left tail.

- There are numerous variations and extensions of VaR, including conditional VaR (CVaR), incremental VaR (IVaR), and marginal VaR (MVaR) that can provide additional useful information.

- Conditional VaR is the average loss conditional on exceeding the VaR cutoff.

- Incremental VaR measures the change in portfolio VaR as a result of adding or deleting a position from the portfolio or if a position size is changed relative to the remaining positions.

- MVaR measures the change in portfolio VaR given a small change in the portfolio position. In a diversified portfolio, MVaRs can be summed to determine the contribution of each asset to the overall VaR.

- *Ex ante* tracking error measures the degree to which the performance of a given investment portfolio might deviate from its benchmark.

- Sensitivity measures quantify how a security or portfolio will react if a single risk factor changes. Common sensitivity measures are beta for equities; duration and convexity for bonds; and delta, gamma, and vega for options. Sensitivity measures do not indicate which portfolio has greater loss potential.

- Risk managers can use deltas, gammas, vegas, durations, convexities, and betas to get a comprehensive picture of the sensitivity of the entire portfolio.

- Stress tests apply extreme negative stress to a particular portfolio exposure.

- Scenario measures, including stress tests, are risk models that evaluate how a portfolio will perform under certain high-stress market conditions.

- Scenario measures can be based on actual historical scenarios or on hypothetical scenarios.

- Historical scenarios are scenarios that measure the portfolio return that would result from a repeat of a particular period of financial market history.

- Hypothetical scenarios model the impact of extreme movements and co-movements in different markets that have not previously occurred.

- Reverse stress testing is the process of stressing the portfolio's most significant exposures.

- Sensitivity and scenario risk measures can complement VaR; they do not need to rely on history, and scenarios can be designed to overcome an assumption of normal distributions.

- Limitations of scenario measures include the following: Historical scenarios are unlikely to re-occur in exactly the same way; hypothetical scenarios may incorrectly specify how assets will co-move and may get the magnitude of movements wrong; and it is difficult to establish appropriate limits on a scenario analysis or stress test.

- The degree of leverage, the mix of risk factors to which the business is exposed, and accounting or regulatory requirements influence the types of risk measures used by different market participants.

- Banks use risk tools to assess the extent of any liquidity and asset/liability mis-match, the probability of losses in their investment portfolios, their overall leverage ratio, interest rate sensitivities, and the risk to economic capital.

- Asset managers' use of risk tools focus primarily on volatility, probability of loss, or the probability of underperforming a benchmark.

- Pension funds use risk measures to evaluate asset/liability mis-match and surplus at risk.

- Property and casualty insurers use sensitivity and exposure measures to ensure exposures remain within defined asset allocation ranges, economic capital and VaR measures to estimate the impairment in the event of a catastrophic loss, and scenario analysis to stress the market risks and insurance risks simultaneously.

- Life insurers use risk measures to assess the exposures of the investment portfolio and the annuity liability, the extent of any asset/liability mis-match, and the potential stress losses based on the differences between the assets in which they have invested and the liabilities resulting from the insurance contracts they have written.

- Constraints are widely used in risk management in the form of risk budgets, position limits, scenario limits, stop-loss limits, and capital allocation.

- Risk budgeting is the allocation of the total risk appetite across sub-portfolios.

- A scenario limit is a limit on the estimated loss for a given scenario, which, if exceeded, would require corrective action in the portfolio.

- A stop-loss limit requires a reduction in the size of a portfolio, or its complete liquidation, when a loss of a particular size occurs in a specified period.

- Position limits are limits on the market value of any given investment.

- Risk measurements and constraints in and of themselves are not restrictive or unrestrictive; it is the limits placed on the measures that drive action.

Portfolio Management

Economic Analysis, Active Management, and Trading

The first reading in the study session discusses fundamental relationships between economics and investment markets and how the economy affects asset values. The second reading introduces quantitative analysis of active portfolio management and its relevance to portfolio construction and evaluation. The final reading describes developments in equity trading.

READING ASSIGNMENTS

Reading 50	Economics and Investment Markets by Andrew Clare, PhD, and Thomas F. Cosimano, PhD
Reading 51	Analysis of Active Portfolio Management by Roger G. Clarke, PhD, Harindra de Silva, PhD, CFA, and Steven Thorley, PhD, CFA
Reading 52	Algorithmic Trading and High-Frequency Trading by John Bates, PhD

READING

50

Economics and Investment Markets

by Andrew Clare, PhD, and Thomas F. Cosimano, PhD

Andrew Clare, PhD, is at Cass Business School (United Kingdom). Thomas F. Cosimano, PhD, is at the Mendoza College of Business, University of Notre Dame (USA).

LEARNING OUTCOMES

Mastery	The candidate should be able to:
☐	a. explain the notion that to affect market values, economic factors must affect one or more of the following: (1) default-free interest rates across maturities, (2) the timing and/or magnitude of expected cash flows, and (3) risk premiums;
☐	b. explain the role of expectations and changes in expectations in market valuation;
☐	c. explain the relationship between the long-term growth rate of the economy, the volatility of the growth rate, and the average level of real short-term interest rates;
☐	d. explain how the phase of the business cycle affects policy and short-term interest rates, the slope of the term structure of interest rates, and the relative performance of bonds of differing maturities;
☐	e. describe the factors that affect yield spreads between non-inflation-adjusted and inflation-indexed bonds;
☐	f. explain how the phase of the business cycle affects credit spreads and the performance of credit-sensitive fixed-income instruments;
☐	g. explain how the characteristics of the markets for a company's products affect the company's credit quality;
☐	h. explain how the phase of the business cycle affects short-term and long-term earnings growth expectations;
☐	i. explain the relationship between the consumption-hedging properties of equity and the equity risk premium;
☐	j. describe cyclical effects on valuation multiples;
☐	k. describe the implications of the business cycle for a given style strategy (value, growth, small capitalization, large capitalization);

(continued)

LEARNING OUTCOMES

Mastery	The candidate should be able to:
☐	l. describe how economic analysis is used in sector rotation strategies;
☐	m. describe the economic factors affecting investment in commercial real estate.

1   INTRODUCTION

The state of the economy and financial market activity are interconnected. Financial markets are the forums where savers are connected with investors. This activity enables savers to defer consumption today for consumption in the future, allows governments to raise the capital necessary to create a secure society, and permits corporations to access capital to exploit profitable investment opportunities, which, in turn, should help to generate future economic growth and employment. Furthermore, all financial instruments essentially represent claims on an underlying economy. There is, therefore, an important and fundamental connection that runs from the decisions of economic agents, as they plan their present and future consumption, to the prices of financial instruments such as bonds and equities.

The purpose of this reading is to identify and explain the links between the real economy and financial markets and to show how economic analysis can be used to develop ways of valuing both individual financial market securities and aggregations of these securities, such as financial market indices. We begin by reviewing what we refer to as the fundamental pricing equation for all financial instruments. Using this framework, we then move on to explore the relationship between the economy and real default-free debt. From there, we can extend the analysis to the ways in which the economy can influence the prices of the following: nominal default-free debt; credit risky debt (for example, corporate bonds); publicly traded equities; and commercial real estate.

2   FRAMEWORK FOR THE ECONOMIC ANALYSIS OF FINANCIAL MARKETS

The reference point for the analysis of this reading is the present value model of asset valuation. The impact of economic factors on asset values can be studied in the context of that model by examining how economic factors can affect discount rates and future cash flows. These topics are explored in more detail in the following sections.

2.1 The Present Value Model

The value of an asset must be related to the benefits that we expect to receive from holding it; for many assets (e.g., financial securities) these benefits are its future cash flows, which may be specified in the security's contract—as is the case with bonds— or be discretionary—as is the case with ordinary shares. Intuitively, a given amount of money received in the future will be valued less by individual investors than the same amount of money received today. Because an investor can use cash for present consumption, he or she needs an incentive to defer it to the future, and more so as the future becomes less certain. These considerations provide an economic rationale for valuing an asset by discounting its future cash flows to derive its present value.

Equation 1 presents the fundamental present value formula for the value at time t of any financial asset i, V_t^i, which we assume equals its current market price, P_t^i. In general, we will speak of the time t as "today."

$$P_t^i = \sum_{s=1}^{N} \frac{E_t\left[\widetilde{CF}_{t+s}^i\right]}{\left(1 + l_{t,s} + \theta_{t,s} + \rho_{t,s}^i\right)^s} \qquad (1)$$

where:

> P_t^i = the value of the asset i at time t (today)
>
> N = number of cash flows in the life of the asset
>
> $\widetilde{CF}_{t+s}^i$ = the uncertain, nominal cash flow paid s periods in the future
>
> $E_t\left[\widetilde{CF}\right]$ = the expectation of the random variable $\widetilde{CF}$ conditional on the information available to investors today (t)
>
> $l_{t,s}$ = yield to maturity on a real default-free investment today (t), which pays one unit of currency s periods in the future
>
> $\theta_{t,s}$ = expected inflation rate between t and $t + s$
>
> $\rho_{t,s}^i$ = the risk premium required today (t) to pay the investor for taking on risk in the cash flow of asset i, s periods in the future

This expression is general enough to be used to value all financial instruments. The present values of all of the instrument's cash flows are summed from 1 to N. Some assets, such as a five-year zero-coupon bond, may have only one cash flow, and so N would equal five in that case, with cash flows in Periods 1–4 equal to zero. At the other extreme, dividend-paying equities produce cash flows in the form of dividends into the indefinite future, in which case N could, technically, be equal to infinity.

According to Equation 1, effects of the economy on asset prices are transmitted through some combination of influences on the numerator—the asset's expected cash flows—and denominator—the discount rate(s) applied to the asset's expected cash flows.

A factor that typically distinguishes one financial asset class from another is the degree of certainty that investors have about future cash flows. At one extreme there may be little uncertainty. For example, despite losing its AAA rating from Standard & Poor's, investors might still attach a relatively low probability to the prospect of the US Treasury not making the scheduled payments on its debts on time and in full. Investors may regard the probability of the German government defaulting on its debts to be very low, too. At the other extreme, investors may be very uncertain about the size and timing of dividend payments from an equity investment and will also have to consider the prospect of receiving no dividends at all in the event that the company declares bankruptcy.

The uncertainty about future cash flows is reflected in the discount rate in Equation 1. We can think of the discount rate as having three distinct components. The first component is $l_{t,s}$ which effectively represents the return that an investor requires on a real default-free fixed-income security at present time t for a cash flow to be paid s periods in the future. For example, readers can think of this return as being analogous to the return expected on an investment in an inflation-linked bond issued by the government of a developed economy.

The second component in the discount rate, $\theta_{t,s}$, represents the additional return required by investors, above that required from investing in a real default-free investment, for investing in a nominal default-free investment. This additional return is required even though an investor may attach a zero probability to not being paid on time and in full, because future nominal payments will be affected by inflation. In essence, this component of the discount rate represents the compensation that investors demand for the inflation that they expect to experience over the investment horizon. Compensation is demanded because investors are concerned about the real purchasing power of their investments in the future rather than in the nominal value of the future cash flows.

The third component of the discount rate in Equation 1, $\rho_{t,s}^{i}$, represents the additional return that investors expect for investing in financial assets because of uncertainty about the asset's future cash flows. In other words, all securities, even those issued by governments of developed economies and considered risk-free in that there is negligible risk that the issuer will default (as we will see in Section 3), carry some risks for which risk-averse investors will want to be compensated. Indeed the size of this risk premium will vary among asset classes, and this variation is largely responsible for the distinction between one asset class and another.[1]

As we will show throughout this reading, the size and nature of this addition to expected return, $\rho_{t,s}^{i}$, will depend on the characteristics of the asset or asset class in question, which, in turn, will be determined by developments and expected developments in the real economy. This means that the discount rates applied to the cash flows of financial assets will almost certainly vary over time as perceptions of expected economic growth, inflation, and cash flow risk change. In particular during recessions, the risk premium that investors demand on financial assets, especially those that are not default-free, may rise because investors in general may be less willing and able to take on heightened default risk during such periods.

The $\rho_{t,s}^{i}$ component may include more than just the compensation for the uncertainty related to financial cash flows that may be subject to default risk. In particular, $\rho_{t,s}^{i}$ may also reflect other types of risk—for example, liquidity risk. Liquidity risk refers to the possibility that a financial asset cannot be converted quickly into cash at close to its fair value; it is particularly characteristic of investments in commercial real estate and high-yield corporate bonds/loans. And, as many investors learned during the 2008–2009 global financial crisis, some debt instruments, such as mortgage backed securities, can become very illiquid at just the moment when investors become most risk averse and when they want to be holding cash rather than riskier financial assets.

In summary, the expected cash flows for any financial asset, i, can be discounted using the following general expression for the discount rate:[2]

$$1 + l_{t,s} + \theta_{t,s} + \rho_{t,s}^{i} \text{ for } s = 1, \ldots N \tag{2}$$

A major purpose of this reading is to identify the relationship between these elements of the discount rate and the underlying economy, and also to decompose $\rho_{t,s}^{i}$ into its component parts for each asset class.

---

1 We remind the reader of this difference among assets by placing a superscript i to indicate that this premium is specific to the asset under consideration.

2 This additive expression is an approximation to the exact multiplicative expression that includes interaction effects between the terms.

2.2 Expectations and Asset Values

Examining Equation 1 reveals simple but important observations:

- Asset values depend not on past cash flows but on the expectation of future cash flows.

- These expectations are based on (conditional on) current information (indicated by the time subscript t) that may be relevant to forecasting future cash flows. Any information that may contribute to the accuracy or precision of expectations is relevant.

Because asset values are dependent on expectations of future cash flows, information that changes expectations affects asset values and realized returns. Information that has been anticipated is already reflected in asset prices, but information that is different from what was expected constitutes real news that requires expectations to adjust. The adjustment generates a holding-period return that differs from the expected return. This observation about investors' anticipations is important to understanding sometimes seemingly counterintuitive market reactions to economic information releases. Investors judge economic data releases relative to their expectations for the data. Prices may fall (rise) despite "good" ("bad") news if the expectation was for better (worse) news.

Thus, for valuation, one important distinction is information that is "news" or new information and information that has been fully anticipated. Therefore, news is a surprise relative to fully anticipated information.

Although this reading's focus is the effect of economic factors on asset values, investor sentiment (e.g., enthusiasm or despair) can also affect asset values. Economic factors affect asset values through generally direct effects on cash flows and/or discount rates, but investor sentiment affects asset values through direct effects on discount rates via higher or lower risk premiums (and possibly indirect effects on future cash flows).

THE DISCOUNT RATE ON REAL DEFAULT-FREE BONDS

3

Having introduced several fundamental concepts, we can now begin the analysis in detail of economic factors affecting asset values. The first step in understanding the relationship between the economy and investment markets involves noting that the purchase of an investment involves the opportunity cost of lower consumption today. In other words, by buying a financial asset an investor defers some current consumption. The sum of all of these individual saving and consumption decisions are thus going to have an impact on the price of financial assets.

> To explain how investors' concerns for satisfying consumption needs through economic fluctuations affect asset prices, modern finance makes reference to several expressions (Equations 3 through 6) which model how investors evaluate consumption trade-offs. These expressions, and associated (non-testable) calculations, show the analysis behind statements about the relationships between real interest rates, GDP growth, and the volatility of GDP; verbal statements of the intuition behind the relationships are also given that suffice to understand the entire reading.

3.1 Real Default-Free Interest Rates

To demonstrate the importance of the aggregation of these individual saving and investment decisions, we can think through how the aggregated consumption and investment decisions of individuals might determine the real default-free interest rate in an economy—that is, $l_{t,s}$ in Equation 1. Consider a single individual who has to choose between using some portion of his or her wealth to consume today (t) or investing that wealth in default-free bonds that will pay investors one dollar when it matures s periods in the future.

Think of this bond as being issued by a highly rated, developed-economy government, so there is only a negligible prospect of default. Also think of this bond as being inflation index-linked so that investors do not need to concern themselves with the impact of future inflation on the bond's future cash flow. An alternative way of conceptualizing the bond is to assume (only for the moment) that it is issued by this government in a world that has no inflation. In Section 4, we will re-introduce inflation into the pricing problem.

What sort of return would investors require on a bond that is both default-free and unaffected by future inflation? It is tempting to say that an investor would require no return on such a bond because there is no risk of losing money over the investment period in either nominal or real terms. But the choice to invest today involves the opportunity cost of not consuming today. It is the aggregated opportunity cost of all investors that will determine the price of this asset today and its return over the investment horizon.

Think of the return on the asset as the opportunity cost (price) of consuming today. If the return increases, the investor substitutes away from current consumption to future consumption by purchasing an asset. Consequently, as with any other economic decision, an investor must consider the relative prices of the two alternatives. In this case, the investor can

- pay price $P_{t,s}$ today, t, of a default-free bond paying 1 monetary unit of income s periods in the future, or
- buy goods worth $P_{t,s}$ dollars today.

The decision to purchase this bond will be determined by the willingness of individuals to substitute consumption today for consumption in the future. This trade-off is measured by the marginal utility of consumption s periods in the future relative to the marginal utility of consumption today (t). The marginal utility of consumption is the additional satisfaction or utility that a consumer derives from one additional unit of consumption. The ratio of these two marginal utilities—the ratio of the marginal utility of consumption s periods in the future (the numerator) to the marginal utility of consumption today (the denominator)—is known as the **inter-temporal rate of substitution**, denoted $\tilde{m}_{t,s}$.

In "good" economic times, individuals may have relatively high levels of current income so that current consumption is high. In this case, the utility derived from an additional unit of consumption today will be relatively low. Conversely, in "bad" economic times current income and consumption will tend to be relatively low, which means that the utility derived from an additional unit of consumption today will be relatively high. In addition, the marginal utility of consumption of investors diminishes as their wealth increases because they have already satisfied fundamental needs. Thus, investors would receive a larger benefit (utility) from an asset that pays off more in bad economic times relative to one that pays off in good economic times.

The rate of substitution is a random variable because an investor will not know how much she has available in the future from other sources of income, such as salary from working. This uncertainty is present even for an investment that pays a certain amount in one period because the value of this investment is determined by how much utility the investor receives from this investment.

Given this uncertainty, the investor must make the decision today based on her expectations of future circumstances when she receives the payoff from the investment. This expectation is conditional on the information that the investor has when the decision is made. Thus, if the investor wanted to consider an investment in a zero-coupon bond at time t that is certain to pay off one unit of real consumption in s periods, then

$$P_{t,s} = E_t\left[1\widetilde{m}_{t,s}\right] = E_t\left[\widetilde{m}_{t,s}\right] \tag{3}$$

where $\widetilde{m}_{t,s}$ is the investor's marginal willingness to trade consumption at time t for (real) wealth at time $t + s$.[3]

EXAMPLE 1

The Inter-Temporal Rate of Substitution (1 of 3)

Suppose the investor's willingness to trade present for future consumption can be represented as

$$\widetilde{m}_{t,1} = e^{a+b\widetilde{z}}$$

Here, $\widetilde{z}$ is a random shock to the economy that affects the cash flows of the marginal investor; $\widetilde{z}$ is what makes $\widetilde{m}_{t,1}$ a random variable. The exponential form is consistent with assumptions about investor risk aversion and consumption growth often made in finance; a and b are typically negative given those same assumptions.[4] Parameters of the distribution of $\widetilde{z}$ consistent with observed market data can also be established. Suppose that $\widetilde{z}$, assumed to have a mean of zero, takes on one of two values, a negative value indicating a bad state and a positive value indicating a good state. The probabilities of bad and good states are 0.4 and 0.6, respectively.

Using market-consistent values in the exponent in the expression for $\widetilde{m}_{t,1}$, we can calculate the price of a bond promising $1 for sure in one year as the expected value of the investor's willingness to trade present for future consumption:

$$E_t\left[\widetilde{m}_{t,1}\right] = 0.4e^{a+b\times(z \text{ for a bad state})} + 0.6e^{a+b\times(z \text{ for a good state})}$$

$$= 0.4 \times 0.954676 + 0.6 \times 0.954379 = 0.954498$$

---

3 The term $\widetilde{m}_{t,s}$ is technically defined as $(\delta)[MU(C_{t+s})/MU(C_t)]$, where MU denotes marginal utility of consumption, C, and δ is a discount factor that captures the preference for consumption at t rather than later at $t + s$. The discount factor applied to $MU(C_{t+s})$ adjusts it for the time difference of s periods. The tilde on $\widetilde{m}_{t,s}$ indicates it is a random (stochastic) variable and the term may be called the stochastic inter-temporal rate of substitution. As in Example 1, this inter-temporal rate of substitution varies based on the realization of the shock to economic activity, $\widetilde{z}$. In the modern theory of asset pricing, the term m is also referred to as the stochastic discount factor or pricing kernel.

4 The negative exponential function expression reflects constant relative risk aversion utility and lognormally distributed consumption growth. In e^{a+bz}, the expected value is a and standard deviation is z. For an explanation of constant relative risk aversion, see an investments text such as Elton, Gruber, Brown, and Goetzmann (2014).

In the calculation, 0.954676 and 0.954379 are the asset's prices in the bad and good states, respectively.[5] Note the higher value of $1 received in the bad state. Following Equation 3, the investor is willing to buy the risk-free bond today for $0.954498 in exchange for $1 in one year. Also notice that the willingness to invest is smaller for the positive shock, (z for a good state) because an investor is willing to pay less or the bond in the case of a good state. Thus, the positive shock is associated with a higher level of consumption today by the investor.[6]

The investor knows that she cannot affect the price of the bond, and so she must decide whether to buy or sell the bond based on this given price, $P_{t,1}$ (0.954498 from Example 1). If this price of the bond was less than the investor's expectation of the inter-temporal rate of substitution (suppose this is 0.9560), then she would prefer to buy more of the bond today. As more bonds are purchased, today's consumption falls and marginal utility of consumption today rises, so that expectations conditional on current information of the inter-temporal rate of substitution, $E_t\left[\widetilde{m}_{t,s}\right]$, fall. This process continues until the rate of substitution is equal to the bond price shown in Equation 3; that is, equivalently, 0.9560 would fall and converge on 0.954498.

It is worthwhile to emphasize this point: All investors are essentially making investment decisions using Equation 3; some will want to sell their bonds to fund additional, current consumption, whereas others will want to buy bonds and defer some additional consumption until the future. To demonstrate the link between the bond price and these consumption/investment decisions, imagine for the moment that the market price of this bond is too "low" for an individual investor. In this case, the investor with a higher initial inter-temporal rate of substitution (higher $\widetilde{m}_{t,s}$) would buy more of the bond. As a result of this purchase the investor will consume less today leading to an increase in today's marginal utility, but he or she would expect to have more consumption and thus lower marginal utility in the future. Consequently, the inter-temporal rate of substitution would fall.

One investor cannot influence the equilibrium price. But if a substantial group of investors respond this way, then the demand and price of the bond would rise—in the illustration earlier, it would mean that it is possible for the price of the bond, 0.954498, to rise at the same time that the individual investor's inter-temporal rate of substitution was falling. This process would continue until all investors' willingness to invest converges on a single equilibrium value so that Equation 3 is true for all individuals and the market price is determined.

Conversely, if the market price of the bond is too "high" for a group of investors, then the investors with a lower inter-temporal rate of substitution would buy less of the bond. They would have more consumption and lower marginal utility today, but they would expect to have less consumption and higher marginal utility in the future. As a result, the inter-temporal rate of substitution would rise and the demand and price of the bond would fall. This process would again continue until Equation 3 is true for all individuals.

---

5 Values for the random shock are consistent with the level of the yield curve in the United States from January 1999 to January 2014. The derivation of these numbers is beyond the scope of this reading.
6 An exponential function, $f(x) = e^x$ is always increasing in the variable x and increases at an increasing rate as x gets large. For example, $f(0) = e^0 = 1$ and $f(0.05) = e^{0.05} = 1.0513$. If x is negative, the more negative x is the smaller the value of the function. For example, compare $f(-0.05) = e^{-0.05} = 0.9512$ and $f(-0.02) = e^{-0.02} = 0.9802$; the function is still increasing in x.

EXAMPLE 2

The Inter-Temporal Rate of Substitution (2 of 3)

In Example 1, suppose the current market price of the real default-free bond is $9,540 per $10,000, but the investor's inter-temporal rate of substitution is $0.954498 per one dollar promised. The investor would then value the guarantee of $10,000 in one period more than the market, so she would purchase it. As she buys more of the bond, her future income is higher and its marginal utility lower, leading to a fall in her marginal willingness to invest in the risk-free asset. Only if there are many investors with the willingness to trade at $9,544.98 would the market price increase until all investors have the same marginal willingness to invest.

In summary, all investors use Equation 3 to make their investment decisions, so the equilibrium price in the market for these bonds equals the expectation of the inter-temporal rate of substitution of every single investor who participates in the bond market.

If the investment horizon for this bond is one year, and the payoff then is $1, the return on this bond can be written as the future payoff minus the current payment relative to the current payment: [7]

$$l_{t,1} = \frac{1 - P_{t,1}}{P_{t,1}} = \frac{1}{E_t\left[\widetilde{m}_{t,1}\right]} - 1 \qquad (4)$$

Consequently, the return is higher for lower current prices. Equation 4 implies that the one-period real risk-free rate is inversely related to the inter-temporal rate of substitution. That is, the higher the return the investor can earn, the more important current consumption becomes relative to future consumption.

EXAMPLE 3

The Inter-Temporal Rate of Substitution (3 of 3)

Following the circumstances in Example 1, the one-period real risk-free interest rate is $l_{t,1} = \dfrac{1 - 0.954498}{0.954498} = 0.047671$ or 4.7671%.

3.1.1 Uncertainty and Risk Premiums

An investor's expected marginal utility associated with a given expected payoff is decreased by any increase in uncertainty of the payoff; thus, the investor must be compensated with a higher expected return. This result follows from decreasing marginal utility of wealth or income because the loss of utility from lower wealth is larger than the gain from an equivalent increase in wealth. The risk premium compensates the investor for the loss from this fluctuation in future wealth or income. An individual who requires compensation for this uncertainty is called "risk averse." This property was seen in Example 1, in which the inter-temporal rate of substitution was lower in the good state of the economy compared with the bad state.

---

7 The step from the first expression to the second follows from rearranging the first expression $\dfrac{1 - P_{t,1}}{P_{t,1}}$ as $\dfrac{1}{P_{t,1}} - 1$, and then substituting from Equation 3.

For the valuation of cash flows under uncertainty, a second property of most investors' utility is important. In particular, an investor's absolute risk aversion is assumed to fall if he or she has higher wealth or income. (Absolute risk aversion relates to the amount held in risky assets at different levels of wealth;[8] under the assumption of decreasing absolute risk aversion made here, an investor invests larger amounts in risky assets as wealth or income increases.) Consequently, one's marginal utility is always lower as one's wealth or income increases. In this case, the risk premium for a given risk is lower for wealthier individuals because the average loss of marginal utility (slope of utility) from any risk taking is smaller, which means that relative to poorer individuals, wealthier individuals are more willing to take on a given risk. Consequently, wealthier investors are willing to buy more risky assets because they would value the asset more than poorer investors. But the expected marginal utility for wealthier investors will decline as they buy more of the risky asset. Eventually, both the wealthier and poorer investors would have the same willingness to invest in risky assets when the financial market is in equilibrium.

EXAMPLE 4

The Case of Increasing Wealth

This idea can be illustrated by raising the economic shock by a fixed amount regardless of whether the economy is good or bad, which has the effect of increasing the individual's resources and making her wealthier. For example, suppose we add 0.1 to $\tilde{z}$ and thus to the resources of the investor relative to the shock in Example 1. The expected inter-temporal rate of substitution for the investor is now lower for this safe asset (the default-free bond). The expected value of the investor's willingness to trade present for future consumption would then be:

$$E_t\left[\widetilde{m}_{t,1}\right] = 0.4 \times 0.954528 + 0.6 \times 0.954231 = 0.954350$$

Compare this result with Example 1. The inter-temporal rate of substitution is lower under the good and bad shock to the economy. As a result, the expected inter-temporal rate of substitution $E_t\left[\widetilde{m}_{t,1}\right]$ is lower for the wealthier investor by 0.000148 (= 0.954498 − 0.954350). Thus, the wealthier investor will buy the safe bond only at a lower price, and if this lower price is not the equilibrium price, the investor will substitute away from riskless to risky assets.[9]

An individual with decreasing absolute risk aversion would lower the price of safe assets.[10] If the rich individuals are a large percentage of the market, then the equilibrium return on the safe asset increases with the lower price. As a result, the poorer individuals would have incentives to increase their savings with the expected higher return on the safe asset. These savings allow all investors to partially compensate for any additional losses during possible bad times. Consequently, all the investors in the financial market would increase their savings when uncertainty about their future income increases. This higher savings means that the expected marginal utility in the

---

8 Absolute risk aversion is in contrast to relative risk aversion, which relates to the fraction (not the amount) of wealth held in risky assets at different levels of wealth.

9 Because of decreasing absolute risk aversion with wealth and because their fundamental consumption needs are met, wealthy investors will demand a lower premium than poorer investors for holding risky assets, all else being equal.

10 See Altug and Labadie (2008) for a derivation of this result.

future is lower because the investors' future resources are higher. Thus, the equilibrium price based on Equation 3 is lower, meaning that investors are compensated with a higher expected return when uncertainty in income increases.

3.1.2 Risk Premiums on Risky Assets

The price of other (non-default-free) financial instruments is established relative to the price of the default-free bond. This relationship can be seen by considering a default-free bond with a maturity of s periods (s is greater than or equal to two). Assume that the investor is only holding the security for one period. Its current price is $P_{t,s}$. In this case, the bond has value $\widetilde{P}_{t+1,s-1}$ in one period because the term to maturity of the bond has been reduced by one period relative to its original maturity date. As a result, the investor's decision is now given by

$$P_{t,s} = E_t\left[\widetilde{P}_{t+1,s-1}\widetilde{m}_{t,1}\right] \tag{5}$$

The price in one period is uncertain because the s period bond is sold at the market price before it matures. Also notice that there is no interest payment because the bond promises a payment only at the terminal time. If a coupon is promised at time $t + 1$, then its value would have to be added to the right hand side of Equation 5.

EXAMPLE 5

Pricing a Two-Period Default-Free Bond

In this example, we illustrate how the pricing formula in Equation 5 leads to a risk premium on a two-period default-free bond that is not present in the one-period default-free bond. In these calculations, we use five or six digits to the right of the decimal point because the risk premium is small for a two-period bond relative to a one-period default-free bond.

Suppose the price at time 1 of the two-year default-free bond is given by

$$\widetilde{P}_{t+1,2-1} = e^{a'+b'\widetilde{z}}$$

In this case, the future price can be shown to be

$\widetilde{P}_{t+1,2-1} = 0.839181$ for \$1 at Time 2 with probability $p = 0.4$ and

$\widetilde{P}_{t+1,2-1} = 0.954840$ for \$1 at Time 2 with probability $p = 0.6$

The expected price at time $t + 1$ of a \$1 bond maturing at time $t + 2$ is $0.4 \times 0.839181 + 0.6 \times 0.954840 = \$0.908576$. Without considering the investor's willingness to invest, the current value of the two-period bond is the simple present value using the one period real risk-free interest rate of 4.7671% (from Example 3) as the discount rate. Thus, under the assumption stated, the bond would be worth $\dfrac{E_t\left[\widetilde{P}_{t+1,s-1}\right]}{1+l_{t,1}} = \dfrac{0.908576}{1.047671} = \$0.867234$. But the actual price in the financial markets based on Equation 5 is

$$P_{t,s} = E_t\left[\widetilde{P}_{t+1,s-1}\widetilde{m}_{t,1}\right]$$

$$= 0.4 \times 0.839181 \times 0.954676 + 0.6 \times 0.954840 \times 0.954379$$

$$= 0.867226$$

where 0.954676 and 0.954379 are the asset's prices in the bad and good states, as determined in Example 1. The price based on Equation 5 is smaller than the present discounted value at the risk-free rate; the difference is 0.000008 per 1 principal value (i.e., $0.867234 - 0.867226 = 0.000008$). Thus, the holder of a two-year bond earns a risk premium. The reason for this result can be seen by calculating

$$E_t\left[\tilde{P}_{t+1,s-1}\right]E_t\left[\widetilde{m}_{t,1}\right] = 0.908576[0.4 \times 0.954676 + 0.6 \times 0.954379]$$

$$= 0.867234$$

where 0.908576 is the Time 1 price of the bond as determined earlier. Consequently, we see that

$$E_t\left[\tilde{P}_{t+1,s-1}\right]E_t\left[\widetilde{m}_{t,1}\right] > E_t\left[\tilde{P}_{t+1,s-1}\widetilde{m}_{t,1}\right]$$

To summarize, the price uncertainty of the two-period bond at $t = 1$ gives rise to a risk premium, although the bond is default-risk free.

Example 5 showed how future price uncertainty creates a discount for risk. We now derive an alternative expression for the pricing relationship in Equation 5 that explains the nature of that discount and sheds further light on the conclusion of Example 5. In statistics texts, the following relationship between expected values and covariance is proven:

$$E_t\left(\tilde{x}\tilde{y}\right) = E_t\left(\tilde{x}\right)E_t\left(\tilde{y}\right) + \text{cov}\left(\tilde{x},\tilde{y}\right)$$

Here, $\text{cov}_t\left(\tilde{x},\tilde{y}\right)$ refers to the conditional (on information at time t) covariance of the random variable $\tilde{x}$ with $\tilde{y}$. Thus, from Equation 5,

$$P_{t,s} = E_t\left[\tilde{P}_{t+1,s-1}\widetilde{m}_{t,1}\right] = E_t\left[\tilde{P}_{t+1,s-1}\right]E_t\left[\widetilde{m}_{t,1}\right] + \text{cov}\left[\tilde{P}_{t+1,s-1},\widetilde{m}_{t,1}\right]$$

But from Equation 4, $1 + l_{t,1} = \dfrac{1}{E_t\left[\widetilde{m}_{t,1}\right]}$. So, an alternative way to view the pricing relationship in Equation 5 is

$$P_{t,s} = \frac{E_t\left[\tilde{P}_{t+1,s-1}\right]}{1 + l_{t,1}} + \text{cov}_t\left[\tilde{P}_{t+1,s-1},\widetilde{m}_{t,1}\right] \tag{6}$$

where $\text{cov}_t\left[\tilde{P}_{t+1,s-1},\widetilde{m}_{t,1}\right]$ represents the covariance between an investor's inter-temporal rate of substitution, $\widetilde{m}_{t,1}$, and the random future price of the investment at $t + 1$, $\tilde{P}_{t+1,s-1}$, based on the information available to investors today (t). The subscript is reduced by one because an investment with time to maturity s at time t becomes an investment with time to maturity $s - 1$ at time $t + 1$.[11]

Equation 6 expresses the value of a risky asset as the sum of two terms. The first term is the asset's expected future price discounted at the risk-free rate. It may be called the risk neutral present value because it represents a risky asset's value if investors did not require compensation for bearing risk.[12] In Example 5, this value is 0.867234.

The covariance term is the discount for risk. Note that with a one-period default-free bond, the covariance term is zero because the future price is a known constant ($1) and the covariance of a random quantity with a constant is zero; and, intuitively, its value is given by the first term. Consequently, Equation 6 reduces to Equation 3

---

11 See Cochrane (2005).
12 Notice the parallel with the fundamental pricing Equation 1 if it had one cash flow and no risk premium.

for the one-period default-free bond. But with the two-period default-free bond, the future price of $1 two periods in the future is known with certainty, but the price one period in the future is not. Consequently, the covariance term is not zero.

In general with risk-averse investors, the covariance term for most risky assets is expected to be negative. That is, when the expected future price of the investment is high, the marginal utility of future consumption relative to that of current consumption is low. Alternatively, during bad economic times, investors expect a smaller labor income in the future, so the marginal utility of future consumption, and hence the inter-temporal rate of substitution, is higher. This relationship leads investors to demand a higher required rate of trade-off of future for current consumption—as in bad economic times when the labor market contracts. Bad economic times also tend to be associated with declining risky asset pay-outs (declining earnings and dividends for ordinary shares and defaults for bonds) leading to declining asset prices. The result is that the covariance term for risky assets is typically negative, so the price of the asset is lower. This negative covariance term results in a positive risk premium, $\rho_{t,s}^i$, in Equation 1 because a lower price today leads to a higher return over time. Holding all else constant, the risk premium term and the required return for an asset should be higher, and its current market price is lower the larger the magnitude of the negative covariance term.

EXAMPLE 6

An Alternative Method to Evaluate the Price Discount for Risk

The covariance between the investor's willingness to invest and the price of the two year bond next period can also be computed as follows:[13]

$$\text{cov}_t\left[\widetilde{m}_{t,1}, \widetilde{P}_{t+1,2-1}\right] = 0.4(0.954676 - 0.954498) \times (0.839181 - 0.908576) + $$
$$0.6(0.954379 - 0.954498) \times (0.954840 - 0.908576)$$

$$= -0.000008$$

In the bad state of the economy, the willingness to invest (0.954676) is above its average (0.954498), yet the bond price (0.839181) is below its average (0.908576). The reverse is true in the good state. Thus, the covariance between the inter-temporal rate of substitution and the price of the asset is negative. This result means the investor finds this investment inferior to one with a payoff that is independent of her willingness to invest. In particular, we have

$$P_{t,s} = -\frac{E_t\left[\widetilde{P}_{t+1,s-1}\right]}{1 + l_{t,1}} = -0.000008$$

With a lower price, the return on the two-year bond is higher.

In this example, the price discount is not too large because the risk between a one- and two-year US government bond is not that crucial. However, more risky assets, such as equity, will have a higher discount. In addition, the higher risk premium on equity still follows from the covariance between the cash flow and the investor's willingness to invest over the time horizon of the investment. Thus, a higher risk premium for stocks arises from a larger value for this covariance.

---

[13] Recall the standard formula for covariance is: $\text{cov}(\tilde{x}, \tilde{y}) = \Sigma p_i[x_i - E(x)][y_i - E(y)]$.

The risk premium can be computed as follows: The expected holding period return on the s period bond through time $t + 1$, using the results of Example 5, is given by

$$r_{t,s} = \frac{E_t\left[\widetilde{P}_{t+1,s-1}\right] - P_{t,s}}{P_{t,s}}$$

(7)

$$= \frac{0.908576 - 0.867226}{0.867226} = 0.047681 \text{ or } 4.7681\%$$

so the risk premium $\rho^i_{t,s} = r_{t,s} - l_{t,1} = 0.047681 - 0.047671 = 0.00001$.

Alternatively, Equations 7 and 6 can be manipulated so that[14]

$$r_{t,s} - l_{t,1} = \frac{E_t\left[\widetilde{P}_{t+1,s-1}\right]}{P_{t,s}} - \left(1 + l_{t,1}\right) = -\frac{\left(1 + l_{t,1}\right)}{P_{t,s}}\text{cov}_t\left[\widetilde{m}_{t,1}, \widetilde{P}_{t+1,s-1}\right]$$

$$= -\left(1 + l_{t,s}\right)\text{cov}_t\left[\widetilde{m}_{t,1}, \frac{\widetilde{P}_{t+1,s-1}}{P_{t,s}}\right] = -\frac{\left(1 + 0.047671\right)}{0.867226} \times \left(-0.000008\right)$$

(8)

$$= 0.00001 = \rho^i_{t,s}$$

which is the return premium demanded by investors because of the uncertain Time 1 price of the riskless two-period bond.

This relationship implies that an asset's risk premium, $\rho^i_{t,s}$ in Equation 1, is driven by the covariance of its returns with the inter-temporal rate of substitution for consumption, and can exist even for a default-free bond because of the uncertainty of its price before maturity. Most risky assets have returns that tend to be high during good times, when the marginal value of consumption is low, and low during bad times, when the marginal value of consumption is high, and so bear a positive risk premium. Any asset that tended to have relatively high returns when the marginal utility of consumption was high would provide a type of hedge against bad times and bear a negative risk premium and have a relatively high price and low required rate of return.

3.2 Default-Free Interest Rates and Economic Growth

From the previous discussion, it is a relatively small conceptual step to understand the relationship between an economy's GDP growth and real default-free interest rates. If there is a known independent change in the real GDP growth, or a change that can be forecasted perfectly, then an increase in real GDP growth should lead to an increase in the real default-free rate of interest because more goods and services will be available in the future relative to today. The result is that investors' willingness to substitute across time will fall, resulting in less saving and more borrowing, so that the real default-free interest rate increases, as in Equation 4.

But GDP growth from one period to the next cannot be perfectly anticipated. Under these uncertain circumstances, the interest rates will still be positively related to the expected growth rate of GDP, but additionally it will be positively related to the expected volatility of GDP growth.

---

14 Notice that simultaneously multiplying Equation 6 by $(1 + l_{t,1})$ and dividing by $P_{t,s}$ gives

$$\left(1 + l_{t,1}\right) = \frac{E_t\left[\widetilde{P}_{t+1,s-1}\right]}{P_{t,s}} + \left(1 + l_{t,1}\right)\text{cov}_t\left[\widetilde{m}_{t,1}, \frac{\widetilde{P}_{t+1,s-1}}{P_{t,s}}\right],$$

so we can write $\dfrac{E_t\left[\widetilde{P}_{t+1,s-1}\right]}{P_{t,s}} - \left(1 + l_{t,1}\right)$ in Equation 8 as

$$\frac{E_t\left[\widetilde{P}_{t+1,s-1}\right]}{P_{t,s}} - \frac{E_t\left[\widetilde{P}_{t+1,s-1}\right]}{P_{t,s}} - \left(1 + l_{t,1}\right)\text{cov}_t\left[\widetilde{m}_{t,1}, \frac{\widetilde{P}_{t+1,s-1}}{P_{t,s}}\right] = -\left(1 + l_{t,1}\right)\text{cov}_t\left[\widetilde{m}_{t,1}, \frac{\widetilde{P}_{t+1,s-1}}{P_{t,s}}\right].$$

The Effect of Volatility on Prices

One can see the effect of volatility by doubling the standard deviation of the random variable $\tilde{z}$ from what was assumed in Example 1. In this case, the price of the one-period bond in Example 1 would be

$$E_t\left[\widetilde{m}_{t,1}\right] = 0.4 \times 0.954855 + 0.6 \times 0.954260 = 0.954498$$

Notice that the expected value is the same as in Example 1, but that the prices in each state are more dispersed, reflecting the doubling of the standard deviation. For the two-period default free bond, continuing with the parameter values (a' and b') from Example 5, we would compute

$$E_t\left[\widetilde{P}_{t+1,2-1}\right] = 0.4 \times 0.776625 + 0.6 \times 1.005451 = 0.913921$$

Notice that doubling the volatility leads to the somewhat unrealistic price greater than 1 (implying a negative yield) in the good state, even though the expected price is less than 1.

Then,

$$P_{t,s} = E_t\left[\widetilde{P}_{t+1,2-1}\widetilde{m}_{t,1}\right]$$
$$= 0.4 \times 0.776625 \times 0.954855 + 0.6 \times 1.005451 \times 0.954260 = 0.872303$$

The risk neutral price is $\dfrac{E_t\left[\widetilde{P}_{t+1,2-1}\right]}{1 + l_{t,1}} = \dfrac{0.913921}{1.047671} = 0.872336$.

So, from Equation 6, $\text{cov}_t\left[\widetilde{m}_{t,1}, \widetilde{P}_{t+1,2-1}\right] = 0.872303 - 0.872336 = -0.000033$.

As a result, the holding period return on a two-period bond for one year is higher [i.e., $(0.913921 - 0.872303)/0.872303 = 4.771\%$, compared with 4.768% in Example 6], and because of the higher volatility, investors require a higher premium.

There are two practical implications of this analysis for the values of real default-free interest rates:

- An economy with higher trend real economic growth, other things being equal, should have higher real default-free interest rates than an economy with lower trend growth. We should thus expect to find that real default-free interest rates in fast growing developing economies, such as India and China, are higher than in slower growing, developed economies, such as Western Europe, Japan, and the United States. The higher rate of economic growth occurs for developing economies because a developing economy is typically below its steady state growth, so it grows faster to catch up. During these periods, the marginal product of capital (the additional output resulting from the addition of one unit of capital, holding all else constant) would be expected to be higher, so the real default-free interest rate should also be expected to be higher. Of course, this advantage will dissipate as the economy matures, as in the case of Japan and Western Europe from 1950 to 2000.

- Again, other things being equal, the real interest rates are higher in an economy in which GDP growth is more volatile compared with real interest rates in an economy in which growth is more stable.

EXAMPLE 8

The Present Value Model and Macroeconomic Factors

1 An asset's risk premium is high when:

   A there is no relationship between its future payoff and investors' marginal utility from future consumption.

   B there is a positive relationship between its future payoff and investors' marginal utility from future consumption.

   C there is a negative relationship between its future payoff and investors' marginal utility from future consumption.

2 The relationship between the real risk-free interest rate and real GDP growth is:

   A negative.

   B neutral.

   C positive.

3 The relationship between the real risk-free interest rate and the volatility of real GDP growth is:

   A negative.

   B neutral.

   C positive.

4 A risky asset offers high positive returns during business downturns. A colleague argues that the nominal required rate of return on the asset may be less than the nominal risk-free rate. Is the colleague correct?

   A Yes.

   B No, the return must be higher than the nominal risk-free rate.

   C No, the relationship between the asset's nominal return and the nominal risk-free rate is indeterminate.

5 Suppose you are analyzing the expected impact of an increase in real GDP growth above trend on overall equity market valuation. Assume real growth in income of the corporate sector follows real GDP growth. Assume also that there is no impact of the increase on inflation. On the basis of theory and holding all else constant, explain why the impact of the assumed increase in real GDP growth on overall equity market valuation is ambiguous.

Solution to 1:

C is correct. An asset's risk premium is determined by the relationship between its future payoff and the marginal value of consumption as given by the covariance between the two quantities. When the covariance is negative—that is, payoffs are low and expected utility from consumption is high—or equivalently, when times are expected to be bad in the future and the value of an extra unit of consumption is high, the risk premium will be high. When the covariance term is zero (there is no relationship), the asset is risk free. When the covariance term is positive, the asset is a hedge and will have a rate of return less than the risk-free rate.

Solution to 2:

C is correct. The real risk-free rate is positively related to real GDP growth. An increase in real GDP growth reduces the need for investors to save for future consumption because more goods and services will be available to them in the future relative to today as a result of higher expected income in the future. A higher real rate of interest is needed to induce individuals to save for future consumption in such circumstances.

Solution to 3:

C is correct. The real risk-free rate is positively related to the volatility of real GDP growth. An increase in volatility of real GDP growth means that there is greater risk that the income available for consumption will be lower than expected. Therefore, risk-averse investors will require a higher real rate of return in compensation.

Solution to 4:

A is correct. For the required return to be less than the risk-free rate, the asset's risk premium would need to be negative. Because the asset supplies relatively high returns in economic conditions in which the marginal utility of consumption is relatively high, the covariance term in Equation 6 is positive and the asset thus bears a negative risk premium.

Solution to 5:

Equation 1 can be applied to the overall equity market, which is the aggregate of individual equity securities. The increase in real GDP growth would be expected to affect both the numerator and denominator of Equation 1 in offsetting ways, so the overall effect on equity market value is ambiguous. The impact of an increase in real GDP growth on expected corporate earnings is positive by assumption, which by itself would suggest an increase in equity market value by a larger numerator value in Equation 1. However, the increase in real GDP should also increase the real risk-free rate, which by itself would suggest a decrease in equity market value by increasing the rate at which expected cash flows are discounted. We cannot infer which effect will dominate from the information given. The overall effect on equity market value is ambiguous, under the assumptions given.

3.3 Real Default-Free Interest Rates and the Business Cycle

One of the crucial insights that macro-finance provides is that there should be a connection between the real risk-free rate of interest available in an economy and the underlying trend rate of economic growth in the same economy. We explored the roots of this relationship in Sections 3.1 and 3.2. To recap briefly, the willingness of investors to substitute future wealth for current consumption will be inversely related to the change in real GDP growth. In a world where GDP growth could be forecasted perfectly, there will be a positive relationship between the real risk-free rate and real GDP growth. But GDP growth is not perfectly predictable. Because of this unpredictability, we also concluded that the real risk-free rate would not only be positively related to real GDP growth but also positively related to the volatility of real GDP growth.

Equation 1 shows that the real default-free required return, $l_{t,s}$, is a component of the discount rate that we apply to the cash flows generated by all financial instruments.

3.3.1 *Economic Growth and Real Yields*

For evidence of the relationship between real interest rates and GDP growth, we could focus on the yields available from inflation-linked bonds issued by governments in developed economies. These bonds pay a "real" return (or yield) plus a return that is linked directly to an index of consumer prices. Index-linked bonds are issued by many governments in developed economies, including Canada, France, Germany, Italy, Sweden, the United Kingdom, and the United States, and also by some developing countries, such as Brazil. In some markets, for example the United Kingdom's index-linked gilt market, both the coupon and principal payments from these bonds are indexed to a measure of consumer prices. In other markets—for example, the US Treasury Inflation-Protected Securities (TIPS) market—the principal payment is indexed and the coupon is a function of the indexed principal. In both cases, any increase in the level of the consumer price index over time (that is, positive inflation) leads to an increase in both the coupon payment and eventual principal payment.[15] Although the details of the indexation vary from bond market to bond market, for all practical purposes, we can think of these bonds as being inflation protected.

Given the discussion in Sections 3.1 and 3.2, other things being equal, we would expect the (real) yields on inflation-indexed bonds to be higher for those countries with high growth, such as India and China, relative to those issued by, say, the UK or US governments where economic growth is much lower. Other things being equal, we should also expect to see real yields on short-dated index-linked bonds issued by governments of economies that are very volatile to be higher than those issued by governments of economies that are less volatile.

Although many index-linked government bond markets are relatively new, we can examine the cross-sectional relationship between economic growth and real risk-free yields relatively easily. Panel A of Exhibit 1 shows the real yields on a set of short-dated index-linked government bonds in 2007, immediately prior to the 2008–2009 global financial crisis. The real yield on short-dated Japanese government bonds at that time were lower than elsewhere, whereas Panel B shows that Japanese growth had been historically very low and not very volatile up to that point in time. Of the developed-economy bond yields in this exhibit, those issued by the Australian government offered the highest yield, perhaps reflecting the relatively strong Australian economic growth shown in Panel B.

---

15 Interestingly, for most index-linked bonds, a fall in the relevant consumer price index does not lead to a decline in the bond's nominal payments; so although inflation will cause the bond's nominal payments to rise, deflation does not cause them to fall. Investors can therefore benefit from an inflation "floor" of zero.

Exhibit 1   Real Yields, GDP Growth, and Volatility for Various Countries

A. Real Yields, July 2007

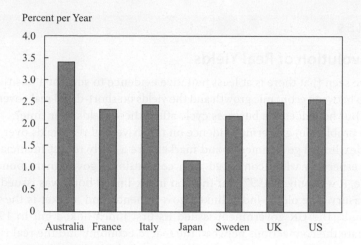

B. Growth and Volatility, 1996–2007

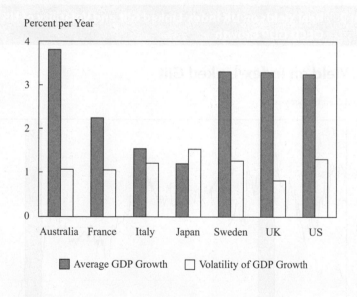

Sources: Based on data from Thomson Reuters and the authors' calculations.

It is difficult to discern a very clear pattern between historic economic growth, the volatility in that growth, and short-term real yields. Nonetheless, it is interesting to note that the correlation between this limited set of bond yields (Panel A of Exhibit 1) and historic growth (gray bars in Panel B of Exhibit 1) is 0.57, but the correlation with historic volatility (white bars in Panel B) is 0.74. So there does appear to be some support for the prediction of macro theory, although this sample is of course very limited. One of the reasons why there is perhaps not a clearer relationship is that the real yield data are forward looking. The real yield data represent the required real return on these bonds based on expected future growth and volatility in that growth, whereas the GDP-based variables represent historic growth and volatility. If investors use the past as a guide to the future, they might expect a reasonably high correlation between past growth and current real yields. But the past may be a very bad guide to the future, particularly in the case of rapidly developing countries, such as Brazil or China, or following the sort of major shock to global economic growth that occurred following the collapse of Lehman Brothers.

EXAMPLE 9

The Evolution of Real Yields

We have seen that there is at least tentative evidence to suggest a positive relationship between economic growth and the yields on short-dated real government bonds. But how does the business cycle affect these yields over time?

The problem in gathering evidence on the drivers of real yields over time is that index-linked government bond markets are a fairly recent financial innovation, especially when compared with conventional government bonds. For example, it was only in 1997 that the first index-linked bond was issued by the US Treasury. The oldest index-linked government bond market is the United Kingdom's. The UK government issued its first index-linked gilt in 1981. To investigate the connections between the macro economy and the real risk-free rate over time, we can focus on the UK's index-linked gilt market.

Exhibit 2	Real Yields on UK Index-Linked Gilt and Volatility of UK and OECD GDP Growth

A. Yield on Index-Linked Gilt

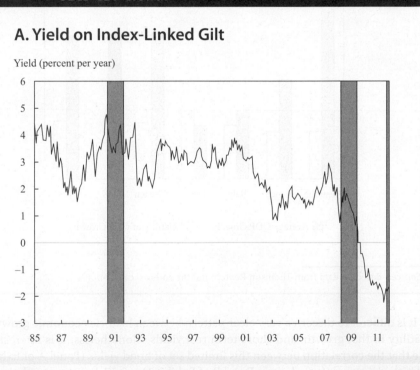

Yield (percent per year)

Exhibit 2   (Continued)

B. Volatility of GDP Growth

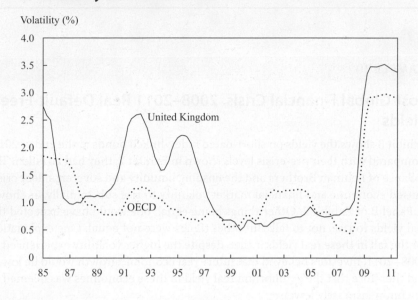

Notes: GDP growth is represented by a three-year moving standard deviation of the variable. Shaded areas in Panel A indicate UK recessions
Sources: Based on data from Thomson Reuters and the authors' calculations.

Panel A of Exhibit 2 shows the real yield on a short-dated constant maturity UK index-linked gilt. We will begin by focusing on the period from 1985 to 2007. Although fairly volatile, there is a clear downward trend in this yield from 1985 to 2007. One explanation for this decline could be a commensurate decline in expectations about UK economic growth. However, real economic growth between 1985 and 1999 averaged 2.8%, and between 2000 and 2007 it averaged 2.7%. There was very little change in average growth at a time when real yields were falling and, therefore, it is probably fair to assume that expectations of future growth were relatively stable over this time too. Panel B of Exhibit 2 shows the volatility of UK real GDP growth as represented by a three year moving standard deviation of this variable. It shows that the volatility of UK economic growth declined quite dramatically from 1995 to 2007. This decline in UK GDP volatility was also experienced elsewhere in the global economy. The same chart shows the decline in GDP volatility for OECD countries. This decline in economic volatility has been called "the great moderation"—that is, a period when the global economy and its financial markets were characterized by relatively low levels of volatility. Therefore, one plausible explanation for the declining level of real interest rates in the United Kingdom is that they were driven down by the moderation in economic volatility between the early 1990s and 2007.

The evidence in Exhibit 2 suggests that declining levels of economic volatility led to declining levels of the real default-free interest rate in the United Kingdom between 1999 and 2007. However, the absence of such markets elsewhere over this sample period does not mean that the same phenomenon was absent or irrelevant in other developed-economy bond markets. The yield on a conventional government bond includes a number of components, one of which is the real default-free rate of return. So, in all likelihood, declining global economic volatility led to declines in the real rates of return required by investors else-where, which, in turn, may have contributed to the decline in conventional government bond yields.[16]

EXAMPLE 10

Post Global Financial Crisis, 2008–2011 Real Default-Free Yields

Exhibit 3 shows the yields on short-dated index-linked bonds at the end of 2011. Compared with their pre-crisis levels shown in Exhibit 2, they had all fallen. The collapse of Lehman Brothers and the ensuing liquidity and sovereign debt crisis caused economic and financial market volatility to rise substantially, as shown in Panel B of Exhibit 2. Other things being equal, one would have expected the real yields to rise, not to fall. But other things were not equal. One explanation for the fall in these real yields is that, despite the higher volatility experienced in 2008–2011, investors believed that future real economic growth would be lower, and therefore that the equilibrium real yield in these economies was deemed to be commensurately lower.

Exhibit 3	Real Yields on Short-Dated Index-Linked Bonds, December 2011

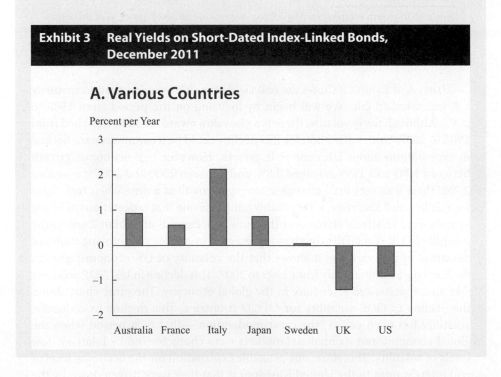

A. Various Countries

16 See Example 10 for an illustration of how the global financial crisis affected real short rates. We will focus on the drivers of conventional government bond yields relative to index-linked government bond yields in Section 4.

Exhibit 3 (Continued)

B. US TIPS and UK Gilts

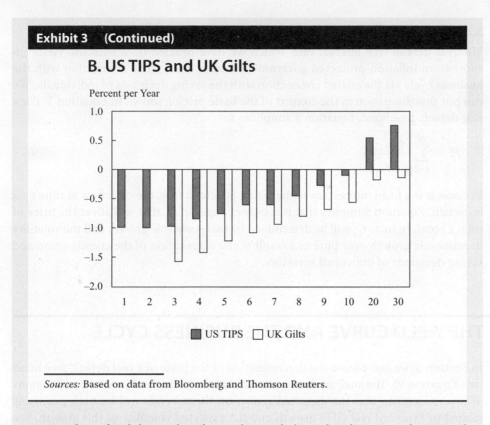

Percent per Year

Sources: Based on data from Bloomberg and Thomson Reuters.

Panel A of Exhibit 3 also shows that real short-dated rates in the United Kingdom and United States were not just lower than they were in the immediate pre-crisis period, but that they were negative, too. Panel B shows that most inflation-linked bonds issued by the US government (TIPS) and all inflation-linked bonds issued by the UK government (index-linked gilts) at this time were also negative.[17] One explanation for the lower yields may have been the fear among some investors of very high levels of inflation in the future. Arguably the easy monetary policy, including both formal (US and UK) and informal (eurozone) quantitative easing programs, implemented because of the collapse of Lehman Brothers along with other events may have led enough investors to believe that inflation-linked government bonds offered the inflation protection they needed despite the low historic and even negative real yields.

But it is also important to remember that index-linked bonds issued by developed-economy governments are not only quite special, given the credit and inflation protection that they provide, but also they are often in very limited supply. These characteristics mean that in times of crisis and of great uncertainty, investors may see them as a safe haven for their capital, which can, in turn, drive down their yields.

---

17 We will explore in more detail the term structure of interest rates in Section 4.

3.3.2 *Real Default-Free Interest Rate Summary*

The real default-free interest rate, which we have proxied here with the yields on short-term inflation-protected government bonds, has a close connection with the business cycle via the related connection with the saving decisions of individuals. We can put this discussion in the context of the basic pricing shown in Equation 1. For a real default-free bond, Equation 1 simplifies to

$$P_t^i = \sum_{s=1}^{N} \frac{CF_{t+s}^i}{\left(1 + l_{t,s}\right)^s} \tag{9}$$

Because it is a fixed interest investment that is default free, the cash flow at time $t + s$ is certain. Equation 9 implies that it is only changes in $l_{t,s}$ that will affect the price of such a bond. In turn, $l_{t,s}$ will be determined by real economic growth and the volatility in economic growth over time as a result of the aggregation of the consumption and saving decisions of individual investors.

4 THE YIELD CURVE AND THE BUSINESS CYCLE

In Section 3, we considered the determination of the price of a real default-free bond (see Equation 9). The analysis demonstrated that the saving and investment decisions of investors mean that the expected return on these bonds will be both positively related to expected real GDP growth and the expected volatility of this growth. We now move on to consider the price of a default-free bond that pays a fixed nominal (currency) amount when it matures. We will consider, for example, a bond issued by a government in a developed economy where the prospect of default is so negligible that it is ignored.

What factors would affect the price of such a bond? First, we consider a world without inflation. In this world, investors would still be giving up current consumption by investing in this bond today, in which case Equation 9 would be appropriate. But of course, deferring consumption at time t in a world with positive inflation will have an impact on the quantity of goods that can be bought at time $t + s$ when the bond matures. Investors will want to be compensated by this bond for the inflation that they expect between t and $t + s$, which we define as $\theta_{t,s}$. If investors can forecast inflation perfectly, they would demand a return given by $l_{t,s} + \theta_{t,s}$ to compensate them for the expected inflation and ensure the real level of consumption. But unless the investment horizon is very short, investors are unlikely to be very confident in their ability to forecast inflation accurately. Because we generally assume that investors are risk averse and thus need to be compensated for taking on risk as well as seeking compensation for expected inflation, they will also seek compensation for taking on the uncertainty related to future inflation. We denote this risk premium by $\pi_{t,s}$, which is distinct from the risk premium ($\rho_{t,s}^i$) in Equation 1.[18] We can rewrite our basic pricing formula for a default-free nominal coupon-paying bond from Equation 9 as follows:

$$P_t^i = \sum_{s=1}^{N} \frac{CF_{t+s}^i}{\left(1 + l_{t,s} + \theta_{t,s} + \pi_{t,s}\right)^s} \tag{10}$$

---

18 Even though it is a risk premium, we have suppressed the superscript i on the inflation uncertainty risk premium because it is not asset specific and applies across all asset classes.

Note that the bond's payoff is still certain in nominal terms because we are assuming that there is a negligible chance that the issuer (a developed-economy government) will default on its commitments. It is the real value of this payoff that is now uncertain, hence the need for a risk premium, $\pi_{t,s}$, on nominal bonds.

EXAMPLE 11

The Risk Premium for Inflation Uncertainty

Suppose that an analyst estimates that the real risk-free rate is 1.25% and that average inflation over the next year will be 2.5%. If the analyst observes the price of a default-free bond with a face value of £100 and one full year to maturity as being equal to £95.92, what would be the implied premium embedded in the bond's price for inflation uncertainty?

Solution:

The (approximate) implied premium can be calculated as follows:

$$\pi_{t,s} = 0.504\% = \frac{100}{95.92} - \left(1 + 0.0125 + 0.025\right)$$

Having established Equation 10, we will now focus on the relationship between short-term nominal interest rates and the business cycle, in which the nominal bond issued by a government in a developed economy has a very short maturity, for example a US Government Treasury Bill.

4.1 Short-Term Nominal Interest Rates and the Business Cycle

Treasury bills (T-bills) are very short-dated nominal zero-coupon government bonds. T-bills are issued by most developed-economy governments or by their agents to help smooth the cash flow needs of the government. The short-dated nature of T-bills and the fact that they are often used to implement monetary policy means that their yields are also usually very closely related to the central bank's policy rate. Indeed, because of their short-dated nature, the uncertainty that investors would have about the inflation over an investment horizon of, say, s equals three months will usually be relatively low. Therefore, for the purposes of the exposition in this section of the reading, we will assume that $\pi_{t,s}$ is so negligible that we can ignore it. So, we can modify Equation 10 to give Equation 11, which can capture all of the salient features of the pricing dynamics of a T-bill:

$$P_t^i = \frac{CF_{t+s}^i}{\left(1 + l_{t,s} + \theta_{t,s}\right)^s} \tag{11}$$

Note that the summation term is not needed because there is only one payment from a T-bill.

We have already examined the way in which the real default-free rate of interest, $l_{t,s}$, will vary over time with the business cycle and how it may also be affected by its status as a haven in times of economic uncertainty. We now move on to consider how a central bank's policy rate, which is a short-term nominal interest rate, evolves with the business cycle.

4.2 Treasury Bill Rates and the Business Cycle

To summarize briefly, the nominal rate of interest will equal the real interest rate that is required to balance the requirements of savers and investors plus investors' expectations of inflation over the relevant borrowing or lending period. It follows that short-term nominal interest rates will be positively related to short-term real interest rates and to short-term inflation expectations. Other things being equal, we would also expect these interest rates to be higher in economies with higher, more volatile growth and with higher average levels of inflation over time.

Panel A of Exhibit 4 shows the yield on a three month US T-bill, and Panel B shows the yield on an equivalent T-bill issued by the UK government. In each panel of the chart, we also present the inflation rates in these two economies. There is a close correlation between measured inflation and T-bill yields in both economies. Although measured inflation is not the same as expected inflation, it is likely that current inflation plays a big role in the formation of inflation expectations, particularly over the very short investment horizon involved when investing in a T-bill.

Exhibit 4   Treasury Bill Rates and Inflation

A. United States

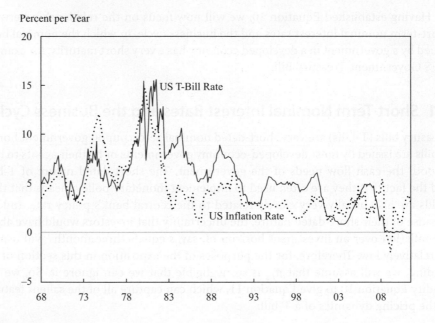

Exhibit 4   (Continued)

B. United Kingdom

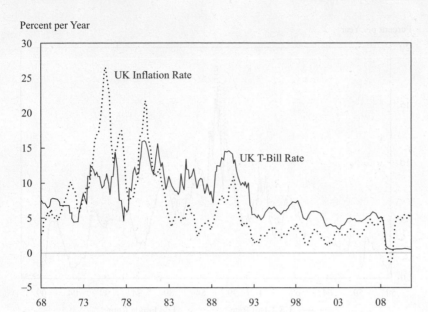

Source: Based on data from Thomson Reuters.

Exhibit 4 clearly shows that the inflation environment is a key driver of short-term interest rates. The central banks and monetary authorities responsible for setting interest rates in an economy do so in response to the economy's position in the business cycle—cutting their policy rates when activity and/or inflation are judged to be "too low" and raising rates when activity and/or inflation are judged to be "too high." In other words, a responsible central bank or monetary authority will usually set its policy rate with reference to the level of expected economic activity and the expected rate of increase of prices—that is, inflation. Exhibit 5 shows the close relationship between the yields on short-term default-free T-Bills in the United States and United Kingdom and the policy rates of their respective central banks.

Exhibit 5   Interest Rates and Policy Rates

A. United States

Percent per Year

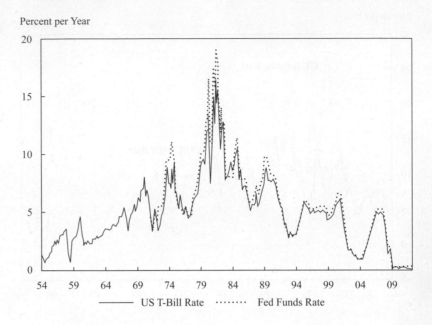

US T-Bill Rate .... Fed Funds Rate

B. United Kingdom

Percent per Year

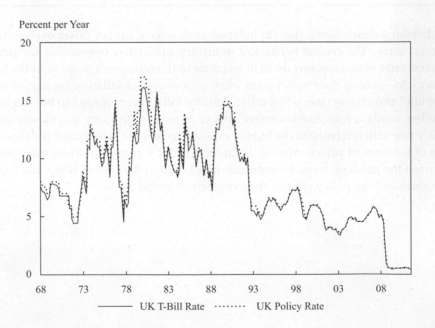

UK T-Bill Rate .... UK Policy Rate

Source: Based on data from Thomson Reuters.

A US economist, Professor John Taylor,[19] devised a rule for setting policy rates, a rule that could help rate setters gauge whether their policy rate is at an "appropriate" level. This rule is known as the Taylor rule, and it takes the following form:

$$pr_t = l_t + \iota_t + 0.5\left(\iota_t - \iota_t^*\right) + 0.5\left(Y_t - Y_t^*\right)$$

$$= l_t + 1.5\iota_t - 0.5\iota_t^* + 0.5\left(Y_t - Y_t^*\right)$$

(12)

where pr_t is the policy rate at time t, l_t is the level of real short-term interest rates that balance long-term savings and borrowing in the economy, ι_t is the rate of inflation, ι_t^* is the target rate of inflation, and Y_t and Y_t^* are, respectively, the logarithmic levels of actual and potential real GDP. The difference between Y_t and Y_t^* is known as the "output gap," which is essentially measured in percentage terms. When the output gap is positive, it implies that the economy is producing beyond its sustainable capacity. This situation is similar to a marathon runner that sets off way too fast at the start of a race; in the end, they will overheat and break down unless they reduce their running pace. Conversely, when the output gap is negative, it implies that the economy is producing below its sustainable capacity. This situation is similar to a marathon runner that sets off too slowly. If he wants to win the race at some point, he will have to use up conserved energy and speed up. Positive output gaps are usually associated with high and/or rising inflation, whereas negative output gaps are usually accompanied by high levels of unemployment. Generally, the policy rule should have a larger weight on inflation (1.5) relative to the weight on output (0.5). The purpose is to stabilize inflation over the longer term near the targeted inflation rate.[20] When inflation is close to the targeted or preferred rate, and when the output gap is zero, the appropriate policy rate will be equal to the level of the short-term real interest rate, l_t, that balances long-term savings and borrowing in the economy, plus the targeted/preferred rate of inflation. This level of the policy rate is often referred to by economists as the neutral policy rate—that is, the policy rate that neither spurs on nor impedes real economic activity. Other things being equal, when inflation is above (below) the targeted level, the policy rate should be above (below) the neutral rate; and when the output gap is positive (negative), the policy rate should also be above (below) the neutral rate. For example, if l_t is 2.0%, ι_t is 3.0%, ι_t^* is 2.0%, and the output gap is 2.0%, then the "appropriate" policy rate implied in the Taylor rule would be 6.5%.

Using fairly conservative parameters, including inflation targets when they are known, and a measure of the output gap estimated by the OECD, we have calculated policy rates based on the Taylor rule for three developed economies back to 1990, as shown in Exhibit 6. The policy rates based on the Taylor rule for the United States, shown in Panel A, seem to track the Fed's actual policy rates fairly closely, until the collapse of the high tech bubble in the early 2000s. According to the Taylor rule, the Fed kept policy rates "too low for too long" between 2002 and 2005. A similar picture emerges for Canada, as shown in Panel B. There is less evidence that policy rates were kept "too low for too long" after the collapse of the high tech bubble in the United Kingdom, as shown in Panel C. More recently, in response to the liquidity and credit crisis, all three central banks cut their policy rates sharply. According to the Taylor rule for all three economies, policy rates were "too low" by the end of 2013.

---

19 Taylor (1993).
20 The reason for the weightings is because the inflation rate appears twice in the equation (see the first line of Equation 12).

Exhibit 6   Policy Rates and Taylor Rule Calculations

A. United States

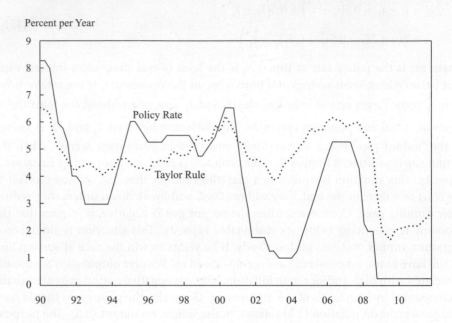

B. Canada

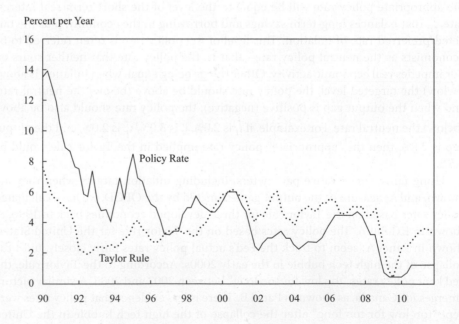

Exhibit 6   (Continued)

C. United Kingdom

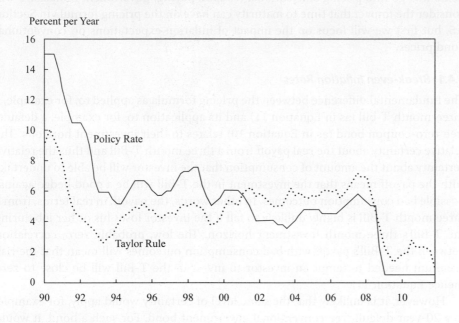

Sources: Based on data from each country's central bank and the authors' calculations.

The notion that short-term interest rates can be at too high or too low a level implies that the relationship between short-term interest rates and the business cycle are interdependent. In other words, instead of moderating the business cycle over time with deft changes to the policy rate, central bankers can exaggerate any cycle by not responding optimally to economic conditions—that is, by committing policy errors. For example, setting rates too low for too long risks creating a credit bubble, whereas setting them too high for too long could lead to recessionary or even depression-like economic conditions.

4.3 Short-Term Interest Rate Summary

Short-term default-free interest rates tend to be very heavily influenced by the inflation environment and inflation expectations over time. But they will also be influenced by real economic activity, which, in turn, is influenced by the saving and investment decisions of households. But these interest rates will also be affected by the central bank's policy rate, which, in turn, should fluctuate around the neutral policy rate as central banks respond over time to deviations in inflation from a preferred or target rate and to developments in the output gap. Finally, it is important to remember that the neutral rate will also vary with the level of real economic growth and with the expected volatility of that growth. In addition, the neutral rate might also change if the level of inflation targeted or preferred by the central bank changes.[21]

In the next section of this reading, we will focus on the relationship between the underlying economy and longer-term nominal default-free government bonds.

---

21 Between 1992 and 1997, the UK inflation target was between 2% and 4%; in 1997, the target became 2.5% with a 1 percentage point allowance around this target. Finally the target was changed in 2003 to 2.0% and to a different definition of inflation, with a 1 percentage point allowance around this target.

4.4 Conventional Government Bonds

The pricing equation shown in Equation 10 can be used to highlight the key components that go into pricing conventional (coupon paying) government bonds. We will consider the impact that time to maturity can have on the pricing formula in Section 4.5, but first we will focus on the impact of inflation expectations on conventional bond prices.

4.4.1 Break-even Inflation Rates

The fundamental difference between the pricing formula as applied to, for example, a three-month T-bill (as in Equation 11) and its application to, for example, a default-free zero-coupon bond (as in Equation 10) relates to their investment horizons. The relative certainty about the real payoff from a three month T-Bill and thus the relative certainty about the amount of consumption that the investor will be able to undertake with the payoff means that the investment in the T-Bill will be a good hedge against possible bad consumption outcomes. In other words, the payoff, in real terms, from a three month T-Bill is highly unlikely to fall if the investor loses his or her job during the T-Bill's three month investment horizon. The low, probably zero, correlation between the T-Bill's payoff with bad consumption outcomes will mean that the risk premium needed to tempt an investor to invest in the T-Bill will be close to zero (hence Equation 11).

However, it is unlikely that the same level of certainty would apply, for example, to a 20-year default-free conventional government bond. For such a bond, it would seem reasonable to assume that the risk premium would be higher than that related to a one- or three-month T-Bill. Note that the cash flow in Equation 10 is still certain, but only in nominal terms. Because investors will naturally have less confidence in their ability to form views about future inflation over 20 years relative to their abilities to form those views over three months, the greater uncertainty about the real value of the bond's payoff will cause investors to demand a premium in compensation for this uncertainty, represented by $\pi_{t,s}$ in Equation 10.

The difference between the yield on, for example, a zero-coupon default-free nominal bond and on a zero-coupon default-free real bond of the same maturity is known as the break-even inflation (BEI) rate. It should be clear from the discussion earlier that this break-even inflation rate will incorporate the inflation expectations of investors over the investment horizon of the two bonds, $\theta_{t,s}$, plus a risk premium that will be required by investors to compensate them predominantly for uncertainty about future inflation, $\pi_{t,s}$. Although the evolution of real zero-coupon default-free yields over time should be driven mainly by the inter-temporal rate of substitution, the evolution of their nominal equivalents will, in addition, be driven by changing expectations about inflation and changing perceptions about the uncertainty of the future inflation environment. We can see this evolution by plotting the constant maturity zero-coupon break-even inflation rates over time.

Panels A, B, and C of Exhibit 7 show the 10-year break-even inflation rates derived from three government bond markets in developed economies where index-linked government bonds have been available for some time now—Australia, the United Kingdom, and the United States—along with the respective inflation rates of each economy. The UK and Australian data, which are available for longer historic periods, show the gradual decline in break-even inflation rates since the mid-1980s. This decline was probably driven by the changing inflation environment in these economies. Between 1985 and 1990, inflation averaged approximately 6.0% and 7.5% in the United Kingdom and Australia, respectively. Between 2000 and 2011, having fallen steadily during the 1990s, inflation averaged 3.0% and 3.2% in the United Kingdom and Australia, respectively. Ten-year break-even rates in the United States were only available from 1997, a period when US inflation was relatively low and stable. Panel

D of Exhibit 7 highlights the impact of the liquidity and credit crisis of 2008–2009 on break-even rates for a range of economies. It shows that for all of these developed economies, 10-year break-even inflation rates fell in response to the weaker global economic environment and weaker inflationary backdrop. The weaker inflationary pressure arises from the lower demand for resources in an economic downturn, so that cost and prices do not rise as fast. For example, 10-year Italian break-even inflation rates fell from 2.3% to 0.8%, reflecting the effect of the eurozone crisis on the Italian economy at that time.

Exhibit 7   Break-even Inflation Rates and Inflation

A. United Kingdom

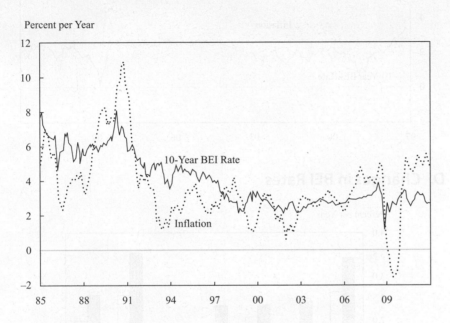

B. Australia

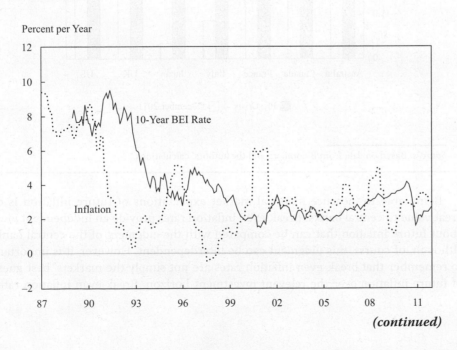

(continued)

Exhibit 7   (Continued)

C. United States

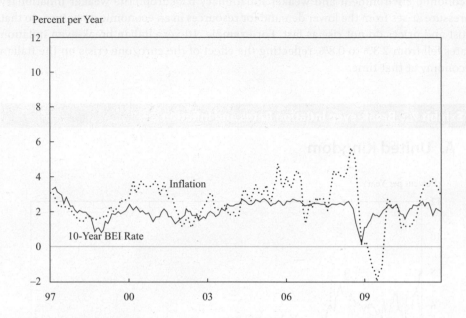

D. Changes in BEI Rates

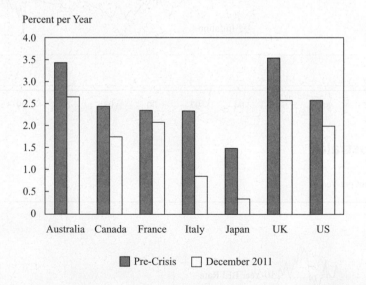

Sources: Based on data from Bloomberg and the authors' calculations.

Being able to measure financial market expectations of future inflation is of great value to central banks. Break-even inflation rates provide an independent view about future inflation that can be compared with the judgment of the central bank; although, of course, this judgment can be interdependent. However, it is important to remember that break-even inflation rates are not simply the markets' best guess of future inflation over the relevant investment horizon. Break-even inflation rates will also include a risk premium to compensate investors for their uncertainty largely about future inflation, and therefore, the uncertainty about the quantity of goods and services that they will be able to consume in the future.

4.5 The Default-Free Yield Curve and the Business Cycle

So far we have discussed the fundamental pricing relationship for default-free real and nominal bonds and short-term nominal interest rates. We now elaborate on these relationships over different investment horizons. We have already indicated that the maturity of a bond will have an impact on the way that investors price it. We now focus on this relationship more specifically. But first consider Panel A in Exhibit 8, which shows the US zero-coupon Treasury curve on three different dates. From July 2007 (just prior to the wider financial crisis) to the end of 2011, the US Treasury curve shifted down by between 3 and 4 percentage points and also became steeper. The short end of the curve was clearly influenced by the reduction in the Fed's policy rate over this period, which fell from 5.25% to virtually 0%. Panel B shows that there was a similar decline in the short end of the gilt curve, as the UK central bank gradually cut its policy rate from 5.75% to 0.50% in response to the same crisis.

Panel A shows that the Treasury curve was upward sloping on each of these dates. Panel B shows that by the end of 2011 the UK government and US government curves looked very similar, but what is interesting is that the UK government curve was downward sloping in July 2007. This slope meant that the UK government could borrow 1-year money at 6.25% but 30-year money at 4.8%. In fact, on the same date the UK government could borrow 50-year money at just over 3.0%. What economic factors could explain not only the fall in Treasury and gilt yields over this period, and elsewhere in the developed world, but also the very negative slope of the gilt curve in the summer of 2007?

Exhibit 8   US and UK Government Bond Yields and Break-even Inflation Rates for July 2007, December 2010, and December 2011

A. US Treasury Curve

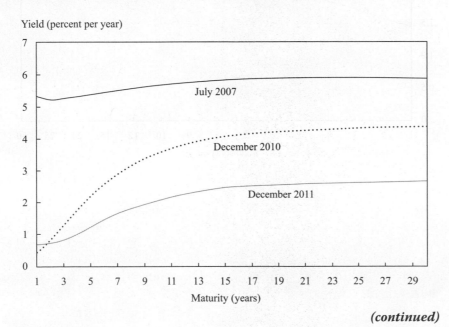

(continued)

Exhibit 8   (Continued)

B. UK Gilt Curve

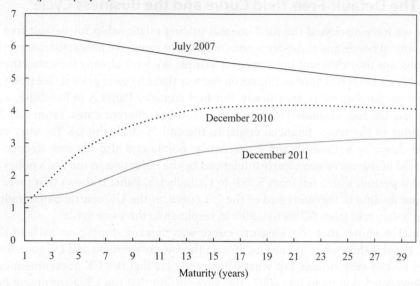

C. US BEI Rates

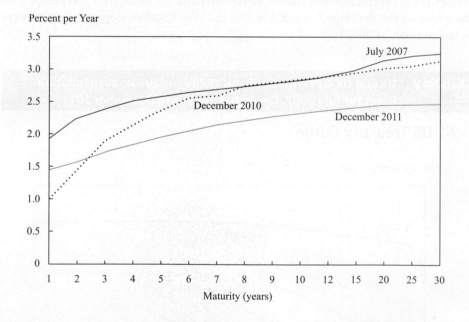

Exhibit 8   (Continued)

D. UK BEI Rates

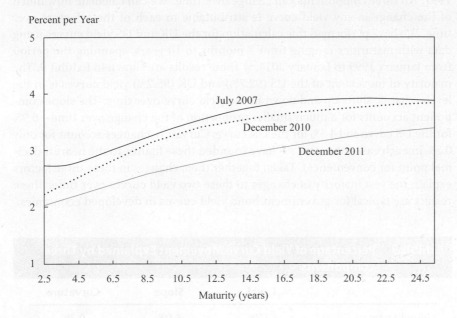

Percent per Year

Sources: Based on data from the Bank of England and Thomson Reuters.

Panels A and B of Exhibit 8 show how the shape of the default-free yield curves shifted in response to the financial crisis precipitated by the collapse of Lehman Brothers. Panels C and D of the exhibit show how break-even inflation rates shifted over the same period. When there is a significant shift in the yield curve, it is often very informative to break down the change into the real and inflationary components. Over this period, the US and UK break-even curves both shifted by just less than a full percentage point across the entire maturity spectrum. This fact could be taken to indicate that as the global recession gathered pace, US and UK government bond investors gradually "priced in" lower and lower levels of future inflation. But crucially, Panels A and B show that the nominal curves shifted down by more than 1 percentage point. For example the US curve fell by as much as 3 percentage points. These facts suggest that market participants saw the financial crisis as potentially having a bigger impact on economic growth than on inflation. Indeed, by December 2011 the US and UK break-even inflation curves were both upward sloping.

This dissection of default-free yield curves and the interpretations that are often made by analysts based on the relative movements of the real and break-even components can be very informative, but the analysis presupposes either that there is no risk premium embedded in investors' return expectations or that any risk premium is constant over time. But the risk premium is unlikely to be zero or constant over time.

EXAMPLE 12

Level, Slope, and Curvature of the Yield Curve

The yield curves shown in Exhibit 8 all have three distinct characteristics. These characteristics are referred to as *level*, which indicates whether rates are high or low, on average; *slope*, which is an indicator of the steepness of the curve, or how quickly or slowly rates change with maturity; and *curvature*, an indicator of how much the curve is different from a straight line. These characteristics were first noted in rates by Steeley in 1990 and Litterman and Scheinkman in 1991. All three components can change over time. We can calculate how much of the change in any yield curve is attributable to each of these factors over time. We have performed this calculation for the UK and US yield curves using data with maturities ranging from 3 months to 10 years, spanning the period from January 1999 to January 2014.[22] These results are shown in Exhibit 9. The majority of movement of the US (92.7%) and UK (95.2%) yield curves is in the level—that is, shifts up and down in the yield curve over time. The slope component accounts for a much smaller proportion of the change over time—6.9% for the US curve and 4.5% for the UK curve. Curvature changes account for only 0.3% in each case (note that we have rounded these figures to the nearest decimal point for convenience). Taken together then, changes in these three factors explain the vast majority of changes to these two yield curves over time. These results are typical for government bond yield curves in developed economies.

Exhibit 9	Percentage of Yield Curve Movement Explained by Three Components		
	Level	**Slope**	**Curvature**
United States	92.7%	6.9%	0.3%
United Kingdom	95.2%	4.5%	0.3%

Sources: Based on data from Bloomberg and the authors' calculations.

Exhibit 10 presents another way of viewing the dynamics of the US yield curve since 1999. The chart shows the way in which the level, slope, and curvature of the US Treasury curve has changed over time.

Exhibit 10	The US Yield Curve Since 1999

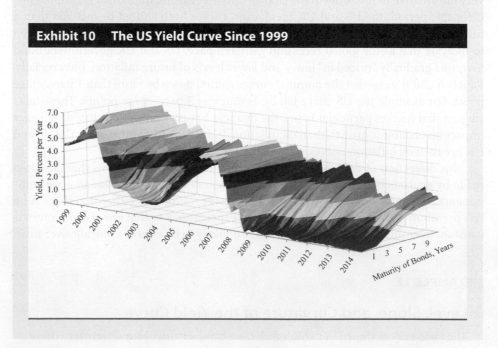

We would expect the level of economic activity to influence yield curve levels. We would also expect that views of future inflation will determine the level of these yield curves because these are nominally dominated bonds. The slope of the yield curve will be influenced by the magnitude of the risk premium in Equation 5 between the price of the bond and the inter-temporal rate of substitution over the investor's time horizon. A positive slope would be a reflection of this risk premium. However, it is not the only variable that affects the slope of the yield curve. The policy rate of the central bank is set based on Taylor rule–like considerations (that is, consideration of the components that make up the rule) so that short rates will tend to be lower during recessions because central banks tend to lower their policy rate in these times.[23] But the impact of monetary policy on longer-term rates will not be as strong because the central bank will usually be expected to bring short-term rates back to normal as the recession recedes and the risk-free rates will increase as economic growth recovers. Thus, the slope of the yield curve will increase during the recession. Finally, if investors anticipate that policy rates as well as short-term risk-free rates will revert back to normal as the recession recedes, then the yield curve will become steeper for the short-term maturities but flatter for the long-term maturities so that the curvature can increase as well. As a result, the shape of the yield curve and its three factors can provide valuable information for both central banks and investors.

4.5.1 *The Slope of the Yield Curve and Investor Expectations*

The required return on future default-risk-free cash flow was explained as consisting of a real interest rate, a premium for expected inflation, and a risk premium demanded by risk-averse investors for the uncertainty about what inflation will actually be (see Equation 10). Thus, referring to government yield curves, expectations of increasing or decreasing short-term interest rates might be connected to expectations related to future inflation rates and/or the maturity structure of inflation risk premiums.

Expectations of declining short-term interest rates can explain the downward sloping UK gilt curve in the summer of 2007. If bond market participants expect interest rates to decline, then reinvestment of the principal amounts of maturing short-term bonds at declining interest rates would offset the initial yield advantage of the shorter-dated bonds. These expectations caused the UK's yield curve to be downward sloping or inverted.

Thus, the variation in short rates over time—in particular, the central bank's policy rate—can influence the shape of the yield curve. These short rates are, in turn, driven by the positive relationship between the real rate of interest that balances investment and saving decisions over time and by the level of and volatility in GDP growth, as well as by the variation of the rate of inflation around the central bank's target, or preferred, level.

4.5.2 *The Term Spread and the Business Cycle*

Exhibit 11 shows the time variation in the slope of the US and UK government yield curves since 1900. In both cases, the slopes have been calculated as the difference (spread) between a long-dated government bond and the yield on an equivalent one-year bond.

---

23 We are not suggesting that central banks slavishly follow the Taylor rule. However, the rule neatly encapsulates two of the key macroeconomic considerations that go into the process of setting the interest rate.

Exhibit 11   US and UK Government Yield Curve Spreads, 1900–2010

A. US Treasury

Term Spread (percent per year)

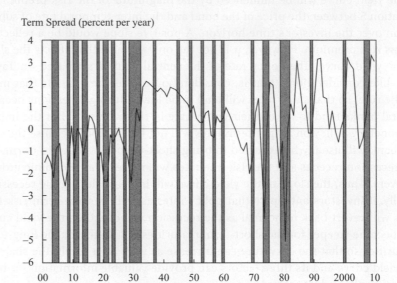

B. UK Gilt

Term Spread (percent per year)

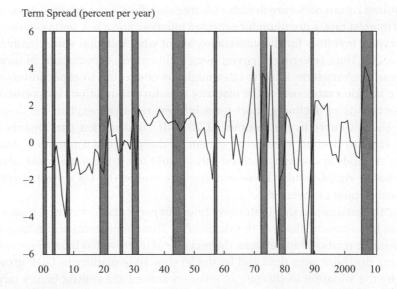

Note: Shaded areas indicate recessions.
Sources: Based on data from NBER and Bank of England.

In both markets, there are times when the curves were very steep. For example, in the mid-1970s the steep slope implied expectations of a sharp increase in interest rates. This was a time when both inflation and inflation expectations were high following the first oil shock of 1973.

But there are times when both curves are steeply inverted—for example, in 1979–1980. The inverted curves in these times implied an expectation of sharply falling inflation and future interest rates. In both economies, the nominal policy rates were extremely high: policy rates peaked at 17.5% in the United States in

December 1980 and at 17% in the United Kingdom in November 1979; during this period, the Fed chairman, Paul Volcker, and Margaret Thatcher had raised policy rates in their respective economies in response to the second oil shock of 1979 and administrations on both sides of the Atlantic came to the conclusion that the defeat of inflation should be the number one policy objective. The inverted curves in both markets suggest that investors expected rates to come down once the causes of high current inflation had been removed. Generally speaking, Exhibit 11 also reveals that a recession is often preceded by a flattening, or even an inversion, in the yield curve. In general, the late stages of a business expansion are often characterized by a peak in inflation and thus relatively high short-term interest rates. If longer maturity yields reflect lower inflation rates and diminished business credit demand, the yield curve would tend to flatten or invert. An inverted yield curve, in particular, is often read as being a predictor of recession.

EXAMPLE 13

Interest Rates, the Yield Curve, and the Business Cycle

1   What financial instrument is best suited to the study of the relationship of real interest rates with the business cycle?

   A   Default-free nominal bonds

   B   Investment-grade corporate bonds

   C   Default-free inflation-indexed bonds

2   Suppose investors forecast an unanticipated increase in real GDP growth and the volatility of GDP growth for a particular country. The effect of such a forecast would be for the coupon payments of an inflation-indexed bond issued by the government of the country:

   A   to rise.

   B   to fall.

   C   to be indeterminate.

3   The yield spread between non-inflation-adjusted and inflation-indexed bonds of the same maturity is affected by:

   A   a risk premium for future inflation uncertainty only.

   B   investors' inflation expectations over the remaining maturity of the bonds.

   C   both a risk premium for future inflation uncertainty and investors' inflation expectations over the remaining maturity of the bonds.

4   State an economic reason why inverted yield may predict a recession.

Solution to 1:

C is correct. These bonds' prices are sensitive to changes in real interest rates because the payments are adjusted for changes in the price of goods.

Solution to 2:

A is correct. The coupon payments would be expected to increase reflecting an increase in the real interest rate.

Solution to 3:

C is correct. The difference between the yield on a zero-coupon default-free nominal bond (such as US government STRIP) and on a zero-coupon default-free real bond of the same maturity (such as US government TIPS) is called the break-even inflation rate. The break-even inflation rate should incorporate investors' inflation expectations over the remaining maturity plus a risk premium for uncertainty about future inflation as in Equation 10.

Solution to 4:

The late stages of business cycles are often characterized by relatively high inflation and high short-term interest rates. To the extent that longer-term yields reflect expectations of declining inflation and a slackening in demand for credit, the yield curve would be expected to flatten or invert.

4.5.3 *Evidence on Risk Premiums for Default-Free Bonds*

If, as seems likely, most investors want to be compensated for taking on risk, then the yield curve, as well as containing information about the interest rate expectations of investors, will also embody a risk premium.

We have already explained why investors would value investments that paid off more in bad times relative to those investments that paid off less in these times, or produced negative returns. This preference tends to drive the expected return down and the price of these favored investments up relative to those with prices that are more positively correlated with bad times. The average slopes of the US and UK government curves from 1900 to 2011 were 0.24% and 0.14%, respectively; in the post 1945 period, they were 0.50% and 0.40%, respectively. This difference suggests that, on average, investors have been willing to pay a premium for shorter-dated US and UK government bonds, which, in turn, means that longer-dated bonds may not be such a good hedge against economic bad times. One interpretation of an upward-sloping yield curve is that short-dated bonds are less positively (or more negatively) correlated with bad times than are long-dated bonds.

Exhibit 12 presents information on the relationship of government bonds with a range of maturities from a selection of countries. Panel A shows that the average yield difference (longer minus shorter) between different bond maturities, with one exception, are all positive. These facts suggest that the bond risk premium generally rises with maturity, which is why it is often referred to as the term premium. Panel B presents the total return on these government bonds by maturity. Over the sample periods, the total returns achieved rise with maturity in each of the bond markets. But why have government bond investors generally been rewarded for holding longer-dated government bonds relative to shorter-dated bonds?

In Panel C, we present the correlation between the (1) total return on bonds with various maturities and (2) the economic growth of the relevant economy. The first thing to notice is that the correlations are all negative. This fact suggests that government bonds in these markets tend to pay off in bad times, which means that investors are willing to pay a relatively high price for them. Therefore, investors should be willing to accept a relatively low return from government bonds because they are at least a partial hedge against "bad" consumption outcomes. Second, the correlation between short-dated government bond returns and economic growth in Australia, Canada, and the United Kingdom is more negative than the equivalent correlations for long-dated government bonds. For example, the correlation between 2-year bond returns in Canada and Canadian economic growth is −30.95%, but the equivalent correlation for 30-year Canadian government bonds is −12.50%. These facts indicate that short-dated bonds have been more reliable hedges against bad economic times than long-dated bonds, which, in turn, means that the bond risk premium should be higher for long-dated government bonds than for their short-dated equivalents. The yield curve should be upward sloping to reflect as a result. In the US Treasury market, the correlation falls (in absolute value) between 5- and 30-year maturities, suggesting that the longer-dated Treasury bonds are less useful as a hedge against bad times over the sample period chosen here. However, two-year Treasuries were a less useful hedge than five-year Treasuries because the correlation between their total return and US GDP growth was less negative.

Exhibit 12 Government Bond Spreads, Total Returns, and GDP Growth Correlations for Four Markets

A. Spreads

Years	5 vs. 2	10 vs. 5	30 vs. 10
Australia	—	0.34%	0.21%	—
Canada	—	0.43%	0.38%	0.37%
United Kingdom	—	0.21%	0.15%	−0.24%
United States	—	0.54%	0.39%	0.32%

B. Total returns

	2	5	10	30
Australia	8.12%	9.52%	10.61%	—
Canada	6.78%	7.94%	9.22%	10.73%
United Kingdom	8.54%	8.83%	10.96%	11.28%
United States	6.96%	8.27%	9.01%	9.97%

C. Correlation with GDP growth

	2	5	10	30
Australia	−42.80%	−43.29%	−35.64%	—
Canada	−30.95%	−37.10%	−28.44%	−12.50%
United Kingdom	−23.82%	−19.79%	−18.24%	−5.11%
United States	−14.85%	−25.52%	−22.24%	−19.73%

Note: The sample period for the United Kingdom and the United States is January 1980 to December 2011. For Australia, it is January 1987 to December 2011, and for Canada, it is January 1985 to December 2011.
Sources: Thomson Reuters and authors' calculations.

The results shown in Exhibit 12 suggest that government bond risk premiums

- are positive;
- are probably related to the consumption hedging benefits of government bonds; and
- are positively related to bond maturity, which means that the "normal" shape for the yield curve is upward sloping.

The last point also helps to explain why the US Treasury curve was generally upward sloping between the summer of 2007 and the end of 2011: A significant portion of the slope was probably related to the existence of a positive risk premium on US Treasuries that increased with maturity.

However, bond risk premiums ($\pi_{t,s}$), like other risk premiums, will not be constant over time. In times of economic uncertainty, investors will tend to value assets more that pay off in bad times—government bonds—which will force their prices up as the risk premium demanded falls. Unfortunately, it is impossible to say how big or small this premium really is, or should be, or how it evolves with the business cycle. But we can get some idea by performing the following experiment. Suppose we can assume that the real return on an index-linked government bond is a good proxy for the real rate of interest that balances savings and investment in an economy over time. If we subtract the yield on an index-linked government bond from the yield on a conventional government bond with a similar maturity, and then subtract from this amount a survey-based measure of inflation expectations, what is left over is the bond risk premium. That is, the extra yield investors require for holding a conventional government bond over and above the real required return and the return in compensation for expected inflation.

Exhibit 13   Bond Risk Premiums (BRP)

A. UK Government BRP

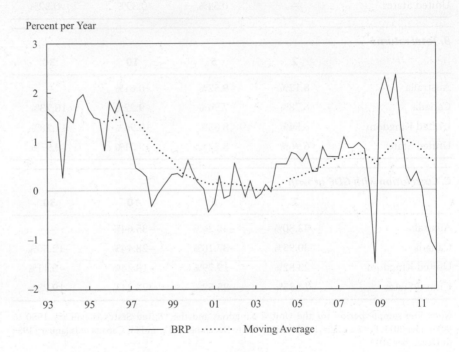

B. Change in Government BRP, 2007–2011

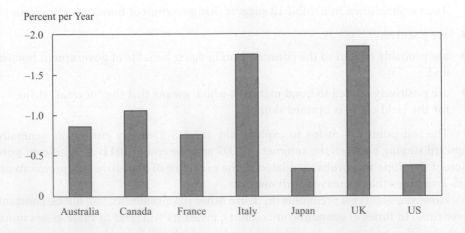

Note: The period 1993–1997 in Panel A was before the inflation-targeting regime.

Panel A of Exhibit 13 presents a calculation of this kind for the UK government bond market. There are a number of points worth noting with respect to this particular representation of the bond risk premium. First, it is certainly imperfect because it shows that the bond risk premium is negative at times. A negative bond risk premium implies that investors are willing to pay for assuming risk, which is inconsistent with risk aversion. Second, putting aside these negative values for the moment, we can see that the bond risk premium varies over time. Between 1993 and mid-1997, the risk premium on UK government bonds averages just less than 1.5%; from mid-1997 to 2005, it averages around 0.25%; and from 2005 to 2011, it averages around 0.75%.

Panel B in Exhibit 13 is based on similar estimates for the bond risk premiums for a range of markets and shows the change in the bond risk premiums from July 2007 to December 2011. For all the government bond markets for which we could make these calculations, the bond risk premium fell—in some cases, quite substantially. This fact implies that investors placed a greater value on the consumption hedging properties of government bonds as a result of the financial crisis. Other things being equal, this implies that they were willing to pay a higher price for these bonds compared with the price they were willing to pay before the crisis. This also implies that bond risk premiums will tend to rise in times when investors place less value on the consumption-hedging properties of government bonds.

4.5.4 Other Factors

In practice, the shape of the yield curve and the relative performance of bonds with different maturities over the business cycle depends on a complex mixture of interest rate expectations and risk premiums considerations. For example, a downward-sloping curve is probably largely the result of investor expectations of future declines in interest rates. The drivers of an upward-sloping curve are more ambiguous. For example, the existence of bond risk premiums that are positively related to maturity means that an upward-sloping curve may not embody expectations of future rate increases. Conversely, it could imply a combination of expected rate increases and risk premiums, or even expected rate cuts that are more than offset by the existence of positive risk premiums.

We have to acknowledge that there will also be times when other factors play a part in shaping the yield curve. Developed-economy government bonds are technically default free because these governments can, in principle, always print cash to meet the promised payments.[24] In this sense, they are very special financial instruments. These markets can also be influenced by supply and demand factors that seem to move yields in ways that do not appear to be consistent with the business cycle. Consider the following examples:

- In the late 1990s, fiscal surpluses in the United States led some investors to take the view that the supply of Treasuries would shrink as the US government paid back its debts (leading to the Treasury scare of 2000). This perceived reduction in future supply was said to have been responsible for the decline in yields as investors bought up these bonds in anticipation of their future scarcity.

---

24 It is important to note that eurozone governments cannot simply print cash to meet their obligations; this fact has led many financial market participants to reevaluate the risks embodied in bonds issued by eurozone governments. Although, if cash is printed, it is a *de facto* partial default in terms of real purchasing power to investors.

- In the early 2000s, Treasury yields were apparently being pushed down by Asian central banks that were using their growing trade surpluses to purchase US Treasuries.

- Regulatory factors can also play an important role in determining government bond yields. This influence is particularly clear in the gilt market. In 1997, the UK government passed legislation that effectively compelled UK pension funds to buy long-dated gilts. This legislation appears to have been one of the main drivers of the inversion of the long end of the UK's yield curve (see Exhibit 8, Panel B). Since that time new accounting rules for pensions—FRS17 followed by IAS19—forced UK pension schemes to increase their demand for long-dated UK government bonds further still. These actions created a vicious circle because the new accounting rules required the schemes to discount their liabilities using the long-dated yields as the discount rate. Consequently, UK pension funds bought long-dated bonds, forcing their yields down; the decline in yields caused the present value of pension liabilities to rise relative to the value of scheme assets, creating deficits; to achieve a better match between assets and liabilities, schemes tried to buy more long-dated gilts, causing their yields to fall further and liabilities to rise further.[25]

There is no doubt that supply and demand considerations along with poorly thought out regulatory or accounting rules can have an impact on government bond markets. But determining the extent of these effects is very difficult. Nevertheless, it is difficult to explain the very inverted shape of the long end of the gilt curve, which has persisted for many years now, without reference to such factors.

EXAMPLE 14

The Japanese Yield Curve and Business Cycle 1990–2012

During the 1980s, real Japanese GDP growth averaged more than 4.60% per year. During the 1990s and 2000s, it averaged around 1.5%. The catalyst for the decline in growth was the collapse of Japan's property bubble and stock crash in the early 1990s. Exhibit 14 shows Japan's real annual GDP growth over the post bubble period, which incorporates the global financial crisis of 2008–2009. The exhibit also shows how real short-term policy rates fell steadily from 4% to 5% in 1990, finally becoming negative by 1997. Since that time, real rates have generally been negative as Japan's central bank, the Bank of Japan, has tried to stimulate its economy by cutting its nominal policy rate to (near) zero.

---

25 A similar phenomenon affected core eurozone bond and swap markets. For more than three years, the yield spread between 10- and 30-year Dutch government bonds (30 minus 10) was negative. It was argued that the negative spread was a direct result of the hedging activities of Dutch pension funds, which had over €1 trillion worth of pension liabilities. The buying pressure on a government bond market that was only around 60% the size of these liabilities thus caused long-dated Dutch government bond prices to rise.

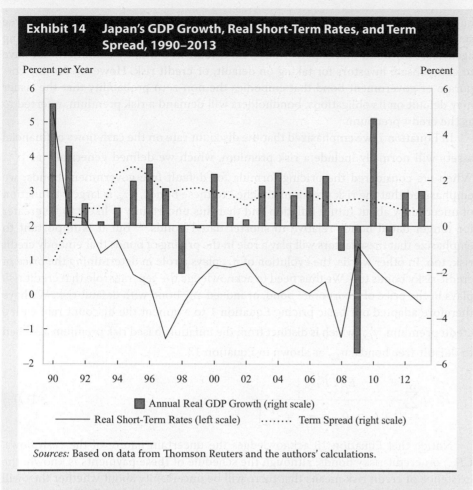

Exhibit 14 Japan's GDP Growth, Real Short-Term Rates, and Term Spread, 1990–2013

Percent per Year

Percent

- ■ Annual Real GDP Growth (right scale)
- —— Real Short-Term Rates (left scale)
- ········ Term Spread (right scale)

Sources: Based on data from Thomson Reuters and the authors' calculations.

Exhibit 14 also shows the term spread over this period—that is, the slope of the yield curve (created by subtracting the policy rate from 10-year Japanese government bonds). At the start of the period, as the Bank of Japan cut its policy rate from just over 8.0% at the end of 1990 to 0.45% by the end of 1995, the curve steepened—from –1.63% at the end of 1990 to 2.59% by the end of 1995. The sharp steepening of the curve in response to the cuts in the policy rate arguably indicated the markets' view that the policy stimulus would work—that is, the yields on longer dated Japanese government bonds embedded some expectation of positive growth and inflation in the future. However, since the mid-1990s, despite cutting its policy rate to zero and enacting programs of quantitative easing, the term spread has fallen steadily. By the end of 2013, it was around 0.60%. The weak economic growth and inflation environment in Japan since the collapse of the property bubble is reflected in the fall and flattening of the Japanese yield curve.

CREDIT PREMIUMS AND THE BUSINESS CYCLE

5

In Section 4, we discussed the economic drivers of what we have referred to as default-free interest rates and bond yields. But the financial crisis has caused many to question what "default free" really means. The bonds issued by many European governments, including those issued by France and Italy as well as those issued by the Greek, Portuguese, Irish, Belgian, and Spanish governments, were all thought to be default free before the euro financial crisis from 2010–2012. Even the default-free status of US Treasuries has now been questioned by both investors and credit rating agencies. Any bond that is perceived to be default-free will, by definition, not have to compensate investors for taking on default, or credit risk. However, for any corporate or government bond that embodies the non-zero probability that the issuer may default on its obligations, bondholders will demand a risk premium, referred to as the credit premium.

In Equation 1, we emphasized that the discount rate on the cash flows of financial assets will normally include a risk premium, which we defined generically as $\rho_{t,s}^{i}$. When we considered the pricing formula for default-free government bonds, we emphasized that the risk premium attached to these bonds, $\pi_{t,s}$, is largely a function of uncertainty about future inflation and that this uncertainty is likely to be greater for longer-dated bonds relative to shorter-dated bonds.[26] But it is important to emphasize that these factors will play a role in the pricing of bonds that embody credit risk, too. In other words, the evolution of $\pi_{t,s}$ plays a role in determining the price of credit-risky bonds too. We thus need to acknowledge the separate role that credit risk plays in the price of a corporate bond, or indeed any bond with default risk. We have therefore adapted our basic pricing Equation 1 to augment the discount rate with a credit premium, $\gamma_{t,s}^{i}$, which is distinct from the inflation-based risk premium attached to default-free bonds, $\pi_{t,s}$, as shown in Equation 13.

$$P_t^i = \sum_{s=1}^{N} \frac{E_t\left[\widetilde{CF}_{t+s}^i\right]}{\left(1 + l_{t,s} + \theta_{t,s} + \pi_{t,s} + \gamma_{t,s}^i\right)^s} \tag{13}$$

Notice that Equation 13 acknowledges the uncertain nature of the cash flows, $CF_{t,s}$, on credit-risky bonds; although the schedule of these payments is known, the existence of credit risk means that there will be uncertainty about whether they will be paid as scheduled. In the event of a default, the amount that the bond investor receives will depend on the recovery rate, which will also be an unknown quantity. The risk premium demanded by investors because of these uncertainties is represented by $\gamma_{t,s}^i$ in Equation 13.

In this section, we will focus on the credit premium, $\gamma_{t,s}^i$, and in particular on the relationship between the business cycle and the credit premium on corporate bonds.

EXAMPLE 15

The Credit Risk Premium

Suppose that an analyst estimates that the real risk-free rate is 1.25%, average inflation over the next year will be 2.5%, and the premium required by investors for inflation uncertainty is 0.50%. If the analyst observes the price of corporate bond with a face value of £100, with one full year to maturity, as being equal to £94.21, what would be the implied credit premium embedded in the bond's price for inflation uncertainty?

---

26 Recall that this risk premium ($\pi_{t,s}$) is distinct from the addition to return that investors require based on their expectations of inflation over the investment horizon, $\theta_{t,s}$ (see Equation 1).

Solution:

The (approximate) implied premium can be calculated as follows:

$$\gamma_{t,s}^i = 1.90\% = \frac{100}{94.21} - \left(1 + 1.25\% + 2.50\% + 0.50\%\right)$$

5.1 Credit Spreads and the Credit Risk Premium

The difference between the yield on a corporate bond and that on a government bond with the same currency denomination and maturity is generally referred to as the credit spread. It is demanded by investors in compensation for the additional credit risk that they bear compared with that embodied in the government bond.

As Equation 13 shows, credit risky bonds share the same risk as default-free bonds, which market participants often refer to as interest rate risk, but they also embody credit risk, $\gamma_{t,s}^i$. Other things being equal a parallel shift up in the yield curve will have an almost identical proportionate impact on the prices of, say, a five-year government bond and a five-year corporate bond. And over time, again other things being equal, the interest rate component of a corporate bond will be driven by the same factors that drive government bond yields and returns. In other words, they are both subject to interest rate risk.

It is the credit risk component of a corporate bond, $\gamma_{t,s}^i$, and the evolution of bond spreads that will cause corporate and comparable government bond returns to diverge over time. It would seem sensible to assume that the premium demanded would tend to rise in times of economic weakness, when the probability of a corporate default and bankruptcy is highest. Exhibit 15 confirms this view. The exhibit shows a representative spread on both AAA/Aaa and BBB/Baa rated US corporate bonds over US Treasuries.[27] First, the Baa spread is always higher than the Aaa spread, reflecting the lower credit quality of Baa bonds relative to Aaa rated bonds. Second, the US recession periods shaded grey in the chart indicate that both low- and higher-grade corporate bond spreads do tend to rise in the lead up to and during a recession, and to decline once the economy comes out of recession.

---

27 The AAA rating category in "AAA/Aaa" is the rating category used by both Standard & Poor's and Fitch Ratings' Services; Aaa is the equivalent rating category used by Moody's Investors Services. These categories are seen as reflecting similar levels of credit risk. Similarly, the BBB rating category is the Standard & Poor's and Fitch equivalent of Moody's Baa rating.

Exhibit 15   Credit Spreads and the Business Cycle

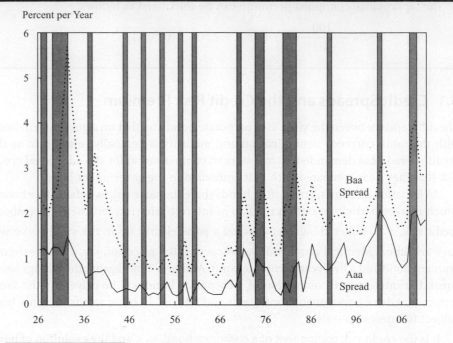

Percent per Year

Note: Shaded areas indicate recessions.
Source: Based on data from Moody's Investors Service.

As expected, the business cycle has a profound effect on credit spreads, but what are the basic components of the credit spread? If we assume that investors are risk neutral, then they will simply demand a return (yield) on their corporate bond investments sufficient to compensate them for the possible loss that they could incur from holding a corporate bond. In turn, this expected loss will depend on the probability of default and the expected recovery rate in the event of default, as shown in Equation 14:

Expected loss = Probability of default × (1 − Recovery rate)   **(14)**

In the instance where investors are risk neutral, the expected return on, say, a 10-year government bond would be equal to the loss-adjusted expected return on a comparable 10-year corporate bond. In practice, however, investors are risk averse, in which case the expected return on a corporate bond will be higher than that on a comparable government bond, even if a significant amount of the credit risk can be mitigated by holding a diversified portfolio of corporate bonds. One of the main reasons why investors continue to be exposed to considerable market risk even in a well-diversified portfolio is that defaults tend to cluster around downturns in the business cycle. Panels A and B of Exhibit 16 show this quite clearly. Panel A shows the number of US corporate defaults per year since 1920, and Panel B shows annual default rates over the same period. Both charts show that there are often long periods of time when there are very few defaults. However, the US depression of the 1930s and the recessions in the 1980s, 1990s, and 2000s were all associated with relatively high default levels and rates. The historic default rates on different ratings classes are sometimes used by analysts as a proxy for the probability of default in Equation 14 for expected loss.

Exhibit 16   US Corporate Defaults, Default Rates, Recovery Rates, and Loss Rates

A. Number of Defaults

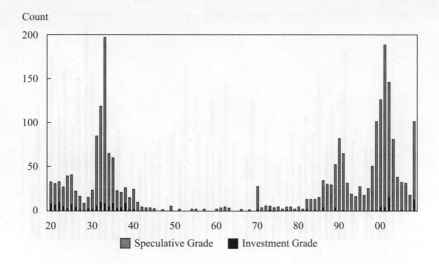

B. Default Rates

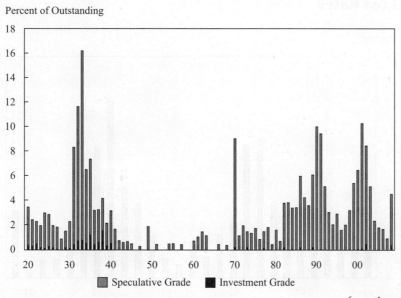

(continued)

Exhibit 16   (Continued)

C. Recovery Rates

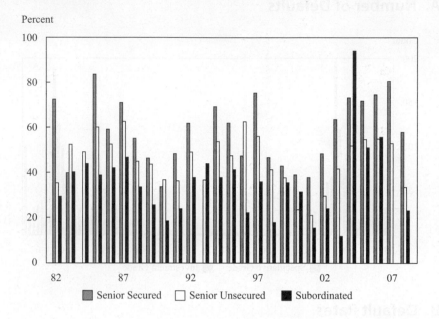

D. Loss Rates

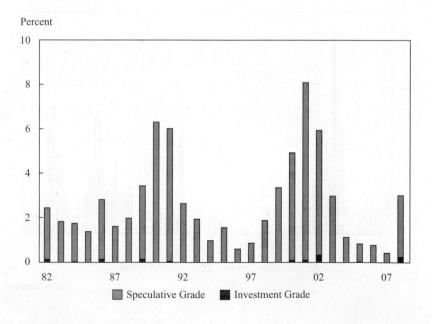

Source: Based on data from Moody's Investors Service.

Panel C of Exhibit 16 shows the evolution of recovery rates on three types of corporate bonds: senior secured, senior unsecured, and subordinated. Senior secured debt, as the name suggests, is secured by a lien or other claim against some or all of the company's assets, whereas senior unsecured debt has no explicit claim to the company's assets in the event of bankruptcy. This explains why recovery rates are generally higher for secured as opposed to unsecured debt holders. Subordinated debt holders, as the name suggests, have an inferior claim on the company's assets compared with senior debt holders, and unsurprisingly, recovery rates are often very low. The recovery rate ranking is interesting, but we can also see from Panel C that recovery rates tend to be higher when the economy is expanding and lower when it is contracting. The reason is because assets that can be sold in order to recover value for bond holders are likely to fetch a higher price in a buoyant rather than in a stagnant economic environment. Finally, Panel D shows the loss rates on US corporate debt since 1982. These loss rates are the net result of the defaults and recovery rates over time. Unsurprisingly, these loss rates are counter-cyclical with regard to the business cycle, meaning that they tend to rise as economic activity declines.

5.2 Industrial Sectors and Credit Quality

Although spreads will evolve with the business cycle, Exhibit 17 illustrates that spreads between corporate bond sectors with different ratings will often have very different sensitivities to the business cycle. Panel A presents a shorter, but finer picture of the relative performance of US corporate bonds by Moody's rating category. The graph shows that when spreads are narrowing relative to government bonds, the spreads between higher- and lower-rated bond categories also narrow. In these times, although corporate bonds will generally outperform government bonds, lower-rated corporate bonds will tend to outperform higher rated bonds. The converse is true as spreads widen, a phenomenon that is illustrated most graphically following the collapse of Lehman Brothers in 2008. The spread on speculative, or high-yield, debt rose from a pre-Lehman's low of around 2.8% to a peak of just more than 20.0%. Over the same period, Baa rated debt spreads rose from around 1.1% to 8.5% and Aaa corporate bond spreads rose from 0.6% to 4.5%.

Exhibit 17   US Credit Spreads and the Business Cycle

A. Moody's Rating

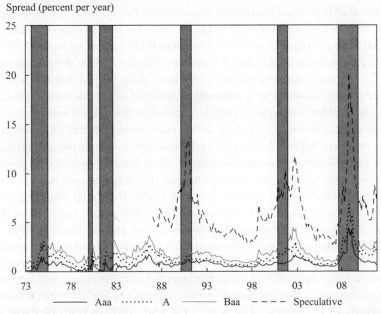

(continued)

Exhibit 17   (Continued)

B. Industrial Sector

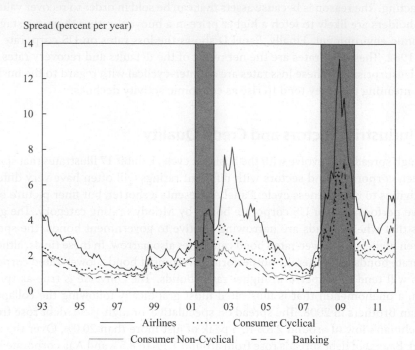

Spread (percent per year)

Note: Shaded areas indicate recessions.
Sources: Based on data from Thomson Reuters and the authors' calculations.

Panel B in Exhibit 17 illustrates another determinant of credit spreads: industrial sector. Analysis by industrial sector addresses the question of how the type of goods and services that individual companies produce may be related to credit quality. Some industrial sectors are more sensitive to the business cycle than others. This sensitivity can be related to the types of goods and services that they sell or to the indebtedness of the companies in the sector. Panel B shows evidence of only the divergent performance of corporate bond sectors over a relatively short period, but the performance of the four sectors shown is very different in times of economic stress. First, in both of the recessions that this period covers (indicated by the shaded areas in the exhibit), the spread on the consumer cyclical sector rose more dramatically than it did for corporate bonds in the consumer non-cyclical sector. For example, the spread on the consumer cyclical sector peaks at just under 4.0% in 2003 compared with around 2.5% for the consumer non-cyclical sector. Second, the graph shows how sensitive the airline sector's credit spread is to the business cycle. The sharp widening of spreads in this sector as a result of both recessions is probably also a function of the lower credit quality on average of companies in the airline sector. Third, the recession of the early 2000s had only a mild impact on the spreads of banks, but a much larger impact in the post-Lehman period, when the sector spread peaked at nearly 7.5%. This difference highlights the fact that the last recession and crisis was first and foremost a banking crisis. But perhaps the most interesting feature is the narrowing of sector spreads in the summers of both 1998 and 2007. In both of these periods, investors were content to receive virtually the same credit spread, $\gamma_{t,s}^{i}$, on airline company debt as on debt issued by companies in the consumer non-cyclical sector.

5.3 Company-Specific Factors

Corporate bond spreads will be driven over time by the business cycle, but the impact of the economic environment on spreads will depend on issuers' industrial sector and rating. When spreads widen, the spreads on bonds issued by corporations with a low credit rating and/or that are part of a cyclical sector will tend to widen the most. Company-specific factors will also play a part in determining the difference in the yield of an individual corporate issuer and that of a government bond with the same maturity. Issuers that are profitable, have low debt interest payments, and that are not heavily reliant on debt financing will tend to have a high credit rating because their ability to pay is commensurately high.

Exhibit 18 provides summary statistics on financial statements for companies across a range of Moody's rating categories. Pre-tax interest coverage is calculated by dividing total pre-tax earnings by total debt interest payments. On average, Aaa companies had $17.60 worth of pre-tax earnings for every $1 of interest payment to which they were committed. By contrast, on average, Baa companies had only $2.50, whereas the average B and Caa rated companies could not cover their interest payments with current period pre-tax earnings. The ratio of free operating cash flow to total debt gives another indication of the profitability and financial flexibility of a company relative to its outstanding debt. There is again a clear deterioration in this metric as average rating quality declines. Finally, the ratio of total debt to total capital gives an idea of the overall indebtedness of a company. Together these and other ratios allow analysts and credit rating agencies to determine a company's ability to meet its debt obligations as they come due. If this ability declines relative to other issuers in their sector, then the spread demanded on their debt will rise, relative to the sector average, and their rating may be lowered by the rating agency.

Exhibit 18 Ratings and Financial Ratios							
	Aaa	Aa	A	Baa	Ba	B	Caa
Pre-tax interest coverage (×)	17.6	7.6	4.1	2.5	1.5	0.9	0.7
Free operating cash flow/Total debt (%)	42.3	28	13.6	6.1	3.2	1.6	0.8
Total debt/Total capital (%)	21.9	32.7	40.3	48.8	66.2	71.5	71.2

Source: Based on data from Moody's Investor Services.

5.4 Sovereign Credit Risk

So far we have discussed the risk premium demanded by investors on both default-free and corporate debt. But credit premiums have always been an important component of the expected return on bonds issued by governments in developing or emerging economies. Even though many of these governments can print money to meet their debt obligations *in extremis*, meaning that they could technically avoid defaulting on these debts, many developing-economy governments have defaulted on their debts in the past. For example, the Russian government defaulted on its debt in 1998, and many others, including Argentina, Brazil, and Mexico, have defaulted in recent years. Such defaults are often very country specific in character, but the global economic environment, oil prices, and the evolution of global trade will often play a part in precipitating such sovereign defaults.

The credit risk embodied in bonds issued by governments in emerging markets is normally expressed by comparing the yields on these bonds with the yields on bonds with comparable maturity issued by the US Treasury. Panel A of Exhibit 19 shows the evolution of this spread for three emerging market bond indices. The impact of the credit crisis is clear; spreads rise in response to the uncertain economic environment globally. But the volatility of the spreads from 1998 to 2003 is a function of the Asian financial crisis in 1997, the Russian debt crisis in 1998, and the recession in developed economies in 2001–2002 following the collapse of the high-tech bubble. What is interesting is the decline in spreads to US Treasuries to 2007, along with the much narrower spreads between the regions at this time. Strong global economic growth between 2003 and 2007 convinced investors that they did not need such a high reward for emerging market default risk, nor that they needed to differentiate much between regions.

Exhibit 19	Sovereign Credit Spreads

A. Emerging Markets

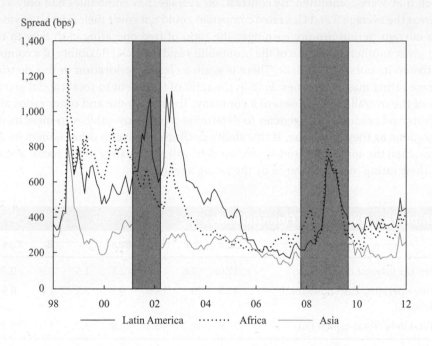

Exhibit 19   (Continued)

B. Developed Economies

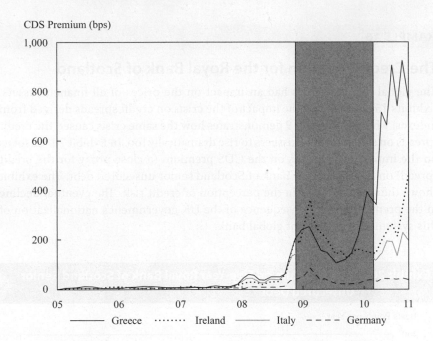

CDS Premium (bps)

Legend: —— Greece ········ Ireland —— Italy − − − − Germany

Note: Shaded areas indicate US recessions.
Sources: Based on data from Thomson Reuters and the authors' calculations.

The 2008–2009 global financial crisis has caused many investors now to question what is meant by the term default-free. Until that time, there was thought to be a set of developed-economy government issuers for which the likelihood of debt default was so low that it could almost be ignored. In other words, investors did not demand meaningful compensation for assuming this risk. Panel B of Exhibit 19 shows how this perception changed dramatically for the debts of a set of eurozone economies during the crisis. The chart shows the cost that an investor would have to pay for insuring themselves against a sovereign default on German, Italian, Irish, and Greek government debt over the next five years through the purchase of credit default swaps (CDS).[28] For example, in January 2006 that cost was 2, 10, 2, and 14 bps, respectively. So, to insure oneself against a default on bonds issued by these governments with, say, a notional value of €10 million, would have cost €2,000, €10,000, €2,000, and €14,000, respectively, per year. However, by the end of 2010 this insurance cost had risen to €38,960, €196,695, €458,270, and €775,280, respectively. Although the causes of this reassessment of sovereign credit risk inherent in developed-economy debt were complex, the basic reason for the increase in the credit risk premium was a reassessment by investors of these sovereign issuers' ability to pay and the likelihood that they might default. The perception of their ability to pay deteriorated dramatically as private-sector debts were absorbed onto sovereign balance sheets. And so, to some extent,

---

28 In simplest terms, the seller of a CDS, in return for a regular premium that can be likened to an insurance premium, agrees to compensate the buyer of the swap when a predefined credit event, such as a borrower defaulting on a loan or bond, occurs.

the rise in this insurance cost was related to the balance sheets of these sovereign nations in much the same way that a deterioration in the quality of the balance sheet of a corporate borrower would cause its credit spread to widen.

EXAMPLE 16

The Credit Premium for the Royal Bank of Scotland

The global financial crisis had an impact on the prices of all financial assets. Exhibits 15 and 17 show the impact of the crisis on credit spreads derived from indexes, whereas Exhibit 19 demonstrates how the same crisis caused the credit spreads on some sovereign issuers to rise dramatically too. In Exhibit 20, we focus on the impact of the crisis on the CDS premium (a close proxy for the credit spread) on five-year Royal Bank of Scotland senior unsecured debt. The exhibit shows the same increase in the perception of credit risk. The eventual decline in the premium was a consequence of the UK government's nationalization of this systemically important global bank.

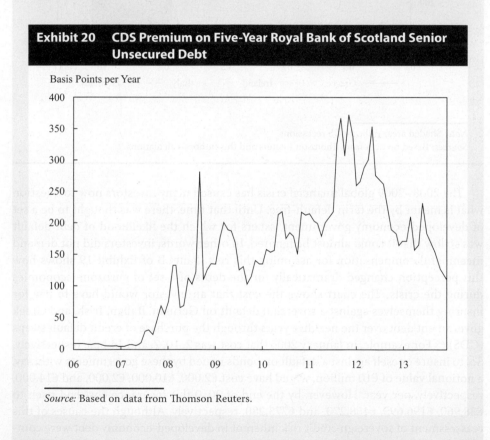

Exhibit 20   CDS Premium on Five-Year Royal Bank of Scotland Senior Unsecured Debt

Source: Based on data from Thomson Reuters.

5.5 Credit Premium Summary

The credit premium ($\gamma_{t,s}^{i}$) is the additional yield required by investors over and above the yield required on comparable default-free debt that investors demand for taking on credit risk. It will tend to rise and fall with the business cycle, mainly because credit risk will tend to rise as an economy turns down and to fall as an economy turns up. However, when credit spreads are generally narrowing, the rate of improvement will tend to be greater for those bonds issued by entities with a relatively weaker ability to pay. At these times too, investors seem to be less discerning among issuers with weak and strong credit credentials. But as the business cycle turns down, and spreads widen, those issuers with a good credit rating tend to outperform those with lower ratings as the spread between low and higher quality issuers widens. This relationship between the economic cycle and defaults means that credit risky bonds (corporate or sovereign) tend to perform poorly in bad economic times, and because of tendency, investors demand a credit premium.

EQUITIES AND THE EQUITY RISK PREMIUM

6

In Section 5, we discussed the credit risk embedded in a bond that has been issued by either a corporation or government, which might not honor its promise to pay the coupons and principal payment in full and on time. Investors can thus not be certain that they will receive the future scheduled cash flows from credit risky bonds. However, when investors purchase bonds that embody credit risk, normally they at least know the proposed schedule of payments and how they are to be determined. But there are other financial instruments in which both the size and timing of the cash flows are uncertain and, indeed, where the cash flows may not materialize at all. The best example of a security that has cash flows with these characteristics is equity because the dividend payment is not promised, can rise and fall over time, and in the event that the issuing corporation becomes bankrupt, can cease altogether.

For equities, we can rewrite the generic pricing Equation 1 as follows:

$$P_t^i = \sum_{s=1}^{\infty} \frac{E_t\left[\widetilde{CF}_{t+s}^i\right]}{\left(1 + l_{t,s} + \theta_{t,s} + \pi_{t,s} + \gamma_{t,s}^i + \kappa_{t,s}^i\right)^s} \tag{15}$$

Notice that it is essentially the same as that for credit risky bonds (Equation 13), but there is no maturity to the cash flows, so investors are essentially buying cash flows (dividends) into perpetuity (∞). In addition, we now have a new term in the discount rate, $\kappa_{t,s}^i$, which is the additional return that investors require for investing in equities, over and above what they require for investing in credit risky bonds $\left(l_{t,s} + \theta_{t,s} + \pi_{t,s} + \gamma_{t,s}^i\right)$

$\kappa_{t,s}^i$ is essentially the equity premium relative to credit risky bonds. This is not the way the equity risk premium is usually expressed. We have expressed it this way for the moment because of the following reasons:

- if a company experiences financial difficulties because the company's debt holders have the senior claim on the company's cash flow, the equity holders will receive the residue, which could be zero; and

- in the event that a company's financial difficulties become so bad that the company is forced into bankruptcy, both bond and equity investors will lose. But depending on the quality of the company, investors in the corporate bond can usually expect to get some of their investment back. The equity investors, however, will normally lose all of their investment. Both debt and equity investors are exposed to risk, but the potential loss is greater for the equity investor.

These are the reasons why investors will require a risk premium, $\kappa_{t,s}^i$, over and above the one that they would require on the corporation's debt, $\gamma_{t,s}^i$. Equation 15 shows that both corporate bond and equity holders face what we might define as corporate risk. It is the combination of this risk that is usually referred to as the equity risk premium. Because the risk associated with equities is normally expressed relative to default-free debt of the same currency, we can rewrite Equation 15 as follows:

$$P_t^i = \sum_{s=1}^{\infty} \frac{E_t\left[\widetilde{CF}_{t+s}^i\right]}{\left(1 + l_{t,s} + \theta_{t,s} + \pi_{t,s} + \lambda_{t,s}^i\right)^s} \qquad (16)$$

where the equity risk premium, $\lambda_{t,s}^i$, is equal to $\gamma_{t,s}^i + \kappa_{t,s}^i$. That is, it is the addition to return required by investors over and above the compensation for risk that they require for holding a default-free government bond of the same currency.[29]

6.1 Equities and Bad Consumption Outcomes

Equity investors will demand an equity risk premium if the consumption hedging properties of equities are poor—that is, if equities tend not to pay off in bad times. Our arguments earlier indicate that the equity risk premium should be positive, and therefore implicitly, that equities are a bad hedge for bad consumption outcomes. However, tying down the exact relationship between equity performance and consumption over time has proved to be very difficult. But we can get some idea of the relationship if we consider a very long history of the real returns produced by equities.

Exhibit 21   Annual Real Equity Returns, 1900–2010

A. United States

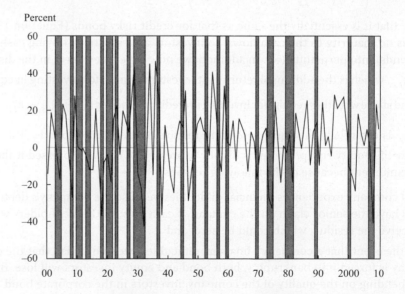

---

29 Technically, a very long-dated, plain-vanilla, coupon-paying, default-free bond.

Exhibit 21   (Continued)

B. United Kingdom

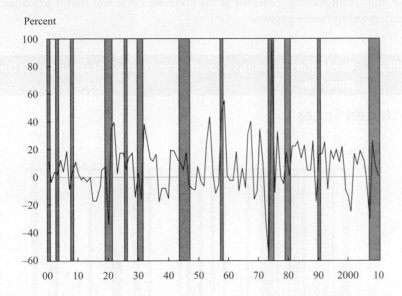

Note: Shaded areas indicate recessions.
Sources: Based on data from Shiller (2000), the Bank of England, and the authors' calculations.

Exhibit 21 shows the annual real (inflation-adjusted) returns generated by both US (Panel A) and UK (Panel B) equities since 1900. Generally speaking, sharp falls in equity prices are associated with recessions—bad times. For example, real UK equity prices more than halved as a recession hit the United Kingdom in 1972, and real US equity prices fell by more than 40% during the Great Depression. More recently, real UK and US equity prices fell by 30% and 40%, respectively, in 2009. Given this evidence, it is difficult to argue that equities are a good hedge for bad consumption outcomes. We would thus expect the equity risk premium to be positive, and given the scale of the declines in prices possible in bad times, we might expect it to be quite large.

Before we consider how large the equity premium should be, we will first focus on the cash flow that equities generate. It is the nature of this cash flow that leads investors to demand an equity risk premium in the first place.

6.2 Earnings Growth and the Economic Cycle

The uncertainty about—and time variation in—future dividends, as represented by the numerator in Equation 15, is a key feature of equity investment. Panels A and B of Exhibit 22 show a long history of US real earnings growth and a shorter history of UK real earnings growth respectively. The exhibit shows that a sharp decline in real earnings nearly always coincides with a recession, which is to be expected; recessions are associated with declines in employment, incomes, output, and subsequently, profitability. US real earnings fell dramatically during the Great Depression, and more recently by nearly 60% in 2009. Conversely, sharp increases in profit growth occur at the end of a period of recession, but in some cases, while recession conditions still persist. Thus, corporate profitability can lead an economy out of recession as well as into it: A negative demand shock can cause demand and corporate profits to shrink. In response, companies lay off workers, reducing their cost base, and thereby adding to the recessionary backdrop. When an upturn in demand occurs, perhaps in response to monetary policy stimulus, demand growth on a lower cost base can lead to a sharp increase in corporate profits, which then leads companies to invest and hire more staff, and so on. Some analysts thus consider corporate profitability to be an important leading indicator of the business cycle and that it provides useful information about future growth.

Exhibit 22	Real Equity Earnings Growth in the United States and the United Kingdom

A. United States

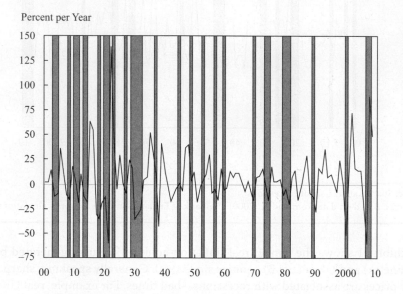

B. United Kingdom

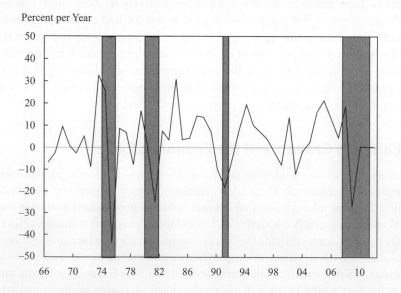

Note: Shaded areas indicate recessions.
Sources: Based on data from Shiller (2000) and the Bank of England.

Equity analysts spend the majority of their time focusing on the numerator in Equation 15—that is, forming views about expected earnings and, therefore, about dividends and free cash flow. Given the close relationship between aggregate earnings, or profits, and the business cycle shown in Exhibit 22, an understanding of the business cycle is crucial for earnings projections, particularly in the short term. However, the business cycle will not affect the corporate profits of every company in the same way. The type of product sold or service provided by the company will have an impact on earnings and consequently on equity performance over the business cycle.

Some companies make products or provide services that are relatively insensitive to general economic conditions. Toothpaste might fall into this category. Because the cost of toothpaste usually only represents a small proportion of the overall household budget, people will generally still want to keep their teeth clean even if the economy is in recession, and because they are unlikely to want to clean their teeth more often simply because the economy is booming, the demand for toothpaste will remain fairly stable over the business cycle. Companies and equity sectors that produce such products are referred to as non-cyclical, or defensive investments. By contrast, some companies, such as airlines, will produce goods or provide services that are extremely sensitive to the business cycle. In difficult economic conditions, consumers are much more likely to postpone or cancel their vacations, or to vacation at home, than to reduce their consumption of toothpaste, and businesses are likely to cut back on airline travel. Generally speaking, an annual family vacation will constitute a large proportion of the household budget and most people do not need a vacation in the same way that they need toothpaste or soap. Businesses may rely on alternatives to expensive travel for meetings, such as video conferencing. By contrast, in good times when real incomes are rising people are more likely to take more vacations, or more expensive ones, and the increase in business activity may necessitate more meetings in new, often distant markets. Economists and investment strategists may view a rise in the earnings of cyclical companies after a period of decline as an indicator of a likely improvement in wider economic growth in the future.

Exhibit 23 shows the annual growth rates (year over year) of real GDP and of the consumption of both durable and non-durable goods for Canada (Panel A) and the United States (Panel B). Both panels of the exhibit show how sensitive durable goods consumption is to the economic cycle. We can expect then that the profits of companies that produce durable as opposed to non-durable goods to be commensurately more volatile too.

Exhibit 23   Year-Over-Year Growth Rate of GDP and the Consumption of Durable and Non-Durable Goods

A. Canada

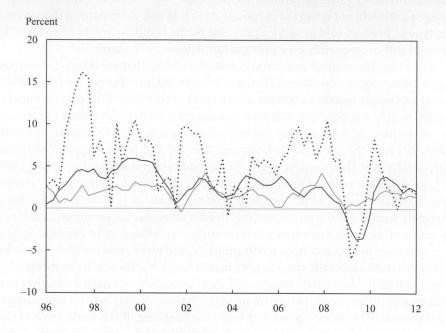

B. United States

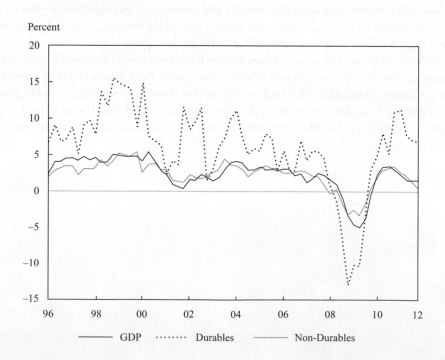

Source: Based on data from Thomson Reuters.

Stock market participants often classify stocks as being cyclical and non-cyclical. Exhibit 24 shows the real earnings growth of the non-cyclical and cyclical goods sectors of both the United States (Panel A) and the United Kingdom (Panel B). The cyclical sectors in this case are represented by companies that produce discretionary consumer goods, whereas the non-cyclical index is represented by an index that includes companies that produce staple (or less discretionary) consumer goods. Panel A shows the clearest evidence of the greater sensitivity to business conditions of the cyclical sector. Real earnings growth rises and falls dramatically over the business cycle. By contrast, although the real earnings of non-cyclical companies vary across the business cycle, the peaks and troughs are less extreme. The time variation in UK real earnings over the business cycle is also evident from the exhibit. However, the difference between the real earnings growth of the UK's cyclical and non-cyclical sectors is less clear, although the cyclical sector tended to experience more significant troughs in real earnings growth over this period.

Exhibit 24   The Real Earnings Growth of Discretionary and Staple Consumer Goods Companies

A. United States

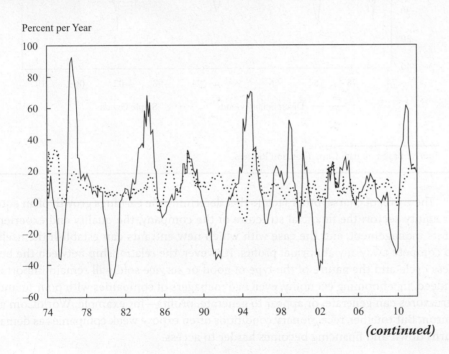

(continued)

Exhibit 24   (Continued)

B. United Kingdom

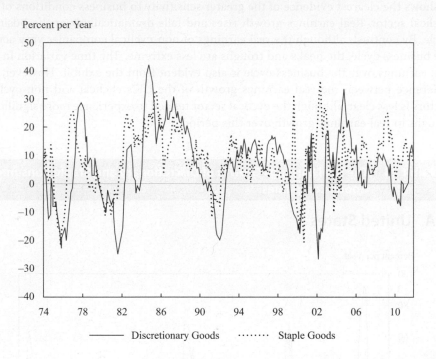

Percent per Year

┌─ Discretionary Goods   ········ Staple Goods

Source: Based on data from Thomson Reuters.

There are, of course, other factors that determine the earnings growth of an equity or equity sector: the financial structure of the company, the quality and experience of its management, and the ease with which new entrants can establish themselves to compete away any abnormal profits. However, the relationship between the business cycle and the nature of the type of good or service sold will remain important. Indeed, in a booming economy, even bad managers of companies with poor financial structures can generate, or appear to generate, profits—for example, WorldCom and Enron. But tougher, recessionary conditions often expose weak companies as demand turns down and financing becomes harder to access.

6.3 How Big is the Equity Risk Premium?

The real earnings of companies are clearly affected by the underlying economy. This relationship is positive in that when the economy turns down, so normally do corporate profits. But it is in these times that investors need their investments to offset these bad times. Because of the pro-cyclicality of economies and corporate profits (in aggregate), equities are not a good hedge against bad consumption outcomes, which, in turn, means that investors will require a risk premium. But how big should this premium ($\lambda_{t,s}^{i}$) be?

It is impossible to quantify the equity risk premium *ex ante*. But we can at least look at its *ex post* value using very long runs of data. Exhibit 25 shows the real annual return on equities and government bonds over the period of 1900–2010 for a range of developed economy equity markets. Over this very long period, equities in each country have outperformed government bonds. The bars representing the *ex post* equity risk premium range from 2.1% per year in Switzerland to 6.0% per year in Australia.

US equities, which comprise the world's largest equity market, have outperformed US Treasuries by 4.5% per year on average over the past 110 years, whereas the global equity market has produced an equity risk premium of 3.9% per year. Of course, there is no guarantee that a premium earned in the past will be earned in the future, but this long span of data show that the *ex ante* equity risk premium for developed-economy equity markets could be somewhere between 3% and 5% per year.

Exhibit 25	*Ex-Post* Real Returns on Equities, Bonds, and Equity Risk Premiums

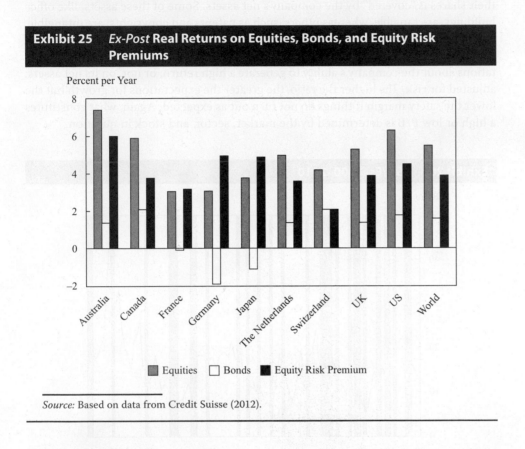

Source: Based on data from Credit Suisse (2012).

6.4 Valuation Multiples

Analysis of company earnings prospects is usually the central focus of equity analysts and strategists. To help compare equities within and among sectors, they will generally monitor valuation multiples, such as the price-to-earnings ratio (P/E) or the price-to-book ratio (P/B). P/E is calculated as the ratio of the current share price to the earnings per share (EPS) generated by the company. This ratio tells investors the price they are paying for the shares as a multiple of the company's earnings per share. Investors use this ratio to compare the valuations attributed to individual equities, sectors, and markets. For instance, if a stock is trading with a low P/E relative to the rest of the market, it implies that investors are not willing to pay a high price for a dollar's worth of the company's earnings. The reason may be because the market believes that the prospect of strong earnings growth in the future is low. Alternatively, a share trading with a very high P/E relative to the rest of the market indicates that investors are willing to pay a higher price for each dollar's worth of the company's earnings. They may be willing to do so because they expect this company's earnings to grow rapidly in the future. When the EPS used to estimate the ratio refers to last year's earnings, the P/E is referred to as being a historical or a trailing P/E. However, when the EPS is based on an estimate of future earnings, it is referred to as the leading or forward P/E. If a company's EPS is expected to grow, then its historic P/E will be greater than its forward P/E. However, what constitutes a high or low P/E very much depends on the market, sector, or company in question and, in particular, on the economic backdrop. US P/Es between 1900 and 2010 are shown in Exhibit 26.

Another popular valuation multiple is the price to book ratio (P/B), which measures the ratio of the company's share price to its net assets or its assets minus liabilities attributed to each share. The P/B tells investors the extent to which the value of their shares is "covered" by the company's net assets. Some of these assets, like office buildings, are tangible, whereas others, such as patents and copyrights, are intangible. Furthermore, some of the assets are actually on the balance sheet and hence part of book value, whereas others are not. It also indicates the strength of investors' expectations about the company's ability to generate a high return, or not, on its net assets, adjusted for risk. The higher the ratio, the greater the expectations for growth but the lower the safety margin if things do not turn out as expected. Again, what constitutes a high or low P/B is determined by the market, sector, and stock in question.

Exhibit 26   US P/Es, 1900–2010

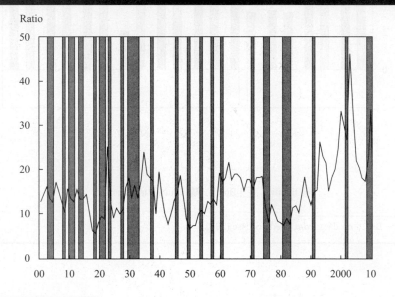

Note: Shaded areas indicate recessions.
Sources: Based on data from Shiller (2000) and Thomson Reuters.

One of the problems for equity strategists is to ascertain whether the P/E (or P/B) is high or low. The average trailing US P/E between 1900 and 1990 was 13.5, indicating that investors were willing to pay $13.5 for a dollar's worth of the previous year's earnings; by the late 1990s and early 2000s they were willing to pay $45. The expansion in the US equity market's P/E during the 1990s was a global phenomenon. Equity strategists justified the rise in the price of earnings with many ad hoc explanations—for example, the end of the cold war, better macro-policy that would ensure that major recessions were a thing of the past, and the internet revolution, to name but a few. However, with regard to the basic pricing relationship, shown in Equation 15, the high P/E could be the result of a number of factors, including

a   an increase in expectation of future real earnings growth $\left(E_t\left[\widetilde{CF}^i_{t+s} \right] \right)$;

b   falling real interest rates $(l_{t,s})$, possibly associated with falling volatility in real GDP growth;

c   a fall in inflation expectations $(\theta_{t,s})$;

d a decline in uncertainty about future inflation ($\pi_{t,s}$); or

e a fall in the equity risk premium ($\lambda_{t,s}^i$).

Other things being equal, any one of these changes, or all of them combined, could justify higher equity prices (P) relative to current earnings (E) and thus higher equilibrium P/Es. There were some investors, however, who were not convinced that such high P/Es relative to historical levels were justifiable, particularly on the grounds of much higher future earnings growth. The US Federal Reserve Board Chairman, Alan Greenspan, alarmed by the rise in P/Es, described the valuation of equity markets in 1996 as essentially the result of "irrational exuberance" on the part of equity investors.

Robert Shiller has proposed an alternative valuation multiple—the real cyclically adjusted P/E (CAPE). The CAPE is derived in the same way as the P/E, but the 'P' represents the real (or inflation-adjusted) price of the equity market and the 'E' is a 10-year moving average of the market's real (or inflation-adjusted) earnings. Deflating the real equity price by a moving average of real earnings irons out the short-term volatility in this indicator over time. Exhibit 27 shows this ratio for the United States from 1900 to 2011. The very high price that equity investors were willing to pay for equities in 1929 and in 1999 and, to a lesser extent in 1965, is still apparent. It is worth noting that the average real return on US equities in the 10 years following the peaks in the CAPE in 1929, 1965, and 1999 were −0.3% per year, −5.4% per year, and −4.1% per year, respectively. Conversely, the average real return over the 10-year period after the two lowest values of the CAPE in 1921 and 1980 were 12.3% per year and 7.3% per year, respectively.

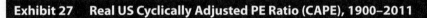

Exhibit 27   Real US Cyclically Adjusted PE Ratio (CAPE), 1900–2011

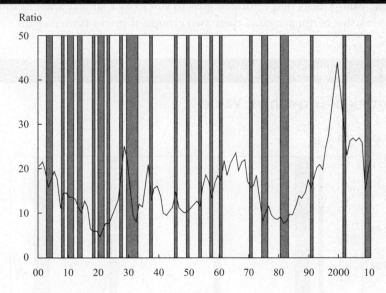

Note: Shaded areas indicate recessions.
Source: Based on data from Shiller (2000).

6.5 Investment Strategy

Various equity investment styles have emerged over the years as a result of the belief that particular groups of stocks sharing one of a number of common characteristics can outperform the broader equity market over the course of the business cycle. Some investors focus on growth stocks while others believe that value stocks will perform best over the longer term.

Growth stocks are so called when investors believe that the prospects for strong earnings growth are good. They tend to trade with a high P/E and a very low dividend yield; in fact, they often have very low (or no) earnings. These companies also often sell products in immature markets where the prospects for higher sales in the future are commensurately high. By contrast, value stocks tend to operate in more mature markets where there is a lower perceived likelihood of substantial earnings growth. However, the trade-off is that value stocks tend to produce relatively high and stable earnings streams for their investors. Value stocks typically trade with a low P/E and a high dividend yield relative to the rest of the market.

In Panel A of Exhibit 28, we present the relative performance of US growth versus US value stocks since the 1970s. There are quite clear periods of outperformance of one style over the other. Close inspection of the chart suggests that value tends to outperform growth investing in the aftermath of a recession, and that growth stocks tend to outperform value stocks in times when the economy is expanding. The most impressive period of outperformance of one style over the other was between 1994 and 2000 when growth investing outperformed value investing by a cumulative 85%. This time was the high-tech bubble period when dot-com and technology stocks were in vogue. Being new, many of these stocks had little or no earnings, but were bought in the hope that their earnings would grow rapidly in the future. With the bursting of the bubble, value stocks outperformed growth stocks by a similar amount until 2005 when the relative performance of these two groups of stocks turned again.

Exhibit 28   US Investment Styles

A. Index of Growth vs. Value

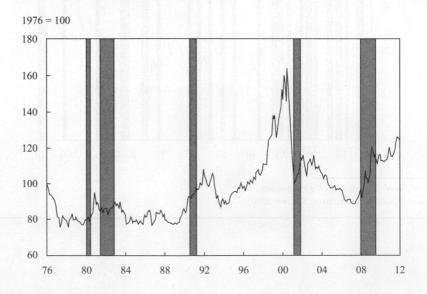

Exhibit 28 (Continued)

B. Index of Small vs. Large

1973 = 100

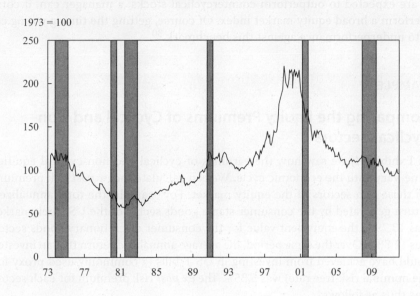

Note: Shaded areas indicate recessions.
Sources: Based on data from Thomson Reuters and the authors' calculations.

Another important focus for equity investors is company size. Some investors focus on small-cap, mid-cap or large-cap stocks. Some also combine this focus with growth and value too—for example, focusing on small-cap growth stocks whereas others might focus on large-cap value stocks. Generally speaking, one might expect small stocks to underperform large stocks in bad times. Almost by definition, small stock companies will tend to have less diversified businesses and have more difficulty in raising financing, particularly during recessions, and will thus be less able to weather an economic storm. If this is true, then other things being equal, one might expect investors to demand a higher equity premium on small, relative to large, stocks.

To understand the differences in prices, consider an increase in uncertainty relative to some other asset. For example, small-company stocks fluctuate more than large-company stocks. For a given level of wealth, the large-company stock would have a risk premium based on decreasing marginal utility of wealth for the investor. The small-company stock would lead to bigger increases and decreases in wealth relative to the investor's initial wealth. Thus, the average expected utility of the investor is lower for the smaller stock, so that smaller stocks require a bigger risk premium.

Panel B of Exhibit 28 shows the relative performance of US small-cap versus large-cap stocks. Even though over the entire sample period of 1973 to 2011, small- and large-cap stocks produced the same performance, there are clear periods when one company size outperforms the other. Between 1982 and 2000, the cumulative outperformance of small stocks over large stocks was almost 400%. But many of these small stocks would also have been high-tech or internet stocks. Since the collapse of the high-tech bubble, however, large companies have outperformed small companies substantially. It should be clear by now that the business cycle can affect the relative performance of different types of equity. Of course, on those occasions when the broad equity market is falling sharply, all equity types fall, and when it is rising sharply, all types will tend to rise in value. But many equity fund managers are benchmarked against a broad equity market index; to outperform this index they need to take over- and underweight positions relative to this benchmark. By rotating into growth stocks when they are expected to outperform value stocks, or small-cap stocks when they are expected to outperform large-cap stocks, or into cyclical stocks when they are expected to outperform countercyclical stocks, a manager can, if correct, outperform a broad equity market index. Of course, getting the timing wrong could lead to underperformance against this benchmark.[30]

EXAMPLE 17

Comparing the Equity Premiums of Cyclical and Non-Cyclical Sectors

In Exhibit 24, we saw how the earnings of cyclical and non-cyclical equities time-vary with the economic cycle. We can calculate the *ex post* risk premium on these two sectors of the equity market. For example, the total annualized return generated by the consumer staple goods sector of the US stock market was 13.79%; the equivalent value for the consumer discretionary goods sector was 11.88%. Over the same period, the average annualized return that an investor could have achieved from investing in US T-bills (a commonly used proxy for the nominal risk-free rate) was 5.35%. The *ex post* risk premium for each sector was thus as follows:

Ex post risk premium on consumer staple goods = 13.79% – 5.35% = 8.44%

and

Ex post risk premium on consumer discretionary goods = 11.88% – 5.35% = 6.53%

To get an idea of the potential value in being able to understand the position of the economy in the business cycle and the impact of this position over time on each of these two stock market sectors, consider Exhibit 29. This exhibit shows the outperformance (the higher *ex post* risk premium) since 1973 of the staples over the discretionary goods sectors.

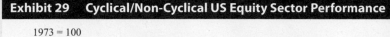

Exhibit 29   Cyclical/Non-Cyclical US Equity Sector Performance

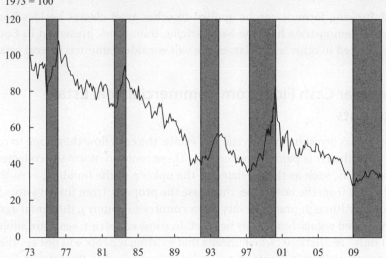

Note: Shaded areas indicate periods where cyclical (discretionary) stocks outperform non-cyclical stocks (staples).
Source: Based on data from Thomson Reuters and the authors' calculations.

An investor that held stocks from the consumer staples sector during those periods in the exhibit that are unshaded but who switched into holding consumer discretionary stocks in those periods that are shaded would have generated a total return of 18.82%, or an *ex post* risk premium of 13.47% (18.82% – 5.35%), over this sample period. Of course, in practice it is very difficult to get the timings of these switches right, but hopefully this example does at least show the potential value for investors of understanding the relationship between the economy and sub-sectors of financial markets, in this case sub-sectors of the US equity market.

EXAMPLE 18

Valuation and the Business Cycle

1 Holding all else constant, what does the observed relationship of equity market price-to-earnings ratios with the business cycle imply about forward-looking equity risk premiums?

2 Characterize the value of equities in hedging bad consumption outcomes.

Solution to 1:

P/Es tend to rise during periods of economic expansion. Holding all else constant, a relatively high P/E valuation level should be associated with a lower return premium to bearing equity risk going forward.

Solution to 2:

Equities tend not to be effective hedges against bad consumption outcomes and, in effect, tend to be bad hedges against recessions.

7   COMMERCIAL REAL ESTATE

The basic pricing formula can be applied to other asset classes besides bonds and equities. To demonstrate how the basic pricing framework presented in Equation 1 can be extended to other asset classes, we will consider commercial real estate.

7.1 Regular Cash Flow from Commercial Real Estate Investments

When investors invest in commercial real estate, the cash flow they hope to receive is derived from the rents paid by the tenants. These rents are normally collected net of ownership costs, such as those related to the upkeep of the building, according to a fixed schedule from the businesses that lease the property from the investors who act as landlords. Although practices vary from country to country, the rental agreement will be reviewed regularly and may be reset. In some countries, rents are subjected to "upward only" restrictions, which means that existing tenants will not see their rents fall, only potentially rise. Rents may also be indexed so that they rise in line with a pre-specified index of (usually) consumer prices.

To a large extent then, the rental income can be viewed as being analogous to the coupon income derived from a bond. Because a well-diversified portfolio of commercial property could be expected to generate a stream of rental income for investors, they might view such a portfolio as being similar to a well-diversified portfolio of bonds. The credit quality of a commercial property portfolio will be determined by the credit quality of the underlying tenants, in much the same way that the credit quality of a bond portfolio will be determined by the credit ratings of the bond issuers of the constituent bonds. Generally speaking, the lower the credit quality of the tenants, the less likely they will be to pay their rent on time or at all.

7.1.1 *The Equity Component of an Investment in Commercial Real Estate*

Investors in commercial real estate will receive regular cash flows derived from the rents paid by tenants, but there is another important element to property investment that is less bond-like. When a bond matures, the investor generally receives the face value of the bond along with the final coupon. But when the lease on a property expires, the investors (acting as landlords) will take back possession of the property and will have to decide whether to re-rent it to another tenant, to sell it to another investor, or to redevelop it for a future sale. The determining factor is likely to be the value of the property at the time. Its value may have risen dramatically over time, or it might now be worth much less. The value of the property will arguably be determined by two key factors: the property's location and the state of the underlying economy. If, during the time of the lease, the area in which the property is situated has become more popular, then the property might be sold at a profit, or it might be worth redeveloping the property. Equally, if the lease expires when general economic activity is high, and thus there is strong demand for property, then the sale or redevelopment option might be worth pursuing. But if, when the lease expires, the location is deemed to be less desirable or the economy is weak, then redevelopment may not be an option, future rents may have to be lower on the property, and investors may come to the view that the property should be sold, even at a loss.

The potential for profit or loss, and the uncertainty related to this profit from redevelopment, adds an equity-like dimension to investment in commercial real estate. In other words, it adds either a positive increment to cash flow or a negative one. To this extent, some investors like to think about the cash flow derived from a commercial real estate portfolio as being part bond, part equity.

7.1.2 *Illiquidity and Investment in Commercial Real Estate*

There is a third aspect to investing in commercial real estate that is also crucial: its illiquidity. Anyone who has sold a home will know that it usually takes a great deal of time and effort to put the property up for sale, to find a buyer, and finally (if a buyer can be found), to finalize the deal. For similar reasons, it can take months, and sometimes years, to exit from a commercial property investment, and the high transactions costs often discourage investors further from liquidating holdings. By contrast, it is relatively easy in normal market conditions to transform a holding in developed-economy government bonds, investment-grade corporate debt, or publicly traded equities into cash. Generally speaking, most of the asset classes that we have considered so far in this reading are liquid relative to an investment in commercial property.

7.2 The Pricing Formula for Commercial Real Estate

Commercial real estate is a "special" asset class, it can be viewed as being part equity, part bond and it is usually very illiquid. However, with some minor adaptions of the generic pricing formula in Equation 1, we can still capture all of the salient features of the price of commercial real estate as follows:

$$P_t^i = \sum_{s=1}^{N} \frac{E_t\left[\widetilde{CF}_{t+s}^i\right]}{\left(1 + l_{t,s} + \theta_{t,s} + \pi_{t,s} + \gamma_{t,s}^i + \kappa_{t,s}^i + \phi_{t,s}^i\right)^s} \tag{17}$$

The pricing formula shown in Equation 17 acknowledges that the expected cash flow from an investment in commercial real estate, $E_t\left[\widetilde{CF}_{t+s}^i\right]$, will be uncertain because tenants may default on the rental agreement. The quality of this rental income will depend on the quality of the tenants, just as the reliability or quality of the coupons from a corporate bond will be dependent on the credit standing of the corporate bond issuer. Furthermore, the property's value in the future cannot be known with certainty.

But what should the discount rate look like? To understand the construction of the discount rate in Equation 17, consider the following tenants and associated rental/leasing agreements:

1 a developed economy government tenant that agrees to pay rental income that is indexed to inflation, $(1 + l_{t,s})$;

2 a developed economy government tenant that agrees to pay fixed nominal rental income, $(1 + l_{t,s} + \theta_{t,s} + \pi_{t,s})$;

3 a corporate tenant that agrees to pay a fixed nominal rental income, $(1 + l_{t,s} + \theta_{t,s} + \pi_{t,s} + \gamma_{t,s}^i)$.

In each case the expressions in parentheses represent the composition of the discount rate that would be applied to the cash flows of bonds issued by these entities: (1) is analogous to the purchase of a real default-free government bond; (2) is analogous to the purchase of a nominal default-free government bond; and (3) is analogous to the purchase of a credit risky nominal bond. In each case, though, we need to add a risk premium to take into account the uncertainty relating to the value of the property at the end of the lease. This premium is analogous to the equity risk premium, $\kappa_{t,s}^i$.

Finally, we have to take into account the illiquidity of a commercial property investment. Because investors cannot easily convert their property investments into cash, there exists the possibility that they will not be able to liquidate their investment in bad economic times. In other words, other things being equal, illiquidity acts to reduce an asset class's usefulness as a hedge against bad consumption outcomes. Because of this, investors will demand a liquidity risk premium, which we have expressed as $\phi^i_{t,s}$ in Equation 17.

The discount rates that investors would apply to an investment in commercial property in each of the three instances previously listed are, therefore,

1 $1 + l_{t,s} + \kappa^i_{t,s} + \phi^i_{t,s}$;

2 $1 + l_{t,s} + \theta_{t,s} + \pi^i_{t,s} + \kappa^i_{t,s} + \phi^i_{t,s}$; and

3 $1 + l_{t,s} + \theta_{t,s} + \pi^i_{t,s} + \gamma^i_{t,s} + \kappa^i_{t,s} + \phi^i_{t,s}$

The relative sizes of the components listed will vary depending on the length of the lease, the quality of the tenant, and the location of the property.

EXAMPLE 19

A Real Estate Investment Decision

An analyst estimates that the real risk-free rate is 1.25%, average inflation over the next year will be 2.5%, and the premium required by investors for inflation uncertainty is 0.50%. He also observes that the yield on a 10-year senior unsecured bond issued by Supermarket plc is 5.75%. From these figures, he deduces that the credit spread on Supermarket plc's 10-year debt is 1.50%.

The same analyst is asked to review for a client (an investor) the opportunity to buy a site currently occupied by Supermarket plc. Once the investor purchases the property, Supermarket plc will lease it back and pay $500,000 annual rent in arrears[31] to the investor. Like the Supermarket bond, the lease on the property has 10 full years to expire. At the end of this period, the property and land will revert to the investor, and the analyst estimates that the resale value of the property after 10 years will be $10 million, net of all transactions costs.

The investor tells the analyst that it normally expects to receive a risk premium of 0.50% on any cash flow from a commercial property investment to compensate it for the uncertainty of the final value of the property and the uncertainty relating to the receipt of rental income, plus a liquidity premium of 1.0% on these cash flows. The investor's required return on the property is thus 7.25% (= 5.75% + 0.5% + 1.0%). If the purchase price of this piece of commercial property is $8.2 million, should the analyst recommend the purchase to the client?

Discount Rate: 7.25%		
Payment Due (years)	Cash Flow	Present Value
1	$500,000	$466,200
2	500,000	434,686
3	500,000	405,301
4	500,000	377,903
5	500,000	352,357
6	500,000	328,538
7	500,000	306,330
8	500,000	285,622

---

31 "Rent in arrears" in this case means that the first annual rental payment is due in 12 months, covering the first year's tenancy, and the second in 24 months, and so on.

	Discount Rate: 7.25%	
Payment Due (years)	**Cash Flow**	**Present Value**
9	500,000	266,314
10	10,500,000	5,214,543
Implied property value		$8,437,796

The cash flows in the table, along with their associated present values, demonstrate that at a discount rate of 7.25%, the property would be priced at $8,437,796. Any asking price above this value would imply a return of less than the investor's hurdle rate of 7.25%, whereas any price below this price implies a return above this hurdle rate. On the basis of this information then, the analyst should recommend that the client goes ahead with the investment.

7.3 Commercial Real Estate and the Business Cycle

The nature of the cash flows from commercial property and the complex structure of the discount rate will all be influenced by the evolution of the underlying economy. Panel A of Exhibit 30 shows the annual growth rate of UK commercial property income over a 30-year period. It is remarkably stable over this period, averaging 6.5% per year; in other words, UK commercial property rental income has grown by approximately 6.5% annually in nominal terms (or 2.5% in real terms) over the last 30 years. The stability of this income stream, across a number of business cycles, suggests that investors might calculate its present value using a very low discount rate. But as well as showing the annual change in rent from a portfolio of UK commercial property, Panel A also shows the annual percentage change in the capital value of the UK's commercial property market. Whereas rental income appears to have been relatively stable (in nominal terms) and almost immune to the business cycle, commercial property capital values are much more sensitive to the economic cycle. Between 1990 and 1992, as the UK economy experienced a deep recession, UK commercial property prices fell by a cumulative 30%. Over the course of the UK's most recent recession, the capital value of the UK's property market fell by 26%. In Panel B of the exhibit, we present the capital value changes in a number of markets across the world between 2008 and 2009. It is clear that the global recession had a significant impact on commercial property prices. For example, in Ireland, one of the developed economies arguably worst hit by the crisis, commercial property prices fell by 55.5%.

Exhibit 30   Commercial Property

A. UK Commercial Property Returns

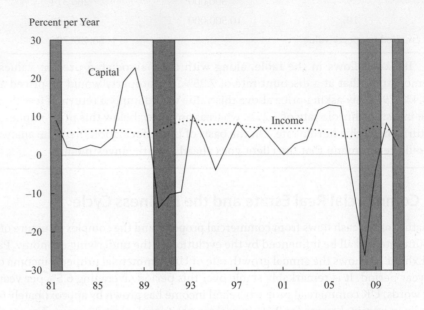

B. UK Commercial Property Value Changes, 2008–2009

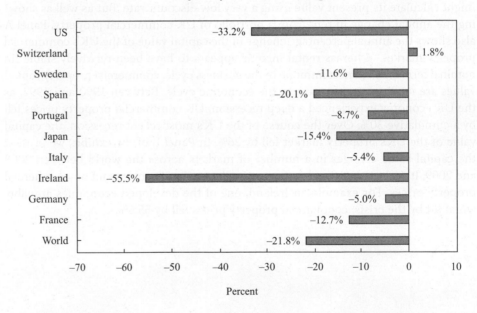

Note: Shaded areas in Panel A indicate recessions.
Source: Based on data from Investment Property Databank (www.ipd.com).

Taken together, the two panels in Exhibit 30 show that even though nominal rental income might be relatively stable, the capital values of commercial property are highly sensitive to the economic environment. A recession will generally cause these values to fall whereas more robust economic conditions will tend to cause commercial property prices to rise, often dramatically. For example, the combination of a recovering and then strong global economy between 2003 and 2006 caused world commercial property prices to rise by nearly 20%. Over the same period they rose by 41% in the United Kingdom and by a staggering 51% in Ireland.[32]

The pro-cyclical nature of commercial property prices means that investors will generally demand a relatively high risk premium in return for investing in this asset class. The reason is because commercial property does not appear to be a very good hedge against bad economic outcomes. In fact, the sharp falls in capital values in recessionary periods resemble the sort of falls that investors in equity experience, although these occurrences are more frequent with equity investment. Arguably then, the sort of risk premium that investors will demand from their commercial property investments will be closer to that demanded on equities than on default-free government bonds.

Finally, although it is difficult to derive a value for the property risk premium, it is likely to vary over time with economic conditions and to be relatively highly and positively correlated with the risk premiums on corporate bonds and equities.

EXAMPLE 20

Valuation and the Business Cycle

Describe how real estate valuation is distinguished from valuation of public equities.

Solution to 1:

Real estate does not trade in public markets.[33] Compared with the valuation of public equities, the valuation of real estate should reflect a discount for relative lack of liquidity.

SUMMARY

In this reading, we have sought to explain the fundamental connection between the prices of financial assets and the underlying economy. The connection should be strong because ultimately all financial assets represent a claim on the real economy. Because all financial assets offer a means of deferring consumption, to make the connection tangible we have explored the relationship between these asset prices and the consumption and savings decisions of economic agents.

- At any point in time, the market value of any financial security is simply the sum of discounted values of the cash flows that the security is expected to produce. The timing and magnitude of these expected cash flows will thus be an integral part of the security's market value. So also will the discount rate applied to these expected cash flows, which is the sum of a real default-free interest rate, expected inflation, and possibly, several risk premiums. Each of these elements will be influenced by the business cycle. It is through these components that the real economy exerts its influences on the market value of financial instruments.

---

32 Data are from Investment Property Databank.
33 Although real estate investment trusts (REITs) do trade in public markets.

- The average level of real short-term interest rates is positively related to the trend rate of growth of the underlying economy and also to the volatility of economic growth in the economy. Other things being equal, these relationships means that we should expect to find that the average level of real short-term interest rates is higher in an economy with high and volatile growth, and lower in an economy with lower, more stable growth.

- On average, over time, according to the Taylor rule, a central bank's policy rate should comprise the sum of an economy's trend growth plus inflation expectations, which might, in turn, be anchored to an explicit inflation target. This policy rate level is referred to as the neutral rate. Other things being equal, when inflation is above (below) the targeted level, the policy rate should be above (below) the neutral rate; and when the output gap is positive (negative), the policy rate should also be above (below) the neutral rate. The policy rate can thus vary over time with inflation expectations and the economy's output gap.

- Short-term nominal rates will be closely related to a central bank's policy rate of interest and will comprise the real interest rate that is required to balance the requirements of savers and investors plus investors' expectations of inflation over the relevant borrowing or lending period. Short-term nominal interest rates will be positively related to short-term real interest rates and to inflation expectations.

- If bond investors were risk neutral, then the term structure of interest rates would be determined by short-term interest rate expectations. But bond investors are risk averse, which means that they will normally demand a risk premium for investing in even default-free government bonds. This risk premium will generally rise with the maturity of these bonds because longer-dated government bonds tend to be less negatively correlated with consumption, and therefore, represent a less useful consumption hedge for investors. Overall, the shape of the curve will be determined by a combination of short-term interest rates and inflation expectations as well as risk premiums. In turn, these factors will be influenced by the business cycle and policymakers.

- The yield differential between default-free conventional government bonds and index-linked equivalents will be driven by inflation expectations and a risk premium. The risk premium will be largely influenced by investors' uncertainty about future inflation.

- The difference between the yield on a corporate bond and that on a government bond with the same currency denomination and maturity is referred to as the measured credit spread. It is conceptually akin (but not equal) to the risk premium demanded by investors in compensation for the additional credit risk that they bear compared with that embodied in the default-free government bond. It tends to rise in times of economic weakness, as the probability of default rises, and tends to narrow in times of robust economic growth, when defaults are less common.

- The uncertainty about and time variation in future equity cash flows (dividends) is a distinct feature of equity investment as opposed to corporate bond investment. This feature also explains why we would expect the equity premium to be larger than the credit premium. In times of economic weakness or stress, the uncertainty about future dividends will tend to be higher and we should thus expect the equity risk premium to rise in such an economic environment.

- Given the uncertain nature of the cash flows generated by equities, investors will demand an equity risk premium because the consumption hedging properties of equities are poor. In other words, equities tend not to pay off in bad times. Because in the event of company failure an equity holder will lose all of his or her investment whereas an investor in the company's bonds may recover a significant portion of their investment, it would be reasonable to assume that a risk averse investor would demand a higher premium on an equity holding than on a corporate bond holding. The two premiums will tend to be positively correlated over time, and will tend to be influenced by the business cycle in similar ways.

- Some companies make products or provide services that are relatively insensitive to general economic conditions. By contrast, other companies will produce goods or provide services that are extremely sensitive to the business cycle. The earnings of the former will tend to be less volatile than those of the latter. As such, when corporate bond and equity investors are expecting economic conditions to deteriorate, they may sell the equities and bonds issued by economically sensitive companies in favor of those financial securities issued by companies whose earnings are less sensitive to economic conditions.

- Small stocks tend to underperform large stocks in difficult economic conditions. The reason is that, almost by definition, small-stock companies tend to have less-diversified earnings streams and have more difficulty in raising financing, particularly during recessions. They will thus be less able to weather economic storms. If this is true, then other things being equal, one might expect investors to demand a higher equity premium on small stocks relative to large stocks. One might also expect this premium to rise in recessions and to fall when the underlying economy is strong.

- The P/E tends to rise during periods of economic expansion and to fall during recessions. A "high" P/E could be the result of a number of factors, including the following: falling real interest rates, a fall in the equity risk premium, an increase in the expectation of future real earnings growth, an expectation of lower operating and/or financial risk, or a combination of all of these factors. All of these components will be influenced by the business cycle.

- The market value of an investment in commercial property can be derived in much the same way as the market value of an investment in equity. The cash flows come in the form of rent, which can be enhanced with additional redevelopment values as leases on properties expire. These cash flows are uncertain, and the uncertainty surrounding them will tend to rise when the economy turns down. We might thus expect the risk premium demanded on commercial property investments to rise in these times.

- The pro-cyclical nature of commercial property prices means that investors will generally demand a relatively high risk premium in return for investing in this asset class. The reason is because commercial property is not a very good hedge against bad economic outcomes. In addition, the illiquid nature of property investment means that investors may also demand a liquidity premium for investing in this asset class.

REFERENCES

Altug, Sumru, and Pamela Labadie. 2008. *Asset Pricing for Dynamic Economies.* Cambridge, UK: Cambridge University Press.

Cochrane, John H. 2005. *Asset Pricing.* Princeton, NJ: Princeton University Press.

Elton, Edward J., Martin J. Gruber, Stephen J. Brown, and William N. Goetzmann. 2014. *Modern Portfolio Theory and Investment Analysis*, 9th Ed. New York, NY: John Wiley & Sons.

Fama, Eugene F., and Kenneth R. French. 1993. "Common Risk Factors in the Returns on Stocks and Bonds." *Journal of Financial Economics*, vol. 33, no. 1 (June): 3–56.

Litterman, R., and J.A. Scheinkman. 1991. "Common Factors Affecting Bond Returns." *Journal of Fixed Income*, vol. 1, no. 1 (June): 54–61.

Shiller, Robert J. 2000. *Irrational Exuberance.* Princeton, NJ: Princeton University Press.

Steeley, James M. 1990. "Modelling the Dynamics of the Term Structure of Interest Rates." *Economic and Social Review*, vol. 21, no. 4 (July): 337–361.

Suisse, Credit. 2012. *Credit Suisse Global Investment Returns Sourcebook 2012.* Zurich: Suisse AG.

Taylor, John B. 1993. "Discretion versus Policy Rules in Practice." *Carnegie-Rochester Conference Series on Public Policy*, vol. 39: 195–214.

PRACTICE PROBLEMS

1 All else equal, which of the following would *most likely* explain the fall in price of a particular company's shares?

   A The expected inflation rate falls.

   B The company's future cash flows are expected to increase.

   C The yield to maturity on real default-free investments rises.

2 The prices of one-period, real default-free government bonds are likely to be *most* sensitive to changes in:

   A investors' inflation expectations.

   B the expected volatility of economic growth.

   C the covariance between investors' inter-temporal rates of substitution and the expected future prices of the bonds.

3 The covariance between a risk-averse investor's inter-temporal rate of substitution and the expected future price of a risky asset is typically:

   A negative.

   B zero.

   C positive.

4 Default-free real interest rates tend to be relatively high in countries with high expected economic growth because investors:

   A increase current borrowing.

   B have high inter-temporal rates of substitution.

   C have high uncertainty about levels of future consumption.

5 Positive output gaps are usually associated with:

   A deflation.

   B high unemployment.

   C economic growth beyond sustainable capacity.

6 All else equal, an investor expects future inflation to increase, but the uncertainty of future inflation to fall. For such an investor the break-even inflation rate:

   A is uncertain.

   B is expected to fall.

   C is expected to rise.

7 The difference between the yield on a zero-coupon, default-free nominal bond and the yield on a zero-coupon, default-free real bond of the same maturity reflects:

   A investors' expectations about future inflation only.

   B a premium for the uncertainty of future inflation only.

   C both, investors' expectations about future inflation and a premium for the uncertainty of future inflation.

8 One interpretation of an upward sloping yield curve is that the returns to short-dated bonds are:

   A uncorrelated with bad times.

B more positively correlated with bad times than are returns to long-dated bonds.

C more negatively correlated with bad times than are returns to long-dated bonds.

9 An analyst, who measures yield as a combination of interest rates and premiums, observes an upward-sloping, default-free government bond nominal yield curve. Which of the following statements is correct?

A Interest rates must be expected to rise in the future.

B Bond risk premiums must be expected to rise in the future.

C Expectations relating to the future direction of interest rates are indeterminate.

10 During a recession, the slope of the yield curve for default-free government bonds is *most likely* to:

A flatten.

B steepen.

C become inverted.

11 A corporate bond has a remaining maturity of 1 year, has a face value of EUR100, and is currently priced at EUR90.90. The real risk-free rate is 3.25%. Inflation is expected to be 2.0% next year, and the premium required by investors for inflation uncertainty is 0.25%.

The implied credit risk premium embedded in the bond's price is *best* described as:

A equal to $(100/90.90) - 1 = 10\%$.

B 10% reduced by the real risk-free rate and expected inflation.

C 10% reduced by the real risk-free rate, expected inflation, and the premium for inflation uncertainty.

12 A decrease in the prices of AAA-rated corporate bonds during a recession would *most likely* be the result of:

A expectations of higher inflation.

B increases in credit risk premiums.

C increases in short-term, default-free interest rates.

13 During an economic period where spreads between corporate and government bonds are narrowing, and spreads between higher and lower rated corporate bond categories are also narrowing, it can be expected that:

A government bonds will outperform corporate bonds.

B lower rated corporate bonds will outperform higher rated corporate bonds.

C higher rated corporate bonds will outperform lower rated corporate bonds.

14 The sensitivity of a corporate bond's spread to changes in the business cycle is *most likely* to be:

A uncorrelated with the level of cyclicality in the company's business.

B positively correlated with the level of cyclicality in the company's business.

C negatively correlated with the level of cyclicality of the company's business.

15 The category of bonds whose spreads can be expected to widen the *most* during an economic downturn are bonds from the:

A cyclical sector with low credit ratings.

B cyclical sector with high credit ratings.

C non-cyclical sector with low credit ratings.

16 When assessing investment opportunities in equities, investors should:

   A assign higher equity risk premiums to non-cyclical companies, relative to cyclical companies.

   B forecast lower volatility in the growth rate of earnings for cyclical companies, relative to non-cyclical companies.

   C forecast higher growth rates in earnings for cyclical companies coming out of a recession, relative to non-cyclical companies.

17 Risk-averse investors demanding a large equity risk premium are *most likely* expecting their future consumption outcomes and equity returns to be:

   A uncorrelated.

   B positively correlated.

   C negatively correlated.

18 Which of the following financial assets is likely to offer the *most* effective hedge against bad consumption outcomes?

   A Equities.

   B Short-dated, default-free government bonds.

   C Long-dated, default-free government bonds.

19 Other things equal, equilibrium price-to-earnings (P/E) ratios will *most likely* decrease if:

   A real interest rates decrease.

   B inflation is expected to increase.

   C there is less uncertainty about future inflation.

20 Which of the following statements relating to commercial real estate is correct?

   A Rental income from commercial real estate is generally unstable across business cycles.

   B Commercial real estate investments generally offer a good hedge against bad consumption outcomes.

   C The key difference in the discount rates applied to the cash flows of equity investments and commercial real estate investments relate to liquidity.

21 With regard to the credit risk of the sovereign debt issued by country governments, which of the following is statements is correct? The credit risk premium on such debt is:

   A zero because governments can print money to settle their debt.

   B negligibly small because no country has defaulted on sovereign debt.

   C a non-zero and positive quantity which varies depending on a country's creditworthiness.

SOLUTIONS

1 C is correct. According to the fundamental pricing equation, the market value of an asset is affected by economic factors that affect the asset's expected future cash flows, default-free interest rates, expected inflation rates or the asset's risk premium. From Equation 1 in Section 2.1, expected cash flows are in the numerator, while expected inflation and the real risk-free rate are in the denominator. Consequently, a rise in the real risk-free rate (the yield to maturity on a default-free instrument) will lead to a fall in the price of a risky asset like stock by increasing the rate at which its cash flows are discounted.

2 B is correct. Only changes in default-free real interest rates will affect the price of real, default-free bonds. The average level of default-free real interest rates is positively related to the volatility of economic growth in the economy; thus, changes in the expected volatility of economic growth would likely lead to changes in real default-free real interest rates, which in turn would affect the prices of real, default-free government bonds.

3 A is correct. For risk-averse investors, when the expected future price of the investment is high (low), the marginal utility of future consumption relative to that of current consumption is low (high). Hence, the covariance of the inter-temporal rate of substitution with asset price is expected to be negative for risk-averse investors.

4 A is correct. The average level of default-free real interest rates is positively related to the expected rate of growth of the underlying economy and also to the volatility of economic growth in the economy. During periods of high expected economic growth, investors are less worried about the future and their consumption abilities in the future—that is, their inter-temporal rate of substitution is low, so they borrow more today and save less. Other things being equal, this means that the average level of default-free real interest rates (the reciprocal of the rate of substitution, see Equation 4) should be higher in an economy with high growth, and lower in an economy with lower, more stable growth.

5 C is correct. An economy operating with a positive output gap—that is, where the level of actual GDP exceeds potential GDP—is producing beyond its sustainable capacity. Positive output gaps are usually associated with high and/or rising inflation, while high levels of unemployment usually accompany negative output gaps.

6 A is correct. The break-even inflation rate is the difference between the yield on a zero-coupon, default-free nominal bond and on a zero-coupon default-free, real bond of the same maturity. The rate incorporates changing expectations about inflation and changing perceptions about the uncertainty of the future inflation environment. Consequently, if inflation is expected to rise, while the uncertainty about future inflation falls, (in Equation 10, $\theta_{t,s}$ rises, but $\pi_{t,s}$ falls) it is unclear in which direction break-even inflation rates will move.

7 C is correct. The difference between the yield on a zero-coupon, default-free nominal bond and the yield on a zero-coupon, default-free real bond of the same maturity is known as the break-even inflation rate. This break-even inflation rate will incorporate the inflation expectations of investors over the investment horizon of the two bonds, plus a risk premium to compensate investors for uncertainty about future inflation. Break-even inflation rates are not simply

the markets' best estimate of future inflation over the relevant investment horizon, as break-even inflation rates also include a risk premium to compensate investors for their uncertainty about future inflation.

8 C is correct. One interpretation of an upward sloping yield curve is that returns to short-dated bonds are more negatively correlated with bad times than are returns to long-dated bonds. This interpretation is based on the notion that investors are willing to pay a premium and accept a lower return for short-dated bonds if they believe that long-dated bonds are not a good hedge against economic "bad times".

9 C is correct. An upward sloping yield curve may be caused by a combination of expected rate increases and positive bond risk premiums. It may also be a combination of expectations that interest rates will be unchanged in the future coupled with positive bond risk premiums. Lastly, an upward sloping yield curve may actually be a reflection of expected rate cuts that are more than offset by the existence of positive bond risk premiums. So, expectations relating to the future direction of interest rates are indeterminate.

10 B is correct. During a recession, short rates are often lower because central banks tend to lower their policy rate in these times because the output gap is likely to be negative. However, the impact of such monetary policy on longerterm rates will not be as strong, so long rates may not fall by as much as short rates. The central bank will usually be expected to bring short term rates back to normal as the recession recedes and the risk free rates will increase as economic growth recovers. Thus, the slope of the yield curve will typically steepen during a recession.

11 C is correct. The implied credit risk premium embedded in the bond's price is the yield (10%) less the default risk-free nominal interest rate, which includes a premium for inflation uncertainty. See Example 15. The credit risk premium can be calculated as 4.51% in this case:

$$\gamma_{t,s}^i = \frac{100}{90.90} - (1 + 0.0325 + 0.02 + 0.0025)$$

$$\gamma_{t,s}^i = 4.51\%$$

12 B is correct. During recessions, the risk premium that investors demand on financial assets, particularly those that are not default-free, such as corporate bonds, may rise because investors in general may be less willing and able to take on heightened default risk during such periods. Specifically, the credit risk premium demanded by investors tends to rise in times of economic weakness, when the probability of a corporate default and bankruptcy is highest.

13 B is correct. When spreads are narrowing, investors seem to be less discerning between issues with weak versus strong credit, and the rate of improvement will tend to be greater for those bonds issued by entities with a relatively weaker ability to pay. Thus, during times when corporate bond spreads are narrowing relative to government bonds, and the spreads between higher and lower rated bond categories also narrowing, corporate bonds will generally outperform government bonds, and lower rated corporate bonds will tend to outperform higher rated corporate bonds.

14 B is correct. The sensitivity of a corporate bond's spread to changes in the business cycle and the level of cyclicality tend to be positively correlated. The greater the level of cyclicality, the greater the sensitivity of the bond's spread to changes in the business cycle.

15 A is correct. During an economic downturn, the spreads of corporate bonds can be expected to widen, as the risk premium that investors demand on risky financial assets will increase. When spreads widen, the spreads on bonds issued by corporations with a low credit rating and that are part of the cyclical sector will tend to widen most.

16 C is correct. During recessions, cyclical companies are likely to experience sharp declines in earnings, more so than non-cyclical companies. In contrast, while coming out of a recession, cyclical companies are likely to generate higher earnings growth relative to non-cyclical companies.

17 B is correct. If investors demand high equity risk premiums, they are likely expecting their future consumption and equity returns to be positively correlated. The positive correlation indicates that equities will exhibit poor hedging properties, as equity returns will be high (e.g., pay off) during "good times" and will be low (e.g., not pay off) during "bad times". In other words, the covariance between risk-averse investors' inter-temporal rates of substitution and the expected future prices of equities is highly negative, resulting in a positive and large equity risk premium. This is the case because, in good times, when equity returns are high, the marginal value of consumption is low. Similarly, in bad times, when equity returns are low, the marginal value of consumption is high. Holding all else constant, the larger the magnitude of the negative covariance term, the larger the risk premium.

18 B is correct. The relative certainty about the real payoff from short-dated, default-free government bonds, and therefore the relative certainty about the amount of consumption that the investor will be able to undertake with the payoff, indicates that an investment in such bonds would be a good hedge against bad consumption outcomes.

19 B is correct. Other things being equal, an increase in inflation expectations would result in lower equity prices relative to current earnings. This would result in lower equilibrium P/E ratios.

20 C is correct. To arrive at an appropriate discount rate to be used to discount the cash flows from a commercial real estate investment, a liquidity premium is added to the discount rate applicable to equity investments. The added liquidity premium provides additional compensation for the risk that the real estate investment may be very illiquid in bad economic times.

21 C is correct. Credit premiums have been an important component of the expected return on bonds issued by countries (sovereign debt). The credit premium varies from country to country depending on how creditworthy investors consider it to be. The fact that countries have both printed money to pay back debt and/or defaulted on it gives rise to non-zero credit risk premium.

READING

51

Analysis of Active Portfolio Management

by Roger G. Clarke, PhD, Harindra de Silva, PhD, CFA, and
Steven Thorley, PhD, CFA

Roger G. Clarke, PhD, is at Analytic Investors (USA). Harindra de Silva, PhD, CFA, is at Analytic Investors (USA). Steven Thorley, PhD, CFA, is at the Marriott School, BYU (USA).

LEARNING OUTCOMES

Mastery	The candidate should be able to:
☐	a. describe how value added by active management is measured;
☐	b. calculate and interpret the information ratio (*ex post* and *ex ante*) and contrast it to the Sharpe ratio;
☐	c. state and interpret the fundamental law of active portfolio management including its component terms—transfer coefficient, information coefficient, breadth, and active risk (aggressiveness);
☐	d. explain how the information ratio may be useful in investment manager selection and choosing the level of active portfolio risk;
☐	e. compare active management strategies (including market timing and security selection) and evaluate strategy changes in terms of the fundamental law of active management;
☐	f. describe the practical strengths and limitations of the fundamental law of active management.

INTRODUCTION

1

The Markowitz (1952) framework of what was originally called modern portfolio theory (MPT) has now become the prominent paradigm for communicating and applying principles of risk and return in portfolio management. Much of the mathematics and terminology of mean–variance portfolio theory was subsequently combined with the notion of informational efficiency by Sharpe (1964) and other financial economists to develop equilibrium models, such as the traditional capital asset pricing model. Separately, the tools of MPT were applied by Treynor and Black (1973) to guide investors in their selection of securities when prices differ from their equilibrium values.

The application of portfolio theory to active management was further developed by Grinold (1989) in "The Fundamental Law of Active Management" and by Black and Litterman (1992).

This reading summarizes the principles of active portfolio management using the terminology and mathematics of the fundamental law introduced by Grinold (1989) and further developed by Clarke, de Silva, and Thorley (2002). Active management theory deals with how an investor should construct a portfolio given an assumed competitive advantage or skill in predicting returns. Thus, active management relies on the assumption that financial markets are not perfectly efficient. In addition, although investors might ultimately care about total risk and return, when asset management is delegated to professional investors in institutional settings (e.g., pension funds) the appropriate perspective is risk and return relative to a benchmark portfolio. In addition to the principal–agent problem in delegated asset management, the availability of passively managed portfolios requires a focus on value added above and beyond the alternative of a low-cost index fund.

This reading assumes an understanding of basic portfolio theory, including the mathematics of expected values, variances, and correlation coefficients, as well as some familiarity with the related disciplines of mean–variance optimization and multi-factor risk models. Section 2 of this reading introduces the mathematics of value added through active portfolio management, including the concepts of active weights, relative returns, and performance attribution systems. Section 3 compares the well-known Sharpe ratio for measuring the total risk-adjusted value added with the information ratio for measuring relative risk-adjusted value added. Section 3 also makes a distinction between *ex ante*, or expected, risk and return versus *ex post*, or realized, risk and return and explains that the information ratio is the best criterion for evaluating active investors. Section 4 introduces the fundamental law that describes how relative skill, breadth of application, active management aggressiveness, and the constraints in portfolio construction combine to affect value added. Section 5 provides examples of active portfolio management strategies in both the equity and fixed-income markets. Section 6 describes some of the practical limitations of the fundamental law, and Section 7 summarizes the concepts and principles discussed in this reading.

2   ACTIVE MANAGEMENT AND VALUE ADDED

The objective of active management is to add value in the investment process by doing better than a benchmark portfolio. Value added is a relative performance comparison to investing in the benchmark portfolio, often called passive investing. If the investor outperforms the benchmark portfolio, value added is positive. If the investor underperforms the benchmark portfolio, value added is negative. Specifically, in the latter case, the investor would have been better off during the measurement period by simply holding the benchmark portfolio, particularly net of fees and expenses. Examples of indices that are used as benchmark portfolios include the MSCI All Country World Index and the Barclays Global Aggregate Bond Index, which represent the performance of global equities and global bonds, respectively.

2.1 Choice of Benchmark

A benchmark or passive portfolio should have a number of qualities to serve as a relevant comparison for active management:

■ The benchmark is representative of the assets from which the investor will select.

- Positions in the benchmark portfolio can actually be replicated at low cost.
- Benchmark weights are verifiable *ex ante*, and return data are timely *ex post*.

An available security market index is often used as the benchmark portfolio. The most common market indices weight the individual assets by their market capitalization. Capitalization weighting has played a prominent role in the development of capital market theory because such indices are generally self-rebalancing and can be simultaneously held by many investors. Float-adjusted market capitalization-weighted indices represent an incremental improvement over non-float-adjusted indices by accounting for the percentage of a security or asset that is not privately held and thus available to the general investing public. One important consequence of using a float-adjusted capitalization-weighted market index as the benchmark is that when all relevant assets are included in the market, the value added from active management becomes a zero-sum game with respect to the market. Because the market portfolio represents the average performance across all investors that own securities before costs, active investors as a group cannot outperform the market (i.e., active management is a zero-sum game). For benchmarks that have a narrower definition than the total market, active management would not generally be a zero-sum game with respect to the narrower benchmark because investors might invest in assets outside the benchmark.

The return on the benchmark portfolio, R_B, is based on the returns to the individual securities and the weights of each security in the portfolio:

$$R_B = \sum_{i=1}^{N} w_{B,i} R_i \tag{1}$$

where R_i is the return on security i, $w_{B,i}$ is the benchmark weight of security i, and N is the number of securities. Similarly, the return on an actively managed portfolio, R_P, is a function of the weights of the securities i held in the portfolio, $w_{P,i}$, and the returns to the individual securities:

$$R_P = \sum_{i=1}^{N} w_{P,i} R_i \tag{2}$$

Of course, there might be securities in the benchmark that are not part of the actively managed portfolio and that would have a weight of zero by definition or simply be left out of the calculation in Equation 2. Similarly, an investor could include securities in the active portfolio that are not in the benchmark and would have a benchmark weight of zero in Equation 1.[1]

2.2 Measuring Value Added

The value added or "active return" of an actively managed portfolio is typically calculated as the simple difference between the return on that portfolio and the return on the benchmark portfolio,

$$R_A = R_P - R_B$$

and can thus be either positive or negative. A risk-adjusted calculation of value added, which we will refer to as the managed portfolio's alpha, incorporates some estimate of the managed portfolio's risk relative to the benchmark, often captured by the portfolio's

---

[1] For simplicity, the same notation, N, is used in the summation in the expression for the managed portfolio return and the benchmark return, although there may be fewer or more securities in the managed portfolio compared with the benchmark.

beta, $\alpha_P = R_P - \beta_P R_B$. Unfortunately, the term *alpha* in practice is also often used to refer to active return, which implicitly assumes that the beta of the managed portfolio relative to the benchmark is 1.

Equations 1 and 2 can be combined to illustrate the important principle that value added is ultimately driven by the differences in managed portfolio weights and benchmark weights: $\Delta w_i = w_{P,i} - w_{B,i}$. These values are called the active weights of the managed portfolio, and the symbol Δ (Greek letter delta) is used to indicate the difference from the benchmark weights. Combining Equations 1 and 2 and employing this definition for active weights yields the conceptually important result that value added is the sum product of the active weights and asset returns:

$$R_A = \sum_{i=1}^{N} \Delta w_i R_i$$

Given that the sum of the active weights is zero, we can also write the value added as the sum product of active weights and active security returns:

$$R_A = \sum_{i=1}^{N} \Delta w_i R_{Ai} \qquad (3)$$

where $R_{Ai} = R_i - R_B$. Equation 3 indicates that positive value added is generated when securities that have returns greater than the benchmark are overweighted and securities that have returns less than the benchmark are underweighted.

Whereas many applications of value added focus on individual securities as the assets, we first illustrate the concept with a simple numerical example of a composite portfolio that has just two assets—a stock portfolio and a bond portfolio. Suppose the benchmark is a 60/40 weighted composite portfolio of stocks/bonds. The investor believes that over the next year stocks will outperform bonds, so the investor holds a portfolio that is weighted 70% stocks and 30% bonds. The managed portfolio is said to be *overweight* stocks by 10 percentage points and *underweight* bonds by 10 percentage points (an active weight of −10 percentage points on bonds). Assume that *ex post* (i.e., "after the fact"), the return on the stock market turned out to be 14.0% and the return on the bond market turned out to be just 2.0%. As a result, the return on the managed portfolio is 0.70(14.0) + 0.30(2.0) = 10.4% and the return on the benchmark is 0.60(14.0) + 0.40(2.0) = 9.2%.

From these final numbers, one could directly calculate the value added as 10.4 − 9.2 = 1.2%. But using Equation 3, a more informative calculation of value added showing the contributions from each segment is $R_A = 0.10(14.0 - 9.2) - 0.10(2.0 - 9.2)$ = 0.5 + 0.7 = 1.2%. This breakout suggests that a 0.5% return relative to the benchmark was generated by being overweight stocks and a 0.7% return was generated by being underweight bonds, for a total of 1.2%. Of course, the actual returns might have been different, with the stock market return being lower than the bond market return, resulting in negative value added in the managed portfolio. For example, if the stock market had a return of −14.0% instead of +14.0%, then the value added from this single overweight/underweight decision would have been $R_A = 0.10(-14.0) - 0.10(2.0) = -1.6\%$.

EXAMPLE 1

Value Added and Country Equity Markets

Consider the MSCI EAFE Index as the benchmark for an actively managed portfolio that includes allocations to individual countries, as given in the exhibit below. The portfolio (both benchmark and managed) weights are for the beginning of 2013. The portfolio manager actively manages country allocations, but does not engage in security selection.

Country	Benchmark Weight	Portfolio Weight	2013 Return
United Kingdom	22%	16%	20.7%
Japan	21%	14%	27.3%
France	10%	8%	27.7%
Germany	9%	24%	32.4%
Other Countries	38%	38%	18.8%

Source: Data from MSCI.

1   Which countries have the largest overweight and largest underweight in the managed portfolio compared with the benchmark portfolio? What are the active weights for these two countries?

2   Using active weights and total returns, what was the value added of the managed portfolio over the benchmark portfolio in the calendar year 2013?

Solution to 1:

Germany has the largest overweight at $24 - 9 = +15\%$, and Japan has the largest underweight at $14 - 21 = -7\%$.

Solution to 2:

The value added is $-0.06(20.7) - 0.07(27.3) - 0.02(27.7) + 0.15(32.4) = 1.2\%$. Note that the "Other Countries" active weight is zero, so this asset does not contribute anything to the portfolio's active return for any realized asset return. The value added can also be calculated using relative returns in Equation 3 with the same net result.

2.3 Decomposition of Value Added

In contrast to the previous simple example, performance attribution systems often attempt to decompose the value added into *multiple* sources. The most common decomposition is between value added due to asset allocation and value added due to security selection. Consider a composite portfolio of stocks and bonds where the asset allocation weights differ from a composite benchmark *and* each asset class is actively managed by selecting individual securities. The total value added is the difference between the actual portfolio return and the benchmark return:

$$R_A = \sum_{j=1}^{M} w_{P,j} R_{P,j} - \sum_{j=1}^{M} w_{B,j} R_{B,j}$$

The first summation has both portfolio weights and the returns on actively managed portfolios, designated by the "P" subscript. The second summation has both benchmark weights and benchmark returns, designated by the "B" subscript. The subscript $j = 1$ to M counts the number of asset classes, leaving the notation subscript $i = 1$ to N for use elsewhere to count the securities within each asset class.

We can rewrite the total value added as the sum of the active asset allocation decisions and the weighted sum of the value added from security selection, $R_{A,j} = R_{P,j} - R_{B,j}$, within each asset class:

$$R_A = \sum_{j=1}^{M} \Delta w_j R_{B,j} + \sum_{j=1}^{M} w_{P,j} R_{A,j} \tag{4}$$

although this formulation arbitrarily assigns an interactive effect to security selection.[2] The performance attribution system in Equation 4 may be easier to conceptualize with just two asset classes, stocks and bonds (in other words, with $M = 2$). Using *stocks* and *bonds* as the subscripts, Equation 4 becomes:

$$R_A = \left(\Delta w_{stocks} R_{B,stocks} + \Delta w_{bonds} R_{B,bonds} \right) + \left(w_{P,stocks} R_{A,stocks} + w_{P,bonds} R_{A,bonds} \right)$$

The first (parenthetical) term above is the value added from the asset allocation decision. The second term is the value added from security selection within the stock and bond portfolios. The active weights in the first term refer to differences from the policy portfolio. For example, the long-term policy portfolio might be 60/40 stocks versus bonds, and the investor deviates from this policy portfolio from year to year based on beliefs about the returns to each asset class.

To give a numerical example, consider the fund returns for the calendar year 2013 in the following table.

Fund	Fund Return (%)	Benchmark Return (%)	Value Added (%)
Fidelity Magellan	35.3	32.3	3.0
PIMCO Total Return	−1.9	−2.0	0.1
Portfolio Return	23.4	18.6	4.8

Specifically, the Fidelity Magellan mutual fund had a return of 35.3%, compared with a 32.3% return for its benchmark, the S&P 500 Index. In the same year, the PIMCO Total Return Fund had a return of −1.9%, compared with a −2.0% return for its benchmark, the Barclays US Aggregate Index. Consider an investor who invested in both actively managed funds, with 68% of the total portfolio in Fidelity and 32% in PIMCO. Assume that the investor's policy portfolio (strategic asset allocation) specifies weights of 60% for equities and 40% for bonds.

- As shown in the table, Fidelity Magellan added value of $R_A = R_P - R_B = 35.3\% - 32.3\% = 3.0\%$ and PIMCO Total Return Fund Fidelity Magellan added value of $R_A = R_P - R_B = -1.9\% - (-2.0\%) = 0.1\%$. These value added numbers represent the funds' skill in security selection.

---

2 As first discussed by Brinson, Hood, and Beebower (1986), the interaction effect between asset allocation and security selection can be separated out by a third term in the formula, $R_A = \sum_{j=1}^{M} \Delta w_j R_{B,j} + \sum_{j=1}^{M} w_{B,j} R_{A,j} + \sum_{j=1}^{M} \Delta w_j R_{A,j}$, leaving the second term as a security selection effect that excludes the interaction effect.

- Using the actual weights of 68% and 32% in the Fidelity and PIMCO funds, the combined value added from security selection was 0.68(3.0%) + 0.32(0.1%) = 2.1%.

- The active asset allocation weights in 2013 were 68% – 60% = +8% for equities and –8% for bonds, so the value added by the active asset allocation decision was 0.08(32.3%) – 0.08(–2.0%) = 2.7%. The total value added by the investor's active asset allocation decision *and* by the mutual funds through security selection was 2.1% + 2.7% = 4.8%. To confirm this total value added, note that the return on the investor's portfolio was 0.68(35.3%) + 0.32(–1.9%) = 23.4% and the return on the policy portfolio was 0.60(32.3%) + 0.40(–2.0%) = 18.6%, for a difference of 23.4% – 18.6 = 4.8%.

Performance attribution systems can be expanded to include several asset classes—for example, stocks, bonds, real estate, and cash (in other words, with $M = 4$ in Equation 4). For a given asset class, the performance attribution system might also include value added from the selection of industries or sectors relative to the benchmark. For example, an equity portfolio might measure value added from over- and underweighting different industry sectors, as well as individual stock selection within those sectors, and a fixed-income portfolio might decompose value added from the mix of sovereign government bonds versus corporate bonds, as well as individual bond selection.

In summary, deviations from portfolio benchmark weights drive the value added by active portfolio management. If every asset in the managed portfolio is held at its benchmark weight, there would be no value added relative to the benchmark. The total value added can be decomposed into various sources that capture the contribution from different decisions, such as asset allocation and security selection.

COMPARING RISK AND RETURN

3

The risk–return trade-off of a portfolio can be represented in either *absolute* or *relative* terms. The Sharpe ratio provides an absolute expected (*ex ante*) or realized (*ex post*) reward-to-risk measure. As we have noted, however, value added is a relative return comparison. The information ratio provides a benchmark relative expected (*ex ante*) or realized (*ex post*) reward-to-risk measure.

3.1 The Sharpe Ratio

The Sharpe ratio is used to compare the portfolio return in excess of a riskless rate with the volatility of the portfolio return. The ratio provides a measure of how much the investor is receiving in excess of a riskless rate for assuming the risk of the portfolio. The Sharpe ratio, SR_P, is calculated for any portfolio, either actively managed or a benchmark, using the formula

$$SR_P = \frac{R_P - R_F}{STD(R_P)}$$

(5)

where R_P is the portfolio return, R_F is the risk-free rate, and $STD(R_P)$ is the standard deviation of the portfolio return. In this context, the standard deviation of the portfolio return is often called either volatility or total risk. The Sharpe ratio can be used as an *ex ante* measure of *expected* return and risk, in which case the general formula in Equation 5 would have the expected portfolio return, $E(R_P)$, minus the risk-free rate in the numerator and a forecast of volatility in the denominator. As subjective forecasts, the expected return and standard deviation of return will likely vary among different investors.

The Sharpe ratio can also be used to measure the *ex post* or *realized* performance of a portfolio over some time period. In that case, when applied to multiple time periods, the numerator in Equation 5 is the difference between the average realized portfolio return, $\overline{R_P}$, and the average risk-free rate, $\overline{R_F}$, and the denominator in Equation 5 is the sample standard deviation. The convention for Sharpe ratios is to annualize both the portfolio average return and the portfolio risk. For example, if the past return data are measured monthly, the average monthly return can be multiplied by 12 and the monthly return volatility can be multiplied by the square root of 12. The logic for multiplying the standard deviation by the *square root* of 12 is that variance (i.e., standard deviation squared), under certain assumptions, increases proportionally with time.[3]

Exhibit 1	Benchmark Sharpe Ratios for 1994–2013 (based on a risk-free rate of 2.8%)				
	MSCI World	S&P 500	Russell 2000	MSCI EAFE	Barclays US Aggregate
Average annual return	8.5%	10.0%	13.4%	7.3%	5.7%
Return standard dev.	15.3%	15.2%	21.1%	16.7%	3.7%
Sharpe ratio	0.37	0.47	0.50	0.27	0.78

Exhibit 1 reports the annualized monthly historical return data (not compounded) in US dollars for several different benchmark portfolios for the 20-year period from 1994 to 2013. Long-term *ex post* Sharpe ratios for equity benchmarks have typically fallen within a range of 0.20–0.50, although over a shorter horizon they will vary over a wider range and can be either negative or positive. The Sharpe ratio for the Barclays US Aggregate fixed-income benchmark in Exhibit 1 is particularly high because of the secular decline in interest rates over this 20-year period. Exhibit 2 reports historical return data and Sharpe ratios from 1994 to 2013 for some well-known actively managed mutual funds over the same period.[4] The Sharpe ratios in both exhibits are based on a risk-free rate of 2.8%, the average annualized US Treasury bill return during this 20-year period. The comparison of Sharpe ratios between funds intentionally uses data from the same measurement period. In other words, it would not be as useful to compare the Sharpe ratio of one fund over one five-year period with that of another fund over a different five-year period.

---

3 Although this scaling convention is common in practice, multiplying monthly returns by a factor of 12 for averages and the square root of 12 for standard deviations ignores the multiplicative (i.e., compound) nature of returns over time (for further details, see Kaplan 2012/2013). Simple multiplication factors (e.g., 250 and the square root of 250 for annualizing trading-day returns) are only technically correct if the underlying returns are independent and continuously compounded or logarithmic. Similarly, annualized compound returns for the two values in the numerator of the Sharpe ratio (i.e., the portfolio return and the riskless rate) may be used instead of the annualized difference of arithmetic returns. The various methodologies produce slightly different results but should not be a serious problem as long as comparisons between different portfolios use the same approach.

4 The selection of funds for illustration in this reading was made without any intended implication, positive or negative, concerning their performance relative to other possible choices.

Exhibit 2	Active Fund Sharpe Ratios for 1994–2013 (based on a risk-free rate of 2.8%)				
	Fidelity Magellan	**Vanguard Windsor**	**Templeton World**	**T. Rowe Price Small Cap**	**JPMorgan Bond**
Average annual return	8.6%	10.4%	9.9%	12.5%	5.9%
Return standard dev.	17.9%	17.3%	16.3%	17.4%	3.8%
Sharpe ratio	0.32	0.44	0.44	0.56	0.82

An important property is that the Sharpe ratio is unaffected by the addition of cash or leverage in a portfolio. Consider a combined portfolio with a weight of w_P on the actively managed portfolio and a weight of $(1 - w_P)$ on risk-free cash. The return on the combined portfolio is $R_C = w_P R_P + (1 - w_P)R_F$, and the volatility of the combined portfolio is just $\text{STD}(R_C) = w_P \text{STD}(R_P)$ because the $(1 - w_P)R_F$ portion is risk free. Applying these two relationships in Equation 5 gives the Sharpe ratio for the combined portfolio as

$$\text{SR}_C = \frac{R_C - R_F}{\text{STD}(R_C)} = \frac{w_P(R_P - R_F)}{w_P \text{STD}(R_P)} = \text{SR}_P$$

which is the same as the Sharpe ratio of the actively managed portfolio. Note that the weight in the combined portfolio, w_P, could be greater than 1, so $(1 - w_P)$ could be negative, indicating that leverage created by *borrowing* risk-free cash and investing in risky assets also does not affect the portfolio's Sharpe ratio.

The proposition that, independent of preferences, investors should form portfolios using two funds—one of which is the risk-free asset and the other the risky asset portfolio with the highest Sharpe ratio—is known as two-fund separation. On the one hand, if the expected volatility of the risky asset portfolio is higher than the investor prefers, the volatility can be reduced by holding more cash and less of the risky portfolio. On the other hand, if the expected volatility of the risky portfolio is lower than the investor desires, the volatility and expected return can be increased by leverage. For example, suppose an investor believes the performance of the Vanguard Windsor mutual fund shown in Exhibit 2 will repeat going forward but the investor desires a volatility of 10%. The investor might invest 58% of assets in the Vanguard Windsor fund and 42% in cash to reduce overall portfolio risk. The expected return of the combined portfolio is 0.58(10.4%) + 0.42(2.8%) = 7.2%. The volatility of the combined portfolio is 0.58(17.3%) = 10.0%. The Sharpe ratio of the combined portfolio is (7.2% − 2.8%)/10.0% = 0.44, the same as the 0.44 Sharpe ratio of the Vanguard Windsor fund shown in Exhibit 2.

EXAMPLE 2

Adjusting Risk and Return Using the Sharpe Ratio

Consider an investor choosing between two risky portfolios: a large-cap stock portfolio and a small-cap stock portfolio. Although forecasts about the future are usually subjectively determined, suppose for simplicity that the investor expects that the future statistics will be equal to the historical S&P 500 and Russell 2000 values and that the current risk-free rate is 2.8%. The forecasted

0.50 Sharpe ratio of the small-cap portfolio is higher than the 0.47 ratio of the large-cap portfolio, but suppose the investor does not want the high 21.1% volatility associated with the small-cap stocks.

	Large Cap	Small Cap
Expected return	10.0%	13.4%
Expected volatility	15.2%	21.1%
Sharpe ratio	0.47	0.50

1 How much would an investor need to hold in cash (in percentage terms) to reduce the risk of a portfolio invested in the small-cap portfolio and cash to the same risk level as that of the large-cap portfolio?

2 Based on your answer to 1, calculate the Sharpe ratio of the small-cap plus cash portfolio.

3 Compare the expected return of the small-cap plus cash portfolio with the expected return of the large-cap portfolio.

Solution to 1:

We want to reduce the 21.1% volatility to 15.2% by adding cash. The weight of small-cap stocks in the combined portfolio must therefore be 15.2/21.1 = 72%, leaving a 28% weight in risk-free cash. With that amount of cash, the volatility of the combined portfolio will be 0.72(21.1%) = 15.2%, the same as the large-cap portfolio.

Solution to 2:

The Sharpe ratio of the combined portfolio is unaffected by the amount in cash, so it remains 0.50.

Solution to 3:

The expected return of the combined portfolio is 0.72(13.4%) + 0.28(2.8%) = 10.4%, 40 basis points (bps) higher than the 10.0% expected return on the large-cap portfolio but with the same risk as the large-cap portfolio. To reconfirm, the Sharpe ratio of the combined portfolio is (10.4% − 2.8%)/15.2% = 0.50, the same as the original 0.50 value.

3.2 The Information Ratio

The simplest definition of the information ratio compares the active return from a portfolio relative to a benchmark with the volatility of the active return, which we call "active risk" or "benchmark tracking risk." The information ratio can be thought of as a way to measure the consistency of active return, as most investors would prefer a more consistently generated value added (low active risk) rather than a lumpy active return pattern. Like the more formal distinction between active portfolio return and alpha, active risk has a more exact beta-adjusted counterpart, which Grinold and Kahn (1999) called "residual risk." This reading will present the information ratio based on the implicit assumption that the beta of the managed portfolio relative to the benchmark is exactly 1.0, although in practice that assumption can be relaxed.[5]

---

5 See Fischer and Wermers (2013) for a recent presentation of the information ratio that does not assume beta is 1. The alternative definition is also known as the Treynor–Black appraisal ratio.

The information ratio tells the investor how much active return has been earned, or is expected to be earned, for incurring the level of active risk. Active return, R_A, is the difference between the managed portfolio return, R_P, and the benchmark portfolio return, R_B. The information ratio of an actively managed portfolio, IR, is calculated by dividing the active return by active risk:

$$\text{IR} = \frac{R_P - R_B}{\text{STD}(R_P - R_B)} = \frac{R_A}{\text{STD}(R_A)} \tag{6}$$

where $\text{STD}(\cdot)$ is the standard deviation function. As with the Sharpe ratio, the typical convention is to annualize both the active return and the active risk. The information ratio can refer to the investor's *ex ante*, or forecasted, active return, in which case the numerator in Equation 6 would be replaced by the expected returns—that is, $E(R_A) = E(R_P) - E(R_B)$. Alternatively, the calculation of an *ex post*, or historical, information ratio would use realized average active returns and the realized sample standard deviation of the active return.

Two investment strategies and the associated terminology can help reinforce the conceptual distinction between the Sharpe ratio and the information ratio. First, a "closet index fund" (a fund that advertises itself as being actively managed but is actually close to being an index fund) will have a Sharpe ratio that is close to the benchmark because the excess return and volatility will be similar to the benchmark. However, the closet index fund will have a small amount of active risk, although positive by definition like any volatility estimate. While there may be little active risk, the information ratio of a closet index fund will likely be close to zero or slightly negative if value added cannot overcome the management fees. Of course, if one has the actual holdings of the fund, closet indexing is easy to detect on the basis of a measurement called "active share."[6] As a second example, the Sharpe ratio and the information ratio for a market-neutral long–short equity fund (a fund with offsetting long and short positions that has a beta of zero with respect to the market) would be identical if we consider the benchmark to be the riskless rate, because the excess return and active return would be the same calculation, as would be total risk and active risk.

Exhibit 3 shows historical information ratios for the mutual funds in Exhibit 2, with the benchmark portfolio for each calculation shown at the bottom of Exhibit 3. The average active return in the first row of Exhibit 3 can be verified by subtracting the specified benchmark average return in Exhibit 1 from the average fund return in Exhibit 2. The active risk is the annualized standard deviation of the return differences from 1994 to 2013, which cannot be verified with just the summary data in Exhibits 1 and 2.

As shown in Exhibit 3, *ex post* information ratios will be negative if the active return is negative. In fact, under the zero-sum property of active management, the average realized information ratio across investment funds with the same benchmark should be about zero. The realized information ratios in Exhibit 3 are within a range of about −0.25 to +0.25, although the range would be much wider over shorter periods. Of course, *ex ante*, or before the fact, if an investor did not expect the information ratio to be positive, he or she would simply invest in the benchmark. Note that ranking by active risk, a relative measure, does not necessarily equate to ranking by total risk, an absolute measure. For example, the relative risk of Fidelity Magellan in Exhibit 3 is slightly lower than the relative risk of Vanguard Windsor, but the absolute risk of Fidelity Magellan in Exhibit 2 is slightly higher.

---

6 The active share of a portfolio—a measure of how similar a portfolio is to its benchmark—was defined by Cremers and Petajisto (2009) as half the sum of the absolute values of the active weights. The active share of a closet index fund is close to zero. In the absence of short selling and leverage, the maximum active share is 100%.

Exhibit 3	Active Fund Information Ratios for 1994–2013				
	Fidelity Magellan	**Vanguard Windsor**	**Templeton World**	**T. Rowe Price Small Cap**	**JPMorgan Bond**
Active return	−1.5%	0.4%	1.4%	−0.9%	0.2%
Active risk	6.1%	7.4%	5.4%	3.4%	1.1%
Information ratio	−0.25	0.05	0.26	−0.26	0.18
Benchmark	S&P 500	S&P 500	MSCI World	Russell 2000	Barclays US Aggregate

Unlike the Sharpe ratio, the information ratio is affected by the addition of cash or the use of leverage. For example, if the investor adds cash to a portfolio of risky assets, the information ratio for the combined portfolio will generally shrink. However, the information ratio of an unconstrained portfolio is unaffected by the aggressiveness of active weights. Specifically, if the active security weights, Δw_i, defined as deviations from the benchmark portfolio weights, are all multiplied by some constant, c, the information ratio of an actively managed portfolio will remain unchanged.

To see this, recall the expression for the active return of a managed portfolio in Equation 3. If each active weight in Equation 3 is multiplied by some constant, c, then the active return on the altered portfolio, R_C, is

$$R_C = \sum_{i=1}^{N} c\Delta w_i R_{Ai} = c\sum_{i=1}^{N} \Delta w_i R_{Ai} = cR_A$$

Similarly, the active risk of the altered portfolio is $c\text{STD}(R_A)$, so the information ratio of the altered portfolio is

$$\text{IR}_C = \frac{cR_A}{c\text{STD}(R_A)} = \text{IR}$$

the same as that of the actively managed portfolio with no proportional increase in the active weights. Specifically, if the active weights in a managed portfolio are all doubled, the expected active return (or realized average active return) would be doubled, along with the expected or realized active risk, leaving the information ratio unchanged.

Of course, an outside investor will not be able to adjust the active risk of an existing fund by changing the individual asset active weight positions, but the same objective can be met by taking positions in the benchmark portfolio. For example, if the active risk of a fund is 5.0%, combining that fund in an 80/20 mix with the benchmark portfolio (i.e., a benchmark portfolio weight of 20%) will result in an active risk of the combined portfolio of 0.80(5.0%) = 4.0%, with a proportional reduction in the active return. Similarly, the investor can short sell the benchmark portfolio and use the proceeds to invest in the actively managed fund to increase the active risk and return. Note that in practice, institutional investors might simply reduce the amount they would have otherwise invested in the benchmark portfolio or other actively managed fund, rather than employ an explicit short sell.

3.3 Constructing Optimal Portfolios

An important concept from basic portfolio theory is that with a risk-free asset, the portfolio on the efficient frontier of risky assets that is tangent to a ray extended from the risk-free rate is the optimal risky asset portfolio in that it has the highest possible Sharpe ratio. Thus, given the opportunity to adjust absolute risk and return with cash or leverage, the overriding objective is to find the single risky asset portfolio with the maximum Sharpe ratio, whatever the investor's risk aversion. A similarly important property in active management theory is that, given the opportunity to adjust active risk and return by investing in both the actively managed and benchmark portfolios, the squared Sharpe ratio of an actively managed portfolio is equal to the squared Sharpe ratio of the benchmark plus the information ratio squared:

$$SR_P^2 = SR_B^2 + IR^2 \qquad (7)$$

Equation 7 implies that the active portfolio with the highest (squared) information ratio will also have the highest (squared) Sharpe ratio. As a consequence, according to mean–variance theory, the expected information ratio is the single best criterion for assessing active performance among various actively managed funds with the same benchmark.[7] For any given asset class, an investor should choose the manager with the highest expected skill as measured by the information ratio, because investing with the highest information-ratio manager will produce the highest Sharpe ratio for the investor's portfolio.

The preceding discussion on adjusting active risk raises the issue of determining the *optimal* amount of active risk, without resorting to utility functions that measure risk aversion. For unconstrained portfolios, the level of active risk that leads to the optimal result in Equation 7 is

$$STD(R_A) = \frac{IR}{SR_B}STD(R_B) \qquad (8)$$

where $STD(R_B)$ is the standard deviation of the benchmark return.[8] This Sharpe ratio maximizing level of active risk or "aggressiveness" comes from the general mean–variance optimality condition that the ratio of expected active return to active return variance of the managed portfolio be set equal to the ratio of expected benchmark excess return to benchmark return variance.

For example, if the actively managed portfolio has an information ratio of 0.30 and active risk of 8.0% and the benchmark portfolio has a Sharpe ratio of 0.40 and total risk of 16.0%, then according to Equation 8 the optimal amount of aggressiveness in the actively managed portfolio is $(0.30/0.40)16.0\% = 12.0\%$. If the actively managed portfolio is constructed with this amount of active risk, the Sharpe ratio will be $(0.40^2 + 0.30^2)^{1/2} = 0.50$, as shown in Equation 7. To verify this Sharpe ratio, note that the actively managed portfolio in this example has an expected active return of $(0.30)12.0\% = 3.6\%$ over the benchmark, or a total expected excess return of $6.4\% + 3.6\% = 10.0\%$. By definition, the total risk of the actively managed portfolio is the sum of the benchmark return variance and active return variance,

$$STD(R_P)^2 = STD(R_B)^2 + STD(R_A)^2$$

so at the optimal active risk of 12.0%, the total portfolio risk is $(16.0^2 + 12.0^2)^{1/2} = 20.0\%$, verifying the maximum possible Sharpe ratio of $10.0/20.0 = 0.50$.

The initial actively managed portfolio has active risk of only 8.0%, whereas the optimal amount required under the assumed information ratio needed to maximize the Sharpe ratio is 12.0%. The actively managed portfolio would thus need to be managed more aggressively to increase the active risk while preserving the same information ratio, or alternatively, the investor could short the benchmark and use the proceeds

---

7 The original insight about the importance of an actively managed portfolio's information ratio can be traced back to Treynor and Black (1973), although the description in this reading has been modified to be consistent with Grinold (1989).

8 Note that the right-hand side of Equation 8 should be multiplied by the benchmark beta of the actively managed portfolio if that value is different from 1.

to increase the size of the actively managed fund. The proportion required to be invested in the actively managed fund would be 12.0/8.0 = 1.5 times while shorting the benchmark by 0.5 times to fund the increase.

For readers familiar with risk–return charts in basic portfolio theory, Exhibit 4 will help illustrate these concepts.

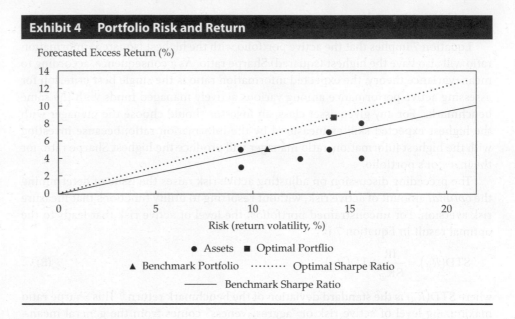

Exhibit 4   Portfolio Risk and Return

Several individual risky assets are plotted in Exhibit 4 in terms of their forecasted return in excess of the risk-free rate ("excess return") on the vertical axis and risk on the horizontal axis. The values for the individual assets are based on subjective assessments supplied by the investor. The theory described in this reading explains how to optimally employ those expectations assuming they are based on reasonable judgment. Using the benchmark portfolio weights (not shown), the risks and expected returns of the individual assets combine into the benchmark portfolio risk and expected return shown in Exhibit 4. Because the expected returns plotted along the vertical axis are in excess of the risk-free rate, the slope of a line that emanates from the origin (zero risk and zero excess return) is the Sharpe ratio of the benchmark portfolio. Specifically, the Sharpe ratio of the benchmark portfolio (i.e., slope of the dark line) in Exhibit 4 is the expected excess return of 5.0% divided by return volatility of 10.8%, or 5.0%/10.8% = 0.46.

Because of diversification, the Sharpe ratio of the benchmark portfolio is higher than those of most of the individual assets, but the benchmark portfolio does not have the highest possible Sharpe ratio of all portfolios that can be constructed from these assets. In fact, the optimal portfolio (i.e., mean–variance efficient frontier portfolio with the highest possible Sharpe ratio) shown in Exhibit 4 has an expected excess return of 8.7% and return volatility of 14.2%, which result in a Sharpe ratio of 8.7%/14.2% = 0.61 (i.e., slope of the dotted line). This higher Sharpe ratio could be retained in a portfolio while adjusting the level of risk through the use of cash or leverage. For example, the risk of the optimal portfolio could be reduced along the dotted line to the benchmark portfolio risk of 10.8% with an expected excess return of 0.61(10.8%) = 6.6%, compared with the benchmark expected excess return of 5.0%.

Exhibit 5   Portfolio Active Risk and Return

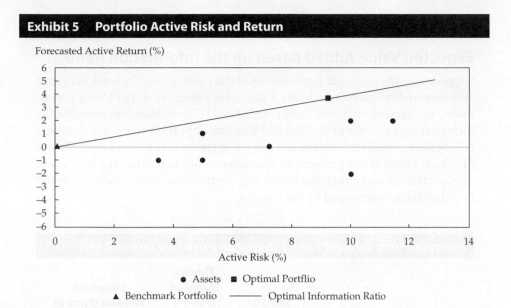

Forecasted Active Return (%)

Active Risk (%)

● Assets   ■ Optimal Portflio

▲ Benchmark Portfolio   —— Optimal Information Ratio

Exhibit 5 plots the same individual assets, the benchmark portfolio, and the optimal portfolio in Exhibit 4 in terms of their expected *active* return on the vertical axis and *active* risk on the horizontal axis. By definition, the benchmark portfolio is plotted at the origin in Exhibit 5 with zero active return and zero active risk. The individual assets have both positive and negative active returns compared with the benchmark portfolio return, whereas the optimal portfolio has a positive active return of 3.8% and active risk of 9.4%. The information ratio of the optimal portfolio is therefore 3.8%/9.4% = 0.40, the slope of the dark line in Exhibit 5. The information ratio of this optimal portfolio is higher than that of any of the individual assets and, in fact, can be shown to be the square root of the sum of the squared values of the individual assets' information ratios, similar to Equation 7, including those assets with negative information ratios. The asset weights required for the construction of this optimal portfolio are the subject of the next section of this reading; they might be negative for negative-IR assets, meaning that short sells of individual assets may be required.

Although the information ratio will remain constant at 0.40, various levels of aggressiveness can be applied to the actively managed portfolio in Exhibit 5 by scaling the optimal active weights or, alternatively, taking a position in the benchmark portfolio, leading to portfolios that plot along the dark line. But to construct the *optimal* actively managed portfolio given the assumed information ratio, the active risk must be adjusted to a level of (0.40/0.46)10.8% = 9.4%, in accordance with Equation 8. Specifically, this level of aggressiveness is required to construct the optimal portfolio in Exhibit 4, and according to Equation 7, the Sharpe ratio of this optimal portfolio is $(0.46^2 + 0.40^2)^{1/2} = 0.61$.

As we will see later, optimal levels of active risk in equity management practice are typically lower than those shown in this numerical example because the underlying portfolios are constrained to be long only, leading to information ratios that are substantially lower. As the information ratio gets close to zero, either because of constraints or because the manager is judged to be less skilled, the optimal amount of active risk in Equation 8 goes to zero, meaning that the optimal portfolio becomes the passive benchmark portfolio.

EXAMPLE 3

Expected Value Added Based on the Information Ratio

Suppose that the historical performance of the Fidelity Magellan and Vanguard Windsor mutual funds in Exhibits 2 and 3 are indicative of the future performance of hypothetical funds "Fund I" and "Fund II." In addition, suppose that the historical performance of the S&P 500 benchmark portfolio shown in Exhibit 1 is indicative of expected returns and risk going forward, as shown below. We use historical values in this problem for convenience, but in practice the forecasted, or expected, values for both the benchmark portfolio and the active funds would be subjectively determined by the investor.

Excerpted from Exhibits 1 and 2 (based on a risk-free rate of 2.8%)			
	S&P 500	Fidelity Magellan (Fund I)	Vanguard Windsor (Fund II)
Average annual return	10.0%	8.6%	10.4%
Return standard dev.	15.2%	17.9%	17.3%
Sharpe ratio	0.47	0.32	0.44

Excerpted from Exhibit 3		
	Fidelity Magellan (Fund I)	Vanguard Windsor (Fund II)
Active return	−1.5%	0.4%
Active risk	6.1%	7.4%
Information ratio	−0.25	0.05
Benchmark	S&P 500	S&P 500

1 State which of the two actively managed funds, Fund I or Fund II, would be better to combine with the passive benchmark portfolio and why.

2 Calculate the possible improvement over the S&P 500 Sharpe ratio from the optimal deployment of a new fund, called "Fund III," which has an expected information ratio of 0.20.

3 Suppose Fund III comes with an active (i.e., benchmark relative) risk of 5.0% but the investor wants to adjust the active risk to 6.5%. Describe how that adjustment would be made. (No calculations required, give a qualitative description.)

4 Again, suppose Fund III comes with an active risk of 5.0%. Determine the weight of the benchmark portfolio required to create a combined portfolio with the highest possible expected Sharpe ratio.

Solution to 1:

Fund II has the potential to add more value as measured by the Sharpe ratio, because Fund II has the higher expected information ratio: 0.05 compared with −0.25.

Solution to 2:

Properly combined with the S&P 500 benchmark portfolio, Fund III has the potential to increase the expected Sharpe ratio from 0.47 for the passive benchmark portfolio to an expected Sharpe ratio of $(0.47^2 + 0.20^2)^{1/2} = 0.51$.

Solution to 3:

To increase the active risk of Fund III to the optimal level, the investor would need to be more aggressive in managing the portfolio, take a short position in the benchmark, or, more simply, invest less than he or she otherwise would have invested in the benchmark or other actively managed fund.

Solution to 4:

According to Equation 8, the optimal amount of active risk is $(0.20/0.47)15.2\% = 6.5\%$, the value proposed in Question 3. The benchmark portfolio weight needed to adjust the active risk in Fund III is $1 − 6.5\%/5.0\% = −30\%$.

Note that at the 6.5% optimal level of active risk, Fund III has an expected active return of $0.20(6.5\%) = 1.3\%$, a total expected excess return of $7.2\% + 1.3\% = 8.5\%$, and a total risk of $(15.2^2 + 6.5^2)^{1/2} = 16.5\%$, for an expected Sharpe ratio of $8.5/16.5 = 0.52$, within rounding error of the 0.51 value calculated for Question 2.

In summary, the information ratio is active return over active risk, in contrast to the excess return-to-risk measure known as the Sharpe ratio. Information ratios help investors focus on the relative valued added by active management. The information ratio is unaffected by the aggressiveness of the active weights (i.e., deviations from benchmark weights) in the managed portfolio, because both the active return and the active risk increase proportionally. The potential improvement in an active portfolio's expected Sharpe ratio compared with the benchmark's Sharpe ratio is a function of the squared information ratio. Thus, the expected information ratio becomes the single best criterion for constructing an actively managed portfolio, and the *ex post* information ratio is the best criterion for evaluating the past performance of various actively managed funds.

THE FUNDAMENTAL LAW OF ACTIVE MANAGEMENT

4

The fundamental law is a framework for thinking about the potential value added through active portfolio management. The framework can be used to size individual asset active weights, estimate the expected value added of an active management strategy, or measure the realized value added after the fact, but the most common use is the description and evaluation of active management strategies. The law itself is a mathematical relationship that relates the expected information ratio of an actively managed portfolio to a few key parameters.

4.1 Active Security Returns

On the basis of the prior section, we assume that the investor is concerned about maximizing the managed portfolio's active return subject to a limit on active risk (also called "benchmark tracking risk"). To this end, the investor uses forecasts for each security of the active return, R_{Ai}, or thus the benchmark relative return,

$$R_{Ai} = R_i - R_B \qquad\qquad\qquad (9)$$

for the N individual assets that might be included in the portfolio. Our notation for the investor's forecasts of the active security returns is μ_i (Greek letter mu). The term μ_i can be thought of as the security's expected active return, $\mu_i = E(R_{Ai})$, referring to the investor's subjective expectation, in contrast to an expectation based on a formal equilibrium model.

Although we focus on the simple definition of active security return in Equation 9, there are several possible choices depending on the assumed risk model (i.e., statistical model of returns) and the desired trade-off between a conceptual treatment and more complex but implementable formulas. For example, Equation 9 can be modified to define the active security return as the residual return in a single-factor statistical model, $R_{Ai} = R_i - \beta_i R_B$, where β_i is the sensitivity of the security return to the benchmark return. Although this expression may appear to be related to the CAPM, the benchmark return may or may not be the market return and the fundamental law does not require the empirical validity of the CAPM, the multi-factor APT (arbitrage pricing theory), or any other equilibrium theory of required returns. The individual security active return can also be defined as the residual return in a multi-factor statistical model:

$$R_{Ai} = R_i - \sum_{j=1}^{K} \beta_{j,i} R_j$$

with K market-wide factor returns, R_j, and security sensitivities, $\beta_{j,i}$, to those factors. The technical appendix covers the most general case with exact implementable formulas, but for now we continue to use Equation 9 to define the asset active returns.[9]

Exhibit 6 provides a conceptual diagram in which to think about the various parameters in the fundamental law of active management. At the three corners of the triangle are the sets of forecasted active returns, μ_i; active portfolio weights, Δw_i; and realized active returns, R_{Ai}. The base of the triangle reflects the realized value added through active management, defined as the difference between the realized returns on the actively managed portfolio and the benchmark portfolio. Value added is the sum of the products of active weights and active returns for the $i = 1$ to N securities

---

9 The technical appendix is available online under "Supplemental Materials" at www.cfainstitute.org. It is not included or assigned as part of the curriculum.

in the portfolio, as shown in Equation 3. The value of this sum is ultimately a function of the correlation coefficient between the active weights, Δw_i, and realized active returns, R_{Ai}.[10]

Exhibit 6   The Correlation Triangle

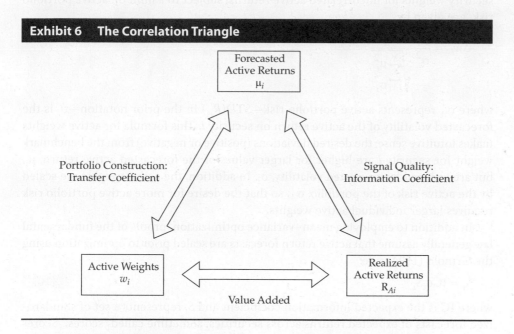

In Exhibit 6, the arrows in the legs of the triangle represent the correlation between the quantities at the corners of the triangle to which the arrows point. While the arrow at the base of the triangle reflects value added, a clearer understanding of the sources and limitations of value added can be obtained by examining the correlations on the two vertical legs. First, there is little hope of adding value if the investor's forecasts of active returns do not correspond at least loosely to the realized active returns. Signal quality is measured by the correlation between the forecasted active returns, μ_i, at the top of the triangle, and the realized active returns, R_{Ai}, at the right corner, commonly called the information coefficient (IC). Investors with higher IC, or ability to forecast returns, will add more value over time, but only to the extent that those forecasts are exploited in the construction of the managed portfolio. The correlation between any set of active weights, Δw_i, in the left corner, and forecasted active returns, μ_i, at the top of the triangle, measures the degree to which the investor's forecasts are translated into active weights, called the transfer coefficient (TC).

---

10 To understand the role of the correlation coefficient, consider the following algebraic expansion of Equation 3 that uses COV, STD, and COR to designate the covariance, standard deviation, and correlation coefficient functions, respectively:

$$R_A = \sum_{i=1}^{N} \Delta w_i R_{Ai}$$
$$= COV(\Delta w_i, R_{Ai})N$$
$$= COR(\Delta w_i, R_{Ai})STD(\Delta w_i)STD(R_{Ai})N$$

The exact equalities in this expansion depend on the fact that the cross-sectional means of active weights and active returns are zero. Specifically, the population covariance between two variables, X and Y, is calculated as $COV(X, Y) = \frac{1}{N}\sum_{i=1}^{N}(X_i - \bar{X})(Y_i - \bar{Y})$ or simply $COV(X, Y) = \frac{1}{N}\sum_{i=1}^{N}X_i Y_i$. Similarly, the population variance for a single variable is $VAR(X) = \frac{1}{N}\sum_{i=1}^{N}X_i^2$ if the mean is zero.

In the following math, we transition to using sigma rather than STD in order to simplify the notational appearance of the fundamental law equations. Formal mathematical proofs are left to the technical appendix, but mean–variance-optimal active security weights for uncorrelated active returns, subject to a limit on active portfolio risk, are given by

$$\Delta w_i^* = \frac{\mu_i}{\sigma_i^2} \frac{\sigma_A}{\sqrt{\sum_{i=1}^{N} \frac{\mu_i^2}{\sigma_i^2}}}$$

where σ_A represents active portfolio risk—STD(R_A) in the prior notation—σ_i is the forecasted volatility of the active return on security i. This formula for active weights makes intuitive sense; the desired deviations (positive or negative) from the benchmark weight for security i are higher for larger values of the forecasted active return, μ_i, but are reduced by forecasted volatility, σ_i. In addition, the active weights are scaled by the active risk of the portfolio, σ_A, so that the desire for more active portfolio risk requires larger individual active weights.

In addition to employing mean–variance optimization, proofs of the fundamental law generally assume that active return forecasts are scaled prior to optimization using the Grinold (1994) rule:

$$\mu_i = IC\sigma_i S_i \tag{10}$$

where IC is the expected information coefficient and S_i represents a set of standardized forecasts of expected returns across securities, sometime called "scores." Scores with a cross-sectional variance of 1 are used in Equation 10 to ensure that the scaling process using the multipliers σ_i (separate values for individual securities) and IC (one value for all securities) result in expected active returns of the correct magnitude. Specifically, if the assumed IC value is low, then the cross-sectional variation of the expected active returns in Equation 10 will be low. However, the exact process for calculating expected active returns may be more involved than the simple rule indicated in Equation 10, depending on how the investor's views on individual asset returns are originally formulated.

Using the Grinold rule shown in Equation 10, the mean–variance optimal active weights are

$$\Delta w_i^* = \frac{\mu_i}{\sigma_i^2} \frac{\sigma_A}{IC\sqrt{BR}} \tag{11}$$

where IC stands for information coefficient and BR, which has replaced the symbol N, stands for breadth, two key fundamental law parameters we discuss in turn below.

As previously stated, IC is the *ex ante* (i.e., anticipated) cross-sectional correlation between the N forecasted active returns, μ_i, and the N realized active returns, R_{Ai}. To be more accurate, IC is the *ex ante risk-weighted* correlation

$$IC = COR\left(\frac{R_{Ai}}{\sigma_i}, \frac{\mu_i}{\sigma_i}\right) \tag{12}$$

where COR($\cdot$) indicates correlation. As a correlation coefficient, IC can take on values anywhere from −1.00 to +1.00, although small positive values less than 0.20 are often the norm. The *ex ante*, or anticipated, IC must be positive or the investor would generally not pursue active management and would simply invest in the passive benchmark. Later, we will discuss the realized, or *ex post*, information coefficient in terms of measuring active management performance after the fact, where the realized information coefficient might be either positive or negative, leading to positive or negative value added.

The other important fundamental law parameter in Equation 11 is BR, or breadth, conceptually equal to the number of independent decisions made per year by the investor in constructing the portfolio. The simplest case for the calculation of breadth is a single-factor risk model where the only source of correlation between the securities is the common market factor, and where decisions about the active return for any given security are independent from one year to the next. In this case, breadth is equal to the number of securities, because each active return is independent from the other active return forecasts for that period and independent from the forecast for that security in subsequent periods.

However, most risk models will incorporate other factors—for example, economic sectors or industries. If the risk model includes the assumption that all the securities within a given industry are positively correlated, then part of the forecast that the active returns for securities in that industry will be higher or lower is based on just one perspective the investor has about the industry and breadth is intuitively lower than the number of securities. Alternatively, breadth can be higher than the number of securities if factors in the risk model suggest that their active returns are negatively correlated. For these more complicated cases, breadth will be a non-integer number, as explained in the technical appendix.

Similarly, if some aspect of a security is fairly constant over time and the investor makes decisions about expected active return based on that characteristic, then breadth over time is lower. Alternatively, if the investor makes quarterly or monthly forecasts about a security that are truly independent over time, then breadth can be as high as the number of securities times the number of rebalancing periods per year.

EXAMPLE 4

Scaling Active Return Forecasts and Sizing Active Weights

Consider the simple case of four individual securities whose active returns are defined to be uncorrelated with each other and have active return volatilities of 25.0% and 50.0%. After some analysis, an active investor believes the first two securities will outperform the other two over the next year, and thus assigns scores of +1 and −1 to the first and second groups, respectively. The scenario is depicted in the following exhibit:

Security	Score	Volatility
#1	1.0	25.0%
#2	1.0	50.0%
#3	−1.0	25.0%
#4	−1.0	50.0%

1 Assume that the anticipated accuracy of the investor's ranking of securities is measured by an information coefficient of IC = 0.20. What are the forecasted active returns to each of the four securities using the scaling rule $\mu_i = IC\sigma_i S_i$?

2 Given the assumption that the four securities' active returns are uncorrelated with each other, and forecasts are independent from year to year, what is the breadth of the investor's forecasts?

3 Suppose the investor wants to maximize the expected active return of the portfolio subject to an active risk constraint of 9.0%. Calculate the active weights that should be assigned to each of these securities using the

formula $\Delta w_i^* = \dfrac{\mu_i}{\sigma_i^2} \dfrac{\sigma_A}{IC\sqrt{BR}}$

Solution to 1:

The forecasted active return to Security #1 is 0.20(25.0%)(1.0) = 5.0%. Similar calculations for the other three securities are shown in the following exhibit.

Security	Score	Active Return Volatility	Expected Active Return
#1	1.0	25.0%	5.0%
#2	1.0	50.0%	10.0%
#3	−1.0	25.0%	−5.0%
#4	−1.0	50.0%	−10.0%

Solution to 2:

If the active returns are uncorrelated with each other and the forecasts are independent from year to year, then the investor has made four separate decisions and breadth is BR = 4, the number of securities.

Solution to 3:

The size of the active weight for Security #1 is $\Delta w_i^* = \dfrac{0.05}{0.25^2}\dfrac{0.09}{0.20\sqrt{4}} = 18\%$.

Similar calculations for the other four securities are shown in the following exhibit.

Security	Expected Active Return	Active Return Volatility	Active Weight
#1	5.0%	25.0%	18.0%
#2	10.0%	50.0%	9.0%
#3	−5.0%	25.0%	−18.0%
#4	−10.0%	50.0%	−9.0%

4.2 The Basic Fundamental Law

On the basis of Equation 3, the anticipated value added for an actively managed portfolio, or expected active portfolio return, is the sum product of active security weights and forecasted active security returns:

$$E(R_A) = \sum_{i=1}^{N} \Delta w_i \mu_i$$

Using the optimal active weights in Equation 11 and forecasted active security returns in Equation 10, the expected active portfolio return is

$$E(R_A)^* = IC\sqrt{BR}\,\sigma_A \tag{13}$$

where the * indicates that the actively managed portfolio is constructed from *optimal* active security weights, Δw_i^*. We remind readers that the algebra for this result assumes that breadth is the number of securities: BR = N. A more general proof where breadth is different from the number of securities is provided in the technical appendix.

The basic fundamental law of active management in Equation 13 states that the optimal expected active return, $E(R_A)^*$, is the product of three key parameters: the assumed information coefficient, IC; the square root of breadth, BR; and portfolio active risk, σ_A. Using Equation 13, we can also express the information ratio of the unconstrained optimal portfolio, $E(R_A)^*/\sigma_A$, as the product of just two terms: $IR^* = IC\sqrt{BR}$.

EXAMPLE 5

The Basic Fundamental Law

Consider the simple case of four individual securities whose active returns are uncorrelated with each other and forecasts are independent from year to year. The active return forecasts, active risks, and the active weights for each security are shown in the exhibit below.

Security	Expected Active Return	Active Return Volatility	Active Weight
#1	5.0%	25.0%	18%
#2	10.0%	50.0%	9%
#3	−5.0%	25.0%	−18%
#4	−10.0%	50.0%	−9%

1 Suppose that the benchmark portfolio for these four securities is equally weighted (i.e., $w_{B,i}$ = 25% for each security) and that the forecasted return on the benchmark portfolio is 10.0%. What are the portfolio weights and the total expected returns for each of the four securities?

2 Calculate the forecasted total return and active return of the managed portfolio.

3 Calculate the active risk of the managed portfolio.

4 Verify the basic fundamental law of active management using the expected active return and active risk of the managed portfolio. The individual security active return forecasts and active weights were sized using an information coefficient of IC = 0.20, breadth of BR = 4, and active risk of σ_A = 9.0%.

Solution to 1:

The portfolio weight for Security #1 is the benchmark weight plus the active weight, 25% + 18% = 43%. The total expected return for Security #1 is the expected benchmark return plus the expected active return, 10.0% + 5.0% = 15.0%. Similar calculations for the other three securities are shown in the following exhibit.

Security	Total Weight	Total Return Forecast
#1	43%	15.0%
#2	34%	20.0%
#3	7%	5.0%
#4	16%	0.0%
	100%	

Solution to 2:

The forecasted total return of the portfolio is the sum of portfolio weights times total returns for each security: 0.43(15.0) + 0.34(20.0) + 0.07(5.0) + 0.16(0.0) = 13.6%. The expected active return of the portfolio is the managed portfolio return minus the benchmark return: 13.6 − 10.0 = 3.6%. Alternatively, the calculation is the sum of active weights times active returns for each security: 0.18(5.0%) + 0.09(10.0%) − 0.18(−5.0%) − 0.09(−10.0%) = 3.6%.

Solution to 3:

The active risk of the managed portfolio is the square root of the sum of active weights squared times the active volatility squared for each security, which gives $[0.18^2 \times 25.0^2 + 0.09^2 \times 50.0^2 + (-0.18)^2 \times 25.0^2 + (-0.09)^2 \times 50.0^2]^{1/2} = 9.0\%$.

Solution to 4:

The basic fundamental law states that the expected active portfolio return is $IC\sqrt{BR}\sigma_A = 0.20 \times 4^{1/2} \times 9.0 = 3.6\%$, which is consistent with the calculation in the Solution to 2. Alternatively, the information ratio of 3.6/9.0 = 0.40 confirms the basic fundamental law that $IR^* = IC\sqrt{BR} = 0.20 \times 4^{1/2} = 0.40$.

4.3 The Full Fundamental Law

Although we were able to derive an analytic (i.e., formula-based) solution for the set of unconstrained optimal active weights in Equation 11, a number of practical or strategic constraints are often imposed in practice. For example, if the unconstrained active weight of a particular security is negative and large, that might lead to a negative absolute weight or short sell of the security. Many investors are constrained to be long only, either by regulation or by preference because of the extra complexity and costs of short selling. For quantitatively oriented investors, optimal solutions for active weights under long-only constraints, limits on turnover, socially responsible screens, or other constraints generally require the use of a numerical optimizer. Alternatively, one can use the fundamental law framework to better analyze the active weights that are subjectively determined by less quantitative techniques.

Let Δw_i (without an *) represent the *actual* active security weights for a constrained portfolio, in contrast to the optimal active weights, Δw_i^*, specified in Equation 11. As explained previously, the transfer coefficient, TC, is basically the cross-sectional correlation between the forecasted active security returns and actual active weights. To be more accurate, for a single-factor risk model, TC is the following *risk-weighted* correlation:

$$TC = COR(\mu_i/\sigma_i, \Delta w_i \sigma_i)$$

Based on the correspondence between optimal active weights and forecasted active returns in Equation 11, the transfer coefficient can also be expressed as the risk-weighted correlation between the optimal active weights and the actual active weights, $TC = COR\left(\Delta w_i^* \sigma_i, \Delta w_i \sigma_i\right)$. The technical appendix discusses the calculation of TC for a more general multi-factor risk model.

As a correlation coefficient, TC can take on values anywhere from −1.00 to +1.00, although TC values are typically positive and range from about 0.20 to 0.90. A low TC results from the formal or informal constraints imposed on the structure of the portfolio. In fact, at TC = 0.00, there would be no correspondence between the active return forecasts and active weights taken and thus no expectation of value added from active management. In contrast, TC = 1.00 (no binding constraints) represents a perfect correspondence between active weights taken and forecasted active returns, allowing the full expected value added to be reflected in the portfolio structure. The portfolio TC could even conceivably be negative if relative weights are negatively correlated with current expected returns because the portfolio needs rebalancing.

Including the impact of the transfer coefficient, the full fundamental law is expressed in the following equation:

$$E(R_A) = (TC)(IC)\sqrt{BR}\sigma_A \qquad \textbf{(14)}$$

where an * is not used because the managed portfolio is constructed from *constrained* active security weights, Δw_i.[11] The full fundamental law of active management shown in Equation 14, which we will refer to simply as the *fundamental law* henceforward, states that the expected active return, $E(R_A)$, is the product of four key parameters: the transfer coefficient, TC; the assumed information coefficient, IC; the square root of breadth, BR; and portfolio active risk, σ_A. Using Equation 14, we can also express the portfolio's information ratio, $E(R_A)/\sigma_A$, as the product of just three terms: $IR = (TC)(IC)\sqrt{BR}$.

The fundamental law as stated in Equation 14, although more practical than Equation 13, is still based on a simple risk model for the individual securities. Specifically, the equations in this section are based on the simplifying assumption of a single-index model, so the active security returns are residual returns and are thus uncorrelated with each other. If we go even further in terms of simplicity and assume that the individual securities all have the same residual volatility, then the correlation formulas for IC and TC do not need to be risk weighted. Alternatively, we could move in the direction of more complexity by using the single-factor risk model with factor sensitivity: $R_{Ai} = R_i - \beta_i R_B$. In quantitative portfolio management practice, even more sophisticated multi-factor risk models are used, with correspondingly more complex fundamental law parameter values—as described in the technical appendix—although the basic form of Equation 14 is preserved.

EXAMPLE 6

The Full Fundamental Law

Consider the simple case of four individual securities whose active returns are uncorrelated with each other, and forecasts are independent from year to year. The securities have a range of active return forecasts, risks, optimal active weights, and actual active weights as given in the exhibit below. The optimal active weights are based on a formula for maximizing the active return of a managed portfolio for a given level of active risk. The actual active weights are the result of a numerical optimizer with a number of constraints, in addition to the active risk constraint of 9.0%.

---

11 To better understand the role of the correlation coefficient, consider the algebraic expansion of the forecasted active return of the managed portfolio under the simplifying assumption that the security active returns are uncorrelated with each other:

$$E(R_A) = \sum_{i=1}^{N}\Delta w_i \mu_i = \sum_{i=1}^{N}(\Delta w_i \sigma_i)(\mu_i/\sigma_i)$$

$$= N\ COV(\Delta w_i \sigma_i, \mu_i/\sigma_i)$$

$$= N\ COR(\Delta w_i \sigma_i, \mu_i/\sigma_i)STD(\Delta w_i \sigma_i)STD(\mu_i/\sigma_i)$$

$$= N \qquad (TC) \qquad \sigma_A/\sqrt{N} \qquad (IC) \qquad = (TC)(IC)\sqrt{N}\sigma_A$$

where the replacement of $STD(\mu_i/\sigma_i)$ with IC is based on the Grinold rule for scaling active returns, shown in Equation 10.

Security	Expected Active Return	Active Return Volatility	Optimal Active Weight	Actual Active Weight
#1	5.0%	25.0%	18%	6%
#2	10.0%	50.0%	9%	4%
#3	−5.0%	25.0%	−18%	7%
#4	−10.0%	50.0%	−9%	−17%

1   Calculate the transfer coefficient (TC) as the risk-weighted correlation coefficient between the four active return forecasts and the four actual active weights. Compare this number with the transfer coefficient for the optimal active weights.

2   The forecasted active return of the optimal portfolio is the sum of the active weights times active returns for each security: $0.18(5.0) + 0.09(10.0) + (−0.18)(−5.0) + (−0.09)(−10.0) = 3.6\%$. The active risk of the optimal portfolio is the square root of the sum of active weights squared times the active volatility squared for each security: $[(0.18)^2(25.0)^2 + (0.09)^2(50.0)^2 + (−0.18)^2(25.0)^2 + (−0.09)^2(50.0)^2]^{1/2} = 9.0\%$. Calculate the forecasted active return and active risk of the managed portfolio using the *actual* rather than unconstrained optimal active weights.

3   Verify the full fundamental law of active management using the active portfolio return, active portfolio risk, and transfer coefficient calculations in Parts 1 and 2. The individual active return forecasts and optimal active weights were sized using an information coefficient of IC = 0.20 and breadth of BR = 4.

Solution to 1:

The transfer coefficient is the correlation between the risk-weighted expected active returns and actual active weights: $TC = COR(\Delta w_i \sigma_i, \mu_i/\sigma_i)$, where COR denotes correlation (for example, you can use the Microsoft Excel function CORREL) with four pairs of numbers. For example, the risk-weighted values for Security #1 are $\Delta w_1 \sigma_1 = 0.06(25.0) = 1.5\%$ and $\mu_1/\sigma_1 = 5.0/25.0 = 20.0\%$. The correlation coefficient across all four securities (calculated in Excel) is TC = 0.58. The transfer coefficient for the optimal active weights is by definition 1.0 but can be verified by the calculated correlation coefficient. For example, the risk-weighted values for Security #1 are then $\Delta w_1 \sigma_1 = 0.18(25.0) = 4.5\%$ and $\mu_1/\sigma_1 = 5.0/25.0 = 20.0\%$.

Solution to 2:

The forecasted active return of the managed portfolio is $0.06(5.0) + 0.04(10.0) + 0.07(−5.0) + (−0.17)(−10.0) = 2.1\%$. The active risk of the managed portfolio is the square root of the sum of actual active weights squared times the active volatility squared for each security, $[(0.06)^2(25.0)^2 + (0.04)^2(50.0)^2 + (0.07)^2(25.0)^2 + (−0.17)^2(50.0)^2]^{1/2} = 9.0\%$, as specified by the active risk constraint.

Solution to 3:

The full fundamental law states that the expected portfolio active return will be $E(R_A) = (TC)(IC)\sqrt{BR}\sigma_A = 0.58 \times 0.20 \times (4)^{1/2} \times 9.0 = 2.1\%$, consistent with the direct calculation in the Solution to 2.

We close this sub-section by noting that the transfer coefficient, TC, also comes into play in calculating the optimal amount of active risk for an actively managed portfolio with constraints. Specifically, with constraints and using notation consistent with expressions in the fundamental law, Equation 8 becomes

$$\sigma_A = TC \frac{IR^*}{SR_B} \sigma_B$$

where IR* is the information ratio of an otherwise unconstrained portfolio. Employing this optimal level of aggressiveness leads to a maximum possible value of the constrained portfolio's squared Sharpe ratio:

$$SR_P^2 = SR_B^2 + (TC)^2 \left(IR^*\right)^2$$

As noted before, the active risk of an actively managed fund can be adjusted to its optimal level while preserving the information ratio by adding long or short positions in the benchmark portfolio. For further insight, we note that with a transfer coefficient of 0.00, the optimal amount of active risk calculated above is zero. In other words, the investor should just invest in the benchmark portfolio.

To illustrate the impact of the transfer coefficient, if the actively managed portfolio has a transfer coefficient of 0.50 and an unconstrained information ratio of 0.30 and the benchmark portfolio has a Sharpe ratio of 0.40 and risk of 16.0%, then the optimal amount of aggressiveness in the actively managed portfolio is 0.50(0.30/0.40)16.0 = 6.0%. If the actively managed portfolio is constructed with this amount of active risk, the Sharpe ratio will be $(0.40^2 + 0.50^2 \times 0.30^2)^{1/2} = 0.43$. If the constrained portfolio has an active risk of 8.0%, the active risk can be lowered to the optimal level of 6.0% by mixing 1 − 6.0/8.0 = 25% in the benchmark and 75.0% in the actively managed fund.

4.4 *Ex Post* Performance Measurement

Most of the fundamental law perspectives discussed up to this point relate to the expected value added through active portfolio management. Actual performance in any given period will vary from its expected value in a range determined by the benchmark tracking risk. We now turn our attention to examining actual performance, the *ex post* analysis of the realized value added.

The key determinant of the sign and magnitude of the realized value added in Equation 3 is the degree to which the portfolio has positive active weights on securities that realize positive relative returns and negative active weights on securities that realize negative relative returns. In other words, actual performance is measured by the relationship between relative weights and realized relative returns. Knowing how actual returns match up with realized returns (the *realized* information coefficient, IC_R) allows the investor to examine what realized return to expect given the transfer coefficient. Specifically, expected value added conditional on the realized information coefficient, IC_R, is

$$E\left(R_A \mid IC_R\right) = (TC)(IC_R)\sqrt{BR}\sigma_A \qquad (15)$$

Equation 15 is similar to the fundamental law, shown in Equation 14; in Equation 15 the realized information coefficient, IC_R, replaces the *expected* information coefficient, IC.

We can represent any difference between the actual active return of the portfolio and the conditional expected active return with a noise term:

$$R_A = E(R_A \mid IC_R) + \text{Noise} \qquad (16)$$

Equation 16 states that the realized value added of an actively managed portfolio can be divided into two parts. The first part comes from the expected value added given the realized skill of the investor that period, and the second part represents any noise that results from constraints that impinge on the optimal portfolio structure.

Equation 15 also leads to an *ex post* (i.e., realized) decomposition of the portfolio's active return variance into two parts: variation due to the realized information coefficient and variation due to constraint-induced noise. Clarke, de Silva, and Thorley (2005) showed that the two parts of the realized variance are proportional to TC^2 and $1 - TC^2$. For example, with a TC value of, say, 0.60, only $TC^2 = 36\%$ of the realized variation in performance is attributed to variation in the realized information coefficient, and $1 - TC^2 = 64\%$ comes from constraint-induced noise. Low-TC investors will frequently experience periods when the forecasting process succeeds but actual performance is poor or when actual performance is good even though the return-forecasting process fails.

EXAMPLE 7

Ex Post Performance

Consider an active management strategy that includes BR = 100 investment decisions (e.g., 100 individual stocks whose active returns are uncorrelated, and annual rebalancing), an expected information coefficient of IC = 0.05, a transfer coefficient of TC = 0.80, and annualized active risk of $\sigma_A = 4.0\%$. Thus, the expected value added according to the fundamental law is

$$E(R_A) = (TC)(IC)\sqrt{BR}\sigma_A = 0.80 \times 0.05 \times \sqrt{100} \times 4.0\% = 1.6\%$$

1 Suppose that the *realized* information coefficient in a given period is −0.10, instead of the expected value of IC = 0.05. In the absence of constraint-induced noise, what would be the value added that period?

2 Suppose that the actual return on the active portfolio was −2.6%. Given the −0.10 realized information coefficient, how much of the forecasted active return was offset by the noise component?

3 What percentage of the performance variance (i.e., tracking risk squared) in this strategy over time is attributed to variation in the realized information coefficient (i.e., forecasting success), and what percentage of performance variance is attributed to constraint-induced noise?

Solution to 1:

The value added, without including constraint-induced noise (which has an expected value of zero) is

$$E(R_A \mid IC_R) = (TC)(IC_R)\sqrt{BR}\sigma_A = 0.80 \times (-0.10) \times \sqrt{100} \times 4.0\% = -3.2\%$$

In other words, conditional on the actual information coefficient, the investor should expect an active return that is negative because the realized information coefficient is negative.

Solution to 2:

The noise portion of the active return is the difference between the actual active return and the forecasted active return: −2.6 − (−3.2) = 0.6%. In other words, the noise component helped offset the negative value added from poor return forecasting. Of course, the constraint-induced noise component could just as easily have gone the other way, exacerbating the negative value added. Note that the negative realized active return of −2.6% is well within the range associated with the tracking error of 4.0% per period.

Solution to 3:

Given the transfer coefficient of TC = 0.80, TC^2 = 64% of the variation in performance over time is attributed to the success of the forecasting process, leaving 36% due to constraint-induced noise.

APPLICATIONS OF THE FUNDAMENTAL LAW

5

In this section, we discuss three specific applications of active portfolio management—one application to a global equity strategy with different sets of active return forecasts and constraints and two applications to US fixed income. These applications will further illustrate how the fundamental law is used to evaluate active portfolio strategies, including security selection and market timing.

5.1 Global Equity Strategy

In our first example, we show how the fundamental law can be used to calculate the expected active return for an actively managed portfolio benchmarked to the MSCI All Country World Index (ACWI). This global equity example focuses on the cross-sectional characteristics of the fundamental law, whereas the US fixed-income examples that follow will also include time-series implications of the law. The investable assets in this example are the individual MSCI country indices, including the 21 EAFE (Europe, Australasia, and the Far East) countries, the United States, and Canada, and the Emerging Markets Index, for a total of 24 assets. "Now" is the beginning of the calendar year 2014. For purposes of illustration, we will assume that the future will be like the past in terms of active risk, and thus we will base our estimates on the US dollar return to the MSCI country indices from 2009 to 2013. In practice, managerial judgment or a commercial model would be used to forecast risk. The various rankings of the countries' forecasted active returns for the calendar year 2014 are hypothetical.

The *ex ante* expected active risk of each asset is equal to the annualized historical standard deviation of beta-adjusted differences between the individual country return and the ACWI return, as shown in the second column of Exhibit 7. For example, the active risk of the United Kingdom is 5.8% and the active risk of Japan is 10.9%. Note that the risk estimates are for active returns, meaning the difference between the individual asset and benchmark returns. The total risk of each country would be higher based on the estimated risk of the benchmark and the benchmark beta.

Exhibit 7   Long–Short Global Equity Fund for 2014 (risk statistics based on MSCI returns from 2009 to 2013)

Country	Score	Active Return Volatility	Expected Active Return	Active Weight	ACWI Benchmark Weight	Portfolio Weight
United Kingdom	2.0	5.8%	1.2%	16.6%	8.2%	24.8%
Japan	0.0	10.9%	0.0%	−2.6%	7.7%	5.1%
France	−2.0	8.9%	−1.8%	−11.4%	3.7%	−7.7%
Germany	0.0	8.7%	0.0%	2.0%	3.5%	5.5%

(continued)

Exhibit 7 (Continued)

Country	Score	Active Return Volatility	Expected Active Return	Active Weight	ACWI Benchmark Weight	Portfolio Weight
Switzerland	2.0	8.5%	1.7%	7.7%	3.3%	11.0%
Australia	0.0	12.0%	0.0%	−1.2%	2.8%	1.6%
Spain	−2.0	19.2%	−3.8%	−4.9%	1.3%	−3.6%
Sweden	0.0	11.9%	0.0%	−2.1%	1.2%	−0.9%
Hong Kong	1.0	13.1%	1.3%	2.9%	1.1%	4.0%
Netherlands	0.0	8.6%	0.0%	1.6%	1.1%	2.7%
Italy	−1.0	15.5%	−1.6%	−1.3%	0.9%	−0.4%
Singapore	0.0	12.7%	0.0%	−2.2%	0.6%	−1.6%
Belgium	1.0	10.5%	1.1%	5.6%	0.4%	6.0%
Denmark	0.0	12.1%	0.0%	−1.2%	0.4%	−0.8%
Finland	−1.0	15.7%	−1.6%	0.0%	0.3%	0.3%
Norway	0.0	13.8%	0.0%	−0.8%	0.3%	−0.5%
Israel	1.0	14.9%	1.5%	1.2%	0.2%	1.4%
Ireland	0.0	15.6%	0.0%	0.7%	0.2%	0.9%
Austria	−1.0	15.5%	−1.6%	−2.0%	0.1%	−1.9%
Portugal	0.0	15.3%	0.0%	1.0%	0.0%	1.0%
New Zealand	1.0	14.6%	1.5%	1.9%	0.0%	1.9%
United States	0.0	4.1%	0.0%	−4.2%	48.4%	44.2%
Canada	−1.0	9.6%	−1.0%	−6.9%	3.6%	−3.3%
Emerging	0.0	9.3%	0.0%	−0.4%	10.7%	10.3%
Total	0.0			0.0%	100.0%	100.0%

Transfer Coefficient	Information Coefficient	Breadth
0.982	0.095	27.0

Active Return	Active Risk	Information Ratio
0.99%	2.00%	0.496

The 24 individual assets in Exhibit 7 are listed by size in the EAFE benchmark, followed by the United States, Canada, and the emerging markets. For example, the United Kingdom has a benchmark weight of 8.2% and Canada has a benchmark weight of 3.6%. Scores representing an active investor's forecasts of the relative performance of each asset during 2014 are assigned to each country. The scores are one of five numerical values that represent a managerial forecast of strong outperformance (2.0), weak outperformance (1.0), neutral performance (0.0), weak underperformance (−1.0), and strong underperformance (−2.0). The number of scores in each of these five categories is based on the requirement that the scores sum to zero and have a cross-sectional standard deviation of 1.

The active return forecasts in the third column of Exhibit 7 are based on the Grinold rule in Equation 10 of "IC times volatility times score," where IC is the *ex ante* information coefficient that measures the assumed accuracy of the investor relative rankings, as illustrated by the right leg of the correlation triangle in Exhibit 6. In this example, we use an assumed information coefficient of 0.10, meaning that forecasted and realized active security returns are expected to have a cross-sectional correlation coefficient of 0.10. For example, the active return forecast for the United Kingdom, which has a score of 2.0, is 0.10(5.8)(2.0) = 1.2%. Alternatively, the active return forecast for Japan is 0.0% because the score is 0. As explained later, the information coefficient used in fundamental law accounting will be adjusted down to 0.095, as shown at the bottom of Exhibit 7, to account for the assignment of scores in this particular example.

The active weights for each country are based on the active return forecast and a numerical optimizer (i.e., Excel Solver) with the objective to maximize the expected active return of the portfolio, subject to a 2.00% constraint on active risk. Note that while the active weights for each country are generally correlated with the forecasted active returns in Exhibit 7, they are not perfectly proportional, for two reasons. First, the optimizer also takes into account the estimated correlations between each country's active return, based on the MSCI monthly return data from 2009 to 2013. Exhibit 8 reports the estimated active return correlations for the eight largest EAFE countries; the full correlation matrix is not reported to conserve space. For example, the correlation coefficient between the United Kingdom (GB) and Japan (JP) is fairly low at 0.004, while the correlation coefficient between France (FR) and Germany (DE) is higher at 0.247. Note that these correlation coefficients are for *active* returns, meaning the differences between the individual country and ACWI benchmark returns. The correlations for *total* country returns would all be positive and much higher—for example, values that range from 0.4 to 0.9.

Exhibit 8	Active Return Correlation Coefficients for Eight Countries (based on MSCI returns from 2009 to 2013)							
Country	GB	JP	FR	DE	CH	AU	ES	SE
GB	1.000	0.004	0.162	0.014	0.098	−0.023	0.219	0.102	...
JP	0.004	1.000	−0.101	−0.073	0.103	−0.090	0.000	−0.069	...
FR	0.162	−0.101	1.000	0.247	0.095	−0.016	0.346	0.059	...
DE	0.014	−0.073	0.247	1.000	0.010	−0.105	0.108	0.047	...
CH	0.098	0.103	0.095	0.010	1.000	0.103	0.070	0.045	...
AU	−0.023	−0.090	−0.016	−0.105	0.103	1.000	0.010	0.072	...
ES	0.219	0.000	0.346	0.108	0.070	0.010	1.000	0.056	...
SE	0.102	−0.069	0.059	0.047	0.045	0.072	0.056	1.000	...
	...	...	...	...	...	...	...	...	...

The second reason that the active weights in Exhibit 7 are not perfectly proportional to the forecasted active returns is that the active weights are constrained by the optimizer to sum to zero. For example, the highest active weight in Exhibit 7 is for the United Kingdom, at 16.6%, and the lowest active weight is for France, at −11.4%. These active weights are added to the benchmark weights to give the total portfolio weights in the last column of Exhibit 7. For example, the total weight for the United States is 44.2%, even though the active weight is −4.2%, because the US benchmark weight in the ACWI is 48.4%. In fact, the optimization in Exhibit 7 is for a relatively unconstrained long–short portfolio where the sum of the positive total weights is about 120% and the sum of the negative total weights is about −20%, what might be called a "120/20 long–short" strategy in practice.

Because the optimization is basically unconstrained, the transfer coefficient or risk-weighted correlation between active return forecasts and active weights shown at the bottom of Exhibit 7 is 0.982, almost perfect. The transfer coefficient in this example takes into account all the risk statistics (i.e., forecasted active volatilities *and* forecasted correlations) but is not exactly 1.0 because of the budget constraint that the active weights sum to zero. Alternatively, if the sum of active weights were allowed to be non-zero, effectively allowing for risk-free cash or leverage in the equity portfolio to meet the budget constraint, the transfer coefficient would be exactly 1.0. The breadth of the strategy shown at the bottom of Exhibit 7 is 27.0, slightly higher than the number of individual assets, 24.0, because the risk model includes active return correlation coefficients that are different from zero. If all the off-diagonal correlations in the extended table in Exhibit 8 were exactly zero, then breadth would be exactly 24.0, instead of 27.0. The technical appendix discusses the calculation of breadth in more detail.[12]

The fundamental law in Equation 14 states that the expected active return on the portfolio is $E(R_A) = (TC)(IC)\sqrt{BR}\sigma_A = 0.982 \times 0.095 \times (27.0)^{1/2} \times 2.00 = 0.97\%$. Alternatively, the expected active return of 0.99% shown at the bottom of Exhibit 7 is calculated as the sum of the active weights times active returns. Thus, the accuracy of the fundamental law is quite high. The fundamental law is often expressed in terms of the information ratio, or forecasted active return over active risk. Using this framework, the validation of the fundamental law is $IR = (TC)(IC)\sqrt{BR} = 0.982 \times 0.095 \times (27.0)^{1/2} = 0.485$, fairly close to actual forecasted active return divided by active risk, $0.99/2.00 = 0.496$. Because the information ratio in this relatively unconstrained portfolio is unaffected by the aggressiveness of the strategy, we would get the same IR value if the active risk were allowed to be higher. For example, if the active risk specified to the optimizer were increased to 3.00%, the forecasted active return would increase to 1.49%, an information ratio of, again, $1.49/3.00 = 0.496$.

Exhibit 9 continues examining the global equity strategy but uses a slightly different assignment of scores than Exhibit 7 to illustrate how this change affects the values in the fundamental law. Specifically, the scores for Germany (DE) and the United Kingdom (UK) have been switched, as well as the scores for Switzerland (CH) and Australia (AU). While the breadth in Exhibit 9 is unchanged at 27.0, the information coefficient has increased slightly to 0.103, compared with 0.095 in Exhibit 7. Even though the assumed IC used to create the expected active returns in Exhibit 9 is still 0.10, the IC used in fundamental law accounting has increased because the new assignment of scores represents a slightly more ambitious forecast. For example, the active (i.e., benchmark relative) returns for France and Germany in Exhibit 9 are now forecasted to go strongly in opposite directions, even though they are positively correlated according to the risk model in Exhibit 8. Given the increase in IC and slight change in TC, the fundamental law calculation for Exhibit 9 is now $IR = (TC)(IC)\sqrt{BR} = 0.995 \times 0.103 \times (27.0)^{1/2} = 0.533$, quite close to the actual value of 0.532.

---

12 See Buckle (2004) for a more in-depth discussion of breadth calculations.

Exhibit 9	Long–Short Global Equity Fund with Different Scores for 2014 (risk statistics based on MSCI returns from 2009 to 2013)

Country	Score	Active Return Volatility	Expected Active Return	Active Weight	ACWI Benchmark Weight	Portfolio Weight
United Kingdom	0.0	5.8%	0.0%	0.7%	8.2%	8.9%
Japan	0.0	10.9%	0.0%	0.2%	7.7%	7.9%
France	−2.0	8.9%	−1.8%	−11.3%	3.7%	−7.6%
Germany	2.0	8.7%	1.7%	12.9%	3.5%	16.4%
Switzerland	0.0	8.5%	0.0%	−2.9%	3.3%	0.4%
Australia	2.0	12.0%	2.4%	7.4%	2.8%	10.2%
Spain	−2.0	19.2%	−3.8%	−4.1%	1.3%	−2.8%
Sweden	0.0	11.9%	0.0%	−1.8%	1.2%	−0.6%
Hong Kong	1.0	13.1%	1.3%	3.4%	1.1%	4.5%
Netherlands	0.0	8.6%	0.0%	3.3%	1.1%	4.4%
Italy	−1.0	15.5%	−1.6%	−1.2%	0.9%	−0.3%
Singapore	0.0	12.7%	0.0%	−2.1%	0.6%	−1.5%
Belgium	1.0	10.5%	1.1%	7.4%	0.4%	7.8%
Denmark	0.0	12.1%	0.0%	−0.4%	0.4%	0.0%
Finland	−1.0	15.7%	−1.6%	−2.4%	0.3%	−2.1%
Norway	0.0	13.8%	0.0%	0.4%	0.3%	0.7%
Israel	1.0	14.9%	1.5%	1.4%	0.2%	1.6%
Ireland	0.0	15.6%	0.0%	0.0%	0.2%	0.2%
Austria	−1.0	15.5%	−1.6%	−2.1%	0.1%	−2.0%
Portugal	0.0	15.3%	0.0%	1.8%	0.0%	1.8%
New Zealand	1.0	14.6%	1.5%	1.6%	0.0%	1.6%
United States	0.0	4.1%	0.0%	−3.6%	48.4%	44.8%
Canada	−1.0	9.6%	−1.0%	−5.3%	3.6%	−1.7%
Emerging	0.0	9.3%	0.0%	−3.4%	10.7%	7.3%
Total	0.0			0.0%	100.0%	100.0%

Transfer Coefficient	Information Coefficient	Breadth
0.995	0.103	27.0

Active Return	Active Risk	Information Ratio
1.06%	2.00%	0.532

We now apply constraints to the global equity strategy to focus on the transfer coefficient. Specifically, Exhibit 10 shows two *constrained* portfolio optimizations using the same score assignments and thus active return forecasts as in Exhibit 7. The first optimization, shown on the left-hand side of Exhibit 10, has two constraints. First, the portfolio is constrained to be long only, meaning that a negative active weight for any given country cannot be bigger than the benchmark weight. For example, France has an active weight of −3.7%, bounded by the benchmark weight of 3.7%, so that the total weight for France in the managed portfolio is zero. Second, the portfolio weights are constrained to not be more than 10.0% over or under the benchmark weight, meaning that the absolute value of any given country active weight cannot be greater than 10.0%. For example, the active weights for the United Kingdom and Switzerland are limited to 10.0% and the active weight for the United States is limited to −10.0%.

Exhibit 10 Constrained Global Equity Funds for 2014 (risk statistics based on MSCI returns from 2009 to 2013)

Country	Active Weight	ACWI Benchmark Weight	Portfolio Weight	Active Weight	ACWI Benchmark Weight	Portfolio Weight
United Kingdom	10.0%	8.2%	18.2%	8.6%	8.2%	16.8%
Japan	−5.0%	7.7%	2.7%	−7.8%	7.7%	−0.1%
France	−3.7%	3.7%	0.0%	−3.7%	3.7%	0.0%
Germany	−2.9%	3.5%	0.6%	−3.5%	3.5%	0.0%
Switzerland	10.0%	3.3%	13.3%	10.0%	3.3%	13.3%
Australia	−2.8%	2.8%	0.0%	−2.8%	2.8%	0.0%
Spain	−1.2%	1.3%	0.1%	−1.2%	1.3%	0.1%
Sweden	−1.2%	1.2%	0.0%	−1.2%	1.2%	0.0%
Hong Kong	5.0%	1.1%	6.1%	9.5%	1.1%	10.6%
Netherlands	−1.0%	1.1%	0.1%	−1.0%	1.1%	0.1%
Italy	−0.8%	0.9%	0.1%	−0.8%	0.9%	0.1%
Singapore	−0.5%	0.6%	0.1%	−0.5%	0.6%	0.1%
Belgium	5.9%	0.4%	6.4%	−0.4%	0.4%	0.0%
Denmark	−0.4%	0.4%	0.0%	−0.4%	0.4%	0.0%
Finland	−0.3%	0.3%	0.0%	−0.3%	0.3%	0.0%
Norway	−0.3%	0.3%	0.0%	−0.3%	0.3%	0.0%
Israel	4.5%	0.2%	4.7%	10.0%	0.2%	10.2%
Ireland	0.8%	0.2%	1.0%	−0.1%	0.2%	0.1%
Austria	−0.1%	0.1%	0.0%	−0.1%	0.1%	0.0%
Portugal	−0.1%	0.0%	−0.1%	−0.1%	0.1%	0.0%
New Zealand	4.6%	0.0%	4.6%	10.0%	0.0%	10.0%
United States	−10.0%	48.4%	38.4%	−10.0%	48.4%	38.4%
Canada	−3.7%	3.6%	−0.1%	−3.7%	3.6%	−0.1%
Emerging	−6.9%	10.7%	3.8%	−10.0%	10.7%	0.7%
Total	0.0%	100.0%	100.0%	0.0%	100.0%	100.0%

Transfer Coefficient	Information Coefficient	Breadth	Transfer Coefficient	Information Coefficient	Breadth
0.724	0.095	27.0	0.574	0.095	27.0

Active Return	Active Risk	Information Ratio	Active Return	Active Risk	Information Ratio
0.71%	2.00%	0.357	0.85%	3.00%	0.283

The long-only and maximum over- or underweight constraints substantially reduce the transfer of active return forecasts into active weights, as shown by the transfer coefficient of 0.724 at the bottom of the left side of Exhibit 10, compared with 0.982 for the same scores and active return forecasts in Exhibit 7. The impact of this transfer coefficient on expected active return according to the fundamental law is $E(R_A) = (TC)(IC)\sqrt{BR}\sigma_A = 0.724 \times 0.095 \times (27.0)^{1/2} \times 2.00 = 0.71\%$, compared with 0.99% for the unconstrained portfolio in Exhibit 7. Similarly, the impact of this transfer coefficient measured by the information ratio is $IR = (TC)(IC)\sqrt{BR} = 0.724 \times 0.095 \times (27.0)^{1/2} = 0.357$, compared with 0.496 for the unconstrained portfolio. In other words, the expected active return and information ratio are reduced by almost a third because of the constraints imposed in portfolio construction.

As previously mentioned, an increase in the allowed active risk from 2.00% to 3.00% in the unconstrained portfolio in Exhibit 7 proportionally increases the active return, leaving the information ratio at about 0.496. However, an increase in allowed active risk to 3.00% does *not* preserve the information ratio of the constrained portfolio, as shown by the optimization on the right-hand side of Exhibit 10. Specifically, the higher active risk leads to more variation in unconstrained active weights, as shown in Equation 11, and the constraints thus become more binding. For example, the active weight for New Zealand, which is 4.6% on the left-hand side of Exhibit 10, is capped at the maximum possible value of 10.0% on the right-hand side of Exhibit 10. The result is a further reduction in the transfer coefficient from 0.724 to 0.574, leading to a reduction in the information ratio to $IR = (TC)(IC)\sqrt{BR} = 0.574 \times 0.095 \times (27.0)^{1/2}$ = 0.283, compared with 0.357 at the lower active portfolio risk of 2.0%.

The key concept is that although an unconstrained IR is invariant to the level of active risk, as shown by the dark line in Exhibit 5, the IR for a *constrained* portfolio generally decreases with the aggressiveness of the strategy. Specifically, the dark line in Exhibit 5 for a constrained portfolio would curve downward from left to right, in accordance with an increasingly lower transfer coefficient. Thus, the constraints that are imposed on the portfolio should inform the decision of how aggressively to apply an active management strategy.

EXAMPLE 8

Compare and Contrast Active Management Strategies

Consider two active management strategies: individual stock selection with a benchmark composed of 100 securities, and industrial sector selection with a benchmark of nine sectors. The active security returns are defined as residuals in a risk model and thus are essentially uncorrelated, and forecasts are independent from year to year. Suppose the individual stock investor is expected to exhibit skill as measured by an information coefficient of 0.05, while the industrial sector investor has a higher information coefficient of 0.15.

1 Conceptually, what is the breadth (i.e., number of independent decisions per year) of each active management strategy?

2 Calculate the expected information ratio for each strategy, under the assumption that each investor's forecasts can be implemented without constraints, such as the long-only constraint or a limit on turnover each year.

3 Suppose the aggressiveness of each active management strategy is established by a portfolio active risk target of 3.0% per year. What is the expected active return to each strategy?

4   Under the more realistic assumption that the individual security selection strategy is constrained to be long only and has turnover limits, the transfer coefficient has a value of 0.60. What is the constrained information ratio and expected active return of the security selection strategy?

5   Suppose the aggressiveness of the constrained individual security selection strategy is increased to a portfolio active risk target of 4.0% per year. Conceptually, what is likely to happen to the information ratio, and why?

Solution to 1:

Given that the active asset returns in each strategy are uncorrelated, and forecasts are independent from year to year, the breadth of the security selection strategy is BR = 100 and the breadth of the sector selection strategy is BR = 9.

Solution to 2:

The expected information ratio of the unconstrained security selection strategy is calculated as $IR = (IC)\sqrt{BR} = 0.05 \times \sqrt{100} = 0.50$, while the information ratio of the industrial sector selection strategy is $IR = (IC)\sqrt{BR} = 0.15 \times \sqrt{9} = 0.45$.

Solution to 3:

The expected active return to the unconstrained security selection strategy is 0.50(3.0) = 1.50%, while the expected active return of the industrial sector selection strategy is 0.45(3.0) = 1.35%.

Solution to 4:

The information ratio of the constrained security selection strategy is $IR = (TC)(IC)\sqrt{BR} = 0.60 \times 0.05 \times \sqrt{100} = 0.30$, rather than 0.50, and the expected active return is 0.30(3.0) = 0.90%, rather than 1.50%.

Solution to 5:

A more aggressive implementation of the constrained security selection strategy will likely result in larger deviations of constrained weights from unconstrained weights and thus a lower transfer coefficient. For example, the transfer coefficient might drop from 0.60 to 0.50, leading to an information ratio of only $IR = (TC)(IC)\sqrt{BR} = 0.50 \times 0.05 \times \sqrt{100} = 0.25$. Thus, instead of a proportional increase in the expected active return associated with an increase in the active portfolio risk from 3.0% to 4.0%, the expected active return would only increase from 0.9% to 0.25(4.0) = 1.0%.

5.2 Fixed-Income Strategies

Two additional examples of the fundamental law in practice are based on the Barclays US fixed-income index returns. Consider first an active management strategy of over- and underweighting credit exposure once a quarter using corporate investment-grade and high-yield bond portfolios as assets. Let the benchmark portfolio be composed of 70% investment-grade bonds and 30% high-yield bonds. Each quarter, the active investor makes a single dichotomous decision either to overweight the investment-grade asset (and thus underweight the high-yield asset) or to overweight the high-yield asset (and thus underweight the investment-grade asset). In addition to switching to a fixed-income example, we are also now moving into a time-series application of the fundamental law, instead of the purely cross-sectional application.

After some thought, we decide to use the historical 2009–2013 returns on exchange-traded funds (ETFs) that track the two bond portfolios for our risk estimates. Specifically, the quarterly return volatility of the IG (investment-grade) asset is 2.84%, and the quarterly return volatility of the HY (high-yield) asset is 4.64%, with an estimated correlation between the two of 0.575. Because there are only three risk parameters in this strategy, a data table is not needed. The *active* risk of this decision is the volatility of the differential returns between the two bond portfolios, $[(2.84)^2 - 2(2.84)(4.64)(0.575) + (4.64)^2]^{1/2} = 3.80\%$. In effect, the active investor assigns a "score" of either +1.0 or −1.0 on credit exposure each quarter, with an *annualized* active risk of $3.80 \times (4)^{1/2} = 7.60\%$. Suppose the fixed-income investor expects to call the market correctly 55% of the time (i.e., 11 out of 20 quarters). If the investor makes the correct call 55% of the time and an incorrect call 45% of the time, then the time-series information coefficient is $0.55 - 0.45 = 0.10$.[13] Without a limit on active risk, the expected active return can be calculated using a simple probability-weighted average: $0.55(3.80) + 0.45(-3.80) = 38$ bps per quarter. But to illustrate the fundamental law, we use the Grinold rule of "alpha equals IC times volatility times score": $0.10(3.80)(1.0) = 38$ bps.

The investor decides to limit the annual active risk to 2.00% and thus sets the active weight (i.e., deviation from the 70/30 benchmark weights) at $2.00/7.60 = 26.3\%$. Under the assumption that active returns are uncorrelated over time, the breadth of this strategy is 4.0, the four quarterly rebalancing decisions made each year. Thus, in quarters when the investor believes credit risk will pay off, the managed portfolio is invested $70.0\% - 26.3\% = 43.7\%$ in investment-grade bonds and $30\% + 26.3\% = 56.3\%$ in high-yield bonds. Alternatively, in quarters where the investor believes credit risk will not pay off, the active portfolio has $70.0\% + 26.3\% = 96.3\%$ in investment-grade bonds and only $30\% - 26.3\% = 3.7\%$ in high-yield bonds. According to the simple form of the fundamental law, the expected annualized active return to this strategy is $E(R_A) = (IC)\sqrt{BR}\sigma_A = 0.10 \times (4.0)^{1/2} \times 2.00 = 40$ bps a year, or 10 bps per quarter. Alternatively, given the active weight of 26.3% motivated by the desire to limit active risk, the expected quarterly return can be calculated more directly as $0.263 \times 38 = 10$ bps. Given the small breadth of this strategy, the annual information ratio is only $IR = (IC)\sqrt{BR} = 0.10 \times (4.0)^{1/2} = 0.20$.

The key concept in this illustration is that the breadth of the strategy is 4, meaning four active management decisions per year. The same small-breadth problem also applies to quarterly tactical asset allocation decisions in a simple strategy that switches between equity and cash. There are so few opportunities to make an active decision in these "market-timing" strategies that the investor's accuracy as measured by the information coefficient must be quite high to achieve even a modest information ratio. A full description of the breadth calculation requires matrix formulas supplied in the technical appendix; one "rule of thumb" described in the technical appendix is that breadth is approximately $BR = N/[1 + (N - 1)\rho]$, where N is the number of securities and ρ is the average correlation between the active security returns. In this fixed-income example, $\rho = 0.0$, so breadth is $BR = 4.0$.

A natural question is whether the expected information ratio can be increased by switching more frequently—say, monthly. Although it is somewhat more complicated to show, the basic answer is yes—*if* the information coefficient of 0.10 can be maintained and *if* the credit exposure decisions in this example are truly independent over time. For example, making monthly calls that do not change during the quarter (i.e., signals of +1.0, +1.0, and +1.0 in January, February, and March) will *not* increase the

---

13 If a time series of T predicted dichotomous (i.e., plus or minus 1.0) scores, $S_{P,t}$, and a time series of T realized dichotomous scores, $S_{R,t}$, both have zero means, then the time-series covariance between the two is $COV(S_P, S_R) = \frac{1}{T}\sum_{t=1}^{T} S_{P,t}S_{R,t}$. The product of the two scores at time period t is 1.0 if the scores have the same sign (i.e., the call is correct) and −1.0 if the scores have different signs (i.e., the call is incorrect). Because the scores have unit variances, the correlation coefficient is equal to the covariance. Thus, the time-series correlation is equal to the number of correct calls minus the number of incorrect calls all over total calls, or, in other words, the percentage correct minus the percentage incorrect.

information ratio of 0.20. However, if the monthly signals are truly uncorrelated with each other, then the information ratio in this example would be $IR = (IC)\sqrt{BR} = 0.10 \times \sqrt{12} = 0.35$. Although somewhat implausible, if an investor made daily decisions (250 trading days a year) that were truly independent and were *still* correct 55% of the time, the expected information ratio could potentially increase to $IR = (IC)\sqrt{BR} = 0.10 \times \sqrt{250} = 1.58$.

The high 1.58 information ratio indicates that the investor could earn an expected active return of 3.16% with active risk of only 2.00%. With such a high information ratio, the investor might be inclined to increase the aggressiveness of the credit risk strategy—for example, doubling to an expected return of $2 \times 3.16\% = 6.32\%$ and active risk of $2 \times 2.00\% = 4.00\%$. Besides the issue of transaction costs, this more aggressive strategy would likely bump up against various constraints. For example, at the higher 4.00% active risk, the required active weights would be plus and minus 4.00/7.60 = 52.6%, meaning that a tilt against credit risk would require a total portfolio weight of 70% + 52.6% = 122.6% in investment-grade bonds, funded by a −22.6% *short* position in high-yield bonds.

The essential logic of this example is not confined to a dichotomous decision, meaning that the same general perspectives would hold if the single credit risk signal were continuous—for example, numbers like −0.57 or 1.32. Then under the more aggressively applied active risk target of 4.0%, a signal of −0.57 would require an active weight of −0.57(4.0)/7.6 = −30.0%. With a benchmark portfolio of 70.0% investment-grade and 30.0% high-yield bonds, this active weight translates into to a 100% position in investment-grade bonds and no position in high-yield bonds. Alternatively, for a positive credit risk signal of 1.32, the required active weight would be 1.32(4.00)/7.60 = 69.5%, meaning 100% in high-yield bonds and almost no position in investment-grade bonds. In other words, for this more aggressive strategy under a long-only constraint, the transfer coefficient would be less than 1 and the full fundamental law, $IR = (TC)(IC)\sqrt{BR}$, would come into play. Under a normal distribution for scores, the transfer coefficient of this strategy is 0.62, so the expected information ratio is only $IR = 0.62 \times 0.10 \times \sqrt{250} = 0.98$, not 1.58.[14] For an active risk of 4.00%, the expected active return is thus only 0.98 × 4.00% = 3.92%, not 6.32%.

For our second fixed-income example, consider an active management strategy using the five US Treasury bond portfolios in Exhibit 11 as the individual assets. We will consider the neutral benchmark to be an equally weighted composite portfolio of the five, or 20% invested in each asset, but with annual rebalancing. In other words, we are now moving back into a purely cross-sectional application of the fundamental law.

---

14 The transfer coefficient in this example is based on the calculation $\Phi(1.32) − \Phi(-0.57) = 0.62$, where $\Phi(S)$ is the cumulative standard normal distribution function. Given long-only limits on positions, the actual active risk of the constrained portfolio would be lower than 4.0%. In other words, the actual active weights (determined by a numerical optimizer) would need to be larger than the simple formula (S)4.0/7.6 to get back up to an actual active risk of 4.0%.

Exhibit 11 Barclays US Treasury Bond Average Returns and Risk (return statistics from 2009 to 2013)

	Treas. 0–1	Treas. 1–3	Treas. 3–7	Treas. 7–10	Treas. 10–20
Avg. Ret.	0.24%	1.11%	2.68%	3.23%	3.60%
Volatility	0.07%	0.86%	3.55%	6.59%	9.24%

Exhibit 12 shows the volatility of the historical return differences between each asset and the equally weighted benchmark. Note that while the absolute volatility of each asset return goes up with maturity in Exhibit 11, the *active* volatility with respect to the benchmark is highest for the assets with the shortest maturity, at 3.90%, and the longest maturity, at 5.34%. Exhibit 12 also shows the estimated active (i.e., benchmark relative) return correlation matrix, which has both positive and negative values, in contrast to the absolute return correlation matrix (not shown), which would only have large positive values. For example, the correlation between the 0–1-year T-bond active return and the 1–3-year T-bond active return in Exhibit 12 is *positive* 0.494, meaning that these shorter-maturity active returns tend to move together. However, the correlation between the 0–1-year active return and the 7–10-year active return is *negative*, at −0.491, meaning that these two diverse maturity active returns tend to move apart.

Exhibit 12 US Treasury Bond Estimated Active Return Risk and Correlations (return statistics from 2009 to 2013)

	Treas. 0–1	Treas. 1–3	Treas. 3–7	Treas. 7–10	Treas. 10–20
Active Vol.	3.90%	3.32%	1.34%	2.69%	5.43%

Active Corr.	Treas. 0–1	Treas. 1–3	Treas. 3–7	Treas. 7–10	Treas. 10–20
Treas. 0–1	1.000	0.494	0.221	−0.491	−0.473
Treas. 1–3	0.494	1.000	0.275	−0.488	−0.487
Treas. 3–7	0.221	0.275	1.000	−0.200	−0.351
Treas. 7–10	−0.491	−0.488	−0.200	1.000	0.454
Treas. 10–20	−0.473	−0.487	−0.351	0.454	1.000

A full description of the calculation requires matrix formulas supplied in the technical appendix, but the breadth associated with the risk estimates in Exhibit 12 is 9.4, even though there are only 5.0 assets. The breadth is different from the number of assets because the off-diagonal values in the correlation matrix are substantially different from zero. Exhibit 13 shows the fundamental law calculations for two sets of scores given an active portfolio risk target of 1.0% per year. The first set of scores has positive values for the shorter-maturity bonds and negative scores for the longer-maturity bonds. The associated active returns are calculated using Grinold rule and an assumed information coefficient of 0.20; for example, the active return for 10–20-year T-bonds is 0.20 × 5.43% × −1.76 = −1.91%. The active weights in Exhibit 13 are calculated by an optimizer given the constraint on active risk of 1.00%. For example, the active weight for the 10–20-year T-bonds is –19.1%, shown in the upper half of Exhibit 13. Given the benchmark weights of 20% for each asset, this results in a total weight of only 20 – 19.1 = 0.9% in the managed portfolio.

Although the information coefficient used to scale the active returns was 0.20, the first set of scores in Exhibit 13 does not represent a very ambitious forecast, so the information coefficient used in the fundamental law calculation is 0.12. The intuition for the large downward adjustment in the information coefficient is that the positive scores for the shorter-maturity bonds and the negative scores for the longer-maturity bonds are all based on essentially one active decision that interest rates will rise. Specifically, the expected active (i.e., benchmark relative) return for the managed fixed-income portfolio is $E(R_A) = (IC)\sqrt{BR}\sigma_A = 0.12 \times (9.4)^{1/2} \times 1.00 = 37$ bps a year.

Exhibit 13	Signals and Weights for a Fixed-Income Portfolio with Breadth of 9.4 and Active Risk of 1.00% (return statistics from 2009 to 2013)

	Treas. 0–1	Treas. 1–3	Treas. 3–7	Treas. 7–10	Treas. 10–20	IC	Active Ret.
Score	0.63	0.67	0.92	–0.46	–1.76	0.12	0.37%
Active Ret.	0.49%	0.45%	0.25%	–0.25%	–1.91%		
Active Wgt.	–1.5%	–2.1%	15.4%	7.4%	–19.1%		
Total Wgt.	18.5%	17.9%	35.4%	27.4%	0.9%		
Score	–0.22	1.20	0.23	0.57	–1.77	0.18	0.55%
Active Ret.	–0.17%	0.80%	0.06%	0.31%	–1.93%		
Active Wgt.	–11.3%	17.0%	–12.8%	24.3%	–17.2%		
Total Wgt.	8.7%	37.0%	7.2%	44.3%	2.8%		

In contrast, the second set of scores in Exhibit 13 is a more ambitious set of active forecasts that specify a modification in the shape of the yield curve. As a result, the information coefficient is 0.18, not much lower than the 0.20 value used to scale the active returns, and the expected active return for the portfolio using the fundamental law is $E(R_A) = (IC)\sqrt{BR}\sigma_A = 0.18 \times (9.4)^{1/2} \times 1.00 = 55$ bps a year. The fundamental law in terms of the expected information ratio for the second set of scores in Exhibit 13 is $IR = (IC)\sqrt{BR} = 0.18 \times (9.4)^{1/2} = 0.55$, alternatively calculated as the expected active return over active risk, 55/100 = 0.55.

At this relatively high information ratio, the investor may be inclined to increase the active risk to, say, 2.00% instead of 1.00%. However, given that the longest-maturity asset has a total weight approaching zero (i.e., 2.8% as shown in the lower right-hand corner of Exhibit 13), such a strategy would likely require shorting, and if short sells are not allowed, the transfer coefficient would be less than 1.00.

EXAMPLE 9

Breadth and Rebalancing in Active Management Strategies

Consider an active portfolio management strategy that involves decisions on overweighting or underweighting four individual assets. For example, the assets might be ETFs for four country equity markets or four different fixed-income ETFs. The active returns to Assets #1 and #2 are positively correlated, as are the active returns to Assets #3 and #4. However, the assumed risk model for active returns has no other non-zero correlations. The correlation structure in this risk model is shown in the 4-by-4 correlation matrix below, and the breadth calculation is BR = 3.2. For simplicity, we will assume that the portfolio management decisions are dichotomous, meaning that each year, the investor forecasts two of the assets to outperform the benchmark and the other two assets to underperform.

Correlations	#1	#2	#3	#4
#1	1.00	0.25	0.00	0.00
#2	0.25	1.00	0.00	0.00
#3	0.00	0.00	1.00	0.25
#4	0.00	0.00	0.25	1.00

1 Conceptually speaking (i.e., exact numbers are not necessary), why is the breadth less than the number of assets for this strategy?

2 Suppose the investor predicts Assets #1 and #2 to outperform and that Assets #3 and #4 will underperform. Conceptually speaking (i.e., exact numbers are not necessary), how will these scores affect the information coefficient in the fundamental law compared with a prediction that Assets #1 and #3 will outperform and Assets #2 and #4 will underperform?

3 Suppose the active investor rebalances monthly instead of just once a year. Explain how this would affect the information ratio of this strategy, clearly stating your assumptions.

Solution to 1:

According to the risk model, the active returns to Assets #1 and #2 tend to move together, with a correlation coefficient of 0.25, as do the active returns for Assets #3 and #4. As a result, the 3.2 breadth of this strategy is lower than the number of assets, $N = 4$.

Solution to 2:

According to the risk model, the active returns to Assets #1 and #2 tend to move together, so a forecast that both will outperform is not as ambitious as a forecast that one will outperform while the other underperforms. As a result, the information coefficient will be adjusted downward by more under the first set of forecasts than under the second set of forecasts.

Solution to 3:

Rebalancing monthly instead of annually could increase the breadth by a factor of 12, but only if the active management decisions for each asset are truly uncorrelated over time. For example, the breadth could increase to as much as $12 \times 3.2 = 38.4$. However, to increase the information ratio, one would have to assume that the information coefficient remains at the same level and that there

> are no constraints to fully implementing the active management decisions (i.e., a transfer coefficient of 1.00). For example, turnover constraints might limit the degree to which the monthly active management decisions could be fully implemented into new active positions, resulting in a lower transfer coefficient.

In summary, the examples above illustrate how the information coefficient, IC, measures the strength of the return-forecasting process, or signal. The information coefficient is the correlation between the forecasted and realized security active returns and is anticipated to be positive or active management is generally not justified. Breadth, BR, measures the number of independent decisions made by the investor each year and is equal to the number of securities only if the active returns are cross-sectionally uncorrelated. Similarly, breadth increases with the number of rebalancing periods only if the active returns are uncorrelated over time.

Like the information coefficient, the transfer coefficient, TC, is a simple multiplicative factor in the fundamental law, and it measures the extent to which constraints reduce the expected value added of the investor's forecasting ability. In the absence of constraints, the transfer coefficient is approximately 1.00, resulting in the basic form of the fundamental law. However, in practice, investors often work under constraints that result in TC values between 0.20 and 0.80. The lower transfer coefficient suggests that average performance in practice is only a fraction (20%–80%) of what would otherwise be predicted by the basic form of the fundamental law.

6   PRACTICAL LIMITATIONS

The limitations of the fundamental law include both practical considerations, such as ignoring transaction costs and taxes, and more conceptual issues, such as dynamic implementation over time. In this section, we focus on two limitations: the *ex ante* measurement of skill using the information coefficient and assumptions of independence in forecasts across assets and over time. The fundamental law extends the mean–variance-optimization approach to relative performance and hence has many of the same limitations of mean–variance optimization. In this reading, we do not deal with the shortcomings of mean–variance optimization in general (e.g., assumptions of normality in return distributions or the degree of risk aversion) or the technical problems associated with the estimation and use of a risk model (e.g., the correct set of risk factors, nonlinearities, and non-stationary returns). The fundamental law takes as given that mean–variance optimization to balance risk and return against a benchmark is the correct objective function and that the investor has a way to adequately model risk.

6.1 *Ex Ante* Measurement of Skill

A core element of the fundamental law is the information coefficient, generally defined as the correlation between the portfolio investor's forecasts and actual outcomes. Active investors assume that the financial market they are trading in is not perfectly efficient in terms of public information and that they have some differential skill in competing with other active investors; otherwise, active management is generally not justified. Behaviorally, one might argue that investors tend to overestimate their own skills as embedded in the assumed IC, but even if that bias did not exist, questions about assessing an accurate level of skill remain. Furthermore, forecasting ability probably differs among different asset segments and varies over time.

For example, Qian and Hua (2004) expanded the basic form of the fundamental law by including the uncertainty about the level of skill, or the reality that the realized information coefficient can vary over time. Specifically, they showed that realized active portfolio risk, σ_A, is a product of both the benchmark tracking risk predicted by the risk model, denoted σ_{RM}, and the additional risk induced by the uncertainty of the information coefficient, denoted σ_{IC}:

$$\sigma_A = \sigma_{IC}\sqrt{N}\sigma_{RM} \tag{17}$$

Their insight about "strategy risk" is derived under the simplifying assumptions that portfolio positions are unconstrained, TC = 1.00, and that breadth is the number of securities, BR = N, but can be expanded to include both refinements. In other words, they suggest that a more accurate representation of the basic fundamental law using the expression in Equation 17 is

$$E(R_A) = \frac{IC}{\sigma_{IC}}\sigma_A \tag{18}$$

The key impact of accounting for the uncertainty of skill is that actual information ratios are substantially lower than predicted by an objective application of the original form of the fundamental law. Specifically, security (i.e., individual stock) selection strategies are analytically and empirically confirmed to be 45%–91% of original estimates using the fundamental law. Like the refinement for implementation issues associated with constraints as measured by the transfer coefficient, strategy risk reduces expected and average realized information ratios. The higher the uncertainty about forecasting ability, the smaller the expected value added is likely to be.

6.2 Independence of Investment Decisions

As we have discussed, the number of individual assets, N, is not an adequate measure of strategy breadth, BR, when the active returns between individual assets are correlated, as defined by the risk model, and forecasts are not independent from period to period. Specifically, decisions to overweight all the stocks in a given industry or all the countries in a given region because they are responding to similar influences cannot be counted as completely independent decisions, so breadth in these contexts is lower than the number of assets. Similarly, when fundamental law concepts are applied to hedging strategies using derivatives or other forms of arbitrage, breadth can increase well beyond the number of securities.

For example, arbitrage of just two securities, say, a country equity market ETF traded on two different exchanges, can have extremely high breadth, meaning that the expected active return on the strategy is large compared with the active risk. To illustrate, Clarke, de Silva, and Thorley (2006) showed that a practical measure of breadth is

$$BR = \frac{N}{1 + (N-1)\rho} \tag{19}$$

where ρ is the same correlation coefficient in all the off-diagonal elements of the risk model. For just two securities, $N = 2$, and a correlation coefficient associated with near-arbitrage opportunities, $\rho = -0.8$, breadth could be BR = 2/[1 − (2 − 1)0.8] = 10.0 so that information ratios are quite high for even modest values of IC or forecasting skill.

Another example of the limitation of the fundamental law due to the lack of decision independence is the active management of fixed-income portfolios. Most descriptions of the fundamental law are based on individual stock selection strategies where the risk of equity securities is decomposed into systematic and idiosyncratic factors by a risk model. Once the systematic risk factors are removed, the active asset returns (defined as the returns on idiosyncratic risks) are essentially independent, so breadth can be more easily determined. In contrast, almost all bonds represent some form of duration risk, as well as credit risk and optionality, so returns are highly correlated in more subtle ways. In addition, the implicit assumption of normality in the realized return distribution of bonds with default risk and embedded options is clearly unwarranted.

The limitation of independent decisions within the fundamental law also affects time-series implementation. In particular, increasing the rebalancing frequency may increase the realized information ratio, but only to the extent that sequential active return forecasts are independent from period to period. Refinements on the concept of breadth—for example, Buckle (2004)—have improved the cross-sectional operationalization of the fundamental law, but more work is needed to provide conceptually useful modifications of the fundamental law in a multi-period, multi-asset setting.

In summary, the fundamental law is a useful conceptual framework in many active management applications and can even produce operational measurements of the essential elements of an active management strategy. But an understanding of the limitations of the law is warranted—particularly the issues of uncertainty in the level of assumed skill and the measurement of breadth in the face of time-dependent rebalancing policies and multi-period optimization.

EXAMPLE 10

Limitations of the Fundamental Law

Consider an active portfolio management strategy of selecting individual stocks in the S&P 500 on a monthly basis. The investor does a quick calculation of the fundamental law based on an information coefficient of IC = 0.05 and BR = 12 × 500 = 6,000, giving an astounding information ratio of IR = 3.87. In other words, at an active portfolio risk of 3.0%, the expected active return would be 3.87(3.0) = 11.6%.

Provide at least two different explanations of *why* the information ratio in this example could be too high, based on practical limitations of the fundamental law.

Solution:

Potential answers include the following:

1   Cross-sectional dependence: The active returns on the 500 stocks in the S&P 500 are probably correlated, so the number of independent monthly decisions is lower than 500. For example, the investor could be forecasting outperformance of all the stocks in a given industrial sector and underperformance of all the stocks in another sector.

2   Time-series dependence: The decisions on any particular stock may be correlated from month to month. For example, the forecasting process might be based on the earnings yield (reported EPS over price), which changes slowly over time. A stock that is forecasted to outperform in one month is likely to retain the outperformance forecast for several months in a row.

3 Uncertainty: Although an information coefficient of 0.05 appears to be modest, the basic form of the fundamental law does not account for uncertainty in the information coefficient or the likelihood that the information coefficient changes over time and could be different for different sets of stocks.

4 Constraints: An answer that involves accounting for such constraints as long only or turnover limits using a transfer coefficient is a weaker answer because the impact of constraints and the transfer coefficient is a well-known refinement of the fundamental law, even though it does not appear to be used in this example.

SUMMARY

This reading covers a number of key concepts and principles associated with active portfolio management. Active management is based on the mathematics and principles of risk and return from basic mean–variance portfolio theory, but with a focus on value added compared with a benchmark portfolio. Critical concepts contained in the reading include the following:

- Value added is defined as the difference between the return on the managed portfolio and the return on a passive benchmark portfolio. This difference in returns might be positive or negative after the fact but would be expected to be positive before the fact or active management would generally not be justified.

- Value added is related to active weights in the portfolio, defined as differences between the various asset weights in the managed portfolio and their weights in the benchmark portfolio. Individual assets can be overweighted (have positive active weights) or underweighted (have negative active weights), but the complete set of active weights sums to zero.

- Positive value added is generated when positive-active-weight assets have larger returns than negative-active-weight assets. By defining individual asset active returns as the difference between the asset total return and the benchmark return, value added is shown to be positive if and only if end-of-period realized active asset returns are positively correlated with the active asset weights established at the beginning of the period.

- Value added can come from a variety of active portfolio management decisions, including security selection, asset class allocation, and even further decompositions into economic sector weightings and geographic or country weights.

- The Sharpe ratio measures reward per unit of risk in absolute returns, whereas the information ratio measures reward per unit of risk in benchmark relative returns. Either ratio can be applied *ex ante* to expected returns or *ex post* to realized returns. The information ratio is a key criterion on which to evaluate actively managed portfolios.

- Higher information ratio portfolios can be used to create higher Sharpe ratio portfolios. The optimal amount of active management that maximizes a portfolio's Sharpe ratio is positively related to the assumed forecasting accuracy or *ex ante* information coefficient of the active strategy.

■ The active risk of an actively managed strategy can be adjusted to its desired level by combining it with a position in the benchmark. Furthermore, once an investor has identified the maximum Sharpe ratio portfolio, the total volatility of a portfolio can be adjusted to its desired level by combining it with cash (two-fund separation concept).

■ The fundamental law of active portfolio management began as a conceptual framework for evaluating the potential value added of various investment strategies but has emerged as an operational system for measuring the essential components of those active strategies.

■ Although the fundamental law provides a framework for analyzing investment strategies, the essential inputs of forecasted asset returns and risks still require judgment in formulating the expected returns.

■ The fundamental law separates the expected value added, or portfolio return relative to the benchmark return, into the basic elements of the strategy:

  ● *skill* as measured by the information coefficient,

  ● *structuring* of the portfolio as measured by the transfer coefficient,

  ● *breadth* of the strategy measured by the number of independent decisions per year, and

  ● *aggressiveness* measured by the benchmark tracking risk.

  The last three of these four elements may be beyond the control of the investor if they are specified by investment policy or constrained by regulation.

■ The fundamental law has been applied in settings that include the selection of country equity markets in a global equity fund and the timing of credit and duration exposures in a fixed-income fund.

■ The fundamental law of active management has limitations, including uncertainty about the *ex ante* information coefficient and the conceptual definition of breadth as the number of independent decisions by the investor.

REFERENCES

Black, Fischer, and Robert Litterman. 1992. "Global Portfolio Optimization." *Financial Analysts Journal*, vol. 48, no. 5 (September/October):28–43.

Brinson, Gary P., L. Randolph Hood, and Gilbert L. Beebower. 1986. "Determinants of Portfolio Performance." *Financial Analysts Journal*, vol. 42, no. 4 (July–August):39–44.

Buckle, David. 2004. "How to Calculate Breadth: An Evolution of the Fundamental Law of Active Portfolio Management." *Journal of Asset Management*, vol. 4, no. 6:393–405.

Clarke, Roger, Harindra de Silva, and Steven Thorley. 2002. "Portfolio Constraints and the Fundamental Law of Active Management." *Financial Analysts Journal*, vol. 58, no. 5 (September/October):48–66.

Clarke, Roger, Harindra de Silva, and Steven Thorley. 2005. "Performance Attribution and the Fundamental Law." *Financial Analysts Journal*, vol. 61, no. 5 (September/October):70–83.

Clarke, Roger, Harindra de Silva, and Steven Thorley. 2006. "The Fundamental Law of Active Portfolio Management." *Journal of Investment Management*, vol. 4, no. 3:54–72.

Cremers, K.J. Martijn, and Antti Petajisto. 2009. "How Active Is Your Fund Manager?" *Review of Financial Studies*, vol. 22, no. 9:3329–3365.

Elton, Edward, and Martin Gruber. 1973. "Estimating the Dependence Structure of Share Prices." *Journal of Finance*, vol. 28, no. 5:1203–1232.

Fischer, Bernd, and Russell Wermers. 2013. *Performance Evaluation and Attribution of Security Portfolios*. Oxford, UK: Elsevier Inc.

Grinold, Richard C. 1989. "The Fundamental Law of Active Management." *Journal of Portfolio Management*, vol. 15, no. 3 (Spring):30–37.

Grinold, Richard C. 1994. "Alpha is Volatility Times IC Times Score, or Real Alphas Don't Get Eaten." *Journal of Portfolio Management*, vol. 20, no. 4 (Summer):9–16.

Grinold, Richard C., and Ronald N. Kahn. 1999. *Active Portfolio Management: A Quantitative Approach for Providing Superior Returns and Controlling Risk*, 2nd ed. New York: McGraw-Hill.

Kaplan, Paul D. 2012/2013. "2013. "What's Wrong with Multiplying by the Square Root of Twelve." *Journal of Performance Measurement*, vol. 17, no. 2 (Winter):16–24.

Markowitz, Harry M. 1952. "Portfolio Selection." *Journal of Finance*, vol. 7, no. 1:77–91.

Qian, Edward, and Ronald Hua. 2004. "Active Risk and Information Ratio." *Journal of Investment Management*, vol. 2, no. 3 (Third Quarter):20–34.

Sharpe, William F. 1964. "Capital Asset Prices: A Theory of Market Equilibrium under Conditions of Risk." *Journal of Finance*, vol. 19, no. 3:425–442.

Treynor, J., and Fischer Black. 1973. "How to Use Security Analysis to Improve Portfolio Selection." *Journal of Business*, vol. 46:66–86.

PRACTICE PROBLEMS

1 Wei Liu makes two statements about active portfolio management:

     Statement 1   The "active return" of an actively managed portfolio is the difference between the portfolio's return and the return on the benchmark portfolio, and is equal to the managed portfolio's alpha.

     Statement 2   The active weights are the differences in the managed portfolio's weights and the benchmark's weights.

Are Liu's statements correct?

   A   Only Statement 1 is correct.

   B   Only Statement 2 is correct.

   C   Both statements are correct.

2 The benchmark weights and returns for each of the five stocks in the Capitol index are given below. The Tukol Fund uses the Capitol Index as its benchmark, and the fund's portfolio weights are also shown in the table.

Stock	Portfolio Weight (%)	Benchmark Weight (%)	2016 Return (%)
1	30	24	14
2	30	20	15
3	20	20	12
4	10	18	8
5	10	18	10

What is the value added (active return) for the Tukol Fund?

   A   0.00%

   B   0.90%

   C   1.92%

3 Consider the following asset class returns for calendar year 2016:

Asset class	Portfolio Weight (%)	Benchmark Weight (%)	Portfolio Return (%)	Benchmark Return (%)
Domestic equities	55	40	10	8
International equities	20	30	10	9
Bonds	25	30	5	6

What is the value added (or active return) for the managed portfolio?

   A   0.25%

   B   0.35%

   C   1.05%

4 Gertrude Fischer mentions two properties of the Sharpe ratio and the information ratio that she says are very useful.

     Property 1   The Sharpe ratio is unaffected by the addition of cash or leverage in a portfolio.

Property 2   The information ratio for an unconstrained portfolio is unaffected by the aggressiveness of the active weights.

Are Fischer's two properties correct?

A   Yes.

B   No. Only Property 1 is correct.

C   No. Only Property 2 is correct.

The following information relates to Questions 5 and 6

	S&P 500	Indigo Fund
Expected annual return	9.0%	10.5%
Return standard deviation	18.0%	25.0%
Sharpe ratio	0.333	0.30
Active return		1.2%
Active risk		8.0%
Information ratio		0.15

5   What is the maximum Sharpe ratio that a manager can achieve by combining the S&P 500 benchmark portfolio and the Indigo Fund?

A   0.333

B   0.365

C   0.448

6   Which of the following pairs of weights would be used to achieve the highest Sharpe ratio and optimal amount of active risk through combining the Indigo Fund and benchmark portfolio, respectively?

A   1.014 on Indigo and −0.014 on the benchmark

B   1.450 on Indigo and −0.450 on the benchmark

C   1.500 on Indigo and −0.500 on the benchmark

7   The benchmark portfolio is the S&P 500. Which of the following three portfolios can be combined with the benchmark portfolio to produce the highest combined Sharpe ratio?

	S&P 500	Portfolio A	Portfolio B	Portfolio C
Expected annual return	9.0%	10.0%	9.5%	9.0%
Return standard deviation	18.0%	20.0%	20.0%	18.0%
Sharpe ratio	0.333	0.350	0.325	0.333
Active return	0	1.0%	0.5%	0
Active risk	0	10.0%	3.0%	2.0%

A   Portfolio A

B   Portfolio B

C   Portfolio C

8 Based on the fundamental law of active management, if a portfolio manager has an information ratio of 0.75, an information coefficient of 0.1819, and a transfer coefficient of 1.0, how many securities are in the portfolio manager's fund, making the assumption that the active returns are uncorrelated.

   A About 2

   B About 4

   C About 17

9 Two analysts make the following statements about the transfer coefficient in the full fundamental law of active management:

   Analyst One says, "The transfer coefficient measures how well the realized returns correlate with the anticipated returns, adjusted for risk."

   Analyst Two says, "The transfer coefficient measures how well the realized returns correlate with the active weights, adjusted for risk."

   Which, if either, analyst is correct?

   A Only Analyst One is correct.

   B Only Analyst Two is correct

   C Neither analyst is correct.

10 The full fundamental law of active management is stated as follows:

$$E(R_A) = (TC)(IC)\sqrt{BR}\sigma_A$$

   Which component on the right hand side represents the extent to which the portfolio manager's expectations are realized? The

   A transfer coefficient, TC.

   B information coefficient, IC.

   C breadth, BR.

11 An analyst is given the following information about a portfolio and its benchmark. In particular, the analyst is concerned that the portfolio is a closet index fund.[1] The T-bill return chosen to represent the risk-free rate is 0.50%.

	Benchmark	Portfolio
Return	8.75%	8.90%
Risk	17.50%	17.60%
Active Return	0.00%	0.15%
Active Risk	0.00%	0.79%
Sharpe Ratio	0.4714	0.4773
Information Ratio	N/A	0.1896

   Which of the following three statements *does not* justify your belief that the portfolio is a closet index?

   I. The Sharpe ratio of the portfolio is close to the Sharpe ratio of the benchmark.

   II. The information ratio of the portfolio is relatively small.

   III. The active risk of the portfolio is very low.

   A Statement I

---

[1] A closet index fund is a fund that advertises itself as being actively managed but is actually close to being an index fund.

B Statement II

C Statement III

12 You are considering three managers for a small cap growth mandate. After careful analysis, you produce the following forward looking expectations about the managers' active risk and active return:

	Manager A	Manager B	Manager C
Active Return	0.7%	0.6%	1.2%
Active Risk	3.2%	3.1%	6.3%

If you intend to rely on the information ratio to make your decision, which manager should you choose?

A Manager A

B Manager B

C Manager C

13 You have a portfolio 100% allocated to a manager with an ex-post active risk at 8.0%. You choose to allocate a 75% position to the active manager and 25% to the benchmark to bring the portfolio back to your target active risk of 6.0%. If the manager's information ratio is 0.50, what happens to the information ratio of the portfolio after the reallocation?

A The information ratio increases because the lower active risk reduces the denominator of the ratio.

B The information ratio remains unchanged because allocations between the active portfolio and the benchmark don't affect the information ratio.

C The information ratio decreases because allocating some of the portfolio to the benchmark means that the external manager generates less active return.

The following information relates to Questions 14 and 15

You are analyzing three investment managers for a new mandate. The table below provides the managers' ex-ante active return expectations and portfolio weights. The last two columns include the risk and the ex-post, realized active returns for the four stocks. Use the following data for the following two questions:

	Manager 1		Manager 2		Manager 3			Realized
	Δw	$E(R_A)$	Δw	$E(R_A)$	Δw	$E(R_A)$	Risk	R_A
Security 1	−0.125	0.03	0.2	0.04	−0.05	0.025	0.17	0.06
Security 2	0.025	0.04	0	0.01	0.05	0.015	0.10	0.07
Security 3	0.075	0.05	−0.1	0	0.05	0.005	0.12	0.04
Security 4	0.025	0.06	−0.1	0.02	−0.05	0.015	0.25	0.02

14 Suppose all three managers claim to be good at forecasting returns. According to the full fundamental law of active management, which manager is the best at efficiently building portfolios by anticipating future returns?

A Manager 1

B   Manager 2

C   Manager 3

15   Suppose all three managers claim to be efficient in portfolio construction. According to the full fundamental law of active management, which manager is the best at building to make full use of their ability to correctly anticipate returns?

    A   Manager 1

    B   Manager 2

    C   Manager 3

---

16   Manager 1 has an information coefficient of 0.15, a transfer coefficient of 1.0, and invests in 50 securities. Manager 2 has a different strategy, investing in more securities, but is subject to investment constraints that reduce his transfer coefficient. Manager 2 has an information coefficient of 0.10, a transfer coefficient of 0.8, and invests in 100 securities. The investment selections of each manager are independent decisions. If both managers target an active risk of 5.0%, which manager will have the greater expected active return?

    A   Manager 1

    B   Manager 2

    C   Both managers will have the same active return.

17   Nick Young is concerned that Goudon Partners, one of his money managers, overestimates its expected active return because Goudon overstates its strategy breadth. Young makes two notes about his concern:

    Note 1   Although Goudon claims that the number of independent asset decisions is high because it uses 200 stocks, many of these stocks cluster in industries where the same general analysis applies to several stocks.

    Note 2   Goudon claims that each stock is independent and evaluated each month, or 12 times per year. These analyses are not independent because some of their strategies, such as favoring a particular industry or favoring value stocks, persist beyond one month. For example, a strategy of favoring low-P/E stocks will persist for several months and the investment decisions are not independent.

    If his judgments are correct, are Young's notes about the overstatement of breadth correct?

    A   Only Note 1 is correct.

    B   Only Note 2 is correct.

    C   Both Notes 1 and 2 are correct.

18   Caramel Associates uses the fundamental law to estimate its expected active returns. Two things have changed. First, Caramel will lower its estimate of the information coefficient because they felt their prior estimates reflected overconfidence. Second, their major clients have relaxed several constraints on their portfolios, including social screens, prohibitions on short selling, and constraints on turnover. Which of these changes will increase the expected active return?

    A   Only the lower information coefficient.

B Only the relaxation of several portfolio constraints.

C Both the lower information coefficient and the relaxation of portfolio constraints.

The following information relates to Questions 19–25

James Frazee is chief investment officer at H&F Capital Investors. Frazee hires a third-party adviser to develop a custom benchmark for three actively managed balanced funds he oversees: Fund X, Fund Y, and Fund Z. (Balanced funds are funds invested in equities and bonds.) The benchmark needs to be composed of 60% global equities and 40% global bonds. The third-party adviser submits the proposed benchmark to Frazee, who rejects the benchmark based on the following concerns:

Concern 1: Many securities he wants to purchase are not included in the benchmark portfolio.

Concern 2: One position in the benchmark portfolio will be somewhat costly to replicate.

Concern 3: The benchmark portfolio is a float-adjusted, capitalization-weighted portfolio.

After the third-party adviser makes adjustments to the benchmark to alleviate Frazee's concerns, Frazee accepts the benchmark portfolio. He then asks his research staff to develop risk and expected return forecasts for Funds X, Y, and Z as well as for the benchmark. The forecasts are presented in Exhibit 1.

Exhibit 1	Forecasted Portfolio Statistics for Funds X, Y, and Z and the Benchmark			
	Fund X	**Fund Y**	**Fund Z**	**Benchmark**
Portfolio weights:				
Global equities (%)	60.0	65.0	68.0	60.0
Global bonds (%)	40.0	35.0	32.0	40.0
Expected return (%)	10.0	11.6	13.2	9.4
Expected volatility (%)	17.1	18.7	22.2	16.3
Active risk (%)	5.2	9.2	15.1	N/A
Sharpe ratio (SR)	0.45	0.50	0.49	0.44

Note: Data are based on a risk-free rate of 2.3%.

Frazee decides to add a fourth offering to his group of funds, Fund W, which will use the same benchmark as in Exhibit 1. Frazee estimates Fund W's information ratio to be 0.35. He is considering adding the following constraint to his portfolio construction model: Fund W would now have maximum over- and underweight constraints of 7% on single-country positions.

Frazee conducts a search to hire a manager for the global equity portion of Fund W and identifies three candidates. He asks the candidates to prepare risk and return forecasts relative to Fund W's benchmark based on their investment strategy, with the only constraint being no short selling. Each candidate develops independent annual forecasts with active return projections that are uncorrelated and constructs a portfolio made up of stocks that are diverse both geographically and across economic sectors. Selected data for the three candidates' portfolios are presented in Exhibit 2.

Exhibit 2	Forecasted Portfolio Data for Equity Portion of Fund W		
	Candidate A	**Candidate B**	**Candidate C**
Rebalancing	Annually	Annually	Annually
Number of securities	100	64	36
Information ratio (IR)	0.582	0.746	0.723
Transfer coefficient (TC)	0.832	0.777	0.548
Information coefficient*	0.07	0.12	0.22

* Information coefficient based on previously managed funds.

Frazee asks Candidate C to re-evaluate its portfolio data given the following changes:

Change 1: Fix the number of securities to 50.

Change 2: Rebalance on a semiannual basis.

Change 3: Add maximum over- or underweight constraints on sector weightings.

19 Which of Frazee's concerns *best* justifies his decision to reject the proposed benchmark?

   A Concern 1

   B Concern 2

   C Concern 3

20 Based on Exhibit 1, the expected active return from asset allocation for Fund X is:

   A negative.

   B zero.

   C positive.

21 Based on Exhibit 1, which fund is expected to produce the greatest consistency of active return?

   A Fund X

   B Fund Y

   C Fund Z

22 Based on Exhibit 1, combining Fund W with a fund that replicates the benchmark would produce a Sharpe ratio *closest* to:

   A 0.44.

   B 0.56.

   C 0.89.

23 If Frazee added the assumption he is considering in Fund W's portfolio construction, it would *most likely* result in:

   A a decrease in the optimal aggressiveness of the active strategy.

B the information ratio becoming invariant to the level of active risk.

C an increase in the transfer of active return forecasts into active weights.

24 Based on the data presented in Exhibit 2, the candidate with the greatest skill at achieving active returns appears to be:

A Candidate A.

B Candidate B.

C Candidate C.

25 Which proposed change to Fund W would *most likely* decrease Candidate C's information ratio?

A Change 1

B Change 2

C Change 3

The following information relates to Questions 26–29

John Martinez is assessing the performance of the actively managed diversified asset portfolio. The diversified asset portfolio is invested in equities, bonds, and real estate, and allocations to these asset classes and to the holdings within them are unconstrained.

Selected return and financial data for the portfolio for 2015 are presented in Exhibit 1.

Exhibit 1	Diversified Asset Portfolio 2015 Portfolio Performance			
	Subportfolio Return (%)	Benchmark Return (%)	Portfolio Allocation (%)	Strategic Asset Allocation (%)
Equities subportfolio	36.9	31.6	63	60
Bond subportfolio	−2.4	−2.6	28	35
Real estate subportfolio	33.4	28.3	9	5

Martinez uses several risk-adjusted return metrics to assess the performance of the diversified asset portfolio, including the information ratio and the Sharpe ratio. Selected risk, return, and statistical data for the portfolio are presented in Exhibit 2.

Exhibit 2	Diversified Asset Portfolio Data, 1996–2015		
	Transfer Coefficient (TC)	Information Coefficient (IC)	Breadth (BR)
Equities subportfolio	0.90	0.091	21
Bond subportfolio	0.79	0.087	23
Real estate subportfolio	0.86	0.093	19

Martinez has recently hired Kenneth Singh to help him evaluate portfolios. Martinez asks Singh about the possible effects on the portfolio's information ratio if cash were added to the diversified asset portfolio or if the aggressiveness of the portfolio's active weights were increased. Singh responds with two statements:

Statement 1   Adding cash to the portfolio would change the portfolio's information ratio.

Statement 2   Increasing the aggressiveness of active weights would not change the portfolio's information ratio.

26 Based on Exhibit 1, the value added to the diversified asset portfolio attributable to the security selection decision in 2015 was *closest* to:

   A   2.3%.

   B   3.9%.

   C   6.1%.

27 Based on Exhibit 1, the value added of the diversified asset portfolio attributable to the asset allocation decision in 2015 was *closest* to:

   A   2.3%.

   B   3.9%.

   C   6.1%.

28 Based on data in Exhibit 2 and using the information ratio as the criterion for evaluating performance, which subportfolio had the best performance in the period 1996–2015?

   A   The bond subportfolio.

   B   The equities subportfolio.

   C   The real estate subportfolio.

29 Which of Singh's statements regarding the information ratio is correct?

   A   Only Statement 1

   B   Only Statement 2

   C   Both Statement 1 and Statement 2

SOLUTIONS

1 B is correct. Although the first part of Statement 1 is correct (active return, or value added, equals the difference between the managed portfolio return and the benchmark return), active return is not the same as alpha. In other words, $R_A = R_P - R_B$, while $\alpha_P = R_P - \beta_P \times R_B$. Statement 2 correctly defines active weights.

2 B is correct. The portfolio active return is equal to the portfolio return minus the benchmark return:

$$R_A = R_P - R_B$$

The portfolio return is $R_P = \sum_{i=1}^{n} w_{P,i} R_i$

$R_P = 0.30(14\%) + 0.30(15\%) + 0.20(12\%) + 0.10(8\%) + 0.10(10\%) = 12.9\%$.

The benchmark return is $R_B = \sum_{i=1}^{n} w_{B,i} R_i$

$R_B = 0.24(14\%) + 0.20(15\%) + 0.20(12\%) + 0.18(8\%) + 0.18(10\%) = 12.0\%$.

The active return is:

$$R_A = R_P - R_B = 12.9\% - 12.0\% = 0.9\%$$

Note that this same correct answer can be obtained in two other equivalent ways. The active weights are the differences between the portfolio and benchmark weights, or $\Delta w_i = w_{P,i} - w_{B,i}$. Computing the active weights from the table above, the active return is:

$$R_A = \sum_{i=1}^{N} \Delta w_i R_i$$

$$= 0.06(14\%) + 0.10(15\%) + 0(12\%) - 0.08(8\%) - 0.08(10\%)$$
$$= 0.9\%$$

Finally, we could express the active security returns as their differences from the benchmark return, or $R_{Ai} = R_i - R_B$. Computing the active security returns from the table above, the portfolio active return is the sum product of the active weights and the active security returns:

$$R_A = \sum_{i=1}^{N} \Delta w_i R_{Ai}$$

$$= 0.06(2\%) + 0.10(3\%) + 0(0\%) - 0.08(-4\%) - 0.08(-2\%)$$
$$= 0.9\%$$

3 C is correct. The active return is equal to the portfolio return minus the benchmark return:

$$R_A = R_P - R_B = \sum_{j=1}^{M} w_{P,j} R_{P,j} - \sum_{j=1}^{M} w_{B,j} R_{B,j}$$

The portfolio return is $R_P = \sum_{i=1}^{n} w_{P,i} R_i = 0.55(10\%) + 0.20(10\%) + 0.25(5\%) = 8.75\%$

The benchmark return is $R_B = \sum_{i=1}^{n} w_{B,i} R_i = 0.40(8\%) + 0.30(9\%) + 0.30(6\%) = 7.70\%$

$R_A = R_P - R_B = 8.75\% - 7.70\% = 1.05\%$

4   A is correct. Both properties are correct. For Property 1, if w_P is the weight of an actively managed portfolio and $(1 - w_P)$ is the weight on risk-free cash, changing w_P does not change the Sharpe ratio, as can be seen in this equation.

$$SR_C = \frac{R_C - R_F}{STD(R_C)} = \frac{w_P(R_P - R_F)}{w_P STD(R_P)} = SR_P$$

For Property 2, the information ratio of an unconstrained portfolio is unaffected by multiplying the active security weights, Δw_i by a constant.

5   B is correct. The highest squared Sharpe ratio of an actively managed portfolio is:

$$SR_P^2 = SR_B^2 + IR^2 = 0.333^2 + 0.15^2 = 0.1334$$

The highest Sharpe ratio is $SR_P = \sqrt{0.1334} = 0.365$

6   A is correct. The optimal amount of active risk is:

$$STD(R_A) = \frac{IR}{SR_B} STD(R_B) = \frac{0.15}{0.333} 18.0\% = 8.11\%$$

The weight on the active portfolio (Indigo) would be 8.11%/8.0% = 1.014 and the weight on the benchmark portfolio would be 1 − 1.014 = −0.014.

We can demonstrate that these weights achieve the maximum Sharpe ratio (of 0.365). Note that 8.11% is the optimal level of active risk, and that Indigo has an expected active return of 1.014(1.2%) = 1.217% over the benchmark (and a total excess return of 6.0% + 1.217% = 7.217%. The portfolio total risk is

$$STD(R_P)^2 = STD(R_B)^2 + STD(R_A)^2 = 18.0^2 + 8.111^2 = 389.788$$

Taking the square root, $STD(R_P) = 19.743$, and the optimal Sharpe ratio is indeed 7.217/19.743 = 0.365.

7   B is correct. The active portfolio that is optimal is the portfolio with the highest Information ratio, the ratio of active return to active risk. The IRs for the three active portfolios are:

$IR_A = 1.0/10.0 = 0.10$

$IR_B = 0.5/3.0 = 0.167$

$IR_C = 0/2.0 = 0.00$

Portfolio B has the highest IR and is the best active portfolio; it is therefore the best portfolio to combine with the benchmark.

8   C is correct. Using the equation $IR^* = IC \times \sqrt{BR}$ and assuming that breadth can be interpreted as number of securities in the portfolio, solving for breadth in the equation above yields $\left(\frac{0.75}{0.1819}\right)^2 = 17.000$.

9   C is correct. The transfer coefficient measures how well the anticipated (ex-ante), risk adjusted returns correlate with the risk-adjusted active weights. This is also expressed in the equation for the transfer coefficient: $TC = COR(\mu_i/\sigma_i, \Delta w_i \sigma_i)$.

10 B is correct. The IC measures an investment manager's ability to forecast returns.

11 B is correct. A closet index will have a very low active risk and will also have a Sharpe ratio very close to the benchmark. Therefore, Statements I and III are consistent with a closet index portfolio. A closet index's information ratio can be indeterminate (because the active risk is so low), and often negative due to management fees.

12 A is correct. Manager A has the highest information ratio. The information ratio is defined as $IR = \dfrac{\text{active return}}{\text{active risk}}$. The managers in this example have the following information ratios:

	Manager A	Manager B	Manager C
Information ratio	0.7/3.2 = 0.219	0.6/3.1 = 0.194	1.2/6.3 = 0.190

13 B is correct. The information ratio is unaffected by rebalancing the active portfolio and the benchmark portfolio. In this case, the active return and active risk are both reduced by 25%, and the information ratio will be unchanged.

14 C is correct. The proper statistic to calculate is the information coefficient, and it is defined as follows:

$$IC = COR\left(\frac{R_{Ai}}{\sigma_i}, \frac{\mu_i}{\sigma_i}\right)$$

A manager is a good forecaster if his or her ex-ante active return expectations (forecasts) are highly correlated with the realized active returns. The information coefficient requires that these forecasts and realized returns be risk-weighted. When this is done for the three managers, the risk-weighted forecasts and realized returns are:

	Risk-weighted forecasts, μ_i/σ_i			R_{Ai}/σ_i
	Manager 1	Manager 2	Manager 3	Realized
Security 1	0.176	0.235	0.147	0.353
Security 2	0.400	0.100	0.150	0.700
Security 3	0.417	0.000	0.042	0.333
Security 4	0.240	0.080	0.060	0.080

The ICs are found by calculating the correlations between each manager's forecasts and the realized risk-weighted returns. The three managers have the following ICs:

	Manager 1	Manager 2	Manager 3
Information coefficient	0.5335	0.0966	0.6769

Manager 3 has the highest IC.

15 B is correct. The proper statistic to calculate is the transfer coefficient and it is defined as follows:

$$TC = COR(\mu_i/\sigma_i, \Delta w_i \sigma_i)$$

The TC is the cross-sectional correlation between the forecasted active security returns and the actual active weights, adjusted for risk.

	Risk-weighted forecasts, μ_i/σ_i			Risk-adjusted weights, $\Delta w_i\sigma_i$		
	Manager 1	Manager 2	Manager 3	Manager 1	Manager 2	Manager 3
Security 1	0.1765	0.2353	0.1471	−0.0213	0.0340	−0.0085
Security 2	0.4000	0.1000	0.1500	0.0025	0.0000	0.0050
Security 3	0.4167	0.0000	0.0417	0.0090	−0.0120	0.0060
Security 4	0.2400	0.0800	0.0600	0.0063	−0.0250	−0.0125

The three managers have the following TCs:

	Manager 1	Manager 2	Manager 3
Transfer coefficient	0.7267	0.8504	−0.0020

Manager 2 has the highest TC.

16 A is correct. Manager 1's IR = TC × IC × $\sqrt{BR}$ = 1.0 × 0.15 × $\sqrt{50}$ = 1.06.
Manager 2's IR = 0.8 × 0.10 × $\sqrt{100}$ = 0.80. Manager 1's active return is 1.06(5.0)
= 5.3% and Manager 2's expected active return is 0.80(5.0) = 4.0%. Manager 1
has the greater expected active return.

17 C is correct. If the decisions about each of the 200 stocks are not independent,
and if the decisions about a stock from one month to the next are not independent, then Goudon Partners is overstating its estimates of its breadth and its
expected active returns.

18 B is correct. Although the relaxation of portfolio constraints will increase the
transfer coefficient (and expected active returns), the lower information coefficient reduces the information ratio and the expected active return.

19 A is correct. Because the benchmark does not contain many assets that Frazee
wants to invest in, the benchmark may not be representative of his investment
approach. Concern 2, as stated, is less important because it does not imply that
the cost of replicating the benchmark is a serious concern. Finally, Concern 3
actually states a generally positive feature of the benchmark.

20 B is correct. Active return from asset allocation is derived from differences
between the benchmark weight and the portfolio weight across asset classes.
For Fund X, the expected active return from asset allocation is calculated as:

Active Return from Asset Allocation

$$= \sum_{j=1}^{M} \Delta w_j R_{B,j} = (60 - 60)R_{B,e} + (40 - 40)R_{B,b} = 0$$

Where Δw_j is the difference in the active portfolio and the benchmark asset
weights, $R_{B,e}$ is the benchmark's return from global equities, and $R_{B,b}$ is the
benchmark's return from global bonds.

Because Fund X has the same asset weights as the benchmark across the two
asset classes (60% global equities, 40% global bonds), the expected active return
from asset allocation is zero.

21 C is correct. The IR measures the consistency of active return. The IR is calculated for the three funds as follows:

$$IR = \frac{R_P - R_B}{STD(P_P - R_B)} = \frac{R_A}{STD(R_A)}$$

IR for Fund X = (10.0 − 9.4)/5.2 = 0.6/5.2 = 0.12

IR for Fund Y = (11.6 − 9.4)/9.2 = 2.2/9.2 = 0.24

IR for Fund Z = (13.2 − 9.4)/15.1 = 3.8/15.1 = 0.25

Fund Z has the largest IR and thus is expected to produce the greatest consistency of active return.

22 B is correct. Given the IR for Fund W of 0.35 and the benchmark's SR of 0.44, the combination of the benchmark portfolio and Fund W would produce an SR of 0.55, calculated as follows:

$$SR_P^2 = SR_B^2 + IR^2$$

$$SR_P = (0.44^2 + 0.35^2)^{0.5} = 0.56$$

23 A is correct. The new assumption adds constraints to Fund W. The IR for a constrained portfolio generally decreases with the aggressiveness of the strategy because portfolio constraints reduce the transfer of active return forecasts into active weights. Furthermore, the optimal active risk is given by the following formula:

$$\sigma_A = TC\frac{IR}{SR_B}\sigma_B$$

The addition of portfolio constraints reduces the TC, thus also reducing the optimal active risk.

So, having maximum over- and underweight constraints on single-country positions decreases the optimal aggressiveness of the active management strategy.

24 B is correct. The IR measures the consistency of active return generation. A higher ratio generally indicates better managerial skill at achieving active returns on a risk-adjusted basis. The IR for Candidate B (0.746) is higher than the IR for Candidate A (0.582) and Candidate C (0.723).

Thus, Candidate B appears to have the greatest skill as indicated by the highest IR of 0.746.

25 C is correct. The IR is calculated as $IR = (TC)(IC)\sqrt{BR}$, where BR is breadth. Change 3, establishing new constraints of caps on the over- and underweight of sectors, reduces the correlation of optimal active weights with the actual active weights, which results in a decreased TC and thus a decrease in the IR. Change 1 (increasing portfolio size from 36 to 50) and Change 2 (increasing the frequency of rebalancing from annually to semiannually) would both likely have the effect of increasing the BR of the portfolio, which would increase the IR.

26 B is correct. Based on the differences in returns for the portfolio and benchmark in Exhibit 1, the value added by each asset class within the portfolio is shown in the following table:

	Subportfolio Return (%)	Benchmark Return (%)	Value Added (%)	Portfolio Allocation (%)
Equities subportfolio	36.9	31.6	5.3	63
Bond subportfolio	−2.4	−2.6	0.2	28
Real estate subportfolio	33.4	28.3	5.1	9

The value added from security selection is calculated as the sum of the actual portfolio weights multiplied by each subportfolio's value added measure. Thus, the value added from security selection is calculated as: Value added from security selection = 0.63(5.3%) + 0.28(0.2%) + 0.09(5.1%) = 3.9%.

A is incorrect. It represents the value added from asset allocation.

C is incorrect. It represents the total value added (3% + 3.9% = 6.1%).

27 A is correct. The value added from asset allocation is calculated as the sum of the differences in the weights between the strategic (benchmark) allocation and the actual subportfolio allocation multiplied by each subportfolio's benchmark return.

	Benchmark Return (%)	Actual Asset Allocation (%)	Strategic Asset Allocation (%)	Actual – Strategic Asset Allocation (%)
Equities subportfolio	31.6	63	60	+3
Bond subportfolio	−2.6	28	35	−7
Real estate subportfolio	28.3	9	5	+4

Thus, the value added by the active asset allocation decision is calculated as:

Value added from asset allocation decision = 0.03(31.6%) − 0.07(−2.6%) + 0.04(28.3%) = 2.3%.

B is incorrect. It is the value added from security selection.

C is incorrect. It is the total value added.

28 B is correct. The information ratio for a portfolio can be expressed as follows:

$$IR = (TC)(IC)\sqrt{BR}$$

The information ratios for the three subportfolios are calculated as follows:

	Information Ratio
Equities subportfolio	$0.90 \times 0.091 \times (21)^{0.5} = 0.38$
Bond subportfolio	$0.79 \times 0.087 \times (23)^{0.5} = 0.33$
Real estate subportfolio	$0.86 \times 0.093 \times (19)^{0.5} = 0.35$

Based on the information ratio, the equities subportfolio outperformed the real estate subportfolio. The information ratio for the equities subportfolio of 0.38 was higher than the information ratio for the real estate subportfolio of 0.35 and the bond subportfolio of 0.33.

29 C is correct. The information ratio for a portfolio of risky assets will generally shrink if cash is added to the portfolio. Because the diversified asset portfolio is an unconstrained portfolio, its information ratio would be unaffected by an increase in the aggressiveness of active weights.

READING

52

Algorithmic Trading and High-Frequency Trading

by John Bates, PhD

John Bates, PhD, is at Judge Business School, University of Cambridge (United Kingdom).

LEARNING OUTCOMES	
Mastery	**The candidate should be able to:**
☐	**a.** define algorithmic trading;
☐	**b.** distinguish between execution algorithms and high-frequency trading algorithms;
☐	**c.** describe types of execution algorithms and high-frequency trading algorithms;
☐	**d.** describe market fragmentation and its effects on how trades are placed;
☐	**e.** describe the use of technology in risk management and regulatory oversight;
☐	**f.** describe issues and concerns related to the impact of algorithmic and high-frequency trading on securities markets.

INTRODUCTION

1

It is estimated that 75% of US stock trades are not placed by humans but by computer algorithms. This figure has been expanding over time and is expected to continue to do so. More trading is done by machines than humans because the human brain cannot process the volumes of information needed to make trading decisions and place trades before a competitor does. Algorithms can process millions of pieces of data per second, make sub-millisecond decisions, and take autonomous actions.

A trading algorithm may be as straightforward as an *execution algorithm* that is programmed to intelligently slice up large trades on behalf of a buy-side firm (such as a pension fund or mutual fund) to minimize market impact. But an algorithm can get as complex as a self-learning, *high-frequency algorithm* that makes decisions on what, when, and how to trade and executes these trades itself, without any human input.

Adapted from a 2010 submission to the CFTC Technology Advisory Committee on Algorithmic and High-Frequency Trading. Dr. Bates is a member of the CFTC Technology Advisory Committee.

It is not just equities that are traded by algorithms; the same algorithmic trading trend is evident in other electronically traded asset classes: futures, foreign exchange (FX), bonds, energy, and so on. In all of these asset classes, algorithms are autonomously managing more and more of the trading decisions. And this trend is occurring in all trading markets around the world. There is, in fact, a high-frequency algorithmic war raging: Algorithms compete to find the best opportunities and execute on them first. This has been a concern to some parties who are worried that certain market participants have an "unfair advantage." But humans are still needed as the creators of algorithms and arbiters of good sense. It has not yet become possible to digitize the instincts of a really good trader!

Algorithms have a life cycle: from research to implementation to testing to tuning. Sometimes algorithms go wrong, which can be extremely costly. There is, therefore, increased interest in using compliance algorithms to monitor trading algorithms, with a view to detecting aberrant behavior.

2   THE BASICS OF ALGORITHMIC TRADING

At its most basic, an algorithm is "a sequence of steps to achieve a goal," and **algorithmic trading** is "using a computer to automate a trading strategy."[1] In almost all cases, algorithms encode what traders can do by watching the market and manually placing orders. But in the time it takes for a trader to take in information, decide on a trade, and enter a trade, algorithms can make and execute thousands of trading decisions.

There are two types of trading algorithms: algorithms for execution and algorithms for high-frequency trading (HFT).

2.1 Execution Algorithms

Execution algorithms are used to break down large orders and execute them over a period of time. The smaller trades can then be released at irregular intervals to reduce the probability of the trading strategy being detected by other market participants. The goal is to minimize the impact that a large order has in the market and to achieve a benchmarked price. Examples of execution algorithms include the **volume-weighted average price (VWAP)**,[2] **implementation shortfall**, and **market participation algorithms**. These algorithms take various approaches to determine how to break down a large order. The VWAP uses the historical trading volume distribution for a particular security over the course of a day and divides the order into slices, proportioned to this distribution. Implementation shortfall dynamically adjusts the schedule of the trade in response to market conditions to minimize the difference between the price at which the buy or sell decision was made and the final execution price. Market participation slices the order into segments intended to participate on a pro-rata basis with volume throughout the course of the execution period.

A typical use of an execution algorithm is the case in which a buy-side participant, such as a mutual fund, pension fund, or hedge fund, sends a broker an order to be executed algorithmically. The buy-side participant may want to execute a large order (such as building a new portfolio position or selling an entire position) and wants to achieve a benchmarked price, minimize the cost of execution, and minimize the

---

1 The term "algorithmic trading" is sometimes used more narrowly to describe what is subsequently defined as execution-only strategies or broker algorithms.
2 The VWAP is calculated by multiplying the number of shares traded during the day by the price at which they traded and then dividing that result by the total number of shares traded on that day.

likelihood of other market participants front running the order, thus driving the price higher (in the case of a buy order) or lower (in the case of a sell order). Rather than having a trader execute this order manually, the institution may elect to use a broker algorithm (a trading algorithm managed by a broker rather than the buy-side participant). The order can be transmitted either by phone or in an automatic way from a buy-side **execution management system (EMS)** as a **FIX** (financial information exchange) order.[3] The buy-side participant provides all the information, such as the specific instrument, whether the order is a buy or a sell order, the quantity, and the algorithm to use; this is called the **parent order**. An *instance* (a running version) of the execution algorithm is then *instantiated* (created and started to run with the relevant input parameters of the parent order) within the broker environment to trade the order. It is also possible to run these algorithms within the buy side and just send the **child orders** (a subset of the total order) straight to the market through **direct market access (DMA)**, which is the ability for a buy-side institution to trade directly using the exchange membership of a **sell-side** firm (its brokerage firm). To achieve this execution, some EMS have built-in algorithms and some institutions have built their own algorithms using such technologies as **complex event processing**, described in more detail later.

2.2 High-Frequency Trading Algorithms

Although execution algorithms are about automating "how to trade"—that is, how to place orders in the market—high-frequency trading algorithms add "when to trade" and even sometimes "what to trade." Execution algorithms are about minimizing market impact and trying to ensure a fair price, whereas HFT algorithms are about profit. The "high frequency" refers to the tracking of high-frequency streams of data (such as market data feeds or news feeds), making decisions based on patterns in those data that indicate possible trading opportunities, and automatically placing and managing orders to capitalize on those opportunities.

Market data feeds stream directly from trading venues, such as stock or futures exchanges, foreign exchange markets, or bond markets. The streams are made up of *events*, which describe a change in the state of the market, such as *quote events*, *trade events*, and *news events*. A quote event is a new bid or offer in the market for a certain instrument at a certain price level and with a certain available quantity (volume). A trade event shows a new trade that has taken place at a certain price and a certain volume. A news event contains news related to particular instruments or economic indicators. Although all news offers value, some news is more relevant than other news. If the news contained in a news event merely confirms pre-existing expectations, that event is likely to have a lesser impact than news "surprises." Algorithms gather data from these feeds and look for patterns that indicate interesting trading opportunities.

A term commonly associated with HFT is **statistical arbitrage** (or "stat arb"). Stat arb algorithms monitor instruments that are known to be statistically correlated with the goal of detecting breaks in the correlation that indicate trading opportunities. For example, consider the relationship (called the delta 1:1) between a bond, such as the 10-year government bond on ICAP (Brokertec), and a derivative of it on the Chicago Board of Trade (CBOT). These instruments tend to move together, but

---

3 The FIX protocol is an electronic communications protocol for the real-time global exchange of securities transactions and market information.

if that relationship breaks for a few milliseconds, there is an opportunity to buy one and sell the other at a profit. There are a variety of types of HFT algorithms for stat arb trading, including the following:

- *Pairs trading*—looking for breaks in the correlated relationships between pairs of instruments.

- *Index arbitrage*—monitoring for breaks in the correlated relationships between instruments and the index of its sector (e.g., Ford against the automotive sector or a stock index future against one or more of its underlying component elements).

- *Basket trading*—applying stat arb techniques to custom baskets of instruments rather than to individual instruments. The value of the basket is constantly recalculated by weighting the relative prices and holdings of each instrument in the basket and calculating an overall basket value as if it were a single instrument. This basket can then be used as part of a more complex strategy, such as pairs trading or index arbitrage.

- *Spread trading*—a related form of stat arb that is particularly popular in the futures market. The trading is based on taking positions, usually one long and one short, on instruments, with the profitability of the trade determined by movements in the spread (difference) between the two. Examples include the purchase of July corn and the sale of December corn (intra-market spread), the purchase of February lean hogs and the sale of February live cattle (inter-market spread), and the purchase of March Kansas City wheat and the sale of March Chicago wheat (inter-exchange spread). More complex inter-exchange multi-legged spreads include *crack spreads* (trading the differential between the price of crude oil and petroleum products), *spark spreads* (trading the theoretical gross margin of a gas-fired power plant derived from selling a unit of electricity against the price of the fuel required to produce this unit of electricity, including all other costs of operation, maintenance, and capital and other financial costs), and *crush spreads* (the purchase of soybean futures and the sale of soybean oil and soybean meal futures).

- *Mean reversion*—the underlying assumption that if an instrument moves too far from its average price over some recent time period, it will trade back toward that average (revert to the mean). The gap between the current price and the expected price represents a buying or selling opportunity. Mean reversion algorithms use real-time analytics to spot these buying and selling opportunities.

- *Delta neutral strategies*—strategies used in derivatives trading to earn a profit that is independent of the direction of price movement in the underlying asset. (When calculating options prices, five components called "the Greeks" are used. "Delta" is the amount by which an option's price is expected to move in proportion to a price movement in the underlying asset.) Delta neutral trading is a strategy in which multiple positions are taken to hedge the risk of price movements in the underlying asset. By combining the delta values of options and/or stocks to achieve an overall delta value of 0 (or very close to it), the trader can profit from the time decay of the option or from changes in volatility, irrespective of the direction in price of the underlying security.

In HFT strategies, low latency is very important. **Latency** is the time difference between stimulus and response. In a trading algorithm context, it is the amount of time taken for market data to be received, a pattern to be identified, a decision to be made, and trades to be placed. Low latency is important to get first mover advantage and to act on an opportunity before a competitor does. Latency needs to be considered end to end (i.e., an HFT algorithm should use low latency market data streaming from a trading venue as rapidly as possible, low latency analysis and decision making, and a low latency order execution channel directly to the trading venue). All of these things can add to the expense of running a trading firm. When an algorithm is particularly sensitive to latency and trades with only one trading venue, firms may co-locate their algorithms with that trading venue to reduce the distance that data must travel to and from the venue. We discuss more on what components must be considered in end-to-end latency below.

Low latency decision making is particularly relevant when placing multiple trades as part of a stat arb strategy. This process is called a *multi-legged* trade, in which each trade is a leg. First, it is important to act quickly on the liquidity opportunity seen in the market; fast reaction is important if the trader wants to beat a competitor to the opportunity. Second, it is important not to get "legged out," with one leg of the strategy executing but another leg being confronted with a market that has moved, which means the opportunity is lost. There are, of course, mitigating actions that can be taken in such cases, either automatically or manually.

HFT algorithms are typically used in bank proprietary trading groups, hedge funds, and proprietary trading firms. A pairs trading algorithm, for example, can be used to trade many different pairs of instruments. Creating a new pairs trade is called instantiating a new instance of an algorithm. The new trading strategy instance is given a set of key parameters. For example, it needs to know the instruments, e.g., Microsoft (MSFT) and Oracle (ORCL), and specific trading thresholds, such as at what level of correlation deviation should one be bought and the other sold. Once initiated, HFT algorithms often run with little human intervention. Typically, traders monitor the status, profit and loss (P&L), and other key parameters on real-time dashboards and can intervene when or if they believe it is necessary. In the case of spread trading, traders often use specialized tools called **spreaders** to model, implement, and manage spread trading.

The HFT algorithm types described are just a subset of the algorithms in the market, but they illustrate many of the principles. A selection of other areas in which high-frequency algorithmic techniques are used include the following:

- *Liquidity aggregation* and *smart order routing*. Markets have become increasingly fragmented as the number of venues trading the same instruments has proliferated. This phenomenon is known as market fragmentation and creates the potential for price and liquidity disparities across venues. As market fragmentation has continued, algorithmic techniques have been used to aggregate liquidity across markets and use smart order routing to send orders to the venues with the best price and liquidity. These techniques (described later in more detail) can be used by high-frequency algorithmic traders to operate more effectively in a fragmented environment.

- *Real-time pricing of instruments*. Algorithmic techniques have also been used in the real-time pricing of such instruments as bonds, options, and foreign exchange. Traditional pricing techniques use slower-moving pricing analytics and fundamentals to price instruments. However, higher-frequency algorithmic techniques can improve on these approaches to pricing by using information on what is happening in the aggregated market (i.e., given the current liquidity, whether the broker can make money by increasing the spread) and the tier and history of the customer the price is being published for (i.e., how should the spread be adjusted given the importance of this customer). High-frequency pricing can thus influence prices and spreads based on the up-to-millisecond view of the market and the tier of the customer.

- *Trading on news*. In the last couple of years, there has been increasing interest from HFT firms in incorporating news into HFT algorithms. The concept is that firms can trade automatically on news, such as economic releases, announcement of a war, or unexpected weather events, before a human trader can react. They can also correlate with and respond to patterns, such as the way in which news can be expected to affect price movements. For a number of years, a handful of highly innovative firms have been experimenting with news in HFT. More recently, this interest is growing with the introduction of new types of structured high-frequency news feeds. News providers are including tags in the feeds that enable algorithms to quickly extract key information, such as data associated with an economic release.

■ *Genetic tuning.* Another interesting technique is genetic tuning, in which many thousands of permutations of algorithms are run in parallel and fed with real market data but are not necessarily trading live in the market. The algorithms that have the most profitable theoretical P&L profile can be put into the market to trade live. Over time, live algorithms may become less profitable and can be deactivated. The profitable branches of algorithms can be grown, and the less profitable branches killed off. This model of *Darwinian trading* allows self-evolving systems to discover profitable opportunities through evolutionary processes, with some seeding and guidance by human experts. These techniques are still exploratory and are only used in a few advanced firms.

■ The ultimate goal of algorithmic trading and HFT is the "money machine"—an algorithm that figures out what to trade and the strategy to trade it and then continuously self-evolves to remain profitable and outwit competitors. Although there are many somewhat smart algorithms out there, most still require human expertise and oversight.

The Latency War

In all forms of algorithmic trading—but particularly in HFT—minimizing latency is a key factor in success. Specifically, trading groups are concerned with end-to-end latency—the total delay from the market data being generated at the trading venue(s) and being delivered to an algorithm, a decision being taken by an algorithm, and the necessary orders being placed and filled in the venue(s). When several firms are competing for the same opportunity, the one with the lowest latency wins. We describe many other aspects important to the success of algorithmic and high-frequency trading, but clearly, latency is very important. There are several components in the low latency value chain:

■ *Market data.* Traditionally, such firms as Thomson Reuters were the preferred one-stop-shop way of delivering market data. But market data intermediaries can add significant latency, and firms focused on HFT are interested in connecting directly to the trading venues through their market data application programming interfaces (APIs). Market data firms have responded by creating lower latency versions of their products, and new vendors have emerged.

■ *Algorithmic and high-frequency trading engine.* The traditional approach in top-tier firms was to hire the top talent and build algorithms in-house by hand using a traditional programming language, such as C++. These algorithms were tuned to minimize latency in response to patterns in market data. However, with the requirement for quicker time to market for new algorithms, such new technologies as complex event processing (CEP)—which combines rapid development with low latency response to complex patterns in market data—have become popular. CEP is discussed more fully in Section 5.

■ *Order execution.* In recent years, many trading venues have adopted the FIX protocol as the standard way to place orders. To minimize latency, many institutions connect directly to the venues and place and manage orders over FIX.

- *Physical connection*. Some firms have become focused on the physics of reducing latency—making the physical connection over which market data and orders are transmitted as fast as possible. There are a number of suppliers that can provide a dedicated network that is already wired into trading venues around the world.

- *Co-location*. At the extremes of reducing the latency physics is **co-location** (co-lo), in which firms actually install their algorithms next to or in the facilities of a trading venue. Several companies have built businesses around providing hosting platforms to allow trading firms to install their software in these co-lo facilities. The challenge with co-location comes for firms that run cross-market, cross-asset, or cross-border algorithms that might involve trading with multiple venues that are not geographically co-located. These algorithms usually should be hosted at a location with fast interconnect to all the necessary venues.

The Life Cycle of an Algorithm

OPTIONAL
SEGMENT

Proprietary algorithms, or customized versions of more common algorithms, are the key differentiator among both brokers that offer execution algorithms and HFT shops; if everyone has the same algorithms, there is no competitive advantage. In practice, there is not a tremendous difference between different brokers' VWAP algorithms or different proprietary trading firms' pairs trading algorithms, but each firm usually has its own "secret ingredient" that makes the algorithm slightly different. There are also obscure algorithmic approaches unique to individual firms, which are closely guarded secrets.

Once a trading opportunity has been discovered, there are several stages of development before an algorithm can go live.

- *Authoring and customization*. A discovered pattern must be translated into an algorithm that can trade in the market. A traditional approach has been to use an army of developers to code a strategy. This approach is disadvantaged by slow time to market; the possibility that the algorithm does not fulfill the trading strategy the business sought; and the danger of complex, convoluted code ("spaghetti code") that can be understood and maintained by only a few people, who may eventually leave the organization. Modeling tools have been developed that enable a strategy to be laid out in terms of state flow (control logic), rules, and analytics and that can generate an executable strategy to be loaded into an algorithm engine. An in-house build often creates a **black box**—an algorithm with hidden workings—that is only understood by a few technical wizards. The concept of a **white box** algorithm is becoming popular; a white box algorithm is built on a model whose logic is clearly visible to the business and can be easily changed.

- *Back testing and simulation*. Using recorded historic data, the author of the algorithm can determine how it would have performed under market conditions ranging from a bull market to a bear market or, more specifically, target its behavior using test data from days with certain known phenomena, such as a non-farm payroll or other economic releases or the market crash of 6 May 2010 (the "flash crash"), when US equity and futures prices dropped nearly 10% in a matter of minutes. Some blue-chip shares briefly traded at a penny, only to recover most of the lost ground before the end of the trading day. Simulation involves creating hypothetical simulated markets using historical asset prices and then running the algorithms as if they had been live during that historical period.

- *User acceptance testing*. Most trading groups believe that back testing and simulation are not substitutes for real use because reality can present scenarios that were not considered in back testing. Often, the algorithm will be tested in live markets with a small group of select early-adopter traders. Real-time pre-trade risk precautions can be built into all algorithmic platforms to provide additional protection against unforeseen circumstances.

■ *Production.* When an algorithm goes live—receives real market data, makes trading decisions, and places live orders in the market—it is said to be "in production." Algorithms usually need to be certified using the firm's internal certification procedures before they are put into production.

■ *Analysis and tuning.* Once an algorithm has been running live, its performance can be analyzed to detect ways in which it can be fine-tuned to be made more profitable or more efficient or respond more intelligently to certain risk scenarios. This continuous analysis may also reveal that an HFT algorithm is no longer profitable enough and should be modified or discontinued.

■ In addition to the run-time concerns around minimizing latency described earlier, there are other important drivers of the demand for rapid research and development in algorithmic trading. Research by Aite Group indicates that many trading algorithms have a lifespan of less than three months.[4] In fact, during the highly volatile markets of late 2008, some firms changed their algorithms on a daily basis to anticipate and respond to daily opportunities. Thus, *alpha discovery*—finding new patterns in the market that might be viable to trade on—is critical to the survival of a HFT firm.

■ *First-mover advantage.* The markets are constantly changing, and new patterns emerge around which algorithms can be built. It is key to be able to build, test, and deploy a new algorithm quickly because competitors may have spotted the same opportunity and may be trying to trade on it first.

■ *Adapting to change.* Changes in the market can impact the effectiveness of existing algorithms. An HFT algorithm that was trading on a phenomenon that only one firm had spotted initially may eventually lose its effectiveness as competitors spot the pattern and mine it more effectively. Thus, the original HFT algorithm might now be ineffective or even create a loss. The trading firm must be able to detect this quickly and either switch off or enhance the algorithm.

■ *Reverse engineering.* It is possible for other trading firms to **reverse engineer** a competitor's algorithm: Watch the pattern of orders, determine what triggers an algorithm to trade, and then create a competing algorithm to out-perform them.

END OPTIONAL SEGMENT

3   THE EVOLUTION OF ALGORITHMIC AND HIGH-FREQUENCY TRADING

The use of algorithms in the financial markets first gained footing as advances in technology offered capital market firms a trading edge. The evolution to electronic markets allowed traders to implement trading tools through open application programming interfaces (APIs). Algorithms, which can process more information and act more quickly than a human, were an obvious avenue for traders to explore to gain that additional edge. Over time, a number of factors have caused algorithmic trading to evolve further. This section explores that evolution.

One can compare algorithmic trading and HFT to gold mining. When gold is discovered in a new territory, it is often lying around on the surface of the ground. When more people hear about the gold, a gold rush ensues and everyone descends on the territory. Over time, those seeking gold have to pan for it in rivers or dig to

---

4 Aite Group, "The World According to Quants: Enter Alpha Generation Platforms," impact report, (July 2008).

find the hidden seams of gold. In algorithmic trading, and particularly in HFT, trading firms are always seeking new opportunities and trying to mine them before others descend on them.

Key drivers in the evolution of algorithmic trading and HFT over the past 15 years include the following:

- *Market fragmentation.* As the number of trading venues has proliferated, trading in any given instrument has been split (or fragmented) across these multiple venues. As a result, the available liquidity on any one exchange represents just a small portion of the aggregate liquidity for that instrument. Trading strategies have had to adapt to this fragmented liquidity to avoid intensifying the market impact of a large trade. Many asset classes have experienced fragmentation, and this trend shows no signs of fading. In the United States alone, order flow in exchange-listed equities is divided among 11 exchanges and 40 alternative trading systems.[5] Algorithmic techniques, such as **liquidity aggregation** and smart order routing, have evolved to capitalize on the challenges and opportunities presented by fragmentation. Liquidity aggregators create a "super book" that combines liquidity on a per symbol or currency pair basis. This offers a global-ordered view of market depth for each instrument regardless of which trading venue offers the liquidity. For example, the best bid for a Eurodollar future may be on the Chicago Mercantile Exchange (CME) and the second best may be ELX Markets, a fully electronic futures exchange. Smart order routing sends the order to the relevant market(s) on which the quote is displayed. Low latency and rapid update are clearly important to avoid trading on stale liquidity information.

- *Opportunities in new asset classes.* Initially, exchange-traded equities and futures markets were the focus of algorithmic trading because of three factors: fully electronic markets, open access to connect algorithms, and market fragmentation. As the foreign exchange and bond markets have become increasingly electronic, open, and fragmented, algorithmic trading and HFT have expanded in those markets as well. More recently, HFT involving energy trading has increased in popularity.

- *Opportunities in cross-asset class trading.* As new asset classes became more accessible to algorithmic trading, some firms added capabilities in cross-asset class trading for both profit opportunities and hedging purposes. An example of a cross-asset, profit-oriented trading opportunity is statistical arbitrage across futures and bonds: A US Treasury 10-year government bond listed on ICAP/ Brokertec is determined to have a correlation relationship with the US 10-year future listed on the CBOT. A slight deviation from this correlation relationship creates an opportunity to buy one and sell the other.

- *Opportunities in new geographies.* Algorithmic trading and HFT started predominantly in the US and UK markets but have spread geographically over time, first to other major trading centers, such as Tokyo, Sydney, Hong Kong, Toronto, and across Europe, and then to such locations as South Korea and Singapore. One of the hottest new markets is Brazil, where both futures and

---

5 Mary Jo White, "Enhancing Our Equity Market Structure," Presentation given at the Securities and Exchange Global Exchange and Brokerage Conference, New York (5 June 2014).

equities are now widely traded algorithmically on BM&FBOVESPA. At each stage, algorithms have to be tailored to the characteristics of the local markets. Each new market presents new trading opportunities.

- *Opportunities in cross-border trading.* As more instruments are listed in multiple countries, statistical arbitrage strategies can capitalize on any pricing disparities that arise as a result. This cross-border trading introduces a foreign exchange component into the strategy, requiring algorithms to convert the relative bids and offers in real time.

4   ALGORITHMIC AND HIGH-FREQUENCY TRADING PLATFORMS AND TECHNOLOGIES

Many firms still use in-house development for the custom creation of algorithms. However, because of the need to create, evolve, back test, and tune algorithms rapidly, as well as to accommodate connections to new trading venues, firms are increasingly using third-party products to accelerate their trading life cycle. Some key technologies integral to algorithmic trading include the following:

- *Execution management systems*—front-end trading systems that allow access to broker algorithms as well as access to custom algorithms integrated with the EMS.

- *Complex event processing*—a platform specifically designed for complex analysis and response to high-frequency data. CEP platforms incorporate graphical modeling tools that can rapidly capture and customize strategies and a trading engine connected to any combination of cross-asset market data and trading venues. CEP is used widely for algorithmic trading, HFT, liquidity aggregation, smart order routing, pre-trade risk analysis, and market surveillance.

- *Tick database*—a real-time time-series database designed to capture and store high-frequency market data for analysis and back testing.

5   USE OF ALGORITHMIC TECHNIQUES AS A SAFETY NET

The tools and techniques developed to facilitate algorithmic and high-frequency trading have proven useful for risk management of the algorithm itself and in the regulatory oversight of markets generally. The same techniques used in algorithmic trading—continuous data analysis, pattern recognition, self-learning, data visualization tools (e.g., graphical dash-boarding), and alerting—are now being built into many commercial tools used by regulators, exchanges, and trading firms.

5.1   Risk Management Uses of Trading Algorithms

HFT can scale the capabilities of a trader hundreds or thousands of times. However, it can also increase trading risk. To complement high-frequency trading, high-frequency pre-trade risk capabilities are needed. Many firms embraced this concept some time ago. However, some groups turned off their pre-trade risk management because it increased latency. They believed any potential downside was outweighed by the potential upside of trading first. That shortcut is used much less often following the 2008 market decline and with increased regulatory scrutiny.

Two approaches being successfully used to mitigate trading risk are the following:

- *Real-time pre-trade risk firewall.* It is possible to continuously recalculate risk exposures on positions while monitoring trades as they go to market and determining what impact they would have on pre-defined risk limits. In the event exposures would breach a pre-established risk threshold, trades can be blocked from going to market. It is also possible to monitor for erroneous trades, such as **fat finger trades** (trading errors like buying 1 share at $1,000 instead of 1,000 shares at $1), and block them. This capability is useful not only for trading groups but also for brokers offering **sponsored access**. Sponsored access enables direct market access (DMA) for clients of the broker who want to trade using the broker's exchange memberships. Doing so means, however, that the broker has liability if the client does something against regulations. Ideally, the broker will monitor this trading activity on a client-by-client basis. Using the latest technology platforms, such as CEP, enables pre-trade checks to be performed with minimal latency.

- *Back testing and market simulation.* As stated earlier, it is highly beneficial to test algorithms with a variety of real historical and pre-planned scenarios before putting them to work live to see how they can be expected to perform. This process can be done in conjunction with realistic and tunable market simulators.

5.2 Regulatory Oversight: Real-Time Market Monitoring and Surveillance

Several regulators around the world have recognized that real-time market monitoring and surveillance allows more rapid response to potential crises and market abuse, potentially allowing rapid action to prevent or minimize any market impact. The former UK regulator of the financial services industry, the Financial Services Authority (FSA), was one of the first to speak up on this issue and specify a system to achieve more real-time monitoring by using CEP. Now other regulators around the world are looking at similar approaches. Many trading venues have had real-time surveillance technologies for a long time, but there is a lack of consistency across the market. Brokers can also benefit from this kind of technology to prevent abuse in their trading operations and ensure their good reputations.

The goal of real-time monitoring is to detect anomalous market movements (e.g., price or volume spikes for a particular security on one or more exchanges). It provides an early warning system to potential market problems and enables rapid response.

The goal of real-time market surveillance is to detect potential market abuse while it is happening. The FSA drew an analogy that "traders are driving Ferraris and regulators are trying to catch them on bicycles." Using the same technology used in HFT for real-time surveillance and monitoring gives regulators "Ferraris as police cars" to enable them to keep up with the high-frequency markets. The kinds of patterns that can be detected include the following:

- *Insider trading.* A form of market abuse in which traders gain access to information that they should not be party to. An example of activity that might be subject to regulatory scrutiny is an unusually large trade by a trader who does not usually trade that particular instrument followed closely by a news event that moves the market in that instrument. Was it luck or inside information at work? If it happens several times, then it might be investigated, including monitoring message networks to see whom the trader has been speaking to.

■ *Front running orders.* A situation in which a trader with knowledge of a large buy-side order trades ahead of that order in anticipation of its market impact. Algorithms can be used to detect unusual and coincidental orders from a proprietary trader just prior to an event that moves the market, such as a large client order being placed by a trader in a brokerage with whom the proprietary trader has just been exchanging messages.

■ *Painting the tape.* A practice in which a trader manipulates the top of the book to make the market price go in one direction before executing its own trade at the more favorable price. For example, a trader continuously takes the best offer in the market in a particular instrument to drive the price up. Repeatedly taking the best offer is a fairly cost-effective way to drive the price up and may not involve buying a large quantity of the instrument. The trader then *sells* a large quantity of the same instrument.

■ *Fictitious orders.* A form of market abuse in which a trader sends orders with the intent of manipulating the price and thereby luring algorithms to respond. The term **quote stuffing** refers to one such practice in which large quantities of fictitious orders are rapidly entered into the market by an algorithm and then just as quickly cancelled. These orders distract other algorithms because they must be processed and analyzed; meanwhile, the source algorithm can ignore this activity and trade ahead of others or act on the pricing anomalies the fictitious orders created. Algorithms may also try to lure other algorithms into behaving in a particular way, slowing down other market participants. **Layering** is one such strategy designed to ignite a rapid price movement up or down by placing a legitimate order on one side of the market and layering multiple illegitimate orders on the other side to try to bait participants to trade with the real order. **Spoofing** is another strategy to manipulate prices; the algorithm places limit orders that are not intended to be executed.

■ *Wash trading.* A form of manipulation in which an investor simultaneously buys and sells the same financial instruments to generate trading volume and thus interest and perceived demand in instruments the trader wants to sell.

■ *Trader collusion.* A form of market abuse in which traders cooperate to deliberately manipulate the market in their favor. Two examples include the manipulation of Libor (London Interbank Offered Rate) and the foreign exchange benchmark rates through trader collusion. Libor is calculated by averaging the interbank borrowing interest rate estimates from major banks in London. In 2012, it was determined that traders had been colluding to inflate or deflate the rates to their advantage. In foreign exchange, the benchmark WM/Reuters FX rate is set daily based on a specific 60-second time window every day. Traders colluded to send through trades before and during the time window to manipulate the rates to their advantage. These incidents have led to increased surveillance of phone, messaging, and trader behavior.

Keeping an audit trail of market data and potential abuse cases is important. Tick databases can be used. Surveillance systems built on business analytics platforms can also be used to research new abuse patterns.

IMPACT OF ALGORITHMIC AND HIGH-FREQUENCY TRADING ON THE SECURITIES MARKETS

6

Algorithmic and high-frequency trading present both positive and negative repercussions for the markets as a whole. The positive impacts include the following:

- *Minimized market impact of large trades.* As already described, algorithmic trading provides an automated and intelligent way to break down large orders into smaller chunks to minimize their impact on the market while achieving a benchmarked price. Market statistics illustrate the impact: For all global markets, the average order size has fallen whereas the number of orders has risen significantly.

- *Lower cost of execution.* The use of algorithms, rather than more expensive traders, and the competition between brokers continue to drive down margins and help the buy side achieve a significantly reduced cost of execution.

- *Improved efficiency in certain markets.* Many emerging statistical arbitrage opportunities are usually quickly identified by firms, and algorithms can be created to exploit these opportunities and reduce such inefficiencies.

- *More open and competitive trading markets.* Although the large, top-tier firms are perceived as dominating the market, such technologies as CEP, widely available low latency market connectivity, and hosting environments enable small teams to run an advanced quant trading operation.

- *Improved and more efficient trading venues.* Increased competition for liquidity between trading venues is putting pressure on exchange costs, thereby accelerating the level of technological advancement provided by trading venues. Lower matching latency, improved order throughput, and more value-added services, such as co-location, have become more widely available.

Concerns surrounding the impact of algorithmic and high-frequency trading on securities markets include the following:

- *Fear of an unfair advantage.* There is a strong perception among members of the US Congress and the public at large that algorithmic traders have an unfair advantage relative to other market participants. Because they are often co-located with the trading venues and have super-fast algorithms, it is perceived that they can see market movements milliseconds before other participants and thus perhaps "front run" the ordinary investor. Many also contend that such behavior as spoofing is widespread. The flash crash, Knight Capital Group fiasco, Libor manipulation, and FX manipulation are some events among many that have been attributed—rightly or wrongly—to high-frequency traders. Because algorithmic firms have access to order book data, they can learn from and back test strategies by using information that is not readily available to other investors. And lastly, it is perceived that regulators are lagging in their capability to monitor the activity of high-frequency traders.

- *Acceleration and accentuation of market movements.* Algorithms have no emotion; they are looking for pre-programmed opportunities and will ruthlessly execute against them. Although algorithms did not cause the flash crash, it is likely they accelerated and accentuated it. Market panic in particular instruments can trigger stop-losses and a rapidly declining price, which may lead an algorithm to short those instruments to buy them back at a profit.

- *Gaming the market.* With millions of autonomous algorithms looking for opportunities, it is easier to spoof the market by sending in anomalous quotes to try to trigger certain behavior in algorithms. It is also easier to carry out potential market abuse, such as wash trades or painting the tape, because finding that abuse in a high-frequency, fragmented world is challenging.

- *Increased risk profile.* Although algorithms can make an individual trader hundreds or thousands of times more productive, they can also increase the risk profile of that trader by hundreds or thousands of times. Because algorithms are moving very fast, without proper pre-trade risk precautions, critical exposure levels can be quickly exceeded and errors, such as fat finger trades, can be quickly accentuated.

- *Algorithms gone wild.* Trading firms have varying standards of certification for algorithms before they can go live, and in some cases, some logic may be incorrect or missing. Also, algorithms may encounter scenarios they are not prepared for. For these reasons, algorithms can go wrong or behave contrary to their intended specification, which can result in incorrect orders being placed and a large potential loss. Worse still, it can result in a stream of spurious orders being placed. There have been a number of such cases covered in the press in recent years—most notably, the Knight Capital algorithm that went out of control and lost the firm $440 million in 30 minutes in 2012. Algorithms run at very high speed, and detecting these problems can be challenging. One way to catch them is to have a live, human trader watching positions and the behavior of the algorithm in real time. A well-designed algorithmic platform will have a "kill switch" to pull one or all algorithms from the market. Although traders often prefer to hedge undesired positions manually, a more effective approach to out-of-control algorithms is to have a real-time pre-trade risk firewall capability that can block incorrect or spurious trades if they fall outside a particular behavior, break policies, or exceed particular risk exposures.

Knight Capital Says Trading Glitch Cost It $440 Million

"The Knight Capital Group announced on Thursday that it lost $440 million when it sold all the stocks it accidentally bought Wednesday morning because of a computer glitch. … The problem on Wednesday led the firm's computers to rapidly buy and sell millions of shares in over a hundred stocks for about 45 minutes after the markets opened. Those trades pushed the value of many stocks up, and the company's losses appear to have occurred when it had to sell the overvalued shares back into the market at a lower price."

Source: Nathaniel Popper, *New York Times DealBook* (2 August 2012).

- *Potential for market denial-of-service-style attacks.* There have been a number of incidents when out-of-control algorithms have fired streams of orders into the market in quick succession. Such an incident can act in the same way as a network "denial of service" attack in which an IT network firewall spends all its time rejecting fraudulent packets and thus cannot accept any real data packets. The market can experience a significant slowdown as it attempts to handle this fast-paced, high-volume activity.

- *Additional load on trading venues.* Many algorithms adjust their bids and offers nearly continuously—canceling current orders and replacing them with modified orders—as they respond to small changes in the markets. This process also has the potential to slow down the markets. Many trading venues have considered charging for excessive order cancellations because of the additional load that it creates.

■ *Increased difficulty of policing the market.* Regulators' efforts to monitor the markets and ensure their effective functioning are challenged by the multitude of high-frequency algorithms, market fragmentation, cross-asset trading, and **dark pools** (trading venues that do not publish their liquidity and are only available to selected clients). Although new technologies and techniques, such as CEP-powered real-time surveillance, can help here, the situation is still complex.

There is also one deeply fundamental question surrounding HFT that is the subject of continued debate among market participants:

> Do algorithmic and high-frequency trading disadvantage the smaller trading firms and other market participants?

Much has been made in the mainstream press of the unfair advantage of HFT compared with techniques available to smaller firms and the ordinary investor. The techniques described in this article, as well as the market and news event data purchased by HFTs, are available to any firm; in fact, asset managers use trading algorithms on behalf of their clients, the ordinary investor. However, these techniques are quite costly to develop and run, and many investors cannot afford them, creating unequal access to information. A 2013 review of HFT research literature[6] contains some indications that smaller investors are disadvantaged by this unequal access to information but also strongly supports the assertion that HFT has led to the narrowing of bid–ask spreads, lower transaction costs, and an increase in liquidity and price efficiency—without an increase in volatility.

SUMMARY

Algorithmic and high-frequency trading are important factors in today's markets. Just like electronic terminals replaced open outcry (trading by shouting and waving bits of paper in the trading pits of stock exchanges), so algorithms are replacing the humans that operated the electronic trading terminals in various forms of trade execution. Key points to remember regarding algorithmic trading include the following:

■ There are two main types of algorithms: execution algorithms, which minimize the market impact of large orders, and high-frequency algorithms, which constantly monitor real-time market data and look for patterns to trade on.

■ Algorithms can adapt to market fragmentation by incorporating liquidity aggregation and intelligent smart order routing capabilities.

■ Algorithms can be used for real-time pricing of instruments.

■ Low latency is important and latency at each layer of the end-to-end latency equation must be considered: the physical connections to the market, the market data feeds, the algorithmic engine, and the order execution feed to a trading venue.

■ The life cycle of an algorithm includes alpha discovery to find new patterns, algorithm implementation, back testing, production, and tuning.

---

6 See https://secure.fia.org/ptg-downloads/HFT_Literature_Review_0913.pdf.

- Algorithms are used in many asset classes, including equities, futures, foreign exchange, bonds, and energy. Algorithms will likely be developed to exploit additional areas as new types of assets migrate to electronic trading.

- Surveillance algorithms can be used to spot potential market abuse and compliance breaches.

- The broad market impact of algorithmic trading is largely positive. Research shows that HFT has led to tighter bid–ask spreads, lower transaction costs, increases in liquidity, and improved pricing efficiency.

- The primary concerns regarding HFT are the potential for HFT to accentuate and accelerate market movements: the risk posed by an out-of-control algorithm, the ability of a trader to manipulate the market through spoofing or quote stuffing, the increased complexity of regulatory oversight, and the impact of unequal access to information.

GLOSSARY

Algorithmic trading	The use of computer algorithms to place and manage orders in the market. Some algorithms operate on behalf of a human trader; others are completely autonomous.
Basket trading	Trading not with single instruments but with multiple instruments (a basket), with the value of the basket being continuously recalculated in real time.
Black box	An algorithm for which the workings are hidden.
Child order	An order generated by a trading algorithm and put in the market to execute part of the overall parent order.
Co-location (co-lo)	The act of locating trading algorithms next to a trading venue or in a site with very low latency connections to a trading venue in order to reduce overall end-to-end trade latency.
Complex event processing (CEP)	A platform specifically designed for complex analysis and response to high-frequency data. CEP platforms typically include modeling tools, a CEP engine, and market data connectors.
Dark pools	Trading venues that do not publish their liquidity and are only available to selected clients.
Direct market access (DMA)	A way for buy-side firms (such as hedge funds) to trade using the exchange membership of a sell-side firm. The buy-side firm sends the trades directly to market over a DMA connection to the sell-side firm. In this way, a buy-side firm can run its own proprietary algorithms without having to rely on or share knowledge with the sell-side firm. (See also "sponsored access.")
Execution algorithms	Execution algorithms operate on behalf of a trader to break down large orders intelligently to minimize market impact. They are typically used by or on behalf of buy-side institutions.
Execution management system (EMS)	Software applications used by traders and designed to display market data and provide fast access to trading venues for transacting orders. They may also make local algorithms available or provide access to broker algorithms.
Fat finger trades	Trades in which order entry mistakes are made, such as buying 1 share at $1,000 instead of 1,000 shares at $1.
Front running of orders	A form of insider trade that involves a trader being party to a large buy-side order that it should not know about and then trading ahead of that order in anticipation of its market impact.
FIX	The financial information exchange (FIX) protocol, a messaging protocol used by financial institutions to communicate trade information.
Market fragmentation	The development of multiple markets in a given asset class that each list the same instruments. For example, there are many US equities venues listing the same stocks.

(continued)

High-frequency trading (HFT) algorithms	High-frequency trading uses autonomous algorithms that analyze and respond to real-time market data to decide what, how, and when to trade. Typically, they are fast-moving algorithms that analyze thousands of market events per second and make sub-millisecond trading decisions. Often, the holding time for stocks is very short—potentially intra-day holding or even holding for only a few seconds!
Implementation shortfall algorithm	An algorithm that minimizes the trade-off between the market impact of immediately executing an order versus the risk of market drift if the order takes too long to execute.
Index arbitrage	Monitoring for breaks in the correlated relationships between instruments and the index of its sector (e.g., Ford against the automotive sector or a stock index future against one or more of its underlying component elements).
Insider trading	A form of market abuse in which traders gain information that they should not be party to and trade using that information (e.g., good or bad news on a company).
Latency	The time difference between stimulus and response. In a trading algorithm context, it is the amount of time from the market data being received, a pattern being identified, a decision being made, and trades being placed. In algorithmic trading, the lowest end-to-end latency possible is desirable.
Layering	Using fictitious orders on one side of the market to manipulate algorithms to buy a real order on the other side of the market.
Liquidity aggregation	Monitoring multiple trading venues in a fragmented market and combining their order books into a "super book" so a trader or algorithm can always find the best price and liquidity combination. (See also smart order routing.)
Market participation algorithm	An algorithm that executes an order as a percentage of volume trading in the markets.
Painting the tape	A manipulative practice in which a trader continuously takes the best offer in the market in a particular instrument to drive the price up; then the trader sells a large quantity of the same instrument.
Parent order	An execution algorithm is given a parent order (e.g., execute 100,000 shares of Apple), and then it uses logic to divide it up into child orders that are fed into the market.
Pairs trading	Looking for breaks in the correlated relationships between pairs of instruments.
Quote stuffing	Sending large quantities of fictitious orders into the market to distract other algorithms.
Reverse engineering	Being able to work out how an algorithm works from its behavior in the market and replicating its behavior.
Sell side	The part of the financial industry involved with the creation, promotion, analysis, and sale of securities. It includes investment bankers who serve as intermediaries between issuers of securities and the investing public, analysts who perform stock research and make ratings, and the market makers who provide liquidity in the market.

Smart order routing	An algorithm to route an order to the trading venue with the best price and liquidity at a certain point in time.
Spoofing	Using fictitious limit orders to manipulate prices.
Sponsored access	A service provided by a broker to certain clients that enables direct market access for those clients to trade using the broker's exchange memberships.
Spread trading	Taking positions, usually one long and one short, on instruments with profitability being determined by the spread (difference) between the two. (See also spreaders.)
Spreaders	Specialized tools used by traders to model, implement, and manage spread trading.
Statistical arbitrage (stat arb)	A trading strategy designed to detect and trade on breaks in the correlation between instruments that are known to be statistically correlated.
Tick database	A real-time time-series database designed to capture and store high-frequency market and trade data for analysis and back testing.
Trader collusion	Market manipulation in which traders cooperate to deliberately manipulate the market in their favor.
Wash trading	A form of market manipulation in which an investor simultaneously buys and sells the same financial instruments to generate trading volume and thus interest and perceived demand in instruments the trader wants to sell.
White box	An algorithm whose workings are exposed and can be modified or customized.
Volume-weighted average price (VWAP)	An execution algorithm that seeks to achieve a benchmarked price at or better than the VWAP. The VWAP is calculated by adding the price traded for every transaction (price multiplied by volume traded) and then dividing by the total volume traded for the day. A VWAP algorithm places orders over a time period based on the historic volume distribution, with the aim of meeting or beating the VWAP.

Glossary

Abandonment option   The ability to terminate a project at some future time if the financial results are disappointing.

Abnormal earnings   See *residual income.*

Abnormal return   The return on an asset in excess of the asset's required rate of return; the risk-adjusted return.

Absolute convergence   The idea that developing countries, regardless of their particular characteristics, will eventually catch up with the developed countries and match them in per capita output.

Absolute valuation model   A model that specifies an asset's intrinsic value.

Absolute version of PPP   The extension of the law of one price to the broad range of goods and services that are consumed in different countries.

Accounting estimates   Estimates used in calculating the value of assets or liabilities and in the amount of revenue and expense to allocate to a period. Examples of accounting estimates include, among others, the useful lives of depreciable assets, the salvage value of depreciable assets, product returns, warranty costs, and the amount of uncollectible receivables.

Accumulated benefit obligation   The actuarial present value of benefits (whether vested or non-vested) attributed, generally by the pension benefit formula, to employee service rendered before a specified date and based on employee service and compensation (if applicable) before that date. The accumulated benefit obligation differs from the projected benefit obligation in that it includes no assumption about future compensation levels.

Acquirer   The company in a merger or acquisition that is acquiring the target.

Acquiring company   The company in a merger or acquisition that is acquiring the target.

Acquisition   The purchase of some portion of one company by another; the purchase may be for assets, a definable segment of another entity, or the purchase of an entire company.

Active factor risk   The contribution to active risk squared resulting from the portfolio's different-than-benchmark exposures relative to factors specified in the risk model.

Active return   The return on a portfolio minus the return on the portfolio's benchmark.

Active risk   The standard deviation of active returns.

Active risk squared   The variance of active returns; active risk raised to the second power.

Active share   A measure of how similar a portfolio is to its benchmark. A manager who precisely replicates the benchmark will have an active share of zero; a manager with no holdings in common with the benchmark will have an active share of one.

Active specific risk   The contribution to active risk squared resulting from the portfolio's active weights on individual assets as those weights interact with assets' residual risk.

Adjusted funds from operations   Funds from operations (FFO) adjusted to remove any non-cash rent reported under straight-line rent accounting and to subtract maintenance-type capital expenditures and leasing costs, including leasing agents' commissions and tenants' improvement allowances.

Adjusted present value   (APV) As an approach to valuing a company, the sum of the value of the company, assuming no use of debt, and the net present value of any effects of debt on company value.

Adjusted R^2   A measure of goodness-of-fit of a regression that is adjusted for degrees of freedom and hence does not automatically increase when another independent variable is added to a regression.

Administrative regulations or administrative law   Rules issued by government agencies or other regulators.

Advanced set   The reference interest rate is set at beginning of the settlement period.

Advanced settled   An arrangement in which the settlement is made at the beginning of the settlement period.

Agency costs   Costs associated with the conflict of interest present when a company is managed by non-owners. Agency costs result from the inherent conflicts of interest between managers and equity owners.

Agency costs of equity   The smaller the stake that managers have in the company, the less is their share in bearing the cost of excessive perquisite consumption or not giving their best efforts in running the company.

Agency issues   Conflicts of interest that arise when the agent in an agency relationship has goals and incentives that differ from the principal to whom the agent owes a fiduciary duty. Also called *agency problems* or *principal–agent problems.*

Agency problem   A conflict of interest that arises when the agent in an agency relationship has goals and incentives that differ from the principal to whom the agent owes a fiduciary duty.

Alpha   The return on an asset in excess of the asset's required rate of return; the risk-adjusted return.

American Depositary Receipt   A negotiable certificate issued by a depositary bank that represents ownership in a non-US company's deposited equity (i.e., equity held in custody by the depositary bank in the company's home market).

Analysis of variance (ANOVA)   The analysis of the total variability of a dataset (such as observations on the dependent variable in a regression) into components representing different sources of variation; with reference to regression, ANOVA provides the inputs for an *F*-test of the significance of the regression as a whole.

Arbitrage   1) The simultaneous purchase of an undervalued asset or portfolio and sale of an overvalued but equivalent asset or portfolio, in order to obtain a riskless profit on the price differential. Taking advantage of a market inefficiency in a risk-free manner. 2) The condition in a financial market in which equivalent assets or combinations of assets sell for two different prices, creating an opportunity to profit at no risk with no commitment of money. In a well-functioning financial market, few arbitrage opportunities are possible. 3) A risk-free operation that earns an expected positive net profit but requires no net investment of money.

Arbitrage-free models　Term structure models that project future interest rate paths that emanate from the existing term structure. Resulting prices are based on a no-arbitrage condition.

Arbitrage-free valuation　An approach to valuation that determines security values that are consistent with the absence of arbitrage opportunities.

Arbitrage opportunity　An opportunity to conduct an arbitrage; an opportunity to earn an expected positive net profit without risk and with no net investment of money.

Arbitrage portfolio　The portfolio that exploits an arbitrage opportunity.

Asset-backed securities　A type of bond issued by a legal entity called a *special purpose vehicle* (SPV), on a collection of assets that the SPV owns. Also, securities backed by receivables and loans other than mortgage loans.

Asset-based approach　Approach that values a private company based on the values of the underlying assets of the entity less the value of any related liabilities.

Asset-based valuation　An approach to valuing natural resource companies that estimates company value on the basis of the market value of the natural resources the company controls.

Asset beta　The unlevered beta; reflects the business risk of the assets; the asset's systematic risk.

Asset purchase　An acquisition in which the acquirer purchases the target company's assets and payment is made directly to the target company.

Asymmetric information　The differential of information between corporate insiders and outsiders regarding the company's performance and prospects. Managers typically have more information about the company's performance and prospects than owners and creditors.

At market　When a forward contract is established, the forward price is negotiated so that the market value of the forward contract on the initiation date is zero.

At-the-money　An option in which the underlying value equals the exercise price.

Autocorrelation　The correlation of a time series with its own past values.

Autoregressive model (AR)　A time series regressed on its own past values, in which the independent variable is a lagged value of the dependent variable.

Available-for-sale investments　Debt and equity securities not classified as either held-to-maturity or fair value through profit or loss securities. The investor is willing to sell but not actively planning to sell. In general, available-for-sale securities are reported at fair value on the balance sheet.

Backward integration　A merger involving the purchase of a target ahead of the acquirer in the value or production chain; for example, to acquire a supplier.

Backwardation　A condition in futures markets in which the spot price exceeds the futures price; also, the condition in which the near-term (closer to expiration) futures contract price is higher than the longer-term futures contract price.

Bankruptcy　A declaration provided for by a country's laws that typically involves the establishment of a legal procedure that forces creditors to defer their claims.

Basic earnings per share　(EPS) Net earnings available to common shareholders (i.e., net income minus preferred dividends) divided by the weighted average number of common shares outstanding during the period.

Basis　The difference between the spot price and the futures price.

Basis trade　A trade based on the pricing of credit in the bond market versus the price of the same credit in the CDS market. To execute a basis trade, go long the "underpriced" credit and short the "overpriced" credit. A profit is realized when the price of credit between the short and long position converges.

Bear hug　A tactic used by acquirers to circumvent target management's objections to a proposed merger by submitting the proposal directly to the target company's board of directors.

Bear spread　A spread that becomes more valuable when the price of the underlying asset declines.

Benchmark　A comparison portfolio; a point of reference or comparison.

Benchmark value of the multiple　In using the method of comparables, the value of a price multiple for the comparison asset; when we have comparison assets (a group), the mean or median value of the multiple for the group of assets.

Bill-and-hold basis　Sales on a bill-and-hold basis involve selling products but not delivering those products until a later date.

Blockage factor　An illiquidity discount that occurs when an investor sells a large amount of stock relative to its trading volume (assuming it is not large enough to constitute a controlling ownership).

Bond indenture　A legal contract specifying the terms of a bond issue.

Bond yield plus risk premium method　An estimate of the cost of common equity that is produced by summing the before-tax cost of debt and a risk premium that captures the additional yield on a company's stock relative to its bonds. The additional yield is often estimated using historical spreads between bond yields and stock yields.

Bonding costs　Costs borne by management to assure owners that they are working in the owners' best interest (e.g., implicit cost of non-compete agreements).

Book value　Shareholders' equity (total assets minus total liabilities) minus the value of preferred stock; common shareholders' equity.

Book value of equity　Shareholders' equity (total assets minus total liabilities) minus the value of preferred stock; common shareholders' equity.

Book value per share　The amount of book value (also called carrying value) of common equity per share of common stock, calculated by dividing the book value of shareholders' equity by the number of shares of common stock outstanding.

Bootstrapping　A statistical method for estimating a sample distribution based on the properties of an approximating distribution.

Bottom-up approach　With respect to forecasting, an approach that usually begins at the level of the individual company or a unit within the company.

Bottom-up investing　An approach to investing that focuses on the individual characteristics of securities rather than on macroeconomic or overall market forecasts.

Breakup value　The value derived using a sum-of-the-parts valuation.

Breusch–Pagan test　A test for conditional heteroskedasticity in the error term of a regression.

Brokerage　The business of acting as agents for buyers or sellers, usually in return for commissions.

Bull spread   A spread that becomes more valuable when the price of the underlying asset rises.

Buy-side analysts   Analysts who work for investment management firms, trusts, and bank trust departments, and similar institutions.

Calendar spread   A strategy in which an investor sells (or buys) a near-dated call and buys (or sells) a longer-dated one on the same underlying asset and with the same strike.

Callable bond   Bond that includes an embedded call option that gives the issuer the right to redeem the bond issue prior to maturity, typically when interest rates have fallen or when the issuer's credit quality has improved.

Cannibalization   Cannibalization occurs when an investment takes customers and sales away from another part of the company.

Cap rate   See *capitalization rate*.

Capital charge   The company's total cost of capital in money terms.

Capital deepening   An increase in the capital-to-labor ratio.

Capital rationing   A capital rationing environment assumes that the company has a fixed amount of funds to invest.

Capital structure   The mix of debt and equity that a company uses to finance its business; a company's specific mixture of long-term financing.

Capitalization of earnings method   In the context of private company valuation, valuation model based on an assumption of a constant growth rate of free cash flow to the firm or a constant growth rate of free cash flow to equity.

Capitalization rate   The divisor in the expression for the value of perpetuity. In the context of real estate, the divisor in the direct capitalization method of estimating value. The cap rate equals net operating income divided by value.

Capitalized cash flow method   In the context of private company valuation, valuation model based on an assumption of a constant growth rate of free cash flow to the firm or a constant growth rate of free cash flow to equity. Also called *capitalized cash flow model*.

Capitalized cash flow model   In the context of private company valuation, valuation model based on an assumption of a constant growth rate of free cash flow to the firm or a constant growth rate of free cash flow to equity. Also called *capitalized cash flow method*.

Capitalized income method   In the context of private company valuation, valuation model based on an assumption of a constant growth rate of free cash flow to the firm or a constant growth rate of free cash flow to equity.

Capped floater   Floating-rate bond with a cap provision that prevents the coupon rate from increasing above a specified maximum rate. It protects the issuer against rising interest rates.

Carried interest   A share of any profits that is paid to the general partner (manager) of an investment partnership, such as a private equity or hedge fund, as a form of compensation designed to be an incentive to the manager to maximize performance of the investment fund.

Carry arbitrage model   A no-arbitrage approach in which the underlying instrument is either bought or sold along with an opposite position in a forward contract.

Carry benefits   Benefits that arise from owning certain underlyings; for example, dividends, foreign interest, and bond coupon payments.

Carry costs   Costs that arise from owning certain underlyings. They are generally a function of the physical characteristics of the underlying asset and also the interest forgone on the funds tied up in the asset.

Cash available for distribution   Funds from operations (FFO) adjusted to remove any non-cash rent reported under straight-line rent accounting and to subtract maintenance-type capital expenditures and leasing costs, including leasing agents' commissions and tenants' improvement allowances.

Cash-generating unit   The smallest identifiable group of assets that generates cash inflows that are largely independent of the cash inflows of other assets or groups of assets.

Cash offering   A merger or acquisition that is to be paid for with cash; the cash for the merger might come from the acquiring company's existing assets or from a debt issue.

Cash-secured put   An option strategy involving the writing of a put option and simultaneously depositing an amount of money equal to the exercise price into a designated account.

Cash settled   A procedure used in certain derivative transactions that specifies that the long and short parties engage in the equivalent cash value of a delivery transaction.

Cash settlement   A procedure used in certain derivative transactions that specifies that the long and short parties engage in the equivalent cash value of a delivery transaction.

Catalyst   An event or piece of information that causes the marketplace to re-evaluate the prospects of a company.

CDS spread   A periodic premium paid by the buyer to the seller that serves as a return over Libor required to protect against credit risk.

Chain rule of forecasting   A forecasting process in which the next period's value as predicted by the forecasting equation is substituted into the right-hand side of the equation to give a predicted value two periods ahead.

Cheapest-to-deliver   The debt instrument that can be purchased and delivered at the lowest cost yet has the same seniority as the reference obligation.

Clean surplus accounting   Accounting that satisfies the condition that all changes in the book value of equity other than transactions with owners are reflected in income. The bottom-line income reflects all changes in shareholders' equity arising from other than owner transactions. In the absence of owner transactions, the change in shareholders' equity should equal net income. No adjustments such as translation adjustments bypass the income statement and go directly to shareholders equity.

Clean surplus relation   The relationship between earnings, dividends, and book value in which ending book value is equal to the beginning book value plus earnings less dividends, apart from ownership transactions.

Clientele effect   The preference some investors have for shares that exhibit certain characteristics.

Club convergence   The idea that only rich and middle-income countries sharing a set of favorable attributes (i.e., are members of the "club") will converge to the income level of the richest countries.

Cobb–Douglas production function   A function of the form $Y = K^\alpha L^{1-\alpha}$ relating output (Y) to labor (L) and capital (K) inputs.

Cointegrated   Describes two time series that have a long-term financial or economic relationship such that they do not diverge from each other without bound in the long run.

Collar   An option position in which the investor is long shares of stock and then buys a put with an exercise price below the current underlying price and writes a call with an exercise price above the current underlying price.

Collateral return   The component of the total return on a commodity futures position attributable to the yield for the bonds or cash used to maintain the futures position. Also called *collateral yield*.

Commercial real estate properties   Income-producing real estate properties, properties purchased with the intent to let, lease, or rent (in other words, produce income).

Commodity swap   A type of swap involving the exchange of payments over multiple dates as determined by specified reference prices or indexes relating to commodities.

Common size statements   Financial statements in which all elements (accounts) are stated as a percentage of a key figure such as revenue for an income statement or total assets for a balance sheet.

Company fundamental factors   Factors related to the company's internal performance, such as factors relating to earnings growth, earnings variability, earnings momentum, and financial leverage.

Company share-related factors   Valuation measures and other factors related to share price or the trading characteristics of the shares, such as earnings yield, dividend yield, and book-to-market value.

Comparables   Assets used as benchmarks when applying the method of comparables to value an asset. Also called *comps*, *guideline assets*, or *guideline companies*.

Compiled financial statements   Financial statements that are not accompanied by an auditor's opinion letter.

Comprehensive income   All changes in equity other than contributions by, and distributions to, owners; income under clean surplus accounting; includes all changes in equity during a period except those resulting from investments by owners and distributions to owners; comprehensive income equals net income plus other comprehensive income.

Comps   Assets used as benchmarks when applying the method of comparables to value an asset.

Conditional convergence   The idea that convergence of per capita income is conditional on the countries having the same savings rate, population growth rate, and production function.

Conditional heteroskedasticity   Heteroskedasticity in the error variance that is correlated with the values of the independent variable(s) in the regression.

Conditional VaR (CVaR)   The average loss conditional on exceeding the VaR cutoff; sometimes referred to as the *expected tail loss* or *expected shortfall*.

Conglomerate discount   The discount possibly applied by the market to the stock of a company operating in multiple, unrelated businesses.

Conglomerate merger   A merger involving companies that are in unrelated businesses.

Consolidation   The combining of the results of operations of subsidiaries with the parent company to present financial statements as if they were a single economic unit. The assets, liabilities, revenues and expenses of the subsidiaries are combined with those of the parent company, eliminating intercompany transactions.

Constant dividend payout ratio policy   A policy in which a constant percentage of net income is paid out in dividends.

Constant returns to scale   The condition that if all inputs into the production process are increased by a given percentage, then output rises by that same percentage.

Contango   A condition in futures markets in which the spot price is lower than the futures price; also, the condition in which the near-term (closer to expiration) futures contract price is lower than the longer-term futures contract price.

Contingent consideration   Potential future payments to the seller that are contingent on the achievement of certain agreed on occurrences.

Continuing earnings   Earnings excluding nonrecurring components. Also referred to as *core earnings*, *persistent earnings*, or *underlying earnings*.

Continuing residual income   Residual income after the forecast horizon.

Continuing value   The analyst's estimate of a stock's value at a particular point in the future.

Control premium   An increment or premium to value associated with a controlling ownership interest in a company.

Conventional cash flow   A conventional cash flow pattern is one with an initial outflow followed by a series of inflows.

Convergence   The property of forward and futures contracts in which the derivative price becomes the spot price at expiration of the derivative.

Conversion period   For a convertible bond, the period during which bondholders have the right to convert their bonds into shares.

Conversion price   For a convertible bond, the price per share at which the bond can be converted into shares.

Conversion ratio   For a convertible bond, the number of shares of common stock that a bondholder receives from converting the bond into shares.

Conversion value   For a convertible bond, the value of the bond if it is converted at the market price of the shares. Also called *parity value*.

Convertible bond   Bond with an embedded conversion option that gives the bondholder the right to convert their bonds into the issuer's common stock during a pre-determined period at a pre-determined price.

Convexity   A measure of how interest rate sensitivity changes with a change in interest rates.

Core earnings   Earnings excluding nonrecurring components. Also referred to as *continuing earnings*, *persistent earnings*, or *underlying earnings*.

Corporate governance   The system of principles, policies, procedures, and clearly defined responsibilities and accountabilities used by stakeholders to overcome the conflicts of interest inherent in the corporate form.

Corporate raider   A person or organization seeking to profit by acquiring a company and reselling it, or seeking to profit from the takeover attempt itself (e.g., greenmail).

Corporation   A legal entity with rights similar to those of a person. The chief officers, executives, or top managers act as agents for the firm and are legally entitled to authorize corporate activities and to enter into contracts on behalf of the business.

Correlation analysis   The analysis of the strength of the linear relationship between two data series.

Cost approach   Approach that values a private company based on the values of the underlying assets of the entity less the value of any related liabilities. In the context of real estate, this approach estimates the value of a property based on what it would cost to buy the land and construct a new property on the site that has the same utility or functionality as the property being appraised.

Cost of debt   The cost of debt financing to a company, such as when it issues a bond or takes out a bank loan.

Cost of equity   The required rate of return on common stock.

Covariance stationary   Describes a time series when its expected value and variance are constant and finite in all periods and when its covariance with itself for a fixed number of periods in the past or future is constant and finite in all periods.

Covered call   An option strategy in which an investor who already owns the underlying asset sells a call option giving someone else the right to buy the asset at the exercise price.

Covered interest rate parity   Relationship among the spot exchange rate, forward exchange rate, and the interest rates in two currencies that ensures that the return on a hedged (i.e., covered) foreign risk-free investment is the same as the return on a domestic risk-free investment. Also called *interest rate parity*.

Cox–Ingersoll–Ross model   A partial equilibrium term structure model that assumes interest rates are mean reverting and interest rate volatility is directly related to the level of interest rates.

Credit correlation   The correlation of credits contained in an index CDS.

Credit curve   The credit spreads for a range of maturities of a company's debt; applies to non-government borrowers and incorporates credit risk into each rate.

Credit default swap   A derivative contract between two parties in which the buyer makes a series of cash payments to the seller and receives a promise of compensation for credit losses resulting from the default.

Credit derivative   A derivative instrument in which the underlying is a measure of the credit quality of a borrower.

Credit event   The outcome that triggers a payment from the credit protection seller to the credit protection buyer.

Credit protection buyer   One party to a credit default swap; the buyer makes a series of cash payments to the seller and receives a promise of compensation for credit losses resulting from the default.

Credit protection seller   One party to a credit default swap; the buyer makes a series of cash payments to the seller and receives a promise of compensation for credit losses resulting from the default.

Credit ratings   Ordinal rankings of the credit risk of a company, government (sovereign), quasi-government, or asset-backed security.

Credit risk   The risk that the borrower will not repay principal and interest. Also called *default risk*.

Credit scoring   Ordinal rankings of a retail borrower's credit riskiness. It is called an *ordinal ranking* because it only orders borrowers' riskiness from highest to lowest.

Credit spreads   The difference between the yields on default-free and credit risky zero-coupon bonds.

Current exchange rate   For accounting purposes, the spot exchange rate on the balance sheet date.

Current rate method   Approach to translating foreign currency financial statements for consolidation in which all assets and liabilities are translated at the current exchange rate. The current rate method is the prevalent method of translation.

Curvature   One of the three factors (the other two are level and steepness) that empirically explain most of the changes in the shape of the yield curve. A shock to the curvature factor affects mid-maturity interest rates, resulting in the term structure becoming either more or less hump-shaped.

Curve trade   Buying a CDS of one maturity and selling a CDS on the same reference entity with a different maturity.

Cyclical businesses   Businesses with high sensitivity to business- or industry-cycle influences.

Data mining   The practice of determining a model by extensive searching through a dataset for statistically significant patterns.

"Dead-hand" provision   A poison pill provision that allows for the redemption or cancellation of a poison pill provision only by a vote of continuing directors (generally directors who were on the target company's board prior to the takeover attempt).

Debt ratings   An objective measure of the quality and safety of a company's debt based upon an analysis of the company's ability to pay the promised cash flows, as well as an analysis of any indentures.

Decision rule   With respect to hypothesis testing, the rule according to which the null hypothesis will be rejected or not rejected; involves the comparison of the test statistic to rejection point(s).

Default intensity   Gives the probability of default over the next instant $[t, t + \Delta]$ when the economy is in state X_t.

Default probability   See *probability of default*.

Default risk   See *credit risk*.

Defined benefit pension plans   Plan in which the company promises to pay a certain annual amount (defined benefit) to the employee after retirement. The company bears the investment risk of the plan assets.

Defined contribution pension plans   Individual accounts to which an employee and typically the employer makes contributions, generally on a tax-advantaged basis. The amounts of contributions are defined at the outset, but the future value of the benefit is unknown. The employee bears the investment risk of the plan assets.

Definition of value   A specification of how "value" is to be understood in the context of a specific valuation.

Definitive merger agreement   A contract signed by both parties to a merger that clarifies the details of the transaction, including the terms, warranties, conditions, termination details, and the rights of all parties.

Delta   The relationship between the option price and the underlying price, which reflects the sensitivity of the price of the option to changes in the price of the underlying. Delta is a good approximation of how an option price will change for a small change in the stock.

Dependent variable   The variable whose variation about its mean is to be explained by the regression; the left-hand-side variable in a regression equation.

Depository Trust and Clearinghouse Corporation   A US-headquartered entity providing post-trade clearing, settlement, and information services.

Depreciated replacement cost   In the context of real estate, the replacement cost of a building adjusted different types of depreciation.

Derivative   A financial instrument whose value depends on the value of some underlying asset or factor (e.g., a stock price, an interest rate, or exchange rate).

Descriptive statistics   The study of how data can be summarized effectively.

Diluted earnings per share (diluted EPS) Net income, minus preferred dividends, divided by the weighted average number of common shares outstanding considering all dilutive securities (e.g., convertible debt and options); the EPS that would result if all dilutive securities were converted into common shares.

Dilution A reduction in proportional ownership interest as a result of the issuance of new shares.

Diminishing marginal productivity When each additional unit of an input, keeping the other inputs unchanged, increases output by a smaller increment.

Direct capitalization method In the context of real estate, this method estimates the value of an income-producing property based on the level and quality of its net operating income.

Discount To reduce the value of a future payment in allowance for how far away it is in time; to calculate the present value of some future amount. Also, the amount by which an instrument is priced below its face value.

Discount factor The present value or price of a risk-free single-unit payment when discounted using the appropriate spot rate.

Discount for lack of control An amount or percentage deducted from the pro rata share of 100 percent of the value of an equity interest in a business to reflect the absence of some or all of the powers of control.

Discount for lack of marketability An amount of percentage deducted from the value of an ownership interest to reflect the relative absence of marketability.

Discount function Discount factors for the range of all possible maturities. The spot curve can be derived from the discount function and vice versa.

Discount rate Any rate used in finding the present value of a future cash flow.

Discounted abnormal earnings model A model of stock valuation that views intrinsic value of stock as the sum of book value per share plus the present value of the stock's expected future residual income per share.

Discounted cash flow (DCF) analysis In the context of merger analysis, it is an estimate of a target company's value found by discounting the company's expected future free cash flows to the present.

Discounted cash flow method Income approach that values an asset based on estimates of future cash flows discounted to present value by using a discount rate reflective of the risks associated with the cash flows. In the context of real estate, this method estimates the value of an income-producing property based by discounting future projected cash flows.

Discounted cash flow model A model of intrinsic value that views the value of an asset as the present value of the asset's expected future cash flows.

Discriminant analysis A multivariate classification technique used to discriminate between groups, such as companies that either will or will not become bankrupt during some time frame.

Diversified REITs REITs that own and operate in more than one type of property; they are more common in Europe and Asia than in the United States.

Divestiture The sale, liquidation, or spin-off of a division or subsidiary.

Dividend coverage ratio The ratio of net income to dividends.

Dividend discount model (DDM) A present value model of stock value that views the intrinsic value of a stock as present value of the stock's expected future dividends.

Dividend displacement of earnings The concept that dividends paid now displace earnings in all future periods.

Dividend imputation tax system A taxation system which effectively assures that corporate profits distributed as dividends are taxed just once, at the shareholder's tax rate.

Dividend payout ratio The ratio of cash dividends paid to earnings for a period.

Dividend policy The strategy a company follows with regard to the amount and timing of dividend payments.

Dividend rate the annualized amount of the most recent dividend.

Dominance An arbitrage opportunity when a financial asset with a risk-free payoff in the future must have a positive price today.

Double taxation system Corporate earnings are taxed twice when paid out as dividends. First, corporate earnings are taxed regardless of whether they will be distributed as dividends or retained at the G-13 corporate level, and second, dividends are taxed again at the individual shareholder level.

DOWNREIT A variation of the UPREIT structure under which the REIT owns more than one partnership and may own properties at both the REIT level and the partnership level.

Downstream A transaction between two related companies, an investor company (or a parent company) and an associate company (or a subsidiary) such that the investor company records a profit on its income statement. An example is a sale of inventory by the investor company to the associate or by a parent to a subsidiary company.

Due diligence Investigation and analysis in support of a recommendation; the failure to exercise due diligence may sometimes result in liability according to various securities laws.

Dummy variable A type of qualitative variable that takes on a value of 1 if a particular condition is true and 0 if that condition is false.

Duration A measure of the approximate sensitivity of a security to a change in interest rates (i.e., a measure of interest rate risk).

Dutch disease A situation in which currency appreciation driven by strong export demand for resources makes other segments of the economy (particularly manufacturing) globally uncompetitive.

Earnings surprise The difference between reported EPS and expected EPS. Also referred to as *unexpected earnings*.

Earnings yield EPS divided by price; the reciprocal of the P/E ratio.

Economic growth The expansion of production possibilities that results from capital accumulation and technological change.

Economic obsolescence In the context of real estate, a reduction in value due to current economic conditions.

Economic profit See *residual income*.

Economic sectors Large industry groupings.

Economic value added (EVA®) A commercial implementation of the residual income concept; the computation of EVA® is the net operating profit after taxes minus the cost of capital, where these inputs are adjusted for a number of items.

Economies of scale A situation in which average costs per unit of good or service produced fall as volume rises. In reference to mergers, the savings achieved through the consolidation of operations and elimination of duplicate resources.

Edwards–Bell–Ohlson model A model of stock valuation that views intrinsic value of stock as the sum of book value per share plus the present value of the stock's expected future residual income per share.

Effective convexity Sensitivity of duration to changes in interest rates.

Effective duration Sensitivity of the bond's price to a 100 bps parallel shift of the benchmark yield curve, assuming no change in the bond's credit spread.

Embedded options Contingency provisions found in a bond's indenture or offering circular representing rights that enable their holders to take advantage of interest rate movements. They can be exercised by the issuer, by the bondholder, or automatically depending on the course of interest rates.

Enterprise value (EV) Total company value (the market value of debt, common equity, and preferred equity) minus the value of cash and investments.

Enterprise value multiple A valuation multiple that relates the total market value of all sources of a company's capital (net of cash) to a measure of fundamental value for the entire company (such as a pre-interest earnings measure).

Entry price The price paid to acquire an asset.

Equilibrium The condition in which supply equals demand.

Equity carve-out A form of restructuring that involves the creation of a new legal entity and the sale of equity in it to outsiders.

Equity charge The estimated cost of equity capital in money terms.

Equity REIT A REIT that owns, operates, and/or selectively develops income-producing real estate.

Equity swap A swap transaction in which at least one cash flow is tied to the return on an equity portfolio position, often an equity index.

Error autocorrelation The autocorrelation of the error term.

Error term The portion of the dependent variable that is not explained by the independent variable(s) in the regression.

Estimated parameters With reference to a regression analysis, the estimated values of the population intercept and population slope coefficient(s) in a regression.

Ex ante tracking error A measure of the degree to which the performance of a given investment portfolio might be expected to deviate from its benchmark; also known as *relative VaR*.

Ex ante version of PPP Hypothesis that expected changes in the spot exchange rate are equal to expected differences in national inflation rates. An extension of relative purchasing power parity to expected future changes in the exchange rate.

Ex-dividend Trading ex-dividend refers to shares that no longer carry the right to the next dividend payment.

Ex-dividend date The first date that a share trades without (i.e., "ex") the dividend.

Ex-dividend price The price at which a share first trades without (i.e., "ex") the right to receive an upcoming dividend.

Excess earnings method Income approach that estimates the value of all intangible assets of the business by capitalizing future earnings in excess of the estimated return requirements associated with working capital and fixed assets.

Exchange ratio The number of shares that target stockholders are to receive in exchange for each of their shares in the target company.

Exercise date The date when employees actually exercise stock options and convert them to stock.

Exercise value The value of an option if it were exercised. Also sometimes called *intrinsic value*.

Exit price The price received to sell an asset or paid to transfer a liability.

Expanded CAPM An adaptation of the CAPM that adds to the CAPM a premium for small size and company-specific risk.

Expectations approach A procedure for obtaining the value of an option derived from discounting at the risk-free rate its expected future payoff based on risk neutral probabilities.

Expected holding-period return The expected total return on an asset over a stated holding period; for stocks, the sum of the expected dividend yield and the expected price appreciation over the holding period.

Expected loss The probability of default multiplied by the loss given default; the full amount owed minus the expected recovery.

Expected shortfall See *conditional VaR*.

Expected tail loss See *conditional VaR*.

Exposure to foreign exchange risk The risk of a change in value of an asset or liability denominated in a foreign currency due to a change in exchange rates.

Extendible bond Bond with an embedded option that gives the bondholder the right to keep the bond for a number of years after maturity, possibly with a different coupon.

External growth Company growth in output or sales that is achieved by buying the necessary resources externally (i.e., achieved through mergers and acquisitions).

External sustainability approach An approach to assessing the equilibrium exchange rate that focuses on exchange rate adjustments required to ensure that a country's net foreign-asset/GDP ratio or net foreign-liability/GDP ratio stabilizes at a sustainable level.

Factor A common or underlying element with which several variables are correlated.

Factor betas An asset's sensitivity to a particular factor; a measure of the response of return to each unit of increase in a factor, holding all other factors constant.

Factor portfolio See *pure factor portfolio*.

Factor price The expected return in excess of the risk-free rate for a portfolio with a sensitivity of 1 to one factor and a sensitivity of 0 to all other factors.

Factor risk premium The expected return in excess of the risk-free rate for a portfolio with a sensitivity of 1 to one factor and a sensitivity of 0 to all other factors. Also called *factor price*.

Factor sensitivity See *factor betas*.

Failure to pay When a borrower does not make a scheduled payment of principal or interest on any outstanding obligations after a grace period.

Fair market value The market price of an asset or liability that trades regularly.

Fair value The amount at which an asset (or liability) could be bought (or incurred) or sold (or settled) in a current transaction between willing parties, that is, other than in a forced or liquidation sale; as defined in IFRS and US

GAAP, the price that would be received to sell an asset or paid to transfer a liability in an orderly transaction between market participants at the measurement date.

Financial contagion   A situation where financial shocks spread from their place of origin to other locales; in essence, a faltering economy infects other, healthier economies.

Financial distress   Heightened uncertainty regarding a company's ability to meet its various obligations because of lower or negative earnings.

Financial risk   The risk that environmental, social, or governance risk factors will result in significant costs or other losses to a company and its shareholders; the risk arising from a company's obligation to meet required payments under its financing agreements.

Financial transaction   A purchase involving a buyer having essentially no material synergies with the target (e.g., the purchase of a private company by a company in an unrelated industry or by a private equity firm would typically be a financial transaction).

First-differencing   A transformation that subtracts the value of the time series in period $t - 1$ from its value in period t.

First-order serial correlation   Correlation between adjacent observations in a time series.

Fitted parameters   With reference to a regression analysis, the estimated values of the population intercept and population slope coefficient(s) in a regression.

Fixed-rate perpetual preferred stock   Nonconvertible, noncallable preferred stock with a specified dividend rate that has a claim on earnings senior to the claim of common stock, and no maturity date.

Flip-in pill   A poison pill takeover defense that dilutes an acquirer's ownership in a target by giving other existing target company shareholders the right to buy additional target company shares at a discount.

Flip-over pill   A poison pill takeover defense that gives target company shareholders the right to purchase shares of the acquirer at a significant discount to the market price, which has the effect of causing dilution to all existing acquiring company shareholders.

Floored floater   Floating-rate bond with a floor provision that prevents the coupon rate from decreasing below a specified minimum rate. It protects the investor against declining interest rates.

Flotation cost   Fees charged to companies by investment bankers and other costs associated with raising new capital.

Forced conversion   For a convertible bond, when the issuer calls the bond and forces bondholders to convert their bonds into shares, which typically happens when the underlying share price increases above the conversion price.

Foreign currency transactions   Transactions that are denominated in a currency other than a company's functional currency.

Forward curve   The term structure of forward rates for loans made on a specific initiation date.

Forward dividend yield   A dividend yield based on the anticipated dividend during the next 12 months.

Forward integration   A merger involving the purchase of a target that is farther along the value or production chain; for example, to acquire a distributor.

Forward P/E   A P/E calculated on the basis of a forecast of EPS; a stock's current price divided by next year's expected earnings.

Forward price   The fixed price or rate at which the transaction scheduled to occur at the expiration of a forward contract will take place. This price is agreed to at the initiation date of the contract.

Forward pricing model   The model that describes the valuation of forward contracts.

Forward rate   An interest rate that is determined today for a loan that will be initiated in a future time period.

Forward rate agreement   A forward contract calling for one party to make a fixed interest payment and the other to make an interest payment at a rate to be determined at the contract expiration.

Forward rate model   The forward pricing model expressed in terms of spot and forward interest rates.

Forward value   The monetary value of an existing forward contract.

Franking credit   A tax credit received by shareholders for the taxes that a corporation paid on its distributed earnings.

Free cash flow   The actual cash that would be available to the company's investors after making all investments necessary to maintain the company as an ongoing enterprise (also referred to as free cash flow to the firm); the internally generated funds that can be distributed to the company's investors (e.g., shareholders and bondholders) without impairing the value of the company.

Free cash flow hypothesis   The hypothesis that higher debt levels discipline managers by forcing them to make fixed debt service payments and by reducing the company's free cash flow.

Free cash flow method   Income approach that values an asset based on estimates of future cash flows discounted to present value by using a discount rate reflective of the risks associated with the cash flows.

Free cash flow to equity   The cash flow available to a company's common shareholders after all operating expenses, interest, and principal payments have been made, and necessary investments in working and fixed capital have been made.

Free cash flow to equity model   A model of stock valuation that views a stock's intrinsic value as the present value of expected future free cash flows to equity.

Free cash flow to the firm   The cash flow available to the company's suppliers of capital after all operating expenses (including taxes) have been paid and necessary investments in working and fixed capital have been made.

Free cash flow to the firm model   A model of stock valuation that views the value of a firm as the present value of expected future free cash flows to the firm.

Friendly transaction   A potential business combination that is endorsed by the managers of both companies.

Functional currency   The currency of the primary economic environment in which an entity operates.

Functional obsolescence   In the context of real estate, a reduction in value due to a design that differs from that of a new building constructed for the intended use of the property.

Fundamental factor models   A multifactor model in which the factors are attributes of stocks or companies that are important in explaining cross-sectional differences in stock prices.

Fundamentals   Economic characteristics of a business such as profitability, financial strength, and risk.

Funds available for distribution   Funds from operations (FFO) adjusted to remove any non-cash rent reported under straight-line rent accounting and to subtract maintenance-type capital expenditures and leasing costs, including leasing agents' commissions and tenants' improvement allowances.

Funds from operations   Accounting net earnings excluding (1) depreciation charges on real estate, (2) deferred tax charges, and (3) gains or losses from sales of property and debt restructuring.

Futures price   The price at which the parties to a futures contract agree to exchange the underlying (or cash). In commodity markets, the price agreed on to deliver or receive a defined quantity (and often quality) of a commodity at a future date.

Futures value   The monetary value of an existing futures contract.

FX carry trade   An investment strategy that involves taking on long positions in high-yield currencies and short positions in low-yield currencies.

Gamma   A measure of how sensitive an option's delta is to a change in the underlying. The change in a given instrument's delta for a given small change in the underlying's value, holding everything else constant.

Generalized least squares   A regression estimation technique that addresses heteroskedasticity of the error term.

Going-concern assumption   The assumption that the business will maintain its business activities into the foreseeable future.

Going-concern value   A business's value under a going-concern assumption.

Goodwill   An intangible asset that represents the excess of the purchase price of an acquired company over the value of the net identifiable assets acquired.

Grant date   The day that stock options are granted to employees.

Gross domestic product   A money measure of the goods and services produced within a country's borders over a stated time period.

Gross lease   A lease under which the tenant pays a gross rent to the landlord who is responsible for all operating costs, utilities, maintenance expenses, and real estate taxes relating to the property.

Growth accounting equation   The production function written in the form of growth rates. For the basic Cobb–Douglas production function, it states that the growth rate of output equals the rate of technological change plus α times the growth rate of capital plus $(1 - \alpha)$ times the growth rate of labor.

Growth capital expenditures   Capital expenditures needed for expansion.

Growth option   The ability to make additional investments in a project at some future time if the financial results are strong. Also called *expansion option*.

Guideline assets   Assets used as benchmarks when applying the method of comparables to value an asset.

Guideline companies   Assets used as benchmarks when applying the method of comparables to value an asset.

Guideline public companies   Public-company comparables for the company being valued.

Guideline public company method   A variation of the market approach; establishes a value estimate based on the observed multiples from trading activity in the shares of public companies viewed as reasonably comparable to the subject private company.

Guideline transactions method   A variation of the market approach; establishes a value estimate based on pricing multiples derived from the acquisition of control of entire public or private companies that were acquired.

Harmonic mean   A type of weighted mean computed by averaging the reciprocals of the observations, then taking the reciprocal of that average.

Hazard rate   The probability that an event will occur, given that it has not already occurred.

Hazard rate estimation   A technique for estimating the probability of a binary event, such as default/no default, mortality/no mortality, and prepay/no prepay.

Health care REITs   REITs that invest in skilled nursing facilities (nursing homes), assisted living and independent residential facilities for retired persons, hospitals, medical office buildings, or rehabilitation centers.

Held for trading investments   Debt or equity securities acquired with the intent to sell them in the near term.

Held-to-maturity investments   Debt (fixed-income) securities that a company intends to hold to maturity; these are presented at their original cost, updated for any amortization of discounts or premiums.

Herfindahl–Hirschman Index (HHI)   A measure of market concentration that is calculated by summing the squared market shares for competing companies in an industry; high HHI readings or mergers that would result in large HHI increases are more likely to result in regulatory challenges.

Heteroskedastic   With reference to the error term of regression, having a variance that differs across observations.

Heteroskedasticity   The property of having a nonconstant variance; refers to an error term with the property that its variance differs across observations.

Heteroskedasticity-consistent standard errors   Standard errors of the estimated parameters of a regression that correct for the presence of heteroskedasticity in the regression's error term.

Historical exchange rates   For accounting purposes, the exchange rates that existed when the assets and liabilities were initially recorded.

Historical simulation method   The application of historical price changes to the current portfolio.

Ho–Lee model   The first arbitrage-free term structure model. The model is calibrated to market data and uses a binomial lattice approach to generate a distribution of possible future interest rates.

Holding period return   The return that an investor earns during a specified holding period; a synonym for total return.

Homoskedasticity   The property of having a constant variance; refers to an error term that is constant across observations.

Horizontal merger   A merger involving companies in the same line of business, usually as competitors.

Hostile transaction   An attempt to acquire a company against the wishes of the target's managers.

Hotel REITs   REITs that own hotel properties but, similar to health care REITs, in many countries they must refrain from operating their properties themselves to maintain their tax-advantaged REIT status.

Human capital   The accumulated knowledge and skill that workers acquire from education, training, or life experience.

Hybrid approach   With respect to forecasting, an approach that combines elements of both top-down and bottom-up analysis.

Hybrid REITs   REITs that own and operate income-producing real estate and invest in mortgages as well; REITs that have positions in both real estate assets and real estate debt.

I-spreads   Shortened form of "interpolated spreads" and a reference to a linearly interpolated yield.

Illiquidity discount   A reduction or discount to value that reflects the lack of depth of trading or liquidity in that asset's market.

Impairment   Diminishment in value as a result of carrying (book) value exceeding fair value and/or recoverable value.

Impairment of capital rule   A legal restriction that dividends cannot exceed retained earnings.

Implied volatility   The standard deviation that causes an option pricing model to give the current option price.

In-sample forecast errors   The residuals from a fitted time-series model within the sample period used to fit the model.

Income approach   Valuation approach that values an asset as the present discounted value of the income expected from it. In the context of real estate, this approach estimates the value of a property based on an expected rate of return; the estimated value is the present value of the expected future income from the property, including proceeds from resale at the end of a typical investment holding period.

Incremental cash flow   The cash flow that is realized because of a decision; the changes or increments to cash flows resulting from a decision or action.

Incremental VaR (IVaR)   A measure of the incremental effect of an asset on the VaR of a portfolio by measuring the difference between the portfolio's VaR while including a specified asset and the portfolio's VaR with that asset eliminated.

Indenture   A written contract between a lender and borrower that specifies the terms of the loan, such as interest rate, interest payment schedule, maturity, etc.

Independent projects   Independent projects are projects whose cash flows are independent of each other.

Independent regulators   Regulators recognized and granted authority by a government body or agency. They are not government agencies per se and typically do not rely on government funding.

Independent variable   A variable used to explain the dependent variable in a regression; a right-hand-side variable in a regression equation.

Index CDS   A type of credit default swap that involves a combination of borrowers.

Indexing   An investment strategy in which an investor constructs a portfolio to mirror the performance of a specified index.

Industrial REITs   REITs that hold portfolios of single-tenant or multi-tenant industrial properties that are used as warehouses, distribution centers, light manufacturing facilities, and small office or "flex" space.

Industry structure   An industry's underlying economic and technical characteristics.

Information ratio   (IR) Mean active return divided by active risk; or alpha divided by the standard deviation of diversifiable risk.

Informational frictions   Forces that restrict availability, quality, and/or flow of information and its use.

Initial public offering   (IPO) The initial issuance of common stock registered for public trading by a formerly private corporation.

Inter-temporal rate of substitution   The ratio of the marginal utility of consumption s periods in the future (the numerator) to the marginal utility of consumption today (the denominator).

Interest rate parity   See *covered interest rate parity*.

Interest rate risk   Risk that interest rates will change such that the return earned is not commensurate with returns on comparable instruments in the marketplace.

Internal rate of return   (IRR) Rate of return that discounts future cash flows from an investment to the exact amount of the investment; the discount rate that makes the present value of an investment's costs (outflows) equal to the present value of the investment's benefits (inflows).

Internal ratings   Credit ratings developed internally and used by financial institutions or other entities to manage risk.

International Fisher effect   Proposition that nominal interest rate differentials across currencies are determined by expected inflation differentials.

Intrinsic value   The value of an asset given a hypothetically complete understanding of the asset's investment characteristics; the value obtained if an option is exercised based on current conditions. The difference between the spot exchange rate and the strike price of a currency.

Inverse price ratio   The reciprocal of a price multiple, e.g., in the case of a P/E ratio, the "earnings yield" E/P (where P is share price and E is earnings per share).

Investment objectives   Desired investment outcomes; includes risk objectives and return objectives.

Investment strategy   An approach to investment analysis and security selection.

Investment value   The value to a specific buyer, taking account of potential synergies based on the investor's requirements and expectations.

ISDA Master Agreement   A standard or "master" agreement published by the International Swaps and Derivatives Association. The master agreement establishes the terms for each party involved in the transaction.

Judicial law   Interpretations of courts.

Justified (fundamental) P/E   The price-to-earnings ratio that is fair, warranted, or justified on the basis of forecasted fundamentals.

Justified price multiple   The estimated fair value of the price multiple, usually based on forecasted fundamentals or comparables.

Key rate durations   Sensitivity of a bond's price to changes in specific maturities on the benchmark yield curve. Also called *partial durations*.

kth order autocorrelation   The correlation between observations in a time series separated by k periods.

Labor force   Everyone of working age (ages 16 to 64) that either is employed or is available for work but not working.

Labor force participation rate   The percentage of the working age population that is in the labor force.

Labor productivity   The quantity of real GDP produced by an hour of labor. More generally, output per unit of labor input.

Labor productivity growth accounting equation   States that potential GDP growth equals the growth rate of the labor input plus the growth rate of labor productivity.

Lack of marketability discount   An extra return to investors to compensate for lack of a public market or lack of marketability.

Law of one price   A principle that states that if two investments have the same or equivalent future cash flows regardless of what will happen in the future, then these two investments should have the same current price.

Leading dividend yield   Forecasted dividends per share over the next year divided by current stock price.

Leading P/E   A P/E calculated on the basis of a forecast of EPS; a stock's current price divided by next year's expected earnings.

Legal risk   The risk that failures by company managers to effectively manage a company's environmental, social, and governance risk exposures will lead to lawsuits and other judicial remedies, resulting in potentially catastrophic losses for the company; the risk that the legal system will not enforce a contract in case of dispute or fraud.

Legislative and regulatory risk   The risk that governmental laws and regulations directly or indirectly affecting a company's operations will change with potentially severe adverse effects on the company's continued profitability and even its long-term sustainability.

Level   One of the three factors (the other two are steepness and curvature) that empirically explain most of the changes in the shape of the yield curve. A shock to the level factor changes the yield for all maturities by an almost identical amount.

Leveraged buyout   (LBO) A transaction whereby the target company management team converts the target to a privately held company by using heavy borrowing to finance the purchase of the target company's outstanding shares.

Leveraged recapitalization   A post-offer takeover defense mechanism that involves the assumption of a large amount of debt that is then used to finance share repurchases; the effect is to dramatically change the company's capital structure while attempting to deliver a value to target shareholders in excess of a hostile bid.

Libor–OIS spread   The difference between Libor and the overnight indexed swap (OIS) rate.

Linear association   A straight-line relationship, as opposed to a relationship that cannot be graphed as a straight line.

Linear regression   Regression that models the straight-line relationship between the dependent and independent variable(s).

Linear trend   A trend in which the dependent variable changes at a constant rate with time.

Liquidation   To sell the assets of a company, division, or subsidiary piecemeal, typically because of bankruptcy; the form of bankruptcy that allows for the orderly satisfaction of creditors' claims after which the company ceases to exist.

Liquidation value   The value of a company if the company were dissolved and its assets sold individually.

Liquidity preference theory   A term structure theory that asserts liquidity premiums exist to compensate investors for the added interest rate risk they face when lending long term.

Liquidity premium   The premium or incrementally higher yield that investors demand for lending long term.

Liquidity risk   The risk that a financial instrument cannot be purchased or sold without a significant concession in price due to the size of the market.

Local currency   The currency of the country where a company is located.

Local expectations theory   A term structure theory that contends the return for all bonds over short time periods is the risk-free rate.

Locational obsolescence   In the context of real estate, a reduction in value due to decreased desirability of the location of the building.

Lockout period   Period during which a bond's issuer cannot call the bond.

Log-linear model   With reference to time-series models, a model in which the growth rate of the time series as a function of time is constant.

Log-log regression model   A regression that expresses the dependent and independent variables as natural logarithms.

Logit model   A qualitative-dependent-variable multiple regression model based on the logistic probability distribution.

Long/short trade   A long position in one CDS and a short position in another.

Look-ahead bias   A bias caused by using information that was not available on the test date.

Lookback period   The time period used to gather a historical data set.

Loss given default   The amount that will be lost if a default occurs.

Macroeconomic balance approach   An approach to assessing the equilibrium exchange rate that focuses on exchange rate adjustments needed to close the gap between the medium-term expectation for a country's current account balance and that country's normal (or sustainable) current account balance.

Macroeconomic factor model   A multifactor model in which the factors are surprises in macroeconomic variables that significantly explain equity returns.

Macroeconomic factors   Factors related to the economy, such as the inflation rate, industrial production, or economic sector membership.

Maintenance capital expenditures   Capital expenditures needed to maintain operations at the current level.

Managerialism theories   Theories that posit that corporate executives are motivated to engage in mergers to maximize the size of their company rather than shareholder value.

Marginal investor   An investor in a given share who is very likely to be part of the next trade in the share and who is therefore important in setting price.

Marginal VaR (MVaR)   A measure of the effect on portfolio VaR of a small change in a position size.

Market approach   Valuation approach that values an asset based on pricing multiples from sales of assets viewed as similar to the subject asset.

Market conversion premium per share   For a convertible bond, the difference between the market conversion price and the underlying share price, which allows investors to identify the premium or discount payable when buying a convertible bond rather than the underlying common stock.

Market conversion premium ratio   For a convertible bond, the market conversion premium per share expressed as a percentage of the current market price of the shares.

Market efficiency   A finance perspective on capital markets that deals with the relationship of price to intrinsic value. The **traditional efficient markets formulation** asserts that an asset's price is the best available estimate of its intrinsic value. The **rational efficient markets formulation** asserts that investors should expect to be rewarded for the costs of information gathering and analysis by higher gross returns.

Market timing   Asset allocation in which the investment in the market is increased if one forecasts that the market will outperform T-bills.

Market value   The estimated amount for which a property should exchange on the date of valuation between a willing buyer and a willing seller in an arm's-length transaction after proper marketing wherein the parties had each acted knowledgeably, prudently, and without compulsion.

Market value of invested capital   The market value of debt and equity.

Mature growth rate   The earnings growth rate in a company's mature phase; an earnings growth rate that can be sustained long term.

Maximum drawdown   The worst-returning month or quarter for the portfolio or the worst peak-to-trough decline in a portfolio's returns.

Mean reversion   The tendency of a time series to fall when its level is above its mean and rise when its level is below its mean; a mean-reverting time series tends to return to its long-term mean.

Merger   The absorption of one company by another; two companies become one entity and one or both of the pre-merger companies ceases to exist as a separate entity.

Method based on forecasted fundamentals   An approach to using price multiples that relates a price multiple to forecasts of fundamentals through a discounted cash flow model.

Method of comparables   An approach to valuation that involves using a price multiple to evaluate whether an asset is relatively fairly valued, relatively undervalued, or relatively overvalued when compared to a benchmark value of the multiple.

Minority Interest   The proportion of the ownership of a subsidiary not held by the parent (controlling) company.

Mispricing   Any departure of the market price of an asset from the asset's estimated intrinsic value.

Mixed offering   A merger or acquisition that is to be paid for with cash, securities, or some combination of the two.

Model specification   With reference to regression, the set of variables included in the regression and the regression equation's functional form.

Molodovsky effect   The observation that P/Es tend to be high on depressed EPS at the bottom of a business cycle, and tend to be low on unusually high EPS at the top of a business cycle.

Momentum indicators   Valuation indicators that relate either price or a fundamental (such as earnings) to the time series of their own past values (or in some cases to their expected value).

Monetary assets and liabilities   Assets and liabilities with value equal to the amount of currency contracted for, a fixed amount of currency. Examples are cash, accounts receivable, accounts payable, bonds payable, and mortgages payable. Inventory is not a monetary asset. Most liabilities are monetary.

Monetary/non-monetary method   Approach to translating foreign currency financial statements for consolidation in which monetary assets and liabilities are translated at the current exchange rate. Non-monetary assets and liabilities are translated at historical exchange rates (the exchange rates that existed when the assets and liabilities were acquired).

Monetizing   The conversion of the value of a financial transaction into currency.

Monitoring costs   Costs borne by owners to monitor the management of the company (e.g., board of director expenses).

Monte Carlo simulation   A method of estimating VaR in which the user develops his or her own assumptions about the statistical characteristics of the distribution and uses those characteristics to generate a distribution that represents hypothetical returns to a portfolio with the specified characteristics.

Mortgage-backed securities   Asset-backed securitized debt obligations that represent rights to receive cash flows from portfolios of mortgage loans.

Mortgage REITs   REITs that invest the bulk of their assets in interest-bearing mortgages, mortgage securities, or short-term loans secured by real estate.

Mortgages   Loans with real estate serving as collateral for the loans.

Multi-family/residential REITs   REITs that invest in and manage rental apartments for lease to individual tenants, typically using one-year leases.

Multicollinearity   A regression assumption violation that occurs when two or more independent variables (or combinations of independent variables) are highly but not perfectly correlated with each other.

Multiple linear regression   Linear regression involving two or more independent variables.

Multiple linear regression model   A linear regression model with two or more independent variables.

Mutually exclusive projects   Mutually exclusive projects compete directly with each other. For example, if Projects A and B are mutually exclusive, you can choose A or B, but you cannot choose both.

n-Period moving average   The average of the current and immediately prior $n - 1$ values of a time series.

Naked credit default swap   A position where the owner of the CDS does not have a position in the underlying credit.

Negative serial correlation   Serial correlation in which a positive error for one observation increases the chance of a negative error for another observation, and vice versa.

Net asset balance sheet exposure   When assets translated at the current exchange rate are greater in amount than liabilities translated at the current exchange rate. Assets exposed to translation gains or losses exceed the exposed liabilities.

Net asset value   The difference between assets and liabilities, all taken at current market values instead of accounting book values.

Net asset value per share   Net asset value divided by the number of shares outstanding.

Net lease   A lease under which the tenant pays a net rent to the landlord as well as an additional amount based on the tenant's pro rata share of the operating costs, utilities, maintenance expenses, and real estate taxes relating to the property.

Net liability balance sheet exposure   When liabilities translated at the current exchange rate are greater assets translated at the current exchange rate. Liabilities exposed to translation gains or losses exceed the exposed assets.

Net operating income   Gross rental revenue minus operating costs, but before deducting depreciation, corporate overhead, and interest expense. In the context of real estate, a measure of the income from the property after deducting operating expenses for such items as property taxes, insurance, maintenance, utilities, repairs, and insurance but before deducting any costs associated with financing and before deducting federal income taxes. It is similar to earnings before interest, taxes, depreciation, and amortization (EBITDA) in a financial reporting context.

Net operating profit less adjusted taxes (NOPLAT)   A company's operating profit with adjustments to normalize the effects of capital structure.

Net present value (NPV)   The present value of an investment's cash inflows (benefits) minus the present value of its cash outflows (costs).

Net regulatory burden   The private costs of regulation less the private benefits of regulation.

Net rent   A rent that consists of a stipulated rent to the landlord and a further amount based on their share of common area costs for utilities, maintenance, and property taxes.

Network externalities   The impact that users of a good, a service, or a technology have on other users of that product; it can be positive (e.g., a critical mass of users makes a product more useful) or negative (e.g., congestion makes the product less useful).

No-arbitrage approach   A procedure for obtaining the value of an option based on the creation of a portfolio that replicates the payoffs of the option and deriving the option value from the value of the replicating portfolio.

No-growth company   A company without positive expected net present value projects.

No-growth value per share   The value per share of a no-growth company, equal to the expected level amount of earnings divided by the stock's required rate of return.

Non-cash rent   An amount equal to the difference between the average contractual rent over a lease term (the straight-line rent) and the cash rent actually paid during a period. This figure is one of the deductions made from FFO to calculate AFFO.

Non-convergence trap   A situation in which a country remains relative poor, or even falls further behind, because it fails to t implement necessary institutional reforms and/or adopt leading technologies.

Non-monetary assets and liabilities   Assets and liabilities that are not monetary assets and liabilities. Non-monetary assets include inventory, fixed assets, and intangibles, and non-monetary liabilities include deferred revenue.

Non-renewable resources   Finite resources that are depleted once they are consumed; oil and coal are examples.

Nonconventional cash flow   In a nonconventional cash flow pattern, the initial outflow is not followed by inflows only, but the cash flows can flip from positive (inflows) to negative (outflows) again (or even change signs several times).

Nonearning assets   Cash and investments (specifically cash, cash equivalents, and short-term investments).

Nonlinear relation   An association or relationship between variables that cannot be graphed as a straight line.

Nonstationarity   With reference to a random variable, the property of having characteristics such as mean and variance that are not constant through time.

Normal EPS   The EPS that a business could achieve currently under mid-cyclical conditions. Also called *normalized EPS*.

Normalized earnings   The expected level of mid-cycle earnings for a company in the absence of any unusual or temporary factors that affect profitability (either positively or negatively).

Normalized EPS   The EPS that a business could achieve currently under mid-cyclical conditions. Also called *normal EPS*.

Normalized P/E   P/E based on normalized EPS data.

Notional amount   The amount of protection being purchased in a CDS.

NTM P/E   Next twelve months P/E: current market price divided by an estimated next twelve months EPS.

Off-the-run   A series of securities or indexes that were issued/created prior to the most recently issued/created series.

Office REITs   REITs that invest in and manage multi-tenanted office properties in central business districts of cities and suburban markets.

On-the-run   The most recently issued/created series of securities or indexes.

One-sided durations   Effective durations when interest rates go up or down, which are better at capturing the interest rate sensitivity of bonds with embedded options that do not react symmetrically to positive and negative changes in interest rates of the same magnitude.

Operating risk   The risk attributed to the operating cost structure, in particular the use of fixed costs in operations; the risk arising from the mix of fixed and variable costs; the risk that a company's operations may be severely affected by environmental, social, and governance risk factors.

Operational risk   The risk of loss from failures in a company's systems and procedures, or from external events.

Opportunity cost   The value that investors forgo by choosing a particular course of action; the value of something in its best alternative use.

Optimal capital structure   The capital structure at which the value of the company is maximized.

Option-adjusted spread   (OAS) Constant spread that, when added to all the one-period forward rates on the interest rate tree, makes the arbitrage-free value of the bond equal to its market price.

Option combination   An option strategy that typically uses both puts and calls, an example of which is the straddle, which involves buying one call and one put.

Option spread   The investor buys one call and writes another with a different exercise price or expiration or buys one put and writes another with a different exercise price or expiration.

Orderly liquidation value   The estimated gross amount of money that could be realized from the liquidation sale of an asset or assets, given a reasonable amount of time to find a purchaser or purchasers.

Organic growth   Company growth in output or sales that is achieved by making investments internally (i.e., excludes growth achieved through mergers and acquisitions).

Other comprehensive income   Changes to equity that bypass (are not reported in) the income statement; the difference between comprehensive income and net income.

Other post-employment benefits   Promises by the company to pay benefits in the future, such as life insurance premiums and all or part of health care insurance for its retirees.

Out-of-sample forecast errors   The differences between actual and predicted value of time series outside the sample period used to fit the model.

Out-of-the-money   Options that, if exercised, would require the payment of more money than the value received and therefore would not be currently exercised.

Pairs trading   An approach to trading that uses pairs of closely related stocks, buying the relatively undervalued stock and selling short the relatively overvalued stock.

Par curve   A hypothetical yield curve for coupon-paying Treasury securities that assumes all securities are priced at par.

Par swap   A swap in which the fixed rate is set so that no money is exchanged at contract initiation.

Parameter instability   The problem or issue of population regression parameters that have changed over time.

Parametric method   A method of estimating VaR which uses the historical mean, standard deviation, and correlation of security price movements to estimate the portfolio VaR. Generally assumes a normal distribution, but can be adapted to non-normal distributions with the addition of skewness and kurtosis. Sometimes called the *variance–covariance method* or the *analytical method*.

Partial equilibrium models   Term structure models that make use of an assumed form of interest rate process. Underlying risk factors, such as the impact of changing interest rates on the economy, are not incorporated in the model.

Partial regression coefficients   The slope coefficients in a multiple regression. Also called *partial slope coefficients*.

Partial slope coefficients   The slope coefficients in a multiple regression. Also called *partial regression coefficients*.

Partnership   A business owned and operated by more than one individual.

Payout amount   The payout ratio times the notional.

Payout policy   The principles by which a company distributes cash to common shareholders by means of cash dividends and/or share repurchases.

Payout ratio   An estimate of the expected credit loss.

Pecking order theory   The theory that managers take into account how their actions might be interpreted by outsiders and thus order their preferences for various forms of corporate financing. Forms of financing that are least visible to outsiders (e.g., internally generated funds) are most preferable to managers and those that are most visible (e.g., equity) are least preferable.

PEG   The P/E-to-growth ratio, calculated as the stock's P/E divided by the expected earnings growth rate.

Pension obligation   The present value of future benefits earned by employees for service provided to date.

Perfect capital markets   Markets in which, by assumption, there are no taxes, transactions costs, or bankruptcy costs, and in which all investors have equal ("symmetric") information.

Performance appraisal   The evaluation of risk-adjusted performance; the evaluation of investment skill.

Perpetuity   A perpetual annuity, or a set of never-ending level sequential cash flows, with the first cash flow occurring one period from now.

Persistent earnings   Earnings excluding nonrecurring components. Also referred to as *core earnings*, *continuing earnings*, or *underlying earnings*.

Pet projects   Projects in which influential managers want the corporation to invest. Often, unfortunately, pet projects are selected without undergoing normal capital budgeting analysis.

Physical deterioration   In the context of real estate, a reduction in value due to wear and tear.

Physical settlement   Involves actual delivery of the debt instrument in exchange for a payment by the credit protection seller of the notional amount of the contract.

Poison pill   A pre-offer takeover defense mechanism that makes it prohibitively costly for an acquirer to take control of a target without the prior approval of the target's board of directors.

Poison puts   A pre-offer takeover defense mechanism that gives target company bondholders the right to sell their bonds back to the target at a pre-specified redemption price, typically at or above par value; this defense increases the need for cash and raises the cost of the acquisition.

Pooling of interests method   A method of accounting in which combined companies were portrayed as if they had always operated as a single economic entity. Called pooling of interests under US GAAP and uniting of interests under IFRS. (No longer allowed under US GAAP or IFRS).

Portfolio balance approach   A theory of exchange rate determination that emphasizes the portfolio investment decisions of global investors and the requirement that global investors willingly hold all outstanding securities denominated in each currency at prevailing prices and exchange rates.

Position delta   The overall delta of a position that contains some combination of assets and derivatives.

Positive serial correlation   Serial correlation in which a positive error for one observation increases the chance of a positive error for another observation, and a negative error for one observation increases the chance of a negative error for another observation.

Potential GDP   The maximum amount of output an economy can sustainably produce without inducing an increase in the inflation rate. The output level that corresponds to full employment with consistent wage and price expectations.

Preferred habitat theory   A term structure theory that contends that investors have maturity preferences and require yield incentives before they will buy bonds outside of their preferred maturities.

Premise of value   The status of a company in the sense of whether it is assumed to be a going concern or not.

Premium leg   The series of payments the credit protection buyer promises to make to the credit protection seller.

Present value model   A model of intrinsic value that views the value of an asset as the present value of the asset's expected future cash flows.

Present value of growth opportunities   The difference between the actual value per share and the no-growth value per share. Also called *value of growth*.

Present value of the expected loss   Conceptually, the largest price one would be willing to pay on a bond to a third party (e.g., an insurer) to entirely remove the credit risk of purchasing and holding the bond.

Presentation currency   The currency in which financial statement amounts are presented.

Price momentum   A valuation indicator based on past price movement.

Price multiples   The ratio of a stock's market price to some measure of value per share.

Price return   Measures the price appreciation or percentage change in price of a security or the securities in an index or portfolio.

Price-setting option   The operational flexibility to adjust prices when demand varies from forecast. For example, when demand exceeds capacity, the company could benefit from the excess demand by increasing prices.

Priced risk   Risk for which investors demand compensation for bearing (e.g., equity risk, company-specific factors, macroeconomic factors).

Principal–agent problem   A conflict of interest that arises when the agent in an agency relationship has goals and incentives that differ from the principal to whom the agent owes a fiduciary duty.

Principal components analysis   (PCA) A non-parametric method of extracting relevant information from high-dimensional data that uses the dependencies between variables to represent information in a more tractable, lower-dimensional form.

Principle of no arbitrage   In well-functioning markets, prices will adjust until there are no arbitrage opportunities.

Prior transaction method   A variation of the market approach; considers actual transactions in the stock of the subject private company.

Private market value   The value derived using a sum-of-the-parts valuation.

Probability of default   The probability that a bond issuer will not meet its contractual obligations on schedule.

Probability of survival   The probability that a bond issuer will meet its contractual obligations on schedule.

Probit model   A qualitative-dependent-variable multiple regression model based on the normal distribution.

Procedural law   The body of law that focuses on the protection and enforcement of the substantive laws.

Production-flexibility   The operational flexibility to alter production when demand varies from forecast. For example, if demand is strong, a company may profit from employees working overtime or from adding additional shifts.

Project sequencing   To defer the decision to invest in a future project until the outcome of some or all of a current project is known. Projects are sequenced through time, so that investing in a project creates the option to invest in future projects.

Prospective P/E   A P/E calculated on the basis of a forecast of EPS; a stock's current price divided by next year's expected earnings.

Protection leg   The contingent payment that the credit protection seller may have to make to the credit protection buyer.

Protective put   An option strategy in which a long position in an asset is combined with a long position in a put.

Proxy fight   An attempt to take control of a company through a shareholder vote.

Proxy statement   A public document that provides the material facts concerning matters on which shareholders will vote.

Prudential supervision   Regulation and monitoring of the safety and soundness of financial institutions to promote financial stability, reduce system-wide risks, and protect customers of financial institutions.

Purchasing power gain   A gain in value caused by changes in price levels. Monetary liabilities experience purchasing power gains during periods of inflation.

Purchasing power loss   A loss in value caused by changes in price levels. Monetary assets experience purchasing power loss during periods of inflation.

Purchasing power parity (PPP)   The idea that exchange rates move to equalize the purchasing power of different currencies.

Pure expectations theory   A term structure theory that contends the forward rate is an unbiased predictor of the future spot rate. Also called the *unbiased expectations theory*.

Pure factor portfolio   A portfolio with sensitivity of 1 to the factor in question and a sensitivity of 0 to all other factors.

Putable bond   Bond that includes an embedded put option, which gives the bondholder the right to put back the bonds to the issuer prior to maturity, typically when interest rates have risen and higher-yielding bonds are available.

Qualitative dependent variables   Dummy variables used as dependent variables rather than as independent variables.

Quality of earnings analysis   The investigation of issues relating to the accuracy of reported accounting results as reflections of economic performance; quality of earnings analysis is broadly understood to include not only earnings management, but also balance sheet management.

Random walk   A time series in which the value of the series in one period is the value of the series in the previous period plus an unpredictable random error.

Rational efficient markets formulation   See *market efficiency*.

Real estate investment trusts (REITS)   Tax-advantaged entities (companies or trusts) that typically own, operate, and—to a limited extent—develop income-producing real estate property.

Real estate operating companies   Regular taxable real estate ownership companies that operate in the real estate industry in countries that do not have a tax-advantaged REIT regime in place or are engaged in real estate activities of a kind and to an extent that do not fit within their country's REIT framework.

Real exchange rate   The relative purchasing power of two currencies, defined in terms of the *real* goods and services that each can buy at prevailing national price levels and nominal exchange rates. Measured as the ratio of national price levels expressed in a common currency.

Real interest rate parity   The proposition that real interest rates will converge to the same level across different markets.

Real options   Options that relate to investment decisions such as the option to time the start of a project, the option to adjust its scale, or the option to abandon a project that has begun.

Rebalance return   A return from rebalancing the component weights of an index.

Reconstitution   When dealers recombine appropriate individual zero-coupon securities and reproduce an underlying coupon Treasury.

Recovery rate   The percentage of the loss recovered.

Reduced form models   Models of credit analysis based on the outputs of a structural model but with different assumptions. The model's credit risk measures reflect changing economic conditions.

Reference entity   The borrower on a single-name CDS.

Reference obligation   A particular debt instrument issued by the borrower that is the designated instrument being covered.

Regime   With reference to a time series, the underlying model generating the times series.

Regression coefficients   The intercept and slope coefficient(s) of a regression.

Regulatory arbitrage   Entities identify and use some aspect of regulations that allows them to exploit differences in economic substance and regulatory interpretation or in foreign and domestic regulatory regimes to their (the entities) advantage.

Regulatory burden   The costs of regulation for the regulated entity.

Regulatory capture   Theory that regulation often arises to enhance the interests of the regulated.

Regulatory competition   Regulators may compete to provide a regulatory environment designed to attract certain entities.

Relative-strength indicators   Valuation indicators that compare a stock's performance during a period either to its own past performance or to the performance of some group of stocks.

Relative valuation models   A model that specifies an asset's value relative to the value of another asset.

Relative VaR   See *ex ante tracking error*.

Relative version of PPP   Hypothesis that changes in (nominal) exchange rates over time are equal to national inflation rate differentials.

Renewable resources   Resources that can be replenished, such as a forest.

Rental price of capital   The cost per unit of time to rent a unit of capital.

Replacement cost   In the context of real estate, the value of a building assuming it was built today using current construction costs and standards.

Reporting unit   For financial reporting under US GAAP, an operating segment or one level below an operating segment (referred to as a component).

Reputational risk   The risk that a company will suffer an extended diminution in market value relative to other companies in the same industry due to a demonstrated lack of concern for environmental, social, and governance risk factors.

Required rate of return   The minimum rate of return required by an investor to invest in an asset, given the asset's riskiness.

Residential properties   Properties that provide housing for individuals or families. Single-family properties may be owner-occupied or rental properties, whereas multi-family properties are rental properties even if the owner or manager occupies one of the units.

Residual autocorrelations   The sample autocorrelations of the residuals.

Residual dividend policy   A policy in which dividends are paid from any internally generated funds remaining after such funds are used to finance positive NPV projects.

Residual income   Earnings for a given time period, minus a deduction for common shareholders' opportunity cost in generating the earnings. Also called *economic profit* or *abnormal earnings*.

Residual income method   Income approach that estimates the value of all intangible assets of the business by capitalizing future earnings in excess of the estimated return requirements associated with working capital and fixed assets.

Residual income model   (RIM) A model of stock valuation that views intrinsic value of stock as the sum of book value per share plus the present value of the stock's expected future residual income per share. Also called *discounted abnormal earnings model* or *Edwards–Bell–Ohlson model*.

Residual loss   Agency costs that are incurred despite adequate monitoring and bonding of management.

Restructuring   Reorganizing the financial structure of a firm.

Retail REITs   REITs that invest in such retail properties as regional shopping malls or community/neighborhood shopping centers.

Return on capital employed   Operating profit divided by capital employed (debt and equity capital).

Return on invested capital   A measure of the after-tax profitability of the capital invested by the company's shareholders and debt holders.

Reverse carry arbitrage   A strategy in involving the short sale of the underlying and an offsetting opposite position in the derivative.

Reverse stress testing   A risk management approach in which the user identifies key risk exposures in the portfolio and subjects those exposures to extreme market movements.

Reviewed financial statements   A type of non-audited financial statements; typically provide an opinion letter with representations and assurances by the reviewing accountant that are less than those in audited financial statements.

Rho   The change in a given derivative instrument for a given small change in the risk-free interest rate, holding everything else constant. Rho measures the sensitivity of the option to the risk-free interest rate.

Riding the yield curve   A maturity trading strategy that involves buying bonds with a maturity longer than the intended investment horizon. Also called *rolling down the yield curve*.

Risk budgeting   The allocation of an asset owner's total risk appetite among groups or divisions (in the case of a trading organization) or among strategies and managers (in the case of an institutional or individual investor).

Risk decomposition   The process of converting a set of holdings in a portfolio into a set of exposures to risk factors.

Risk factors   Variables or characteristics with which individual asset returns are correlated. Sometimes referred to simply as *factors*.

Risk reversal   An option position that consists of the purchase of an out-of-the-money call and the simultaneous sale of an out-of-the-money put with the same "delta," on the same underlying currency or security, and with the same expiration date.

Robust standard errors   Standard errors of the estimated parameters of a regression that correct for the presence of heteroskedasticity in the regression's error term.

Roll   When an investor moves from one series to a new one.

Roll return   The component of the return on a commodity futures contract attributable to rolling long futures positions forward through time. Also called *roll yield*.

Rolling down the yield curve   A maturity trading strategy that involves buying bonds with a maturity longer than the intended investment horizon. Also called *riding the yield curve*.

Root mean squared error (RMSE)   The square root of the average squared forecast error; used to compare the out-of-sample forecasting performance of forecasting models.

Sales comparison approach   In the context of real estate, this approach estimates value based on what similar or comparable properties (comparables) transacted for in the current market.

Scaled earnings surprise   Unexpected earnings divided by the standard deviation of analysts' earnings forecasts.

Scatter plot   A two-dimensional plot of pairs of observations on two data series.

Scenario analysis   Analysis that involves changing multiple assumptions at the same time.

Screening   The application of a set of criteria to reduce a set of potential investments to a smaller set having certain desired characteristics.

Seasonality   A characteristic of a time series in which the data experiences regular and predictable periodic changes, e.g., fan sales are highest during the summer months.

Securities offering   A merger or acquisition in which target shareholders are to receive shares of the acquirer's common stock as compensation.

Security selection risk   See *active specific risk.*

Segmented markets theory   A term structure theory that contends yields are solely a function of the supply and demand for funds of a particular maturity.

Self-regulating organizations   Private, non-governmental organizations that both represent and regulate their members. Some self-regulating organizations are also independent regulators.

Sell-side analysts   Analysts who work at brokerages.

Sensitivity analysis   Analysis that shows the range of possible outcomes as specific assumptions are changed; involves changing one assumption at a time.

Serially correlated   With reference to regression errors, errors that are correlated across observations.

Service period   For employee stock options, usually the period between the grant date and the vesting date.

Settled in arrears   An arrangement in which the interest payment is made at the end of the settlement period.

Settlement   In the case of a credit event, the process by which the two parties to a CDS contract satisfy their respective obligations.

Shaping risk   The sensitivity of a bond's price to the changing shape of the yield curve.

Shareholders' equity   Total assets minus total liabilities.

Shark repellents   A pre-offer takeover defense mechanism involving the corporate charter (e.g., staggered boards of directors and supermajority provisions).

Shopping center   REITs that invest in such retail properties as regional shopping malls or community/neighborhood shopping centers.

Single-name CDS   Credit default swap on one specific borrower.

Sinking fund bond   A bond which requires the issuer to set aside funds over time to retire the bond issue, thus reducing credit risk.

Sole proprietorship   A business owned and operated by a single person.

Spin-off   A form of restructuring in which shareholders of a parent company receive a proportional number of shares in a new, separate entity; shareholders end up owning stock in two different companies where there used to be one.

Split-off   A form of restructuring in which shareholders of the parent company are given shares in a newly created entity in exchange for their shares of the parent company.

Split-rate tax system   In reference to corporate taxes, a split-rate system taxes earnings to be distributed as dividends at a different rate than earnings to be retained. Corporate profits distributed as dividends are taxed at a lower rate than those retained in the business.

Spot curve   The term structure of spot rates for loans made today.

Spot price   The current price of an asset or security. For commodities, the current price to deliver a physical commodity to a specific location or purchase and transport it away from a designated location.

Spot rate   The interest rate that is determined today for a risk-free, single-unit payment at a specified future date.

Spot yield curve   The term structure of spot rates for loans made today.

Spurious correlation   A correlation that misleadingly points toward associations between variables.

Stabilized NOI   In the context of real estate, the expected NOI when a renovation is complete.

Stable dividend policy   A policy in which regular dividends are paid that reflect long-run expected earnings. In contrast to a constant dividend payout ratio policy, a stable dividend policy does not reflect short-term volatility in earnings.

Standard deviation   The positive square root of the variance; a measure of dispersion in the same units as the original data.

Standard of value   A specification of how "value" is to be understood in the context of a specific valuation.

Standardized beta   With reference to fundamental factor models, the value of the attribute for an asset minus the average value of the attribute across all stocks, divided by the standard deviation of the attribute across all stocks.

Standardized unexpected earnings   (SUE) Unexpected earnings per share divided by the standard deviation of unexpected earnings per share over a specified prior time period.

Static trade-off theory of capital structure   A theory pertaining to a company's optimal capital structure; the optimal level of debt is found at the point where additional debt would cause the costs of financial distress to increase by a greater amount than the benefit of the additional tax shield.

Statistical factor model   A multifactor model in which statistical methods are applied to a set of historical returns to determine portfolios that best explain either historical return covariances or variances.

Statistically significant   A result indicating that the null hypothesis can be rejected; with reference to an estimated regression coefficient, frequently understood to mean a result indicating that the corresponding population regression coefficient is different from 0.

Statutes   Laws enacted by legislative bodies.

Statutory merger   A merger in which one company ceases to exist as an identifiable entity and all its assets and liabilities become part of a purchasing company.

Steady state rate of growth   The constant growth rate of output (or output per capita) which can or will be sustained indefinitely once it is reached. Key ratios, such as the capital–output ratio, are constant on the steady-state growth path.

Steepness   One of the three factors (the other two are level and curvature) that empirically explain most of the changes in the shape of the yield curve. A shock to the steepness factor changes short-term yields more than long-term yields.

Sterilized intervention   A policy measure in which a monetary authority buys or sells its own currency to mitigate undesired exchange rate movements and simultaneously offsets the impact on the money supply with transactions in other financial instruments (usually money market instruments).

Stock purchase   An acquisition in which the acquirer gives the target company's shareholders some combination of cash and securities in exchange for shares of the target company's stock.

Stop-loss limit   Constraint used in risk management that requires a reduction in the size of a portfolio, or its complete liquidation, when a loss of a particular size occurs in a specified period.

Storage REITs   REITs that own and operate self-storage properties, sometimes referred to as mini-warehouse facilities.

Straddle   An option strategy involving the purchase of a put and a call on the same underlying with the same exercise price and expiration date. If the put and call are held long, it is a long straddle; if they are held short, it is a short straddle.

Straight bond   An underlying option-free bond with a specified issuer, issue date, maturity date, principal amount and repayment structure, coupon rate and payment structure, and currency denomination.

Straight-line rent   The average annual rent under a multi-year lease agreement that contains contractual increases in rent during the life of the lease. For example if the rent is $100,000 in Year 1, $105,000 in Year 2, and $110,000 in Year 3, the average rent to be recognized each year as revenue under straight-line rent accounting is ($100,000 + $105,000 + $110,000)/3 = $105,000.

Straight-line rent adjustment   See *non-cash rent*.

Strategic transaction   A purchase involving a buyer that would benefit from certain synergies associated with owning the target firm.

Stress tests   A risk management technique which assesses the portfolio's response to extreme market movements.

Stripping   A dealer's ability to separate a bond's individual cash flows and trade them as zero-coupon securities.

Structural models   Structural models of credit analysis build on the insights of option pricing theory. They are based on the structure of a company's balance sheet.

Subsidiary merger   A merger in which the company being purchased becomes a subsidiary of the purchaser.

Substantive law   The body of law that focuses on the rights and responsibilities of entities and relationships among entities.

Succession event   A change of corporate structure of the reference entity, such as through a merger, divestiture, spinoff, or any similar action, in which ultimate responsibility for the debt in question is unclear.

Sum-of-the-parts valuation   A valuation that sums the estimated values of each of a company's businesses as if each business were an independent going concern.

Sunk cost   A cost that has already been incurred.

Supernormal growth   Above average or abnormally high growth rate in earnings per share.

Survivorship bias   Bias that may result when failed or defunct companies are excluded from membership in a group.

Sustainable growth rate   The rate of dividend (and earnings) growth that can be sustained over time for a given level of return on equity, keeping the capital structure constant and without issuing additional common stock.

Swap curve   The term structure of swap rates.

Swap rate   The interest rate for the fixed-rate leg of an interest rate swap.

Swap rate curve   The term structure of swap rates.

Swap spread   The difference between the fixed rate on an interest rate swap and the rate on a Treasury note with equivalent maturity; it reflects the general level of credit risk in the market.

Synthetic CDO   Created by combining a portfolio of default-free securities with a combination of credit default swaps undertaken as protection sellers.

Synthetic long position   A combination of options (buying a call and writing a put) having the same expiration date and the same exercise price, which is approximately equivalent to a long position in the stock.

Synthetic short position   A derivatives strategy that creates the same performance as a short position in the underlying.

Systematic risk   Risk that affects the entire market or economy; it cannot be avoided and is inherent in the overall market. Systematic risk is also known as non-diversifiable or market risk.

Systemic risk   The risk of failure of the financial system.

Tail risk   The risk that losses in extreme events could be greater than would be expected for a portfolio of assets with a normal distribution.

Takeover   A merger; the term may be applied to any transaction, but is often used in reference to hostile transactions.

Takeover premium   The amount by which the takeover price for each share of stock must exceed the current stock price in order to entice shareholders to relinquish control of the company to an acquirer.

Tangible book value per share   Common shareholders' equity minus intangible assets reported on the balance sheet, divided by the number of shares outstanding.

Target   The company in a merger or acquisition that is being acquired.

Target capital structure   A company's chosen proportions of debt and equity.

Target company   The company in a merger or acquisition that is being acquired.

Target payout ratio   A strategic corporate goal representing the long-term proportion of earnings that the company intends to distribute to shareholders as dividends.

Technical indicators   Momentum indicators based on price.

TED spread   A measure of perceived credit risk determined as the difference between Libor and the T-bill yield of matching maturity.

Temporal method   A variation of the monetary/non-monetary translation method that requires not only monetary assets and liabilities, but also non-monetary assets and liabilities that are measured at their current value on the balance sheet date to be translated at the current exchange rate. Assets and liabilities are translated at rates consistent with the timing of their measurement value. This method is typically used when the functional currency is other than the local currency.

Tender offer   A public offer whereby the acquirer invites target shareholders to submit ("tender") their shares in return for the proposed payment.

Term premium   The additional return required by lenders to invest in a bond to maturity net of the expected return from continually reinvesting at the short-term rate over that same time horizon.

Terminal price multiples   The price multiple for a stock assumed to hold at a stated future time.

Terminal share price   The share price at a particular point in the future.

Terminal value of the stock   The analyst's estimate of a stock's value at a particular point in the future. Also called *continuing value of the stock*.

Termination date   The date of the final payment on a swap; also, the swap's expiration date.

Theta   The change in a derivative instrument for a given small change in calendar time, holding everything else constant. Specifically, the theta calculation assumes nothing changes except calendar time. Theta also reflects the rate at which an option's time value decays.

Time series   A set of observations on a variable's outcomes in different time periods.

Tobin's *q*   The ratio of the market value of debt and equity to the replacement cost of total assets.

Top-down approach   With respect to forecasting, an approach that usually begins at the level of the overall economy. Forecasts are then made at more narrowly defined levels, such as sector, industry, and market for a specific product.

Top-down investing   An approach to investing that typically begins with macroeconomic forecasts.

Total factor productivity (TFP)   A multiplicative scale factor that reflects the general level of productivity or technology in the economy. Changes in total factor productivity generate proportional changes in output for any input combination.

Total invested capital   The sum of market value of common equity, book value of preferred equity, and face value of debt.

Tracking error   The standard deviation of the differences between a portfolio's returns and its benchmark's returns; a synonym of active risk. Also called *tracking risk*.

Tracking risk   The standard deviation of the differences between a portfolio's returns and its benchmark's returns; a synonym of active risk. Also called *tracking error*.

Trailing dividend yield   Current market price divided by the most recent annualized dividend.

Trailing P/E   A stock's current market price divided by the most recent four quarters of EPS (or the most recent two semi-annual periods for companies that report interim data semi-annually.) Also called *current P/E*.

Tranche CDS   A type of credit default swap that covers a combination of borrowers but only up to pre-specified levels of losses.

Transaction exposure   The risk of a change in value between the transaction date and the settlement date of an asset of liability denominated in a foreign currency.

Trend   A long-term pattern of movement in a particular direction.

Triangular arbitrage   An arbitrage transaction involving three currencies which attempts to exploit inconsistencies among pair wise exchange rates.

Unbiased expectations theory   A term structure theory that contends the forward rate is an unbiased predictor of the future spot rate. Also called the *pure expectations theory*.

Unconditional heteroskedasticity   Heteroskedasticity of the error term that is not correlated with the values of the independent variable(s) in the regression.

Uncovered interest rate parity   The proposition that the expected return on an uncovered (i.e., unhedged) foreign currency (risk-free) investment should equal the return on a comparable domestic currency investment.

Underlying earnings   Earnings excluding nonrecurring components. Also referred to as *continuing earnings*, *core earnings*, or *persistent earnings*.

Unexpected earnings   The difference between reported EPS and expected EPS. Also referred to as an *earnings surprise*.

Unit root   A time series that is not covariance stationary is said to have a unit root.

Uniting of interests method   A method of accounting in which combined companies were portrayed as if they had always operated as a single economic entity. Called pooling of interests under US GAAP and uniting of interests under IFRS. (No longer allowed under US GAAP or IFRS).

Unlimited funds   An unlimited funds environment assumes that the company can raise the funds it wants for all profitable projects simply by paying the required rate of return.

Unsterilized intervention   A policy measure in which a monetary authority buys or sells its own currency to mitigate undesired exchange rate movements and does not offset the impact on the money supply with transactions in other financial instruments.

Upfront payment   The difference between the credit spread and the standard rate paid by the protection if the standard rate is insufficient to compensate the protection seller. Also called *upfront premium*.

Upfront premium   See *upfront payment*.

UPREITs   An umbrella partnership REIT under which the REIT owns an operating partnership and serves as the general partner of the operating partnership. All or most of the properties are held in the operating partnership.

Upstream   A transaction between two related companies, an investor company (or a parent company) and an associate company (or a subsidiary company) such that the associate company records a profit on its income statement. An example is a sale of inventory by the associate to the investor company or by a subsidiary to a parent company.

Valuation   The process of determining the value of an asset or service on the basis of variables perceived to be related to future investment returns, or on the basis of comparisons with closely similar assets.

Value additivity   An arbitrage opportunity when the value of the whole equals the sum of the values of the parts.

Value at risk (VaR)   The minimum loss that would be expected a certain percentage of the time over a certain period of time given the assumed market conditions.

Value of growth   The difference between the actual value per share and the no-growth value per share.

Variance   The expected value (the probability-weighted average) of squared deviations from a random variable's expected value.

Vasicek model   A partial equilibrium term structure model that assumes interest rates are mean reverting and interest rate volatility is a constant.

Vega   The change in a given derivative instrument for a given small change in volatility, holding everything else constant. A sensitivity measure for options that reflects the effect of volatility.

Venture capital investors   Private equity investors in development-stage companies.

Vertical merger   A merger involving companies at different positions of the same production chain; for example, a supplier or a distributor.

Vested benefit obligation   The actuarial present value of vested benefits.

Vesting date   The date that employees can first exercise stock options.

Visibility   The extent to which a company's operations are predictable with substantial confidence.

Weighted average cost of capital   (WACC) A weighted average of the after-tax required rates of return on a company's common stock, preferred stock, and long-term debt, where the weights are the fraction of each source of financing in the company's target capital structure.

Weighted harmonic mean   See *harmonic mean*.

White-corrected standard errors   A synonym for robust standard errors.

White knight   A third party that is sought out by the target company's board to purchase the target in lieu of a hostile bidder.

White squire   A third party that is sought out by the target company's board to purchase a substantial minority stake in the target—enough to block a hostile takeover without selling the entire company.

Winner's curse The tendency for the winner in certain competitive bidding situations to overpay, whether because of overestimation of intrinsic value, emotion, or information asymmetries.

Write-down A reduction in the value of an asset as stated in the balance sheet.

Yield curve factor model A model or a description of yield curve movements that can be considered realistic when compared with historical data.

Z-spread The constant basis point spread that needs to be added to the implied spot yield curve such that the discounted cash flows of a bond are equal to its current market price.

Zero A bond that does not pay a coupon but is priced at a discount and pays its full face value at maturity.

Zero-coupon bond A bond that does not pay a coupon but is priced at a discount and pays its full face value at maturity.

Index